DISABILITY & THE POLITICS OF EDUCATION

PETER LANG
New York • Washington, D.C./Baltimore • Bern
Frankfurt am Main • Berlin • Brussels • Vienna • Oxford

DISABILITY & THE POLITICS OF EDUCATION

AN INTERNATIONAL READER

EDITED BY
SUSAN L. GABEL & SCOT DANFORTH

PETER LANG
New York • Washington, D.C./Baltimore • Bern
Frankfurt am Main • Berlin • Brussels • Vienna • Oxford

Library of Congress Cataloging-in-Publication Data

Disability and the politics of education: an international reader /
edited by Susan L. Gabel, Scot Danforth.
p. cm.
Includes bibliographical references.
1. People with disabilities—Education. 2. Education and state.
3. Comparative education. 4. Inclusive education.
I. Gabel, Susan L. (Susan Lynn). II. Danforth, Scot.
LC4019.D55   371.904—dc22   2008000240
ISBN 978-0-8204-8895-0 (hardcover)
ISBN 978-0-8204-8894-3 (paperback)

Bibliographic information published by **Die Deutsche Bibliothek**.
Die Deutsche Bibliothek lists this publication in the "Deutsche
Nationalbibliografie"; detailed bibliographic data is available
on the Internet at http://dnb.ddb.de/.

Cover design by Clear Point Designs
Cover art, *The Big Dance*, by Judith Sheldon
Photo of cover art by S. Kay Young, Inc.

The paper in this book meets the guidelines for permanence and durability
of the Committee on Production Guidelines for Book Longevity
of the Council of Library Resources.

© 2008 Peter Lang Publishing, Inc., New York
29 Broadway, 18th floor, New York, NY 10006
www.peterlang.com

All rights reserved.
Reprint or reproduction, even partially, in all forms such as microfilm,
xerography, microfiche, microcard, and offset strictly prohibited.

Printed in the United States of America

For Dad with love
—Susan

To MaryEllen and Hope, my dear comrades on this journey
—Scot

About THE Cover Artist

The cover is a photograph of an original work of art—The Big Dance—by Judith Sheldon, who creates vibrant cloth collages. In this one, she uses colorful fabric and flags to represent what she calls the "joy of dance and drum that moves us to a new place inside ourselves." Hers is an aesthetic of inclusion and diversity—an aesthetic of existence. She is drawn to differences and to the immeasurable possibilities they imply. "When we share our unique ways of being," she says, "our differences form a unified expression. The differences become instruments of expression, making the music richer and deeper and the dance revelatory and surprising. Surrounded by the sound of the universe, we fly through space and time." The Big Dance was first exhibited at the Arts Club of Chicago during the Seventh Annual Second City Disability Studies in Education Conference in 2007.

Judith is a visual artist and dancer in Detroit, Michigan. Judith and her partner, Baba Issa Abramaleem, a visual artist and percussionist, create innovative inclusion programs such as Musical Chairs, a dance education program that partners students who use wheelchairs with students who do not, and Heart of Hearing, a music education program for Deaf and hearing impaired learners. Additional information is available at www.firstcircleinc.com. Photograph by S. Kay Young, Inc.

Editorial Board

Julie Allan
University of Stirling
Stirling, Scotland

Beth Ferri
Syracuse University
Syracuse, New York, USA

Anita Ghai
College of Jesus and Mary
New Delhi, India

Valerie Harwood
University of Wollongong
Wollongong, New South Wales, Australia

Susan Peters
Michigan State University
East Lansing, Michigan, USA

Table of Contents

Foreword
  Len Barton xvii
Acknowledgements. xxi

Chapter 1. Disability and the International Politics of Education
  Susan L. Gabel and Scot Danforth. 1

Section I. Inclusive Education

Chapter 2. Teachers' Dominant Discourses of Inclusion and Disability:
  A Case Study at a Semi-rural Township School in the Province
  of KwaZulu-Natal, South Africa
  Jabulani Ngcobo and Nithi Muthukrishna 19

Chapter 3. Inclusion in Italy: What Happens When Everyone Belongs
  Beth A. Ferri 41

Chapter 4. An Analysis of Inclusive Education Policy Implementation
  in Zimbabwe: Challenges for Learner Support
  Auxilia Badza, David Chakuchichi, and Robert Chimedza 53

Chapter 5. Inclusion in Indian Education
    Susan L. Gabel and Jagdish Chander 69

Chapter 6. Inclusion?
    Linda J. Graham and Roger Slee 81

Chapter 7. Reading Stories of Inclusion: Engaging with
    Different Perspectives towards an Agenda for Inclusion
    Andrew Azzopardi 101

Chapter 8. Research in Inclusive Education as a Possible Opening
    to Disability Studies in Education
    Geert Van Hove, Griet Roets, Kathleen Mortier,
    Elisabeth De Schauwer, Mieke Leroy, and Eric Broekaert 121

Chapter 9. Doing Inclusive Education Research
    Julie Allan and Roger Slee 141

Section II. Policy

Chapter 10. An Analysis of the Impact of Advocacy and Disability
    Rights on the Quality of Life of People with Disabilities in Zimbabwe
    Robert Chimedza, Auxilia Badza, and David Chakuchichi.....................165

Chapter 11. Disability Education in the People's Republic of China:
    Tradition, Reform, and Outlook
    Qing Shen, Helen McCabe, and Zhaoyang Chi.................................177

Chapter 12. The Role of Residential Schools in Shaping the
    Nature of the Advocacy Movement of the Blind in India
    Jagdish Chander..201

Chapter 13. Politics, Inclusion, and Disabled Children:
    The Colombian Context
    Marisol Moreno Angarita and Susan L. Gabel 225

Chapter 14. Inclusive Education and School Choice:
    Democratic Rights in a Devolved System
    Liz Gordon and Missy Morton...237

Chapter 15. Private Troubles or Public Issues? The Social Construction
of "The Disabled Baby" in the Context of Social Policy
and Social and Technological Changes
Dóra S. Bjarnason 251

Chapter 16. Czech Republic: Empowerment
of D(/d)eaf Community through Education (1945–2006)
Jitka Sinecka. 275

Chapter 17. Reframing Global Education from a Disability
Rights Movement Perspective
Susan Peters, Kimberly Wolbers, and Lisa Dimling. 291

Chapter 18. A Model for Policy Activism
Susan L. Gabel. 311

Section III. Theorizing Disability

Chapter 19. "I Got Trouble with My Reading": An Emerging Literacy
Tanya Titchkosky. 337

Chapter 20. Deleuze, Guattari, and the Boundaries
of Intellectual Disability
Anna C. Hickey-Moody. 353

Chapter 21. Taking Exception: Discourses of Exceptionality
and the Invocation of the "Ideal"
Valerie Harwood and Nici Hymphry 371

Chapter 22. Using Metaphors to Research the Cultural
and Ideological Construction of Disability
Scot Danforth. 385

Chapter 23. Double Trouble: Disability and Disability Studies in Education
Rod Michalko. 401

Chapter 24. Cartographies of Eugenics and Special Education:
A History of the (Ab)normal
Phil Smith 417

Chapter 25. Caring Power and Disabled Children:
  The Rise of the Educational Élan in Europe, in Particular in Belgium
  and the Netherlands
    Annemieke van Drenth 433

Chapter 26. Not So Strange Bedfellows:
  The Promise of Disability Studies and Critical Race Theory
    David J. Connor 451

Chapter 27. Disability Studies and Psychology:
  Emancipatory Opportunities
    Dan Goodley and Rebecca Lawthom 477

Chapter 28. A Comparison: Difference, Dependency, and Stigmatization
  in Special Education and Disability Studies
    Kathryn Young and Emily Mintz 499

Section IV. Higher Education

Chapter 29. Disability in the German, Swiss, and
  Austrian Higher Education Systems
    Justin J. W. Powell, Kai Felkendorff, and Judith Hollenweger 517

Chapter 30. The Reasonable Adjustments Duty for Higher
  Education in England and Wales
    Kim Marshall 541

Chapter 31. Moving in from the Margins:
  From Accommodation to Universal Design
    Sheryl Burgstahler and Rebecca Cory 561

Chapter 32. Adapting Disability Studies within Teacher
  Education in Singapore
    Levan Lim, Thana Thaver, and Kenneth Poon 583

Chapter 33. Disability Narratives, Social Models,
  and Rights Perspectives as Higher Education Imperatives
    Christopher Johnstone, Alex Lubet, and Leonard Goldfine 599

Appendix A	619
Appendix B	627
Appendix C	631
Appendix D	647
Contributors	655

Foreword

To read the chapters in this collection is to reinforce the perennial significance of a critical, questioning approach to inclusive thinking, disability issues, and research and practice. The questions that the contributors raise in each chapter provide a powerful stimulus for further reflection and active critical engagement. My awareness and appreciation of an informed understanding of current ideas, concerns, interpretations, and indications of possible future directions of interests in this field of study were enhanced through the process of preparing these comments. The process also had the important consequence of encouraging me to think about the silences in these accounts, what questions were not being asked, and thus need to be raised and pursued. Revisiting the question of the nature and relationship between "inclusive education" and "disability studies" through these themes and contexts was particularly important. Although the readings offer a wealth of insights and ideas, they also provide a necessary and powerful reminder of the extent of the work that still needs to be undertaken conceptually, theoretically, and empirically in relation to meanings, values, processes, and outcomes and their interrelationship as well as the question of developing effective strategies for change.

These chapters also strengthened my recognition of the crucial importance of developing and maintaining an informed understanding of how the ideas and issues involved in these themes are being explored within different societies.

We have so little awareness and knowledge of the nature of such work and of the dangers of the unquestioning dominance of Western ideas. What can we learn about ways of thinking differently that challenge our own presuppositions and perspectives but that have their origins in different sociohistorical, cultural, and social contexts? What forms of language do we need to be able to engage in meaningful cross-border discussions? This process of reciprocal informed exchange involving a respectful recognition of points of commonality and difference provides a much richer, sensitive, complex knowledge and understanding of the issues, ideas, and challenges that have been, are being, and still need to be engaged with. It reminded me of our responsibility for more comprehensive thinking and understanding. Reading these chapters also raised the issue of how to seriously reflect such material in my own work and how to introduce students to this increasingly rich range of insights and ideas.

My reading of the chapters reinforced the centrality of critical analysis and change in relation to the pursuit of more inclusive thinking and practice. Change is complex, multilayered, and the barriers to becoming able to think, behave, and interact differently are varied and deeply rooted in the culture and taken-for-granted nature of everyday life. Change is not easily achieved and maintained. Thus the focus of critical analysis extends well beyond such factors as single-impairment concerns, attitudes, and resources. Inclusion is based on a recognition of the profoundly serious understanding of the nature of exclusion and discrimination, which involves the perennial task of identifying, challenging, and ultimately removing all the complex, varied barriers to inclusive participation. It requires us to adopt a zero-tolerance attitude to all forms of exclusion. The stakes are high in this process and relate to the significance of the effective realization of equity, social justice, active citizenship, and nondiscriminatory conditions and relations in the lives of all individuals. This requires a dynamic, serious conception of exclusion in which the extent of the changes and the difficulties of meeting the challenges of the removal of all the barriers to inclusion, are not underestimated or treated as less than fundamentally significant concerns. With each chapter in this book I became increasingly aware of the political nature of working toward more inclusive thinking and practice and of the urgency and difficulty of engaging with transformative change.

One of the exciting aspects of this collection is the range of topics that the contributors investigate empirically and theoretically. In our work we often consider the position and experience of other people, including children, in our own and other societies. This also involves contextual factors such as the structure and culture of institutions, official discourse, and policy issues. It is a wonderful privilege to be able to work closely with so many people who are willing to share their personal feelings and perspectives with us. These detailed and important studies provide a wealth of insights, informed critical knowledge, and understanding of many aspects of human experience and interactions. They constitute a valuable learning experience about the history, socioeconomic conditions, lives, and experiences of others—both the positive and the negative factors. Reflecting on these readings raised a crucially important but often neglected issue: How much of our developing knowledge and understanding as researchers do we use to promote inclusive developments within the institutions in which we work and within the society in which they are placed? Sometimes in giving so much time and attention to other people and contexts we neglect the very setting in which we work and the people involved. Within our own work contexts and societies there is so much that is unacceptable and exclusionary and needs to be fought over and changed, and we must be part of that critical engagement.

Reflecting on these chapters and my own position as an academic involved in the development of inclusive education and disability studies, I have been drawn to a fundamental question: What is the purpose of our work? We are caught between contradictory and competing factors as the growing pressure to achieve academic status through research and teaching essentially celebrates excessive individualism and personal ambition. Nor is this, for example, merely about obtaining research funding and getting published. It is increasingly about winning support from high-status funding bodies or councils and publishing in the most prestigious journals. The extremely competitive culture of higher education nationally and globally with the increasing pressures of "audit cultures" and comparisons between performance and outcome has made for a divisive process. It has powerful exclusionary impacts on individual academics, departments, and even universities. The emphasis on being marketability is an ever-present reality in terms of who we are and what we produce. These reflections brought forth some troublesome questions: What are the significant motivations informing my work? Who benefits from my thinking, research, and writing? How far is the purpose of my work concerned with advancing the interests, hopes, expectations, and well-being of disabled people and their organizations? The process of learning involved in establishing working relationships with disabled people should challenge issues of power, status, and influence what, how, why we research and write. However, as in so many aspects that we investigate, the extent to which laudable rhetoric is realized in actual practice continues to be challenging.

I have been concerned for some time about the barriers within higher education that inhibit the establishment and maintenance of a debate over these fundamental issues of inclusive thinking and practice. As I read these chapters I found myself asking: What constitutes a debate? How can it be encouraged and maintained? What kinds of relationships will this involve? How far is the current system of publishing counterproductive to this task? We work in a culture increasingly characterized by measurement and control in which image and accountability are crucial. How we think, talk, and understand educational issues and practice has been influenced by the language of business and its vocabulary of targets, efficiency, and effectiveness. Inclusive thinking and practice involve such values as openness, reciprocal respect, trust in which there is a genuine sense of being learners. To what extent do we see evidence of such a thriving, creative, encouraging, and disturbing process in our daily working lives? The contributors here raise for me the serious and urgent question of what conditions and relations within higher education, and in particular my work context, will be necessary in order to facilitate this inclusive practice?

Reading this book has been a demanding, thought-provoking, and valuable experience. The volume is a great resource, providing a rich range of ideas, questions, and interesting sources to be explored. I am sure this has not been an easy task, but the outcome has justified all the hard work. This book deserves to be read by a wide readership and ought to be an important text for courses dealing with these serious themes. I hope that, in engaging with these chapters, readers will take the (unfortunately unusual) step of contacting the authors in order to establish a constructive, critical discussion of such work.

Len Barton
Emeritus Professor of Inclusive Education
Institute of Education
University of London

Acknowledgements

Thanks to our families who steadfastly and without complaint support our work and the time it takes us from them. Our production team, led by Bernadette Shade, has been immensely helpful and professional. Chris Myers, our editor at Peter Lang, has been supportive of this and all books in the book series. The series exists because of him and we owe him an enthusiastic thank you. The authors in this volume have waited patiently for publication. We appreciate their contributions and dedication. Julie Allan, Beth Ferri, Valerie Harwood, and Susan Peters served as thoughtful, thorough editorial board members without whom the process of reviewing and responding to submissions would have been overwhelming. Special thanks to Len Barton, who found time in his busy schedule to endorse the book and write the foreword.

CHAPTER ONE

Disability AND THE International Politics OF Education

SUSAN L. GABEL AND SCOT DANFORTH

INTERNATIONAL AGREEMENTS ON THE RIGHT TO EDUCATION: 1990–2007

Since 1990, global attention has been given to education as a human right through the initiative entitled Education for All (EFA). The goals EFA and its related international agreements have built a political framework for pressing governments to increase universal childhood education, literacy, gender equity, and greater access to higher education. Many of the chapters in this *Reader* reflect the influence of EFA, particularly those chapters describing the situation in countries more recently considering free public education for disabled children and disabled people's access to higher education—that is, China, India, Colombia, South Africa, and Zimbabwe. While numerous international events have occurred since the inception of EFA, we summarize five that are important to the understanding of disability and the international politics of education.

1990: Education for All

Launched in 1990 in Jomtien, Thailand, EFA included a "broad coalition of national governments, civil society groups, and development agencies" (World

Bank, 2007) led by UNESCO that formulated the *World Declaration on Education for All* (Appendix A) (UNESCO, 1990) resulting in six basic goals:

- Expand and improve comprehensive early childhood care and education, especially for the most vulnerable and disadvantaged children.
- Ensure that by 2015 all children, particularly girls, those in difficult circumstances, and those belonging to ethnic minorities, have access to and complete, free, and compulsory primary education of good quality.
- Ensure that the learning needs of all young people and adults are met through equitable access to appropriate learning and life skills programs.
- Achieve a 50% improvement in levels of adult literacy by 2015, especially for women, and equitable access to basic and continuing education for all adults.
- Eliminate gender disparities in primary and secondary education by 2005, and achieve gender equality in education by 2015, with a focus on ensuring girls' full and equal access to and achievement in basic education of good quality.
- Improve all aspects of the quality of education and ensure excellence of all so that recognized and measurable learning outcomes are achieved by all, especially in literacy, numeracy, and essential life skills (World Bank, 2007, ¶ 2).

1994: Salamanca Statement

Four years after the announcement of EFA, specific attention was given to the need for education of disabled children resulting in the *Salamanca Statement and Framework for Action* (Appendix B) (UNESCO, 1994), a critical turning point in the international politics of disability and education. The Salamanca Statement proclaims, among other things, that

- "Children with special needs" must "have access to regular schools which should accommodate them within a child-centred pedagogy capable of meeting those needs."
- "Regular schools with [an] inclusive orientation are the most effective means of combating discriminatory attitudes … building an inclusive society and achieving education for all … " (Section 2).

1998: World Declaration on Higher Education

The EFA agenda for higher education was affirmed at the 1998 World Conference on Higher Education where the *World Declaration on Higher Education*

(Appendix C) document (UNESCO, 1998) was produced. This document holds that "education is a fundamental pillar of human rights, democracy, sustainable development and peace" and that "the solution of the problems faced on the eve of the 21st century will be determined … by the role that is assigned to education in general and to higher education in particular" (Preamble, ¶ 5).

2000: Dakar Framework

Slow progress in the decade after Jomtien led to the 2000 World Education Forum in Dakar, Senegal, and the development of the *Dakar Framework for Action* (see Appendix D) (UNESCO, 2000) in which previous agreements were reaffirmed and a framework for achieving the six EFA goals was outlined.

2007: UN Convention

The 2007 Convention on the Rights of Persons with Disabilities (United Nations, 2007a) has (1) promoted the protection of the human rights of disabled people, "including those who require more intensive support" (Preamble [j]); (2) affirmed the right to make one's own choices; (3) confirmed that "children with disabilities should have full enjoyment of all human rights and fundamental freedoms on an equal basis with other children" (Preamble [r]); and (4) recognized the

> importance of accessibility to the physical, social, economic and cultural environment, to health and education and to information and communication, in enabling persons with disabilities to fully enjoy all human rights and fundamental freedoms (Preamble [v]).[1]

By July, 2007, there have been a hundred signatories to the convention, fifteen signatories to the Optional Protocol,[2] and one ratification (Jamaica) of the Convention.[3] Of the seventeen countries represented by the chapters in this book, thirteen have signed the Convention[4] and five of those have signed the Option Protocol[5] (United Nations, 2007b). The four nonsignatory countries represented in this book are United States, Switzerland, Zimbabwe, and Singapore.

SITUATION CRITICAL

The Convention comes at a critical time. According to UNESCO (1999), reaching its goal of EFA "has been, and remains, one of the most daunting challenges facing the global community today" (10). In spite of the numerous Conventions, Declarations, and Statements issued by international bodies, in spite of the resources behind the multiple international agencies who have invested in EFA,[6] today, millions of the world's disabled children cannot obtain a basic childhood education, particularly in countries with limited resources. Yet, even in the wealthiest countries many disabled children are educationally segregated from nondisabled children, particularly if they are labeled with significant mental retardation or what is also called cognitive impairment. In the United States, for example, rather than making progress for students with this label in the last decade, inclusion actually has been decreasing (Smith, 2007). The postsecondary situation also is discouraging. It is certain that a large percentage of the world's 900 million illiterate adults (UNICEF, 2000) are disabled as well as unemployed and poor, with inadequate health care and little or no access to assistive technology or simple assistive devices such as manual wheelchairs. In countries where a large percentage of the population attends a postsecondary institution, inequities remain. For example, disabled adults in the United States are underrepresented in postsecondary education in spite of antidiscrimination legislation and reasonable accommodation requirements (Reid & Knight, 2006).

POLITICS OF SILENCE?[7]

Of course, World Declarations and Statements and UN Conventions are only as good as their impact on the lives of disabled people and an example from India yields discouraging evidence on this matter. Rather than demonstrating an open commitment to EFA's concern for disabled children through action in the field, Mithu Alur (2007) reports a disturbing ambivalence about disability among international agencies consulting on the development of India's Integrated Child Development Services (ICDS) in the 1990s. She describes the international agencies as silent on the issue of its consequences for disabled children. She observes that "representatives of international agencies—although aware of international policy declarations—failed to raise the issue [of including disabled students in the scheme] from the outset." Her conclusion is that "it suited the vested interests from the West to remain silent and avoid controversy." Furthermore, she observes that "international agencies such as UNICEF, the World Food Programme, CARE (US) and the World Bank … remain silent on the matter of inclusion in their programmes of children with disability" (97). It is unclear to us to what extent Alur's observations are representative of EFA agencies' work around the world but it seems unlikely that the responses from agency representatives working with Indian activists is significantly different from responses in other national contexts. Further research is needed to determine whether such "politics of silence" (Slee, 2007) has been documented globally in relation to EFA initiatives.

INTERNATIONAL POLICY "SOLUTIONS"?

Internationally, EFA signatories have engaged in policy borrowing, the "conscious adoption in one context of policy observed in another" (Phillips & Ochs, 2004, 774) as a result of the EFA political imperative. The policies borrowed often attempt to replicate what is done in the United Kingdom or United States; however policy borrowing can create problems as well as solve them. Barton and Armstrong (2007) argue "that we cannot just apply the language of 'inclusion' uncritically, assuming that meanings will be shared across cultures—or even within the same national context or educational authority" (1). Borrowed policies can be "culturally biased toward Anglo-European concepts and constructs" (Meyer, 2003, 33), placing governments in the position of imposing policies, procedures, and political processes on educational institutions that do not fit the cultural context.

In particular, policy borrowing can impose constructions of disability that are in direct conflict with the cultural notions into which they are interjected. Armstrong and Barton (2007) caution against such impositions, noting the "complexities and contradiction involved in imposing new discourses on deeply rooted traditions and practices" (9). While it could be argued that such interjections may impose a construct that is less oppressive and more emancipatory, it is also possible, even likely, that the conflicts between indigenous practices and borrowed policy result in no changes at all due to the persistence of indigenous belief systems. In this case, the ultimate goal of policy borrowing—indigenization or internationalization (Phillips & Ochs, 2004)—is unlikely to be achieved.

INTEGRAZIONE OR INCLUSION?

D'Alessio (2007) provides an example of the dilemma described in the previous paragraph. She reports the discomfort among Italian educators in response to the international pressure to use the term inclusion.

> We prefer to use the term *integrazione*, because in our language, it acquires a positive meaning when compared with the broader terminology provided by pressing international organisations. (Canevaro, cited in D'Alessio, 55)

Within the Italian context, *integrazione* connotes a "long established tradition of strongly committed struggle for the civil rights of disabled people that are embedded in the word … and that would disappear if the word inclusion were to be used instead" (D'Alessio, 55). Regardless of the EFA discourse on inclusion, it is clear that it would be counterproductive to require Italian educators to substitute *integrazione* with inclusion, given the history of Italian progress regarding *integrazione*.

WEST IS BEST?

From the perspective of countries only recently attending to the issue of access to education for disabled children and adults, "colonialism may officially have come to an end," writes Mithu Alur. "[B]ut a new era of neo colonialism has taken over … by Western 'experts.'" She continues: "One legacy of colonialism is a deeply entrenched belief that 'West is best' and consequently there is a tendency at every level to turn to the Western consultant for help" (Alur, 2007, 98). This leaves the troubling realization that the almost twenty years of global attention to the education of disabled people has, to an extent, perpetuated oppressive relationships between West and East/North and South.

Critiques of Western models of educational service delivery for disabled people would support Alur's implication that West is *not* necessarily the best. U.S. federal policy, the Individuals with Disabilities Education Improvement Act (IDEIA) (U.S. Department of Education, 2004), has been criticized for its inherent ableism (Beratan, 2006) and its use of the medical model of disability (Gabel, Chapter 18, this volume). An unintentional consequence of this highly touted U.S. federal policy has been the resegregation of schools through the overrepresentation of African Americans in special education (Blanchett, 2006). Neither have other attempts at avoiding a classification system similar to the one utilized by the IDEIA achieved the desired ends. For example, Armstrong and Barton (2007) note that the British choice of "special educational needs" (SEN), an effort to "replace categories of impairment" with providing statements of educational need, has had disappointing results. They write:

> Paradoxically, although the term focused on educational needs rather than individual impairments it [SEN] also became a mega-category denoting difference or learning difficulty which co-existed with the established categories of impairment. (9)

Broad-scale school reform based on the paradigm of the market economy, often has the opposite effects of those intended by policymakers. New Zealand's efforts are an example of the disappointing results of reform for inclusive education (Wills, 2006). Gordon and Morton (Chapter 14, this volume) have shown that privatization, school choice, and local control have not resulted in inclusive schools:

> In a devolved schooling system, and one in which it will be difficult for the democratic and inclusive classroom to flourish, there appears to be no clear direction, and little evidence of leadership, to ensure that the national policy of inclusion is actually implemented in schools. (246)

Not only is there confusion and a lack of leadership to provide guidance, but "in New Zealand inclusion has to be won, classroom by classroom, school by school."

Even worse, "once won, it can also be lost again, if a dedicated teacher leaves or other circumstances change." Disappointingly, "from a policy perspective, then, inclusion is slippery and difficult, even when it can be recognized, defined and implemented" (246).

GLOBALIZING EDUCATIONAL POLICY AND POLITICS

Tamatea's (2005) critique of the discourse in the Dakar Framework echoes Alur's criticism of the "West is best" tendency in responses to EFA goals and illustrates one of the driving concerns about the globalization of educational policy and politics. He asserts that the Framework's ideology of "neoliberal capitalism" constructs education "along corporate business line[s]" authorizing who can "talk about education, when and how" (314). The official theme of the Framework, continues Tamatea, is a liberal-humanist one ostensibly interested in "rights, self-development and dignity" but its hidden curriculum "hold[s] the potential to bring about significantly less human-centered 'outcomes,' which are not always signaled 'up front.'" According to Tamatea, the hidden curriculum (his phrase) of the Framework results in the "imposition of a highly surveillance orientated, coercive, punitive, regulatory and disciplinary grid comprising a number of strategic axes of discursive and material control" found in Western educational systems. This causes education in non-Western countries to "become a site for reconstruction" based on a neoliberal world order in which the world economy authoritatively dictates the purposes and processes of schooling and "strategies for compliance" (317) monitored by "supranational funding agencies and their conduit states" (318).

Tamatea's account holds that the technologies used to bring states under control include "definition, delimitation and redefinition of 'traditional' educational concepts, and the use of concepts from outside of education reloaded with corporate managerial semantic content" (ibid.) in what Tamatea considers a panopticon-like effect that subordinates compliant states to multinational agencies in the enforcement of "quality," "transparency," and "accountability."

DOUBLESPEAK AND MCDONALDIZATION

According to Tamatea, the Framework's paradoxical use of two competing discourses are like "Orwellian doublespeak" that produces the reality of the future (323) and a "McDonaldization" of school. These are harsh critiques of a *Framework* that purports to benefit humankind.

Goldstein (2004) takes a similar position in his description of what he calls the "dysfunctional consequences" of the Framework's emphasis on high stakes testing systems and learning targets—consequences Tamatea alludes to but does not explicate. These include "the tendency to demotivate pupils and increase their test anxiety" (10), the difficulty of using a "common measurement instrument that obtains 'comparable' scores across individuals and sites (8), and the lack of correlation between improved test scores and actual learning. The importance of these consequences goes beyond their impact on schools or children to whether development projects are funded based on the World Bank's determination of "aid-worthiness" (UNESCO, 2002).

EFA requires curriculum change in addition to high-stakes testing. Here, Goldstein notes, curriculum development bodies, testing companies, and textbook publishers with international reputations are inevitable stakeholders; Educational Testing Service (ETS) in the United States, University of Cambridge Local Examinations Syndicate (UCLES) in England, and the Australian Council for Educational Research (ACER) are among others some examples. Consequently, argues Goldstein, "we may also expect the direction taken by EFA to reflect, in part, the global interests of such corporations" (12).

The Framework speaks of the provision of monetary resources in addition to curriculum, assessment, and monitoring but Tamatea's criticism about doublespeak is validated by textual references to finances. Point #10 in the Framework (2000) affirms "that no countries *seriously committed* to education for all will be thwarted in their achievement of this goal by a lack of resources" (emphasis added). Point #11 promises the mobilizing of "resources needed to provide effective support to national efforts" including "increasing *external finance* for education," "greater predictability in the flow of *external assistance*," "more effective *donor* coordination," "earlier, more extensive and broader *debt relief and/or debt cancellation*," "regular *monitoring of progress* toward EFA goals and targets, including *periodic assessments* (emphases added, Point 11. i–iii, v–vi). Point #21 in the Framework again urges financial commitments:

> Achieving Education for All will require additional financial support by countries and increased *development assistance* and debt relief for education by *bilateral and multilateral donors*, estimated to cost in the order of $8 billion a year. It is therefore essential that new, concrete financial commitments be made by national governments and also by bilateral and multilateral *donors including the World Bank and the regional development banks*, by civil society and by *foundations*. (Point 21, emphases added)

The above excerpts simultaneously create ambiguity and communicate clear but implicit messages about control of EFA goals and outcomes. The definition and measurement of "serious commitment to education" are quite murky, as are phrases such as "regular monitoring of progress" and "predictability in the flow of resources." Who decides whether a country has demonstrated a "serious commitment to education" and how is this measured? If a country fails to meet learning targets or does poorly on assessments, does this demonstrate a lack of serious commitment or a greater need for resources? Who will conduct the "regular monitoring of progress," what instruments will be used in this activity, and who will analyze the results? How will the flow of resources be structured and who will decide how much each country receives and when?

Alur, Goldstein, and Tamatea have answered these questions. The answer also is in the Framework text: "bi-lateral and multi-lateral donors," "including the World Bank, regional development banks," civil society, foundations—most of these representing external assistance or charity in the form of "debt relief or debt cancellation." This situation puts countries struggling to achieve EFA but in need of resources they cannot muster alone in a double bind: on one hand, they may hope to achieve EFA in spite of some unreasonable goals[8] but on the other hand, they cannot do so without external assistance that comes at the cost of neutralizing or supplanting cultural traditions in pedagogy, purpose, and process as well as what Tamatea calls panopticon-like surveillance (e.g., "monitoring of progress," "periodic assessment") and the reconstruction of a neoliberal world order.

EVOLVING POLITICS OF DISABILITY

These critiques beg the question of where to turn next. What options are left? If international agreements, measurable benchmarks, and financial incentives are not the answer to the problem of providing free public education to all children, particularly disabled children, then what is the answer? How can states with limited resources fund universal education and equal access for disabled people without the aid from bi- or multinationals? Should the international community leave the decision of whether or not to provide equal access to education to states? What should be the response if some states refuse or have no resources to provide education to disabled people, as has happened and is happening? How does the international Disability Rights Movement proceed forward if disabled people are left to struggle at a local level without external support when it is needed? Remembering those 900 million illiterate adults, millions of whom are disabled—how do they access the information needed for informed political action; who speaks with them?

Signatory states are not the only stakeholders in a double bind. The Disability Rights Movement in some countries is in the double bind described by Alur: needing resources the state cannot or will not provide, including external political pressure and financial assistance, but wanting control over the rights agenda for their own people, including the maintenance of important cultural features. A culturally sensitive approach is needed and can be extrapolated from the UN Convention's description of disability as an "evolving concept" that "results from the interaction between persons with impairments and attitudinal and environmental barriers that hinders [sic] their *full and effective participation in society on an equal basis with others* (emphasis added, United Nations, 2007a, Preamble [e]). Setting aside the argument that impairment is socially constructed and likely to differ across cultural spaces, and accepting that environmental barriers are fairly universal (i.e., not being able to get into a building has similar consequences regardless of the country in which the building is located), consider the cultural basis for the interplay between attitudes and "full and effective participation in society." EFA and its subsequent agreements including the Dakar Framework speak to the issue of "full and effective participation in society" but the enactment, goal setting, and assessment of progress have been geopolitically biased, as Alur (2007) has pointed out and Barton and Armstrong have cautioned against (2007). This artifact of colonialism neglects taking cultural or social histories, traditions, and expertise into account, as was the case in the Italian example of *integrazione* and the Indian example of Westerners serving as "expert" consultants.

Proposals for real solutions go well beyond the scope of this book and our current research. We can, however, pose two questions that might prompt future work that could be taken up by researchers in Disability Studies in Education. First, what does the current situation—the globalization of educational policy and politics—require of researchers and scholars around the world who are concerned about suffering, injustice, and the exclusion of disabled people from full participation in their own societies? This question should be paired with the caveat that researchers and scholars must avoid the neocolonialism reported in this chapter. One answer to the first question is in the text of EFA in four issues closely linked to disability: gender equity, early childhood education, literacy, vulnerable and disadvantaged children and ethnic minorities. Strategically situating disability as indivisible from such issues—which it is, of course—could be a persuasive approach for confronting the politics of silence. For example, equity for girls is closely linked to equity for disabled people, in part not only because many girls are disabled but also because of the risk to one vulnerable group when another vulnerable group is disenfranchised or made invisible.

Second, what roles could researchers and scholars play in supporting the development and dissemination of an international record of what Geertz (1985) might call local knowledge—broad disability rights discourses of justice that make sense within specific cultural contexts. How could this record be made available to stakeholders (e.g., EFA agencies, states, activists, etc.), what is the best form for communication with each stakeholder group, and what local and international political actions are needed to get agencies to take notice of and break out of the politics of silence? Similarly, how can international allies support local Disability Rights activists in their local work—speaking with but not for them?

Both of the above questions demand a politics of solidarity that unites disabled people and their allies, practitioners and researchers, activists and representatives of EFA agencies. Given the globalization of educational policy and the international politics of silence, Barton's (2001) call for "hope at the center of the struggles for inclusivity" (3) seems more necessary now than ever before.

NOTES

1. The Convention affirmed eight principles, which can be found at "Guiding Principles of the Convention," Retrieved January 20, 2008 from http://www.un.org/esa/socdev/enable/convinfoguide.htm.
2. The Optional Protocol includes eighteen Articles that outline additional responsibilities and procedures for signatories. The Optional Protocol is likely to be more difficult to pass governmental approval since it requires agreement to procedures and policies for action, whereas the Convention requires acknowledgment of shared values with no requirements for fulfilling them.
3. Ratification requires signing onto the Convention and the Optional Protocol.
4. South Africa, Australia, Canada, Malta, Belgium, Iceland, China, Colombia, India, New Zealand, Netherlands, Germany, United Kingdom.
5. South Africa, Malta, Belgium, Germany, Iceland.
6. Five international agencies are collaborating on EFA: United Nations Educational, Scientific and Cultural Organization (UNESCO); United Nations Children's Fund (UNICEF); United Nations Population Fund (UNFPA); United Nations Development Programme (UNDP); and the World Bank.
7. The phrase "politics of silence" is borrowed from R. Slee, "It's a fit-up! Inclusive education, higher education, policy and the discordant voice," in L. Barton & F. Armstrong, eds., *Policy, experience and change: Cross cultural reflections on inclusive education* (Dordrecht: Springer, 2007), pp. 177–188.
8. Examples of unreasonable goals include requirements of 50% improvement in literacy, universal education for all children, and gender equality in education by 2015, a mere fifteens years from the signing of the Dakar Framework.

REFERENCES

Alur, M. (2007). The lethargy of a nation: Inclusive education in India. In L. Barton & F. Armstrong, eds., pp. 91–106, *Policy, experience and change: Cross-cultural reflections on Inclusive education*. Dordrecht: Springer.

Armstrong, F. & Barton, L. (2007). Policy, experience and change and the challenge of inclusive education: The case of England. In L. Barton & F. Armstrong, eds., pp. 5–18, *Policy, experience and change: Cross-cultural reflections on inclusive education*. Dordrecht: Springer.

Barton, L. (2001). Disability, struggle and the politics of hope. In L. Barton, ed., pp. 1–10, *Disability politics and the struggle for change*. London: David Fulton Publishing.

Barton, L. & Armstrong, F. (2007). Introduction. In L. Barton & F. Armstrong, eds., pp. 1–4, *Policy, experience and change: Cross-cultural reflections on inclusive education*. Dordrecht: Springer.

Beratan, G. (2006). Institutionalizing ableism: Ableism, racism, and IDEA 2004. *Disability Studies Quarterly 26*(2). Retrieved March 28, 2006 from http://www.dsq-sds.org/current_issue.html.

Blanchett, W. J. (2006). Disproportionate representation of African American students in special education: Acknowledging the role of White privilege and racism. *Educational Researcher 35*(6), 24–28.

D'Alessio, S. (2007). *Integrazione scolastica and the new vision of inclusive education*. In L. Barton & F. Armstrong, eds., pp. 53–72, *Policy, experience and change: Cross-cultural reflections on inclusive education*. Dordrecht: Springer.

Geertz, C. (1985). *Local knowledge: Further essays in interpretive anthropology*. New York: Basic Books.

Goldstein, H. (2004). Education for all: The globalization of learning targets. *Comparative Education 40*(1), 7–14.

Meyer, L. H. (2003). Wanted: Internationally appropriate best practices. *Research and Practices for Persons with Severe Disabilities 28*(1), 33–36.

Philips, D. & Ochs, K. (2004). Researching policy borrowing: Some methodological challenges in comparative education. *British Educational Research Journal 30*(6), 773–784.

Reid, D. K. & Knight, M. G. (2006). Disability justifies exclusion of disabled students: A critical history grounded in disability studies. *Educational Researcher 35*(6). Retrieved July 7, 2007 from http://www.aera.net/uploadedFiles/Publications/Journals/Educational_Researcher/3506/05ERv35n6_Reid.pdf.

Slee, R. (2007). It's a Fit-Up! Inclusive education, higher education policy and the discordant voice. In L. Barton & F. Armstrong, eds., pp. 77–88, *Policy, experience and change: Cross-cultural reflections on inclusive education*. Dordrecht: Springer.

Smith, P. (2007). Treading water: Including students with intellectual disabilities in education. Paper presented at the annual meeting of the American Educational Research Association, Chicago, Illinois.

Tamatea, L. (2005). The Dakar Framework: Constructing and deconstructing the global neo-liberal matrix. *Globalisation, Societies and Education 3*(3), 311–334.

UNESCO (1990). *World declaration on education for all*. Retrieved July 13, 2007 from http://www.unesco.org/education/efa/ed_for_all/background/world_conference_jomtien.shtml.

UNESCO (1994). *Slamanca statement and framework for action on special needs education*. Salamanca, Spain. Retrieved July 10, 2007 from http://www.un.org/esa/socdev/enable/disovlf.htm.

UNESCO (1998). *World declaration on higher education for the twenty-first century: Vision and action*. Retrieved July 8, 2007 from http://www.unesco.org/education/educprog/wche/declaration_eng.htm.

UNESCO (1999). Salamanca five years out. A review of UNESCO activities in the light of the *Salamanca statement and framework for action on special needs education*. Paris: UNESCO.

UNESCO (2000). *Dakar framework for action*. Retrieved July 13, 2007 from http://unesdoc.unesco.org/images/0012/001211/121147e.pdf.

UNESCO (2002). *Education for all: An international strategy to put the Dakar framework for action on education for all into operation*. Paris: UNESCO.

UNICEF (2000). *Education and literacy*. Retrieved July 12, 2007 from http://www.unicef.org/specialsession/about/sgreport-pdf/sgrep_adapt_part2b_eng.pdf.

United Nations (2007a). *Convention on the rights of persons with disabilities.* Retrieved July 13, 2007 from http://www.un.org/esa/socdev/enable/rights/convtexte.htm.

United Nations (2007b). List of signatory states and regional integration organizations. Retrieved July 13, 2007 from http://www.un.org/esa/socdev/enable/conventionsign.htm.

United States Department of Education (2004). *Individuals with disability educational improvement act.* Washington, DC: U.S. Department of Education.

Section I
Inclusive Education

Uttering the word "inclusion" in educational circles can yield strong reaction, a composite of polysemy and heightened emotions, a wide distribution of interpretations combined with amplified sentiments on all possible sides. It appears that many educators have a strong, almost visceral reaction to the idea of inclusive education, particularly if it means that disabled and nondisabled students will be educated in the same classrooms. Yet, the idea of inclusive education in the world's schools and postsecondary institutions is more multiple than single, more wandering than static, more obscure than a clear program of educational programming, school reform, or pedagogical activity. Internationally speaking, inclusive education is in flux and the chapters in this section reveal that while there is hope there is also disappointment.

Multiple factors have contributed to the impassioned confusion and practical stalemates; this section explores three. First are the often overlooked sociohistorical contexts in which education is practiced. Viewed in this light, inclusive education is best recognized as embedded in the beliefs, rituals, and values of a culture as well as in the resources, policies, politics, and development priorities of a nation. For example, in their analysis of the discourse of educators in South Africa, Jabulani Ngcobo and Nithi Muthukrishna (chapter 2) conclude that medicalized constructions of disability as deficit or pathology play powerful roles in educators' thoughts and actions. This is the case in spite of the fact that the (Western) medicalization of disability is a philosophical import. Shifting to Italy, Beth Ferri's (chapter 3) chapter illustrates how school policies and practices in Italy reflect deeply cherished cultural understandings. Here, inclusive education within shared values of family and relationships is developed to a level of enviable success. In Zimbabwe, a grassroots disability rights movement has been documented for years (Peters and Chimedza, 2000), yet Auxilia Badza, David Chakuchichi, and Robert Chimedza (chapter 3) find that inclusive education policies have too little influence on the actual organizational and pedagogical practices in Zimbabwean schools. Susan Gabel and Jagdish Chander (chapter 5) explore culture, development priorities, and universal education in India. They show that although the Indian government recently made magnanimous commitments to "Education for All," it is stymied by a lack of reliable demographic data, limited resources, and cultural resistance.

Second, despite the extensive, high-quality international scholarship already available that articulates inclusive education in terms of school reform efforts, social justice missions, globalization, or national development, at its most basic, inclusion can be understood as a linguistic vessel that gains ideological positioning and practical fulfillment only when situated within macropolitical (i.e., national and regional education authorities) and micropolitical structures (i.e., schools and communities). Linda Graham and Roger Slee (chapter 6) demonstrate this vividly with their analysis of inclusive education reforms adopted in Queensland, Australia. Their deconstruction illustrates the ways in which ideology confers political status onto different categories of children. They ask who benefits from an inclusive system that creates a hierarchy of social identities resulting from the very processes of including. This recalls Slee and Allan's (2001) "Excluding the Included" in which they deconstruct a foible of inclusion—that it has to be called something at all. Further emphasizing the distance between policy rhetoric and the lived struggles of those actively devalued and pressed to the margins, Andrew Azzopardi (chapter 7) offers narratives of inclusion and exclusion in Malta. He finds that the meanings of inclusion in Maltan contexts involve extremes of hope and despair, a fitting and unsettling reminder of what is at stake in the semantic and ultimately ethical instability of inclusive education. Geert Van Hove, Griet Roets, Kathleen Mortier, Elisabeth De Schauwer, Mieke Leroy, and Eric Broekaert's (chapter 8) extensive work with Belgian parents of disabled children illustrates another perspective in the discourse of inclusion. While they argue "that everything starts with the plan that a family has for its child," the parents' narratives demonstrate that their children are "pigeonholed" as infants and that once in school the "person-centered planning" so lauded in early intervention is absent and their children are likely to be excluded with limited curricular options.

In the third and perhaps the most vivid example of the confusion and stalemates of the inclusion debates, Julie Allan and Roger Slee (chapter 9) investigate researchers whose work is "done under the rubric of inclusive education" and discover that they, too, are conflicted. It would seem that the problems of and concerns about inclusion occur at every social level, within most political systems, and are shared by almost all stakeholders.

It is interesting that the example of success in Italy demonstrates one of the primary criticisms of the practice of inclusive education. Ferri observes that Italian inclusion works in part because it operates within a single system of education. In contrast, Slee (1997) reminds us that in a dual system, the same special education personnel charged with managing social exclusion are the ones responsible for inclusion. The result in countries such as the United States, the United Kingdom, and others has been a creative and confounding effort to defend the status quo practices of often segregating disabled students while simultaneously embracing a new rhetoric of inclusive education. Slee (2001, 167) describes this as "resilience through linguistic dexterity," a strategy of retaining traditional ideological commitments and professional practices through the appropriation of a vocabulary that masks segregationism behind progressive terminology.

Central to this segregationist strategy is the framing of inclusion as a classroom placement decision that should be based on empirical research. In its rhetoric, *full* inclusion—for some, a fear-loaded term stirring images of general education classrooms overwhelmed by social diversity (Danforth and Morris, 2006)—is often positioned in opposition to a continuum of classroom placement options matching student needs and classroom resources, a construction ringing with themes of balance and reasonableness (Brantlinger, 1997). While full inclusion is described as failing empirical tests of effectiveness, the continuum of placement options is described as facilitating the professional address of individual student needs. What remain external to this framing of inclusive education are questions of ethical and political concern (Rice, 2005). Questions such as *How shall the members of diverse societies live and learn together?* and *What are our priorities for the distribution of resources and who gets to make these decisions?* are effectively marginalized by rhetorical renderings that subsume ethical and political considerations beneath the authority of a special education science and the bureaucratic tradition of individualized placement decision making.

Armstrong and Barton (2007) refer to inclusive education as a "flagship idea" that has been used to "transform cultures and practices … in celebration of diversity" while it simultaneously has been "colonized, hollowed out and transformed into an empty signifier" (5). This juxtaposition brings things full circle, back to the realization that when it comes to inclusive education there is hope and disappointment and that these usually exist in tandem. Whether the portrait is of national governmental initiatives or of classrooms in local communities, the view is like a hologram—what you see depends on where you stand in relation to it; however, regardless of the image represented, you know that with slight movement it will change.

Other authors in this volume address themes or topics related to inclusive education including: Shen, McCabe, and Zhaoyang (chapter 11); Moreno Angarita and Gabel (chapter 13); Gordon and Morton (chapter 14); Sinecka (chapter 16); Harwood and Humphrey (chapter 21); Powell, Felkendorff, and Hollenweger (chapter 29); Marshall (chapter 30); and Burgstahler and Cory (chapter 31).

REFERENCES

Armstrong, F., and Barton , L. (2007). Introduction. In L. Barton and F. Armstrong (Eds.), *Policy, experience and change: Cross-cultural reflections on inclusive education,* 5–18. Dordrecht: Springer.

Brantlinger, E. (1997). Using ideology: Cases of nonrecognition of the politics of research and practice in special education. *Review of Educational Research,* 67, 425–459.

Danforth, S., and Morris, P. (2005). Orthodoxy, heresy, and the inclusion of American students considered to have emotional/behavioral disorders. *International Journal of Inclusive Education,* 10, 2/3, 135–148.

Peters, S., and Chimedza, R. (2000). Conscientization and the cultural politics of education: A radical minority perspective. *Comparative Education Review,* 44, 3, 245–271.

Rice, N. (2005). Guardians of tradition: Presentations of inclusion in three introductory special education textbooks. *International Journal of Inclusive Education,* 9, 5, 405–429.

Slee, R. (2001). Social justice and the changing directions in educational research: The case of inclusive education. *International Journal of Inclusive Education,* 5, 2/3, 167–177.

Slee, R. (1997). Imported or important theory? Sociological interrogations of disablement and special education. *British Journal of Sociology of Education,* 18, 3, 407–419.

Slee, R., and Allan, J. (2001). Excluding the Included: A recognition of inclusive education. *International Studies in Sociology of Education,* 11, 2, 173–191.

CHAPTER TWO

Teachers' Dominant Discourses OF Inclusion AND Disability: A Case Study AT A Semi-rural Township School IN THE Province OF KwaZulu-Natal, South Africa

JABULANI NGCOBO AND NITHI MUTHUKRISHNA

INTRODUCTION

For decades, throughout the world disabled children and many others who experience a range of barriers to learning have traditionally been excluded from or marginalised within schools (Ainscow & Haile-Giorgis, 1998). These may include children who are already enrolled in education but for a range of reasons do not achieve adequately, those who are not enrolled in schools but who could participate if schools were more flexible in their responses toward them, and the relatively small group of children with more severe impairments who may have a need for some form of additional support.

It is a universally recognised fact that the prime objective of any education system in a society governed by the democratic ethos should be the provision of quality education to all learners so as to enable them to realise their full potential, rendering them able to meaningfully contribute to and participate in that society throughout their lives. This calls for the education system to ensure that the right to education is upheld as a fundamental constitutional right, and that it sets up systems and mechanisms to ensure the creation of equal opportunities in the education provision for effective learning by all learners irrespective of their differences. Article 28 of the Convention on the Right of the Child (United Nations, 1989) asserts the right of every child to education and requires that this should be provided for on the basis of equality of opportunity. A logical consequence of this right is that all children have the right to receive the kind of education that does not discriminate on grounds of disability, ethnic origin, religion, language, gender, race, capabilities, sex, socio-economic status, sexual orientation, age, and so on.

The major challenge for any country engaged in an effort to realise this imperative ambition is to ensure that the broad vision of Education for All (EFA) as an inclusive concept is reflected in all government policies. Education for All "… must take cognisance of the needs of the poor and the most disadvantaged, including working children, remote rural dwellers and nomads, and ethnic and linguistic minorities, children, young people and adults affected by conflict, HIV/AIDS, hunger and poor health and disabled persons …" (UNESCO, 2000b:19).

It is recognised that current strategies and programmes have largely been insufficient and/or inappropriate for meeting the needs of children and youth who are vulnerable to marginalisation and social exclusion. Where programmes targeting various marginalised and excluded groups do exist, they have functioned outside the mainstream—special programmes, specialised institutions, and specialist educators. Notwithstanding the best intentions, too often the result has been social exclusion, "second-rate" educational opportunities that do not guarantee the possibility to continue studies, or differentiation, becoming yet another form of discrimination, leaving children with various needs outside the mainstream of school life and later, as adults, outside community social and cultural life in general (UNESCO, 1999).

Despite encouraging developments there are still an estimated 113 million primary school-going children not attending school (International Consultative Forum on Education for All, 2000). Ninety percent of them live in low and lower middle income countries, and over 80 million of children out-of-school live in Africa, and of those who do enrol in primary school, large numbers drop out before completing their primary education (UNESCO, 2001). Reasons for this wastage are numerous, but there is also an emerging understanding that this could partly be attributed to the fact that our education systems lack the capacity, for a myriad of reasons, to adequately accommodate the diversity of needs of the learner population. As a response to this challenge, there have been encouraging developments in Southern Africa in setting up inclusive systems of education, aiming at meeting the needs of all learners irrespective of their differences within the mainstream education (UNESCO, 2002). These developments have been made visible in various ways: for instance, the 18th Conference of the Heads of State and Government of the Organisation of African Unity, held in Nairobi, Kenya, on the 27 June 1981, adopted the African Charter on Human and People's Rights (Organisation of African Unity, 1981); the Assembly of Heads of State and Government of the Organisation of African Unity, held in Addis Ababa, Ethiopia, in July 1990, adopted the African Charter on the Rights and Welfare of the Child (Organisation of African Unity, 1990); the African Union declared the first decade of the new millennium as the African Decade of Disabled People. This decade will be marked by a process of designing and implementing programmes for the development of disabled people in Africa.

South Africa did not participate in the Jomtien World Conference in 1990 because of its international isolation due to its apartheid policies. After its first democratic elections in 1994, South Africa was invited to participate in the EFA process, and was welcomed at the Mid-decade Review on EFA that was held in Amman, Jordan, in 1996. South Africa has, as a result, embraced the EFA principles, goals, targets, and guidelines contained in both the Declaration and the Framework for Action. In line with the international trend of ensuring the provision of quality education within mainstream education, South Africa has made significant strides towards the realisation of this goal. For the past ten years, South Africa has paid diligent attention to the fact that institutions of learning need to introspect and reflect on their roles and experiences in terms of what they are offering their learners and whether it meets the diverse range of needs of the learner population.

The ongoing transformation in South Africa has brought about numerous educational issues in sharp focus, resulting in the development of many new laws, policies, and practices. Since 1994, when the new democratic government came into power, South Africa has engaged in far-reaching and fundamental education reforms, thereby breaking decisively with the apartheid past.

The Constitution of the Republic of South Africa Act 108 of 1996 (Republic of South Africa, 1996a) is billed as one of the most progressive constitutions in the world, and codifies and safeguards the rights of all citizens. It reflects the struggles faced by the majority of South Africans and, consequently, to that effect comprises a Bill of Rights that ensconces the right of all learners, irrespective of race, gender, sex, pregnancy, marital status, ethnic or social origin, age, sexual orientation, disability, religion, conscience, belief, culture, language and birth, to basic education, and equal access to educational institutions (ibid.). This section of the constitution recognises sixteen different identities, with the intention of including them all constitutionally in the workings of the South African society (Carrim, 2002). The Bill of Rights lists equality as a substantive right, which, together with principles of human dignity and freedom, influences the interpretation of all other rights in the Bill of Rights. The constitution is founded on the fundamental values of equality, freedom, and non-racism. All the subsequent education legislation and policies are founded on the constitution, and accordingly recognise diversity and the provision of quality education to all learners within a non-segregated education system. These laws and policies provide a framework for the process of building an inclusive education and training system and are the initial strides towards inclusive education in South Africa (Donald, Lazarus, & Lolwana, 1997).

The *White Paper on Education and Training of 1995* (Department of Education, 1995) situates a particular importance on redressing educational inequalities amongst people who suffered particular injustices and all vulnerable groups including disabled persons. The South African Schools Act 84 of 1996 (Republic of South Africa, 1996b), which replaced Education acts of the apartheid regime, stresses the need for all public schools to provide quality education to all learners regardless of their difference: "a public school must admit learners and serve their educational requirements without unfairly discriminating in any way" (5[1]). An overarching policy in South Africa on disability issues is the *White Paper on an Integrated National Disability Strategy of 1997* (Office of the Deputy President, 1997) that acknowledges the fact that a human rights and development approach to disability has significant implications for the way in which education is provided in South Africa. This policy provides a blueprint for integration and inclusion of disability issues into every aspect of governance. Most centrally, it articulates a paradigm shift from dealing with disability-related issues as solely health and welfare issues to a rights-based integrated approach. *Education White Paper 6: Special Needs Education: Building an Inclusive Education and Training System of 2001* (Department of Education, 2001) outlines what an inclusive education and training system is, and how the Education Ministry intends to build it. It also spells out a new categorising principle: that of categorising by the level of support required rather than by a form of disability. This is a landmark policy paper which, as the minister of education points out, would cut our ties with the past and recognise the vital contribution that disabled people, in particular, are making and must continue to make, but as part of and not isolated from the flowering of our nation (ibid.). This legislative framework in South African education underscores the removal of disparities in education that seeks to equalise educational opportunity by attending to the specific needs of those who have been denied equality and access so far. Thus it is clear that there are discernable attempts, in terms of the policy framework, at "operationalizing the comprehensive inclusivity" (Carrim, 2002) contained in the Constitution of the Republic of South Africa.

Furthermore, at an international level, South Africa has ratified a number of international conventions that directly and/or indirectly protect the rights of disabled people, for instance, the Convention on the Rights of the Child (United Nations, 1989), Universal Declaration of Human Rights (United Nations, 1948), World Declaration on Education for All: Meeting Basic Learning Needs (UNESCO, 2000a), Convention against Discrimination in Education (UNESCO, 1960), to name but a few. The United Nations Standard Rules on the Equalisation of Opportunities for Persons with Disabilities (United Nations, 1993) have certainly been useful as a tool in assisting the process of policymaking in South Africa (McCain, 2002).

South Africa has demonstrated committed intention in that all her education policies, programmes and legislation that have emerged accentuate principles of social justice, quality education for all, the right to basic education, equality of opportunity, and redress of past educational disparities. This is indicative of political will to facilitate the transformation of the education system of South Africa. However, South Africa still faces major challenges in making a clean break with the legacy of the apartheid past, despite all these developments it has instituted to redress the imbalances and injustices of the past. In pursuing the process of confronting this legacy, in 1997 the minister and the Department of Education appointed the National Commission on Special Needs in Education and Training (NCSNET) and National Committee for Education Support Services (NCESS) to investigate and make recommendations on all aspects of "special needs and support services" in education and training in South Africa. The NCSNET/NCESS Report (Department of Education, 1997) reveals that the history of education for learners with disabilities in South Africa, like much of the history of our country, reflects massive deprivation and lack of provision for the majority of people. These inequities could be directly attributed to social, economic, and political factors that featured in the history of South African society during apartheid years. These factors had an adverse impact on educational opportunities for many learners from disadvantaged backgrounds. The highly inefficient and fragmented educational bureaucracy excluded and marginalised these learners and excluded them from the mainstream education provision, through entrenching inequalities by institutionalising racial segregation, labeling disabled learners, and separating them from their peers in mainstream schools.

The inequities in the racially determined provision of education for disabled learners, in particular, were exacerbated with the implementation in 1948 of the policy of separate development. The institutionalised apartheid in every aspect of South African life had a significant impact on special needs education. The establishment of the homeland system, the promulgation of Bantu Education Act (Department of Education, 1953), the Indian Education Act (Department of Education, 1965), and the Coloured Persons Education Act (Department of Education, 1963), all entrenched racial disparities and contributed to the massive inequalities and deprivation in educational provision that featured in the National Education Policy Investigation (NEPI) Report of 1992. The divisions in the education system were also reinforced during the apartheid regime by separate education departments being governed by different legislations. The special education area was doubly fragmented—on the one hand, by legislation and policy that enforced separation along racial lines and on the other, by a separation between "ordinary" learners in the mainstream system and learners with "special needs" in a secondary system.

Although South Africa has taken giant strides towards the development of an inclusive education and training system, the traces of the previous system still remain, as special education still exists as an elaborate second system that serves a small minority of learners. Provision of services and resources for black disabled children particularly in rural areas in KwaZulu-Natal remains largely inadequate. Because of the earlier history of racially segregated education in South Africa, such provision is either grossly lacking or non-existent (Perumal, 2005).

In South Africa, although inclusion of disabled children is now an option for parents, the country still faces stark realities as outlined above. *Education White Paper 6: Special Needs Education* (Department of Education, 2001) has legislated that placement in mainstream schools be an option for children with disabilities. This is accurately captured in the following clause:

> 1.3.7 In an inclusive education and training system, a wider spread of educational support services will be created in line with what learners with disabilities require. This means that learners who require low-intensive support will receive this in ordinary schools and those requiring moderate support will receive this in full-service schools. Learners who require high-intensive educational support will continue to receive such support in special schools. (ibid.:15)

However, research conducted by the NCSNET and the NCESS (Department of Education, 1997) indicates that despite the introduction of compulsory education, through the South African Schools Act (Department of Education, 1996) and other legislation, by the democratic government, there is still a mismatch between policy and practice, as many disabled children still remain excluded from formal education (many of them are still in community-run day care centres without appropriate educational provision), and that teachers often respond negatively to the inclusion of a disabled child in the classroom, and that disabled learners are not valued in the school environment. This is an indication of the fact that educational change is not simply a matter of redrafting legislation and restructuring services. The complexity of educational reform requires a more systematic and considered approach to the process of implementing change that targets both the culture and processes of organisational arrangements (Ball, 1987; Fullan, 1990 cited in Ainscow, 1999).

The study discussed in this chapter aimed at listening to the voices of teachers on how they position themselves within socially constructed discourses of disability and inclusion in a mainstream setting that has integrated disabled learners. This chapter explores the challenge of how teacher constructions of their experiences of inclusion of disabled learners shape their professional lives, beliefs, and practices, and questions the contradictions, contestations, and tensions embedded in these dominant discourses. In essence, the chapter seeks to analyze the interactional dynamics of inclusion and exclusion.

The key research questions of the study were: How do teachers position themselves within socially constructed discourses of disability and inclusion? How do teachers' constructions of their experiences of inclusion of disabled learners shape their professional lives, beliefs, and practices? What are the contradictions, contestations, and tensions embedded in these dominant discourses?

RESEARCH METHOD

Semi-structured interviews were held with five class teachers (one special education teacher and four general education teachers), and the school principal. The teachers ranged in age between thirty-one and fifty years. These teachers were all professionals who had a minimum teaching qualification of matric plus three years teacher training, and who had all done a one-year certificate course in special needs education. Two of them were studying for an honours degree in special needs education. The teachers had a teaching experience ranging from six to thirty years, and they had been teaching at this school for a minimum of six years. An interview guide was used to facilitate the interview process. The interview guide was important as it set out "a list of things to be sure to ask about" (Lofland & Lofland, 1995). The thinking behind using semi-structured interviews was to let the participants speak freely in their own words about how they experience a schooling environment that has integrated disabled learners.

Participants were interviewed one by one on different days. An hour was allocated per participant, and participants were allowed to respond in the language in which they were most comfortable. Most responses were given in IsiZulu, whilst in some cases, a mixture of IsiZulu and English was used. The principal was interviewed last, as the intention was to integrate issues raised by teachers in the interview with the principal. All interviews were audio taped and transcribed.

Observations were done in four classrooms three full days each to try and get a sense of interactions between disabled learners, able-bodied learners and, in particular, their teachers in general. We focussed on four classrooms because we wanted to observe lived experiences of disabled learners and their teachers in mainstream classrooms. Non-participatory observation was used to reduce any interaction with the participants and to focus the attention on the events (Burns, 2000). Observations were conducted at three staff meetings to listen to the conversations teachers held about their experiences with learners, and with disabled learners in particular. During observations, field notes were taken, cross-checked with the teachers at times to ensure that interactions and activities were correctly interpreted.

Although some documentation was regarded as confidential, the school was willing to allow us access to its documents on condition that they remained confidential. A careful examination was made of the relevant documents, including various school policies, children's workbooks, snap survey reports,[1] admission forms,[2] learners' progress reports, departmental correspondence.[3] Documents and artefacts were used to understand the context and triangulate data elicited through other methods (McMillan & Schumacher, 2001). The information generated from these artefacts provided a perspective on both the learners being written about and the individuals responsible for these documents.

The school where the research was conducted was established in 1973. It is situated in a densely populated semi-rural township in the northern parts of the province of KwaZulu-Natal, more than twenty-five kilometers away from town. The community has high levels of unemployment and poverty, and those who have jobs have to work in factories and mines far away from their homes. The annual household income for this community is low with 56% of the households earning Rs. 9,600 per annum or less (Rs. 800 per month or less), which would qualify these households for Indigent Support in terms of the Municipality's Indigent Policy. Twenty six percent (26%) of households could be classified as average income households with the remaining 18% being from the higher income category. Many of the learners at the school, therefore, come from working-class households; 368 learners (Male: 188; Female: 180) receive a child support grant; 1-rural29 learners (Male: 53 have only mother and 39 only father; Female: 37 have only mother) are raised by single parents. Although the school is within a walking distance from the tar road, the road leading to the school is a dirt road in a very poor condition—more like a footpath than a road.

The school has a learner population of 1250 with an age range of 3–17, and runs from crèche to grade 4. There are 95 over-age learners, who actually should be at high school according to the departmental regulations for admission. These include learners with disabilities. All the disabled learners in this school were included when the school took a conscious decision to open itself for the admission of disabled learners. The school has integrated 93 learners classified as learners with special needs: 10 deaf; 2 epileptic; 4 physically disabled; 3 cerebral palsied; 1 autistic and 73 experiencing various learning difficulties. These learners ranged in age as follows: deaf: 6–2; epileptic: 10–16; physically disabled: 8–14; cerebral palsied: 12–13; autistic: 9; and experiencing learning difficulty: 6–17, and they have been integrated in four grades, that is, grades 1–4. All learners are African, and most come from the area where the school is situated, whilst a few others from as far as outside the province of KwaZulu-Natal. The language of learning (LOL) at the school is English for hearing learners and the South African Sign Language for deaf learners. The home languages for learners range from SiSwati, South African Sign Language, IsiZulu to Sesotho.

DISCUSSION OF FINDINGS: THE DISCOURSE OF DIFFERENCE

In this study, the analysis focussed on identifying discourses in teachers' constructions of their experience of inclusion at a mainstream school that has integrated disabled learners, in particular, on whether these discourses are legitimated and whether they impact certain knowledges and practices while silencing or challenging others.

BEING "NORMAL": MYTHS AND MISCONCEPTIONS

Teachers' narratives revealed that they had not had any close interaction with a person with a disability before their experience at the school; they only "saw them from a distance." They started interacting closely with disabled persons after the school's decision to admit disabled children. Teachers' practices and thoughts were predominantly shaped by the way in which society sees difference. Using the "normal" as an ideal, teachers saw their understanding of difference as normal and natural. They reported experiencing mixed feelings on their first encounter with disabled learners. "I was happy for them, but at the same time I felt this was a challenge." Some reported that they were afraid of a learner with a disability: "I must speak for myself. I was afraid of them. There was a child who I taught, Sambo; he was disabled and I was very scared of him."

Some teachers thought that being close to disabled children would cause problems in their personal lives: "I think … I was scared that I was going to get a child like that." There were also feelings of not knowing what to do about teaching them—of confusion. This led to a range of reactions towards disabled children. For instance, one teacher reported that

> "… There was a physically disabled child … you could see from the face of the teacher that when the child approaches …, it was like the teacher wanted to push him away …"

Some teachers reported that all their lives they had been separated from disabled people, with disabled people receiving their education in special schools, and not in mainstream schools. Teachers believed that this was a "natural" arrangement of how life should be, and were, therefore, not socialised to want to be associated with disabled learners because theirs was not a special school: " … we know that if you go to [name of special school] … we know that those children are like that, … so the presence of them here … we did not need this …" Most of these teachers had been effectively shaped and deprived by the normalizing gaze of the opportunity to resist these social constructions of difference. As a result, they seemed to have no desire to revolt against the deficit construction of difference.

PATHOLOGISING DIFFERENCE

Despite having spent more than four years with disabled children, discourses of difference as deficit still emerged in the way teachers constructed learner identities. Learners were often constructed as not meeting some pre-established norm or standard of the "real" child as found in the study by Reay (2004: 32). Teachers' narratives revealed that the learner with a disability was receiving judgement that they were different, marked, or inferior. Two of the teachers reported,

> They [disabled children] are very short-tempered. They are easily irritable … This other boy, Sizwe, he is bully—he beats others.

> … most of them [disabled children] are very disruptive. They are disruptive even in the classroom.

So, when the school was opened to learners with disabilities, these constructions of difference that hold individuals in a "mechanism of objectification" (Foucault, 1977: 187) continued to exist. This constructed disabled learners as individual objects to be "treated," "changed," "improved," "trained or corrected," and "normalised" (ibid.: 191). Within this context, teachers' narratives revealed that teachers understood their role as helping disabled learners do ordinary things, in order for them to gain the required amount of social capital, to become "more like us." As one teacher expresses the notion:

> … they can now fit in the mainstream classroom …

The problematic dimension of this is that if teachers are out to make disabled learners "more like us," the unique abilities and potentials of learners are likely to be disregarded, promoting human helplessness as power is stripped from the learner (Clark, Dyson, & Millward, 1998).

CONTRADICTIONS AND SILENCES IN AN UNEQUAL SOCIETY

Teachers' narratives seemed to construct difference into dichotomies that functionally erased ambiguities of membership and stigmatised disabled learners. Teachers were still using particular terms such as "right," "normal," "capable," "able," "complete" to refer to able-bodied learners. These terms are directly contrastable with "wrong," "abnormal," "incapable," "unable," and "incomplete." However, there were silences in teachers' voices with regard to references to disabled learners. Teachers would refer or imply disabled learners by referring to able-bodied learners. For instance, one teacher thought that we must,

> mix them [disabled learners] with those that are "normal" in the mainstream class …

Teachers would not articulate the fact that they considered disabled learners as "abnormal" or "not normal," but would imply that by referring to able-bodied learners as "normal." The main tactic used by teachers here was to try to pretend that everything was normal, avoiding all direct reference to disability (Allan, Brown, & Riddell, 1998). As Michalko (1999) argues, the problematic dimension of this dichotomous construction was that in each case, one "side" of the dichotomy was stigmatised. For example, in the constructed binary of disabled/able-bodied, the assumption was that disabled is "adversity," and able-bodied is "trouble free." In such a case, difference from the normative measure was socially constructed as "deficit" rather than an alternate ontology (Gordon & Rosenblum, 2001). This was a problematic view because whatever disabled learners thought of themselves, they were constantly given a negative, devalued, stigmatised identity by society, and much of their social life was a struggle against this imposed image. On the other hand, difficulties that the so-called trouble-free, able-bodied child might be experiencing were concealed and could not be interrogated. This shows how difficult it was for these teachers to challenge dominant discourses and to participate in the construction of alternate ones. Teachers were often caught in the web of the gaze of normalcy characterised by a tissue of myths, fears, and misunderstandings that society attaches to the status of people who are disabled.

INCLUSION, EMPATHY, OR FEAR?

Teachers' narratives revealed that the biggest difference between disability and other stigmatised statuses such as black, female, and so on, is that, in the other cases, the non-stigmatised have little or no fear of suddenly joining the ranks of the stigmatised (ibid., 2001). For instance, white people do not worry about becoming black; men do not worry about becoming women. The fact that disability is always a potential status was evident in expressions such as "… anyone can find himself like them. The situation can change at any time. I could be disabled the time I go out of that door."

Teachers mentioned a number of situations that might cause a person to be disabled, including the one in which one might be involved in a car accident, and in that way become disabled:

> "… sometimes you find that when the child was born he was right, and he was involved in a car accident and was hurt in the head … we had a child … he was not born disabled … he was involved in a car accident";

Life situations that affect people's mental status negatively:

There are situations here … which affect one's state of mind to an extent that one could develop a mental illness … I may find myself crazy and picking up papers …

Accidents that happen during learning and teaching:

> During learning, let's say we are conducting a scientific experiment, I may have a certain dangerous chemical substance blowing into my eyes and end up being blind.

For these teachers, a variety of things could lead to disability for anyone at any time. However, their constructions of being disabled as being pitiful, helpless, and unfortunate, resembled a recoiling to workings of the discourse of charity.

AGAINST WHOSE STANDARDS?

Narratives of teachers who had a disabled child in their classroom presented disabled learners as heroes who are able to beat oppression and do better than those who have more access to social power. This is how one teacher described Sabelo, an epileptic learner, in her class:

> This boy, Sabelo, is very good. He even beats those that are normal.

There are three problematic dimensions of this view. The first one has to do with the measure or standard against which disabled learners are being measured. This view brings disabled learners under the measure of dominant culture (Young, 2000). The second concern is linked to the first one. The fact that disabled learners' performance was seen to be above some pre-established standard is likely to cause the school not to interrogate its norms, beliefs, and values of operation and to carry on business as usual. The third one has to do with those disabled learners and able-bodied learners who do not have adequate "means of control" to handle the situation of being oppressed (Quin, 2004). There is high probability that teachers might think that just because a certain learner can do well, why cannot others like him or her or those that are "more normal" than him or her do as well?

EDUCATION FOR ALL: POLICY-PRACTICE TENSIONS

Enabling Mechanisms?

The policy commitment of the Department of Education suggests that specific enabling mechanisms and processes are needed to enable the education system to address, minimise, and prevent barriers to learning and development that may exist or arise (Department of Education, 1997; 2001). Teachers in this study reported as their major concern the lack of capacity and vision in some departmental officials in providing the required services to assist them in ensuring quality education for all learners. This is how some of the teachers expressed tensions in working with departmental officials:

> … sometimes I find that some departmental officials' views obstruct what I am trying to do here …

> My prayer is that if people could learn not be crazy about promotions and want to be promoted to offices before they are mature and experienced, because you find that once people are in these offices, they do not know what to do and how to do it. You find that if you need help and you call these people to the school, they have no clue how to go about dealing with your case …

> … PGSES [Psychological, Guidance and Special Education Services] does not visit our school … you call them, they do not come … that frustrates us a lot …

> The Department does conduct workshops, but facilitators lack in-depth knowledge of inclusive education—you see this when a person is talking about something that he does not understand. The bad thing is that we expect something better from these people; they are our seniors. …

> … it should only be [name of the official] who visits our school, because other officials are unable to assist us, and we should wait for [name of the official] …

> Sometimes you find that they do not invite us … I do not understand why they sometimes sideline us as if we do not belong in this district … that frustrates us … having our progress working against us.

The above excerpts, first, paint a picture of departmental officials who lack awareness, are demoralised, have fear, and lack confidence and competence in dealing with a diverse range of learner needs. This suggests a dearth of skills and knowledge, and highlights a system that is unable to meet a diversity of learner needs despite policy imperatives. If becoming an effective school happens to be riddled with so many tensions, how are other schools going to be motivated to work towards becoming inclusive schools? Landsberg, Kruger, and Nel (2005) argue that support is the cornerstone of successful inclusive education. Poor service and support make it impossible to operate schools and classrooms as centres of care and support, with an ethos that everyone belongs, is accepted, welcomed, and supported. If left unattended to, this lack of support for teachers could result in further marginalisation, exclusion, and alienation of disabled learners placed in mainstream schools.

Second, special education has, for many years, been the responsibility of the directorate of PGSES. With the new policy of inclusion, educational inclusion has to be an issue for the entire education system. So, seeing the issue of educational inclusion as the issue for the PGSES only, and not the business of the entire education system, certainly will not help transform the entire education system into an inclusive education system where everyone in the Department of Education works to ensure unrestricted access for all learners. Furthermore, this view could lead to individuals seeing the problem of oppression as an issue for certain sections of society, for certain sections of the education department, for certain schools, for certain learners, for certain teachers, for certain parents, as is the case in this school, where disabled learners could be placed or accommodated only in classrooms of certain teachers, and not others.

Moreover, according to the narratives of teachers, the major difficulty that the school had was that the education system did not seem ready to support their schools to implement policy. In discussing the UK system, Ainscow (99) alludes to the fact that "there is a major problem of how to redesign a system of education that still bears many of the features of the purpose for which it was originally formulated," that of educating those who are "normal" in mainstream schools and those who are disabled in special schools, and orchestrating all provisioning norms within such framework. The teachers alluded to the same tension in South Africa. Teachers reported that their school had had to face not being able to get teachers who are qualified to deliver a curriculum for all—a curriculum characterised by unrestricted access, non-discrimination, flexibility, participation, responsiveness, and sensitivity to the diverse needs of the learner population. The principal reported that the school had often been left with no alternative but to appoint anyone who, most often, had to learn along the way. The feeling was that this was putting learners at further risk of failure.

In addition to the above, teachers' narratives also revealed that some teachers saw the issue of educational exclusion and inclusion only in relation to special needs education. Their views were not able to "go beyond those of disablement"

(Barton, 1999: 58). Teachers' narratives seemed to be dominated by references to disabled learners. Teachers' voices about able-bodied learners were silent. For instance, when teachers were asked to suggest features of what they would consider an inclusive school, their responses were littered with phrases and statements such as "… you should see signs … of deaf people …"; "… there was a child who was wheelchair-bound …"; "… if we are to accommodate those that are on wheelchairs …"; "There are children who walk on crutches …"; "There must also be those who have speech and hearing problems"; "That is why we said every parent who has a disabled child should bring him to the school." Barton argues for placing the issue of disability alongside all forms of oppression in a human rights framework. This will facilitate a process of addressing the needs of all learners, assist in developing an equitable education system that echoes and reflects fundamentals of an equitable society (Dyson, 1999). Within such a framework, educational inclusion would be premised on the principle of "education for all pupils" (Slee, 2001: 115).

According to the South African policy of inclusive education as enshrined in *Education White Paper 6: Special Needs Education: Building an Inclusive Education and Training System* (Department of Education, 2001), disability is not presented as the "barrier to learning and development," but as one of the barriers to learning and development that the policy identifies. A number of writers agree that for all learners to be fully accommodated, teachers need to shift from one set of assumptions, beliefs, values, norms, relationships, behaviours, and practices to another that entails a fundamental reculturing of teaching and learning (Hargreaves, 1994: 255; 1997: 1; Miller, 1998: 530; Fullan, 1998: 226 cited in Pettipher, 2000).

THE RED GROUP, THE ORANGE GROUP, AND THE GREEN GROUP: AN INCLUSIVE CURRICULUM?

As part of the study, three days were spent observing one of the classes that had included disabled learners. In this class, children were arranged predominantly according to their assumed abilities to participate in the teaching and learning process. Children were divided into three groups here. We call these groups the red group, the orange group, and the green group. The red group included children seen as having lower ability and as struggling with many aspects of their work. This group also included disabled learners, whom the teacher referred to as "LSEN," an acronym for learners with special educational needs. Because most disabled learners at the school were over-age, owing to having no access in their local mainstream schools, all over-age disabled learners were categorised and placed in the red group with the assumption that they were behind with their work. The orange group comprised children of medium ability, who would do well or do badly depending on their circumstances at a particular point in time. The green group comprised children who were seen as having higher ability, who appeared to have good self-esteem, and who were always called upon by the teacher to demonstrate tasks to other children.

The children were clearly aware of how they came to be in their respective groups. For example, after a spelling task, Khetha broke down and cried. There was absolute quiet in the classroom. When asked why he was crying, he replied still crying, "I do not want to belong to that group anymore. I did not even obtain a single correct answer." When probed further, the child mentioned that his parents had brought him to the school because he was repeating classes at his previous school. So, he knew why he had been brought to this school, and why the teacher had placed him in the red group.

When asked about this arrangement of children, the teacher explained that such grouping makes organisation, planning, and teaching easier because, "I know exactly who I am dealing with." All learning and teaching activities were synchronised on the basis of this group arrangement of children. During the entire period of observation in this classroom, the children never operated outside these groups.

The observations also revealed that the teacher played a significant role in further stigmatising the red group, by making it known to children who and why they belonged in the red group. For example, Billy, in the green group, was continuously disrupting the class. To try and stop this behaviour, the teacher said to him, "If you continue disrupting the class like this, I will be forced to move you to that group," pointing in the direction of the red group. Comments such as this one made it easy for children to identify who belongs to the red group and why. This marked, marginalised, and stigmatised learners who belonged to the red group. For the three days of observation in this classroom, the teacher would everyday first teach and give tasks to the orange and the green groups, and the red group would be last to receive attention. In the minds of most children, first means important and better, and last means unimportant and bad. Questions should be asked about how easy it is for children in the red group to improve their performance. For children who do not have enough means of control (Quin, 2004), reclaiming their status in the green group is a myth. In South Africa, numerous factors render children vulnerable, and as a result, for most disabled children the exit door out of the "red group" is always locked whilst the entrance door is always wide open.

Contrary to what happened in this classroom, for teachers to teach and organise their classrooms in a way that accommodates diversity, there needs to be flexibility in classroom organisation. Teachers need to experiment with a range of class groupings. These include mixed ability groups, cross-grade groupings and multi-age groupings. Learners should be regarded as an invaluable resource in the teaching and learning process, because they have diverse backgrounds, differing prior learning experiences, differing cultural experiences, different learning styles and so on. Use of co-operative approaches based on the thinking that learners learn from each other would help facilitate this. Co-operative learning involves structuring learning tasks so that learners work in small groups and each learner's efforts contribute to the group's goals (Pettigrew & Akhurst, 1999). In this sense, learners are the centre of the learning and teaching process, and are seen as a source of knowledge, and the teacher is not the only source.

CONCLUSION

Since 1994, the new democratic government of South Africa has embarked on a mission to develop an education system that is able to respond to a diverse range of needs of the learner population. The study presented in this chapter revealed a number of challenges that teachers still faced to be able to accommodate the interests of all learners. Although they should be lauded for embracing an innovation in their school, most of the teachers indicated that they were not yet ready to implement the inclusive education policy. The major lesson that could be learned is that successful implementation of any policy, particularly in a developing context, is not an easy process. It has a myriad of contextual factors. In education these could include, inter alia, the education system itself, education support services, infrastructural backlog and inequity, socio-economic conditions, and so on.

One key barrier that needs to be removed to meet the challenge of ensuring a quality education that fulfils the needs of all learners, particularly in South Africa, is the perception that inclusive education can be implemented within the current education system with minor changes (Lloyd, 2000). Reasons for this kind of thinking often emanate from the limited financial resources within which most of the developing world has to operate. South Africa, as a developing country, is no exception to this rule. However, there is no way new policies could be implemented in a context that was originally designed to fulfil very different goals. For instance, the South African education system was originally designed to serve as an arm of the apartheid state machinery. Therefore, for successful implementation of inclusive education policy in South Africa, radical changes in the education system as a whole have to be made, because South African society now wants to use the education system for a very different purpose.

As inclusion is not simply an add-on to the current operations of a school or an education system, significant restructuring and reculturing processes are needed in the area of how teachers do their work. However, South Africa needs to face up to significant realities to achieve this imperative. One of the major challenges that South Africa continues to face is the re-training and upgrading of the teacher cadre to enable them to provide quality education to all learners. Teachers and their work are one of the crucial ingredients of the successful implementation of the new policy of inclusive education. The responsibility of making the imperatives of the policy of inclusive education visible in the South African schools and classrooms rests, to a significant extent, on the shoulders of teachers who are often ill-equipped for this very important task. It must be borne in mind that South African teachers in the past have not been trained to respond to a wide range of barriers to learning and development (Department of Education, 1997; 2001), including disability. Nor have most of them been equipped to understand and respond to other aspects of diversity in the learner population, for example, those with exceptional ability, living and affected with HIV and AIDS, who abuse substances, who have been traumatised by violence, who come from unstable family conditions, and so on. As a result, they often find it threatening to have to change their tried and tested teaching methods to accommodate disabled children—they have a fear of not being able to manage diversity in the classroom.

A number of school reform initiatives in South Africa have led to the call for the restructuring and reculturing of education to include in school and community life those children who, in the past, have been excluded. This requires communities to build a school environment in which the needs of every child are accommodated and success is fostered for all. This means that all children, irrespective of the type or severity of their perceived educational, physical, or psychological challenge, are valued; and school personnel, family members, friends and the community at large work together to develop and support caring learning communities that acknowledge and celebrate difference.

NOTES

1. Statistical data on learners in a particular school for a specific year.
2. Forms that have to be filled in when learners are being admitted to a school.
3. Circulars written by the Department of Education to schools.

REFERENCES

Ainscow, M. (1999). *Understanding the Development of Inclusive School.* London & Philadelphia: Falmer Press.

Ainscow, M., & Haile-Giorgis, M. (1998). *The Education of Children with Special Needs: Barriers and Opportunities in Central and Eastern Europe.* Florida: United Nations Children's Fund, International Child Development Centre.

Allan, J., Brown, S., & Riddell, S. (1998). Permission to Speak: Theorising Special Education Inside the Classroom. In C. Clark, A. Dyson, & A. Millward (Eds.), *Theorising Special Education* (pp. 21–31). London: Routledge.

Ball, S.J. (1987). *The Micro-politics of the School.* London: Methuen.

Barton, L. (1999). Market Ideologies, Education and the Challenge for Inclusion. In H. Daniels & P. Gartner (Eds.), *Inclusive Education, World Yearbook of Education* (pp. 54–62). London.

Burns, R.B. (2000). *Introduction to Research Methods.* London: Sage Publications.

Carrim, N. (2002). *Inclusion/Exclusion in South African Education: A Discussion Paper.* Unpublished manuscript. University of Sussex, Sussex.

Clark, C., Dyson, A., & Millward, A. (Eds.) (1998). *Theorising Special Education.* London: Routledge.

Department of Education. (1953). *Bantu Education Act.* Pretoria: Government Printer.

Department of Education. (1963). *Coloured Persons Education Act.* Pretoria: Government Printer.

Department of Education. (1965). *Indian Education Act.* Pretoria: Government Printer.

Department of Education. (1995). *White Paper on Education and Training of 1995.* Pretoria: Government Printer.

Department of Education. (1997). *Quality Education for All: Overcoming Barriers to Learning and Development. Final Report of National Commission on Special Needs in Education Training (NCSNET) and National Committee on Education Support Services (NCESS).* Pretoria: Government Printer.

Department of Education. (2001). *Education White Paper 6: Special Needs Education: Building an Inclusive Education and Training System.* Pretoria: Government Printer.

Donald, D., Lazarus, S., & Lolwana, P. (1997). *Educational Psychology in Social Context: Challenges of Development, Social Issues, and Special Need in Southern Africa.* Cape Town: Oxford University Press.

Dyson, A. (1999). Inclusion and Inclusions: Theories and Discourses in Inclusive Education. In H. Daniels & P. Garner (Eds.), *Inclusive Education* (pp. 36–53). London: Kogan Page.

Foucault, M. (1977). *Discipline and Punish: The Birth of the Prison.* Harmondsworth: Penguin.

Fullan, M. (1990). *Implementation and Change.* Milton Keynes: Open University Press.

Fullan, M. (1998). The Meaning of Educational Change: A Quarter of a Century of Learning. In A. Hargreaves, A. Lieberman, M. Fullan, & D. Hopkins (Eds.), *International Handbook of Educational Change. Part 1* (pp. 214–228). London: Kluwer Academic Publishers.

Gordon, B.O., & Rosenblum, K.E. (2001). Bringing Disability into the Sociological Frame: A Comparison of Disability with Race, Sex and Sexual Orientation Statuses. *Disability & Society, 16*(1), 5–19.

Hargreaves, A. (1994). *Changing Teachers, Changing Times. Teachers' Work and Culture in the Postmodern Age.* London: Cassell.

Hargreaves, A. (1997). Rethinking Educational Change: Going Deeper and Wider in the Quest for Success. In A. Hargreaves (Ed.), *Rethinking Educational Change with Heart and Mind* (pp. 1–26). Alexandria, Virginia: Association for Supervision and Curriculum Development.

International Consultative Forum on Education for All. (2000). *Global Synthesis. Education for All Year 2000 Assessment.* Paris: UNESCO Publishing.

Kriegler, S., & Farman, R. (1994). Redistribution of Special Education Resources in South Africa: Beyond Mainstreaming Towards Effective Schools for All. *International Journal of Special Education, 9*(1), 1–12.

Landsberg, E., Kruger, D., & Nel, N. (Eds.) (2005). *Addressing Barriers to Learning: A South African Perspective.* Pretoria: Van Schaik Publishers.

Lloyd, C. (2000). Excellence for *All* Children—False Promises! The Failure of Current Policy for Inclusive Education and Implications for Schooling in the 21st Century. *International Journal of Inclusive Education, 42*(2), 133–153.

Lofland, J., & Lofland, L.H. (1995). *Analyzing Social Settings: A Guide to Qualitative Observation and Analysis.* California: Wadsworth Publishing Company.

McCain, C. V. (2002). Governance and Legislation in South Africa; A Contemporary Overview, *Disability World 12,* 1–6.

McMillan, J.H., & Schumacher, S. (2001). *Research in Education: A Conceptual Introduction.* New York: Longman.

Michalko, R. (1999). *The Two in One: Walking with Smokie, Walking with Blindness.* Philadelphia, PA: Temple University Press.

Miller, L. (1998). Redefining Teachers, Reculturing Schools. Connections, Commitments and Challenges. In A. Hargreaves, A. Lieberman, M. Fullan, & D. Hopkins (Eds.), *International Handbook of Educational Change. Part 1* (pp. 529–543). London: Kluwer Academic Publishers.

Office of the Deputy President (1997). *White Paper on an Integrated Disability Strategy.* Pretoria: Government Printers.

Organisation of African Unity. (1981). *African Charter on Human and People's Rights.* Nairobi, Kenya: OAU Publishing.

Organisation of African Unity. (1990). *African Charter on the Rights and Welfare of the Child.* Addis Ababa, Ethiopia: OAU Publishing.

Perumal, J. (2005). *Towards Inclusive Education: Exploring Policy, Context and Change through an Ethnographic Study in a Rural Context in KwaZulu-Natal.* Ph.D. dissertation, University of KwaZulu-Natal, Durban, South Africa.

Pettigrew, L., & Akhurst, J. (1999). *Learning and Teaching: Psychological Perspectives.* Pietermaritzburg: School of Education, Training and Development, University of Natal.

Pettipher, R. (2000). *Jack of All Trades for Manager of All: Roles of the Inclusive Principal.* Paper presented at ISEC 2000.

Quin, J. (2004). *Social Issues in Education.* Pietermaritzburg: School of Education, Training and Development, University of KwaZulu-Natal.

Reay, D. (2004). Finding or Losing Yourself? Working-Class Relationships to Education. In S.J. Ball (Ed.), *Sociology of Education.* London: Routledge/Falmer Press.

Republic of South Africa. (1996a). *Constitution of the Republic of South Africa (Act 103 of 1996).* Pretoria: Government Printer.

Republic of South Africa. (1996b). *South African Schools Act 84 of 1996.* Pretoria: Government Printer.

Slee, R. (2001). "Inclusion in Practice": Does Practice Make Perfect? *Educational Review, 53*(2), 113–123.

UNESCO. (1960). *Convention against Discrimination in Education.* Paris: UNESCO.

UNESCO. (1999). *Welcoming Schools: Students with Disabilities in Regular Schools.* Paris: UNESCO.

UNESCO. (2000a). *The Dakar Framework for Action. Education for All: Meeting Our Collective Commitments.* Retrieved January 6, 2006, from http://www2.unesco.org/wef/en-conf/dakframeng.shtm.

UNESCO. (2000b). *World Declaration on Education for All: Meeting Our Basic Learning Needs.* Paris: UNESCO.

UNESCO. (2001). *The Open File on Inclusive Education.* Paris: UNESCO.

UNESCO. (2002). *Inclusive Education in Southern Africa: Responding to Diversity in Education.* Harare: UNESCO.

United Nations. (1948). *Universal Declaration of Human Rights.* Geneva: United Nations Department of Public Information.

United Nations. (1989). *Convention on the Rights of the Child.* Geneva: United Nations Publishing.

United Nations. (1993). *United Nations Standard Rules on the Equalisation of Opportunities for Persons with Disabilities.* Geneva: United Nations Department of Public Information.

Young, I.M. (2000). Five Faces of Oppression. In M. Adams, W.J. Blumenfeld, R. Castaneda, H.W. Hackman, M.L. Peters, & X. Zuniga (Eds.), *Readings for Diversity and Social Justice* (pp. 35–49). New York: Routledge.

CHAPTER THREE

Inclusion IN Italy: What Happens WHEN Everyone Belongs

BETH A. FERRI

Two decades after the historic *Brown v. Board of Education* decision in the United States in 1954, the 1970s marked a watershed decade for policies ensuring the right to education for children with disabilities. Like the United States, which passed Public Law 94–412 in 1975 (reauthorized as the Individuals with Disabilities Education Act or IDEA in 1990), Italy also enacted progressive, groundbreaking laws affecting students with disabilities during this time. What distinguishes Italian educational policy, however, is its early implementation of full inclusion—beginning more than twenty years before the *Salamanca Statement and Framework of Action on Special Needs Education* (UNESCO, 1994), which called for the universal implementation of inclusion. In this chapter, I highlight the major differences between the Italian and U.S. inclusion policies and practices. I then review relevant research on teacher attitudes regarding inclusion. Finally, I share insights from observations and interviews with teachers and administrators conducted during a month-long study of inclusion in Italy. I conclude with lessons that U.S. educators can take away from the Italian approach to inclusive education.

A TALE OF TWO COUNTRIES: INCLUSION IN ITALY AND THE UNITED STATES

In the 1970s Italy began passing important legislation assuring the right to education for students with disabilities. In 1971, for example, National Law 118 guaranteed the right to a public education for children with disabilities in general education classes. Circulare 227, which was passed in 1975, stated that the severity of disability could not be used as a reason to prevent integration. Finally, in 1977, Italian National Law 517 outlined specific guidelines for including students with disabilities in general education classrooms—reforms that were instrumental in transforming all of education in Italy. For example, National Law 517 reduced the maximum size of an integrated (or inclusive) class to twenty; limited the number of students with disabilities per class to no more than two; and, integrated special services for students with disabilities in the general education classroom. The law, in addition to abolishing special classes and special schools, also ended the practice of ability tracking (Berrigan, 1988), which has been linked to multiple and long-standing forms of educational inequity (Oakes, 1985; Oakes, Wells, Jones, & Datnow, 1997).

In the United States, the Education of All Handicapped Children Act of 1975 stipulated that eligibility for services and determination of an appropriate educational placement were to be made on the basis of a clinical evaluation of the child. A team of professionals, in consultation with the parent(s) or guardians of the child, was entrusted with the task of considering the most appropriate placement among a continuum of service options.[1] Placement options ranged from the general education class to special school placements, although most commonly they involved special classes organized around particular disability labels for either part or all of the school day. Although the concept of *least restrictive* in the U.S. policy seems to ensure a range of choices, it functions in such a way as to legitimize restrictive placements (Taylor, 1988). Thus, by codifying the idea of *least* restrictive, the law simultaneously suggests that a certain degree of restrictiveness is necessary and appropriate. In the decades following the passage of this law (later renamed IDEA), scholars began to document and question the overrepresentation of students of color and the restrictiveness of their placements (Harry & Klingner, 2006; Losen & Orfield, 2002; Wang, Reynolds, & Walberg, 1986).

While the Education of All Handicapped Children Act of 1975 (Public Law 94–142) guaranteed a free and appropriate public education in the *least restrictive environment*, Italian Law 118 (1971) went a step further by specifying the right of children with disabilities to be educated *in regular classes*. Thus, while the U.S. policies created and then maintained a dual system of general education and special education, the Italian system merged and transformed the two into an entirely new system of education. Because of their early implementation, Italy has long been regarded as a model for inclusive education by such agencies as the United Nations Educational, Scientific and Cultural Organization (UNESCO) and the Organisation for Economic Co-operation and Development (OECD). As

Zambelli and Bonni (2004) contend, Italy is an example of an "advanced model of inclusion" (p. 352). They write that embracing inclusion has meant, "above all, accepting difference and operating in such a way that these [differences] are not transformed into injustices" (p. 351).

Another important aspect of the Italian system of inclusion is the *sostegno*, or support teacher, who serves as a partner to the general education teacher. Roughly equivalent in training to a dual certified teacher in the United States, the *sostegno* is assigned to a whole class, not to an individual child. He/she collaborates with the regular education teacher, modifying curricula as necessary and providing instructional support for all children in the classroom. The *sostegno* does not have a separate classroom and typically is assigned to an inclusive class from six to twenty-two hours per week. His or her caseload is generally between two and four students, although a caseload of two students is more typical (Cornoldi, Terreni, Scruggs, & Mastropieri, 1998). It is important to note that only students with significant learning needs are identified in Italy—students with learning disabilities, for example, are not labeled. In the United States over half of the students identified for special education services are labeled learning disabled (LD). In Italy, any additional services required by students with dyslexia or other learning disabilities are served using a consultation model or by the *sostegno* who is assigned to the class. When asked why students with LD were not identified, Giancarlo Cottoni (interview) replied, "Dyslexia is a *real* disability… [but] we expect variation in speaking, writing, reading, etc." A teacher outside of Rome commented that any teacher "worth their salt" should be able to support a student with a mild learning disability (personal conversation). Because of the educational background and instructional role in the classroom, the *sostegno* is a fully certified co-teacher and therefore *not* comparable to the paraprofessional in the United States. Compared to the United States, paraprofessionals are used infrequently in Italy; they work primarily as assistants to students with physical needs (such as toileting or feeding supports); they are not given instructional roles (Palladino, Cornoldi, & Vianello, 1999).

The blurring of responsibility between the *sostegno* and general education teacher in the Italian model of inclusion departs significantly from typical arrangements between general and special educators in the United States. In fact, when observing inclusive classrooms in Italy it is very difficult to determine which teacher is the general education teacher and which one is the *sostegno*. This is quite intentional. I found that if you inquire as to which teacher is the *sostegno*, your question may well be met by sly grins from both teachers or they might simply ask you to guess! It was obvious that the teachers I met in Italy prided themselves on sharing responsibility for all students in the class and did not see the need to differentiate their roles.

Despite the fact that co-teaching has been associated with increased academic achievement and greater access to the general education curriculum (Walsh & Jones, 2003), this level of co-teaching is much more rare in U.S. classrooms, where special education teachers often function more like teacher aids, playing only ancillary roles to the *real* classroom teacher (Magiera, Smith, Zigmond, & Gebauer, 2005; Walsh & Jones, 2003; Wood, 1998). As Magiera et al. found in their study of inclusive secondary mathematics classes, special education teachers are most often given the task of monitoring student progress or assisting individual students. Special education teachers in inclusive classrooms almost never take a primary role in delivering instruction to either small or large groups of students. Moreover, many general education teachers in the United States defer much of the responsibility and accountability related to students who receive special education supports to the special education teacher, who they see as the experts on such matters. Special education teachers participate in this relationship by shielding the general education teacher from any specific educational responsibilities for the child (Wood, 1998). In this arrangement, the general education teacher and special education teacher maintain very discrete roles and responsibilities in the classroom. Nonetheless, as Walther-Thomas, Bryant, and Land (1996) argue, when co-teaching is most successful, it is virtually impossible to distinguish between general education and special education teachers or to identify which students are labeled.

To summarize, the Italian system of inclusion was marked by the immediate, widespread integration of students with disabilities beginning in 1971. This initial period, from the passage of National Law 188 and continuing until the passage of National Law 518 in 1977 is often referred to as a time of *integrazione selvaggio* or "wild integration." As Nora Ferro, an administrator in Rome commented, the movement went forward without us knowing all the answers. "We were convinced of the rightness of integration and if we waited to know all the answers, we might never have begun and meanwhile lives were being wasted" (Berrigan, 1995). Insisting that despite criticisms from some special educational professionals and disability-related organizations, Ferro argues that any social change requires very strict implementation. She advises that change takes effort and even pain, because systems seek to preserve the status quo. She suggests, that if Italy had not been as strict in implementing inclusion, "the old paradigm would have prevailed" (Ferro, interview).

Conversely, in the United States inclusion progressed in an incremental fashion by maintaining a continuum of educational settings and implementing inclusion gradually. Moreover, rather than national guidelines for inclusion, placement decisions in the United States continued to be made in a more individual or case-by-case fashion. The result of these two different approaches is clear. Whereas virtually all students with disabilities in Italy are educated in inclusive classrooms, the so-called push for inclusion in the 1990s has not led to widespread inclusion in the United States or elsewhere. In fact, Vislie (2003) finds that instead of seeing a fostering of more inclusive educational settings, we have actually seen a "reproduction of special education paradigms and rituals" and an expanding system of special education (p. 30) in countries outside Italy. In other words, despite the contention that there is a growing international consensus about every child's basic and fundamental right to be included (UNESCO, 1994) we have not gained much ground in implementing such policies (Vislie, 2003).

So, the question remains, how do teachers in Italy view this sweeping educational policy? Have their attitudes changed over the thirty years since these laws were enacted? In other words, how is it going?

TEACHER ATTITUDES: A SHARED PHILOSOPHY AND COMMITMENT

There have been several studies of attitudes of Italian teachers (general education and special education teachers) and parents toward school inclusion of students with disabilities. These studies, based on survey research, report an almost universal preference among Italian teachers for inclusive classrooms. Cornoldi et al., for example, researched teacher attitudes twenty years after first implementing inclusion. In a survey of 523 teachers in ten schools in northern and central Italy, researchers found that teachers expressed overwhelming support for inclusion. In fact, fewer than 5% of the teachers they surveyed disagreed with inclusion. Teachers reported that they saw positive gains in academic achievement and social skills, as well as increased autonomy of students with disabilities. They also found that nondisabled students gained a great acceptance of diversity. Teachers in this study, however, reported a need for better materials and resources and more time allotted to support teachers in the classroom. Similarly, Balboni and Pedrabissi (2000) sent a questionnaire to 1,325 parents, teachers, and support teachers. They found that both general education and support teachers favored inclusion, but that special education teachers were the most supportive of the policy. Of all the factors they analyzed, it was found that having direct experience with disabled students led to more favorable attitudes toward inclusion for both parents and teachers. Italian teachers, according to Balboni et al., "are very much in favor of inclusion and extremely willing to accept disabled students in their classes" (p. 149).

Studies of teacher attitudes toward inclusion in the United States are more mixed. Several studies report over half of their respondents holding negative attitudes toward inclusion (Van Reusen, Shoho, & Barker, 2000–2001) or predicting that inclusion will not succeed (Monahan, Marino, & Miller, 1996). Mastropieri and Scruggs (2001) synthesized twenty-eight studies and find that although the majority of teachers in these studies support inclusion in theory, less than 30% report having adequate training or expertise to implement inclusion. Schrumm and Vaughn (1995) reviewed eighteen studies conducted in a five-year period and report a similar lack of training as a major obstacle for implementing inclusion. In a study of 326 graduate and undergraduate preservice teachers enrolled in a survey course on disabilities, Shippen, Crites, Houchins, Ramsey, and Simon (2005) find that although the course lessens prospective teachers' reported levels of anxiety and hostility toward having students with disabilities in their class, these gains are only marginal for general education teachers. As several reports demonstrate, knowledge and direct and sustained experience with students with disabilities leads to greater confidence and greater confidence leads to a more positive attitude toward inclusion (Meijer et al., 1994; Van Reusen et al., 2000–2001). Other studies have found that administrative support, collaboration, and shared vision are also key predictors of positive attitudes toward inclusion (Villa & Thousand, 2003).

From the beginning, teachers and administrators in Italy believed that inclusion would yield benefits to everyone (Berrigan, 1988). Today many believe that inclusion has led to much progress and that there are "many more opportunities for people with disabilities" as a result (Patrizia Ridella, interview). Giancarlo Cottoni (interview) explained that although they knew that inclusion would add complexity, they felt that such complexity would lead to an improved society and a richer experience for everyone. Certainly the Italian approach put into practice many of the key factors associated with successful inclusion that are outlined by Lipsky and Gartner (1998), including visionary leadership, parental support, and collaboration of key constituents. In addition, they collectively "bought into" inclusion as simply the right thing to do. Finally, subsequent inclusion policies took into account many of the concerns that teachers had about including students with disabilities by changing the nature of supports and the way they were organized, as well as making necessary adjustments to the way general education classrooms were configured by lowering class size, limiting the number of students with significant learning needs served by any one classroom, and facilitating team teaching. Thus, inclusion in Italy is not simply a *special education* policy; it represents a complete restructuring of the educational system as a whole.

With these findings in mind, in the late spring of 2003, I traveled with a group of students to Italy. We visited schools in Rome, Florence, and Parma. Besides wanting to see how this policy was being implemented, I was very much hoping to find out from teachers themselves how inclusion was going and what they thought about it.

AN ETHIC OF FULL PARTICIPATION: THE CLASSROOM AS FAMILY

What was most remarkable in visiting Italian classrooms and talking to teachers, administrators, and even cafeteria workers was the almost seamless vision about the "rightness" of inclusive education. A common theme that emerges when talking to educators and administrators in Italy is that inclusion is a "moral issue, which is more important than a legal mandate" (Berrigan, 1988). In general, I found that most teachers and administrators that I met talked about inclusion, not so much in terms of civil rights, but rather as a moral imperative. Moreover, teachers often described the classroom as a family or a community (Nutbrown & Clough, 2004). When asked why they support inclusion for *all* students with disabilities, teachers I spoke to would often say things such as, "Of course we include everyone. You wouldn't push someone out of the family—why would we push someone out of the classroom?" I found as I traveled around the country that as Norra Ferro explained, inclusion in Italy has become "rooted, [it is now] very routine" to the point that it is almost "taken-for-granted" (interview).

The schools I visited seemed to share an "uncompromising commitment and belief in inclusion" (Kugelmass & Ainscow, 2004). They shared many of the values identified by Kugelmass and Ainscow (2004) in their case study of three inclusive schools in England, Portugal, and the United States. Like the school leaders and teachers in their study, Italian teachers and administrators made it known that everyone was valued for their individuality. When teachers described students, they often did so in very holistic ways, discussing their difficulties, but also their creativity, their social skills, their energy, enthusiasm, or playfulness. As a preschool teacher in Parma explained, "We now think differently about the disabled child. We think of disability only as difference—not as deficit or lack. Each child is respected as a whole and unique individual" (interview). They shared a commitment to teach everyone that seemed to be unwavering.

Although the shared vision and the legal aspects of inclusion in Italy are unparalleled, in practice there are always challenges that remain. As Giancarlo Cottoni (director of a research center in Parma) explained, Italy has "a perfect law," and the task now was to grow into these laws—to "adjust ourselves to this perfection" (Cottoni, interview). He described full inclusion as a utopian ideal that they keep in their sight—"although we may never arrive at perfection, we continue to walk toward it." According to Cottini, one of the biggest challenges is the lack of sanctions for schools that are not implementing inclusion adequately or appropriately.

We observed other tensions regarding the implementation of the law. Some of the people we talked to commented that disability-specific accommodations, such as Braille and sign language, were not adequately met by support teachers, who were more globally or superficially trained (Maragn, interview). This lack of disability-specific training led some parents to send their children to private schools for the blind or deaf, where they would be sure to receive training in Braille and sign language. This tension over communication rights was brought into high relief when our group met at a renowned high school for the arts in Florence a support teacher for Deaf[2] students who did not know sign language. Despite the fact that we were obviously taken aback by this revelation, she did not seem to view this as a problem and implied that if she signed to Deaf students it would "isolate" them socially. Of course, this was a clear example of how even in what appears to be a very successful climate of inclusion, there remain areas of exclusion that must be continually addressed. Elena Radutzky, the director of the Mason Perkins Deafness Fund, provided some important background to this issue of communication rights. She said that as in the United States, sign language was banned in Italian schools in the 1880s. She also explained that there is a long-standing cultural valuing of speech, which is evident by the Italian saying, "gesture kills the word." Although sign is not yet considered an official language in Italy, for the first time lawmakers are consulting with disabled activists, and parents are pushing for guarantees that all Deaf children will be given communication assistants in their classes. However, it remains a continued struggle in Italy (and in the United States) to find support teachers who have adequate training in sign language or Braille. Thus, despite the fact that Italy leads the world in inclusion, it must be considered an unfinished mandate as long as students who are deaf or blind cannot be guaranteed full communication rights.

Anna DeMela, an administrator in Florence, also cited support teacher shortages and increased immigration in Italy as continuing challenges (interview). Italy, like the United States, also struggles with issues such as school failure, dropout rates, irregular attendance, and behavioral problems. In the 1980s, only thirty out of every hundred Italian students who entered school finished their high school education. In recent decades, dropout rates have been reduced and now 79.5% of students are attending upper secondary school and 65.3% are earning their certificate compared with only 8% in the 1980s (Beccegato & Elia, 1998). Problems such as dropout rates and behavior issues, however, are not typically characterized as individual student problems, but rather as evidence of school breakdown and failure to fully engage students (ibid.). As Cottoni (interview) remarked, it is not the child that must adapt to the school, but rather it is the school that must adapt to meet the needs of the child.[3] Thus, proposed solutions are often about how the school must change to better reconnect with the child (ibid.).

Others spoke of problems students with disabilities faced finding well-paid jobs, despite the fact that Italy passed a law in 1999 that requires businesses to hire at least one person with a disability for every fifteen nondisabled employees. The government also offers incentives such as tax breaks and salary reimbursements for businesses that hire individuals with more significant disabilities. It is too soon to know about the impact of this law, but in 2000, the Italian government began following the progress of students with disabilities after high school.

Finally, teachers in both U.S. and Italian contexts often report the need for more resources and training (Balboni & Pedrabissi, 2000; Buell, Hallam, Gamel-McCormic, & Scheer, 1999; Cornoldi et al., 1998; Shippen et al., 2005; Van Reusen et al., 2000–2001). A key difference is that in schools with a strong inclusive orientation, teachers and administrators show a willingness to struggle with these imperfections and their commitment to inclusion is sustained through such difficulties (Kugelmass & Ainscow, 2004). In other words, resources are not used as an excuse for why schools cannot include students, but rather a way to further support their efforts to support all students. This was certainly true in the schools that I visited; there seemed to be an understanding that "inclusion is always evolving" (DeMela, interview).

LEARNING FROM EXPERIENCE: IMPLICATIONS FOR POLICY AND PRACTICE

Despite inevitable imperfections, there is much to learn from the Italian approach to inclusion. First, beyond simply implementing a generic policy, the Italian model demonstrates the importance of fostering a shared vision that resonates within a particular cultural context. Whereas U.S. disability policies tend to focus on civil rights, for example, the Italian teachers I spoke with, framed inclusion in terms of an ethic of care or concern—viewing the classroom as a family where everyone is valued and belongs. The model of inclusion in Italy is consistent with a strong familial orientation of Italian culture and heritage. In their study of three inclusive schools in England, Portugal, and the United States, Kugelmass and Ainscow (2004) found that these kind of shared values were often communicated in a public way through slogans or displayed visually throughout the school. The lesson here is that policymakers would be wise to consider framing (and even marketing) educational policy in ways that resonate with specific cultural values and ethos to foster more "buy in" from teachers and other school personnel. In other words, while someone operating from a civil rights-based orientation might see the lack of access to sign language as violating Deaf and blind students' communication rights, policymakers might get further in Italy by thinking about how denying someone access to disability-specific communication systems isolates them from meaningful integration and a sense of belonging to the group. This practice also puts the onus of adapting on the child to adjust to nondisabled modes of interaction rather than adapting the context to welcome disability-specific ways of communicating.

Another lesson we can draw by contrasting the U.S. and Italian approach to inclusion is the limited effects of incremental change. Simply looking at the differences between the numbers of students included in Italy compared with the rest of the world suggests that there is a huge difference between incremental approaches to educational reform adopted outside Italy and a full inclusion, no excuses model within Italy. Whereas 99% of students with disabilities are included in Italy, the majority of students in the United States, for example, continue to spend significant portions of time in resource rooms and self-contained classrooms, despite the fact that both countries adopted disability-related educational policies in the 1970s.

Finally, and perhaps most importantly, the Italian model demonstrates the need for policies that account for the whole educational system, rather than a single population or aspect of reform. As Wedell (2005) notes, inclusion policies often aim only to "soften the blow" (p. 4) of rigid and inaccessible educational systems, rather than transform those very systems to be more welcoming of all learners. Instead of simply including students into the same educational structures that excluded them in the first place, we need to examine what it is about our educational structures that are failing more and more students each year. We would do well to think about inclusion as a way to support the full range of diversity in our schools, including race, ethnicity, language and class differences, as well as ability. By enacting inclusion policies whose scope was more wide-reaching—focusing on lowering class size, instituting models of co-teaching, and limiting the number of students with special needs included in any one class, the Italian policy transformed the whole educational system in ways that was beneficial to everyone. This also may account for parent's general support for inclusion. As one *sostegno* remarked, "Parents of nondisabled children see inclusion as adding to the quality of the class," not taking away from it.

Perhaps the central idea is that the Italian and U.S. models began with a different starting point. As Giancarlo Cottoni said in a meeting with my students, we begin with the idea that the "child is fine and that it is the school that needs to remediate itself" (Cottoni, interview). Thus, he explained, the object of remediation is the classroom, not the child. The philosophy of inclusion that I heard expressed by all the administrators, teachers, and early advocates of inclusion, such as Cottoni with to whom I spoke echo key tenets outlined in the *Salamanca Statement and Framework of Action on Special Needs Education*, which was adopted by the World Conference on Special Needs Education in 1994. This framework, adopted by ninety-two governments and twenty-five international organizations establishes *every* child's right to an inclusive education as the most effective way to combat discrimination and build a more inclusive and welcoming society. The framework asserts that each child is unique and therefore differences in characteristics, interests, and abilities among learners should be expected and accommodated. In other words, as Cottoni would certainly agree, learning environments should be "adapted to the needs of the child" rather than some "preordained assumption" or norms (UNESCO, 1994, p. 7). This is certainly a different starting point from the prevailing U.S. model, which is more steeped in a medical model view that locates the deficit within the child (Wedell, 2005, p. 5)—a view of disability that is ultimately "dysfunctional to the realization of inclusion" (Vislie, 2003, p. 30).

NOTES

1. Although the law was designed to ensure parental participation and collaboration, in practice parents are rarely seen or treated as equal partners in the process.
2. Many people within the Deaf community use a capital (D) when referring to aspects of Deaf culture or Deaf identity and lower case (d) when referring to deafness as an impairment. In this paper I will use a capital when I am referring to Deaf students and lower case when I am speaking of deafness as an impairment.
3. As one of the editors of this book rightly pointed out, if the school fully adjusted to the child it would support the disability-specific communication needs of children who are deaf or blind, rather than expecting a deaf or blind child to function without full communication rights.

REFERENCES

Balboni, G. & Pedrabissi, L. (2000). Attitudes of Italian teachers and parents toward school inclusion of students with mental retardation: The role of experience. *Education and Training in Mental Retardation and Developmental Disabilities.* 35(2), 148–159.

Beccegato, L.S. & Elia, G. (1998). School failure in Italy: Explanations and strategies for intervention. *European Journal of Teacher Education.* 21(2–3), 261–270.

Berrigan, C. (1988, February). Integration in Italy: A dynamic movement. *TASH Newsletter.* (pp. 6–8).

Berrigan, C. (1995). Schools in Italy: A national policy made actual. *Center on Human Policy Newsletter.* (pp. 24–27).

Buell, M.J., Hallam, R., Gamel-McCormic, M. & Scheer, S. (1999). A survey of general and special education teachers' perceptions and inservice needs concerning inclusion. *International Journal of Disability, Development, and Education.* 46(2), 143–156.

Cornoldi, C., Terreni, A., Scruggs, T.E., & Mastropieri, M.A. (1998). Teacher attitudes in Italy after twenty years of inclusion. *Remedial and Special Education.* 19(6), 350–356.

Cottoni, G. (2003, June 3 & 5). Interview. Parma, Italy.

DeMela, A. (2003, April 28). Interview. Florence, Italy.

Ferro, N. (2003, May 14). Interview. Rome, Italy.

Harry, B. & Klingner, J. (2006). *Why are so many minority students in special education? Understanding race and disability in schools.* New York: Teachers College Press.

Kugelmass, J. & Ainscow, M. (2004). Leadership for inclusion: A comparison of international practices. *Journal of Research in Special Education Needs.* 4(3), 133–141.

Lipsky, D. & Gartner, A. (1998). Taking inclusion into the future. *Educational Leadership.* 58, 78–81.

Losen, D. J. & Orfield, G. (2002). *Racial inequity in special education.* Cambridge, MA: Harvard University Press.

Magiera, K., Smith, C., Zigmond, N., & Gebauer, K. (2005). Benefits of co-teaching in secondary mathematics classes. *Teaching Exceptional Children.* 37(3), 20–24.

Maragn, S. (2003, May 14). Interview. Rome, Italy.

Mastropieri, M.A. & Scruggs, T.E. (2001). Promoting inclusion in secondary classrooms. *Learning Disability Quarterly.* 24, 265–274.

Meijer, C. J. W., Piji, S. J., & Hegarty, S. (Eds.). (1994). *New perspectives in special education.* London: Routledge.

Monahan, R.G., Marino, S.B., & Miller, R. (1996). Teacher attitudes toward inclusion: Implications for teacher education. *Education.* 117, 316–320.

Nutbrown, C. & Clough, P. (2004). Inclusion and exclusion in the early years: Conversations with European educators. *European Journal of Special Needs Education.* 19(3), 301–315.

Oakes, J. (1985). *Keeping track: How schools structure inequality.* Binghamton, NY: Vail-Ballou Press.

Oakes, J. Wells, A.S., Jones, M., & Datnow, A. (1997). Detracking: The social construction of ability, cultural politics, and resistance to reform. *Teachers College Record.* 98(3), 482–510.

Palladino, P., Cornoldi, C., & Vianello, R. (1999). Paraprofessionals in Italy: Perspectives from an inclusive country. *JASH.* 24(4), 254–258.

Radutzky, E. (2003, May 14). Interview. Rome, Italy.

Ridella, P. (2003, June 5). Interview. Cooperative Sociale la Bula, Parma, Italy.

Schumm, J. S., & Vaughn, S. (1995). Getting ready for inclusion: Is the stage set? *Learning Disability Research and Practice.* 10(3), 169–179.

Shippen, M.E., Crites, S.A., Houchins, D.E., Ramsey, M.L., & Simon, M. (2005). Preservice teachers' perceptions of including students with disabilities. *Teacher Education and Special Education.* 28(2), 92–99.

Taylor, S. (1988). Caught in the continuum: A critical analysis of the principle of the least restrictive environment. *Journal of the Association of Persons with Severe Handicaps.* 13, 41–53.

UNESCO (1994, June 7–10). *Salamanca Statement on Principles, Policy, and Practice in Special Needs Education and Framework for Action.* Salamanca, Spain.

Van Reusen, A.K., Shoho, A.R., & Barker, K.S. (2000–2001, December–January). High school teachers' attitudes toward inclusion. *The High School Journal.* 84(2), 7–20.

Villa R.A. & Thousand, J.S. (2003). Making inclusive education work: Successful implementation requires commitment, creative thinking, and effective classroom strategies. *Association for Supervision and Curriculum Development.* 61(2), 19–23.

Vislie, L. (2003). From integration to inclusion: Focusing on global trends and changes in the Western European societies. *European Journal of Special Needs Education.* 18(1), 17–35.

Walsh, J. & Jones, B. (2003). New models of cooperative teaching. *Teaching Exceptional Children.* 36(5), 14–20.

Walther-Thomas, C., Bryant, M., & Land, S. (1996). Planning for effective co-teaching: The key to successful inclusion. *Remedial and Special Education.* 17, 255–264.

Wang, M.C., Reynolds, M.C., & Walberg, H.J. (1986). Rethinking special education. *Educational Leadership.* 44(1), 26–31.

Wedell, K. (2005). Dilemmas in the quest for inclusion. *British Journal of Special Education.* 32(1), 3–11.

Wood, M. (1998). Whose job is it anyway? Educational roles in Inclusion. *Exceptional Children.* 64(2), 181–195.

Zambelli, F. & Bonni, R. (2004). Beliefs of teachers in Italian schools concerning the inclusion of disabled students: A Q-sort analysis. *European Journal of Special Needs Education.* 19(3), 351–366.

CHAPTER FOUR

An Analysis OF Inclusive Education Policy Implementation IN Zimbabwe: Challenges FOR Learner Support

AUXILIA BADZA, DAVID CHAKUCHICHI, AND ROBERT CHIMEDZA

INTRODUCTION

The concept of inclusion or inclusive education is usually associated with the child's right to attend their neighborhood regular school. This is the school in which the siblings, friends, and neighbors of the child with disabilities go. It is not child with disabilities that needs to be adapted or changed but the school environment and its support systems so that the school recognizes and is able to serve the diversity in the society in which it exists. Children with disabilities are part of that diversity. The concept "inclusion" is therefore broader and includes inclusive societies, communities, families, and schools. Savolainen, Kokkala, and Alasuutari (2000) view inclusive education as a concept that tries to put into effect the right to education, equal opportunity, and to participation by people with disabilities. It is not just about the access of people with disabilities or some traditionally excluded group of students to education; it is about transforming the entire regular education system to attend to the diverse educational needs of the students.

In developing countries such as Zimbabwe, the concept of inclusion is learned from developed countries and at international fora such as the United Nations, but may not mean the same thing or get implemented in exactly the same way.

The social context of disability helps to define disability and its related concepts. Ingstad and Whyte (1995) observed that attempts to universalize the category "disability" (and related concepts) run into conceptual problems because such definitions should take into consideration the economic, social, political, historical, and cultural contexts. For instance, Mpofu (2001: 13) urges that the concept "mental retardation" is not indigenous to any African country and that the terms used do not mean the same as used in the West. He gives the example of Talle (1995) who observed that the Maasai of Kenya had no word for mental retardation, and the Western conceptualization of mental retardation was equivalent to the Maasai term "olmodai," which translates to fool. Similarly in Zimbabwe the two major languages (Shona and Ndebele) do not have the same conceptualization of mental retardation as in the West (see Chimedza & Peters, 2001 for more details). In the current discussion, it is important therefore to understand and appreciate inclusive education in its political, social, and historical context. In this respect the sociocultural perspective to disability could be correct in asserting that disability is a social construct and not an objective condition (Edgerton, 1993; Trent, 1994).

Inclusive education is about the right of every child to education. Governments have a responsibility to ensure citizens enjoy their rights as enshrined in the country's constitution, laws, acts of parliament, and through policies and practices. In Zimbabwe schools are divided into two categories. These are government and nongovernment schools. Government schools are run completely by the state while parents make small contributions by way of school fees. These schools seem to have all the basic facilities and resources. The nongovernment schools include church mission schools, council schools, municipal schools, and private trust schools. The church schools were established by missionaries a long time ago. The council and municipal schools are in the majority and also the poorly resourced schools. On the other hand, the private trust schools are high-fee paying and therefore have the best resources and facilities. It is important to note that in Zimbabwe nongovernment schools by far outnumber state schools and also have a variety of authorities who may not accept all state policies and regulations. In other words, the state finds it difficult to enforce inclusion in schools that belong to other owners and authorities. The discussion that follows examines the dilemmas of policy implementation, curriculum, and pedagogical issues relating to inclusive education in Zimbabwean schools.

POLICY AND POLICY IMPLEMENTATION AND LEARNER SUPPORT

Special Education policy in Zimbabwe and elsewhere in Africa is a culmination of a number of declarations passed by the United Nations General Assembly such as the Convention on the Rights of the Child (1989), the World Declaration on Education for All (UNESCO, 1990), and Standard Rules on Equalization of Opportunities for Persons with Disabilities (SREOPD) (United Nations, 1993). The aim was to make governments recognize children with disabilities as active participants in their communities with rights to education, training, healthcare and rehabilitation services, vocational training, and recreation opportunities. The SREOPD further stipulates that quality of education for individuals with disabilities should reflect the same standards and ambitions as of general education. Thus children with disabilities should be afforded the same share of educational resources as those without disabilities.

The Zimbabwe Education Act of 1987 (amended in 1991) emphasized that every child shall have the right to education and that no child shall be denied access to education on the grounds of race, tribe, color, religion, creed, place of origin, and political or social status of parents. It can only be assumed that discrimination against disability is implied, but it is clear that it was not specifically mentioned. This is leaving things to chance and may explain why, to date, education for children with disabilities is seen more as a charity than as a rights issue. However, the Ministry of Education adopted inclusive education as a policy for the education of children with disabilities at all levels, from preschool to tertiary levels (Hadebe, 1996). The move was in response to the Salamanca Statement and Framework of Action (1994). Adoption of policy without effective implementation systems impacts negatively on the otherwise noble cause.

In an attempt to facilitate the process of inclusion, the Ministry of Education, Sport and Culture, working through the Department of Schools Psychological Services and Special Needs Education (SPS & SNE), emphasized a multidisciplinary approach that involved the collaboration of different ministries, local authority boards, NGOs, and parents. However, attempts to implement an unclear policy of inclusion have posed a number of challenges. The current Education Act emphasizes education for all without discussing the educational needs of these learners. The act emphasizes that every child in Zimbabwe shall have the right to education (Part II, Section 4[1]). The act further emphasizes that "no child shall be refused admission to any school on the grounds of race, tribe, color, religion, creed, place of origin, political or social status of parent" (Part II, Section 4[2]). Part II, Section 10, stresses the child's "right to enrolment at the school nearest to the place where he/she is ordinarily resident." In this case, the assumption is that inclusion is subsumed in EFA (Education for All). A number of learners with different disabilities are now in the regular schools (Policy Circular Number 3 of 2006). Although learners with disabilities are embraced in the Education for All Act of 1987, Zimbabwean experience shows that the learners are still marginalized in terms of provisions and meeting their special needs in the mainstream.

Unclear policy on inclusion has resulted in inadequate provision of equipment and materials for the education of learners with disabilities. The Zimbabwe Education and Training Commission (Zimbabwe Ministry of Education, 1999) reported a clamor for a clearly stated policy on education for persons with disabilities reflecting same standards and ambitions as the mainstream education. To overcome these policy limitations, the Ministry of Education in Zimbabwe has reviewed existing related statutory instruments to facilitate inclusion. For example Policy Circular Number 3 of 2006 outlines guidelines on providing equal access to the education of learners with disabilities. Other such statutory instruments focus on public examination, infrastructure, and enrolment procedures. However, the need for the development of a comprehensive and clear inclusive policy statement might help to illustrate the differences in educational needs. Merely placing students with disabilities in regular schools without clearly outlining the inclusive education policy is not what inclusion means (Ainscow, 2000).

Another fundamental principle of inclusion is collaboration of all parties involved in preparing students for life in more inclusive societies. Collaboration as defined by Dettmer, Dyck, and Thurston (1999) is laboring together, working jointly in an endeavor. Collaboration can therefore involve uniting and assisting each other for the same cause. The challenges for Zimbabwe pertaining to collaboration are therefore highlighted in the discussion in the pages that follow.

COLLABORATION AMONG STAKEHOLDERS

Successful inclusion presumes that no single teacher can or ought to be expected to have the expertise required to meet the educational needs of all students in the classroom (Dettmer et al., 1999). This calls for collaboration among teachers. A whole school approach to the education of all learners whereby all teachers share responsibility for all students' achievement and behavior is adopted. Consequently teachers would refer to "our students or class" rather than "your" or "my" students or class as is often observed in schools. All members adopt a sense of ownership for all students including those with disabilities. A challenge to the Zimbabwean schools is to develop structures and conditions that encourage collaboration. This would also include the empowerment of individuals and collaborative groups—thus promoting all members to share the responsibilities of monitoring and evaluating the quality of the school activities.

Apart from teachers and administrators, a range of different professionals are involved in the education of learners with disabilities. These include educational psychologists, social welfare workers, medical doctors, nurses, physiotherapists, ophthalmologists, and optometrists, just to name a few. These professionals have diverse roles ranging from quality monitoring, whole school development, staff and student support, to meeting the needs of all children (Lacey, 2000; Roffey, 2001). It is important to note that none of these roles is exclusive, and the roles are therefore interdependent. In Zimbabwe the collaboration among professionals is hindered by subtle rivalry by the players as each individual tries to protect their turf. For example school psychologists would want to have the ultimate decision on school placements of students with disabilities without due regard to other professionals already mentioned. One other contributory factor to unsuccessful collaboration impacting negatively on inclusion is the limited number of qualified personnel in the country. For inclusion to succeed in Zimbabwe, collaboration among these professionals is critical and needs to be seen as strength rather than a potential source of conflict and confusion to learner support. The country could come up with policies that facilitate collaboration among the different professionals to enhance inclusion program.

Parents often blame teachers for their children's failure, while teachers put the blame on parents for failing to provide for and have interest in their children's education and development. As a result, homes and the education system end up functioning in isolation. For a long time, parents have played a passive role in the education of their children with disabilities except for perhaps just bringing the children to the schools (then mostly special schools). Experiences in Zimbabwe show that parents in fact dumped the children at the institutions leaving them to depend on good will of the institutions and meager support from the government. Furthermore the Zimbabwean culture toward disability influenced parental involvement in the education of learners with disability. The presence of people with disability was associated with beliefs such as witchcraft, angered ancestral spirits, and bad omen. To parents having children in special schools was a way of getting rid of them. Learner support for inclusion requires that parents work together collaboratively with teachers and other professionals. Parents play an important role, since they are the first and most enduring educators of their children and hence the need for collaborating with them. Findings of a study of preschools showed greater benefits when parents were involved in the program than when they were not (Mittler, 2000). The situation is the same in Zimbabwe. Programs in which parents are involved do much better than those in which parental involvement is limited to fund-raising activities without any input in the child's learning and social activities. For example, the Harare Hospital Children's Rehabilitation Unit runs workshops for parents of deaf children to assist them to understand their child, be able to communicate with him or her, and effectively get involved in the education of their children. The unit runs this program together with schools for the deaf. This has helped to make these parents get involved in the learning process of their children. The program has cascaded into some of the schools such as Emerald Hill School for the Deaf. Parental involvement in the education of their children with disability should not be left to chance especially in situations such as in Zimbabwe where for a long time parents had the attitude that the education of such children is best left to the teachers who are not only the experts but god-sent saviors of their plight. However, it is evident that collaboration with parents of learners with and without disabilities facilitates inclusion.

AVAILABILITY OF RESOURCES

While factors that militate against the progress toward the practice of inclusion in Zimbabwe maybe varied, unavailability of resources has proven to be the key one (Badza, 2003). These resources range from school infrastructure, funding, teaching and learning material, assistive devices (e.g., hearing aids, wheelchairs, calipers, white canes), to trained personnel. One of the challenges of inclusion is the vested interest ranged against it at all levels of the education system (Dyson, 2000). The development of policies and legislations will not be effective if there is limited political will at all levels—from national, regional down to school and community to provide for all children. Inclusive education in Zimbabwe calls for rethinking the allocation, adaptation, and utilization of existing resources by the government. Local authorities and other stakeholders could chip in to complement government efforts. It is common practice to have resources allocated to institutions for people with disabilities as an afterthought by central government. In Zimbabwe legislation and policies come from central government, but their implementation in school is difficult as the state owns only part of the schools, and local authorities have hardly any resources to effect anything for the benefit of people with disabilities.

Besides inadequate resource allocation, lack of adaptation of physical environments to make buildings and playgrounds more accessible to students with disabilities is a challenge to successful inclusion. This is one of the major reasons why parents still opt for institutional settings as best educational settings for their children (Chimedza, 2006). The landscape and distance from school especially in rural areas makes it impossible for learners with disabilities to commute from home to school. For instance, roads may be sandy and rocky, unsuitable for wheelchair use. Concerns have been raised about the safety of these learners with disabilities by teachers, the community, and parents. In one study, one of the teachers remarked, "It means I have to accompany them all the time wherever they want to go." However, this situation is not unique to Zimbabwe. Studies elsewhere have also shown that restructuring of the physical environments enhanced successful inclusion (Arbeiter & Hartley, 2002; Center & Ward, 1987).

Badza (2003) and Mushoriwa (2001) observed the need for adequate financial support by government for inclusion in Zimbabwe to become a reality. Although the government allocates grants to schools and fee assistance in the form of Basic Education Assistance Module (BEAM) (Zimbabwe Educational Policy Circular Number 6 of 2004), this has proved to be inadequate to meet the costs of equipment, materials, transport, and sometimes medication, and the day-to-day running of the schools.

LEARNER SUPPORT AND TRAINING IN SPECIAL EDUCATION

One of the critical problems facing the implementation of inclusion is inadequacy of teaching personnel for special education both qualitatively and quantitatively. Generally teacher education in Zimbabwe should prepare teachers for teaching and managing learners with disabilities in regular classrooms; however limited availability of trained personnel in disability has hampered the practice. Yet, it is common knowledge that instruction in an inclusive setting requires inherently differentiated teaching based on the needs of the learner. Teachers may not have all the skills and time to provide adequate support to all learners with diverse needs in their class at the same time and hence the need for support in terms of training. Galloway and Goodwin (1987) argue that an attempt to meet the needs of learners can be successful if the needs of their teachers are also understood and met. Support for teachers is in most cases not available and where available it is mostly minimal or inconsistent. Zimbabwe has only one college that trains teachers of learners with visual, hearing, and mental disabilities. The eighteen months-training equips teachers with the theory and practice in special education and specialization in one of the areas highlighted above. The number of graduates is however too small to meet the demand for specialist teachers. Perhaps an approach that could be used to prepare teachers for inclusion in Zimbabwe is school-based staff development in the form of discussions, workshops, and seminars. Regular teacher education programs need redesigning to include pedagogy of special needs education and other inclusive approaches that cater to a greater diversity of learners in the education system.

ATTITUDINAL CHANGE AS A PREREQUISITE FOR LEARNER SUPPORT

Experience in Zimbabwe has shown that neither provision of resources nor development of policies makes an impact on inclusion unless supported by genuine commitment within the school system. Dyson views success of inclusion as rooted in social and educational struggles in which the proponents of inclusion fight against those who support exclusive practices, attitudes, and structures in the education system. Thus resistance to the implementation of inclusion is not something that is entirely unanticipated. Even in this age, people hold on to their beliefs and practices regarding disability and players in inclusion are no exception to this. Teachers are still skeptical about having learners with disabilities in their regular classes. The local beliefs, superstition, and customs cause people to look down upon people with disabilities. In Africa, superstition, spiritual beliefs, and traditional attitudes, all contribute toward societal attitudes toward people with disabilities (Laan & Vayrynen, 1996). In Zimbabwe the birth of a child with disabilities is still viewed negatively and with suspicion. The cause of disability is believed to include a whole range of explanations such as contacts, transgression of previous lives, unfaithfulness, witchcraft, incest, evil spirits, or lack of proper attention to ancestral spirits (Chimedza, 2000; Mushoriwa 2001; Peresuh 1998).

Zindi (1986) in his study of mainstream children's attitudes toward children with disability in Zimbabwe revealed that superstitious beliefs about disability are still strong in Zimbabwe; participants of this study also believed that people born with disability are being punished for their parents' or family's misdeeds.

Although programs on disability awareness are carried out to facilitate attitudinal change toward inclusion, continuous awareness is imperative for learner support.

ADEQUACY OF LEARNER SUPPORT IN INCLUSION

There are exclusionary practices that are subtle in inclusion that require structured mediation through learner support. The education sector needs to be aware of such exclusionary practices and must seek ways to strengthen learner support to increase access and equity in education. The South African Education White Paper on Special Needs Education (2001) classifies people with disabilities according to intensity of learner support. The student with minimal disability would be classified as low intensity support implying that they require little support in inclusion. Students with moderate level of disability fall into the category of intermittent support. In this case, the student is given support as and when needed to ensure functionality of the individual. Those in the severe to profound category are placed in the high intensity support group where they receive care and support continuously. While the approach to educating people with disabilities outlined in the South African White Paper on Special Education seems plausible, it is the practical application of the concept that needs to be interrogated. Zimbabwe has come out with recent legislation that seems to draw influence from the South African concept of service delivery to people with disability. The Zimbabwean Education Policy Number 3 of 2006 (Government of Zimbabwe, 2006) has the following guiding principles for learner support:

- Every child has a right to education
- Schools should accommodate all children regardless of their physical, intellectual, social, emotional, linguistic, and other conditions
- The diversity of individual differences among learners should be recognized and accommodated in all educational programs including sports and cultural aspects.

While these principles serve as a guide, there is need to redefine actual learner support strategies on school placement, learner support, and resource allocation. It is therefore pertinent to say that, people in inclusion require learner support that will mitigate the impact of physical, social, and cultural barriers in accessing the curriculum.

LEARNER SUPPORT AND GENDER ISSUES

Gender refers to male and female roles as they affect the growing-up and functioning of individuals in society. Generally the girl child is disadvantaged in her educational, and psychosocial development. In Zimbabwe and indeed in other developing countries, the girl child has to do certain chores such as drawing water or food preparation before going to school. After school she has more work to do before going to bed. It appears the sociocultural expectations from the girl child place a heavier burden on her than on the boy child in a manner that systemically disadvantages her from school learning. The biological makeup of the girl child (at pubescence and adolescence she goes through menstruation every month) affects her participation in school activities. In Zimbabwe it is most common for a girl child to absent herself from school during the period she is having menstruation. The days of absence implies that she actually misses out on class instruction. The absences from school that are not really necessary are caused by lack of knowledge and sanitary resources and facilities. There is a culture of silence in Zimbabwe on issues of sexual maturation because of the breakdown of the extended family system as noted by Mugenda (2001)

> ... the extended family played a major role of educating youngsters on the physiology of sexual maturation and sexual controls in African society. Today, this role has been left to parents who feel embarrassed to tackle this delicate subject. To a large extent this role has been shifted to the teacher ... (Shumba et al., 2005: 167).

These biological and cultural aspects surrounding the girl child's sexual maturation process cause inequitable access to the school curriculum in a manner that disadvantages her inadvertently.

To mitigate the impact of biocultural factors on the education of the girl child, the school and families should come up with support measures to enable her to access the school curriculum. Learner support for the girl child could essentially include growing-up and sexual maturation education, counseling, and the provision of adequate toilet facilities (FEMED, 2001). The schools in Zimbabwe generally do not have toilet facilities for the girl child to change sanitary pads when she menstruates at school. Sanitary pads are generally too expensive for the majority of the children. In the meantime the Forum for African Women Educationalists (FAWE) has lobbied for tax concession on sanitary products. This effort has borne fruit and sanitary pads now are exempted from taxation. Learner support for girls and women should not be seen as a mere disaggregation of schemes to create access but the formulation and implementation of integrated strategies that empower women through education based on equalization of opportunities for both sexes (Aggarwal, 2004: 435).

LEARNER SUPPORT IN EDUCATION OF LEARNERS WITH SENSORY IMPAIRMENTS

In Zimbabwe students with sensory disabilities, including students with hearing and visual impairments and those who are deaf-blind, access education in special schools that have over the years acquired resources they need. It is therefore difficult for such children to be accepted in the regular school, as the regular school does not have adequate learner support in terms of teacher expertise and resources. Students with disabilities require defined learner support to facilitate their access to the curriculum in an inclusive setting. Deaf students for instance, would need provision of Zimbabwe sign language and use of interpreters where necessary. Those with usable residual hearing would need hearing aids to access the curriculum. Provision of hearing aids and other electro-acoustic equipment should include service and maintenance. Students with visual impairments require learner support in the form of braille materials and audio equipment. Mobility and orientation training is necessary learner support for people with visual impairment. For low vision students, provision of enlarged print and magnifying glasses are indispensable aspects of learner support.

Learner support in the context of sensory impairments should also include adaptation of the curriculum to make it responsive to the unique needs of individual students.

LEARNER SUPPORT TO STUDENTS WITH PHYSICAL AND MOTOR CHALLENGES

In Zimbabwe students with physical and motor challenges have problems of access to the physical environment, because most school facilities do not have structures to accommodate them. For example, the school toilets in most rural areas are made in such a way that a student on a wheel chair cannot even get into, it let alone use it because the doors are usually too small and squatter holes placed in quite difficult corners. Learner support should include mobility and physiotherapy training to improve access to facilities. Problems of access for students with physical and motor disabilities emanate from physical barriers of the education facilities and the social barriers inherent in the negative attitudes and expectations of the community. Physical barriers are not readily noticeable by able-bodied persons but Magama's experience at the University of Zambia says it all. "There were steps everywhere. There were steps at the dining hall, so I could not go into the dining room unless I went through the kitchen … the lab tables were about six to nine inches above my head so I couldn't conduct the experiments on the table" (Chimedza & Peters, 2001: 140). These physical problems should be mitigated to ensure access to school curriculum for people with physical and motor disabilities. Social barriers are manifested in varied ways in social interactions as experienced by Magama, "Initially people I encountered in Philippines would look at me with pity. They would say 'Oh shame. How could God let this happen?' The Filipinos are very religious, so they would look at me in the context of God having let me acquire a disability" (ibid.: 141).

Learner support in the context of physical and motor disabilities should contest negative attitudes and social expectations as well as removal of physical barriers and modification of the structural environment to enable equitable participation in all aspects of life by people with physical and motor disabilities. Access to all social amenities should be seen as a human right thus making the provision of learner support mandatory. Through adequate learner support, especially supportive attitudes, people with physical disability will be able to meaningfully participate and contribute to their communities. Participation and making a contribution to society build self-esteem in people with disabilities, which allows them "to believe they are included as members of society …" (Nagler, 1993: 1). Community belongingness is the very essence of inclusion.

LEARNER SUPPORT FOR STUDENTS WITH INTELLECTUAL DISABILITIES

In Zimbabwe people with intellectual disabilities include those commonly referred to as mentally retarded and those with learning difficulties/disabilities.

This category also requires learner support for real inclusion to take place. The nature of learner support while taking account of the intensity of need per individual should focus on negative aspects of societal expectations and attitudes especially in education, employment, and community interaction such as rejection by peers and or looking down on people with disabilities. Students with intellectual disabilities require adequate support in terms of education and programs that enhance their acceptance and participation in and contribution to society where interdependence skills are vital. Adequate learner support for people with intellectual disabilities should include training in social skills, cognitive skills, and prevocational skills. Training in these skills should enhance the building of self-esteem in people with intellectual disabilities. It is the change in attitudes of society that enables the accommodation of these people as integrally belonging to the community. Gearheart, Weishahn, and Gearheart (1992) assert that the goal of education is to foster successful functioning in society. In this respect, adequate learner support should seek to facilitate a situation where functionality in society is maximized through instructional approaches and strategies. Aggarwal points out that "the task of education for a handicapped child is to prepare him for adjustment to a social cultural environment," designed to make him an integral part of that society (416). This notion influences the way we view the curriculum in such a way that its modification and flexibility should be accounted as essential learner support.

Learner Support for Minority Groups

To appreciate the learner support needs of students of minority groups, we have to understand who are the minority groups. These are students who are the children of people who are in the minority in any given social setup by reason of race, language, ethnicity, and or other socially devised divide. Minority groups would therefore include immigrants and ethnic minorities, victims of trafficking, particularly children, those living in substandard accommodation, the homeless, people living with disabilities, and single parents. In Zimbabwe minority groups include the people with disabilities, the refugees, and minority language groups such as the Tonga, Nambia, Kalanga, Ndau, Venda, and Korekore. The Education Act of 1987 seeks to embrace the learning needs of minority groups but there are other factors that impede progress. For example, the language of school instruction policy often adopts the majority or dominant cultures. Such a setup obviously disadvantages the minority groups to such an extent that they are marginalized and therefore require protection by human rights focused legislation and empowerment.

To give the requisite learner support to the various categories of minority groups, focus on the following issues is needed: (1) literacy and language training for people in minority linguistic groups; (2) training for teachers of students for whom English is a second language as well as ongoing training for teachers in schools who provide English language support to such learners; (3) migration and interculturalism training for teachers as a special initiative to sustain progress in inclusion of minority groups (http://www.socialinclusion.ie/documents/ minority groups). The strategies, it is hoped, would wipe out racial and tribal discrimination, xenophobic tendencies, and intolerant practices that marginalize the minority groups.

Information provision to the disadvantaged groups is another learner support strategy that seeks to empower minority groups with knowledge to survive in a given socioeconomic environment. Learner support essentially mitigates the impact of social marginalization of the disadvantage minority groups.

CONCLUSION

Inclusive education needs to be anchored in appropriate and adequate learner support. The situation common in developing countries where students with disabilities are physically placed in regular education classes without adequate support could actually lead to segregation. Learner support should take cognizance of the social, cultural, political, and economic situations of the country. It should also meet the needs of the learner that make the student function in the regular school system. Governments should come up with programs that are properly backed by policy and budgets. Most initiatives in developing countries, particularly on disability, are left to charity and this has destroyed even very brilliant programs since charity has no legal commitment and it can be withdrawn anytime depending on the prevailing relationships and common understanding between the giver and the receiver.

REFERENCES

Aggarwal, J.C. (2004). *Development and Planning of Modern Education* (8th ed.). Vikas, New Delhi.
Ainscow, M. (2000). Reaching Out to all Learners: Some Opportunities and Challenges. In H. Daniels (Ed.) *Special Education Re-formed beyond Rhetoric* (pp. 85–100). London, Falmer Press.
Arbeiter, S. and Hartley, S. (2002). Teachers and Pupils Experiences of Integrated Experiences in Uganda. *International Journal of Disability Development and Education. 49, 1,* 61–78.
Badza, A. (2003). *Towards Inclusion of Children With VI in Regular Preschools: A Case Study of Regular and Special Needs Preschool Teachers' Attitudes in Zimbabwe.* Unpublished Master of Philosophy Thesis. University of Oslo, Norway.
Center, Y. & Ward, J. (1987). Teachers Attitudes towards the Integration of Disabled Children in Regular Schools. *The Exceptional Child. 34,* 41–57.

Chimedza, R. (2000). *A Study on Children and Adolescents with Disabilities in Zimbabwe*. Harare, UNICEF.
Chimedza, R. (2006). Disability and Inclusive Education in Zimbabwe. In L. Barton & F. Armstrong (Eds.) *Policy Experience and Change: Cross-Cultural Reflections on Inclusive Education*. New York, Springer-Verlang.
Chimedza, R. & Peters, S. (2001). *Disability and Special Needs Education in an African Context*. Harare, College Press.
Dettmer, P., Dyck, N.E., & Thurston, L.P. (1999). *Consultation, Collaboration and Teamwork for Students with Special Needs* (3rd ed.). Boston, Allyn and Bacon.
Dyson, A. (2000). Questioning, Understanding and Supporting the Inclusive school. In H. Daniels (Ed.) *Special Education Re-formed beyond Rhetoric* (pp. 85–100). London, Falmer Press.
Edgerton, R. B. (1993). *The Cloak of Competence: Revised and Updated*. Berkeley, University of California Press.
FEMED (2000). Femshuleni—Rockefeller Foundation Female Education Exploratory Case Studies in Kenya, Uganda and Zimbabwe.
Galloway, D. & Godwin, C. (1987). *The Evaluation of Disturbing Children*. London, Longman.
Gearheart, B.R., Weishahn, M.W., & Gearheart, C.J. (1992). *The Exceptional Student in a Regular Class* (5th ed.). New York, Merrill.
Government of Zimbabwe, the Education Act (1987). Harare, Government Printers.
Government of Zimbabwe (1999). *Zimbabwe Report of the Presidential Commission of Inquiry into Education and Training*. Harare, Government Printers.
Government of Zimbabwe (2006). *Education Policy Circular Number 3 of 2006 Guidelines on Providing Equal Access to Education for Learners with Disabilities*. Harare: Government Printers.
Government of Zimbabwe (2006). *Education Policy Circular Number 6 of 2004. Basic Educational Assistance Module (BEAM): Procedural Guidelines for Application of Learners with Special Needs (Disabilities)*. Harare, Government Printers.
Government of Zimbabwe (2006). *Ministry of Education Policy Circular Number 3 of 2006 Guidelines on Providing Equal Access to Education for Learners with Disabilities*. Harare, Government Printers.
Hadebe, M. (1996). *School Psychological Services and Special Needs Education: Present State of Affairs and Vision Year 2020*. Harare, Ministry of Education.
http://www.socialinclusion.ie/documents/minority groups, pdf.pdf. Retrieved on 29.05.06.
Ingstad, B. & Whyte, S.R. (1995). *Disability and Culture*. Berkeley, University of California Press.
Lacey, P. (2000). Multidisciplinary Work: Challenges and Possibilities. In H. Daniels (Ed.) *Special Education Re-formed beyond Rhetoric* (pp. 157– 172). London, Falmer Press.
Laan, A. & Vayrynen, S. (1996) Integration in Special Needs in Zimbabwe. *Zimbabwe Journal of Educational Research. 8*, 19–33.
Mpofu, E. (2001). Mental Retardation in Cross Cultural Perspective. In R. Chimedza & S. Peters (Eds.) *Disability and Special Needs Education in an African Context* (pp. 98–137). Harare, College Press.
Mugenda, O. (2001) *An Exploratory Study of Sexual Maturation Process and Practices among Pupils in Selected Primary Schools in Kenya*. Nairobi, Kenyatta University.
Mushoriwa, T. (2001). A Study on Attitude of Primary School Teachers in Harare towards the Inclusion of Blind Children in Regular Classes. *African Journal of Special Needs Education. 6, 2*, 107–113.
Nagler, M. (1993). *Perspectives on Disability. 2nd Education Health Markets Research*. Hamilton.
Peresuh, M. (1998). Post-independence Education in Zimbabwe. Achievements, Constraints and Way Forward. *Journal of Practice in Education for Development. 3, 3*, 129–136.

Roffey, S. (2001). *Special Needs in Early Years. Collaboration, Communication and Coordination* (2nd ed.). London, David Fulton Publishers.

Savolainen, K., & Alasuutari (2000). *Meeting Special and Diverse Educational Needs: Making Inclusive Education a Reality*. Helsinki, Ministry of Foreign Affairs Finland and Niilo Maki Institute.

Shumba, O., Kaziboni, T., Manokore, V., Chakuchichi, D., Silitshena, P., Sango, G., Dhlomo, T., & Dube, R. (2005) Knowledge, Perceptions and Attitudes about Growing Up and Sexual Maturation among Primary School Children. *Zimbabwe Journal of Educational Research. 17, 2*, 165–191.

South Africa Department of Education (2001). Education White Paper 6. Special Needs Education. Building an Inclusive Education and Training System. Pretoria.

South Africa Department of Education (2004). Summary Outline of the Draft National Strategy for Screening, Identification, Assessment and Support. Pretoria, Directorate of Inclusive Education.

Talle, A. (1995). A Child Is a Child. Disability and Equality among the Maasai. In B. Ingstad & S.R. Whyte (Eds.) *Disability and Culture* (pp. 56–74). Berkeley, California University Press.

Trent, J. W. (1994). *Inventing the Feeble Mind. A History of Mental Retardation in the United States.* Berkeley, University of California Press.

UNESCO (1990). *The World Declaration on Education for All. Paris,* UNESCO.

UNESCO (1994). *The Salamanca Statement and Frame for Action on Special Needs Education.* Paris, UNESCO.

United Nations (1989). *The United Nations Convention on the Rights of the Child*. New York, United Nations.

United Nations (1993). *The Standard Rules on the Equalization of Opportunities for Persons with Disabilities*. New York, United Nations.

Zimbabwe Ministry of Education (1999). *Report of the Presidential Commission of Inquiry into Education and Training*. Harare, Zimbabwe.

Zindi, F. (1986). Mainstreaming in Zimbabwe. *African Journal of Special Needs Education. 1, 1,* 1–7.

CHAPTER FIVE

Inclusion IN Indian Education

SUSAN L. GABEL AND JAGDISH CHANDER

India's population of 1.1 billion (World Bank, 2007) is the second largest in the world, yet its has one-third of the world's poor people (ibid., 2004). "Twenty percent of the world's out-of-school children" live in India and these children have little access to medical care or economic security. In terms of gender, "the overall picture remains one of stark inequality" according to the World Bank (ibid.), although the government's most recent initiatives focus strongly on increasing access to education for girls. Stark inequality also describes the situation for disabled people, whose illiteracy has been estimated at a staggering 55% (Government of India, 2005b). On the other hand, this "vibrant democracy … has been making progress on a scale, size, and pace that is unprecedented in its own history" (ibid., 2006). This suggests that the issues we discuss in this chapter—inclusion in elementary, secondary, and higher education—should be understood from the point of view of an evolving "vibrant democracy."

One aspect of India's democratic evolution has been its increasing focus on inclusive education. The National Plan for Education adopted under former prime minister Rajiv Gandhi (1986) stipulated that

> the objective should be to integrate the physically and mentally handicapped with the general community as equal partners, to prepare them for normal growth and to enable them to face life with courage and confidence (Pandey & Advani, 1995, 82).

Even before the enunciation of the National Policy in 1986, the Ministry of Welfare initiated a centrally sponsored plan called the Integrated Education of the Disabled Children (Government of India, 1986). The plan is now handled by the Ministry of Human Resource Development. In its revised form, this scheme purported to provide educational opportunities for disabled children in common schools, or the same schools as other children.

In recent years, Indian educators, politicians, and policymakers have engaged in several North-South Dialogues that have helped "place the issue of inclusive education on the national educational development agenda" (Mitra, 2005). One issue of debate within these dialogues has been whether inclusive education should focus on disabled children or "treat all marginalized children as equal" (ibid., ¶ 4). The *Kochi Declaration* (2003), drafted at the North-South Dialogue III in Kerala, India, defines inclusion as "quality education for all, based on the principle of equal opportunities and access." In fact, many of the sources we have cited use a definition similar to that of the *Kochi Declaration*. We agree with this definition, particularly when it is applied to India, but because of our emphasis, most of our chapter will focus on disabled children and adults.

In this chapter we begin by describing some of the difficulties of collecting reliable demographic data on disability in India. The data are provided not only to give basic information about disability but also to contextualize the challenges facing the country in identifying the individuals who need to be included and measuring success in achievement of disability rights. We then briefly touch on legislation of significance pertaining to the rights of disabled Indians—the Persons with Disabilities Act of 1995 (PWD Act). From there we proceed to an overview of issues related to access to elementary and secondary education and then segue into governmental conversations about teacher education reform. We conclude with a discussion of governmental commitments to higher education reform, comparing that commitment to the reality uncovered by research.

DEMOGRAPHICS OF DISABILITY IN INDIA

Problems of counting

To date, no comprehensive survey of disability has been carried out in India. Consequently, there is a lack of authentic and reliable statistics on disability. According to the 2001 census, a mere 2.13% (21 million) of the population of India is disabled (Registrar General of India, 2001; Government of India, 2005b). However, if the yardstick applied by international organizations such as the United Nations is used to determine the incidence of disability in India, the numbers would be much higher. Over ten years ago, Pandey and Advani estimated that up to 20% of the population was disabled, which would have amounted to about 200 million people. More recently, Pinto and Sahu (2001) estimate the number lower, at about 90 million. In 2003, Major H. P. S. Ahluwalia, Chairman of the

Rehabilitation Council of India, estimated the number of disabled Indians at 60 million, a drastically different figure from the ones provided by Pinto and Sahu and Pandey and Advani. Regardless of the exact number, Pintu and Sahu estimate that the disabled population might include up to 78% of the rural population, where poverty, malnutrition, and insufficient medical care are rampant. This seems quite high but it must be understood within the context of a massive rural population in extreme poverty. The World Bank (2004, 2007) identifies overrepresentation of disability among the poor of the developing world as a problem where "social exclusion and isolation are a frequent part of … daily experience" (1) in which people are often "deprived of productive work, become even more impoverished, and fall prey to malnutrition, lack of health care, and poor if any education" (ibid.).

Researchers are left with estimations of the incidence of disability rather than reliable statistics, for several reasons. First, while exposure to people with disabilities is a daily occurrence on the streets of India, the context in which these encounters happen is quite different from that in the West. In spite of their visibility, "[p]ersons with disabilities constitute a highly marginalized group," note Pinto and Sahu (12), and "most adult Indians have not attended school with people with disabilities since integration is only beginning to be implemented in Indian schools" (12).

Problems of definition

Of course, the statistics quoted earlier in this chapter depend upon the definitions used to determine disability. The problem of defining disability is related to the problem of grasping the full impact of disability. To do so, there must be a degree of national agreement on what counts as disability. Agreement between the government and the general public, is not possible in India at this time, as we discuss in the next section. Srivastava, Tripathi, and Misra (1995), Sen (1992), and Gabel, Vyas, Patel, and Patel (2001) have demonstrated this problem in relation to intellectual disability. For example, it is difficult to apply Western concepts associated with intellectual disability (e.g., intelligence, IQ) to a culture in which beliefs about intellectual disability exist concomitantly with caste traditions and Hindu philosophy. In India, learning disability, for example, has no consistent meaning (Vyas, 1996), making it quite difficult to measure its incidence. Bhanushali (n.d.) well summarizes the definitional problem and research challenge:

> No single standard exists in India in order to evaluate disability. In common parlance, different terms such as disabled, handicapped, crippled, physically challenged are used inter-changeably. (Section 2, ¶ 1)

Even governmental documents reflect the problem of the mismatch between Western and Indian concepts due to the adoption of Western definitions of disability in comprehensive disability legislations such as the PWD Act (1995). In its *Draft National Policy for Persons with Disabilities,* the government states:

> ... [I]t is well accepted that there are serious difficulties in the survey of persons with disabilities in the country since the information is collected by non-medical field-investigators on the aspects which are defined in terms of medical conditions. (Government of India, 2005b, 4)

The next excerpt refers to the fact that census takers must attempt to translate the nonmedical way families talk about their members who may be disabled into the way the government classifies disability for the purposes of the census.

> The most difficult aspect of a survey ... is to ensure that the enumerators understand non-medical definitions and are able to co-relate them to the manifestation of the disability. (ibid.)

Shame and stigma

The shame and stigma associated with disability in India exacerbates the problems of counting and definition. India is basically a religious society. The overwhelming majority of the Indian population adheres to the faith of Hinduism and the majority of the Indian population exists in an agrarian rural society in which traditional Hindu religious beliefs persist. One of the most important principles of Hinduism is the concept of *karma* theory. *Karma* is a Sanskrit word that means action. According to this theory, privileges and deficits of the current life are to be attributed to the actions of past lives. If one has any kind of impairment, it is attributed to the sins of one's past lives. Likewise, if one enjoys a privileged life, it is attributed to the good deeds of his/her previous lives. This fatalism and linkage of disability to *karma* is found in many studies of disability in India, including the first author's (Gabel, 2004; Gabel et al., 2001) study of Hindi-speaking Hindu-Indian immigrants to the United States. Similarly, in 1994 Dr. Rita Agrawal summarized it well:

> For a vast majority of people living on the Indian subcontinent, disability thus is irrevocable, since the cause is believed supernatural. While the disabled were objects of pity and sympathy, prevention was considered unthinkable and rehabilitation not possible. Families of disabled persons also resigned themselves to their fate and suffered in silence. (187–188)

As mentioned early in this chapter, India has been "making progress on a scale, size, and pace that is unprecedented in its own history" (World Bank, 2006) and this progress includes progress in thought. Many Indians, particularly those who live in India's urban centers (e.g., Mumbai, Delhi, Kolkatta), now realize that disability is not the result of supernatural intervention. When census takers visit families weighed down by shame and stigma, it can be difficult to obtain any information at all about disabled individuals. Pinto and Sahu confirm this by noting that "in some villages, people with disabilities are shunned, abused, or abandoned at birth, since parents are ashamed of their disabled child, [they] cannot envision a viable future for the child, and fear social isolation themselves" (ibid.).

The demographics of disability in India, confounded by the problems of defining and counting disabled people in spite of the shame and stigma attached to them, frame the social context for the next section on the PWD Act of 1995. Keeping in mind that the PWD Act purports to create the right of access to education, including higher education, questions remain about how it can be determined whether the PWD Act has made a difference in the lives of disabled Indians.

THE PERSONS WITH DISABILITIES (EQUAL OPPORTUNITIES PROTECTION OF RIGHTS AND FULL PARTICIPATION) ACT OF 1995

The PWD Act of 1995 was the first major disability rights legislation in India with coverage extending to all of India with the exception of the state of Jammu and Kashmir (Government of India, 1996). It requires widespread reform of educational and employment opportunities, the establishment of national and state Coordinating Committees composed of stakeholder groups, creation of access to built environments, and provision of assistive devices for students. The following requirements of the PWD Act are the most relevant to this chapter.

- Free education for disabled children up to the age of eighteen (Section 26 [A], Chapter V).
- Development of "teachers' training programmes specializing in disabilities so that requisite trained manpower is available for special schools and integrated schools for children with disabilities" (Section 29, Chapter V).
- Equal access (including physical access) by disabled people to all levels of education including higher education and vocational education (Section 30, Chapter V).
- Reservation of a minimum of 3% of all public educational institutions' admissions at all levels (Section 39, Chapter VI).

The PWD Act's impact on higher education is found in two areas we explore in this chapter: access to higher education and special education teacher preparation. First, we examine inclusion in elementary and secondary education.

INCLUSION IN ELEMENTARY AND SECONDARY EDUCATION

Context of inclusion

In India, inclusion must be understood within a broad context, including the large number of marginalized social groups. For example, the Indian Constitution did not assure elementary education as a fundamental right for *all* children ages, six to fourteen, until 2002. Historically, the only children assured of a good education were those from wealthy families who could afford private education. Poor or lower-caste children inevitably received little or no education and the few disabled children who were educated attended segregated NGO schools. It was not until the installation of the United Progressive Alliance (UPA) Government in 2004 that broad governmental attention was given to inclusive education. In its report to the Forty-seventh session of the International Conference on Education in Geneva (Government of India, 2004), the UPA "expressed its resolve and commitment to the Indian ethos of truly inclusive development" (3) and announced its National Common Minimum Programme (NCMP) in which disparities in access, improvement of the quality and content of education, and devolution of educational policy were key features. To achieve these and other goals of the NCMP, the UPA promised to increase economic security and ensure full equality of opportunity in education and employment. While much of the early text centered on the need for these goals in relation to women and girls, rural villagers, and "Scheduled Castes, Tribes, Other Backward Classes (OBCs) and religious minorities" (4), the text of the Programme later includes disabled children in the list of disadvantaged groups. Inclusive elementary education, universal secondary education, and access to higher education are listed as priorities for these "disadvantaged" groups. Furthermore, "Integrated Education for Disabled Children," a government/NGO partnership program, was initiated "to integrate children with mild to moderate disability in mainstream education" (66).

Dr. Nidhi Singal (2005) argues that while highlighting marginalized social groups based on gender, caste, disability, and so on, "as being in need of specific attention may ensure that their needs are being met," it reproduces the very problem of marginalization in societies in which disability rights have been won to some extent. It makes them "stand apart [and] also exposes them to marginalisation from mainstream developments." She continues,

> For instance, a large number of children with disabilities are the responsibility of a different minority are catered [to] in narrowly focused programmes, but are not explicitly accounted for within the framework of general education. This highlights

the classic dilemma of difference discussed by Minow (1990, 20), which states that the stigma of difference may be recreated both by ignoring and by focusing on it. (Section 7, ¶ 2)

While we agree in theory with Minow's critique referenced above, we do not address it further for two reasons. First, while important, elaboration on such a critique is outside the scope of this chapter. Our goal is to attempt to document some of the progress being made even though that progress is occurring within a context of extreme challenges. Second, to integrate Minow's claim with our goal leaves us wondering pragmatically—what alternatives are immediately available in the Indian context, given its complexities and conflicts, other than focusing on the marginalized groups identified above by the UPA? We have yet to consider the answer to this question.

NCMP interventions

Two interventions announced in the NCMP and its National Report on the Development of Education delivered at the 2004 International Conference on Education in Geneva (Government of India, 2004) are related to elementary and secondary education. The first major intervention is directed at enrolment and retention of all children with disabilities in the mainstream education system. To achieve this objective, the action plan seeks to review implementation of existing programs and identify factors leading to success or failure of the drive toward enrolment and retention of disabled children. Considering the difficulties of defining and counting disability, it is questionable whether this objective will be measurable. The second major intervention is to provide need-based educational and other supports in mainstream schools so that the appropriate curricula and teaching strategies are available for all children.

Discouraging research

In spite of such efforts, *India Together*, the online publication of the Civil Society Information Exchange of India, estimates that 90% of India's disabled children are out of school, numbering around at 40 million (Chatterjee, 2003). The National Centre for Promotion of Employment of Disabled People's (NCPEDP) (2005) Survey of mainstream schools in India (n = 89)[1] reveals the stark situation for disabled children. "A mere 0.51% of the student population consisted of disabled students, again negligible as far as the 3% reservation by the law is concerned" reports the Centre (Section 3). Even more disturbing, eighteen (20%) of the schools admitted they do not accept students with disabilities and eighteen (not necessarily the same schools) were not aware of the PWD Act. Sadly, of the 55 schools that admit disabled students, "only 20 ... employ special educators and only 12 provide training for teachers for working with disabled students" (ibid.).

In addition to the above statistics, "a 2004 government study revealed that only 0.51% disabled students are in mainstream educational institutions" in India (UNICEF, n.d.). In response, Human Resource Development Minister Arjun Singh says, "It should, and will be our objective, to make mainstream education not just available but accessible, affordable and appropriate for students with disabilities" (Government of India, 2005c, Section 2). Sadly, many promises have been made over the years through official statements by various ministers, yet so little concrete action has been taken that many disability rights activists view such promises as empty and reflecting little political will to follow through.

INCLUSION IN HIGHER EDUCATION

Access

As a result of the PWD Act, universities are encouraged to develop special education teacher training programs, to provide "equal education opportunities and experiences to disabled persons in higher education institutions," and to "equip higher education institutions with the facilities to provide access to disabled persons" (Kumar, 2006, Section 1, ¶4). In 2005 the UPA announced its *Comprehensive Action Plan on the Inclusive Education of Children and Youth with Disabilities* (Government of India, 2005a) in which it was claimed that "all schools in the country will be made disabled friendly by 2020" (Section 2, ¶6). Prepared against the backdrop of the poor educational opportunities available to disabled Indians, the action plan seeks to make four major interventions. One intervention is related to higher and vocational education but this intervention was announced seven years after another important commitment that seemed to get lost in the policy shuffle.

In 1998, a mere three years after the PWD Act was enacted, UNESCO held an International Conference on Adult Education in Mumbai at which the *Mumbai Statement on Lifelong Learning, Active Citizenship, and the Reform of Higher Education* (UNESCO, 1998) was developed. This statement committed the signatories to open the doors of higher education to men and women and adapt their "programmes and learning conditions to meet their needs" (ibid., ¶3), implying that adapting programs and meeting needs could include disabled students. Confirmation of this can be found in the *Mumbai Statement's* reiteration of the Hamburg Declaration, which was developed at the UNESCO International

Conference on Adult Education in 1997. The Hamburg Declaration reads, in part, that "learning throughout life," including learning that occurs in institutions of higher education as well as other settings, requires the "rethinking of content to reflect such factors as age, gender equality, *disability*, language, culture and economic disparities" (ibid., ¶1, emphasis added).

To go back to the 2005 Action Plan of UPA, the NCPEDP in India conducted a survey of three levels of educational institutions: (1) universities; (2) colleges; and (3) elementary, middle, and high schools in India. Of the 322 universities in India 119 (36.9%) responded. The following data, the result of university surveys in a country of 1.1 billion people, are extremely disheartening (NCPEDP, 2005).[2]

- 1635 disabled students were enrolled.
- 24 universities (20%) admittedly did not follow the 3% reservation rule.
- 1203 students with physical impairments were enrolled and only 18 universities (15%) reported providing appropriate desks and chairs for students with physical impairments.
- 311 students with visual impairments were enrolled and only 16 universities had assistive software and only 10 universities provided books in Braille.
- 38 students with hearing impairments were enrolled and only 10 universities provided sign language interpreters.
- 76.3% of the disabled students in all 119 universities were male and only 23.7% were female.

Teacher education

The PWD Act requires the development of "teacher training programmes specializing in disabilities so that requisite trained man power is available for special schools and integrated schools for children with disabilities (PWD Act, Section 29, Chapter V). It follows that if disabled children are attending schools, then special education teachers are needed. However, the statistics reported by the NCPEDP in the previous section call into question the claim that disabled children are attending school. Teacher education has been identified as central to the success of the government's plans, which include the modification of teaching methodologies. For the first time the government is considering developing national norms for inclusive education and special education teachers "to enable them to work with children with disability in an inclusive education system" (Mukul, 2005). India's attempts at inclusive education are attempts at making it possible for disabled children to attend public school rather than stay at home or attend segregated NGO schools. For India, this is an important first step.

CONCLUSION

In 1994, for example, Mazurek and Winzer (1994) categorized Indian special education as "emerging" and based on the data we report in this chapter, it still appears to be emerging, particularly as related to preparing teachers for disabled children in the classroom. One of the roadblocks to inclusive education is the "attitude of charity and service to the destitute," the "fair degree of fatalism rooted in the philosophy of *karma*," and the "belief that actions in this life decide one's future reincarnation" (Agrawal, 1994, 187). Another roadblock is the lack of reliable demographic information that will allow the government to identify disabled people and measure the success of inclusive education initiatives. Even now, it is unclear how many disabled Indians—adult or child—need access to education, although it is very clear that the number is extremely large. The data in the NCPEDP surveys, then, must be understood in the context of these unreliable statistics.

On the other hand, the initiatives of the Government of India are, indeed, landmarks in disability rights movement in India and could go a long way in transforming the societal attitude toward disabled people, particularly if the initiatives are implemented and disabled people are seen learning and succeeding in elementary and secondary schools, colleges, and universities. While the World Bank (2006) claim that India is "making progress on a scale, size, and pace that is unprecedented in its own history" is heartening, our hope is that the same scale, size, and pace of economic progress will be applied to inclusive education also.

NOTES

1. Surveys were sent to 318 schools and only 89 responded.
2. Data on students with mental illness or cognitive impairment are not available.

REFERENCES

Ahluwalia, H. P. S. (2003). Training for rehabilitation: Interview with major H. P. S. Ahluwalia. *Frontline 29*(10). Retrieved July 1, 2007 from http://www.hinduonnet.com/fline/fl2010/stories/20030523004311100.htm.

Bhanushali, K. (n.d.). Dimensions of disability in India. In Disability India Network. Retrieved May 18, 2007 from http://www.disabilityindia.org/djartjan06A.cfm.

Chatterjee, G. (2003). The movement for inclusive education. *India Together*. Retrieved July 2, 2007 from http://www.indiatogether.org/2003/apr/edu-inclusive.htm.

Gabel, S. L. (2004). South Asian cultural orientations toward mental retardation. *Mental Retardation 42*, 12–25.

Gabel, S. L., Vyas, S., Patel, H., & Patel S. (2001). Problems of methodology in cross-cultural disability studies: An India immigrant example. In S. N. Barnartt & B. M. Altman, Eds., Exploring theories and expanding methodologies: Where we are and where we need to go. *Research in Social Science and Disability 2*, 209–228.

Government of India (1986). *National Policy on Education*. New Delhi: Ministry of Human Resource Development.

Government of India (1996). *The Persons with Disabilities (Equal Opportunities, Protection of Rights and Full Participation Act, 1995)*. New Delhi: Government of India.

Government of India (2004). India: National report on the development of education. The Indian education system at the beginning of the 21st century: An overview. Retrieved July 1, 2007 from http://www.ibe.unesco.org/International/ICE47/english/Natreps/reports/india.pdf.

Government of India (2005a). *Comprehensive action plan for inclusive education of children and youth with disabilities*. New Delhi: Ministry of Human Resource Development. Retrieved July 1, 2007 from http://education.nic.in/INCLUSIVE.asp.

Government of India (2005b). *Draft national policy for persons with disabilities*. New Delhi: Ministry of Social Justice and Empowerment. Retrieved July 1, 2007 from http://socialjustice.nic.in/Draftpolicy.pdf.

Government of India (2005c). Inclusive education. Retrieved July 1, 2007 from http://education.nic.in/INCLUSIVE.asp.

Kumar, A. (2006). India's Jawaharlal Nehru University: Special education. *Mobility International USA*. Retrieved May 18, 2007 from http://www.miusa.org/ncde/intlopportunities/india.

Mazurek, K., & Winzer, M. A., Eds. (1994). *Comparative studies in special education*. Washington, DC: Gallaudet University Press.

Minow, M. (1990). *Making all the difference: Inclusion, exclusion and American law*. Ithaca: Cornell University Press.

Mitra, M. N. (2005). Swift response triumph. *Education World: The Human Development Magazine*. Retrieved July 2, 2007 from http://www.educationworldonline.net/eduworld/article.php?choice=prev_art&article_id=344&issueid=29.

Mukul, A. (2005). HRD ministry's agenda for the disabled. *The Times of India*, September 14. Retrieved July 1, 2007 from http://timesofindia.indiatimes.com/articleshow/1230177.cms.

National Centre for Promotion of Employment of Disabled People (2005). Status in universities. Retrieved July 1, 2007 from http://www.ncpedp.org/eductn/ed-resrch.htm#univ.

North-South Dialogue III (2003). *The Kochi Declaration*. Kochi, Kerala, India. Retrieved July 2, 2007 from http://www.inclusion-international.org/site_uploads/1119008867197086195.pdf.

Office of the Registrar General of India (2001). Census of India 2001. Retrieved December 31, 2006 from http://censusindia.net/results/disabled_main.html.

Pandey, R. S., & Advani, L. (1995). *Perspectives on disability and rehabilitation*. Delhi: Vikas Publishing House.

Pinto, P. E., & Sahu, N. (2001). *Working with persons with disabilities: An Indian perspective*. Buffalo: Center for International Rehabilitation Research Information and Exchange.

Sen, A. (1992). *Mental handicap among rural Indian children*. New Delhi: Sage Publications.

Singal, N. (2005). Responding to difference: Policies to support "inclusive education" in India. Paper presented at the Inclusive and Supportive Education Congress and the International Special Education Conference. Glasgow, Scotland.

Srivastava, A. K., Tripathi, A. M., & Misra, G. (1995). Western and Indian perspectives on intelligence: Some reflections. *Indian Education Review 30*(2), 30–45.

UNESCO (1998). *The Mumbai statement on lifelong learning, active citizenship and the reform of higher education.* Retrieved July 1, 2007 from http://www.unesco.org/education/uie/confintea/mumbeng.shtml.

UNICEF (n.d.). Government of India announces plan to make education disabled-friendly by 2020. Retrieved July 1, 2007 from http://www.unicef.org/india/media_610.htm.

Vyas, S. (1996). Special education in Indian educational organizations: The social construction of learning disabilities in schools in Bombay. Paper presented at the American Educational Research Association. San Diego, CA.

World Bank (2004). Poverty in India. Issue brief. Retrieved July 1, 2007 from http://siteresources.worldbank.org/INTINDIA/Data%20and%20Reference/20283013/Poverty_India_Brief.pdf.

World Bank (2007). India data profile. Retrieved July 1, 2007 from http://devdata.worldbank.org/external/CPProfile.asp?PTYPE=CP&CCODE=IND.

CHAPTER SIX

Inclusion?

LINDA J. GRAHAM AND ROGER SLEE

INTRODUCTION

Whilst inclusive education is a relatively recent advance in our thinking about schooling and pedagogy, it is a rapidly establishing movement simultaneously reflected in and refracted by education policy, research, and scholarship. This is manifest in the proliferation of policy texts and programmes generated by education jurisdictions globally and locally, and in the burgeoning number of scholarly texts, academic conferences, and research grants dedicated to inclusive education.

As a result, familiarity with the terminology of inclusive education has grown considerably. Somewhat problematically though, there exist competing discourses through which meaning and understandings differ. On the surface these differences are concealed by the continued use of generalised terms within the schooling vernacular. These are terms that assume a benign commonality, but this is a dangerous assumption. Elsewhere Slee (1996) has drawn on Said's depiction of travelling theories to capture the "domestication" and "taming" of subversive theories that have been appropriated and popularized by others to articulate the colonisation of inclusive education philosophy. Originally, inclusive education was offered as a protest; a call for radical change to "traditional" schooling. Increasingly, it is being used as a means for explaining and protecting the status quo.

At least this is what we see happening in the Australian state of Queensland,[1] where the implementation of practices to promote the inclusion of students with disabilities is understood as the achievement of an inclusive education system. One could reasonably argue however, that "[w]e are *still* citing inclusion as our goal; *still* waiting to include, yet *speaking* as if we are already inclusive" (Slee & Allan, 2001, p. 181, emphasis added). This premature articulation, if you will forgive the expression, reveals the underlying disparity in the discourse/s of inclusion. Education Queensland states a commitment "guaranteeing inclusiveness" (Education Queensland, 2002, p. 4); however, we contend that to include is not necessarily to *be* inclusive. The Queensland model, like experiments elsewhere (Allan, 2003), fails to secure inclusiveness due to the existence and extension of uninterrogated normative assumptions that shape and drive policy (Popkewitz & Lindblad, 2000).[2] These assumptions about identity, difference, and academic trajectories inform the construction of reform agendas that do no more than tinker at the edges to produce an *appearance* of more inclusive schools, whilst privileged notions of a "mainstream" persist.

According to this logic, for others to be "included," accommodations have to be made and concessions granted. Benevolent humanitarianism (Ware, 2002), is hard to criticise because attitudes can so easily swing the other way. For example in Australia, indigenous peoples have struggled for justice in a racist pro-white society, winning small concessions and accommodations over the years. However, their call for an apology from the nation has met with intractable opposition from government, inflamed by race-card politics at both state and federal levels. This is being fuelled at the highest level by the take-up of discourse/s that position the historical dispossession, discrimination, and genocide of Aborigines as a "black arm band" view of Australian history (Grattan, 2006). Suddenly, the accommodations and concessions appear too generous and retreat from justice legitimate (Barry, 2006).

There is much scholarly work that points to the tactics, physical and discursive, overt and covert (see Marx, 2003; McCarthy, 2003), that people from dominant groups adopt when they feel their positions of power and privilege are being threatened. Our prime minister's 2006 "Australia Day" address and right-wing political conservatism are exemplars of such resistance. To critique the move to include is a similarly risky affair. However, avoidance may mean that we tolerate systems that profess to be inclusive but in reality engage in practices that are anything but. In this chapter we argue that the discursive politics of "inclusion," which comes to be accompanied by cosmetic adjustments to traditional schooling (Slee & Allan, 2001) simply works to (re)secure an invisible centre from which constructions of Otherness and the designation of marginal positions become possible (Ferguson, 1990). It is hoped that this chapter will provoke consideration of and renewed debate over

- what is meant by talk of inclusion,
- how this may differ from being inclusive, and
- whose interests may be served by practices that seek to include.

Perhaps in this way we can jettison the rhetorical inertia of instrumentalist gestures "*towards* inclusion" (Slee & Allan, 2001), by making visible and deconstructing the centre from which all exclusions derive.

EXORCISING PRESENCES AT CENTRE

> It is in general a question of method: instead of moving from an apparent exteriority to an essential "nucleus of interiority" we must conjure up the illusory interiority in order to restore words and things to their constitutive exteriority. (Deleuze, 1988, p. 43)

As Deleuze suggests, we must look to words and things for how they might work to constitute exteriority. Correspondingly, Graham argues that the term inclusion suggests a *bringing in*; for it arguably presupposes a whole into which something (or someone) can be incorporated. Thus, it is reasonable to argue that there is an implicit centred-ness to the term *inclusion*, for it discursively privileges notions of the pre-existing by seeking to include the Other into a prefabricated, naturalised space. Thus Derrida's statement that "language bears within itself the necessity of its own critique" (Derrida, 1967, p. 358) is particularly pertinent to inclusive education, for the movement is troubled by the multiplicity of meanings that lurk within the discourses that surround and carry it.

There isa need to question "inclusion's need to speak of and identify otherness" (Harwood & Rasmussen, 2002, p. 5), as this works to produce both centre and margin through the privileging of "universal categories and a romanticized, universalised subject" (Lather, 2003, p. 260). As the term inclusion arguably presupposes the already-begun, perhaps the term inclusive is less likely to bring about the sense of foreclosure that appears inherent to inclusion. To "liberate the repressed contradictions always-already present" (Trifonas, 2000, p. 274) in the terms include and inclusion, we argue for the *deliberate use* of the term "inclusive" but following Derrida, "let us use quotation marks to serve as a precaution" (Derrida, 1967, p. 351). This may remind us that the centre into which we talk of including is but a barren and fictional place.

If we must talk of inclusion, then we argue for an invocation of the Derridean concept of writing under erasure which is,

> … to keep something visible but crossed out, to avoid universalizing or monumentalising it, a form of a warning of an irreducibility outside of intentional control in the play of the world, keeping a term as both a limit and resource, opening it up to margins. (Lather, 2003, p. 263)

Spivak explains, "[S]ince the word is inaccurate, it is crossed out. Since it is necessary, it remains legible" (Spivak, 1997, p. xiv). The benefit to writing under erasure as opposed to devising new words is that the word signifies the meaning we are all used to, but the crossing out adds a political message, a dimension of criticality that a whole new word would fail to achieve. Indeed, Spivak cautions against (re)inventing language in an attempt to escape that-which-has-gone-before, stating, "[T]o make a new word is to run the risk of forgetting the problem or believing it solved" (p. xv). Fittingly then, reference to "inclusive" in inclusive education scholarship and research can challenge the centred-ness implicit in limited or tokenistic attempts to "include" the marginalised Other. Such limited notions of inclusion are characterised by incremental accommodations for alterity within an otherwise "mainstream" education system (Graham, 2006).

Perhaps the question now is not so much how do we move "*towards* inclusion" (Slee & Allan, 2001, p. 180, emphasis in original), but what do we do to disrupt the construction of centre from which exclusion derives? This is not as simple as it may seem.

It is relatively easy to point to exclusion and the excluded (Stiker, 1999) but much harder to dismantle the structural and political arrangements determining their position at the margins. However, when we do seek to address exclusion, we make visible the conditions of exclusion by pointing to exceptional characteristics as the markers of difference. And so we go around in circles, for the question to-come but which has not-yet-come in inclusive education research and scholarship is: Different from *what*? What we do not question (but should) are the assumptions that enable us to think in terms of exceptionalities. What normative circuitry may we be drawing on to do this and what circuit breakers might we deploy to avoid turning "desire for assimilation into a norm that supports the perception of disability [and difference] as an alien or exceptional condition" (ibid., p. xi)?

Stiker argues that "a community's marginality is implicitly underscored by the request for inclusion itself" and calls for an examination of the different forms of social inclusion. He states,

> The dilemma, exclude or include, hides a whole series of exclusions that are not all the same and of inclusions which are not all commensurate. We could just as well say that the dilemma is *illusory*. What are societies doing when they exclude in one way or another and when they integrate in this fashion or that? What do they say about themselves in so doing? The study of everything that we could call the marginalized allows us to bring out previously ignored or neglected dimensions of that society. (pp. 16–17, emphasis added)

It can be argued that an authentically inclusive education invites the denaturalisation of "normalcy" to arrive at a ground-zero point from which we banish idealisations of centre. In this way, the language of special and regular education is rendered redundant. If we listen to teachers, education administrators, and academics as they discuss inclusive education and the range of kids who present for schooling, we soon hear that we are a long way from where inclusive schooling should take us. There remains a firmly embedded notion of what a regular school is and more particularly, who it is for. Others may be allowed in, but theirs remains a conditional entry and tenure (Slee, 1996), for inclusion by no means "guarantees inclusiveness" (Education Queensland, 2002, p. 4).

After further conceptualising the theoretical terrain, we will return to this point to interrogate the local context and discuss the problem/s with labelling later in this chapter. In the meantime we argue that limited notions and models of inclusion, realised through what Sleedubs "resources equations" (p. 6), simply work to ensure the objectivisation of individual difference. This results not only in an ever more complex and insidious exclusion but also in refining schooling as a field of application for disciplinary power (Graham, 2006).

In seeking to know the particularities of individual school children, resourcing mechanisms such as Education Queensland's Ascertainment/EAP[3] (Education Queensland, 2002) and Appraisement Intervention[4] (Education Queensland, 2001), allow for the differentiation between and validation/invalidation of different ways of being. Such normalising lenses, ushered into schools under the pretext of better resourcing "the included,"[5] further open-up schools to a technique of government that Foucault calls "discipline-normalisation" (Foucault, 1975a, p. 52), thus providing the means by which we make judgements about the character, ability, and future of different school children.

The deployment of a post-structural analysis relating to disciplinary power can provide a helpful lens to look differently, "think otherwise" (Ball, 1998), and in this way, interrogate the conjoined nature of inclusion/exclusion. In this chapter, we do not simply critique limited notions of inclusion (Graham, 2005) and the inevitable exclusions that result. Instead, we aim to look not beyond but *before*; to make explicit and interrogate the normative assumptions that lead us to think we can even talk of "including."

NORMATIVE CONNECTIVITY

For the differentiation, categorisation, and spatialisation of individuals to become possible, one must have a common referent to consult. This was achieved by the human sciences through the construction of the norm (Foucault, 1972, 1975b, 1977) securing psychology's role in "governing the soul" through techniques of normalisation and the strategic stimulation of subjectivity, anxiety, and desire (Rose, 1990, p. 4). Under the sustained and combined influence of the medical and psychological disciplines, teachers and education administrators have become used to thinking in terms of the norm and categorising educational endeavour according to abstract notions of intelligence (Flynn, 1997) and developmental age/stage theory (Walkerdine, 1984). As Ewald points out, though such "normative individualisation comes about without reference to any nature or essence in subjects ... it is purely comparative" (Ewald, 1992, p. 172). It can be unsettling to acknowledge that the norm is a fiction; however, normalisation is a man-made grid of intelligibility that attributes value to culturally specific performances and in doing so, privileges particular ways of being. Similarly, Ewald reminds us that "it is not the exception that proves the rule. Rather, the exception is *within* the rule" (ibid., p. 173, emphasis added).

Although predicated as natural and true, the rule of the norm is statistically derived, negating the diversity to be found within nature and the naturalness of diversity. Educational use of the norm and normative judgement is disturbingly pervasive as the psychological notion of the norm has acquired legitimacy through a parasitic effect producing its own truth within powerful domains of knowledge production, such as special education and educational psychology. Macherey speaks to this effect when he states, "[I]f the norm is not exterior to its field of application, this is not only because ... it produces it but because it produces itself in it as it produces it" (Macherey, 1992, p. 187).

Correspondingly, Ewald stipulates that "the norm, or normative space, knows no outside" (Ewald, 1992, p. 187). This may seem an irreconcilable argument in an attempt at theorising inclusion/exclusion or experiences of interiority and exteriority; however, this can be understood by returning to Foucault's premise that there is nothing outside of power. That is, there are domains of interiority (centricity) and domains of exteriority (ex-centricity), but neither is free from the effects of "discipline-normalisation" (Foucault, 1975b, p. 52); that is, every*thing* is within the realm of disciplinary power. Even those at centre are shaped through subjectivation and are positioned, their tenuous presence being held in check by normative prescriptions of what is right or what is normal.

Indeed, it could be said that the pervasiveness of disciplinary power is assured by the *proliferation* of centre/s which presents multiple opportunities for the workings of discipline-normalisation through the experiencing of multiple subjectivities. In describing power as diffuse, Foucault cautions against theorising a centralised power (Foucault, 1980a), as in state power or state control, or dare we say, the education civil service. Therefore, a theorisation of *centre* must not be confused with the centralisation of power. There are no headquarters for disciplinary power and thus problematically and no head to cut off, which explains to some degree, the *power* of power and the perplexing endurance of inclusion/exclusion.

Foucault argues we must "eschew the model of Leviathan in the study of power" and "instead base our analysis of power on the study and tactics of domination" (Foucault, 1980, p. 102). He insists "power must be analysed as something that circulates ... through a net-like organisation" (Foucault, 1980b, p. 98). This organisation functions via disciplines (hospitals, prisons, schools, etc.) as carriers of an arbitrating discourse, although Foucault points out that, whilst this discourse speaks of a rule, the code these disciplines come to define "is not that of law but that of normalisation" (p. 107). Tying the disciplines together in a diffuse but cohesive network of power are the sinuous threads of normative discourses through which disciplinary society communicates with itself (Ewald, 1992), producing both "the elements on which it acts" and "the means to control these elements" (Macherey, 1992, p. 178). This is a "form of power that makes individuals subjects" (Foucault, 1983, p. 214), where the use of discursive dividing practices "categorizes the individual, marks him by his own individuality, attaches to him his own identity, imposes a law of truth on him that he must recognize and others have to recognize in him" (ibid.). This results in the compartmentalisation of individuals into spatialised domains and we illustrate this in Figure 1 below.

In the educational context these domains, constructed by virtue of psychological and special education knowledge claims, become filled by so-called target groups for inclusion—disabled children, learning disabled children, disruptive or disordered children, ESL (English as a Second language) children, disadvantaged and at-risk children, and Indigenous children (Education Queensland, 2004a, 2004b, 2004c).[6] In this process of individuation (Foucault, 1975b, 1977), schooling operates as a field of application for disciplinary power (Allan, 1999). This occurs through the production of normative domains as comparative grids of intelligibility that are not only constitutive of exteriority but protective of the centre from which they emanate.

Normalisation produces these domains through normalising discourses that affirm or negate particular ways of being. These discourses can be drawn as two

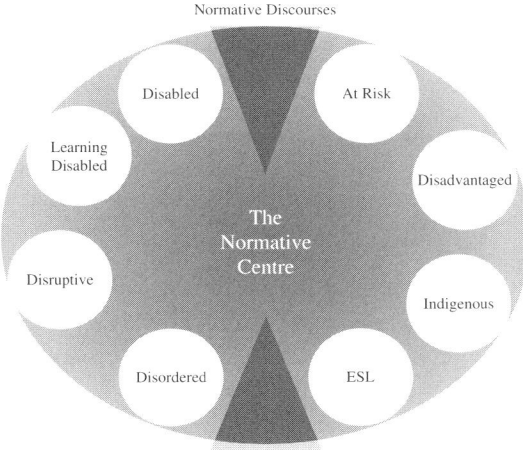

Figure 6.1. Production of spatialised domains.

poles of division (Macherey, 1992, p. 177). On one side, as depicted in Figure 1 below, we have normative discourses comprising valorisation and affirmation of statements of the desirable and the normal subject. On the other, we have statements of deficit and conceptualisations of the other than normal, discourses that demarcate the abnormal object. As a result of the constitutive pressure of these two discursive poles denoting consistent subject and object of error, we can visualise a discursive centre and conceptualise a place representative of normative action and anonymous expressions of disciplinary power.

Within this centre we find the privileged notion of "the permissible and the normal" (ibid., p. 177), outside of which but always within a relational existence is the negative characterised by the pathological, the minority, the Other. The subject's relationship to the norm is dependent upon whether the subject as object is internalised within the boundary of the norm or externalised as beyond its limit. Conversely, the abnormal is defined through transgression of these limits through practices of identification and disqualification, recognition and non-recognition and is a way of being that exists at the margins, held in an external relationship to privileged social norms. It is here that we can find domains of interiority and exteriority within an ostensibly inclusive education environment. From this, we can start to conceptualise how it is that education, as a field of application of normalising judgement, both sets up and is beset by the conjoined nature of inclusion/exclusion.

NORMATIVE (IN)VISIBILITY

Inclusion can thus be theorised as a discursive strategy in a political game that constructs not simply position (modes of interiority/exteriority) but the play by which borders and limits are conceived (Derrida, 1967).

> Play is always play of absence and presence, but if it is to be thought of radically, play must be conceived of before the alternative of presence and absence. Being must be conceived of as presence or absence on the basis of the possibility of play and not the other way around. (p. 369)

However, Ferguson points out that "the place from which power is exercised is often a hidden place. When we try to pin it down, the centre always seems to be somewhere else" (Ferguson, 1990, p. 9). This is perhaps because, as Derrida argues, there *is no* centre but instead an *absence* of centre for which infinite substitutions are made, for there is no natural essence, origin or "invariable presence" (Derrida, 1967, p. 353), supporting a legitimate claim to centre.

> The substitute does not substitute itself for anything which has somehow existed before it. Henceforth, it was necessary to begin thinking that there was no centre,

that the centre could not be thought of in the form of a present-being, that the centre had no natural site, that it was not a fixed locus but a function, a sort of nonlocus in which an infinite number of sign-substitutions came into play. (pp. 353–354)

Highlighting the artificial constitution of centred-ness, Derrida points to "a lack which must be *supplemented*" (p. 367, emphasis in original) through the addition of a sign which (re)places the centre. Thus, when lacking "a natural site" (p. 353) and faced with an absence of centre that is needed in a gyroscopic sense to limit "the play of the structure" (p. 352), we discursively inscribe signifiers of centred-ness producing a *ghostly* centre. This is an apparition that eludes critical examination, for it has no essence, presence, or definitive claim to Being. However this substitution of sign, substituting presence (i.e., singularity/normality/whiteness/able-bodiedness etc.) for absence (multiplicity/diversity), prepares the ground for the deployment of relations of power therein because, as Derrida argues, in "orienting and organizing the coherence of the system, the centre of a structure permits the play of its elements inside the total form" (p. 352). This confers privilege on those whose characteristics align with predicated social norms. In a movement that speaks of the eternal return, the same individuals in positions of power who gaze from the vantage of privilege set the parameters of normality and manage the markers of difference.[7] Thus, those at centre ride the boundaries determining centricity and ex-centricity. However, privilege and position at centre are dependent upon the subjection and marginalisation of the other. The maintenance of positions of power through discursive dividing practices as rhetorical strategies (Nakayama & Krizek, 1995) that (re)secure domination and privilege results in the reinstatement of the politic of the powerful. This goes some way towards explaining the conjoined and stubborn nature of inclusion/exclusion.

WORDS AND THINGS

The realisation of the "structurality of structure" according to Derrida was "the moment when language invaded the universal problematic, the moment when, in the absence of a centre or origin, everything became discourse" (Derrida, 1967, pp. 353–354). Recognising the primacy of discourse (Foucault, 1972) in constructions of centre and margin and thus, the implication of discourse in the conjoined nature of inclusion/exclusion, we seek to interrogate the discourse of inclusion as "a play of substitutions" (Derrida, 1967, p. 365); a play that substitutes an appearance of presence in the absence of a fixed and universal essence. It could also be said that the discourse of inclusion functions to substitute another appearance of presence, that of the Other, whose "presence" obscures the absence of genuine inclusiveness. In this way, the discourse of inclusion may indeed function as strategic rhetoric (Nakayama & Krizek, 1995) that supports this "movement of supplementarity" (Derrida, 1967, p. 365) by obscuring the constructedness and territoriality of a normative, fictional centre (Deleuze & Guattari, 1987).

This occurs through the use of dominant discourses that invoke a mythical norm (Ferguson, 1990), creating both centre and margin by defining and universalising "tacit standards from which specific others can then be declared to deviate" (p. 9). This perpetuates a shadowy and (un)articulable place for those whose interests it serves (Deleuze, 1988; Ewald, 1992); an invisible nerve-centre from which socio-political relations of power that strengthen existing structural arrangements are strategically and anonymously deployed. Realised through technologies that make visible particular objects of scrutiny (Graham, 2006), inclusion functions as a panoptic mechanism through techniques that allow "the assignment to each individual his 'true' name, his 'true' place, his 'true' body, his 'true' disease" (Foucault, 1977, p. 198).

Thus, when realised through normative practices that identify and make visible difference as forms of alterity to include, inclusion works to (re)secure the position and "invisibility of the centre" (Ferguson, 1990, p. 11) through the *normalisation* of culturally specific performances as particular expressions of academic, physical, creative ability; and the *naturalisation* of particular ways of being which are characterised by whiteness, maleness, able-bodiedness and so on. It is our contention that such limited notions of inclusion (Graham, 2005) qualify as strategy within a political project that fundamentally is "more about the disablement of conflict than the recognition of rights" (Rose, 1990, p. 123). Moreover resourcing mechanisms that "measure, supervise and correct" (Foucault, 1997, p. 199), such as Queensland's Ascertainment/EAP and Appraisement Intervention,[8] operate as an exercise in what Foucault describes as "binary division and branding" (p. 199). This results in an illusory interiority; an apprehended inclusion, where the maintenance of notions relating to normality, mainstream, natural and majority ensures that certain children exist as the "included" Other.

THE POWER OF LANGUAGE, THE LANGUAGE OF POWER

As discussed earlier, Derrida argues that the desire for a centre to "orient and organise the coherence of a system" (p. 352), leads to the supplementation of a central signifier that is played off against other signifiers in a system of differences. The maintenance of this central signifier results in an *appearance* of centred-ness within the social imaginary that is spoken into existence through tactical statements that allude to a natural human essence by discursively constructing an/other. This movement establishes a socio-political pivot to secure dominant relations of power, fulfilling "humankind's common desire … for a stable centre, and for the assurance of mastery—through knowing and possessing" (Spivak, 1997, p. xi).

Derrida's notion of *différance* speaks to this movement. *Différance* is a play on the French word *différer*, which means either to differ or to defer. *Différance* suspends by simultaneously differing *and* deferring. In the context of this discussion, interiority and exteriority, or centricity and ex-centricity (Hutcheon, 1988) occur through the movement of *différance* where the naming or signification of the other obtains meaning only through the effacement of other meanings. Thus, for one meaning to prevail, it must not only differ from other meanings but also suspend them entirely; it must *defer*. Derrida notes, "[D]ifferences are 'produced'—deferred—by *différance*" (Derrida, 1982, p. 14). Thus, it can be argued that signification (in this case, naming or labelling) brings about a double movement, working not only to differentiate but also to defer. In this, labelling works to bring certain characteristics to the fore, making them visible. At the same time, the play of *différance* defers—effacing and naturalising—in effect, achieving invisibility for *that-which-is-not named*.

THE PROBLEM/S WITH LABELLING

Perhaps it is here that we can return to a theorisation of inclusion/exclusion in education and question—What else we might be doing when we identify groups that we must work to "include." For example, in a School Report for "Kilternan State School"[9] in the Australian state of Queensland, the school is identified as a "co-educational community based primary school," which

> … includes a Special Education Unit (these students are mainly diagnosed as having Autistic Spectrum Disorder and/or Intellectual Impairment). "Kilternan" is a diverse community where inclusive practices are paramount. Some cultural backgrounds include Indigenous Australians, Serbian, Ethiopian, Arabic, Thai, Japanese and Malaysian. (School Report, Researcher Archive, 2005)

Arguably, this report elucidates how naming of the Other to facilitate or demonstrate their "inclusion" functions to naturalise normalised ways of being. In this example, alterity (difference in behavioural or intellectual performances, colour, culture, appearance, first language) is named and when we do this, "we point up a difference" (Stiker, 1999, p. 5). Once again, however, we return to the question: Different from *what*? Existing un-named in this tokenistic play in the "pure politics of identity" (Said, 1993, p. 310) are the characteristics held by dominant groups, which in Australia can be said to include whiteness, able-bodiedness, English as a first language, and so on.

We see striking correlations here with Sleeter's (1993) description of how race comes to be pedagogically constructed:

> Americans of color were lumped with immigrants who were collectively defined as "other," bringing customs that are, at best, interesting to learn about and share when there is time. "Whiteness" was taken as the norm, as natural ... multidimensional representations of whiteness throughout the school were treated as a neutral background not requiring comment. (p. 167)

However, in the "Kilternan" School Report, *other* culture is not the only form of Otherness being named, as performative anomalies relating to notions of "normalcy" are also identified, as depicted in Figure 2 below. Here, normalcy is established through an unsaying; an *absence* of descriptions of what it is that constitutes normalcy, although it is arguably conceived as a way of being that is underpinned by the taken-for-granted "nature" of whiteness, able-bodiedness, ability, and so on.[10]

This play of differences succeeds through the movement of *différance* (Derrida, 1982), in which the differing and deferring of difference results in an uncontested, naturalised domain at centre.

Naturalisation effaces. In naturalising a particular mode of existence, we construct a universalised space free from interrogation, a ghostly centre that eludes critical analysis and thus recognition of the power relations embodied within notions of normalcy that exert influence over other ways of being (Nakayama & Krizek, 1995). When we identify categories of children, whether we refer to children at risk or children with a disability or children whose first language is not

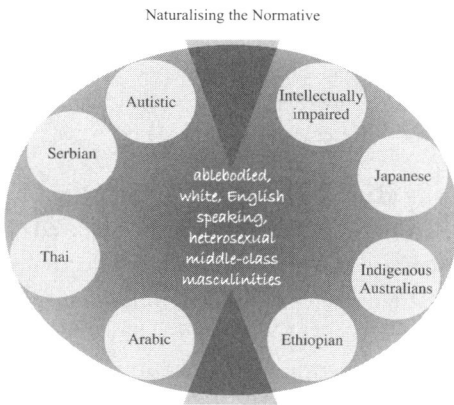

Figure 6.2. Conjuring up the illusory interiority of limited notions of inclusion.

English, we not only make difference *visible* but work to maintain power imbalances and structural inequity by reifying *unnamed* attributes that carry social, political, and cultural currency. Popkewitz and Lindblad (2000) speak to this manoeuvre when discussing the normalisation and reification of schooling performances under the rubric of urban/rural normativities:

> When one examines the education of the poor and groups that have been socially and politically marginalized in the US there are also the inscriptions of universals that go unnamed … Yet even with the absence of categories about which the normativity of the urban child is constructed, everyone knows "who" is being talked about. What is named and what goes unnamed is an effect of power. (p. 9)

Correspondingly, Popkewitz and Lindblad refer to Nicholson's argument that "such discursive practices are the effects of power where those with power can depict others but not themselves as possessing 'ethnicity' and in which men more than women see themselves as without gender" (Nicholson, 1999, p. 130 as cited in Popkewitz & Lindblad, 2000, p. 9).[11] In naming *other* "cultural backgrounds" or minority ethic groups (Indigenous Australians, Serbian, Ethiopian, Arabic, Thai, Japanese, and Malaysian) but *not-naming* the dominant group (Caucasian or European Australian), the "Kilternan" School Report fails to acknowledge the "ethnicity" of the dominant group; that is, "ethnicity" comes to be a characteristic of the Other and the "diverse community" produced by the presence of that Other is particularised as a cultural zoo. Here the project of inclusive schooling derails into "symbolic colonization" (Grinberg & Saavedra, 2000, p. 422).

Unfortunately, such erotification of *other* culture in Australian society is not new and despite the abolition of the White Australia Policy some thirty years ago, racism still runs deep.[12] Problematically though, not only does "language sustain all ideologies, including racial-nationalism" (Tavan, 2005, p. 236), but it also produces the subjects and objects about which these ideologies circulate and the subject-positions (interiority/exteriority, centre/margin) they come to inhabit. In addition, the discursive play of *différance*, which involves the differentiation and deferral of signs, leads to normative (in)visibilities. This offers up particular individuals to the full force of the gaze whilst leaving others in the relative but contingent safety of the shade.[13] In this way, in the words of Ferguson, we are,

> … returned to the invisibility of the centre. In our society dominant discourse tries never to speak its own name. Its authority is based on absence. The absence is not just that of the various groups classified as "other," although members of these groups are routinely denied power. It is also the lack of any overt acknowledgment of the specificity of the dominant culture, which is simply assumed to be the all-encompassing norm. (Ferguson, 1990, p. 11)

WHEREFORE INCLUSION?

This chapter aims to pick up the conversation from Bernadette Baker when she questions the "hunt for disability" by asking,

> What power relations inhere the production of categories such as normal and abnormal? Are these relations worthy of perpetuation? And finally, whether intended or not, is labelling a way of morphing "disability" into the assumptions of an ableist normativity, with all its racial-cultural overtones, rather than questioning certain privileged ontologies and epistemologies to begin with? (Baker, 2002, p. 689)

Our contribution to the debate is simple and to make our point, we refer back to the local context.[14] Education Queensland is committed to fostering inclusiveness. This is commendable. It must be acknowledged that Queensland education has taken giant steps in the development of the New Basics Project, Productive Pedagogies, and inclusive education initiatives and practices. It is a mistake, however, to argue that education in Queensland is authentically inclusive, since the development of inclusivity in Queensland has been attempted via methods of identification and categorisation that make visible ways of being designated as Other. As discussed, the problematic here is twofold. First, as Stiker argues, "when we name, we point up a difference" (Stiker, 1999, p. 5). Second, identification and naming of Others function to preserve existing relations of power in a reified mode of invisibility; which exists "unnamed and unexplored" (Allen, 1999, p. 5) as the *natural* way of being.

In other words, institutional attempts to "include" through processes that identify an/other result in an illusory interiority due to the adoption of discourses and practices that arenormative while at the same time conferring exteriority (Deleuze, 1988). Such limited notions of inclusion result in a forced and ever more strange *inclusion* (Foucault, 1975) which further opens up schools to techniques of "discipline-normalisation" (Foucault, 1975a, p. 52), legitimising judgements about the character, ability, and future of different school children as "ideal" citizens-in-the-making (Popkewitz & Lindblad, 2000; Baker, 2002; Popkewitz, 2004). The subsequent validation/invalidation of different ways of being normalises and naturalises schooling performances that are in accordance with accepted social norms whilst particularising, objectifying, and compartmentalising those that are not.

Baker conceives of this as an "outlaw ontology" that subjects the errant child to a "controlling logic of ableism" through the use of "perfecting technologies" (p. 675). Coupled to this logic is the inexorable push-pull of normalisation. Whilst we agree that "alterity is brought back to the centre to reinforce it" (p. 675), we would qualify that this does not mean that ex-centricity suddenly achieves or is granted centricity, as the discourse of inclusion would imply. Instead, we argue that the maintenance of notions of normalcy results in an exercise of disciplinary power where alterity is subjected to rehabilitation through an intensification of normalising practices (Ewald, 1992). Perhaps this is inclusion, but it is not inclusive. First, only those occupying a position of privilege at centre can "talk" of "including." Second, that talk seldom revolves around recognising and dismantling that vantage and the relations of power and domination sustaining it. Third, talk has constitutive and material effects that can function either as cultural work in a refusal of what is (Foucault, 1980a), or as strategic rhetoric that functions to obscure and (re)secure the existing order of things (Graham, 2005). Regardless of how well-intended (Baker, 2002), talk of "including" that involves what Slee calls a "technical fix" cannot help but bring into play all of the negative ontologies and discursive effects of which we have spoken here.

As Slee and Allan point out, the distinction between inclusion/exclusion (not to mention able/disabled) is discursive. Recognising the dangers in the discourses of inclusion and noting such suspicion by writing under erasure are critical steps in the realisation of an inclusive schooling ecology where "inclusion is no longer cited, but has passed spectrally into our language and processes" (Slee & Allan, 2001, p. 181). It is not enough to evaluate what was planned or what we intended to do. We must also acknowledge and bridge the gaps arising from our efforts to include. Fundamentally, we must ask what assumptions might inform our personal and collective philosophies in relation to inclusive education? What do we *mean* when we talk of including? What *happens*? *Whose* interests are being served? And most of all, into *what* do we seek to include?

NOTES

1. In Australia, education remains the authority of state governments. This means each state has a separate educational system and differences in pedagogy, governance, and structure can be found between each. Currently, one point of difference relating to the Queensland system is that the compulsory school age does not begin until the year the child turns six years of age at which point children enter grade 1. Queensland currently offers twelve years of formal schooling, whereas in other states, such as New South Wales, thirteen years of formal schooling is offered and children enter kindergarten around five years of age to commence their first compulsory year of schooling. In 2007 Queensland has implemented a full-time Preparatory year to bring this state system more into line with other Australian states; however enrolment in Prep will not be compulsory. In addition, Queensland differs in that the Primary years include grades 1–7 and Secondary school includes grades 8–12. New South Wales, for example, Primary includes K–6 and Secondary is from 7 to 12. The assessment/assessment practices and final examination schema are also unique to each state.

2. In this chapter we are cognisant of the research problematic of which Popkewitz and Lindblad (2000) speak: "When social policy and research coincide in classification of groups to be included, such research conserves the political systems of reference through accepting the practices of reform. The problem of research investigates only the effects of the given social relationships, not how those social relations may themselves be the effects of power" (see p. 8 in Popkewitz & Lindblad, [2000] Educational Governance and Social Inclusion and Exclusion: some conceptual difficulties and problematics in policy and research. *Discourse: studies in the cultural politics of education,* 21:1, pp. 5–44).
3. Ascertainment is a resourcing model that aims to appropriately provide support services to students with disabilities in schools. Ascertainment is currently being phased out in Queensland, over three years from 2005. The replacement model is Education Adjustment Program or EAP. The report findings from the Ministerial Taskforce on Inclusive Education (Students with Disabilities) were instrumental in Queensland's redevelopment of Ascertainment, and a number of the Taskforces recommendations were heeded. However, relevant to the argument being made here is that EAP is no different from Ascertainment in its reliance upon deficit/medical model descriptions of impairment and the restrictive recognition of six relatively narrow categories of disability: Intellectual Impairment, Physical Impairment, Vision Impairment, Hearing Impairment, Speech/Language Impairment, and Autistic Spectrum Disorder.
4. Appraisment Intervention is similarly an identification/resourcing model used in Queensland schools to identify and support children with learning difficulties and/or learning disability.
5. We wish to acknowledge the impact of Robin M. Smith's comment, made during an AERA 2005 Disability Studies in Education SIG session, on the construction of this paper. Robin, a disabled scholar/activist made the powerful statement during that session discussion, that she did nt want to be one of "the included." Thank you, Robin. It made us think. We hope you are pleased with the result.
6. Reference to the original inhabitants of the country now known as Australia comes most often under the title Indigenous people or Indigenous Australians. The term "Aboriginal and Torres Strait Islander peoples" attempts to acknowledge that the original inhabitants of this country are not a homogenous group but a diverse multiplicity.
7. This includes, for example, those who decide what is pathological behaviour and entextualise constructions of normality/abnormality in the DSM-IV-TR(Diagnostic and Statistical Manual of Mental Disorders, IV Text revision); those who make decisions in psychiatric offices about whether parent/teacher reports of problematic child behaviour fits any of these evolving categories; to individual teachers who interpret certain classroom behaviours as normal/acceptable, and others as abnormal/unacceptable.
8. For a more detailed analysis of how Education Queensland resourcing mechanisms and testing regimens work to pinpoint a difference and therefore contribute to exclude, see Graham (2006).
9. School name is a pseudonym. Brisbane is the capital city of Queensland, a north-easterly state of Australia.
10. Here again, following Derrida we use quotation marks to serve as a precaution, for there is nothing natural about white ascendancy and systems of domination.
11. For further discussions in the area of discursive strategies that work to (re)secure white dominance, see the 2003 special issue in *International Journal of Qualitative Studies in Education,* 16:1.
12. This cultural "exotic-fication" is uncomfortably reminiscent of an enduring White Australia sentiment that in 1901 culminated in the White Australia Policy that was aimed at restricting

immigration to particular Western European cultural groups. Heavily influenced by eugenics and racial determinism theory, the White Australia Policy endured until the mid-1970s. Until the late 1960s, Aboriginal peoples were not allowed to vote and until the 1968 referendum were not considered citizens and were counted as fauna. Finally after the 1968 referendum, Aboriginal and Torres Strait Islanders were counted in the national census. However, even after the Policy was abolished, Australian immigration sought to avoid "the difficult social and economic problems which may follow from an influx of peoples having different standards of living, traditions and cultures (Tavan, 2005, p. 192) to preserve "social homogeneity" (p. 236).

13. In referring to shade here, we do not claim that those at centre are immune to the gaze nor that they reside in the safety of darkness. Instead, consistent with Foucault's discussion of "intensification" and "redoubled insistence" (Foucault, 1977; Ewald, 1992), we suggest that there are proximal-zones of scrutiny and that the force of the gaze and intensity of light increases incrementally upon one's deviance from the "norm."

14. However, in doing so we must stipulate that the argument being made can be extrapolated to any educational context using policy that relies on the psychological notion of the "norm" and the identification and spatialisation of children according to varying degrees of individual deficit.

REFERENCES

(2001). *Appraisement Intervention: Literacy and Numeracy*. Brisbane: Education Queensland: Queensland Government. Available at: www.education.qld.gov.au.

(2002). *Ascertainment Revised Procedures and Support Materials*. Brisbane: Education Queensland: Queensland Government. 18 March. Available at: www.education.qld.gov.au.

(2004a). *Disability Standards for Education 2004; Disability Discrimination Act Amendment*. P. Ruddock. Canberra: Commonwealth Government.

(2004b). *Educational Adjustment Program for Students with Disabilities (EAP)*. Brisbane: Education Queensland: Queensland Government. Available at: www.education.qld.gov.au.

(2004c). *Inclusive Education: Students with Disabilities*. Brisbane: Education Queensland. 12 October. Available at: http://education.qld.gov.au/curriculum/learning/students/disabilities/

Allan, J. (1999) *Actively seeking inclusion: Pupils with special needs in mainstream Schools* (London, Falmer Press).

Allan, J. (2003) *Inclusion, participation and democracy: What is the purpose?* (Dordrecht, Kluwer Academic Publishers).

Allen, R. L. (1999) The hidden curriculum of whiteness: White teachers, white territory and white community. *Proceedings in American Education Research Association, April 19–23*, Montreal, Quebec, Canada.

Baker, B. (2002) The hunt for disability: The new eugenics and normalization of school children. *Teacher's College Record,* 104:4, pp. 663–703.

Ball, S. (1998) Educational studies, policy entrepreneurship and social theory, in: R. Slee, G. Weiner, & S. Tomlinson, *School effectiveness for whom?* (London, Falmer Press).

Barry, B. (2006) *Why social justice matters* (Cambridge, Polity Press).

Deleuze, G. (1988) *Foucault* (Minneapolis, University of Minnesota Press).

Deleuze, G. & Guattari, F. (1987) *A thousand plateaus: Capitalism & schitzophrenia* (Minneapolis, University of Minneapolis Press).

Derrida, J. (1967) Structure, sign and play in the discourse of the human sciences, in: *Writing and difference* (London, Routledge).
Derrida, J. (1982) *Differance*, m*argins of philosophy* (Sussex, Harvester Press).
Ewald, F. (1992) A power without an exterior, in: T. J. Armstrong, *Michel Foucault: Philosopher* (New York, Harvester Wheatsheaf).
Ferguson, R. (1990) Introduction: Invisible centre, in: R. Ferguson, *Out there: Marginalization and contemporary cultures* (New York and Cambridge, New Museum of Contemporary Art and MIT Press), pp. 9–14.
Flynn, M. (1997) The concept of intelligence in psychology as a fallacy of misplaced concreteness. *Interchange,* 28:2, pp. 231–244.
Foucault, M. (1972) *The archaeology of knowledge* (New York, Pantheon Books).
Foucault, M. (1975a) 12 February 1975, in: V. Marchetti, A. Salomoni, F. Ewald, & A. Fontana, *Abnormal: Lectures at the College de France 1974–1975* (London, Verso), pp. 137–166.
Foucault, M. (1975b) 15 January 1975, in: V. Marchetti, A. Salomoni, F. Ewald, & A. Fontana, *Abnormal: Lectures at the College de France 1974–1975* (London, Verso), pp. 31–54.
Foucault, M. (1977) *Discipline and punish: The birth of the prison* (London, Penguin Books).
Foucault, M. (1980a) Questions of method, in: J. D. Faubion, *Michel Foucault: Power* (New York, New Press), pp. 223–238.
Foucault, M. (1980b) Two lectures, in: C. Gordon, *Power/knowledge: Selected interviews & other writings 1972–1977* (New York, Pantheon Books), pp. 78–108.
Foucault, M. (1983) The Subject and Power, in: H. Dreyfus, L. & P. Rabinow (Eds.), *Michel Foucault: Beyond Structuralism and Hermeneutics* (2nd ed.) (Chicago, University of Chicago Press), pp. 208–226.
Graham, L. J. (2005). (Re)Visioning the centre: QSE-2010 and the quest for the cosmopolitan child. *Philosophy in Education Society of Australasia (PESA) Annual Conference, Hong Kong.* Available at: http://www.pesa.org.au/html/04cal.htm.
Graham, L. (2006) Caught in the net: A Foucaultian interrogation of the incidental effects of limited notions of "inclusion." *International Journal of Inclusive Education,* 10:1, pp. 3–24.
Grattan, M. (2006) Howard claims victory in national culture wars. *The Age*, Melbourne. January 26, p. 3, Available online at: http://www.theage.com.au/articles/2006/01/25/1138066861163.html?page=2.
Grinberg, J. & Saavedra, E. R. (2000) The constitution of bilingual/ESL education as a disciplinary practice: Genealogical explorations. *Review of Educational Research,* 70:4, pp. 419–441.
Harwood, V. & Rasmussen, M. L. (2002). Inspiring methodological provocateurs in inclusive educational research. *American Educational Research Association, Work in Progress presented for Foucault in Education SIG*, New Orleans, AERA.
Hutcheon, L. (1988) *A poetics of postmodernism: History, theory, fiction* (London, Routledge).
Lather, P. (2003) Applied Derrida: (Mis)Reading the work of mourning in educational research. *Educational Philosophy and Theory,* 35:3, pp. 257–270.
Macherey, P. (1992) Towards a natural history of norms, in: T. J. Armstrong, *Michel Foucault: Philosopher* (New York, Harvester Wheatsheaf), pp. 176–191.
Marx, S. (2003) Reflections on the state of critical white studies. *International Journal of Qualitative Studies in Education,* 16:1, pp. 3–5.
McCarthy, C. (2003) Contradictions of power and identity: Whiteness studies and the call of teacher education. *Qualitative Studies in Education,* 16:1, pp. 127–133.
Nakayama, T. K. & Krizek, R. L. (1995) Whiteness: A strategic rhetoric. *Quarterly Journal of Speech,* 81, pp. 291–309.

Popkewitz, T. S. (2004) The reason of reason: Cosmopolitanism and the government of Schooling, in: B. M. Baker & K. E. Heyning, *Dangerous coagulations: The uses of Foucault in the study of education* (New York, Peter Lang).

Popkewitz, T. & Lindblad, S. (2000) Educational governance and social inclusion and exclusion: Some conceptual difficulties and problematics in policy and research. *Discourse: Studies in the Cultural Politics of Education,* 21:1, pp. 5–44.

Rose, N. (1990) *Governing the soul: The shaping of the private self* (London, Routledge).

Said, E. (1993) Politics of knowledge, in: C. McCarthy & W. Crichlow, *Race, identity and representation in education* (New York, Routledge).

Slee, R. (1996) Inclusive schooling in Australia? Not yet! *Cambridge Journal of Education,* 26:1, pp. 19–33.

Slee, R. & Allan, J. (2001) Excluding the Included: A recognition of inclusive education. *International Studies in Sociology of Education,* 11:2, pp. 173–191.

Sleeter, C. E. (1993) How white teachers construct race, in: C. McCarthy & W. Crichlow, *Race, identity and representation in education* (New York, Routledge).

Spivak, G. C. (1997) Translator's preface, *Of grammatology* (Baltimore, John Hopkins University Press).

Stiker, H. J. (1999) *A history of disability* (Ann Arbour, Michigan University Press).

Tavan, G. (2005) *The long, slow death of white Australia* (Carlton North, Scribe Publications).

Trifonas, P. (2000) Jacques Derrida as a philosopher of education. *Educational Philosophy and Theory,* 32:3, pp. 271–281.

Walkerdine, V. (1984) Developmental psychology and the child-centred pedagogy: The insertion of Piaget into early education, in: J. Henriques, W. Holloway, C. Urwin, C. Venn, & V. Walkerdine, *Changing the subject: Psychology, social regulation and subjectivity* (London, Methuen & Co.), pp. 153–202.

Ware, L. (2002) A moral conversation on disability: Risking the personal in educational contexts. *Hypatia,* 17:3, pp. 143–174.

CHAPTER SEVEN

Reading Stories OF Inclusion: Engaging WITH Different Perspectives towards AN Agenda FOR Inclusion

ANDREW AZZOPARDI

PREAMBLE

"Inclusion" is an encompassing term within a whole assemblage of events. In this chapter I fluctuate from reading "inclusion" as an isolated notion to speaking about "inclusion" in a focussed applied concept in education, a contestable idiom seasoned with a mass of "currents and beliefs" (Clough and Corbett 2000). An annotation I need to make at this point is that within the local context, " inclusive education" is turning out to be a cliché—a politically correct term that is used by politicians in their speeches and for policy-makers to silence all woes. Service providers cover the tracks that often lead to a different direction than that of socio-educational "inclusion" (ibid.).

THE COMPLEX DISCOURSE OF "INCLUSION": POSITIONING THE DEBATE

The discourse of inclusive education has its own particular characteristics and has been hijacked by concerns for quality and "achievement." "Inclusion" is one vital factor that brings this conflict to the forefront based on the principle of social integrity. The essence of inclusive education is the ability to respond to diversity. It is a process by which children are given a voice (Dunn 2001; Moore 2001). The *National Minimum Curriculum* (Ministry of Education 1999) and other reforms at state level in Malta have been responsible for the restructuring in the education system conditioned by a competitive stance (Armstrong and Barton 1999). "Inclusion" needs to find its position primarily within this trajectory—engaging with the concept of success that is not engrossed in and gripped by a discourse on competition. "Inclusion" cannot remain a neutral and an apolitical discourse. It is an event located in a social experience (Camilleri 1999). The value of schooling lies in its capacity to prepare students for a life that is gripped by continuous decision making and the will to cultivate a social commitment (Ministry of Education 1999).

The transformative agenda may be cautiously identified as the ability of a disabled person not only to engage with his/her story but also to find ways in which this complex notion brings a practical understanding to life. Being transformative is localised in the social model theory (Oliver 1996; UPIAS 1976). Transformation is best seen when people are telling us about themselves as they are narrating their own stories. It is the ability to respond to the changes around them and to condition their destiny that is unfortunately more often than not cemented in paternalism, professionalisation, invisibility, voicelessness, and an absence of citizenship.

DEFINING (OR "DEFILING") "INCLUSION"

It is a very convoluted state of affairs to develop a mood that is coherent with a reality that is continually altering seemingly faster than one's own thinking. All schools seem to have an agenda to make their students subject to a wide array of rules and restrictions. These regulations prevent the students who have a diversity label from having a voice and "we" assume that the characteristic that distinguishes them prevents their involvement in regular schooling. For disabled children these trivial rules are further compounded by the existing legislation that not only refuses to recognise their voice, but assumes that it is the child's behaviour or impairment that is "the problem" or "the difficulty" preventing their participation in mainstream education (Kenworthy and Whittaker 2000, p. 220).

FICTIONAL NARRATIVES

From the stories I captured in my daily interface with exclusion in my role as a teacher in a marginalised region of the country, characterised by social exclusion, material deprivation, and lack of equal opportunities for children, youth, and adults, I compiled five semi-fictitious narratives to reflect those experiences. These narratives are an assortment of facts, fiction, and issues drawn from other stories/experiences I have come across in my assignation with excluded students.

Stories lie in the blueprint of narrators. Empirical work in the study of diversity typically values narratives and story telling as a form of emancipation, of "giving a voice" to otherwise silenced groups. In emancipatory research, the central purpose of research is seen as supporting the empowerment of service users, and the making of broader social change (Azzopardi 2000; Clough and Corbett 2000). If emancipatory research emphasises the equalisation of research relationships, changed social relations of research production, empowerment, and social change, the focus of user-controlled research lies with whoever originates and makes decisions about research and evaluation. The general contention is that such control is rarely positioned with the (disadvantage and oppressed) groups that are most liable to become informants (Barton and Armstrong 1999; Moore 2000). Stories are the way in which people seem to communicate all the time. Stories and storytelling have been a neglected part of educational research. However, a number of researchers have thankfully realised that "stories are oral literature whose meanings, forms and functions are rooted in cultural contexts, scenes and events that give meaning to action" (Cohen, Manion, and Morrison 2000, p. 302). Stories have been known to carry affluent, valid, and reputable information. *These are the stories*:

STORY 1: CHRIS AND THE BLADE

Chris and the Blade, is about this physically disabled boy, Chris. He is a young student coming from a particular part of the country, a region where I used to work as a teacher. It is a geographical area I know well, a part of the country characterised by poverty. The manifestation and the bringing together of the collective experience contribute to the weaving of a tapestry where the occurrences and the informants are brought together to deliver a message (Azzopardi 2000). In this situation, we can understand better the way students live and think, and the form interaction takes. It is a discourse that takes us well into what is being engaged with in our daily interactions.

These students know interaction through the pain of exclusion.

> I think that what brings them together is something that is a matter of culture. The culture that what's different is to be kept different *(Omar, Teacher)*.

Chris is waiting in front of his home, his face pressed between his two hands, his eyes sticky after a good night's sleep. He's as still as most things in St. Thomas Street, a narrow lane in the centre of a clamped up town with the gantry and tower cranes at one end and the fifty-year-old slums at the other. It's a dark path, leading to hell—some would say. The nauseating smell of humidity, mixed with the staunching odour of vegetable soup—a mix-up that makes you feel as if you are at the end of a day in a discounted restaurant kitchen. Piles of rubbish lie at one corner of the road, all muddled up with a colony of kittens struggling their way into this overload of rubbish. From somewhere you could hear a baby crying out from the brown lazy walls. Walking up the lane was what looked like a very normal eleven-year-old, haversack neatly stacked on his back, wearing a freshly washed and ironed white school shirt, moving with a steady pace as if he doesn't want to arrive late for his next appointment.

Rick: Hey mate what's up?
Chris: W-h-a-t-'-s u-p?
Rick: Yeah, you look as if you're off to the dungeons. It's school time man. I was looking forward to school. It was so boring these last two weeks.
Chris: Oh shit, we're late.
Rick: Oh it's OK. The Head's a twat, he won't notice.
Chris: Well my mother will!
Rick: Come on quick, we can get the bay-blades after…
Chris: After what? I'm on transport this year…
Rick: Oh don't tell me…
Chris: Yeah, don't tell me! She said it's too much for my scoliosis, too much for my arms, too much for my back and the. …
Rick: I suppose it's fair enough…
Chris: No mate it's just crap. My back is fine, I want to play ball and all my mother keeps saying is "watch out love, watch for love, watch them love. …" Oh look there's Mark… Hey Mark quick we're late…
Rick: Mark, look at my blade!
Mark: Cool man … com' on guys let's go … what about the Team, we have a game with 2A tomorrow?
Chris: Can I play?
   [Mark   and Rick look at each other puzzled]
Mark: Quick guys we're late…

Chris is a "typical" in his area. He hardly has a "voice" but still struggles to position himself within a school context that is "a completely different planet" from where he comes from, from parents who treat him as if he is still in hospital coming out of surgery and students who are more sensible than adults think they are. It is a context in which one gets confused about what the real impairment is: Is it about the social constructions of society, the perceptions of the people around this person, or the physical impairment per se? Amongst the issues that stand out is the understanding of "inclusion" tensions as thought out by the boys at school, the normality debate, the restrictive environment, the selectivity that starts even from the cult of play, the anxiety of parents, the condescending way culture decides for "him" or "her" as being "abled" or "disabled" depending on the social mood. The struggles that such individuals have to endure bring into play the way disabling barriers are designed and attitude is cultivated by isolation.

STORY 2: DUSTIN AND THE COUNSELLOR

Dustin and the Counsellor is a story that brings to surface a key issue in Maltese schools, that of the counsellor, a role elaborated within the vocational guidance teacher's "job description." Teachers in Malta are interviewed from central administration and then they are placed according to the vacancies created in schools. There is no consideration for the assortment of cultures and social baggage that teachers and students carry. This story also invokes a debate on the role of other workers/professionals and how they always tend to remain at the peripheries of the "real" social issues. "Helping professions" can turn into statutory oppressive structures. Professionals are liable to think they have a right to take a part of someone's life, dip into that experience, make some money, and move on when the time is ripe for them (Finkelstein 1987; Oliver 1991; Oliver and Sapey 1999).

Counsellor: Hi son! How's it doing at school?
Dustin: It's fine Sir!
Counsellor: You're sure? Been hearing about you quite a lot lately!
Dustin: Oh really! No, I'm cool! Well some of the teachers are litter, junk … I get blamed for everything with them!
Counsellor: Yes? But why?
Dustin: They just see me as their shark bait … I'm sincere, I'm open, so I always own up … the other kids don't … they [the teachers] just keep bragging until I'm told that I either say who it is or I'm in shit! That's not fair! I would never talk about my friends. Some teachers are bums …
Counsellor: You know I've heard things being said about you?
Dustin: Teachers are always telling tales, saying things that are not true …
Counsellor: How are you feeling after being away from this school for these two years? [Dustin has been to a residential school]
Dustin: OK. I like this school better …
Counsellor: Why?
Dustin: The teachers are much better! They talk to us as if we are their friends …
Counsellor: But you said you don't like the teachers …
Dustin: Well, not all of them! Most teachers are OK! I like this school 'cause I have loads of friends … I've been away for two years, but at St. Andrew's, well it wasn't the same … Too much discipline … Too much pressure. If you don't do well, they beat you … they treat you like a pig …
Counsellor: Who?
Dustin: Some of the teachers …

Counsellor:	All of them?
Dustin:	No …
Counsellor:	Most of them?
Dustin:	No just some of them … the drama teacher I hated most. It was a good excuse for him to hit us … he would say it's drama, we need discipline here, we need to … and he hits at us … the fuckin' cunt … I hated him, the bastard …
Counsellor:	Did you speak to the Head?
Dustin:	The Head was one kind of a dick head. He was an ass hole, a real damn bastard. I used to tell him about this at first. … the drama teacher, we used to call him the Caterpillar because he walked the corridor in zigzag, had a really small head and was always wearing a coat bigger than him.[Counsellor and Dustin laugh] … well the Caterpillar told me that the Head had told him what I had said about him. I ended up not doing drama and just getting extra work, more like a copy it was. The ass hole … and the Head was always telling us to go to Mass. I really hate them all. They suck.
Counsellor:	OK, I know this irritates you but easy with the language …
Dustin:	Sorry sir. I used to like our social worker—used to! We talked a lot. At first I didn't trust him. Then I started telling it all. He was cool. He loved the same team I side with, Manchester United. He told me he went to see them once in England. Then all of a sudden he didn't work there anymore. Never heard from him again.

Since then Dustin has been told off by the Head of school. He said that he does like school but he always gets the blame, whatever happens. The Counsellor asked for a case conference. His mother and Aunty came. His mother is rapt in a depression, has a history of domestic violence, and is now a single parent with three other children who are younger than Dustin. Dustin spends most of his time with his Aunty. She is the one who takes care of him. The Head said that Dustin is about to be dismissed from school if things stay as they are. His Aunty asked what is going to happen to him if he is sent away from this school.

Counsellor:	You know you risk being sent away?
Dustin:	Why?
Counsellor:	Your behaviour …
Head:	You've gone wild Dustin … you keep telling lies. Dustin, you keep calling teachers names, you got a flick knife to school the other day and said it's for the fruit …
Dustin:	It was for the fruit …
Head:	So why did you tell me it wasn't for the fruit then?
Dustin:	Uff, come on …
Counsellor:	You're in trouble mate …
Dustin:	Why? [Looking disinterested]
Aunty:	What are we going to do Dustin?
Mum:	This is crazy? Why didn't they keep him at St. Andrew's?
Head:	Yes, what happened there? Do you know? They told us nothing.
Counsellor:	Dustin, you're in trouble …
Dustin:	But why? What did I do?

Head:	You shout all the time, I hear you from my office … don't forget my office is just right by your classroom …
Dustin:	Is it me that shouts only?
Head:	I hear YOU mostly …
Dustin;	But yesterday, I was trying to keep them calm during the History lesson, Paninu [The nick name of the History teacher … meaning "bun"] keeps trying to do a lesson and Joshua kept shooting pins at his face. …
Head:	It's not just yesterday Dustin … Dustin you're in trouble…
Counsellor;	What do you suggest … ? [Looks at relatives] …
Aunty:	Please, give him another chance [Both are in tears].
Mum:	Be a good boy Dustin …
Dustin:	Yes mum, do you have money?
Mum:	No …
Dustin:	[Goes to look in her bag] You see you have—you're a bloody liar!
Head:	That's being rude …
Dustin:	But she lied …
Head:	You see, talking with Dustin is useless …

STORY 3: CLINT AND THE PORTER

What is interestingly worrying in *Clint and the Porter* is the inability of the system to protect the vulnerable members in society, "weak" not as in physical health, but as in the way of poking these persons through our (non-disabled) wrongful attitudes, value impositions, outdated pedagogy, and a thinking process that materialises the failings of the person. The institution becomes an oppressive organisation at all levels. It leaves little opportunity for initiative and protection. Clint can be interpreted as being protected by luck and pushed around by destiny. Like other students he has his own way of being naughty. Disabled people, most of the time, seem to be exempt from waywardness.

	A lot of hullabaloo outside his office …
Counsellor:	OK Paul, see you then … Quick, quick off to class …
Paul:	But. …
Counsellor:	Quick boy quick …
Paul:	Can I have a note sir please?
Counsellor:	[Irritated and snappy] What note son?
Paul:	Well to say I've been here …
Counsellor:	It's OK … tell the teacher you were here. With whom is your lesson? [Before Paul could answer] … She's ok … she won't tell you anything … [Jostles Paul out].

By this time the Counsellor is jammed between Paul's exasperating desire to have a note and a wooden door that is about to smack their backs.

The scene at that time was made up of a crowded foyer with about fifty students going off to their lesson in a buoyant rhythm. Charles the Porter is with a flabbergasted Clint who with a helpless look seems like a puppy about to be whacked by his master. The Counsellor is grappling to find the right words.

Charles: You sod. Pick that fucking God damn cola can from the floor! I saw you throw it away, you know, I saw you lad! [Clint still hanging onto his puppy look]. Now don't you play the handicapped with me, you fuckin' ass hole … I saw you do that … you pick up that tin or I'll flick your silly face mate. [The Porter had his hand raised to the highest level possible, as if he wanted to make sure the slap would be heard all over the school].

Counsellor: Charles, calm down …

Charles: I fucking what?! You know he stepped on my feet? He just did it … yeah he stepped on my goddamn feet … the ass hole. I'm not afraid of this idiot. He just wants to look silly. He's not silly you know, he's just a bastard … I clean, he dirties [Still with his hand raised but now with the counsellor's hand squeezing his elbow in earnest].

Counsellor: Charles he has a shunt …

Charles: A fucking what? [Looking surprised and somewhat confused]

Counsellor: He has a shunt … if you hit it he's dead … you can K-I-L-L- H-I-M … you know, it's one of those things in his brain to keep the liquid flowing … [Charles starts to cool down, coming out of his angry stint. The counsellor keeps at it seeing that Charles seems to start realising what is happening]. He's been operated there a number of times. Got some sort of pipes …

Charles: Shit … oh thanks man… God … I, I lost my temper … I, I, I just couldn't, oh my God. …

Counsellor: It's OK Charles.

Charles: Oh my God …

Counsellor: OK, off to class Clint. … off, off, off …

Clint with a dazzled look, moving on with his unsteady gait, confused look, and with an air of victory stoops off to his next lesson, giving a quick glimpse every ten paces he makes, still feeling the threat of Charles hanging over his head, and a twinkle in his eyes sitting lazily in his twisted specs telling it all. From the end of the corridor you could see his teacher assistant walking towards the victor.

TA: Time for math Clint. Had a good break?
 [Some days later:]
Counsellor: Hey Pete, did you realise what Charles did?
Pete: Did what?
Counsellor: Well the thingy with Clint.
Pete: Damn, that was bad. You know what? I spoke to the bugger?
Counsellor: What bugger?
Pete: Clint … he told me it was his fault …
 [Counsellor opened his eyes with the white showing all around the pupil]
Counsellor: What?
Pete: Yes, Clint threw the can on the floor and he stepped on Charles's feet on purpose …

Counsellor:	Fuck! Goddamn son of a bitch ... but he was going to hit him ... oh and I was about to be slapped myself!
Pete:	Yes, he's a bugger that Charles. He loses it. Fuckin' hell. I mean Clint is handicapped. Not sure these kids should be around. Aren't there special schools for kids like him?
	[The counsellor went out feeling confused, awkward, and tongue-tied ...]

STORY 4: THE CIRCUS IS IN TOWN

The *Circus Is in Town* is a story that I write to manifest the increasing undermining of students and the removal of their identity, distinctiveness, and uniqueness (Barton and Armstrong 1999). There is a concern that people will not listen to students. These students are screaming (at times literally) their heads off trying to find their position and space within society and their communities. Another crucial engagement is the violence that is still part and parcel of our schools life. I have had innumerable conversations with colleagues in my staff room, where people spoke about the need to transform some of our schools into boot camps, re-introducing corporal punishment and removing students who do not abide by regulation and send them to emotional/behavioural disorder (EBD) schools. Schools for these students who carry some diversity label are encapsulated in this establishment, which somehow "throws them up," making them feel that their difference does not suit the society they make "part of." The agony is that this whole notion of violence is no rarity.

A total hustle bustle. A compere plods in whilst the jugglers are still at their games. Others are on the ropes. Some are working the Still Trapeze. Headstand specialists and acrobats. Life-daring stilt walkers. The bars, the poles, the fire-eaters. Clowns, lion-tamers, flying trapeze specialists, make-up, props, costumes and other... This is what it looks like as I pass the science class. No idea of balance or symmetry, discipline or method or order. Down with the pedagogy and up with the restraint! Oh gosh, hang on, this is not it. This shouldn't be it. This is not a Circus we are in—it's the science class—I keep reminding myself!

Teacher 1:	Ok Johnny, I've had enough. Bring your bloody arse back in here. Come down from that window I said! Hey Tom, get that toilet paper roll in here. Get it! Ah, what was that—Oh God! Ok, who threw that?
Peter:	Ron Miss ...
Teacher 1:	Ron, off to the Head.
Ron:	No. It wasn't me... Mark you're a cock face and you look just like the Iguana at Harry's Pet Shop ...
Teacher 1:	Who's the class prefect here? Bring the Head [no one moves]. Who's thrown that olive. ...? Now ... [Screams] Now, somebody has to own up—or you're all grounded for your next football match. [Students expressing their dissent at the top of their voices. Some hanging on to windows, others throwing things at each other and others playing around with the toilet paper roll].

Ron: Hey they're lying ... Paul you're a fucker!
Teacher 1: Ron, you're a damn stupid idiot. The more time passes the more rude you become. You suck.
Ron: Hey teacher, stop the rude words. You cannot call me names.
Teacher 1: Yeah! Says who? Did you hear me say anything rude boys? [Some students nod, others gaze away—none say no]. OK Ron, you know you did wrong. You have been throwing chairs, walking on tables, disturbing other students. You know this isn't fair. This is just not fair and you have to admit [teacher starts getting angry]. You've really piss ... got at my nerves. [Screams outside the classroom—Teacher 1 is now shoving Ron out of the classroom. In the meantime another teacher walks in to help out. Teacher 2 grabs Ron from the elbows and takes him to a quiet and sheltered corner in the school lobby].
Teacher 2: Now it's the two of us Ron. You stop the fucking shit with me. You better behave or I'll kick your ugly face. Now in class we rule—and you go with our rules. [Patting him gently] and keep this in mind—stop the shit or I'll smack your silly face out of the window. You couldn't say anything about this little conversation eh? It's just us—no one will believe you!
Ron: I'm not afraid of you—you're bullying me.
Teacher 2: I'm not, I'm just teaching you the rules of this school. You're new—so you need the help.
Ron: I hate school, I hate teachers. I'm not afraid of you. You cannot touch me. . . . [Screaming heard from the science room ... Teacher1 runs out of the room].
Teacher 1: Call an ambulance someone. Paul has a concussion. He's been knocked down by Darren. Oh my God, Oh my God. ... I just had to leave for two minutes to get the handouts. [Ron looks flabbergasted, as if somebody had really smacked his grin out of the door].
Teacher 2: You'll be OK. I'll tell them you don't usually leave your classroom ... [45 minutes later. Health and Safety teacher comes in the room].
Teacher 3: Paul is fine. He just has a bad headache. I guess going for a check up to hospital will be routine. You'd better go write up an incident report.
Mathew: Hey Miss ...
Teacher 3: Yes ...
Mathew: ... my nose Miss ... it bloody hurts. Shit miss don't touch it.
Teacher 3: I need to have a look Mat.
Mathew: I knocked it against Paul. He was about to fall. Oh shit—it hurts.

STORY 5: THE LITTLE NATIONALS

The Little Nationals, is a story that converges a number of realities in flashbacks. In this story I touch upon various experiences I come across in my professional life (if I can really separate it from my personal). I speak about a visit I made as a social worker to a family that lives in a downtown household. In the process, I recall work I had done at school as a teacher, my role as a researcher, and the whole miscellany that makes up the speckled and varied roles I assume in different parts of the day. I end up reflecting whether my responsibilities are taken over by what I am to gain in this process (mainly money and authority) rather than participating as a supporting actor in this livid and discoloured "reality show" I am engrossed in from morning till night.

Stairs. Loads of stairs. Dark and smelly. A handful of shadows and more stairs. I walked up wearing my tie—feeling uncomfortable, confused, and a bit scared. "God," I kept asking myself, "do these slums still exist?" I don't usually "dress up" for work. I was coming from a meeting, an important meeting at school—a case conference it was. One of our students wasn't behaving well. I told them, "I know what he has!" They all seemed to stop at once. I never managed to have so much eye contact at the same time! "He's got ADHD!" Some lips, some eyes, some cheeks started to quiver and shudder as if they wanted to say, "Thank God, now we can start doing something." On the other hand, they knew, or rather they thought, that there wasn't much to do with this boy—he would be sent away. ... to a special school. They all seemed to agree that a special school "is the most appropriate school for him." The population of the school is just ten students. 'The Headmaster is a "good man bless him" they said. "Oh and what is the name of the school?" I dared to ask. "St. John's EBD" I was told. I could notice a grin under our Head's hand rippling down to his big unsymmetrical belly. He seems to cover his mouth all the time as if he's too shy to show his missing teeth or was he too ashamed of failing to take care of little "Dennis the Menace"? Or is it fear he is engrossed in? And then the. ...

Myself:	*Sorry!—Do you know a family called Zyneb?*
Small boy:	*No.*
Small boy's mum:	*Keep walking up, turn left, walk straight, then turn right and you'll find it. There's a little Madonna in a niche close by.*
Myself:	*Thank you ... [Still confused and struggling hard to get into the social work mode].*

I remember once at school I had a friend of mine, Abdul. He told me to ask the Arabic Language teacher to make a translation for me. I asked why. "You tell her" he told me, "you'll make us all laugh." I remember asking the teacher, "Misses, can I have the translation of "butter in the nest"? Well it didn't sound too bad to me, just silly. "OK darling you're out of class, straight to the Rector and don't come back to this class without your mother." Well I remember asking her, "What did I say wrong? Abdul asked me to ask you this," I continued. She told Abdul to walk out of class with me. I remember being kicked and slapped by Abdul as we walked to the Rector's office. I soon got to know that the literal translation of that phrase in Arabic—it really didn't sound good!

Back to this day and age. I caught sight of the Madonna incubated in a glass coffin standing to attention, waiting for the next pilgrim. I arrived at the top of the stairs. Felt like the stairs would never end. The family I found. All wrapped up in their North African culture, seemingly afraid of the questions I was going to ask, before they actually came to mind. A little Down's syndrome girl looking at me with compassion as if she understood that my heartbeat with all the stairs had shot up. We talked.

As I left the house, I remembered a conversation I had with some students I teach at University some weeks ago. We spoke about diversity, about "inclusion," about people coming from a different culture, about Malta being just at the right point to converge these different cultures. At that time I thought it was a good academic reflection of what is happening—but now it all sounded silly—there's no converging I saw in the slums I'm in! And then my mind shifted to Tarik, a student I teach who was an informant for my thesis.

Myself: Hi Tarik!
Tarik: Hi Sir!
Myself: You know I had to speak to you. I told you about this at the end of the scholastic year last June.
Tarik: Yes, you had to contact me. … You never did! [Looking disappointed]
Myself: Yes [embarrassed] I was busy, well I tried to call, but couldn't get through. Hemm … anyway, you remember what I talked to you about …
Tarik: Yes, you said that you'll be writing a book, a big book and you're going to write about me in this book! [Looking proud]
Myself: OK Tarik … how are you feeling at this school?
Tarik: OK.
Myself: Do you feel bullied?
Tarik: No.
Myself: Ehm. … Do you like school and ….?
Tarik: Oh yes.
Myself: … and the teachers [now looking puzzled]?
Tarik: Yes they're good.
Myself: Do students bully you?
Tarik: No Sir, no.
Myself: Ehm. … not even because of your surname?
Tarik: No.
Myself: But Tarik, last scholastic year you said that you had problems with the other students.
Tarik: No, I am happy at school. They didn't bully me, they were just joking.
Myself: But Tarik you cried and you were very angry.
Tarik: Yes, but now it's fine [Using an irritated tone].
Myself: No it's not OK! If you were bullied, you were. If your friends picked on you it's not right. If they called you names its bad. Look, the other children were treating you badly … badly … there is no question about that. I want to know who was treating you badly. Speak up Tarik, come on speak up. What was wrong?
Tarik: But sir now it's different.
Myself: No son, it's not.
Tarik: But my father was an Arab. He lived in Tunis. My mother lived here alone.

By this time I had arrived outside the slums. The air felt fresh even if bursting with pollution and car fumes. I breathed two, three times to make sure my lungs were full to capacity. I was off to my meeting on inclusion policy. We were going to discuss how Principle 4 of the National Minimum Curriculum could be implemented in schools. Masses of reflections to write tonight in my research diary!

The Little Nationals raises the squandering of our ability to listen to what people at the margins have to say. The principle of active listening however is not enough. We need to move towards eradicating disabling barriers, having a more prominent students' voice, having a national policy on "inclusion," more professional training for teachers, smaller but autonomous schools, a school ethos that positions the students at the centre of all decision-making process, additional parent involvement, less impairment based strategies, a more positive school environment, a managerial group of administrators that are able to map out an effective strategy with the resources they have, better support systems, a stronger grassroots movement, more motivated teachers, and improved training and research at university level. This narrative tells us about the systems in school that do not seem to be functioning, structures that are intended to make students feel "at home" but in reality makes them feel "far from home." Students are thrown out of schools, justified by the rhetoric of professionals and an inability to cope with the diversity that miscellany brings with it. The mechanisms that professionals are so proud of, such as, case conferences, are, at the end of the day, oppressive tools that dish up the barricade of professionalisation (Goodley, Lawton, Clough, and Moore 2004).

"INCLUSION" IS REALISTIC

The responsibility of having an inclusive school community lies primarily with having a school administration that is vigorous (Busher 1998). Schools are expected to create an inclusive culture in an atmosphere that is increasingly demanding and competitive (Farrell and Ainscow 2002). When disabled students are included in regular programmes, the tasks in the programmes need to be attuned to the students' specific requirements. Leadership ultimately rests with the head of school, who has to understand, interpret, and react to the school climate and attitudes of staff towards change. The task of developing "inclusion" strategies will be best facilitated with a knowledgeable administrator who believes that inclusive education is in the best interests of the whole school community. The way that schools are structured reflect the culture and experience of a community and the curriculum is to take account of this reality rather than just account for a traditional chase for credentials. A school institution can bring about an "ideological intent" of oppressing students in already browbeaten contexts (Brown 1999; Freire 1970).

We need to get away from pathologising disability and perceiving it as a welfare dilemma. Disability is an experience of social oppression through political and economic factors that seem to be influenced by a capitalist paradigm. Disability is also interpreted as being a symptom of social oppression, and impairment is the physical representation of this dimension. This social construction is not about or caused by the body (or some impairment), but it collides on the body. Impairment and discrimination have a massive impact on the life of this minority—in different proportions at different times.

We have, each of us, a life story, an inner narrative, whose continuity, whose sense, *is* our life. It might be said that each of us constructs and lives, a "narrative," and that this narrative *is* us, our identity.

> If we wish to know about a man [*sic*], we ask "what is his story—his real, inmost story?"—for each of us *is* a biography, a story. Each of us *is* a singular narrative, which is constructed continually, unconsciously, by, through, and in us—through our perceptions, our feelings, our thoughts, our actions; and not least our discourse, our spoken narrations. Biologically, physiologically, we are not so different from each other; historically, as narratives we are each of us unique. (Sacks 1984, p. 105)

There are concepts that will help make "inclusion" a realistic and practical issue, a vision propagated by the use of narrative research. Education is a mainstream environment that can encapsulate the fundamental principle of "schools for all." Inclusive education must guarantee quality life expectations and should offer lifelong equality of access to all echelons of society. Inclusive education has to adapt to the needs of the student and not vice versa.

"Inclusion" is by no stretch of the imagination, a resolved issue—it can never be. It has not even, in my opinion, permeated our cultural DNA and is still an alien notion to many (Clough and Corbett 2000; Barnes and Mercer 2003). The disabled community has progressed by waging a strenuous struggle against oppression. It is not at all easy to give space within a scenario that disallows the struggle (Oliver 1996). The struggle for inclusive education is part of a wider struggle to bring about an inclusive society in which all individuals and groups enjoy full and equal membership (Barton and Armstrong 1998, p. 262). Schools are idiosyncratic communities, each with their own biographies, circumstances, and profiles. Each school has to develop on its own steam drawing from the most important of resources—the students. There is a need for flexible patterns in schools. We have to develop a critical discourse that does not put us down but encourages the roles and relations within them. Disabled students in our schools are atypical. Their disability is represented as being an impairment, and disability is pathologised in the form of essentialist abjection.

BACK TO SCHOOL

Nonetheless, there are some interesting changes that are starting to take place. Parents, students, teachers, and other professionals are searching for models of positive inclusive practices and are demanding a more active involvement in research which they want to participate in as long as they are in defined roles. We can and need to find out ways how other countries and other societies are making "inclusion" work. We must be creative and find ways how to make it happen. Going back to the school-based "inclusion" debate has been interpreted as a process of extending boundaries. "Inclusion" has or can become the springboard to interpret the existing tensions. There is a dire need to create a network within the wider community to deal with the disadvantage of students' identities without trying to eradicate them from their roots.

This reality threatens the social stability and fosters intransigent attitudes. Given the opportunity, through the adaptation of the curriculum, all students can find themselves a place and an active dynamic and distinct role (Giordmaina 2001). It is up to the school to create the best possible conditions for these changes. "Inclusion" in itself can provide a response to political inventiveness. Students convey their ambitions for the improvement of their education and development, and of the challenges they face in realising these targets within a society that declines their legitimacy. "Inclusion" does not exist in isolation. Students at the margins have a right to equal participation in all aspects of society and in all decisions that concern them. School institutions need to endeavour to be accessible to all. "Inclusion" applies not only to an educational context, employment, and social life, but also to participation in the political processes they are wrapped up in. "Inclusion" in Malta is essentially a contemporary debate in education. Disability is constantly being placed on the fringes of society where tolerance is a rare ingredient. Schools are there to affect change, design an agenda, and engage with these stories—will this happen?

BIBLIOGRAPHY

Ainscow M (1995) "Special needs through school improvement: School improvement through special needs" in Clark C, Dyson A, and Millward A (eds.) *Towards inclusive schools* London: David Fulton Publishers.

Ainscow M (1999) *Understanding the development of inclusive schools* London: Routledge/Falmer Press.

Ainscow M. Booth T, and Dyson A (1999) "Inclusion and exclusion in schools: Listening to some hidden voices" in Ballard K (ed.) *Inclusive education: International voices on disability and justice* London: Falmer Press.

Armstrong F (1999) "Inclusion, Curriculum and the struggle for Space in School" *International Journal of Inclusive Education*, Volume 3 (1): 75–87.

Armstrong F and Barton L (eds.) (1999) *Difference and difficulty: Insights, issues and dilemmas* London: Impact Graphics.

Armstrong F, Armstrong D, and Barton L (eds.) (2000) *Inclusive education—policy, contexts and perspectives* London: David Fulton Publications.

Avramadis E and Norwich B (2002) "Teachers' attitudes towards integration/inclusion: Review of the literature" *The European Journal of Special Needs Education*, Volume 17 (2): 129–147.

Azzopardi A (2000) *Understanding disability politics in Malta: New directions explored*. Unpublished Masters Dissertation, University of Sheffield.

Azzopardi A (2003a) "A case study of a Parents' support group in Malta. The concepts of 'Inclusion. Exclusion and disabling barriers' are analysed in the relationship that parents have with professionals" *Disability and Society*, Volume 15 (7): 1065–1072.

Azzopardi A (2003b) "Inclusive education and the denial of difference: Is this the Cotton era experience? Exploring whether the discourse of inclusive education has been hijacked over standards" *International Journal of Inclusive Education*, Volume 7 (2) (April–June): 159–174.

Bagilhole B (1997) *Equal opportunities and social policy* London: Longman.

Ballard K (ed.) (1999) *Inclusive education: International voices on disability and justice* London: Falmer Press.

Ballard K and MacDonald T (1998) "New Zealand: Inclusive school, inclusive philosophy" in Booth T and Ainscow M (eds.) *From them to us—An international study of inclusive education* London: Routledge.

Barnes C (1997) "A legacy of oppression: A history of disability in Western culture" in Barton L and Oliver M (eds.) *Disability studies: Past, present and future* Leeds: Disability Press.

Barnes C and Mercer G (eds.) (1997) *Doing disability research* Leeds: Disability Press.

Barnes C and Mercer G (2003) *Disability* Cambridge: Polity Press.

Barnes C, Oliver M, and Barton L (eds.) (2002) *Disability studies today* Cambridge: Polity Press.

Bartolo P, Agius Ferrante C, Azzopardi A, Bason L, Grech L, and King M A (2002) *Creating inclusive schools—Guidelines for the implementation of the National Minimum Curriculum policy on inclusive education* Sliema: Salesian Press.

Barton L (2000) "Journeys to inclusive education: Profiles and reflections" in Clough P and Corbett J (eds.) *Theories of inclusive education—A students' guide* London: Paul Chapman Publishing.

Barton L (ed.) (2001) *Disability politics and the struggle for change* London: David Fulton Publishers.

Barton L and Armstrong F (eds.) (1999) *Difference and difficulty: Insights, issues and dilemmas* Sheffield: University of Sheffield Press.

Barton L and Oliver M (eds.) (1997) *Disability studies: Past, present and future* Leeds: Disability Press.

Bassey M (1999) *Case study research in educational settings* Buckingham: Open University Press.

Bauman Z (2001) *Community—Seeking safety in an insecure world* Oxford: Polity Press.

Bayliss P (2004) *"Sam": Proceedings of the 2004 Conference: Disability Studies: Putting theory into practice held at Lancaster University* Exeter, University of Exeter.

Bernstein B (1990) *The structuring of pedagogical discourse* London: Routledge.

Bines H, Swain J, and Kaye J (1998) 'Once upon a time': Teamwork for complimentary perspectives and critique in research on special educational needs" in Clough P and Barton L (eds.) *Articulating with difficulty: Research voices in inclusive education* London: Paul Chapman Publishing Limited.

Black-Hawkings K (1999) *Close encounters of the cultural kind: The significance of culture in understanding processes of inclusion and exclusion in schools* Paper presented at the British Educational Research Association Conference held at the University of Sussex, Sussex, University of Sussex.

Booth T and Ainscow M (1998) *From them to us—An international study of inclusion in education* London: Routledge.

Booth T and Booth W (1993) "Accentuating the positive: A personal profile of a parent with learning difficulties" *Disability, Handicap and Society*, Volume 8 (4).

Booth T and Booth W (1997) "Making connections: A narrative study of adult children of parents with learning disabilities" in Barnes, C and Mercer G (eds.) *Doing disability research* Leeds: Disability Press (pp. 123–141).
Booth T, Swain W, Masterton M, and Potts P (eds.) (1992) *Learning for all–Curricula for diversity in education* London: Routledge and Falmer.
Boswell D M (1994) "The social prestige of residential areas" in Sultana R G and Baldacchino G (eds.) *Maltese society: A sociological enquiry* Malta: Mireva Publications.
Bowles S and Gintis H (1976) *Schooling in capitalist America: Educational reform and the contradictions of economic life* New York: Basic Books.
Brown C (1999) "Parent voices on advocacy, education, disability and justice" in Ballard K (ed.) *Inclusive education: International voices on disability and justice* London: Falmer Press.
Brown S E (1995) "I was born (In a hospital bed)—When I was 31 years old" in *Disability and Society*, Volume 10 (1): 103–109.
Busher H (1998) "Education leadership and management: Contexts, theory and practice" in Clough P (ed.) *Managing inclusive education—From policy to practice* London: Paul Chapman Publishing.
Camilleri J (1999) Disability: A personal odyssey *Disability and Society*, Volume 14 (6): 845–853.
Camilleri J and Callus A M (2001) "Out of the cellars. Disability politics and the struggle for change: The Maltese experience" in Barton L *Disability politics and the struggle for change* London: David Fulton Publishers.
Campbell J and Oliver M (1996) *Disability politics: Understanding our past, changing our future* London: Routledge.
Chan A (2001) *Journey from the edge: challenging central discourses* Paper presented at SCRUTEA, 31st Annual Conference, 3–5 July 2001: University of East London.
Chircop D (1994) "Absenteeism: Deviance, resistance and contestation" in Sultana R and Baldacchino G (eds.) *Maltese society—A sociological enquiry* Malta: Mireva Publications.
Clark C, Dyson A and Millward A (eds.) (1995) *Towards inclusive schools: Mapping the field* London: David Fulton Publishers.
Clough P (ed.) (1998) *Managing inclusive education: From policy to experience* London: Paul Chapman Publishing Limited.
Clough P (2000) "Tales from the edge: Narratives at the borders of inclusive ideology" in Moore M (ed.) *Insider perspectives on inclusion—Raining voices, raising issues* Sheffield: Philip Armstrong Publications.
Clough P (2002) *Narratives and fictions in educational research* Buckingham: Open University Press.
Clough P and Barton L (eds.) (1995) *Making difficulties: Research and the construction of SEN* London: Paul Chapman Publishing Ltd.
Clough P and Barton L (eds.) (1998) *Articulating with difficulty—Research voices in inclusive education* London: Paul Chapman Publishing Limited.
Clough P and Corbett J (eds.) (2000) *Theories of inclusive education* London: Paul Chapman Publications.
Clough P and Nutbrown C (2002) *A students guide to methodology* London: Sage Publications.
Cohen L, Manion M, and Morrison K (2000) *Research methods in education* (5th ed.) London: Routledge/Falmer Press.
Coleridge P (1993) *Disability, liberation and development* London: Oxfam.
Corbett J (1996) *Bad-mouthing—The language of special needs* London: Falmer Press.
Corbett J (1997) "Independent, proud and special: Celebrating our differences" in Barton L and Oliver M (eds.) *Disability studies: Past, present and future* Leeds: Disability Press.

Corbett J (1998) *Special education needs in the twentieth century—A cultural analysis* London: Cassell.
Corbett J and Slee R (2000) "An international conversation on inclusive education" in Armstrong F, Armstrong D, and Barton L (eds.) *Inclusive education: Policy, contexts and comparative perspectives* London: David Fulton Publishers.
Corker M and French S (1999) *Disability discourse* Buckingham: Open University Press.
Davis L (ed.) (1997) *The disability studies—Reader* London: Routledge.
Drake R F (1999) *Understanding disability politics* London: Macmillan.
Dunn K (2001) "Children talk about school" in Dunn K (ed.) *Child development and education: Different experiences, new voices* Sheffield: Philip Armstrong Publications.
Farrell P and Ainscow M (eds.) (2002) *Making special education inclusive* London: David Fulton Publishers.
Finkelstein V (1987) "The naked truth" in *DAIL Magazine* February, 1987.
Finkelstein V (1991) *Working with able-bodied people* Presented by Link TV, 2 May 1991.
Finkelstein V (1999) "A profession allied to the community: The disabled people's trade union" in Stone E (ed.) *Disability and development—Learning from action and research on disability in the majority world* Leeds: Disability Press.
Finkelstein V (2001) *A personal journey in to disability politics* Paper presented at Leeds University centre for disability studies Leeds: University of Leeds.
Freire P (1970) *Pedagogy of the oppressed* (2nd ed.) London: Penguin.
Fulcher G (1999) *Disabling polices? A comparative approach to education policy and disability* Sheffield: Philip Armstrong Publications.
Fullager S and Owler K (1998) "Narratives of leisure: Recreating the self" in *Disability and Society* Volume 13 (3): 441–450.
Geertz C (1973) *The interpretation of cultures: Selected essays* New York: Basic Books.
Geertz C (1983) *Local knowledge: Further essays in interpretative anthropology* New York: Basic Books.
Geertz C (1998) *Works and lives: The anthropologist as author* Stanford, CA: Stanford University Press.
Giordmaina J (2001) *National curriculum on its way: A conference on the implementation of the National Curriculum* Malta: Guttenberg Press Limited.
Goodley D (2000) *Self advocacy in the lives of people with learning difficulties* Buckingham: Open University Press.
Goodley D (2003) "Against a politics of victimisation: Disability culture and self-advocates with learning difficulties" in Riddell S and Watson N (eds.) *Disability, culture and identity* London: Pearson Prentice Hill.
Goodley D and Moore M (2002) *Disability arts against exclusion—People with learning difficulties and their performing arts* Plymouth: BILD Publications.
Goodley D, Lawton R, Clough P, and Moore M (2004) *Researching life stories—Method, theory and analysis in a biographical age* London: Routledge and Falmer Press.
Goodson I and Sikes P (2001) *Life history research in educational settings* Buckingham: Open University Press.
Kenworthy J and Whittaker J (2000) "Anything to declare? The struggle for inclusive education and children's rights" *Disability and Society*, Volume 15 (2): 219–231.
Ministry of Education (1999) *National minimum curriculum—Creating the future together* Malta: Klabb Kotba Maltin.
Moore M (ed.) (2000) *Insider perspectives on inclusion—Raising voices, raising issues* Sheffield: Philip Armstrong Publications.

Moore M (2001) "Children and family life" in Dunn, K. (ed.) *Child development and education: Different experiences, new voices* Sheffield: Philip Armstrong Publications (pp. 47–63).

Morris J (2002a) "Inclusion: Too difficult, expensive and impractical—Or a basic human right" *Special Children* (January 2002): 12–14.

Morris J (2002b) People with physical impairments and mental health support needs: A critical review of the literature. Unpublished.

Oliver M (1988) "The social and political context of educational policy: The case of special needs" in Barton L (ed.) *The politics of special educational needs* London: Falmer Press.

Oliver M (1990a) *The individual and social models of disability* Paper presented at Joint workshop of the living options group and the research unit of the royal college of physicians on People with established locomotor disabilities in hospitals, 23 July 1990.

Oliver M (1990b) *The politics of disablement: Critical texts in social work and the welfare state* London: Macmillan.

Oliver M (ed.) (1991) *Social work—Disabled people and disabling environments* London: Jessica Kingsley Publishers.

Oliver M (1996) *Understanding disability—From theory to practice* London: Macmillan.

Oliver M (2000) *Decoupling education policy from the economy in late capitalist societies: Some implications for special education* Keynote speech in the ISEC 2000 Conference on Some Implications for Special Education.

Oliver M and Barnes C (1998) *Disabled people and social policy: From exclusion to inclusion* London: Longman.

Oliver M and Sapey B (1999) *Social work with disabled people* (2nd ed.) London: Macmillan.

Peters S (2002) "Inclusive education in accelerated and professional development schools: A case-based study of two school reform efforts in the USA" *International Journal of Inclusive Education*, Volume 6 (4): 287–308.

Plummer K (2001) *Documents of life 2—An invitation to a critical humanism* London: Sage Publications.

Potts P (1998) "Knowledge is not enough: An exploration of what we can expect from enquiries which are social" in Clough P and Barton L (Eds) Paul Chapman Publishing Ltd.

Priestly M (1999) *Disability politics and community care* London: Jessica Kingsley Publishers.

Read J (2000) *Disability, the family and society: Listening to mothers* Buckingham: Open University Press.

Reezigt G J and Pijl S J (1998) "The Netherlands: A springboard for other initiatives" in Booth T and Ainscow M (eds.) *From them to us: An international study of inclusion in education* London: Routledge.

Riddell S (2000) "Inclusion and choice: Mutually exclusive principles in special educational needs?" in Armstrong F, Armstrong D, and Barton L (eds.) *Inclusive education: Policy, contexts and comparative perspectives* London: David Fulton Publishers.

Sacks O (1985) "The Man who mistook his wife for a hat and other clinical tales" New York: Summit Books.

Thomas C (1999) "Narrative identity and the disabled self" in Corker M and French S (eds.) *Disability discourse* Buckingham: Open University Press.

Thomas C (2002) "Disability theory: Key ideas, issues and thinkers" in Barnes C, Oliver M, and Barton L (eds.) *Disability studies today* Cambridge: Polity Press.

Thomas S (1995) "Parents' perspectives: Towards positive support for disabled children and those who experience difficulties in learning" in Potts P, Armstrong F, and Masterson M (eds.) *Equality and diversity in education 2: National and international contexts* London: Open University Press.

Thomas G and Glenny G (2002) "Thinking about inclusion" *The International Journal of Inclusive Education*, Volume 6 (4): 345–369.

Thomas G and Loxely A (2001) *Deconstructing special education and constructing inclusion* Buckingham: Open University Press.

Thomas W I and Znaniecki F (1918–1920) *The Polish peasant in Europe and America*, 5 vols. Chicago: University of Chicago Press.

Tregaskis C (2000) "Interviewing non-disabled people about their disability-related attitudes: seeking methodologies" in *Disability and Society*, Volume 15 (2): 343–353.

Tregaskis C (2003) *Constructions of disability* Paper presented at the Disability Studies Conference 2003 at the University of Lancaster Sheffield: University of Sheffield.

Uditsky B (1993) "From integration to inclusion: The Canadian experience" in Slee R (ed.) *Is there a desk with my name on it? The politics of integration* London: Falmer Press.

UPIAS (1976) *Fundamental principles of disability* London: Union of the Physical Impaired against Segregation.

Watterson J (2000) *The voice of mothers of children with disabilities* Paper presented at the Qualitative Evidence-based Practice Conference, Coventry University, May 15–17 2000 Coventry, University of Coventry.

Zaretsky E (ed.) (1996) *The Polish peasant in Europe and America—A classical work in immigration history* Chicago: University of Illinois Press.

CHAPTER EIGHT

Research IN Inclusive Education AS A Possible Opening TO Disability Studies IN Education

GEERT VAN HOVE, GRIET ROETS, KATHLEEN MORTIER, ELISABETH DE SCHAUWER, MIEKE LEROY, AND ERIC BROEKAERT

> Il ne faut pas grand chose pour être heureux, Juste un peu de patience et beaucoup d'amitié.
> [You don't need much to be happy, just a little bit of patience and a lot of friendship.]
>
> —ZITA SWOON, *INTRIGUE*

INTRODUCTION

In this chapter, we try to find a number of links between the research into the practice of inclusive education and reflections on this subject from a critical pedagogical perspective. We, with others (Ware, 2001, p. 112), argue in favour of this approach, as Flemish education still threatens to view "disability" as a static, objectively defined category, a diagnosis that can(not) be treated, a phenomenon that leads to binary (we/them) thinking, a ground for excluding certain children. In other words, in an epistemological sense, we disassociate ourselves from reductionism.

Our inspiration to do so comes from an ongoing learning process and partnership with parents of children with disabilities. For about seven years, we have been working with the children of a large group of parents in the organisation Ouders voor Inclusie (Parents Promoting Inclusion). We are in contact with around 400 families in the Flemish-speaking part of Belgium who have opted for a normal school for their child with a disability. For some "specialists" in our country, the "special needs circuit" becomes such a fixture for children who are designated "special" that their world becomes topsy-turvy. If parents of such children opt for a regular school, this is often regarded as an extraordinary, alternative[1] (in the sense of deviating) choice. We have worked with the children as well as with the parents, on the basis of three major fundamental principles:

> … As a matter of basic sensitivity and good educational practices, educators must presume that the student with a disability can and will change (i.e., develop particular skills, perform in new and interesting ways, engage with the world, demonstrate complexity of thinking and doing). Thus, as for all students, it is important/crucial that educators approach the student from a stance of presuming that he or she is competent, for example intelligent, potentially capable of expression, interaction and leadership… (Biklen, 2000, p. 340).
>
> Special Education is a service and not a place (Giangreco, 1997).
>
> Just like other pupils, children with special needs first and foremost want to participate, make friends, and have a good time in school (Van Hove, Mortier, and De Schauwer, 2005).

We have found that everything starts with the a family's plan for its child. We learned that no longer do researchers have the exclusive right to determine what exists, what reality is. Into this learning process, the term "collaborative teamwork" (Baumgart and Giangreco, 1996, p. 85) has been incorporated. Researchers are forced to leave their desks. They are challenged to (re)define reality in dialogue with the children, their parents, other persons involved, and the local community (Pfeiffer, 2002). This is not a smooth linear process. It is disturbing, complicated, contradictory, and extremely demanding on time, thought, and emotion. (Barton, 1998)

In that sense, the "alternative" preferences of the parents directly pointed to our research group the way to Disability Studies. These "alternative" preferences of parents needed "alternative" paradigmatic thoughts (Goodley and Van Hove, 2005). To make sure that we could work with an interrelated set of ontological, epistemological, and methodological questions, we adopted Freire's interpretation of social phenomena. Freire (1972) expressed his ideas about the ontological position in research as follows: "… For me the concrete reality is something more than isolated facts. The concrete reality consists not only of concrete facts and physical things, but also includes the ways in which the people involved with these facts perceive them. After all facts are not given but constructed by the questions we ask" (Lather, 1991). According to Freire, the way in which reality is viewed may either lead to "silence" or to a collaborative effort. In our daily research practice, this communal action is expressed most clearly when we work together with the parents.

In the next part of this chapter we want to present "key incidents" (Emerson, 2004) that have been written predominantly from the viewpoint of families we have learned to see as our teachers. These key incidents have to be seen as rich descriptions of people and interactions as they exist and unfold in their native habitats (ibid., p. 457). They enable us to understand the risk parents take when they choose inclusive education. We will alter the "short stories"/ "key incidents" with reflections about possible connections to Disability Studies.

As good field researchers, we employ procedures that are simultaneously deductive and inductive. Bulmer (ibid., p. 458) does not call this strict induction but "retroduction": this is moving back and forth between our stories and the theoretical backgrounds of Disability Studies. We were looking for stories that are relevant to our emerging theory and we modified original theoretical statements to fit our stories (ibid., p. 258). So "key incidents" are more than mere observations or events, Emerson (p. 257) suggests that key incidents have to be seen as particular in-the-field events or observations that stimulate or implicate original lines of inquiry and conceptualisation.

KEY INCIDENT 1: HELEN'S STORY

Sometimes parents tell us that the (development) progress made by some of the children is not noticed, because the children are constantly pigeonholed in such a way that their evolution is rendered insignificant. For example, Helen's parents are extremely satisfied with the way in which the school has coached their daughter, and especially with her progress in kindergarten. However, the early intervention team as well as the centre for developmental disorders mainly emphasise the things that Helen is not (yet) capable of—using labels such as "severe intellectual disability," pointing to possible "autism" ... In this manner, Helen's impairments (which the parents certainly do not wish to deny) are mainly used to prevent her from remaining at a regular school. Together with the parents, we want to emphasise that Helen's limitations and possibilities are challenges, and that she needs support if we want to give her the opportunity to participate in the classroom activities alongside her classmates.

The solid, extensive network of special schools in our country conveys the impression that some groups of children really cannot thrive within the standard educational system. In this way, disability is seen as something "pathological" that can be diagnosed objectively. The practices of the system of special education are seen as useful tools to make progress with "these children" (Skrtic, 1995, p. 210).

A Link to Disability Studies in Connection with Key Incident 1

Biklen (2000) asks to conceptualise and practice inclusive schooling in the light of critical disability narratives (p. 337). This offers a lead to the work of colleagues (see, for instance, Bogdan and Taylor, 1989; Booth and Booth, 1996; Corker and French, 1999; Gabel and Peters, 2004; Meekosha, 2004; Pfeiffer, 2002; Skrtic, 1995; Taylor, 2000; Taylor and Bogdan, 1989; Ware, 2001) who have provided important stimuli that have helped shape the field of Disability Studies. Furthermore, the term "critical" seamlessly fits our own Freirian perspective (Freire, 1972, 2004; Gadotti, 1994). Gruenewald (2003) states that "… critical pedagogies are needed to challenge the assumptions, practices and outcomes taken for granted in dominant culture and in conventional education …" (p. 3). Biklen describes critical in relationship to the phenomenon of "disability" as follows: "… the term refers to those works which see disability as occurring within shifting political, economic and social contexts, often highly marginalizing and discriminatory in nature; the critical narratives presume that experiences of people with disabilities cannot be understood simply as a function of individual makeup. These are works that seek to redefine the meanings of disability and to foster participation of people with disabilities in the exercise of power …" (p. 337).

KEY INCIDENT 2: SARAH'S STORY

> *Sarah was due to start her first year at a special school when her parents came to visit me. Until then, these people had been faithful "clientele" of the special educational circuit. In their case, "faithful" did not mean "uncritical." Sarah embarked on her schooling career in a school for children with severe intellectual disability (a type 2 school according to the Flemish classification). In view of the fact that she is completely (physically) dependent on others—Sarah uses a power wheelchair, she has a drain, and receives liquid food through a gastric tube—she was very well looked after. The group of infants that she belonged to was mainly stimulated at a very basic level by teachers and assistants. The parents thought this set-up was not sufficiently challenging for their child; moreover, none of the other children within Sarah's group could provide language stimuli … The parents decided to move Sarah to a type 4 school (special school for children who are physically impaired). In that school, Sarah made good progress, partly because a speech therapist encouraged her to use her non-verbal potential to communicate in a very focused and functional way.*

When Sarah switched from kindergarten to primary school, her parents were made to understand that in all likelihood their child would not be able to handle a primary school at this particular level (type 4). So Sarah's parents now had a child who "did not fit" in a type 2 school because she had too many talents that remained underdeveloped in that environment; but nor would a type 4 school "suit," because "her cognitive abilities' would probably not be adequate ... When they continued to look for a suitable special school for their child, Sarah's parents did not find any other type 4 school in the province that was prepared to give their daughter a chance in primary education. The only real option was to return to a type 2 school ... or— and this is what actually happened—to place Sarah in an regular school ...

Having eight different special school types in the Flemish-speaking part of Belgium implies that some children will "fall by the wayside" because they do not fit in any of the categories. It is as if schools and their experts screen out the naturally grown heterogeneity by forcing the children's needs into the existing practices, or by forcing them out of the system altogether (Skrtic, 1995, p. 202).

A Link to Disability Studies in Connection with Key Incident 2

Our research into inclusion taught us that the road to praxis lies in the genuine "dialogue" with the parents and their children. In Freire's conception, such a "dialogue" is a feature of a "horizontal relationship." The first virtue of dialogue consists of respect for those who are being educated. Another fundamental virtue is to listen to the urgencies and the choices of the pupil (and his or her family). The final virtue is that of tolerance, which is the virtue of living with what is different to be able to argue with what is antagonistic (Gadotti, 1994, pp. 50–51). Dialogue should be regarded as a strategy to respect the knowledge of the pupil and his or her family (ibid., p. 53).

The real needs of Sarah's parents in the above incident were not attended to, because the schools behaved like "colonisers" (in Freire's terms). The "banking pedagogy" that they applied is based on a "vertical relationship" (Freire, 1972). The person who is educated (and his or her family) only needs to listen and obey. The educator (here the professionals) knows and thinks and the pupils do not know and cannot think; the educator speaks and the pupils are listen quietly. It is the educator who makes and prescribes his or her choice and the pupils will follow the prescription. People are asked to live the values, interests, and ideology of the "oppressor" (Gadotti, 1994, p. 52).

Sarah's parents' decision to accept the solution, after a long "quest," to opt for an ordinary school, made us understand Freire's ideas regarding a "dialogic theory" (ibid., p. 55). This kind of theory has characteristics that are diametrically opposed to those of the anti-dialogic theory as seen in following oppositions:

Collaboration (versus conquest): We have learned to meet Sarah's parents as "equal partners"; the plans they have for their daughter are the starting point for a schooling career. These family objectives (e.g., communication and participation in the real world are seen as very important) can guide the school to build a curriculum and a programme of activities for Sarah with obvious links to the family rituals and perspectives.

Union (versus division for domination): We have learned that Sarah's parents are specialists in uniting people around the plans they have with their daughter. They are not interested at all in people who think that power games are of supreme importance.

Organisation (versus manipulation): We have learned that inclusive education practices do need a great deal of communication and exchange in a positive atmosphere. All one's energy is needed to focus on the real goals.

Cultural synthesis (versus cultural invasion): We have learned that the basic ideas about the inclusion of children such as Sarah can be learned from the family experiences/experiments. Professionals do not have to take over; it is more productive to strive for a synthesis of practical (day-to-day) and professional knowledge.

We agree with Smith (2001) that dialogue gives the possibility of unmasking the taken-for-granted. It is a kind of social relation that engages its participants (entailing the same virtues and emotions such as concern, trust, respect, appreciation, affection, and hope).

KEY INCIDENT 3: JEFF'S STORY

Some schools act on the basic assumption that the best way to educate a child with disabilities is full-time in a specialised centre. To a great extent, this practice is bound up with "naïve theories" concerning "best practices" that have evolved in the course of numerous years.

> *For instance, Jeff's parents currently feel under a lot of pressure. The teacher who is deployed by a special school to support their son in his regular school sends out various disturbing messages: Are they aware that Jeff's "motor abilities" would have progressed further if he had had advantage of residing in the*

special centre all the time? Moreover, do they know that a number of the things they presently have to find out for themselves—such as information about specific computer software—could be obtained for them by the special school? And have they not yet understood that Jeff's academic skills would have been more advanced if he had worked with programmes and educational tools specifically adapted for children "suffering from cerebral palsy"? His parents have to bear up under quite a lot of pressure if they want to proceed along the path that they have chosen for Jeff.

A great deal of what is suggested to Jeff's parents is connected with the principles of the "grouping" of children to make sure that the specialists can do their job. As we stated earlier in the text, this kind of causalities are the most important basis for the "othering" and segregation of children such as Jeff (Skrtic, 1995, p. 68).

A Link to Disability Studies in Connection with Key Incident 3

With his basic ideas of "dialogue," "conscientisation," and "breaking the culture of silence," Freire gave us a number of options to resist "the otherness" of persons with labels (Peters, in Corker and French, 1999, p. 103). This framework starts from the proposition that disability may expose a person to discrimination. By daring to discuss (among other things) "the dark side" of day-to-day life in (special) education (Skrtic, 1995, p. xv), we break with a culture of silence where the governing principle seems to be that "… the existing practices are the way they are because they have been that way for years …" This modus operandi carries a substantial risk that people who are "labelled" are manoeuvred into a position in which they are doomed to be as they are seen: incapable, illiterate, dysfunctional, and non-participating members of schools and society (Peters, p. 104). Preferably, the fact that we are shedding light on the darker aspects should be counterweighed with what Lawrence-Lightfoot refers to as "the dimensionality and complexity of goodness." And indeed, social scientists (those working in the field of special education are equally guilty of this) are conspicuous for their tendency to focus exclusively on any negative, and even "pathological" aspects. "The researcher who asks first 'what is good here?' is likely to absorb a very different reality than the one who is on a mission to discover the sources of failure … In examining the dimensionality and complexity of goodness there will, of course, be ample evidence of vulnerability and weakness. In fact, the counterpoint and contradictions of strength and vulnerability, virtue and evil (and how people, cultures and organizations negotiate those extremes in an effort to establish the precarious balance between them) are central to the expression of goodness …" (Lawrence-Lightfoot and Hoffmann Davis, 1997, p. 9).

The authors of this chapter have specifically decided to link "goodness" to the strength of families with disabled children, as well as to the strength of the children themselves. In our opinion, these strengths may predominantly be discovered by means of a "dialogue" with those children and their families. Such a dialogue has to be seen as a tool to realise "conscientisation." According to Peters (p. 105), this praxis organises itself by means of two clearly distinguishable phases:

- unveil the world of oppression, and through praxis come to know themselves as "subject" and commit themselves to transformation;
- transform the reality of oppression in their everyday lives, resulting in an educational pedagogy that ceases to belong to "oppressors" but becomes a pedagogy of all people in an ongoing process of permanent liberation ...[2]

KEY INCIDENT 4: DANNY'S STORY

Danny is a charming teenager who, together with his parents, is fully prepared "to go" for his future. Regardless of his physical impairment and the fact that he is labelled "mild intellectual disabled," he has many plans. He regularly overloads his daily schedule because he tends to feel that trips with his family, as well as his main hobbies—horse-riding and computer games—and his moments of physiotherapy are all equally important and he wants to experience it all with equal enthusiasm.

Lately, he has experienced a number of problems at his school (a special school for children with a physical impairment) because there is no real response to his request to be taught how to use additional computer programmes. A number of times, the teachers have sent him "back to square one" with the message that these programmes are "... not relevant to his curriculum ..." (which prepares him for work in a sheltered environment later on in life). Therefore, on their own initiative, Danny and his parents have found two young IT students who are prepared to teach Danny the finer points of various programmes. This can only take place outside of the curriculum that the school has set for Danny; he does not get any credits for these activities.

Some schools manage to "deprive" children of certain subjects. This is based on the argument that the children (generalisation) will not be able to cope. In other words, the dreams that the children or their parents might have do not play any part in the school curriculum. On the contrary, attempts are made (following

Foucault) to distribute human characteristics in discrete hierarchical relations, including intelligence (Biklen, 2000, p. 351).

A Link to Disability Studies in Connection with Key Incident 4

This incident shows that in certain ways we are very far removed from a practical implementation of "Person Centered Planning" strategies (Holburn and Vietze, 2002). Notwithstanding the fact that this concept is often endorsed, examples show that the actual needs and dreams of the children and their families do not (as yet) always serve as a guideline for implementing support activities. In our opinion, many of these "conflicts" (such as the outlined incident) can be more fully understood if we consider the way families are viewed. Ferguson (in Albrecht, 2001) teaches us in his fascinating chapter that interactions between families and professionals always occur within a social and historical context. Research on families with children with disabilities does not escape the context of assumptions and perspectives specific to a given time and place (pp. 374–375).Our incident is evidence that, regardless of the overt use of certain concepts that are part of a new paradigm, people still (partly) base their practical activities on the old model, and this provokes numerous conflicts. O'Brien and O'Brien (in Holburn and Vietze, 2002) show that families/clients are only really taken into account in cases where a "community of practice" exists (p. 4). They define this as follows: "… groups of people informally bound together by shared expertise and a passion for a joined enterprise …"

The latter is only possible if people take each others' expertise seriously. This is at odds with an educational landscape in which (placement) decisions for children with disabilities are constructed from the authority of professional knowledge. The paradigmatic professional knowledge of (student placement) decisions is based on a theoretical perspective within the culture of professionalism. It creates and maintains professional authority and contributes to the separation between professionals and their clients in determining decisions (of school placement) (Raymond, 2001, p. 32). Educational practices that are genuinely driven by person-centred planning principles will always have to return to the basic premises of these strategies:

- avoiding depersonalizing labels and stigmatizing procedures;
- honouring the voices of the persons who know the person best;
- building relationships;
- increasing choices;
- individualizing supports based on high expectations for the person's development;

- demanding that agencies adopt new forms of service and organisation to provide newly conceived supports (O'Brien and O'Brien, 2002, p. 15).

KEY INCIDENT 5: WALT'S STORY

From the moment their son was born, the parents of Walt, currently a sturdy pre-school child with Down's syndrome, have very actively sought out the "best" solutions and approach. With the assistance of an early intervention team, when Walt was ready for kindergarten they visited a number of kindergartens for children with special needs. Eventually, their search was strongly influenced by the following "incident"... On a nice day, Walt's mum is driving towards a possible school for her son. Walt and his siblings (two sisters and his brother) are sitting on the back seat of the car... The mother decides that the time has come to inform her daughters about the plans she and her husband have made for little Walt... As they slowly drive past the building, she tells the sisters that this is the school where Walt will go after the summer holidays... She adds that this is a special school for children who are a bit different, just like their little brother... After a brief silence, there is a loud protest from the back seat. The sisters do not agree with their parents' choice of school. They want to know why Walt is not allowed to go to their school. "... Walt will be so lonely, mummy..." says the eldest. "... Perhaps he will not have any friends there"... "And be all alone," says the other sister. According to his parents, this has been one of the most defining moments during their quest to find a school. Their own doubts, after visiting several special schools (would this really be the most stimulating environment for Walt?), perfectly converged with the challenging remarks made by Walt's sisters... They embarked on a new search: in the days following this "incident" the parents enquired at the school of their daughters whether Walt would possibly be welcome there...

This incident indicates that any decisions regarding a child who carries the label "disabled," equally concern its siblings, that is, the broader network (Naylor and Prescott, 2004).

A Link to Disability Studies in Connection with Key Incident 5

Many of the data that our research produces are closely connected to what Bogdan and Taylor (1989) have referred to as "the Social Construction of Humanness." In their previous articles (also ibid.), they described the perspective of people who do not stigmatise, stereotype, or reject those with obvious disabilities.

And indeed, it is fascinating to see how Walt's sisters "side with" their brother. However, theirs is no arbitrary action. Taylor and Bogdan seek to understand those who have an "accepting relationship." According to their definition (ibid., p. 27) this relationship is defined as a relationship between a person with a deviant attribute and a non-disabled person, which is long-standing and characterised by closeness ("Walt could go to our school"/"Walt shares the same teachers his brother was having") and affection ("Walt will be so lonely and not make any friends") and in which the deviant attribute does not have a stigmatising or morally discrediting character in the eyes of the non-disabled person.

It is obvious that Walt's siblings view him in a different way; therefore their relationship with him differs from that of the professionals who thought that he would perform better in a special environment. "… Notwithstanding cultural definitions of 'mental retardation' and the treatment in institutional settings of those so labelled, non-disabled people can conduct and form accepting relationships with those who have the most severe disabilities, and construct positive definitions of them as human beings. Those alliances exist and need to be understood as one way to complicate overly deterministic conceptualisations of labelling, stigma, and rejection …" (ibid., p. 138). Consequently, humanness becomes a construct characterised by a number of features:

- "Attributing thinking to the Other." This feature gives a lot of power to those who are not disabled in any way. Attributing thinking is a matter of "reading meaning" into gestures or movements the person makes. People sharpen their perception, so that from clues available, inner intentions can be captured (p. 139). In our key incident, Walt's siblings assume that Walt will start to think about all the friends who are not there when he is in that special school, and that he will be lonely because of this. Evidently, this perception is based on the powerful relationship between Walt and his siblings. "… Relationships are never static—they are dynamic, evolving and fluid. They are negotiated, week by week, day by day …" (Lawrence-Lightfoot and Hoffmann Davis, 1997, p. 135). Walt's siblings have come to know him, and they feel that he *is* able to think; to their mind, he is capable of going to school with the other children in his neighbourhood.
- "Seeing individuality in the Other" (Bogdan and Taylor, 1989, p. 141). The perspective of people who construct humanness use perspectives towards their disabled others that define them as distinct, unique individuals with particular and specific characteristics that set them apart from others. Walt's siblings do not regard Walt as "just a kid who is part of a group of children with a disability, who all go to this specific special

school." He is someone who likes to play with friends/likes to play in the same buildings and special corners of their school. Personality, likes and dislikes, feelings and motives are thus clearly distinguished.
- "Viewing the other as reciprocating." The fact that Walt's siblings view their brother as somebody who is able to make friends, implies that they see him as a fully competent participant in a relationship, and that he has to be seen as contributing something to the partnership (ibid., p. 143).

The aforementioned elements strongly define and determine a person. Because Walt is seen as having the ability to think, someone with individual motives, capable of participating in relationships, the others allocate him a particular place. He belongs in the school where his siblings go to (our school); he will partake in the family rituals and stories connected to the school in question (prepare school bags together, travel to school with his sisters, enter through the same gate, be collected at the same spot, play in the same playground, be taught by ex-teachers of his siblings) (ibid., p. 145). Here, two little girls and a little boy (the siblings) with a large sense of social commitment make short shrift of the tendency to turn people into objects, to tag them as belonging to separate groups. They act starting from a very basic assumption: Walt is first of all our little brother; when will we get rid from the "special" jargon?

KEY INCIDENT 6: PETE'S STORY

Pete and his family live outside the city. The family likes to work in their roomy garden, and they own a number of animals (horses, geese, rabbits …). From the time he was a young boy, Pete has loved looking after the animals as well as the doing strenuous work in the garden. He is remarkably adept at dealing with animals, and he is good at what he does. When he completed his schooling at a "normal" primary school, his choice of training/career seemed obvious. "I want to be a farmer" is one of Pete's favourite sayings. However, when Pete's parents started to look for a school that could provide support for Pete in achieving this dream, they were faced with a number of problems. In view of his Down's syndrome, Pete is expected to do training in preparation for his transfer to a day-care centre. His cognitive capacities are said to be insufficient for a type 3 special secondary school. During introductory visits to various locations in their area, Pete's parents end up in day-care centres with a very limited number of animals in the garden, and some with a small garden … This seems very far removed from Pete's idea "to be a farmer" … Consequently, they once again turn to the regular educational system. For three years, Pete goes to horticultural school, then switches to part-time education. This means that every week he goes to school for a number of days; he also stays at home for one day to work on several courses with a personal supervisor … In addition, he does work placements in horticultural centres. It seems likely that, thanks to the perseverance of his parents, Pete will be able to find a job in a tree nursery close to where he lives. And Pete is very confident about his future. During one of his work placements, at the municipal Parks and Public Gardens Department, it turned out that he impacted very positively on his workmates. For Pete knows a number of people. When they were clearing green waste from public areas, suddenly a lot of his acquaintances stopped to say hello. In this way the entire team of council workers unexpectedly became the centre of interest.

A Link to Disability Studies in Connection with Key Incident 6

This key incident goes back to the importance of the context. In the Flemish system a great deal of attention is given to the "pathology." This focus on pathology frequently leads to a referral to a "specially adapted environment" (a school, a home, the workplace …). We all know (Biklen, 2000, p. 341) that "… performance depends upon context …" Under the pretext of propositions that have not been proven at all, such as "… these pupils like to be among 'their own group' …" or "… there is an enormous difference between the capabilities of children with special needs, and those of other children of the same age-group …" a number of children are in danger of being excluded from the *real* world. In our view, the description by Sara Lawrence-Lightfoot and Hoffman Davis (p. 41) of the concept "context" indicates very clearly the problems and dangers of these propositions. "… By context, I mean the setting—physical, geographic, temporal, historical, cultural, aesthetic—within which the action takes place. Context becomes the framework, the reference point, the map, the ecological sphere; it is used to place people and action in time and space and as a resource for understanding what they say and do. The context is rich in clues for interpreting the experience of the actors in the setting. We have no idea how to decipher or decode an action, a gesture, a conversation, or an exclamation unless we see it embedded in context. Portraitists view human experience as being framed and shaped by the setting …"

We take this statement as our starting point when defining the problems of a (sometimes obligatory) life away from the real world/real school. In a recent article (De Waele and Van Hove, 2005) we managed to expose the "dehumanizing effect" of special settings (in this article we specifically refer to facilities for adults with a disability) through extensive ethnographic research in a Flemish residential facility. Despite our "new" rhetoric and policies we are still confronted with an "oppressing care culture." This lived experience of those who are taken out of the real world is organised with "distance" ("we" versus "them"), "care" (a very specific way of communication, organised passivity, etc.), and "control" (routines, collectivity, etc.) (p. 627).

KEY INCIDENT 7: JIM'S STORY

In Flanders, it is argued strongly that any additional support that is required for children with special needs in ordinary schools should be organised through the special educational system. The adherents of this line of reasoning support this argument, as it is true that special schools are specialised.

> *Jim has cerebral palsy and goes to a regular school. Notwithstanding the fact that he has problems walking, cannot move his hands very swiftly, and speaks somewhat slowly, Jim has a great zest for life. He manages to get others to support him if he feels that he is moving slowly, he turns out to be one of the best readers of his class, and he is reasonably good at sums. At first glance, all of this seems to add up to a successful example of inclusion. Then the parents were allocated a new supervisor for Jim. She was a young, enthusiastic staff member at a special school and it turned out that she was especially interested in possible (consequences of) Cerebral Visual Impairment* (Schenk-Rootlieb, Van Nieuwenhuizen, Van Waes, and Van der Graaf [1992]) *in Jim. This particular interest, in addition to the supervisor's special expertise, quickly led to conflicts with the parents. The latter did not see the use of the tests and exercises that Jim had to do in connection with a possible Cerebral Visual Impairment. They felt that because of these tests and his "therapy" their son was saddled with a new problem. Moreover, his class teacher turned out to be unaware of the content and objectives of this form of "support." And the expert thought it was necessary to take Jim out of the classroom several times per week …*

A Link to Disability Studies in Connection with Key Incident 7

This key incident provides a very interesting link to a Foucauldian perspective. Priestley (2002) shows that Foucault's framework is an excellent instrument for understanding the way in which a person's identity is construed (p. 94). It's constructed in two ways. On the one hand we become known to others through a variety of external disciplines and discourses (many of them institutionally embedded). On the other hand, we make ourselves known through self-knowledge and by speaking about ourselves. In our key incident, Jim is taken out of his classroom—this sets him very much apart from the other children in this fairly traditional school, where most learning takes place in groups. Furthermore, the new/additional diagnosis is an extra burden on Jim. Because of this diagnosis "on top of the known cerebral palsy," his teacher felt more distant from Jim's learning experience. The latter is perfectly in keeping with conclusions from other studies. The level of engagement that general education teachers have with students with disabilities has been identified in the literature as a key factor affecting the success of inclusive educational experiences (Giangreco, Broer, and Edelman, 2001, p. 75). In addition, this approach is diametrically opposed to Biklen's the views (p. 346) on inclusion as a possibility for creating and finding contexts for experiencing competence. Biklen states that teachers have a responsibility to try and find ways of assisting the child in bridging the gap between separation from others and inclusion, between silence or ineffective communication or disordered action and meaningful participation.

CONCLUSIONS

Through our work with families we have learned to appreciate and understand the oeuvre of Paulo Freire and his colleagues much better. While combining this critical pedagogical perspective with Disability Studies, we walk the same road of colleagues as Goodley (s.d.), Mahzer and Reid (2006), and Clear and Hutchinson (2006). Together with them we argue that in (special) education we need to learn to become more *uncertain* by:

- asking new/other questions
- listening to new/other experts
- digging into new/other sources.

Setting up such "risky journeys" can be helpful in digging a hole in the dyke of certainty ("… we know what is good for you …") (Giroux, in Goodley, s.d.). It can help to destabilise judgements that are made about children only from their labels (Mahzer and Reid, 2006, p. 113). Our experiences with inclusive education projects challenge unitary, universalised explanations that are moulded in types of special schools or standard programmes (most of the time based on what children are not able to do).

Our projects with parents, children, and schools open up possibilities of entering a space for permanent and collective learning. Within this space parents are seen as experts, children with and without labels as participants, and teachers as explorers of creative paths instead of bureaucrats. So we can fight oppressive and unjust situations; so we start to plan together journeys without a map; so we learn that using the dialogical pedagogy (as presented by Freire and his colleagues) is more than a technique or a method (Freire, 1998). To us "modest relations"

(Van Hove, Roets, and Goodley, p. 188 in Goodley and Van Hove, 2005) is the central motive. Disability in a pedagogical context becomes a relational concept. Assumptions about "normality" and the reproduction of structural differences are disclosed and mirrored in these modest relationships. In view of this choice, we cannot stay (in research and practice) neutral in a Freirian perspective; this leads to communal activism and resistance to further a longed-for social change (Freire, 2004). In this way our pedagogical work becomes a combination of a political act, a creative act, and an act of knowing (Gadotti, 1998, p. 2).

With help of the above "key incidents" we also learned to understand Freire's category (Freire, 2004, pp. 181–182) of "untested feasibility." Starting with the dreams of families and children, we have seen how they deal with "limit situations." At this point we observe the closest the dialogue between the practice of inclusive education and Disability Studies:

- "problems" get different "definitions": no longer the impairments of the children we worked with have to be seen as "the main problem/the main obstacle." Within a process of conscientisation (Freire, 1972) and liberation, parents and teachers learned to see obstacles in attitudes, school culture, training of experts, and discriminatory practices.
- "solutions" get different "definitions." Objective and detached professionals (with standard solutions) are no longer needed. What is more, the Latin American version of "companions" (Mc Gee) is expected. Companions are needed to support solutions that are built via dialogical action and reflection.
- "positions" get different "definitions." Children with labels (and their families) are no longer docile acceptors of "what is there" (Freire, 2004, p. 182). They learn to perceive problems as challenges and they act to overthrow the limit situations to realise a more humane situation and the concretisation of one of their biggest dreams: to participate.

NOTES

1. (Historical) Context. In 1970, Belgium decided that children with special needs should be entitled to special education in schools specifically set up for that purpose. Nationwide, various schools were recognised and classified. Through these special schools, the government wanted to cater for the specific needs of "children whose development was in danger." In respect of primary education, eight different types were selected that ranged from mild to severe intellectual, physical, or sensory impairment.

   There were no specific infant schools of types 1 or 8 as it was assumed that these children could be educated—at that pre-school level—in ordinary schools.

> Type 1: Schools for children with mild intellectual disability.
> Type 2: Schools for children with moderate to severe intellectual disability.
> Type 3: Schools for children with behavioural and emotional disorders.
> Type 4: Schools for children with a physical impairment.
> Type 5: Schools for children who are ill or suffering from chronic disease.
> Type 6: Schools for children who are visually impaired.
> Type 7: Schools for children who are deaf, or hard of hearing.
> Type 8: Schools for children with a learning disability.

Special secondary education offered four different types of schooling ranging from protected activities and environments to full adherence to the standard secondary curriculum.

From halfway through the 1970s to the end of the 1980s, the percentage of pupils in special

> Type 1: To prepare pupils for a protected lifestyle and activities in a protective environment.
> Type 2: To prepare pupils for activities in a sheltered workshop.
> Type 3: To prepare pupils for a "normal" job and a life as part of mainstream society.
> Type 4: To allow pupils to adhere to a standard curriculum at secondary level in the context of a special school.

schools was around 3%. In the 1990s, the number of pupils attending special schools grew steadily. Obviously, over the past fifteen years the trend has been to exclude, not to include children in the mainstream. During the 1990s, the population in special schools increased by 38%. Nevertheless, it is possible to identify differences between the various levels of schooling. For example, the percentage of infants educated in special schools is relatively small. Of the infants attending school in the educational year 2003–2004, 0.73% were registered at a special school. However, there was a marked increase at primary and secondary education level; 6.32% of the children registered at a primary school in the year 2003–2004 attended a special school; at secondary level, the percentage of children in special education was 3.78% (Mardulier, 2005).
2. Students in our Faculty are trained to become "reflective practitioners."

REFERENCES

Barton, L. (1998). Developing an Emancipatory Research Agenda: Possibilities and Dilemmas. In Clough, P. and L. Barton (eds.), *Articulating with Difficulty. Research Voices in Inclusive Education* (pp. 29–39). London: Paul Chapman Publishing.

Baumgart, D. and Giangreco, M. (1996). Key Lessons Learned about Inclusion. In D. Lehr and F. Brown (eds.), *Persons Who Challenge the System: Persons with Profound Disabilities* (pp. 79–97). Baltimore: Paul H. Brooks Publishing.

Biklen, D. (2000). Constructing Inclusion: Lessons from Critical, Disability Narratives. *International Journal of Inclusive Education*, 4, 4, 337–353.

Bogdan, R. and Taylor, S. (1989). Relationships with Severely Disabled People: The Social Construction of Humanness. *Social Problems*, 36, 2, 135–148.

Booth, T. and Booth, W. (1996). Sounds of Silence: Narrative Research with Inarticulate Subjects. *Disability and Society*, 11, 1, 55–69.

Clear, M. and Hutchinson, F. (2006). Learning from Each Other: A Theoretical and Applied Overview of the Relationship between Disability Studies and Peace Studies. *Review of Disability Studies*, 2, 88–98.

Corker, M. and French, S. (eds.) (1999). *Disability Discourse*. Buckingham-Philadelphia: Open University Press.

De Waele, I. and Van Hove, G. (2005). Modern Times: A Ethnographic Study on the Quality of Life of People with a High Support Need in a Flemish Residential Facility. *Disability and Society*, 20, 6, 625–640.

Emerson, R. (2004). Working with "Key Incidents." In C. Seale, G. Gobo, J. Gubrium, and D. Silverman (pp. 457–472). *Qualitative Research Practice*. London: Sage.

Ferguson, P. (2001). Mapping the Family: Disability Studies and the Exploration of Parental Response to Disability. In G. Albrecht, K. Seelman, and M. Bury (eds.), *Handbook of Disability Studies* (pp. 373–395). Thousand Oaks: Sage Publications.

Freire, P. (1972). *Pedagogy of the Oppressed*. Harmondsworth: Penguin Books.

Freire, P. (1998). *Teachers as Cultural Workers. Letters to Those Who Dare to Teach*. Boulder, CO: Westview Press.

Freire, P. (2004). *Pedagogy of Hope*. London and New York: Continuum.

Gabel, S. L. and Peters, S. (2004). Presage of a Paradigm Shift? Beyond the Social Model of Disability toward Resistance Theories of Disability. *Disability and Society*, 19, 6, 585–600.

Gadotti, M. (1994). *Reading Paulo Freire. His Life and Work*. Albany: State University of New York Press.

Gadotti, M. (1998). The Political-Pedagogical Praxis of Paulo Freire. Lecture on the Paulo Freire Forum, Sao Paulo.

Giangreco, M. (1997). Key Lessons Learned about Inclusive Education: Summary of the 1996 Schonell Memorial Lecture. *International Journal of Disability, Development and Education*, 44, 3, 193–206.

Giangreco, M., Broer, S., and Edelman, S. (2001). Teacher Engagement with Students with Disabilities: Differences between Paraprofessional Service Delivery Models. *Journals of the Association for Persons with Severe Handicaps*, 26, 2, 5–86.

Goodley, D. and Lawthom, R. (2005). Epistemological Journeys in Participatory Action Research: Alliances between Community Psychology and Disability Studies. *Disability and Society*, 20, 2, 135–152.

Goodley, D. and Van Hove, G. (eds.) (2005). *Another Disability Studies Reader? People with Learning Difficulties and a Disabling World*. Antwerp: Garant Publishers.

Goodley, D. (s.d.). Towards Socially Just Pedagogies: Deleuzoguattarian Critical Disability Studies. Submitted to the *International Journal of Inclusive Education*.

Gruenewald, D. (2003). The Best of Both Worlds: A Critical Pedagogy of Place. *Educational Researcher*, 32, 4, 3–12.

Holburn, S., and Vietze, P. M. (eds.) (2002). *Person Centered Planning: Research, Practice and Future Directions*. Baltimore: Paul Brookes.

Lather, P. (1991). *Getting Smart: Feminist Research and Pedagogy with/in the Postmodern*. London: Routledge.

Lawrence-Lightfoot, S. and Hoffmann Davis, J. (1997). *The Art and Science of Portraiture*. San Francisco: Jossey-Bass Publishers.

Lyle O'Brien, C. and O'Brien, J. (2002). The Origins of Person Centered Planning. In S. Holburn, P. Vietze, and Person (eds.), *Centered Planning, Research, Practice and Future Directions* (pp. 3–27). Baltimore: Paul Brookes Publishing.

Mahzer, W. and Reid, K. (2006). Learning Disabilities, the Missing Discussion in Disability Studies: Is There a Possibility for Alliance? *The Review of Disability Studies*, 2, 106–122.

Mardulier, T. (2005). Kan het nog iets meer zijn? Over inclusief onderwijs in Vlaanderen. *Impuls voor onderwijsbegeleiding, 35ste jaargang*, 3, 187–197.

Meekosha, H. (2004). Drifting Down the Gulf Stream: Navigating the Cultures of Disability Studies. *Disability and Society*, 19, 7, 721–734.

Naylor, A. and Prescott, P. (2004). Invisible Children? The Need for Support Groups for Siblings of Disabled Children. *British Journal of Special Education*, 31, 4, 199–206.

O'Brien, C. L. and O'Brien, J. (2002). The Origins of Person Centered Planning: A Community of Practice Perspective. In S. Holburn and P. M. Vietze (eds.), *Person Centered Planning: Research, Practice and Future Directions* (pp. 3–28). Baltimore: Paul Brookes.

Peters, S. (1999). Transforming Disability Identity through Critical Literacy and the Cultural Politics of Language. In M. Corker and S. French (eds.), *Disability Discourse* (pp. 103–115). Buckingham: Open University Press.

Pfeiffer, D. (2002). The Philosophical Foundations of Disability Studies. *Disability Studies Quarterly*, 22, 2, 3–23.

Priestley, M. (2002). Discourse and Identity: Disabled Children in Mainstream High Schools. In M. Corker and Sally French (eds.), *Disability Discourse* (pp. 92–102). Buckingham: Open University Press.

Raymond, H. (2001). Listening Carefully for Inclusion: A Principal's Awakening. *International Journal of Whole Schooling*, 1, 2, 31–43.

Schenk-Rootlieb, A., Van Nieuwenhuizen, O., Van Waes, P., and Van Der Graaf, Y. (1992). The Prevalence of Cerebral Visual Disturbance in Children with Cerebral Palsy. *Developmental Medicine and Child Neurology*, 34, 473–480.

Skrtic, T. (ed.) (1995). *Disability and Democracy. Reconstructing (Special) Education for Postmodernity*. New York and London: Teachers College Press.

Smith, M. K. (2001) Dialogue and Conversation. *The Encyclopaedia of Informal Education*. http://www.infed.org/biblio/b-dialog.htm.

Taylor, S. (2000). You're Not a Retard, You're Just Wise. *Journal of Contemporary Ethnography*, 29, 1, 58–92.

Taylor, S. and Bogdan, R. (1989). On Accepting Relationships between People with Mental Retardation and Non-disabled People: Towards an Understanding of Acceptance. *Disability, Handicap and Society*, 4, 1, 21–36.

Van Hove, G., Mortier, K., and De Schauwer, E. (2005). Onderzoek Inclusief Onderwijs. *Orthopedagogische Reeks Gent*, 25.

Van Hove, G., Roets, G. and Goodley, D. (2005). Disability Studies: About Relationships, Power, and Knowing as Forms of Participation. In D. Goodley and G. Van Hove (eds.) *Another Disability Studies Reader? People with Learning Difficulties and a Disabling World* (pp. 185–198). Antwerp: Garant Publishers.

Ware, L. (2001). Writing, Identity and the Other. Dare We Do Disability Studies? *Journal of Teacher Education*, 52, 2, 107–123.

CHAPTER NINE

Doing Inclusive Education Research

JULIE ALLAN AND ROGER SLEE

INTRODUCTION

Research done under the rubric of inclusive education contains a series of contestations that are often emotive and highly charged. This is captured in recent journal exchanges between traditional special education researchers (Brantlinger, 1997) and those whom they describe variously and loosely as full-inclusionists, postmodernists or adherents to disability studies in education (Kaufman & Hallahan, 1995; Brantlinger, 1997; Kauffman & Sasso, 2006; Gallagher, 2006). To those entering the field as a student or a novice researcher, the attention to positioning must seem bewildering, if not ironic, for a field describing itself as inclusive. This fracture and fragmentation within this research interest is not surprising when considering its origins (Slee, 2006). A relatively recent arrival to the education research and policy lexicon, inclusive education has cross-disciplinary origins and confounding applications. It is little then wonder that students register confusion. But what is potentially more problematic is an absence of an acknowledgement of confusion.

Too often, there is an apparent unwillingness by researchers of inclusive education to reveal their positions, *where they are coming from,* by specifying the foundations of knowledge and assumptions about the nature of reality on which their work is based. At the same time, however, they call for the recognition of the ideological and intellectual traditions from those they critique. This makes it difficult for the outsider, or even the insider, to challenge their position or to engage in debate with them. We contend that the lack of reflexivity across the field of inclusive education limits its capacity to reduce educational and social exclusion.

We wanted to find a way of opening up some of the controversies and counterpoints that characterise inclusive education. Rather than produce yet another piece of commentary, we decided to embark on a research project with individuals who had undertaken key pieces of research and/or scholarship. By *researching the researchers,* we were trying to get inside the research process and explore how decisions were made: for example, the questions to be addressed in the research, who was to be included, how sense was made of the data, writing, and the impact of the work. In undertaking this research project and presenting our findings to students and researchers we wanted readers to engage, albeit mediated by our emphases and interpretations, with the researchers as they reflect upon specific pieces of their work.

In this chapter we discuss the positioning of the researchers and scholars in relation to the field of inclusive education and their engagement with its controversies and counterpoints. Their responses to direct questions about their own positions are the material for this discussion and we attempt to further elaborate their stance in relation to three "meta" questions that we ask of their commentaries:

- What is the problem to which inclusive education has become the solution?
- What is seen as the nature of the "damage" arising from the problem?
- What do the researchers/scholars see as the work's intent?

In introducing the researchers and describing our engagement with them, it is necessary for us to acknowledge tensions in our project design and the anxieties they generated.

INTRODUCING THE RESEARCHERS

As researchers designing a project, inevitably we bring to the workbench our personal and intellectual histories. Research is never disinterested or objective. We receive and interpret the world in ways that are shaped by our individual biography and naturally we have strong views about what a better world looks like and the role of education in contributing to that better world. Reducing educational exclusion and moving towards more inclusive futures for students disadvantaged by the complex interactions of poverty, disability, race, language, sexuality, and gender with pedagogy, curriculum, and the organisation of schooling are at the centre of our educational project. How we apprehend, analyze, and interpret patterns of exclusion is also shaped by the interplay of personal biography and intellectual training inside and outside of the academy. In this respect we are like all the participants in the project, although our views about education and researching may differ significantly.

For us the recent emergence and expansion of inclusive education is both hopeful and troubling. In plotting its trajectory we acknowledge key intellectual moments. Though not referred to as inclusive education at the time, there was an emerging research in the 1970s and 1980s that offered a paradigmatic and political challenge to established special educational perspectives on disability as defectiveness and personal tragedy. In the United Kingdom, researchers such as Ford, Mongon, and Whelan (1982) in their text, *Special Education and Social Control. Invisible Disasters* and Tomlinson (1982) in her *A Sociology of Special Education*, together with disability activists such as Oliver (1985), Barnes (1990), Barton (1988), and Morris (1991) (the list is indicative rather than exhaustive) collectively issued a challenge to the functionalist heartland of special education with its focus on separating defective children from or integrating these children into largely unchanging regular schools for regular children. The critique of special education was not restricted to the United Kingdom. In the United States, special education, pressured by the demands of parents and progressive rights-based litigation (Minow, 1990; Pickering Francis & Silvers, 2000) moved to conditional forms of integration or mainstreaming (Biklen, 1985). During this time traditional special education continued to expand its influence. Indicators of this expansion may be seen in the funding it attracted, the number of students diagnosed with broadening diagnostic schedules, and through its grip on research funding agencies.

A key to this emergent and critical field was the acknowledgement that inclusive education was about *all* children as it shifted its focus to consider the pervasive nature of exclusion in and through education. Consequently, the pursuit of inclusive educational research brought together a broad range of interests and research tools spanning the new sociology of education, critical theory and pedagogy, post-structuralism and postmodern philosophy, feminist research, disability studies, and postcolonial studies. Within this field hybrids formed; researchers drew from the work of school effectiveness and school improvement studies together with popularised management and education leadership writings from Senge (1989), Fullan (1991) and Wenger (1998). This branch of school improvement writing applied a social justice element to its agenda. The effective school, they argue, is the inclusive school (Ainscow, 1991).

Inclusive education gathered traction as a Third Way political imperative (Giddens, 1998) and was taken up globally by international agencies such as UNESCO and the OECD (Pijl, Meijer, & Hegarty, 1997). Governments reorganised to establish inclusive education within their education portfolios. The success of inclusive education as an organising node and funding imperative hastened a general uptake of a new lexicon by special education to describe its activity (Brantlinger, 2004). Brantlinger tracks this through her survey of special educational texts as they added titles and chapters to reflect a new political climate.

The consequence of this is that a large number of researchers contiguously describe themselves as special and inclusive education researchers. The research that appears in search engines as inclusive education spans a range of methodologies including experimental design, ethnography, discourse analysis, action research—and the list goes on. This is not by itself problematic, as the deployment of a range of analytic instruments enables us to represent the nuances of complex social phenomena. What is problematic is the way in which research design carries assumptions about the world and the intentions of its architects. For instance, is the research designed to discover facts about the child to assist the teacher to fit the child into the existing structures, pedagogic, curricular, and physical, of the classroom or is the research examining complex social relations that render some children vulnerable in order to change institutional life? In this milieu, the deconstruction of discourse and attendant practices become critical for the student and neophyte researcher as they traverse what may well be an overextended field.

In establishing our "sample," we wished to avoid typologising the field because of our resistance to the ways in which such rigid categorising fixes people and their work and our sense that we would, in any case, be inaccurate. We also wanted to construct a sample of researchers and/or scholars in relation to their work rather than to themselves as individuals. In spite of ourselves, and our good intentions, our sample of researchers and scholars located them at points on what appears to be a spectrum of research on inclusive education that went from what we termed traditional special educational research to critical research within a sociological framework. Between these two "ends" we located work done by those working within a school improvement/reform paradigm and disability activists. The objective was not to construct a "spectrum" as it may seem to suggest a linear narrative of descending or ascending political and methodological value for their research. While it was necessary at the outset for us to identify different research genres or traditions across the field, we were aware that the descriptions that we imposed on the research and the categories we constructed would, through the research, unravel. In inviting the researchers and scholars to be interviewed, we did not reveal their position on the spectrum to them; this was because we wanted to avoid all the effects we know to be associated with recognition of labelling and we wanted to allow them to position themselves.

Deciding upon researchers to form our cohort was in part a question of logistics and accessibility. Many of the interviews were undertaken at the Annual Meeting of the American Education Research Association in Montreal. Our attendance at this meeting afforded us access to most of our interviewees. The remaining interviews were conducted by telephone and at agreed locations. The interviews were based upon a selection of their work determined by us that was both representative of their research and significant to the broad field of inclusive education. In this way we broadened the definition of inclusive education to the consideration of exclusion according to factors other than disability such as race, gender, and class. The table below identifies the researchers and scholars and the work that we identified as having been significant.

The Researchers and their Work

Special Education Research	*School Improvement/ Reform*	*Disability Activism*	*Critical Research*
Ken Kavale *The Positive Side of Special Education: Minimising Its Fads, Fancies and Follies* (2004, with M. Mostert)	Tony Booth *The Index for Inclusion* (2002, with M. Ainscow)	Len Barton *Disability Studies Today* (2002, with M. Oliver & C. Barnes)	David Gillborn *Rationing Education* (2000, with D. Youdell)
Karen Harris *Making the Writing Process Work* (1996, with S. Graham)	Lani Florian "What Can National Data Sets Tell Us about Inclusion and Pupil Achievement?" (2004, with M. Rouse; K. Black-Hawkins, & S. Jull)	Mike Oliver *Understanding Disability: From Theory to Practice* (1996)	Stephen Ball *Choice, Pathways and Transitions Post-16* (2000, with M. Maguire & S. Macrae)
Kim Cornish "Attention and Language in Fragile X" (2004, with V. Sudhalter & J. Turk)	Alan Dyson "Making Space in the Standards Agenda: Developing Inclusive Practices in Schools" (2003, with F. Gallannaugh & A. Millward)		Ellen Brantlinger *Dividing Classes* (2003)
	Suzanne Carrington "A Case Study of Inclusive School Development" (2004, with S. Robinson)		Sally Tomlinson *A Sociology of Special Education* (1982)

One other researcher was interviewed, but has been omitted from our sample at this stage for technical reasons. In most cases the individuals were well known to us and we carried out the majority of the interviews jointly. The participants were sent a copy of the transcripts for correction, with an invitation to embellish further if they wished. Inaccuracies arising from the international nature of this study, in which a Canadian transcriber found the Scottish and Australian interviewers, at times, "incoherent," were ironed out. The respondents were asked a series of questions relating to the process of research and/or scholarship involved in the specific piece of work that had been identified, from the initial conceptualisation through to writing and impact.

Our analysis was situated within a post-structuralist framework, drawing on some of the key concepts from the work of Foucault (1977, 1988); Derrida (1992); and Deleuze and Guattari (1987). This enabled us to examine, first of all, the content of *what* people said about their research and also to look at *how* people talked, by attending to the images, metaphors, and positioning of themselves and others. The examination of participants' discourses enabled a particular attention to values and to issues of power and revealed to us some of the tensions, controversies, and counterpoints in the researchers' and scholars' work. Our analysis, thus, had three strands. The first of these was the initial framing of the respondents' work—our sample. The second strand was the reading of their representations of their work and our interpretations of how, in the interviews, they had addressed the meta-questions about the nature and purpose of their work. The third strand involved looking at, within, and behind these interpretations, pulling on particular "threads" and watching them unravel.

WHERE ARE THEY COMING FROM?

We asked the participants to indicate where they would locate the specific piece of their work that we had identified for the focus of their interview in relation to inclusive education, special education, and disability studies. For some this was a challenging question because of the lack of clarity associated with these categories and the different types of research that might be done within, for example, disability studies. The respondents positioned their work by elaborating the kind of performance they saw it doing within academic, policy and practice fields and in relation to others. The research and scholarship was differentiated by the individuals as foundational work, building a corpus of knowledge; or as work that established a particular relationship with the policy and practice community. Distinctions emerged in the work in relation to others between that which was undertaken upon others, as *provocations* and that which was carried out with others, through strategic *alignments*. A final kind of work was depicted as nomadic, working between disciplines and policy and practice spaces and having an amorphous identity. The discursive performances of the work are discussed in the pages that follow.

FOUNDATIONS

Mike Oliver and Sally Tomlinson saw their texts *Understanding Disability* (1996) and *A Sociology of Special Education* (Tomlinson, 1982) as foundational performances, establishing new knowledge and new ways of thinking about the "problem" of disability. Mike Oliver outlined the areas of his foundations, disability studies, the social model of disability, and emancipatory research, but expressed dissatisfaction with how these had been understood and received:

> If I think about three areas, if I think about my work as being 1) the kind of theoretical developments that I have made, I wouldn't be unhappy with being the way I am positioned there as one of the intellectual leaders or founding fathers of disability studies, call it what you like … If I think about the way my work around the social model instead, which is an attempt to link theory to practice, if you like, the way I am positioned on that, I am profoundly unhappy because I think with very few exceptions practically everybody who has kind of attempted to grapple what I have said about the social model has misinterpreted or misunderstood … In terms of that area, I would express unhappiness and anger even about the way my work has been and still is being interpreted I think by some people who accuse me of being a kind of naïve social modelist or whatever … The third area, if you think about, not the research that I've actually done, but my attempts to create a different way of doing research, then my argument would be one of about disappointment, I think.

Sally Tomlinson's foundations emerged from within sociology when she undertook groundbreaking work in relation to class and race. The time had come, she felt, when inclusive education had come into existence, and she became convinced of the relevance of the sociology of education for inclusive education:

> I mean originally I thought of it as part of the sociology of education which is now a non-subject or unacceptable, but I've come to regard it, because I've carried on working in the area of race and also education policy generally, but from again sociological structural notions of social class and so on, so I have come to regard it more. I was quite glad when this notion of inclusive education became more popular because it was okay in the 70s and the 80s to look at this particular excluded group, or I was looking at two, because I was also looking at black young people, but then when you put it all together it became more obvious that you couldn't regard special education disability as something other than part of a whole range of inclusions or exclusions and so this is why we now need a sociology of inclusive education.

Sally related how none other than Mary Warnock, the so-called architect of inclusion (CSIE, 2005) had reviewed the book and described her amusement at how she had positioned her:

> She said it was a horribly fascinating tale that I had unfolded. She called me not exactly a Marxist loonie, but Marxist-oriented. But actually I am a Weberian. I sort of go for special interests and look at class status and power in different ways to basically the means of production, although that is very important, you know, but I don't think she knew the difference between Marx and Weber, actually.

Warnock's recent pronouncements on inclusion (2005) suggest some more fundamental confusion (Barton, 2005; Allan, 2008) but that is another matter. Both Mike and Sally saw their work as having performed some knowledge production, but Mike in particular was left with a sense of disappointment at the limited uptake of his foundational social model and emancipatory research. The social model, he argued, had become merely another way for professionals to talk and not act, as he'd intended it to be used:

> I wish people would stop talking about it. The social model is not some kind of conceptual device to debate. The social model is a tool that we should use to try and produce changes in the world, changes in what we do. What I hoped from that was that people would start using it and then what we would actually see was not "what are the theoretical underpinnings of the social model? Mike Oliver says this and Jenny Morris says that and somebody else says that." You know, complete rehashes of that, but this is what I did with the social model. This is how I took it into a particular school or particular social work agency. This is what we did with it and this is whether it worked or not.

Mike Oliver's attempts to engineer emancipatory research had also been disappointing as people seemed to him to be hung up on debates about objectivity and subjectivity and seemed satisfied with experiential accounts of disabled people.

RELATIONAL RESEARCH

A number of researchers and scholars saw their texts as performing work either upon others, in a challenging or provocative way, or with others, the establishment of strategic alignments.

Provocations

Len Barton, Mike Oliver, and Colin Barnes all depicted their texts, *Disability Studies Today* (2002); *Dividing Classes* (Brantlinger, 2003); and *The Positive Side of Special Education: Minimising Its Fads, Fancies and Follies* (Kavale & Mostert, 2004) as working upon mainstream academics and practitioners and, through conceptual provocation (Bains, 2002), trying to change their minds. Len Barton described his work as inherently political and as doing the work of raising questions and challenging:

> I would have to say that I am trying to develop a critical political analysis that is rooted in experience and in the processes of people's everyday lives. How significant, how sensitive one is to the nuances of that and so forth is an issue. Certainly one is attempting to develop alternative ideas, alternative ways of conceiving the field, most importantly, of raising questions … I would say that that is how I would relate certainly to special education because in all sorts of ways, even though I was in the field as a special educator my work has been increasingly and progressively about challenging dominant assumptions about practices and particularly psychological ideas and arguments in the field of disability studies. Again, it's about challenging non-disabled views of the world. I see a great deal of my work in that field is trying to raise questions to that group of people.

The strong element of reflexivity in Len Barton's work, both in relation to his own writing, and what he enjoins others to do, suggests parallels with Foucault's practices of the self. These practices require the utmost scrutiny of one's thoughts and writing through work that is "ethical" and that

> Evokes the care of what exists and might exist; a sharpened sense of reality, but one that is never immobilized before it; a readiness to find what surrounds us strange and odd; a certain determination to throw off familiar ways of thought and to look at the same things in a different way … a lack of respect for the traditional hierarchies of what is important and fundamental. (1988, p. 321)

Ellen Brantlinger portrayed her work as "debunking" the labels associated with children from low-income families and saw it as running parallel to, but distinct from, the work on debunking labels in respect of children with severe disabilities done by such people as Susan Gabel and Phil Ferguson:

> Everything I did tried to counteract that, to say these are typical kids. These are difficult situations where, you know, you overburden teachers, their only recourse is to [label and exclude] so I think just sort of constantly interrogating, questioning and challenging how context and thinking presents real problems for a certain segment of the population who are pretty powerless.

Ellen described herself as radical, but less so than some of her counterparts in the field who championed the disappearance of special education:

> In some ways I didn't feel we should get rid of [special education] and the reason is I do think that any kids who have problems with schools and teachers who have diverse classes need support and I didn't think it was going to come from the inside.

Ellen's work appeared to perform what Foucault (1977, p. 73) termed "transgression," a form of non-positive affirmation, which subverts the norms that operated, and through this piece of work and others, she became recognised as someone who would transgress:

> In terms of the results of this activism, I actually got quite a bit done in my time but I had different reactions from all of these local people—some was just hostility. These people conveyed that attitude that it was rude to bring up social class. You know, their reaction was shut the door on that darn lady. Punish her. Don't let her kids get on the bus. They actually put the bus zone on the other side of my alley and the neighbours were mad at me. I told them let's just go to the bus stop on the first day of school and put our kids on. The bus driver never said a thing. So that solved that.

Ken Kavale described his work as more of a kind of persistence, working on the special education community to persuade them to be a little less special and encouraging the mainstream to recognise and accept the value of specialist instruction:

> I think that the idea is that you have to convince people that some of the traditional ways that we have approached special education in trying to make it special in some sense is actually—might be a bit counterproductive. You know we really don't need many special techniques. What we need is sound instructional methodology that we can adapt for the purposes of special education and those things work ... So I think if you re-iterate those same statements, hopefully it'll somehow, at some point, you know, stick so to speak.

Both Ellen Brantlinger and Ken Kavale may balk at the parallels drawn between their work, especially since each acknowledges the other as on the opposite side of an "ideological split" (Ken Kavale). We will consider these contestations, and their ideological bases, in more detail in our future writing. Here it is the performances *upon* others that we are interested in and where we discern these similarities rather than the positions of the work per se. Their work and that of Len Barton have an intense activism and intent to change what each of them sees, differently of course, as the status quo.

Alignments

The work of five individuals, Mel Ainscow's *Index for Inclusion* (Booth & Ainscow, 2002), Lani Florian's *What Can National Data Sets Tell Us about Inclusion and Pupil Achievement* (Florian, et. al., 2004); Kim Cornish, Vicki Sudhalter, and Jeremy Turk's (2004) "Attention and Language in Fragile X"; Karen Harris and Steven

Graham's (1996) *Making the Writing Process Work*; and Suzanne Carrington and Robyn Robinson's (2004) "A Case Study of Inclusive School Development" was represented as less confrontational and more conciliatory, recognising a reality that the "other"—either special education or inclusive education—would not go away and looking for accommodations and compromises. Mel Ainscow described how this need for compromise diminished his capacity for activism:

> I think basically I see myself as an activist. Someone who is trying to make a contribution, a direct contribution to thinking, to policy, to practice, but I'd like to think, I think this is a weakness in what I do, because you make compromises, but I'd like to think that I'm an activist who occasionally ruffles feathers and challenges and disturbs what is going on. I'd like to be better at that. The trouble is if you are working with the people who are really under pressure—teachers, government people—in order to be better at that you have to make compromises.

Lani Florian acknowledged the formidable presence of special education and the need to find ways of working with it:

> I think that special education has a long way to go … I don't think that the profession is going to go away, maybe what we call it could be different, you know that kind of thing, but I think there will always be a need for some kind of concern and advocacy for—around vulnerable kids, however, we define who those kids are.

She took exception to Mike Oliver's threat, in his keynote address to the Manchester International Special Education Congress, of "dancing on the grave of special education," arguing that this was futile. She saw her own work as providing a "bridge" between disability studies and special education, recognising the need for:

> something called professional knowledge that is important, that needs to be brought to bear in the service of inclusion but we need to think about how we do the work differently.

Suzanne Carrington had used *The Index for Inclusion* as a tool for establishing alliances with stakeholders within schools "to look at what is currently happening and what could happen when we dream about what could be." She was uneasy about her work being located within inclusive education because, for many, this was merely about disability and she saw her work as concerning a wider constituency. She preferred it to be depicted as educational reform or more effective schools. Kim Cornish et al. saw inclusive education as having a more dogged presence and regarded this as unfortunate:

> It serves no purpose, in my view, to have [children with emotional and behavioural difficulties] in inclusive settings because you know, the whole classroom is disrupted,

> the teacher is—feels out of control because they have no proper training on this. You know the student isn't really learning to their potential because the classroom is full of distraction ... You can end up with, you know, a nice warm fuzzy title for it all but at the end of the day, who benefits? Nobody has ever looked ... and I can guess who doesn't benefit ... But when you've got a child with mental retardation, with specific behavioural, cognitive difficulties, then to simply place them in inclusive settings with no appropriate resources, then I think it's just a set-up for failure.

She opted, however, to situate her work within inclusive education, seeing little alternative to this:

> If I were in the UK, if you asked me that three years ago, I would have said ... special needs definitely. Now I would like to say I would like to situate my work in inclusive education because this is exactly what it is. You know it's taken me three years to accept that it's not going to change, that inclusive education in Quebec is here to stay at least for the time being ... I come from a very developmental neuroscience background and that methodology and approach guides my work but I think that the end point of it now would be situated within inclusive education—at least I'd like to think I could do that—to situate within inclusive education and to contribute to that ... I wish [inclusive education} wasn't here in Quebec, but I think it will stay here albeit with no resources.

Karen was also wary of the presence of inclusive education, but sought recognition of "common ground" and a greater appreciation from regular education of the contribution and insights into practice and learning that had come from special education:

> I don't believe that we necessarily need different methods. I do think that one of the things that Special Ed has found and has to offer to General Ed is it's not—it's not special methods, it's effective methods and if it works with kids with LD, it's highly likely to work with most kids. This whole differentiated instruction thing—that General Ed thinks they discovered—that's all out of Special Ed. That's where it all started. Every single concept that they use in differentiated instruction was in Special Ed twenty years before. So that—hopefully now we're finding common ground. So hopefully what we do goes back to just helping the kids who need the help and that's hopefully where we see the work.

NOMADIC WANDERINGS

The work by Stephen Ball, *Choice, Pathways and Transitions Post-16,* and David Gillborn and Deborah Youdell's *Rationing Education* had, by their estimate, a nomadic quality and an in-betweenness. Stephen Ball acknowledged this as one of its strength but it also created difficulties:

> Well, I think one of the problems perhaps is that it is difficult to place. It doesn't fit easily ... I wouldn't say that it's been ignored but don't think it finds a home within

which it becomes an obvious point of reference. It passes by a lot of people I think, so there is a paradox in that sense. And the second part of the paradox is not simply that it doesn't fit kind of conceptually or stylistically into policy debates or academic debates. In trying to take on complexity it crosses a lot of disciplinary boundaries so it doesn't fit neatly into disciplines either. It deals with youth studies and it deals with policy and it deals with the economics of the city and it deals with 14–19 and lifelong learning and it tries to move across all those and so that makes it a problematic text as well.

The book was also, he described, a "reflexive text" because it spoke about research processes. David Gillborn and Deborah Youdell also found that their book could not be put easily into any one "pigeon hole" because it performed in multiple spaces:

> It really achieves a great thing because the Foucauldian notion of discourse suffuses it because we talk about ability as affecting and affected by discourses of intelligence and eugenics etc. etc. So it's Foucauldian and there's a particular data analysis section that's really Foucauldian: the student league table. We do a technologies of disciplinary power analysis but we also draw on the triage and say this is a structure of these social educational processes. So we do that. Absolutely. So, yeah, you couldn't put it in a pigeon hole … But I don't think that is … a problem at all. I think that what it does is to pick what is most effective to answer particular questions.

Their book, as they saw it, was in some ways a "very traditional" piece of critical school ethnography that, however, made use of theoretical tools previously not available within this field moving between structural analysis, symbolic interactionism, and Foucauldian analysis. It also, they said, "picks up the policy scholarship that had come on line more recently." They saw themselves as benefiting personally from this movement, as Dave Gillborn described:

> The book was part of the process of doing both because we had different … I mean the book is totally much more than we could have done separately. And it wasn't either of us trumping the other. We both learned from each other and the book is better than either of us could have done by ourselves and we learned from each other as we did it. I got Foucault working with you in a way that I had never got Foucault before and I think you got, you had a bit more respect for some old-fashioned symbolic interactionisim than you certainly had at the beginning.

The nomadic quality and undecidability (Derrida, 1992) of both these texts had enabled them to perform what Deleuze and Guattari (1987, p. 161) call "deterritorialization," replacing the rigid and striated spaces with smooth ones in which new conversations could take place:

> This is how it should be done: Lodge yourself on a stratum; experiment with the opportunities it offers, find an advantageous place on it, find potential movements of deterritorialization, possible lines of flight, experience them, produce flow

conjunctions here and there, try out continuums of intensities segment by segment, have a small plot of new land at all times.

These new "lines of flight" (ibid.) created "wanderings" into some key policy and practice spaces. *Rationing Education,* or rather one of its authors, had made it into the Committee for Racial Equality, the Select Committee for MPs and Education Select Committee and, via Michael Apple, had hit an American audience and become A level sociology coursework in the United Kingdom. Stephen Ball spoke with a certain pride of how his text had never been selected in the Systematic Reviews undertaken and of how, travelling within the Economic and Social Research Council programme in which it had been located, it had "perplexed" some of the other researchers and how he had enjoyed the transgressive role he had played within this. He had, however, been invited to write a paper for a review of 14–19 provision, sponsored by the Nuffield Foundation, and the merit of his wanderings had been recognised.

WHAT'S THE PROBLEM AND WHERE?

For some of the researchers/scholars, the problem to which inclusive education had become the solution was clearly at the level of the education system and the way it created failure for children and young people. Dave Gillborn/Deborah Youdell's, Ellen Brantlinger's and Sally Tomlinson's critiques of the subjectification process, depicted persuasively how children get manoeuvred out of the system through some systematic and sophisticated processes, for example, through the A-C economy (David Gillborn & Deborah Youdell), "tracking" (Ellen Brantlinger) and "benevolent humanitarianism" (Sally Tomlinson). Lani Florian identified a problem with the permissions granted to schools to exclude individuals, especially those with emotional or behavioural difficulties, who would have detrimental effect on the mainstream population. Stephen Ball's diagnosis focussed on the "presumptions" about young people and choice, and the way in which these closed off rather than opened up opportunities for participation.

Mike Oliver and Len Barton saw the problem as lying with the professionals who were "precious" enough to think they could deny children access to mainstream education or who engaged in hypocrisy:

> What I have been increasingly angry about and I was angry about it in sociology of education and I am angry about it now in the fields I work in, it is people who claim to have an expertise in an area. Their conduct with other people is anything but exemplary. They are quite offensive. They have unacceptable mannerisms, statements, objectionable forms of behavior and so forth. I find that unacceptable and it cannot be tolerated. (Len Barton)

Mel Ainscow and Alan Dyson also identified people as contributing to exclusion, but saw their contexts—schools—as creating these problems by allowing them to engage in exclusionary practices and hold low expectations. Theirs was an optimistic reading in which they saw the potential for changing contexts and the people within them.

For Ken Kavale, Kim Cornish, and Karen Harris, inclusive education was itself the problem, wreaking havoc on children with special needs and their mainstream peers. They used strong language to depict the damage inflicted upon them through such wrong-headedness, causing "sacrifice" (Ken Kavale), creating a "set-up for failure" (Kim Cornish) and kids getting "dumped without the structure and support they needed" who began to "fall apart" and "suffered" (Karen Harris). Suzanne Carrington also saw inclusive education as part of the problem, but for her this was because it narrowed thinking and was restricted, for many, to disability.

CONTROVERSIES AND COUNTERPOINTS

Our reading of the researchers' and scholars' characterisations of their work produced a number of tensions, contradictions, controversies and counterpoints at different moments of the research process. The *conceptualisation* of the research was a source of tension for some of the researchers and scholars, arising from the strategic alignments they sought to forge. For Mel Ainscow and Lani Florian and her team, in order to address the kinds of problems they were interested in, it was necessary to buy into a genre of school effectiveness that they recognised as troubling. Alan Dyson and his research team entered into the Economic and Social Research Council's (the major government funding agency for social research in the United Kingdom) Teaching and Learning Research Programme, which had some expectations he felt unable to deliver on, but still saw it as enabling him to pursue a research agenda that interested him. Kim Cornish also acknowledged the tensions that the Quebec Government's recent pronouncements on inclusive education imply for her research programme.

Stephen Ball and his team were committed to a *methodology* that privileged the voices of young people, but when they took the research into new territories, for example, by talking less about education and more about their life experiences, the team had to decide whether to go with that or to try to pull the research back to the original focus. This became a very productive discussion within their text about the difference between inscribing or representing meaning through the voices of a research cohort.

The *analysis* of the data presented tensions, contradictions, and counterpoints for some of the researchers and the scholars. In Stephen Ball's case, these were highly productive and the "arguments" within the team produced new insights and new "lines of flight." Similarly Dave Gillborn and Deborah Youdell spoke of their joint analysis amounting to something new that was more than the sum of their parts. In both cases, however, the new knowledge they had produced had an amorphous quality and did not fit neatly into any area of educational research.

For all the researchers and scholars *ideology* was deeply troubling and many spoke of their unease with how they were positioned in the debate between special educators and inclusionists. Whilst several offered the plaintive claim that all research on inclusive education was ideological, they engaged in some interesting and often emotive othering, using the language of enmity or of being the victim to defend their own position and vilify those on the other side. Kim Cornish's repositioning of herself on the side of the other, as a special educationist working on inclusive education was a deliberate attempt to ensure her own survival, but she was clearly uneasy about operating in what she perceived as a sometimes hostile and misdirected camp.

Finally, the question directed to all researchers and scholars about the impact of their work produced some serious doubts that they had made any contribution at all. Several researchers and scholars turned the question back on us, inviting us to estimate their work's impact, but we refused this graciously. Mike Oliver was much more certain than others about his failure to make an impact on the social model of disability and on emancipatory research, and recorded his bitter disappointment at this. This was indeed surprising, if not shocking, for us.

As for us, the researchers of the researchers, we have encountered the process so far as gormless stumblings and attempts to avoid a series of pitfalls. As we have done this we have recognised, at this early stage in the analysis, some tensions, contradictions, controversies, and counterpoints. The most troubling of these is our construction of a typology to get the research going and our concern that whilst the intent was that this should be unravelled by the research process, any presentation of this fixes the people and their work in particular ways. Readers of the typology may enhance the fixative gel, but our hope is that they will also shake it up by their own reading and positioning of the researchers' and scholars' work.

A second concern is how our analysis is read. We have already been rattled by a suggestion that we are engaging in performance theory when neither of us knew what this entailed. Our own value positions and the colouring this may give to the analysis continue to trouble us and at least one of the subjects of the research has remarked wryly on our refusal, so far, to position ourselves and reveal our own value positions. We promise to do this once we can work these out. An issue that is perhaps a feature of our long-distance working relationship, between Stirling in Scotland and Montreal, Canada, but one we think we genuinely have to learn about is how one collaborates within a flat hierarchy. And then there is the question of writing about all of this, which scares us senseless at times. So, we may have bitten off more than we can chew and our undertaking to open up our own research processes to scrutiny may come back to haunt us. But we do believe in the importance of surfacing the deep uncertainties that are inherent in research on inclusive education and so will face our own ghosts with a firm resolve.

POSITIONS AND POWER POINTS

We approached the interviews, and the individuals concerned, with some trepidation, fuelled by a concern to allow them to do justice to themselves and a suspicion of ourselves as researchers. That suspicion concerned our own positions and the values we brought to the encounters with the research subjects. The discipline we sought to maintain was to focus on the work rather than the individual, but at times we found ourselves wandering into the lives of people we had respected, and perhaps even revered, over many years. Exercising surveillance over our capacity to be judgmental about the work of some of the subjects, we sometimes emerged from interviews impressed the work's ethical integrity, methodological coherence, and positive intent.

In analysing the interviews we also tried to focus on the work and its discursive performances rather than on the researchers and scholars and hope that we have produced a fair representation. Ours is, of course, a very particular representation, informed by a post-structuralist perspective, which refuses, or attempts to refuse, signifides and essences. We have tried to avoid offering judgements on the relative effectiveness of the different works, but have read the kind of nomadic wandering qualities of the work of Dave Gillborn and Deborah Youdell and Stephen Ball (and his colleagues) as positive, found in the provocations of Len Barton and Ellen Brantlinger elements that are ethical and seen considerable depth in the foundational work of Mike Oliver and Sally Tomlinson. Some of the alignments we have identified have troubled us, though we do not yet understand why. Knowing and describing fields set up particular trajectories for theorising, analysing, and explaining research. Our depictions fix both the intent and the performance of the work in ways that may be foreign, uncomfortable, or even irritating for the individuals concerned. Our own intent, we insist, has not been to irritate, but we genuinely hope that we are providing a kind of intellectual tin opener that prises the lid off the research processes and that will encourage others to follow suit.

REFERENCES

Ainscow, M. (1991) *Effective schools for all.* London: David Fulton.
Allan, J. (2008) *Just inclusion: Putting the philosophers of difference to work.* Dordrecht: Springer.
Bains, P. (2002) Subjectless subjectivities. In B. Massumi (ed.) *A shock to thought: expression after Deleuze and Guattari.* London and New York: Routledge.
Ball, S., Maguire, M., and Macrae, S. (2000) *Choice, pathways and transitions Post-16: New youth, new economies in the global city.* London and New York: Routledge Falmer.
Barnes, C. (1990) *Cabbage syndrome: The social construction of dependency.* London: Falmer Press.
Barton, L. (ed.). (1988) *The politics of special educational needs.* London: Falmer.
Barton, L. (2005) Special educational needs: A new look. Unpublished paper.
Barton, L., Oliver, M., and Barnes, C. (eds.). (2002) *Disability studies today.* Cambridge: Polity Press.
Biklen, D. (1985) *Achieving the complete school: Strategies for effective mainstreaming.* New York: Teachers College Press.
Booth, T. and Ainscow, M. (2002) *The index for inclusion: Developing learning and participation in schools* (2nd ed). Bristol: Centre for Studies in Inclusive Education.
Brantlinger, E. (1997) Using ideology: Cases of nonrecognition of the politics of research and practice in special education. *Review of Educational Research,* 67 (4), 425–459.
Brantlinger, E. (2003) *Dividing classes: How the middle class negotiates and justifies school advantage.* New York: Routledge.
Brantlinger, E. (2004) The big glossies: How textbooks structure (special) education. In D. Biklen (ed.) *Common solutions: Inclusion and diversity at the center.* University of Syracuse.
Carrington, S. and Robinson, S. (2004). A case study of inclusive school development: A journey of learning. *The International Journal of Inclusive Education,* 8 (2), 141–153.
Centre for Studies in Education (CSIE). (2005) News digest, June. Retrieved on 3/3/06 from http://inclusion.uwe.ac.uk/csie/june05.htm.
Cornish, K., Sudhalter, V., and Turk, J. (2004) Attention and language in Fragile X, mental retardation and developmental disabilities. *Research Reviews,* 10, 11–16.
Deleuze, G. and Guattari, F. (1987) *A thousand plateaus: Capitalism and schizophrenia.* London: Athlone Press.
Derrida, J. (1992) *The other heading: Reflections on today's Europe,* trans P. Brault and M. Naas. Bloomington and Indianapolis: Indiana University Press.
Dyson, A., Gallannaugh, F., and Millward, A. (2003) Making space in the standards agenda: Developing inclusive practices in schools. *European Educational Research Journal,* 2, 228–244.
Florian, L., Rouse, M., Black-Hawkins, K., and Jull, S. (2004) What can national data sets tell us about inclusion and pupil achievement? *British Journal of Special Education,* 31 (3), 115–121.
Ford, J., Mongon, D., and Whelan, J. (1982) *Special education and social control. Invisible disasters.* London: Routledge and Kegan Paul.
Foucault, M. (1977) A preface to transgression. In D. Bouchard (ed.) *Language, countermemory, practice: Selected essays and interviews by Michel Foucault.* Oxford: Basil Blackwell.
Foucault, M. (1988) *The care of the self: The history of sexuality, 3.* trans R. Hurley. Harmondsworth: Penguin.
Fullan, M. (1991) *The new meaning of educational change.* London: Cassell.
Gallagher, D. (2006) If not absolute objectivity, then what? A reply to Kauffman and Sasso. *Exceptionality,* 14 (2), 91–107.
Giddens, A. (1998) *The Third Way. The renewal of social democracy.* Cambridge: Polity.

Gillborn, D. and Youdell, D. (2000) *Rationing education: Policy, practice, reform and equity.* Buckingham/Philadelphia: Open University Press.

Harris, K. and Graham, S. (1996) *Making the writing process work: Strategies for competition and self-regulation.* Cambridge, MA: Brookline Books.

Kauffman, J. M. and Hallahan, D. P. (1995) *The illusion of full inclusion: A comprehensive critique of a current special education bandwagon.* Austin: Pro-Ed.

Kauffman, J. M. and Sasso, G. M. (2006) Toward ending cultural and cognitive relativism in special education. *Exceptionality,* 14 (2), 65–90.

Kavale, K. and Mostert, M. (2004) *The positive side of special education: Minimizing its fads, fancies and follies.* Lanham, Md: Scarecrow Education.

Minow, M. (1990) *Making all the difference. Inclusion, exclusion and American law.* New York: Cornell University Press.

Morris, J. (1991) *Pride against prejudice.* London: Women's Press.

Oliver, M. (1985) The Integration—Segregation debate: Some sociological considerations. *British Journal of Sociology of Education,* 6 (1), 75–92.

Oliver, M. (1996) *Understanding disability: From theory to practice.* Basingstoke: Macmillan.

Pickering Francis, L. and Silvers, A. (2000) *Americans with disabilities: Exploring implications of the law for individuals and institutions.* New York: Routledge.

Pijl, S. J., Meijer, C., and Hegarty, S. (1997) *Inclusive education: A global agenda.* London: Routledge.

Senge, P. (1989) *The fifth discipline: The art and practice of the learning organisation.* London: Century.

Slee, R. (2006) Limits to and possibilities for educational reform. *International Journal of Inclusive Education,* 10 (2/3), 109–120.

Tomlinson, S. (1982) *A sociology of special education.* London: Routledge and Kegan Paul.

Warnock, M. (2005) *Special educational needs: A new look. Impact No 11.* London: Philosophy Society of Great Britain.

Wenger, E. (1998) *Communities of practice: Learning, meaning & identity.* New York: Cambridge University Press.

Section II
Policy

The 2003 Report of the United Nations High Commissioner for Human Rights indicates that a "a dramatic shift in perspective in relation to disability" has "taken place in all economic and social systems ... the human rights dimension had been affirmed and emphasized over the past two decades" (2). Policy has served as an instrument of the dramatic shifts the high commissioner references and whether it is situated (as is the case in this section) within the history of an ancient civilization, a developing nation, a market economy, or national social values, the policy milieu offers a glimpse into the inner working of the politics of disability.

Chapters in this section uncover some of the ways policy's ability to shape social life can be harnessed toward the ends of the disabled people's movement but they also reveal some of the consequences of policy initiatives or in contrast, policy inertia. Culture, history, and the challenge of limited resources prove to be important factors in the first chapters in this section. Robert Chimedza, Auxilia Badza, and David Chakuchichi's (chapter 10) study of quality of life in Zimbabwe demonstrates the deep connection between governmental policy and the ability of disabled people to be economically secure, make their own decisions, and live as full members of the community. They paint a portrait of a country with grassroots disability activism contrasted against poverty and limited resources that leave many "people with disabilities begging at street corners and in public buses" China compares closely to India in its development of disability rights. Both countries have evolved from ancient cultures, affirmed human rights by signing onto the UN Convention (United Nations, 2007), and mandated universal education for children. Neither country has achieved universal education. In light of China's emerging place in the world economy, Qing Shen, Helen McCabe, and Zhaoyang Chi (chapter 11) provide a look into the conditions of the world's largest population of disabled people. Their historical contextualization illustrates the challenges of moving beyond the affirmation of disability rights in the face of centuries-old cultural traditions. Jagdish Chander's (chapter 12) historical account of the blind advocacy movement in India illustrates the importance of activism, particularly when governmental and policy attention is on disability rights but resources and motivation might be minimal. Marisol Moreno Angarita and Susan Gabel (chapter 13) provide another example of the need for activism. In their mapping of legislative initiatives in Columbia, it becomes clear that even with legislative attention to inclusive education (in Columbia this can mean giving disabled children a segregated public education), the situation in schools is disappointing at best—in spite of governmental claims to the contrary.

The above chapters beg the question of whether policy created and defined becomes policy implemented. Armstrong and Barton (2007) indicate that this is not necessarily going to be the case because "the barriers to inclusion are stubborn and multi-varied and it is important to recognise the distinction between laudable rhetoric and actual practice" (15). Liz Gordon and Missy Morton's (chapter 14) critique of the devolution of educational policy distilled in the market ideology of neoliberal policies in New Zealand vividly demonstrates this caveat. They show that policy intended to enhance democratic education can backfire for disabled students when it is engulfed by community-run schools and competing agendas.

In addition to the increasing recognition of disability rights on the international scene, "the areas of social life which are subject to policy," writes Yeatman (1998), "have grown extraordinarily" (18). "In all societies," she continues, "social actors think about what they are doing and why" but "in many societies, the grounds of this reflection refers to a body of customary law and practice which requires [interpretation] by those who are seen as closest to its divine source" (18–19). In other words, some social actors are considered more capable of interpreting policy than are others. Dóra Bjarnason (chapter 15) tackles policy from within this tension involving social actors. She reports about parents who have given birth to disabled children and medical professionals whose expertise tends to go unquestioned when families interface with them. Although her chapter is an explicit account of social policy in Iceland, the underlying lessons revealed by her research can be generalized to other policy contexts. Jitka Sincecka (chapter 16) explores another tension between "those who are seen as closest to its divine source"—i.e., oralist educators of the d/Deaf—and d/Deaf people and their families and does so while situating the tension within Czech history and illustrating what happens when policy is received and changed at the grassroots level.

The last two chapters in this section provide potential models for use in activism in the policy arena. We place them last because they offer ideas for action in response to the issues emerging from the previous chapters, including the issues frequent mismatch between governmental rhetoric and action, the stigmatizing cultural notions influencing policy and policy decisions, and the unanticipated consequences of educational policy reform. Noting that "globalization assigns a special role to education" (Stromquist, 2002, 16), Susan Peters, Kimberly Wolbers, and Lisa Dimling (chapter 17) map out a "radical minority perspective" that targets disabled peoples' exclusion from school and argues for a model of global education using a disability rights lens. Susan Gabel (chapter 18) complements Peters et al., with a proposal of a model for policy activism that she defines as "strategic action to influence policy for the purpose of achieving equity and other sociopolitical goals."

Other authors in this volume address themes or topics related to policy including: Ngcobo and Muthukrishna (chapter 2), Ferri (chapter 3), Badza, Chakuchichi, and Chimedza (chapter 4), Gabel and Chander (chapter 5), Smith (chapter 24), van Drenth (chapter 25), Powell, Felkendorff, and Hollenweger (chapter 29), and Marshall (chapter 30).

REFERENCES

Armstrong, F., and Barton, L. (2007). Introduction. In L. Barton and F. Armstrong (Eds.), *Policy, experience and change: Cross cultural reflections on inclusive education*, 5–18. Dordrecht: Springer.

Barton, L., and Armstrong, F. (Eds.) (2007). *Policy, experience and change: Cross cultural reflections on inclusive education*. Dordrecht: Springer.

Stromquist, N. (2002). *Education in a globalized world*. New York: Rowman & Littlefield Publishers, Inc.

United Nations (2003). Report of the United Nations High Commissioner for Human Rights (on progress in the implementation of the recommendations contained in the study on the human rights of persons with disabilities). New York: United Nations. Retrieved on July 4, 2007 from http://www.unhchr.ch/huridocda/huridoca.nsf/(Symbol)/E.CN.4.2003.88.En?Opendocument.

United Nations (2007). Highlights. Office of the United Nations High Commissioner for Human Rights. Retrieved on July 4, 2007 from http://www.ohchr.org/english/issues/disability/index.htm.

Yeatman, A. (Ed.) (1998). *Activism and the policy process*. St. Leonards: Allen & Unwin.

CHAPTER TEN

An Analysis OF THE Impact OF Advocacy AND Disability Rights ON THE Quality OF Life OF People WITH Disabilities IN Zimbabwe

ROBERT CHIMEDZA, AUXILIA BADZA,
AND DAVID CHAKUCHICHI

INTRODUCTION

One of the true measures of the impact of advocacy and disability rights movement on people with disabilities is the quality of life of the individuals with disability. It is not uncommon in Zimbabwe to come across people with disabilities begging at street corners and in public buses. This calls into question and interrogates the quality of life of these people against a background of successful associations of the disabled and disability advocacy groups in the country (for more details, see Peters & Chimedza, 2000). The quality of life concept, started as a political slogan in the 1950s, was eventually adopted in medicine. As a conceptual model it is consistent with the World Health Organization (WHO) definition of health as embracing an individual's physical, psychological, and spiritual functioning; his or her connections with his or her environments and opportunities for enhancing and maintaining skills (Awofeso, 2005). Thus the quality of life concept is really a measure of the well-being and health of an individual in relation to the individual's environment. The construct defines certain individual physical, psychological, and spiritual functioning contextual to appropriateness of living environments and opportunities for well-being. Defined thus, quality of life is simply, "[t]he degree to which a person enjoys the important possibilities of his or her life" (Renwick, Brown, & Nagler, 2002).

CONCEPTUAL FRAMEWORK

The definition of quality of life as the degree to which one enjoys his or her life suggests that the possibilities for success in life differ from person to person depending on their socioeconomic circumstances and biological endowments. First, there are basic considerations such as provision for food, shelter, health, safety, and belongingness that determine one's quality of life. For many people with disabilities in Zimbabwe, meeting these basic needs remains a daily challenge. The second consideration focuses on the range of opportunities available to match the individual's potential. In other words, once basic needs are met, the quality of life indicator examines whether people with disabilities have opportunities to achieve economic security through employment, obtain an adequate education, and contribute to the community. Finally, though equally important is the availability of choice and control in an individual's environment. This indicator analyzes, for example, whether people with disabilities can choose where and with whom they live and whether to have a family; it also tells us whether they have choice in employment or are relegated to menial labor, and whether they have varied leisure experiences to choose from. Felce (in Mpofu, 2003) defines the quality of life construct as comprising the person's objective circumstances and the subjective appraisal of those circumstances in the light of the individual's sociocultural values. Objective circumstances include verifiable situations such as health, economic status, happiness, freedom, and other related conditions. On the other hand, the subjective appraisal focuses on the individual's self-evaluation of his or her situation in life. This self-assessment determines the person's level of happiness. Biersdoff (2001) defines quality of life as those aspects of life that make living worthwhile for the individual. While considering the quality of life for people with disabilities, Biersdorff suggests meaningful activities, opportunities for choice and decision making, and caring relationships in social interaction should be taken into account. Though there is no consensus on the constitutive elements of the quality of life construct, Cummins and Cahill (in Bramston, Bruggerman, & Pretty, 2002) point out that community involvement and integration have often been recorded as elements of the construct. For people with disabilities, community acceptance and connectedness are significant factors indicative of positive life experiences. According to Bramston et al., the quality of life construct includes life satisfaction, well-being, social belonging, empowerment, and control of the decision-making process.

QUALITY OF LIFE IN PEOPLE WITH DISABILITIES IN ZIMBABWE

In disability issues, the quality of life construct generally comprises both the personal and environmental conditions. Baird et al. and Schuessler and Fisher (in Orange, 2002) offer a complex but comprehensive exposition of quality of life concept that has three factors. These are (1) personal satisfaction with life in general (well-being and happiness); (2) personal satisfaction with socioeconomic status (work, finances, health, and relationships); and (3) sociodemographic indicators of environmental opportunities, stressors, and resources. Both intra-individual capacities and environmental factors are important to the quality of life concept.

Advocacy strongly influences the quality of life of people with disability and also the quality of life concept in general. In other words, where there is strong advocacy, there are more chances for people with disabilities to have a better quality of life than where advocacy has little or no impact. Some of the quality of life factors of the level and impact of advocacy include, personal satisfaction, level of independent living, and productivity status (Mpofu, 2003). In Zimbabwe, for people with disability, inclusion, or the full integration of people with disabilities into every aspect of society, is a means for achieving quality of life. Inclusion is designed to foster belongingness, obtain equal opportunities and accommodation in everyday-life activities through positive support. Unfortunately, ill-planned inclusion strategies often backfire, as the people with disabilities often experience exclusion where they are supposed to feel included. For instance, if a wheelchair-user cannot independently get into an office because of steps on a doorway and thus ends up being assisted by able-bodied persons, we should see the very structural environment as excluding the wheelchair-user. It is obvious that in this situation the person with disabilities does not feel personal satisfaction as he or she is made to feel dependent. Yet with the removal of barriers, the individual could easily be independent. Inclusion should be well planned with adequate individualized support to give personal satisfaction to the people with disability. First, in Zimbabwe at the moment, there are no efforts to include features in the design of public and private buildings that facilitate access for people with disabilities. Architects designing new buildings, city engineers and planners planning new roads and buses for public transport, all fail to take into consideration the needs of wheelchair-users and blind people. No adaptations are made to ensure that citizens with disabilities also use these facilities independently. There is no legislation that forces the service providers to include adaptations. What is worrying is that such a situation exists in Zimbabwe despite the presence of a strong advocacy culture through associations of people with disabilities such as the National Council of Disabled Persons Zimbabwe, Zimbabwe National Association of the Deaf, and League of the Blind. Their pleas could be falling on deaf ears for all we know, but it is hoped that with the current inclusion into the legislature of people with disabilities such as Senator Joshua Malinga, these issues will be addressed. It is critical for the advocacy groups to persist in sensitizing not only the nondisabled lawmakers but also to remind those lawmakers with disabilities that disability is one of the constituencies that they represent in parliament or senate.

Second, in Zimbabwe the technocrats and professionals whose work is not directly linked to disability, ignore issues concerning people with disabilities in their planning and designing process mainly out of ignorance. Their training and orientation has left out this important consideration from their curriculum—public sector service provisions. Advocacy groups therefore should include in their agenda the sensitization of training institutions and persuade them to address disability issues in their training programs. This will certainly help professionals to design and plan their work taking into account the needs of people with disabilities.

Independent living is one of the indicators of the quality of life as proposed by DeJong (Mpofu, 2003). It denotes control over one's life and the reduction of reliance on others for basic life arrangements. In a study by DeJong (1981), participants rated living with family as the least restrictive and institutional accommodation as most restrictive. In other studies (Nosek & Fuhrer cited in Mpofu 2003: 78), independent living is considered an indicator of quality of life across disability categories. However a critical look at DeJong's study indicates that independent living is perceived as the ability to live in a family environment, which inevitably becomes interdependent living. Advocacy should therefore focus on interdependence rather than independent living as a measure of the quality of life concept. In Zimbabwe interdependent living is very common especially with the extended family concept in practice. According to this concept, extended members of the family look after each other and help each other in performing village and family chores. Unfortunately people with disabilities do not benefit from this practice, because of the Zimbabwean's negative attitude to disability that comes from the culture and belief system. Family members may live with persons with disability but still treat them as unable to do anything and as minors, and do not accord them their rightful status in the family structure. Also, some people with disabilities still live in institutions and this is contrary to notions of both independent and interdependent living. One way to change attitudes and beliefs is through the education and conscientization of the nondisabled persons so that they are able to live together with people with disabilities in complementary roles as members of the same family. Advocacy groups of people with disabilities in Zimbabwe are well positioned to play this educator's role, given their historical background. Early on in the movement, they had used a similar approach to form national associations of people with disabilities at grassroots level.

Productivity status is yet another vital measure of the quality of life construct. Disability groups and support groups have made numerous advocacy representations for employment opportunities for people with disabilities. In other countries, such as the United States, legislation such as the American Disabilities Act is the result of the work of pressure groups focused on giving people with disability the status of a productive person. Provision of decent accommodation, education, and training enables people with disabilities to seek employment and become productive members of society. In Zimbabwe not many people with disabilities are gainfully employed; most of them are unemployed with little or no social security resources. Therefore they end up being destitute and as beggars, a situation that is of concern to disability advocacy groups in the country. The situation becomes worse when the country is faced with political and economic hardships, as Zimbabwe is at the moment; people with disabilities and other vulnerable groups are hit the hardest.

QUALITY OF LIFE FROM CHARITY TO EMANCIPATION

The quality of life for people with disabilities is closely related to their level of development as a group and the extent to which they influence that development agenda. Coleridge (1993) observed that attitude to development across the world recognizes that charity alone is inadequate and that the only meaningful development is that which involves people in the process of planning and implementing solutions to their problems. Charity is about people remaining victims and being controlled by others, while development (emancipation) is about people understanding the causes of their underdevelopment and working to change their situation with the understanding gained. Yet, for a long time, the service delivery model for people with disabilities in Zimbabwe and other developing countries has been based on the medical and charity models of cure and care or care and cure. As Malinga in Coleridge argues, such an approach has not benefited people with disabilities.

There are a number of social, cultural, normative, and physical obstacles that restrict opportunities for people with disabilities in Africa. Disability issues are almost always in the hands of professionals who are not disabled. This becomes a problem if in trying to resolve issues they ignore the very people who are directly affected by those issues. Emancipation is about challenging, correcting, and breaking barriers and advocacy has a key role to play in this process. The right approach is to empower people with disabilities to be their own liberators and to focus on and correct shortcomings of the environment and mainstream society that do not accommodate people's differences so that in this process their quality of life gets improved.

COLONIAL ERA INFLUENCE

It is important to highlight two key interventions in and philosophies on disability in the colonial era of Zimbabwe in the early 1950s that in a way influenced the quality of life concept among the disabled in the country. These are the contributions of Jairos Jiri, and the Cyrene Mission as portrayed in the film *Pitaniko, the Film of Cyrene* (Devlieger, 1998). Jairos Jiri's concern for disabled people was purely philanthropic but anchored in the philosophy of self-help. His approach and vision were in a way influenced by the self-help for Africans movement of that time, which was mostly characterized by African-controlled initiatives in an environment in which white supremacy reigned. Cyrene Mission's approach, on the other hand, was to reject charity and develop Christian faith and to build an institution to provide opportunities for the disabled rather than rely on self-help as in the Jairos Jiri philosophy. At Cyrene Mission, people with disabilities were instructed in Christianity and trained for professions such as carpentry and art painting so that eventually they became independent. Both approaches finally resulted in establishment of institutions for the disabled and it is from these institutions that the disability movements in Zimbabwe evolved. Today there are several self-help institutions for the disabled in Zimbabwe such as the Working Hands Deaf Cooperative at Juru Growth Point. They are run as business entities and are very successful. They make door frames and window frames, reconstruct damaged bodies of vehicles, make dresses and so on. They have been in operation now for over ten years and many deaf people are earning a living through this self-help initiative.

DISABILITY MOVEMENTS IN ZIMBABWE

Groups such as the National Council of Disabled Persons Zimbabwe, League of the Blind, Zimbabwe National Association of the Deaf, and the National Association of Societies for the Care of the Handicapped have been active in promoting disability issues and trying to create awareness by working with their members at grassroots level, and conscientizing them of their oppressed condition and of the need to liberate themselves from it. As Crewe and Zola (1983: 84) noted, "Significant social movement becomes possible when there is a revision; people looking at some misfortune see it no longer as warranting charitable consideration, but as an injustice which is intolerable in society." Peters and Chimedza discuss in detail the emergence and development of the disability movement in Zimbabwe, which started as political pressure groups and eventually developed into powerful national and regional disability rights associations that influenced policy development in Zimbabwe and in the region. Leaders from the Zimbabwe disability associations took top positions in regional and international associations. For instance, Joshua Malinga and Alexander Phiri from Zimbabwe initially led the Southern Africa Federation of the Disabled. Malinga later took up leadership positions in the Pan-Africa Federation of the Disabled and Disabled Persons International. Such an exposure strengthened the advocacy and disability rights movement in Zimbabwe. The various associations of the disabled continue to fight for their human rights and demand participation in national issues that affect them. Disability issues are therefore no longer viewed as civil rights but as human rights.

CONSCIENTIZATION

Through advocacy, lobbying, and the conscientization processes over the years, people with disabilities have also taken professional and leadership positions in society. In the past, the only time one saw or read about people with disabilities in the media was when they were shown as recipients of donations or when a pathetic story about them was aired. Stories about people with disability that appeared in Zimbabwe press were usually pejorative even as they praised the generous donors. While there is nothing wrong with receiving donations, it is important for the media to balance such reporting by also publishing the achievements and accomplishments of people with disabilities. An example of such an attempt was a television program produced by Rehabilitation International Education Commission Zimbabwean Chapter with financial assistance from the Ministry of Health and the World Health Organization. Once a week for thirteen weeks, this program profiled a day in the life of a person with disabilities who had succeeded in life. Prominent Zimbabweans with disabilities who are lawyers, teachers, counselors, international sports persons, politicians, business persons, and so on featured in this program. The fact that the television presenter Mr. Godfrey Majonga was also disabled enhanced the effectiveness of the program. Such coverage helps to build a positive image of people with disabilities. The public began to see the positive contributions people with disabilities are making to society as opposed to the stigma of people with disabilities always appearing on television as receivers of charity. The presentation made clear that these are examples of what people with disabilities can achieve with adequate support and training. The intention was not to show people with disability as superachievers but to demonstrate their potential. However, it is critical to ensure that such an awareness creation is not an isolated event, but becomes part of the regular media coverage in the country.

TRENDS IN LOCAL LEGISLATION

The right to education, health, shelter, and food are basic human rights and every government or nation must commit itself to the provision of these to all its citizens. The advocates for human rights for people with disabilities ask: To what extent are these basic rights assured by the Government of Zimbabwe to its people with disabilities? Provision for such basic human rights is made through legislation and various acts of parliament that assure the beneficiaries a decent quality of life. It is against this background that this section of the chapter will examine the legal framework of the country for guaranteeing quality of life for people with disabilities.

THE CONSTITUTION

Constitution is the supreme law of a country, and there can be no other law or provisions of the law that can be contrary to or inconsistent with the constitution. All other laws are interpreted according to the constitution. However, it is a matter of great concern that the constitution of Zimbabwe (amended sixteen times since independence in 1980) makes no specific mention of people with disabilities. The assumption is their rights are implicit in references to human rights because basically they are human beings (NASCOH, 2000). For instance, the constitution of Zimbabwe provides its citizens the right to life free from discrimination on the basis of race, tribe, place of origin, or ethnic background (section 23). It does not mention disability as basis for discrimination. This leaves people with disability vulnerable and unprotected by the constitution. At the moment, though according to the constitution, everyone is equal before the law and has equal rights and opportunities, the same constitution could be instrumental in permitting and perpetuating inequalities for people with disabilities in Zimbabwe (NASCOH, 2000). Discrimination on the basis of disability exists as does discrimination based on race or ethnic group. To remain silent on it while highlighting other types of discrimination is to condone it and this is certainly not acceptable. The constitution, on the contrary, should have provisions for affirmative action or positive discrimination in favor of vulnerable groups (including people with disabilities) to help increase opportunities for people with disabilities with a view to improving the quality of their life.

THE DISABLED PERSONS ACT OF 1992

Revised in 1996, the Disabled Persons Act of 1992 (Government of Zimbabwe, 1992) is an attempt at improving the quality of life of people with disabilities by making provisions for their welfare and rehabilitation. Unfortunately, the larger part of the act (7 sections out of 11) dwells on the appointment and setting up of the administrative board and its terms of reference rather than on issues pertaining to disability. It has been observed that the act provides minimal involvement of people with disabilities in policy and decision making on issues related to them. For instance, Section 4 gives more power to the government through the minister who appoints board members including the chairperson and the deputy than to representatives of disabled people. Although ten members of the board are nominated by organizations of and for people with disabilities, there is no guarantee that they would be people with disabilities. Even when people with disabilities have been appointed, the board is dysfunctional and it rarely meets. Such a situation denies empowerment to people with disability to fight for their rights. The major limiting factor of the act and its administrative structures is lack of state funding. Although the act mentions provision of equipment and assistive devices such as hearing aids and wheelchairs, there is no mention of the funding agency. The nonavailability of funds results in the government's inability to enforce the act. Funds are critical, more so in Zimbabwe and other developing countries than elsewhere, as assistive devices are imported and are very expensive in relation to the income of the average Zimbabwean. Most people with disability are unable to buy them since they depend on donations and social welfare funds even for their day-to-day living. Thus financial constraints can drastically restrict the capacity of the board to achieve its goals. In line with the United Nations Standards Rules, Rule 4 (United Nations, 1994), the Zimbabwean government has an obligation to avail itself of finances for procuring equipment and assistive devices for people with disabilities. However, the Rules contain no clauses that specify the role of the government in the provision of such resources and this is a cause for concern for people with disabilities, since on the ground this lacuna has a negative impact on the quality of their life.

The same could be said of other areas covered in the act. Lack of funding and a monitoring structure have rendered the Disability Act ineffective. For instance, though the act provided for a right to access to physical structures for people with disability, many buildings including new ones are still inaccessible to them. Government office buildings, for instance, are without user-friendly elevators and entrances. Persons with physical disabilities often have to get others to run their errands. Such a situation while promoting dependence denies them the right to privacy. Although the act gives the board the responsibility for suing the defaulting building-owners, to sue government institutions such as schools, educational or training institutions, hospitals, and government offices, one must obtain consent from the respective Ministry he or she intends to sue before serving the order (NASCOH, 2000). Section 8 further places the burden on the person with disability to sue for damages, should he or she be denied access to public premises, services, or amenities. Persons with disabilities are further hampered by limited financial resources for any litigation they may contemplate. So far no law suits have been filed by people with disabilities in Zimbabwe. Evidently, disability organizations, advocacy groups, and people with disabilities need to intensify their advocacy efforts for effective enforcement of the Disability Act.

THE EDUCATION ACT OF 1987

The Education Act of 1987 makes education a fundamental children's right in Zimbabwe (Government of Zimbabwe, 1987; Part II, Section 4[11]). Like the Zimbabwean constitution, this act makes no specific reference to children with disabilities. For instance, Part II Section 4(2) emphasizes nondiscriminatory admission of children into schools on "the basis of race, tribe, color, religion, creed, place of origin, political opinion or the social status of his parents." The act also emphasizes the right of every child to be enrolled in schools nearest their homes. Schools are not obliged to provide children with disabilities easy access to the premises. Unlike the Education Laws in developed countries such as United States Britain, and Norway, the schools in Zimbabwe are not mandated to provide special facilities and devices for children with disabilities.

CONCLUSION

Advocacy and disability rights movements can have a strong influence on issues and practices that impact the quality of lives of people with disabilities. Organizations of people with disabilities, human rights organizations, and professionals who advocate for a better quality of life for people with disabilities need to continue exerting pressure on both public and private sector service providers so that people with disabilities get an equal service as that provided to people without disabilities and that both private and public sectors make a conscious effort to provide extra services to bridge the gap between the two groups in access availability. In educational institutions, particularly in tertiary and higher educational institutions, there is need to provide greater and better access for people with disabilities, as at the moment, access is limited. It is only inclusive service provision that will put an end to discrimination against people with disabilities.

REFERENCES

Awofeso, N. (2005). Re-defining "Health." Retrieved 20 September 2006 from http://www.who.int/bulletin/bulletin_board/83/ustun11051/en/index.html.

Biersdorff, K.K.(2001). Quality of Life for People with Profound Disabilities. *Rehabilitation Review*, 12, 1, January, 621–629.

Bramston, P., Bruggerman, K., & Pretty, G. (2002). Community Perspectives and Subjective Quality of Life. *International Journal of Disability, Development and Education*, 13, 385–397.

Coleridge, P. (1993). *Disability, Liberation and Development*. Oxford: Oxfam Publications.

Crewe, N. & Zola, I. (1983). *Independent Living for Physically Disabled People*. San Francisco: Jossey-Bass Publishers.

Devlieger, P.J. (1998). Representations of Physical Disability in Colonial Zimbabwe: The Cyrene Mission and *Pitaniko, the Film of Cyrene*. *Disability & Society*, 13, 5, 709–724.

Government of Zimbabwe. (1987). *Education Act*. Harare: Government Printers.

Government of Zimbabwe. (1996). *Disabled Persons Act Chapter 17: 01 Revised 1996*. Harare: Government Printers.

Mpofu, E. (2003). *Counselling Students with Disabilities II*. Harare: Zimbabwe Open University.

National Association of Societies for the Care of the Handicapped (NASCOH). (2000). Audit Report on the Disabled Persons Act (1992).

Orange, L.M.(2002) *Skills Development for Multicultural Counseling: A Quality of Life Perspective*. California State University.

Peters, S. & Chimedza, R. (2000). Conscientization and the Cultural Politics of Education: A Radical Minority Perspective. *Comparative Education Review*, 44, 3, 245–271.

Renwick, R., Brown, I., & Nagler, M. (eds). (2002). Quality of Life in Health Promotion and Rehabilitation; *Conceptual Approaches, Issues, and Applications. quality. Oflife.utoronto.ca.* Retrieved 16 May 2006.

United Nations. (1994). *The Standard Rules on the Equalisation of Opportunities for Persons with Disabilities*. New York: United Nations.

CHAPTER ELEVEN

Disability Education in the People's Republic of China: Tradition, Reform, and Outlook

QING SHEN, HELEN MCCABE, AND ZHAOYANG CHI

INTRODUCTION

Since 1978, the People's Republic of China (PRC) has seen enormous change in its economy, society, and policy realms. The period known as "Reform and Opening," formally begun in December 1978, has brought about many improvements in the standard of living, educational opportunities, and new, flexible freedoms for the people (*lao bai xing*). These changes should, when looked at from a standpoint of social justice, include all people. Indeed, individuals with disabilities have seen some increased opportunities to participate in society since 1978. However, have the reforms paid enough attention to this population? Are individuals with disabilities truly included in Chinese society today? What connections can we draw between the historical/cultural background and the current social/political/economic situation of Chinese society, and how individuals with disabilities are or are not included? This chapter addresses these questions. To better grasp the impact of reforms on individuals, specific examples are provided about blindness, autism, and inclusion. This will be followed by discussions that consider both the development of new services and limitations in society that continue to place individuals with disabilities outside of the mainstream.

TRADITIONAL BACKGROUND: CARE AND EDUCATION FOR PEOPLE WITH DISABILITIES

Throughout Chinese history, traditional values and family structure have had a great impact on the way in which the society and families support people with disabilities. Confucianism advocates a society of great harmony. Theories in Confucianism promote, at the family level, the notion that harmony should be achieved by the unselfish love between couples, parents. and children. According to Confucianism, the parent-child relationship is the closest relationship of all, and it is the basic element of a harmonious society. To achieve harmony in a family, people are expected to do whatever they can for the other family members, including one's parents and one's children (Wang, 2006).[1] According to Zi (1987), Confucianism's stress on blood ties has "infiltrated all fields of life of the Chinese people and had far-reaching influences on the development of Chinese history" (pp. 444–445).

While family harmony may seem to be only positive, this emphasis in Confucianism has also been seen as a potentially problematic "graded love" (Dubs, 1951, p. 50), where individuals are more caring and loving toward those who have closer relations to them than to those outside the family. Dubs described this potential problematic by citing a later philosopher, Mo-zi, who felt that China was "being destroyed by the continual wars between the great noble clans, all of whom were closely related" (p. 51); thus, graded love was problematic "because their loves are graded so sharply, fixed upon their own persons or their own states, instead of upon all equally" (p. 51). Despite this famous argument of Mo-zi, holding family relationships above all others continued. A later Confucian thinker, Mencius argued that "equal love for all is unnatural" (p. 51), and called for a person's special duties to one's own parents. Dubs argued that this is a "justification of qualified selfishness" (p. 55) that led to nepotism, favoritism, corruption, and the fall of dynasties. This emphasis on the family has affected individuals with disabilities today.

Traditionally communities were called upon to take care of their individual members too. Going back to the ancient times, supporting people with disabilities was seen as the community's responsibility. According to *Li Ji* (the Record of Rites), a classic of Confucianism, Datong Shehui (an internationalized assimilation in which people lead a fairly comfortable life) should be the ultimate state of society. In such a utopian society, young children, the elderly, and people who are sick or disabled can all be supported by the community when they have no blood kin. When we try to determine how well this community support idea has prevailed, however, it is telling that the 1950 Marriage Law obligated *parents* to support their children and children to support their parents. It also stated that neighborhood committees (local community governing bodies) were responsible for the support of individuals with disabilities, as well as the aged and orphans, "if the family fails" (Vermeer, 1979, p. 866). Based on this law, it seems the community is seen only as a backup, when the family, who is closest to an individual with a disability, fails in its duty.

In fact, some traditional philosophies have led to a more negative depiction of disability. Another philosophy having deep roots in the Chinese culture is Taoism. Taoism promotes the belief that a person will gain power and strength if he or she behaves in harmony with the nature of the universe and will suffer later in life if he or she acts against the nature of the universe (Lam, 2000). According to the Tao Te Ching, the most important Taoist text, psychological disturbance is caused by a conflict between human will and the development of the laws of nature. If one is too greedy and aspires for what one does not deserve, one loses the balance of a peaceful mind (Ji, 2005). In other words, one has oneself to blame if one suffers from psychological disorders, because one did not "play right." On the other hand, Buddhism, the most popular religion among Chinese people, argues that a disability is caused by deeds from the past lives (of self, parents, or closely related people) or the past of the current lives that acted against the nature of the universe (Liu, 2001). Traditionally, the purpose of procreation is to pass on family names and extend family lines. Having a child with disability who may not end up marrying or having a child is seen as damaging this function greatly, and is regarded as a shame of the whole family. Therefore, for fear of "losing face," when one member of a family has any "problem," other members tend to seek help from family first, before turning to "strangers" including neighborhood committees, professionals, and government offices.

Clearly, there are various impacts of Chinese traditional culture on views of individuals with disabilities. On the one hand, family and society were both traditionally encouraged to support family members and others who had a disability. On the other hand, other traditional beliefs have led to a feeling that there is shame in having a child with a disability, and thus it is the sole responsibility of family, and *not* society. Given this context, the family continues to be the primary provider of support. However, society is much changed, especially since 1978 when China began the period of Opening and Reform, when the society began to allow privatization, and ceased to provide free medical/health services and lifelong job stability (leading to a rising new problem of unemployment). The interactions between families with individuals with disabilities and societies have changed accordingly.

CURRENT CONTEXT: ECONOMIC AND SOCIAL REFORMS

To understand and analyze the present situation of education and inclusion for individuals with disability in China, this section first presents a brief history of special education, leading up to the post-1978 period of Reform and Opening. We then examine in more detail the economic and social reforms of the past almost three decades that impact this population.

Until missionaries from Europe and the United States came in the nineteenth century, there had been no official special education in China (Epstein, 1988; Yang & Wang, 1994). The first special education school for blind children was founded in 1870, and in 1887 the first school for deaf children was also established, both by Western missionaries (Chen, 1996a). The first school for special education was established by a Chinese was founded in 1916. However, China suffered from consecutive adverse political and economic conditions over the several decades thereafter, which hampered the development of special education as a formal discipline in the country. The ten-year Cultural Revolution between 1966 and 1976 brought turmoil to the country, which not only completely stopped economic development but also brought the education system to a virtual halt. The turning point came when Deng Xiaoping initiated the period of Reform and Opening (*gaige kaifang*) in 1978, which included reforms that led to tremendous progress in various aspects of the economic, social, and cultural life in China.

The reforms that were set in motion in 1978 with the initiation of Deng Xiaoping's Reform and Opening meant that, unlike the period between 1949 and the mid-1970s, the state was no longer responsible for all aspects of a person's life, such as education, employment, medical care, and social welfare. A major feature of the reforms was a change from a state-planned economy to increased emphasis on relying on market forces. Along with economic reforms have come social changes, including changes in the system of lifetime guaranteed employment as provision of social welfare was no longer provided solely by one's work unit (*danwei*) (Howell & Pearce, 2001).[2]

Individuals with disabilities have been impacted by these reforms in the economy and society in a variety of ways. The focus on market forces, in the form of privatization, competition, and depending on oneself (*zifu yingkui*) means that organizations ranging from schools to businesses have a growing concern with profit and income generation. Schools seek ways to charge fees for various services or activities, despite the fact that the Compulsory Education Law of 1986 (National People's Congress, 1986) states that tuition itself is "free" in compulsory education (Grades 1–9). Organizations providing medical or educational services to individuals with disabilities have begun charging ever-increasing fees for services (McCabe, 2004). Moreover, these market forces also limit employment opportunities for individuals with disabilities who are often seen as less efficient workers and thus become undesirable workers.

However, there have also been benefits for individuals with disabilities since the reform period began. Before 1978, under Mao Zedong, a philosophy of "radical egalitarianism" (Kraus, 1976) dominated Chinese society. The Chinese Communist Party's policy goal was "first narrowing, and then eliminating the 'three great differences,' which separate the citizens of China: the distinctions between workers and peasants, between city and country, and between mental and manual labor" (Kraus, 1976, p. 1081). Under Mao Zedong, efforts were made to "build more egalitarian social relationships, to minimize the differences in social status and rewards among the people" (Townsend, 1977, p. 1009). This led to an idea that, aside from obvious sensory impairments, disabilities were not acknowledged; any individual differences were said to be caused by "individual attitudes" (Cleverly, 1991, p. 196).

In the atmosphere of reform since 1978, however, this egalitarianism has been replaced by an atmosphere of allowing and encouraging differences, including economic differences, social differences, and recognition of different individual abilities. The rights of persons with disabilities have been promoted at least in part due to the prestige of the disability rights leader, Deng Pufang (who is the son of the late leader, Deng Xiaoping), who has been disabled since falling from a window during a struggle with Red Guards during the Cultural Revolution. In 1988, Deng Pufang and others established the China Disabled Persons' Federation (CDPF), which is the first government organization that focuses on advocacy for the rights of, and services for, persons with disabilities (Kohrman, 2003). Since the late 1970s, special education schools and classes have been set up in many major cities, in particular for children with visual, hearing, and mild cognitive disabilities. These are also the only three disabilities mentioned in the first law that discussed special education, the Compulsory Education Law. Education for children with moderate or severe cognitive disability, such as children with autism, is very limited, and this population is often excluded from any schooling opportunities (Deng, Poon-McBrayer, Farnsworth, & McCabe, 2001). The actual extent of integrating children with disabilities into the education system is considered in the rest of this chapter. Nevertheless, a first step was taken; the recognition and acceptance of individual differences helped to bring about a system of special education in which students of different abilities are served in different ways. China currently has a range of educational service delivery options, including special schools, special classes, and *suiban jiudu*, a model of inclusion discussed in the pages that follow. However, how inclusive are educational opportunities?

DISABILITY IN CHINA TODAY

The definition of disability recognized in China was adopted from the Disabled Persons' Rights Declaration of the United Nations (UN) ASSEMBLY

(Wilde, 2001) and is addressed in the comprehensive legislation and policy protecting and promoting the rights of disabled people in China—the Law of the People's Republic of China on the Protection of Disabled Persons (National People's Congress, 1990). The law provides that

> A disabled person refers to one who suffers from abnormalities or loss of a certain organ or function, psychologically or physiologically, or in anatomical structure and has lost wholly or in part the ability to perform an activity in the way considered normal. (Article 2)

According to the Chinese Disability Classification Standard (*Zhongguo canji fenlei biaozhun*, n.d.), persons with disabilities are classified according to five types (1) visual disabilities; (2) hearing and speech disabilities; (3) mental retardation; (4) physical disabilities, and (5) psychological disorders. Those with two or more disabilities are classified under multiple disabilities and other disabilities (*Quanguo gelei canjiren shuju*, n.d.). The 1990 Law includes these five categories as well as multiple disabilities and other disabilities (Article 2).

China is a developing country with the largest population in the world. It also has the largest number of persons with disabilities in the world (Qiu, 1998). The CDPF conducted the first national sample survey on China's disabled population in 1987.[3] The results of the 1987 sample survey revealed that there were 51.64 million persons with disabilities in China (current estimates have exceeded 60 million), among which there were more than 8 million children with disabilities age fourteen and under, which was 2.66% of children of the same age group in China (Chinese Children, n.d.).

Three policies call for nine-years of compulsory education, including the Compulsory Education Law (National People's Congress, 1986), the Law of the People's Republic of China on the Protection of Disabled Persons (National People's Congress, 1990), and the Regulations on the Education of Persons with Disabilities (State Council, 1994). However, implementation of universal nine-year of education is not complete. Available statistics provide some information. In 1980, after the period of Reform and Opening had begun, but before any of the relevant education laws were passed, there were 292 special schools serving 33,000 children who were blind, deaf, or had a mild cognitive disability. By 1990, there were 746 special schools, along with 1,885 special classrooms at general education public schools, serving 80,000 students with either sensory or cognitive impairments (Lynch, 1994; National Education Commission, 1991). By the end of 1995, there were 1,379 special education schools, 6,510 special education classes attached to regular schools serving 296,000 students with disabilities (including those attending regular schools) (White Paper of the Government, 1996). According to the 2004 *Quanguo Jiaoyu Shiye Fazhan Tongji*

Gongbao (Report on the Developmental Statistics of China Education, 2005), there were 1560 special schools in China; and there were a total of 371,800 students with disabilities studying at special schools as well as regular schools or special classes affiliated at regular schools. However, with 8.18 million children (aged 0–14) with disabilities in 1987 (Xu, 1994), this was still clearly not enough. To look at these numbers another way, there are simply not enough schools, classrooms, and teachers to serve all children with disabilities; it was estimated that based on available school placements in 1996, 1.8 million new school placements were needed to achieve the national goal of providing education to 80% of children with disabilities (UNESCO, 1998).

There have been efforts from a variety of sectors of society to provide education for individuals with disabilities, resulting in the increasing school enrollment indicated in the figures above. The following sections examine specific examples of implementation of educational policy, including education for individuals with visual impairments/blindness, individuals with autism, as well as at the implementation of *suiban jiudu*, a more inclusive service delivery option for children with disabilities.

BLINDNESS

Blind education has a long history in China, yet few of its details have been documented. The first school for children with visual impairment in China was founded by foreign missionaries; specifically, Mary Gutzlaff, wife of a Pomeranian pioneer missionary to China, who opened a small school in Macau in September 1835, under the auspices of the Society for Promoting Female Education in China, India, and the East, with help also from the Morrison Education Society (Couling, 1917; Miles, 1998). Another person, Rev. Dr. Edward W. Syle (1817–1890), contributed to education for Chinese adults who were blind (Miles, 1998). The first "official" school for the visually impaired in China was founded in 1870 by a Scottish Presbyterian pastor William H. Murray (Hartmann, 1890; Murray, 1890; Nan, 1995). In 1920 it was reestablished in Beijing, and the name was changed to *Qiming* (Morning-Star) Blind School. When the Chinese Communist Party took over the regime in 1949, the school's name again changed to "Beijing Blind Child School" (Nan, 1995).

In the early twentieth century, Chinese people began to establish their own special schools. In 1912, Zhang Jian, the famous Chinese industrialist and philanthropist, established *Nantong Mang Ya Shifan Chuanxi Suo* (Nantong Teacher's School for the Blind and Deaf) in Jiangsu Province. This school was the first to prepare teachers for special schools. In 1916 he established the first

Chinese-established blind school, the *Nantong Mang Ya Xuexiao* (Nantong School for the Blind and Deaf). In 1927 the Chinese government established *Shili Mang Ya Xuexiao* (Nanjing Municipal School for the Blind and Deaf). In the year 1932, three departments (Middle School, Vocational Training, Teachers' Senior High School) were also established in this school (Lin, 1999).

When the Chinese Communist Party came into power in 1949, private education institutions were transformed into state-run schools. The 1951 "Regulations on the Reform of the School System" stated that children with visual impairments were to be provided with six years of education (Government Administration Council of the Central People's Government, 1951). From 1976, primary education for children with visual impairments was changed to a five-year system, and some schools began to provide vocational middle school education. Despite the statement in the 1991, Article 23 Law on the Protection of Disabled Persons that "ordinary educational institutions shall provide education for disabled persons who are able to receive ordinary education," this is not always guaranteed. However, there have been a number of experiments and projects to promote more inclusive service delivery, in the form of *suiban jiudu* (literally, "follow class for study").[4] The beginning of this movement can be traced back to 1986, with the Gold-Key education project, a project begun by Xu Bailun to educate children with visual impairments in general education classrooms. However, children with visual impairment continue to be largely educated in special schools. In 2004, the *Quanguo Jiaoyu Shiye Fazhan Tongji Gongbao* (Report on the Developmental Statistics of China Education, 2005) reported that 41,700 children with visual impairments were studying in blind schools.

As provided by the Law on the Protection of Disabled Persons (National People's Congress, 1991), students at blind schools do not have to pay tuition for Grades 1 to 9, because this is considered compulsory education. Moreover, students at blind schools are provided with free textbooks. As for living expenses, currently there are several projects run by the government, to which the students may apply, and get funding accordingly if they are approved.[5]

Policy requires that "course planning and teaching-standards for special schools should be drawn by the State Council Educational Administration Department; and the provincial ministries of education are responsible for publishing teaching materials" (State Council, 1994). However, according to the teachers from the blind schools, since there is no testing system in place for students in blind schools, and these students do not usually participate in the National College Entrance Exams (NCEE), blind schools "mostly do not follow the national teaching standards in practice, but individual schools decide on their own class planning and teaching standards instead." However, in general, subjects taught in blind schools are not much different from those in general education schools. For example, courses such as chemistry, physics, mathematics, Chinese language, politics, and so on can be seen on a blind school's class schedule as well as a general education school's schedule. In addition, blind schools also have a couple of courses designed specially for blind students, for example, the Walking Class, which teaches the adaptive skill of walking independently.

According to several teachers from the blind schools, their students have been using the "same teaching materials" as in other schools. However, the versions the blind schools are using are actually the ones used in general education schools twenty years ago, which is clearly problematic and is discussed later in this chapter. Textbooks used in most blind schools right now are the Braille version of the general school textbooks, published by Shanghai Publishing House for Blind Children in 1983. Since then, textbooks for general education schools have changed dramatically every year, but the schools for the blind are still teaching the same contents. From 2003, new Braille versions of the current school textbooks have been coming out for Chinese language and mathematics for Grades 1–3. However, this project will take about ten years to finish—by which time the general education school textbooks will have had a lot of changes again. At two high schools for the blind though, in Qingdao and Shanghai, students are taught with the same current textbooks as in general education schools, because these students are geared toward college.

Career choices for people with visual impairments remain limited compared to the growing educational opportunities available, and compared to opportunities for the general public. Currently, all vocational training programs for people with visual impairments, whether high school or college level, are in fields of herbalist or masseur.[6] Generally, students coming out of the vocational training programs do have a good chance of getting employed. Their best choices are to go to government-run hospitals to work in their Chinese Medicine or Physical Therapy departments.

AUTISM

Policy relevant to disability has called for compulsory nine-years of education to be set up and provided for children with disabilities. Children who are blind are mentioned directly in the policies, but children with autism are never mentioned specifically. This has caused difficulties for families seeking educational opportunities for their children with autism; they note that the absence of a direct mention of autism in the law is problematic and schools easily reject these children (McCabe, 2004). However, many articles in these laws call for education for children with disabilities in general, and some advocates of education for children with autism point out that under the Compulsory Education Law and the Law on the Protection of Persons with Disabilities, since children with autism are not explicitly excluded, they must be implicitly included (Cai, 1997). Of course, what advocates believe and what actually occurs are not always the same.

It is not surprising that children with autism are not mentioned in existing policy, as recognition of this disability only began on a very small scale in the early 1980s. Children with autism were first diagnosed in China in 1982, by Dr. Tao Kuo-tai in Nanjing (Tao, 1987). Since that time, educational opportunities for children with autism have been increasing, though they are still far from enough, and these opportunities continue to lag behind those of children who are blind, deaf, or have mild cognitive disability, the three categories of disability first mentioned in policy, in the Compulsory Education Law. While a small number of children with autism in the early 1990s began to attend public special education schools generally geared for children with mild cognitive disability, more specialized (and often short-term) intervention programs began to be established in 1993, beginning with the Beijing Stars and Rain Education Institute for Autism, the Beijing Rehabilitation Association for Autistic Children, and the Nanjing Child Mental Health Research Center. The two Beijing organizations are nonstate entities; indeed, the growth of a nongovernmental sector has led to increased services for children with autism.[7] Before 1993, there were no specialized programs serving children with autism, and very few schools (including special education schools) accepted children with autism (McCabe, Wu, & Zhang, 2005). However, since the three organizations just listed were opened and/or began serving children with autism in 1993, there are a growing number of parents and interested professionals who start educational intervention programs to serve children, mainly young children, and provide instruction that ranges from formal applied behavior analysis and discrete trial teaching, to more general education using a preschool model.

Various policies have promoted these nongovernmental provisions of educational services to children with autism, which have been very important contributors to educating this population. Education policies, including the 1994 Regulations of the People's Republic of China on Education for Persons With Disabilities, call on social forces, social organizations, families, and all sections of society to provide education for children with disabilities (State Council, 1994). Policies on social organizations and private nonprofit, nonenterprise units (NGOs[8]) have also created opportunities and recognition for these nongovernmental organizations to provide social welfare and other services formerly provided only by the government (State Council, 1998a, 1998b). In addition, the current favorable atmosphere for private businesses and organizations has allowed for the creation of other service organizations which, despite their educational focus, are registered as businesses. Unfortunately, these organizations do not receive any government funding, and rely solely on donations and fees for providing services. Efforts in some organizations are made to keep prices as low as possible while still maintaining a stable organization with enough funds to operate, but overall, pay for services indeed limits the ability of many families and children to attend (McCabe, 2004).

Due to the decentralization of responsibility that has occurred in society, and new diversified organizational structures, children with autism in China today are beginning to obtain a variety of educational opportunities, including special education at state-run special education ("cultivate intelligence" *peizhi xuexiao*) schools, special education classes at state-run schools, and private special education schools, as well as at other noneducational settings. For example, at several state-run hospitals/mental health centers, special departments are being set up to provide intervention to children, often in the form of sensory integration therapy, or individual instruction (sometimes based loosely on applied behavior analysis and discrete trial teaching). Finally, private/nongovernmental organizations, are being run by parents, and a small but growing number of children are attending general education classes. Both these types of opportunities are often tied strongly with parent advocacy, as has been seen in other nations around the world.

Despite the existence of a variety of educational or intervention placements, parents of children with autism continue to struggle to find a school to accept their children. Special education schools (*peizhi xuexiao*, cultivate intelligence schools) exist mainly in cities, and they do not have to accept a child with autism. The majority of students in these schools have mild cognitive disabilities, and schools for blind or deaf children are even less likely to accept a child with autism. In spite of the roadblocks, students with autism are beginning to gain access to these schools, including both those who are misdiagnosed as having mild mental retardation, and those with a correct diagnosis of autism (McCabe, Wu, & Zhang, 2005); however even when a special education school does accept a child, it may soon refuse to continue to educate that child because instructors have no background in autism and are "unequipped to meet their needs" (Rubin, 2000, p. 8). The problem of access to education is compounded in smaller towns and villages, where there are often no special education schools or classrooms, and general education schools often refuse to accept children with any learning or behavioral differences. Experiments with more inclusive service delivery models have begun, however, and it is often in those smaller towns where special education schools are not available, that this occurs.

INCLUSION: SUIBAN JIUDU

Policies such as the Compulsory Education Law and the Law of the PRC on the Protection of Disabled Persons do not *mandate* that education be provided to all students, but rather they state that local governments shall provide compulsory (nine years) education to children with and without disabilities, and the national goal is to gradually universalize provision of nine years of education for all. Without a mandate, there is no guarantee that this will occur. However, there are efforts being made, and specifically this call for nine years of education is one of the major reasons why inclusive education models in public general education schools has begun, both in towns and villages, and in urban areas. New inclusive education models are described here, given the knowledge that they are not based on the philosophy of social justice and equal access for all, but rather as a way to comply with the Compulsory Education Law. This phenomenon is discussed in greater detail in the concluding sections.

Suiban jiudu opportunities represent a change from the policy of the Law of the People's Republic of China on the Protection of Persons (National People's Congress, 1990), which states that education in a general education setting is included as one option, but only for those whose disability does not affect their performance in the classroom. Since the mid-1990s, experimental programs have been set up to investigate methods for including children with disabilities (usually mild cognitive and sensory disabilities) (Chen, 1996b, 1997).

Statistics regarding school enrollment have convinced professionals and government leaders to consider a more flexible approach to school placements, not limited to a special school. In 1987, statistics from the National Survey on the Status of Disabilities showed that only 55% of school-age children with disabilities were in school. The national enrollment rate for children without disabilities was much higher, at 97%. *Suiban jiudu* has been seen as a solution for children in areas that do not have, or cannot afford, special schools or programs (Chen, 1996b, 1997). Clearly, this does not satisfy the goal of changing societal beliefs about inclusion and rights of all people. In fact, *suiban jiudu* first began for purely practical reasons, and it started unofficially in rural and remote areas as a function of providing compulsory education; now, when children in rural and remote areas gain access to education, it is primarily at general education schools, where neither special schools nor other educational services for children with disabilities are available. The idea is to increase the integration of students with disabilities in regular schools to contribute to the universalization of compulsory education (Chen & Hua, 1998). One practical issue has been cost; it is not economically feasible to build new schools for the education of children with disabilities in local efforts to universalize compulsory education (Mitchell, 1995; Yang & Wang, 1994). Another factor has been transportation. Poor and rural areas that are unable to build and equip special schools or classrooms have found that *suiban jiudu* is a practical way to provide education for children with disabilities so that they do not need to face inconvenient or nonexistent transportation to a centrally located special education school (Chen, 1996b, 1997; Yang & Wang, 1994).

Both in rural areas and increasingly in more urban areas, education in the general education classroom has become a main channel of education for children with disabilities who are in school for practical reasons. It is unfortunate that most efforts for inclusive practices have been made simply to fulfill practical requirements. However, in many areas there is an acute lack of awareness of a philosophy of equal rights and opportunity for people of all abilities. There continues to be a lack of awareness in society that children with disabilities simply have the same right to opportunities as other children. Many people still doubt that children with disabilities can learn, and see the home as being the responsible institution to teach children with disabilities life-skills and self-care skills (Chen, 1996b). On the other hand, the government laws calling for the provision of compulsory nine years of education to all children do demonstrate some official movement toward committing to the idea that the community, including schools, should in some way provide for all children.

Better teacher training and advocacy by parents and special education professionals are helping to change beliefs regarding inclusive practices. Regarding teacher training, Peng (2003) found that teachers who have received training relevant to *suiban jiudu* have a more positive attitude toward including children with disabilities in their classrooms. In addition, parent and professional advocacy plays an important role in helping children with disabilities gain access to *suiban jiudu*, as evident in examples of many parents of children with autism who have been active in advocating for educational opportunities for their own and other children.

Despite the efforts to provide inclusive educational opportunities, these are still experimental and first steps. Some schools provide joint classes or "counterpart activities" between children with hearing impairments in rehabilitation center preschool classes and children in general education preschool classes (Zhao, Guo & Zhou, 1997; Wu, 1997; Zhou & Cheng, 1995, 1997). Others provide individual instruction within the general education group setting in poor, rural areas with limited resources and children with various abilities and disabilities in one class (Zhao, 1997). In other cases, children with disabilities are gaining access to schools through more unofficial channels. There are an unknown number of children who attend schools in which their relatives are teachers or administrators, or their family has another connection. For example, parents of children with autism often advocate for a spot in a general education preschool or elementary school. Their requirements are minimal—that the teacher allows their child to be in the classroom, and their child learns to sit quietly without disrupting others. There are often very little or no modifications made; compulsory education is based on a national curriculum for all students and it is difficult for a teacher to consider modifying it at all. Students are evaluated on the basis of test scores, and teachers are evaluated on the basis of those scores; thus general education teachers worry not only that a child with a disability will score poorly, but also that accepting students with disabilities will interfere with the achievement of other students (Mitchell, 1995).

Despite the lack of modifications or addressing of children's individual needs, the children who obtain educational placements in settings described above remain the fortunate ones. Notwithstanding policies that call for compulsory education, children with disabilities often still struggle to be accepted into any school at all. There is still no awareness on the ground level in society that children with disabilities have a right to opportunities just as other children have. Many people continue to question providing education for children with disabilities when universal education for children without disabilities has not yet been fully achieved, and they believe that keeping a child with a disability at home makes the most sense (Chen, 1996b). What can we make of the above depiction of disability and special education in China today?

DISCUSSION: TOWARDS AN UNDERSTANDING OF DISABILITY IN CHINA

The above has presented the current state of education and inclusion for students with disabilities in China, with a focus on children with autism and visual impairments. Small steps have been taken toward providing more opportunities to these students. However, is there any reason to believe that individuals with disabilities will be provided with equal educational opportunities in the near, or not so near, future? We critically consider this question by looking at reforms in the overall education system, the challenge faced by special/inclusive education, and overall social awareness and advocacy for people with disabilities.

Hope for Inclusive Practices?: Standardized Exams vs. Suzhi Jiaoyu

One consistent theme in the Chinese education system has been exams. The focus on standardized exams has made ideas of differentiated instruction in an inclusive setting appear impossible to implement. Currently, the most important set of exams a student takes during his/her school life is the NCEE (*gaokao*). The origin of the NCEE is in imperial China (starting from the Sui Dynasty, AD 581–618), when the emperors used the Imperial Examination (*keju*) to select "wise men" (*xianshi*) among ordinary people (*buyi*). The Imperial Exam system developed along with the dynasties, and by the time last two dynasties, the Ming and Qing dynasties, in the Chinese history ended (1911), the Imperial Exam had become highly systematic (Yuan, 1994).

When the People's Republic of China was established, a new systematic exam system, the NCEE was used to select students for higher education, and determine which college they could go to. The Exams were discontinued for a few years during the Cultural Revolution (1966–1976), but the government reinstituted it in 1977 (Yuan, 1994). Over the years, there have been minor reforms of the NCEE, but the Exams have always been highly standardized—students from all over the country take the same set of test papers created by a group of people designated by the Education Bureau (with only one exception for the city of Shanghai, where students are tested with a unique set of papers); and the finished papers are gathered and graded according to one uniform set of "standard solutions." With this standard test as the most important theme and end point of the whole education system, students are judged on their test scores; and schools are evaluated largely on their student's average/top scores.

This situation has made it very difficult for students with disabilities to become mainstreamed, for three reasons. Highly standardized tests geared toward typically developing students mean that all educational activities in the schools are designed with uniform contents and method. Differentiating instruction is not considered. Second, the way the tests are held are also standardized, and any adaptation for students with special needs is considered unfair. Third, in an education system where test scores are the only standard for students' performance, schools are judged by the test scores of their students too. With this pressure present, teachers are asked to focus on increasing the average score of their students, ignoring the performance of students who fall out of the "normal distribution." The motive has always been to find a way to increase test scores more effectively.

However, there seems to be some movement in the way that the education system is set up, a way that could be promising for inclusive practices. In June 1999, a paper, "Decision to Bring Forward Education Reform and Carry out Education for All-Around Development (*suzhi jiaoyu*)" was published by the State Council. This paper required that the education system shift its emphasis from exams to "creativity and practical skills," and it mentioned that education should be adapted according to students' characters and developments (State Council of the People's Republic of China, 1999). However, since the NCEE is still in existence, and continues to be the deciding factor in where a student goes after high school, it has been difficult to really implement the shift from exam scores to all-around development. Up to now, we have not seen much reform done in the education system that can create opportunities for students with disabilities.

The good news is, many people, including researchers, government officials, schools, and parents are calling for reform/abolishment of the NCEE, and there have been a number of discussions on how it should be reformed, or what should replace it, if it is abolished. What will happen to the NCEE? What change will that bring to the whole education system? Is that going to bring better opportunities for students with disabilities to enter into the general education system? These questions remain.

Advocacy

Making change in society, changing beliefs, including becoming a more inclusive society, all these will not occur from policy decisions alone. Rather, change often depends on those at the grassroots level and in particular, those who have a connection with the cause. For disability rights, parents and self-advocates have been the leaders in bringing about equal rights and opportunities in other countries, such as the United States. In China, parents have become the main advocates calling for more opportunities and rights for their children with autism, and self-advocates have been influential in other sectors, such as physical disability (such as CDPF).

In 1951, Dubs wrote, "Chinese family loyalties are sill the source of much in China's sorrows" (1951, p. 55). Today, in 2006, Chinese family loyalties are the source of strength and (advocacy), but indeed the tendency to serve only those close to you can become a negative force. Services for children with autism have come about largely through parent efforts, and new organizations are opened often by parents. Inclusion has not become widespread, and one of the ways in which it does occur is when families have connections. When children remaining at home is seen as an acceptable practice, and the family is seen as the primary provider, the traditional emphasis on family can make things difficult for individuals with disabilities.

Regarding family, another point also needs to be considered. Like in traditional China, the family is essential: parents are the frontlines in terms of seeking more opportunities. However, understanding parent advocacy in China requires understanding not only family traditions, but also the current reform period. In other words, are families bound to each other for cultural reasons only? According to Logan, Bian, and Bian (1998), "The East Asian family is the cornerstone of social support for most Asians, more so than in the West, due to both cultural values and economic practicality" (p. 851). To understand disability in China, we must consider cultural and practical factors. Logan and colleagues' study on co-residence between parents and their adult children found that traditional values were not as important as economic reasons when looking at changes in residency patterns—"behaviors do not always mirror people's values … what appear to be cultural traditions might simply be practical responses to people's daily needs"

(p. 854). In the case of disability, it is clear from interviews with parents that their love for their children, and the traditional bonds of family, are primary factors in their seeking services and opportunities; however, it is also evident that financial and other practical reasons play a part. There are not enough schools, or schools are too expensive, and so families must do much of the work themselves. Understanding family patterns, such as supporting family members with disabilities, "should be interpreted not only in reference to traditional values but also in reference to the impact of state policy" (Logan et al., 1998, p. 854).

Practically speaking, due to a lack of schools and professionals in the People's Republic of China, parents of children with disabilities often are the only teachers of their children. They face an environment that includes, depending on their location, little to no services. Regarding traditional culture, they also face negative social and cultural beliefs about disability, a lack of awareness and understanding of their needs, and a continued belief that disability is to be "dealt with" within the realm of the family. For both practical and cultural reasons, parents are the ones who are making enormous efforts to seek and create services and educational opportunity for their children. This takes time. However, families also see their children as their hopes for the future, and both want to do, and see their responsibility as doing anything to help them obtain whatever is needed.

While this description of parent advocacy might apply loosely in many cultures, the Confucian impact, combined with the impact of the economic reforms of post-1978, make China a country worth examining for its uniqueness regarding disability. Yet another factor that makes disability and family experiences, related to parent advocacy and efforts, unique in China is the family planning policy set by the State Family Planning Commission that requires most couples to have just one child (Attane, 2002). One of the various exceptions to this limitation is when the first child has a disability, in which case, a couple may apply to have a second child. While this is allowed, many families choose to have just one child, or wait many years before having a second child. For example, parents of children with autism often explain that they want to spend all of their time, energy, and finances to support their first child as best they can, and fear a second child will decrease attention needed for the first one. Due to the policy and the societal expectation that most families have just one child, it is very difficult for families to choose to have a second child. The advocacy of parents, and the efforts to secure educational and other opportunities, is often tied to the idea that this is their only child.

Opportunity and Inclusion: Continued Barriers

As discussed earlier, the percentage of students with disabilities being enrolled in compulsory education in China is increasing. With this said, are we really ready to celebrate a more accessible education environment for people with disabilities? There are still causes for concern and three previously mentioned situations provide examples. First, the textbooks used in special schools (e.g., blind schools) are ten or twenty years behind the ones being used in general education. This inevitably hinders the students' opportunities to be included into mainstream education, and increases their difficulty in merging with the society.

Second, although people with visual impairments have increasing education opportunities, and they do have some opportunities to acquire higher education, they have very limited career choices. Almost all vocational training for people with visual impairments is as herbalist or masseur. Therefore if a person goes through the education system and starts a career (which is the most common route), s/he has no other choices but to become a herbalist or a masseur.

Third, government laws began to call for the provision of compulsory nine years of education to all children in 1986, and experimental programs have been set up to investigate methods for including children with disabilities (usually mild cognitive and sensory disabilities). This demonstrates some official recognition that all children, with or without disabilities, should have equal opportunity to education. However, inclusion has begun to serve purely a practical function of universalizing compulsory education: while there are more students with disabilities brought into general education classrooms, and some teachers are provided training to eliminate prejudice against these students (Peng, 2003), there have been minimal efforts to differentiate instruction accordingly, and *suiban jiudu* is not available to all students. We do want to acknowledge a government nod to the importance of education for all, through its policies and construction of special education schools; however, this is not seen as urgent as education for children without disabilities, and constructing special schools remains entirely too segregated a practice.

With a new focus on *suzhi jiaoyu*, perhaps schools will become more accepting of students who do not fit the standardized mold. However, because the population of China is so large, it is extremely difficult for any student to be accepted into university, or even high school. Given the intense competition for higher education, which is one's ticket to a good job, schools are not yet likely to adopt new methods of education that go beyond teaching for the exams.

CONCLUSION

China, though one of the oldest civilizations in the world, remains a developing country that is undergoing enormous change and transition right now. Change is rapid, as seen in the current expression, "*Jihua gan bu shang bianhua*" (Plans cannot keep up with change). However, change in the areas of disability and inclusion has not been as rapid as change in the economy and the infrastructure. Understanding the current state of disability and special education in China necessitates an understanding of the unique context of China during this Reform and Opening period. This chapter has presented this context so that we can examine both new opportunities for individuals with disabilities as well as continued barriers to their equal inclusion in society. Where will China's disability and special education go in the future? We are *shimu yidai* (waiting eagerly and sincerely to see what happens), just as our readers are.

NOTES

1. Confucius asked both parents and children to compromise for the other party's benefits, which was called *fuci zixiao* (father being kind and son being filial). However, later when Confucius' students wrote down his words in the literature, they emphasized the son's filiality because they placed themselves in the position of students (sons) (Wang, 2006).
2. There are great differences between urban and rural China, and this description focuses largely on social change in urban China.
3. A second sample survey was launched in April, 2006, and the results are scheduled to come out in November 2006. In this survey, 2.6 million people (2% of the whole population) will be surveyed in 734 counties and cities in the 31 provinces, autonomous regions and municipalities across the nation (Xianhua News Agency, 2006; Office of the 2nd Sample Survey of People with Disabilities, 2006).
4. *Suiban jiudu*, literally translated as "follow class for study" (www.cosn.net) is the most common expression for this new model of more inclusive service delivery. The other most common phrase is "*yiti hua jiaoyu*," which means "integration." Inclusion (*quanna xing jiaoyu*) is a less used term.
5. Qing Shen, one of the authors of this chapter, has been conducting a series of interviews with teachers from blind schools in China. Some of the information, examples and numbers in this section are from her interview data.
6. Forty-one of the blind schools provide such vocational high school training, sending out approximately 400 graduates every year; and four schools provide 3-year or 4-year college training in the same major. There are currently about 16,500 people with visual impairments working as a masseur, and only 500 of them have received college education (Chinese Disabled Persons' Federation, 2000).
7. Helen McCabe, one of the authors of this chapter, has been conducting research on autism in China for several years. Some of the information, examples and numbers in this section are from her research data.
8. These organizations, and others that are not officially registered as such, are often referred to as NGOs in relevant literature.

REFERENCES

Attane, I. (2002). China's family planning policy: An overview of its past and future. *Studies in Family Planning, 33* (1), 103–113.

Cai, P. (1997, August 12). Wo bie wu xuanze: Yi wei muqin de zishu [I do not have a choice—A mother's account in her own words]. *Zhongguo Qingnian Ribao* [China Youth Daily], p. 8.

Canjiren baohu fa xiugai gongzuo lingdao xiaozu bangongshi [The office of leading group for the revision of the law of the People's Republic of China on the protection of persons with disabilities]. (n.d.). Guanyu canjiren baozhang fa xiugai zongti kuangjia d fangan jiqi shuoming [Proposal and explanation on the revision of the general construction of the law on the protection of disabled persons]. Retrieved April 6, 2006, from China Disabled Person's Federation Web site http://temp.cdpj.cn/bzfxg/2005-04/05/content_3933.htm

Chen, Y.Y. (1996a). *Classroom teaching in suiban jiudu.* Beijing: China International Broadcasting Press.

Chen, Y.Y. (1996b). Making special education compulsory and inclusive in China. *Cambridge Journal of Education, 26* (1), 47–57.

Chen, Y.Y. (1997). Mianxiang weilai, mianxiang shijie de zhongguo yitihua jiaoyu [China's integrated education, facing the future and facing the world]. In Y.Y. Chen (Ed.), *Zhongguo yitihua jiaoyu gaige de lilun yu shijian* [Theory and practice in China's integrated education reform] (pp. 3–17). Beijing: Huaxia.

Chen, Y.Y. (2005). *Policy and development of inclusive education in China.* Paper presented at "A comparative seminar of inclusive education in the Asia-pacific region," Korea Institute for Special Education (KISE), Ansan City, Korea. pp. 45–68.

Chen, Y.Y., & Hua, G.D. (1998). *Teshu ertong de suiban jiudu shiyan: Nongcun de chenggong jingyan* [Experiment in *suiban jiudu* for exceptional children: A successful experience in the countryside.] Beijing: Jiaoyu Kexue Chubanshe.

China Disabled Persons' Federation Publishing Office. (2005). *2004 Zhongguo canjiren shiye fazhan tongji gongbao* [Report on the developmental statistics of China disabled persons' cause]. Retrieved April 10, 2006, from China Disabled Person's Federation Web site: http://www.cdpf.org.cn/shiye/sj-04.htm

China Education Bureau. (2005). *2004 Quanguo jiaoyu shiye fazhan tongji gongbao* [Report on the developmental statistics of China education]. Retrieved April 10, 2006, from http://www.edu.cn/20050728/3144984.shtml

Chinese Children. (n.d.). Retrieved March 5, 2006, from Chinese Culture Web site: http://www.chinaculture.org/gb/en_aboutchina/2003-09/24/content_24144.htm

Cleverly, J. (1991). *The schooling of China* (2nd edition.) North Sydney: Allen & Unwin.

Couling, S. (1917). *Blind in China. Encyclopedia Sinica.* London: Oxford University Press.

Deng, M., Poon-McBrayer, K.F., Farnsworth, E., & McCabe, H. (2001). The development of special education in China: A sociocultural review. *Remedial and Special Education, 22*, 288–298.

Dubs, H.H. (1951). Development of Altruism in Confucianism. *Philosophy East and West, 1* (1), 48–55.

Epstein, I. (1988). Special educational provision in the People's Republic of China. *Comparative Education, 24* (3), 365–375.

Feng, Yuan (1994). From the imperial examination to the National College Entrance Examination: The dynamics of political centralism in China's educational enterprise. *ASHE Annual Meeting Paper.* Washington, DC.

Government Administration Council of the Central People's Government. (1951). *Zhengwuyuan guanyu gaige xuezhi de jueding* [Regulations on the reform of the school system]. Retrieved April 6, 2006, from Xinhua Net Web site: http://news.xinhuanet.com/ziliao/2004-12/16/content_2342125.htm

Hartmann, F. (1890). Orphanages, asylums for the blind, deaf and dumb, and other charitable institutions in China. In *Records of the General Conference of the Protestant Missionaries of*

China (Shanghai, May 7–20, 1890) (pp. 291–302). Shanghai: American Presbyterian Mission Press.

Howell, J., & Pearce, J. (2001). *Civil society and development. A critical exploration*. Boulder: Lynne Rienner.

Ji, Y. F. (2005). *Daojia sixiang dui jingshen fenxi lilun de yidian qishi* [An apocalypse of Taoism to the theory of psychoanalysis]. Retrieved April 7, 2006, from Suxiaopo Xinli Zhensuo [Psychology clinic of Suxiaopo] Web site: http://www.suxb.com/jiyifu1.htm

Kohrman, M. (2003). Authorizing a disability agency in post-Mao China: Deng Pufang's story as biomythography. *Cultural Anthropology, 18* (1), 99–131.

Kraus, R.C. (1976). The limits of Maoist egalitarianism. *Asian Survey, 16,* 1081–1096.

Lam, J. (2000). *Chinese philosophies and religions*. Retrieved April 7, 2006, from Index-China Web site: http://www.index-china.com/index-english/people-religions-s.html

Lin, Z. (1999). 90 Niandai dalu diqu mang jiaoyu zhengce zhi zhixing [Implementation of education policies in Mainland China in 1990s]. *Journal of National Taitung Teachers College, 10,* 105–122.

Liu, G.Z. (2001). *Chinese culture and disability: Information for U.S. service providers*. Retrieved December 3, 2004, from CIRRIE Web site: http://cirrie.buffalo.edu/china.html#_Toc518185189

Logan, J.R., Bian, F., & Bian, Y. (1998). Tradition and change in the urban Chinese family: The case of living arrangements. *Social forces, 76* (3), 851–882.

Lynch, J. (1994). *Provision for children with special educational needs in the Asia region*. Washington, D.C.: The World Bank.

McCabe, H. (2004). *State, society, and disability: Supporting families of children with autism in the People's Republic of China*. Unpublished Ph.D. dissertation, Indiana University.

McCabe, H., Wu, S.X., & Zhang, G.J. (2005). Experiences with autism in the People's Republic of China: Viewing social change through one family's story. *Journal of International Special Needs Education, 8,* 11–18.

Miles, M. (1998). *Blind & sighted pioneer teachers in 19th century China & India*. Retrieved April 10, 2006, from http://www.socsci.kun.nl/ped/whp/histeduc/mmiles/index.html

Mitchell, D.R. (1995). Special education policies and practices in the Pacific Rim Region. Paper presentation at the Annual International Convention of the Council for Exceptional Children, Indianapolis, IN (ERIC Document ED 391261).

Murray, W.H. (1890). Teaching the Chinese blind. In *Records of the General Conference of the Protestant Missionaries of China* (Shanghai, May 7–20, 1890) (pp. 302–306). American Presbyterian Mission Press.

Nar, D.Q. (1995). Special education in Beijing: An Overview. ERIC Document 397 567.

National People's Congress. (1986). *Zhonghua renmin gongheguo yiwu jiaoyu fa* [The Compulsory Education Act of the People's Republic of China]. Retrieved March 3, 2006, from China Education and Research Network Web site: http://www.edu.cn/20050114/3126820.shtml

National People's Congress. (1990). *Zhonghua renmin gongheguo canji ren baozhang fa* [Law of the People's Republic of China on the Protection of Persons with Disabilities]. Retrieved March 3, 2006, from \China Disabled Person's Federation Web site: http://www.cdpf.org.cn/english/info_01.htm

Peng, X.G. (2003). Teshu jiaoyu jiaoshi dui suiban jiudu de taidu diaocha yanjiu. [A study of teachers' attitudes towards suiban jiudu of students with disabilities.] *Chinese Journal of Special Education, 2*.

Persons with Disabilities in China. (2006). Retrieved March 12, 2006, from China Society for Human Rights Studies Web site: http://www.humanrights.cn/zt/magazine/200402004921153911.htm

Qiu, Z. (1998, September). Disability statistics in the People's Republic of China. *Asia and Pacific Journal on Disability, 1* (3). Retrieved March 4, 2006, from Disability INFormation Resources website: http://www.dinf.ne.jp/doc/english/asia/resource/z00ap/003/z00ap00308.htm

Quanguo gelei canjiren shuju [National statistical data on various categories of people with disabilities]. (n.d.). Retrieved March 24, 2006, from China Disabled Person's Federation Web site: http://www.cdpf.org.cn/shiye/sj-000a.htm

Rubin, K. (2000). Chinese charities' Long March. *Chronicle of Philanthropy*, pp. 7–8, 10.

The Situation of Children in China. (1996). Retrieved March 4, 2006, from White Papers of the Government Web site: http://big5.china.com.cn/e-white/children/c-5.htm

State Council. (1994). *Canjiren jiaoyu tiaoli* [Regulations on the education of persons with disabilities]. Retrieved March 3, 2006, from China Disabled Person's Federation Web site: http://www.cdpf.org.cn/zhengce/fl-002.htm

State Council. (1998a). *Shehui tuanti dengji guanli tiaoli* [Regulations on the registration and management of social organizations]. Beijing: Falu Chubanshe.

State Council. (1998b). *Minban feiqiye danwei dengji guanli zhanxing tiaoli* [Provisional regulations on the registration and management of private non-enterprise units]. Beijing: Falu Chubanshe.

State Council. (1999). Decision to bring forward education reform and carry out education for all-around development. Retrieved July 16, 2006, from China Education Online Web site: http://www.cer.net/article/20010101/3053814.shtml

Suiban jiudu ["Follow class for study"]. (2001). Retrieved May 5, 2002, from China Online for the Special Needs Web site: http://www.cosn.net

Tao, K.T. (1987). Brief report: Infantile autism in China. *Journal of Autism and Developmental Disorders, 17* (2), 289–296.

Townsend, J.R. (1977). Chinese populism and the legacy of Mao Tse-Tung. *Asian Survey, 17*, 1003–1015.

UNESCO. (1998). *China: Suiban jiudu in practice.* EFA 2000 Bulletin, 32. Paris: Author.

Vermeer, E.B. (1979). Social welfare provisions and the limits of inequality in contemporary China. *Asian Survey, 19*, 856–880.

Wang, W. (2006). *Lunyu Jiao Women Ruhe Chuli Renji Guanxi* [Theories on inter-personal relationships in Lunyu]. Retrieved April 10, 2006, from Xueshuo Lianxian [Theory online] Web site: http://www.xslx.com/htm/zlsh/zzpj/2006-01-16-19641.htm

Wilde, J.W. (2001). *A comparative study on disability laws of China and the USA: Commissioned by UNICEF office in the P.R. China.* Retrieved March 3, 2006, from John Wilde's Web site: http://fog.ccsf.cc.ca.us/~jwilde/United_Nations_Report.pdf

Wu, H. (1997). Longjian ertong duikou huodong de duozhong jiaoyu xiaoying. [The many types of educational effects of counterpart activities for deaf and healthy children]. In Y.Y. Chen (Ed.), *Zhongguo yitihua jiaoyu gaige de lilin yu shijian* [Theory and practice of the reform of China's integrated education] (pp. 240–245). Beijing: Xinhua Chubanshe.

Xianhua News Agency. (2006). *2nd Sample Survey on China's Disabled Population.* Retrieved March 10, 2006, from China through a Lens Web site: http://arabic.china.org.cn/english/2006/Feb/158123.htm

Xu, Y. (1994). China. In K. Mazurek & M. Winzer (Eds.), *Comparative Studies in Special Education* (pp. 163–178). Washington, D.C.: Galludet University Press.

Yang, H., & Wang, H. (1994). Special education in China. *Journal of Special Education, 28* (1), 93–105.

Zhao, L., Guo, C.F., & Zhou, M. (1997). Jiankang youer yu long youer de duikou jiaoyu huodong shijian [The implementation of counterpart activities for healthy young children and young children who are deaf]. In Y.Y. Chen (Ed.) Zhongguo *yitihua jiaoyu gaige de lilin yu shijian* [Theory and practice of the reform of China's integrated education] (pp. 231–239). Beijing: Xinhua Chubanshe.

Zhongguo canji fenlei biaozhun [Chinese Disability Classification Standard]. (n.d.). Retrieved March 24, 2006, from Guanzhou Disabled Persons' Federation Web site: http://www.gzdpf.gov.cn/asp/shownews.asp?id=990

Zhou, J., & Cheng, X.Q. (1995). Lun xueqian jiaoyu jigou de teshu ertong jiaoyu [A discussion of education for exceptional children at preschool education organizations]. *Teshu Ertong yu Shizi Jiaoyu [Exceptional Children and Teacher Training]*, 3, 2–5.

Zhou, J., & Cheng, X.Q. (1997). Lun xueqian ertong yitihua jiaohua de jiaoxue celue [Educational strategies of integration in pre-school]. *Zhongguo Teshu Jiaoyu (China Special Education)*, 2, 10–14.

Zi, Z. (1987). The relationship of Chinese traditional culture to the modern China: An introduction to the current discussion. *Asian Survey, 27,* 442–458.

CHAPTER TWELVE

The Role OF Residential Schools IN Shaping THE Nature OF THE Advocacy Movement OF THE Blind IN India

JAGDISH CHANDER

Residential schools for the blind played a very crucial role in triggering the broad-based advocacy movement of the blind, and highly influenced the change in its nature in the post-1978 period. This chapter presents an analysis of the role of three such schools, two of which are located in Delhi and the third one in the nearby state of Uttaranchal (which was earlier a part of the State of Uttar Pradesh) in northern India. It was as a result of the contribution of the high school graduates or students of these three schools that the movement acquired a radical character in the post-1978 period when the social base of leadership of National Federation of the Blind (NFB) was widened after a major split in this organization leading to a change of leadership. NFB was founded in 1970 and it is India's first organization of the blind, based on the philosophy of self-advocacy and it continues to be the largest national level advocacy organization for the blind in the country. The majority of its active members have been the high school graduates or current students of these three schools selected as a sample for this chapter, that is, Andha Mahavidyalaya, Government Senior Secondary School for the Blind Boys, and the Model School for the Visually Handicapped. To show the actual geographical location of these schools, a map of India (Figure 12.1) and a map of Delhi (Figure 12. 2) are provided. In the latter, the locations of the schools referred to in this chapter are marked.

METHODOLOGY

I conducted ninety-three interviews with forty-five interviewees from the summer of 2004 to the summer of 2005 for the purpose of my Ph.D. dissertation at Syracuse University. While some newspaper coverage has been used as a part of document analysis for this study, the primary source of information is these interviews in addition to observations deriving from my own experience as a student of two out of three schools covered in this study. Many of the interviewees were the alumni of these three residential schools and most of them were involved in the movement right from their schooldays. Their direct experiences may be the best source for the description of the history of the advocacy movement.

As I grew up for a part of my school life during the late 1970s and the 1980s in two of these residential schools for the blind in Delhi during the peak period of the advocacy movement of the blind in India, I also draw upon my own lived experience in making an analysis of the role of these three schools in the movement. I studied up to the fourth grade in the Government Senior Secondary School for the Blind Boys, Kingsway Camp. Then I joined the Andha Mahavidyalaya, Punchkuian Road, where I studied up to eighth grade and continued to stay there while completing my high school education in an inclusive educational setup. Because of the geographical proximity of the Hostel for College-Going Blind Students located in the premises of the Government Senior Secondary School for the Blind Boys, Kingsway Camp to the campus of Delhi University (where I lived during my college studies), I was able to maintain a close interaction with the blind students living in the hostel. This enabled me to keep a track of the advocacy activities carried out by NFB during my college life in late 1980s through the intense involvement of blind students living in that hostel. Hence, while the primary method of this study is oral history because of the extensive reliance on the interview data, the methods of document analysis and participatory observation have also been used to some extent.

Before analyzing the role of residential schools in of promoting the advocacy movement of the blind, it will be useful to briefly discuss some of the relevant literature on disability to understand the changing perspective on disability advocacy in India.

BACKGROUND LITERATURE

Other than one unpublished master's thesis from the University of Illinois at Chicago on the disability rights movement in India written by Meenu Bhambhani (2004), there has hardly been any study of this subject. Even Bhambhani, who focused on the disability rights movement since the early 1990s, makes only a casual mention of the advocacy movement of the blind in India. She fails to relate the origin of the disability rights movement to the movement of the blind in India.

Nothing about Us without Us

The only publication by an American scholar that I could identify that touches on the issue of the disability rights movement in India is the book by James Charlton, *Nothing about Us without Us* (Charlton, 1998). Charlton devotes part of a chapter to the disability rights movement in India, particularly to the advocacy movement of the blind. However, his portrayal of the advocacy movement of the blind is highly erroneous. As Bhambhani (2004, p. 35) rightly notes, Charlton completely neglects to discuss the Disability Rights Group, a group that has been active since March, 1993 in Delhi. Similarly, he fails to even mention the NFB, the largest advocacy organization of the blind in India. On the contrary, he portrays the National Association for the Blind (NAB) as the largest and the most powerful advocacy organization of the blind (Charlton, 1998, pp. 145–46). The fact is that for most of its existence, NAB has been a service agency in the area of blindness, and until very recently it vehemently opposed the advocacy approach adopted by organizations such as the NFB.

Indian Publications, 1980s

Neither of the two important publications of the 1980s, Chaturvedi (1981) and Mani (1988), mentions a word about the advocacy movement of the blind, its accomplishments, and its approach. A similar line was adopted by Kitchlu (1991) in relation to welfare services for the blind in India in the second half of the twentieth century. While Mani and Chaturvedi dealt with disability issues from a policy angle in a broad way, Kitchlu claimed to analyze the educational and employment measures adopted for the blind by the Welfare State of India. The clear message sent to the readers through these publications was that whatever benefits or discounts offered to the blind or the disabled people were gifted to them as a part of welfare-oriented philosophy of the Indian State and not as a result of the struggle carried out by them for their rights.

Disability Studies

The 1990s witnessed some progress in recognition of the importance of the advocacy approach of the disabled activists. The growing literature in the West based on the disability studies approach gradually started to influence the approach of intellectuals regarding disability in India, though initially in only a very minor and insignificant way. Therefore, there was very little reflection on the incorporation of the minority model (Barnartt & Scotch, 2001; Davis, 2002; Linton, 1998; Russell, 1998; Scotch, 1984; Shapiro, 1993) or the social model (Campbell & Oliver, 1996; Oliver, 1990, 1996) of disability in some of the writings in India in the 1990s. However, three major publications deserve special mention: the book by Ali Baquer (1994) published in the prelegislation days in India; the book by R.S. Pandey and Lal Advani (Pandey & Advani, 1995), also published in the prelegislation period; and the book by Ali Baquer and Anjali Sharma (Baquer & Sharma, 1997), published in the immediate post–disability law period. While the book by Pandey and Advani and the book co-authored by Baquer and Sharma fall in line with the traditional medical model of disability, they make some contribution toward the newly emerging disability rights perspective in India. On the other hand, the earlier book written by Baquer in 1994 was to a greater extent based on analysis of disability issues from a disability studies perspective.

Lately, a beginning has been made of the adoption of a disability studies approach by a few Indian scholars. For instance, Asha Hans and Annie Patri (2003), and Anita Ghai (2003) incorporate the disability studies perspective in the literature on disability in India. However, these are, so far, only two identifiable publications in India that can be put in the category of disability studies. The first is a book compiled and co-edited by Hans and Patri (2003) and the second book authored by Ghai (2003) address issues of marginalization of disabled women and the feminist discourse in India. While Hans and Patri initiated this effort through publication of an edited volume on disabled women's identity from a disability studies perspective, Ghai carried forward this trend of academic discourse based on this perspective. In particular, Ghai's work should inspire young scholars interested in this new approach. Other than these two books that were completed in the last three years, most publications generally fall into the medical model category, presenting status reports on existing disability conditions.

RESIDENTIAL SCHOOLS: THE TRAINING GROUND FOR PREPARING THE LEADERSHIP OF THE MOVEMENT

After family, school is perhaps the second factor that leaves indelible imprints on the personality of any individual, and the blind are no exception. But personalities are influenced in a stronger way if the schools are supplemented with hostels (i.e., residential quarters). Such schools may be similar to what is known as "ashrams" in India, where the teacher-disciple relationship is developed. However, these schools are different from ashrams in the sense that teachers do not share living quarters with students.

Many blind children studying in residential schools often fall into a relatively different age group from their sighted counterparts. Once a child acquires blindness, the initial reaction of every parent is to make every possible attempt to get a treatment for curing this impairment. Moreover, since most blind children come from rural parts of India, their parents often lack information regarding the availability of educational opportunities for them. This takes away a lot of time of during their childhood and puts them much behind their sighted counterparts in the pursuit of school education. Hence, most of these children studying in residential schools are admitted relatively much later as compared to their sighted counterparts owing to lack of information, and time spent in the treatment with the hope of a cure. As a result, the age group of such children ranges from five to twenty-five years. The children who fall within this age group learn their daily activities either under the guidance of the older children or through female aids called *ayahs* (Hindi word for caretakers) who are supervised by female superintendents.

A variety of arrangements, ranging from boarding and lodging to education, is needed for the smooth functioning of residential schools. From my own experience of being a former student of residential schools for the blind, I have observed a trend in the functioning of such schools, namely that that dissatisfaction or resentment over these arrangements is sometimes expressed mildly and sometimes to an extreme degree in the form of a protest that at times develops into a student movement if the demands are not satisfied by the management.

All the three schools selected as a sample for this chapter witnessed the resentment of the students against the management for the poor quality of some arrangements, particularly the quality of food. This resentment often took the form of a protest often leading to movements, which proved to be baptisms for future advocates of rights of the blind. The statement by Santosh Kumar Rungta, a prominent leader of the advocacy movement of the blind in India since the late 1970s cited below, gives a vivid picture of the school environment in which some of the students of the residential schools for the blind were unofficially trained and prepared for future leadership:

> I think that was when I was in the third class. There were lots of problems as one usually faces in residential school. This incident took place in 1964. I was nine years old. There were problems of food and hygiene. One evening, there was a sudden cause for our reacting sharply, and it finally resulted in the first ever strike in the history of school. I was mainly instrumental for the strike. What exactly happened

was that I had caught a cook red-handed when he was taking away prepared food as well as uncooked material. When students went to report to the principal and he refused to take any action, I locked the cook in the kitchen itself. We maintained that unless a district administration's officer comes and registers a case, he would not be set free. Ultimately, this incident led to the constitution of a committee which would look into the entire affairs of the school. We had a hot discussion on the matter because somehow the committee wanted to protect the employees and was favoring the administration. We did not allow it to happen. Ultimately, it was decided that the mess committee (dining management committee) of students would be constituted to decide the menu, control and regulate the functioning of the kitchen. That was the first change that we could bring in. (personal interview, April 4, 2005)

UNIQUE CHARACTERISTICS OF THE THREE RESIDENTIAL SCHOOLS

At present, there are more than 250 residential schools for the blind in the length and breadth of India and most of the schools are for the blind boys and couple of schools are imparting education to the blind girls. (M.K. Rastogi, personal interview, May 18, 2005).

The first school for the blind was opened in 1887 by an Irish Christian Missionary in Amritsar, Punjab and a chain of schools were opened during the last decade of the nineteenth century and first quarter of twentieth century in Mumbai (formerly known as Bombay), Kolkata (formerly known as Calcutta), and other parts of India (Sanyal & Giri, 1985, p. 7).

Three schools selected for the purpose of analysis of their role in the advocacy movement of the blind in India are: (1) Andha Mahavidyalaya located in Delhi; (2) Government Senior Secondary School for the Blind Boys located in Delhi at Kingsway Camp; and (3) Model School for the Visually Handicapped located in Dehradun, district of Uttaranchal, formerly a part of Uttar Pradesh (see Figures 12.1 and 12.2).

Andha Mahavidyalaya

Andha Mahavidyalaya, located in Delhi, is the oldest residential school for the blind in India. It was originally established in Lahore, which is now part of Pakistan and relocated to Delhi at the time of partition of the country in 1947. It is a school for blind boys. For the most part of its existence since the 1960s, the size of the student body has remained in the vicinity of 100 (B.P. Yadav, personal interview, April 17, 2005). The school provides education up to eighth grade and after that, these students are sent to mainstream schools while living in the same

Figure 12.1. Map of India.

school accommodation. The school was initially run entirely on public donations, but during early 1980s, the government took over the school and started providing teachers' salary and office expenses including the salary of the staff. However, the responsibility for lodging, boarding, and other expenses of the students from first to twelfth grade still remains with Blind Social Welfare Society, a privately run not-for-profit organization that was running the school prior to the support received from the government.

Andha Mahavidyalaya is located at Punchkuian Road, an area of New Delhi in the vicinity of most of the high-level central (federal) government offices and within a distance of less than a mile from Cannaught Place, the downtown area of Delhi. The Parliament House, the President's House, and almost all central government offices are located within a distance of approximately two to three miles from the school. This proximity of the school to the central government offices makes it a strategic location and enables the activists of the movement to use it as a base for carrying out their activities. The proximity to the downtown area makes it possible for the students to approach these offices to pressure the government to meet their demands. These students could be used for launching any protest against the government without involving much finance. As a result, the

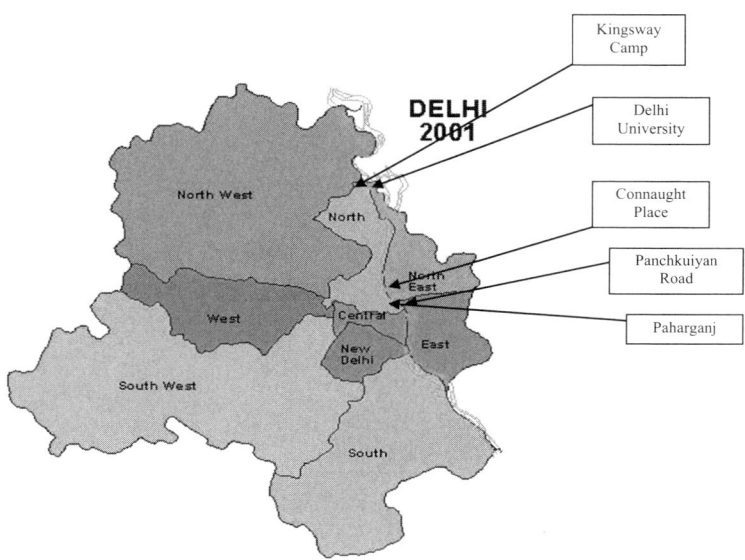

Figure 12.2. Map of Delhi.

students of Andha Mahavidyalaya generally provided a great force for any advocacy activity relating to the blind movement. Added to this, after 1978, the NFB was shifted to Paharganj, Delhi which is less than a mile away from this school.

Government Senior Secondary School for the Blind Boys at Kingsway Camp

In addition to Andha Mahavidyalaya, there is the Government Senior Secondary School for the Blind Boys at Kingsway Camp, a residential school located in Delhi. As explained by its first principal, C.D. Tamboli, this school was established in 1969 and functioned in the low population density area of Delhi called Maharani Bagh and was later moved to a campus of the Delhi Administration located at Kingsway Camp in 1971 (C.D. Tamboli, personal interview, March 25, 2005). The school campus is a part of the Poor House complex, the Beggar Home that provides a temporary shelter to the beggars who are rounded up. Some residents of the Home have been used as casual staff members for this school. Although it is a state government-run institute, the choice of location, the premises of the Poor House, reveals the Delhi Administration's bankruptcy of approach to educational support for blind schoolchildren and college students. However, as a result of a demand presented by the students of the school toe the chief minister of Delhi, the name of the premises was changed from "Poor House" to "The Louis

Complex" on the anniversary of the birth of Louis Braille on January 4, 1994. On the same date, the school was extended from tenth to twelfth grade (C.D. Tamboli, personal interview, March 25, 2005).

Two unique and important factors arising out of the location of the Government Senior Secondary School for the Blind Boys enable it to serve as a training center to prepare future leaders of the advocacy movement: First, it is located at a distance of almost two miles from the main campus of the University of Delhi; second, the school has a hostel for blind college students attached to it. Proximity to the campus of the University of Delhi enables the students of the school to interact with the college-going blind students. At the same time, the location of the Hostel for College-Going Blind Students in the campus of the school enables the children to interact with the college students residing in the hostel on a regular basis. These college-going blind students always form the backbone of the advocacy movement of the blind. Due to a close relationship of the college students living in the hostel with the high school students, the former often recruit the latter in advocacy activities carried out in Delhi.

Model School for the Visually Handicapped

On January 4, 1959, a central government-run school was opened in Dehradun in Uttar Pradesh (L. Advani, personal interview, January 21, 2005). It was initially named the Model School for the Blind Children and is now known as the Model School for the Visually Handicapped, or more popularly known as The Model School. Unlike the other two schools, it is coeducational and its hostels are divided in such a way that boys and girls of similar age groups are able to interact with each other. In the early two decades of its inception, this school was located separately, approximately two miles away from the Training Centre for the Adult Blind (TCAB), which has been providing variety of training to the adult blind who could not manage to get education at an earlier age. By mid-1960s, the school management started involving the students in the decision-making process by forming a mess committee comprising students' representatives. The introduction of this democratic process gave rise to expectations which, if not fulfilled, paved the way for resentment. Moreover, it is worth mentioning that the school was being run by the Ministry of Social Justice and Empowerment then known as "the Ministry of Welfare." The budget of the school used to be affected by wars and the 1960s witnessed two wars—one with China in 1962 and other with Pakistan in 1965. Obviously, owing to the cut in the budget, the standard of the food decreased and, as the students were immature, it was difficult for the administration to explain the situation. This was also one of the causes of resentment. The process of democratization, initiated through the involvement of school students in the mess committee, divided the school into two factions, each opposing each other. This situation became explosive as was seen in the movement of March, 1967 that culminated in the closure of the school sine die in October of the same year. The leadership of the school went to Delhi to plead its case, initially by a direct dialogue with Mrs. Indira Gandhi, the prime minister, and later on by lobbying with some of the opposition leaders and by getting the question raised in parliament. Later on, the school was moved to the campus of the National Institute for the Visually Handicapped (NIVH), an institute which comprises the TCAB, Central Braille Press, Central Braille Library, and Technical Training Center for the Blind. The location of TCAB on the same campus as that of NIVH provided an opportunity for the students of the school to learn life skills and develop a consciousness about their rights from their older peers at the training center, as majority of them used to be older blind people and would have had their lived experiences to offer to their younger counterparts. This became the most important factor in enabling the Model School to develop as a training ground for the future leaders of the advocacy movement of blind.

RESIDENTIAL SCHOOLS AS SEEDBEDS OF ADVOCACY

With this overview of the origin and structure of these three schools, it is now easier to understand the importance of the role of these schools in preparing the future leadership of the advocacy movement of the blind in India. The two schools located in Delhi not only prepared the future leaders of the advocacy movement of the blind, but also served as staging grounds for carrying out the movements over a period of time. In the following pages, I analyze the role of these three schools as the training ground for preparing the future leaders of the advocacy movement of the blind and the overall impact of the role of these schools in shaping its nature in New Delhi, the capital city of India.

Andha Mahavidyalaya

As has been stated, Andha Mahavidyalaya provides education up to the eighth grade and then offers boarding and lodging to its students pursuing education at secondary and higher secondary school level as well as college education. The students have had a variety of experiences of the so-called benevolence arising from religion. Hindu donation is not seen as either help or contribution. It is something more than that. Under Indian customs dominated by the Hindu ethos, donations are given with a view to getting good wishes from the beneficiaries. They may be also given to remove bad omen from the donating families and the receiver is not supposed to object to the quality of the donation. That is why it is popularly said in Hindi *"Daan kee Bachiya ke Dant Nahin Gine Jate"* (no one counts the teeth of the donated calf). This means that if one is getting something in donation, the recipient is always on the receiving end and has no choice in deciding the quality of what he/she is getting.

As students were afraid of punishment, they did not initially raise any objection regarding the quality of services provided to them. But with the passage of time, particularly with the establishment of government-run schools such as the Government Senior Secondary School for the Blind Boys at Kingsway Camp, students of a charity institution such as Andha Mahavidyalaya gained consciousness regarding their right to a decent standard of living and started questioning the quality of the services and goods provided to them as a part of donation. The Government Senior Secondary School for the Blind Boys at Kingsway Camp was fully run by the government and the administration was supposed to maintain a certain minimum standard. As the students of the Government Senior Secondary School for the Blind Boys and Andha Mahavidyalaya, used to interact with each other, they also exchanged their views about the standard of the school in terms of quality of food and other living arrangements. This interaction developed awareness of their rights.

Along with the emergence of the NFB as an organization for self-advocacy, several organizations were initiated in Delhi by the blind in the early 1970s. The high school graduates of Andha Mahavidyalaya started advocating for admission to the university and then for the accommodations necessary to pursue college education. In the spring of 1972, they launched a sustained struggle to pressure the government to direct the colleges of Delhi University to permit the admission of blind students. One of the activists among them, named Baldev Krishna Sharma (B.P. Yadav, April 17, 2005) conducted a hunger strike in front of the residence of the Prime Minister, Mrs. Indira Gandhi. Later on, he was joined by others. The Ministry of Social Justice and Empowerment pressured the principal of the school to take disciplinary action against the students, who were then given corporal punishment (R.M. Vyas, February 3, 2006). At the same time, an organization called Akhil Bharatiya Netraheen Vidyarthi Parishad (All India Council of the Blind Students) was formed in April, 1972 (B.P. Yadav, personal interview, April 17, 2005). It continued with advocacy activities relating to the demand for admission of blind students in the colleges. Owing to some conflicts over financial issues, the Akhil Bharatiya Netraheen Vidyarthi Parishad was closed and a new organization called the National Student Organization of the Blind emerged. This still exists in its dormant form and is managed by the alumni of this school.

Once some of these high school graduates of Andha Mahavidyalaya were in college, they launched a sustained struggle for accommodations at the higher education level, and for this purpose they formed an organization called National Blind Youth Association (NBYA) on November 7, 1974 (B.P. Yadav, personal interview, April 17, 2005). NBYA initially intended to focus on the struggle for the educational needs of blind students at the university level. It was led by Dr. Bharat Prasad Yadav who was one of the high-spirited alumni of this school. Under his leadership, NBYA led many movements at the University of Delhi on various issues such as providing hostel accommodation for blind students, supplying free tapes and tape recorders, throwing open the admission for them into professional degrees such as Bachelor's of Education, and adding a section for Braille books in the university library.

By the late 1970s, NBYA developed the reputation as the most powerful and effective organization in Delhi fighting for the interest of blind students in the University of Delhi, but it could not be developed into an institutionalized organization owing to lack of required funds for its infrastructure and running expenses on regular bases. The leaders could not procure sufficient funding either through the government or public donations. Hardly any government will provide funds for the purpose of advocacy. It was equally hard to procure funding from public donations in the absence of any service delivery activities carried out by the organization. However, it needs to be acknowledged that despite the fact that NBYA could not be developed as an institutionalized force, it continued to exert pressure that succeeded in pushing the University of Delhi to open a separate section for Braille books and make available readers for reading out print books for blind students in the University Library. It also forced the university to permit blind students to gain admission to the Bachelor's of Education program by the end of 1979 (B.P. Yadav, personal interview, April 17, 2005).

In the early 1980s, there was a growing rift in the management of Andha Mahavidyalaya. There were allegations that management was misappropriating funds. NBYA launched a movement on the issue of bringing the management under the control of the Delhi administration. As a result of the partial success of this movement, Andha Mahavidyalaya was converted in to a semiprivate school. The staff salary was then covered by the Delhi administration, while the boarding and lodging remained dependent upon private donations through private management.

It is worth noting here that current students were involved in this effort to bring the school under partial control of the Delhi administration. Hence, it can be regarded as another focused training to fight for an important cause. This was a practical lesson and, in its own way, the beginning of the involvement of the school-going students in the advocacy movement. In fact, the issue of involvement of school students in the advocacy activities has had two dimensions. On the one hand, was the issue of transferring the administrative control of the school from private management to the State Government of Delhi. This was handled by an advocacy organization, that is, NBYA. On the other hand, was the issue pertaining to a school and it was not possible to take up this issue without involving school students. With this, the trend of using the students of residential schools as activists for various movements developed. This trend gave birth to a new controversy popularly known as merit of education versus involvement of students in the politics.

Bharat Prasad Yadav, the prominent leader of NBYA believed, "It was a practical experience to participate in the movement … I feel that there is a need of the involvement of the students in such activities" (B.P. Yadav, April 17, 2005). This trend was questioned in various quarters, as it was considered to be a cause of deterioration of the quality of education imparted in these schools. Whether the accusation was correct or not is beyond the scope of this chapter, but it is clear from this description that the residential schools such as Andha Mahavidyalaya not only became the best training grounds for the future activists of the movement, but also the bases from where the advocacy activities were carried out by the organizations such as NBYA and NFB.

Government School for the Senior Secondary Blind Boys at Kingsway Camp

The Government School for the Senior Secondary Blind Boys at Kingsway Camp in Delhi was inspired by the example of the Andha Mahavidyalaya. Many of the high school graduates of Andha Mahavidyalaya were admitted to various colleges in the University of Delhi and moved to the Hostel for the College-Going Blind Students located in the campus of this school. These residents of the hostel were constantly involved in various advocacy-related activities in the 1980s and 1990s. The success of the experience of the movement led by the students of Andha Mahavidyalaya in acquiring partial government funding stimulated this school to encourage the involvement of the advocacy organizations in the matters of the school. Just as in Andha Mahavidyalaya, there started an era in which NBYA and the NFB intervened in school matters and worked to align students in favor of one or the other organization.

There was a period in the mid-1980s when this school and the hostel for the college-going students witnessed a conflict between various groups supporting one of these two leading advocacy organizations of the blind in Delhi—NBYA and NFB. The conflict between the members of two different organizations arose because each one wished to establish its identity by using the students in one way or the other for the advocacy activities led by them. However, with the change in the leadership of the NBYA, its supremacy was established in this school as well as the hostel by 1987 and the conflict ceased.

The Model School for the Visually Handicapped

The Model School in Dehradun had entirely different experiences with advocacy movements. Being run by the central government, it had a national character to a great extent despite the fact that there has been a predominance of blind students from the northern state of Uttar Pradesh because of its geographical proximity. It is this national character and, as well as the admission of students from a few schools from different parts of northern India that impart education only up to the eighth standard, that fostered a variety of experiences at this school.

The newcomers in higher classes carried different cultures based on their experiences of the schools, which they originally came from. This became evident particularly when a group of middle school students came from different parts of Uttar Pradesh such as Lucknow, Gorakhpur, and Kanpur in the 1960s. It is this group that was more active in their sharp responses to certain unwanted or unacceptable steps taken by the management. A proactive approach was brought to this school by this group and it was exhibited in the form of the first ever-organized movement under the leadership of these students on March 23, 1967 (J. Luthra, personal interview, May 21, 2005; S.K. Rungta, personal interview, April 4, 2005; R.K. Sarin, personal interview, January 30, 2005). This movement was organized on a quotidian issue such as food, but it was a spontaneous issue, which worked like a flint for dry grass. One finds that almost every student took part in that movement. Surprisingly when the police threatened to arrest the protesters, even the children in the 7–8 age group were ready to court arrest ("Blind Children revolt," 1967). Some of the students involved in this incident later participated in the protest of 1973 led by NFB in Delhi. During this protest, these activists adopted the method of polishing shoes of the members of parliament and burning their college degrees to draw attention of policymakers to their plight caused by unemployment despite being highly qualified to work in white-collar jobs (M.K. Rastogi, personal interview, May 18, 2005).

The year 1967 is also important in the Indian politics in terms of rising dissatisfaction with the central government over the issue of leadership, including a leadership struggle between Mrs. Indira Gandhi and Morarji Desai for the position of prime minister. Northern India witnessed an anti-Congress wave (opposition to the ruling Congress Party) in the elections of 1967 (Rudolph & Rudolph, 1987; Vanaik, 1990). In the Model School, there were some teachers who were influenced by the progressive ideology and supported the students' cause. But the fact that the central government intervened in the matter does not mean that the movement was over within three days. In fact, within certain intervals, this movement continued up to the month of October. On October 25, "unity day" was organized and the student leaders gave a call to go to Delhi without informing the principal (R.K. Sarin, personal interview, January 30, 2005). Thirty students left the school in small groups and the next morning all reached Delhi. This put a check on the movement in the school campus and for the first time, the movement was taken to Delhi. The issue of closing the school sine die was raised in the parliament and the government was forced to reopen the school in January, 1968 (R.K. Sarin, personal interview, January 30, 2005). This issue had also become important because of the fact that it was the only residential school for blind that was being run by the central government.

In the post-1967 period, these movements continued over different issues. In a span of one-and-a-half decades, the students of the Model School participated in various movements on issues ranging from proper catering arrangements to autonomy of the then National Centre for the Blind (NCB), of which Model School was a part. It is pertinent here to deal briefly with the controversy over making the NCB an autonomous body and renaming it as NIVH. It was the understanding of the administrators of NCB that this institute should be made autonomous so that one need not approach central government for all petty issues in which finance is involved. They were interested in getting a consolidated fund with some control over it and by making the secretary of the Ministry its ex-officio in charge. At the same time, the administration wanted the liberty to initiate new programs without unnecessary involvement of the central government. On the other hand, the students and the trainees and even some of the staff were of the view that this will pave the way for the dictatorship of the management and will fulfill the dictum "those who hold purse, hold the power."

Initially, the movement regarding the issue of autonomy of the NIVH was organized by the students of the school, but at a later stage, there was regular intervention by the NFB. At this stage, it was the students who approached the NFB. They believed that as some of the officers (board members) of the NFB since the late 1970s had been the high school graduates of the Model School, their case might be pleaded in all genuineness. That proved true and the movement then shifted into the hands of the NFB.

Since the establishment of the NFB Unit in Dehradun in the mid-1970s (H.H. Khan, personal interview, August 2, 2005), almost all the movements were organized by this unit. Although the struggle over the issue of autonomy of NCB and its renaming as the NIVH did not yield favorable results for the students of the Model School and the trainees of the TCAB, they were intensely involved in the struggle led by NFB. Many of the leaders of the second generation of the NFB who gave a radical color to the advocacy movement in the post-1978 period were the high school graduates of the Model School. The most powerful leader of the NFB since 1978, Santosh Kumar Rungta, is also a product of this school.

RESIDENTIAL SCHOOLS AND NATIONAL LEVEL ADVOCACY

The advocacy movement of the blind in India formally began at the national level with the founding of the NFB in Delhi in 1970 (J.L. Kaul, personal interview, February 14, 2005; A.K. Mittal, personal interview, May 16, 2005; B.V. Reddy, personal interview, July 31, 2005). Deriving its name from the NFB in the United States (Jernigan, 1999; Matson, 1990), the organization in India was initially named the NFB Graduates and was originally founded by a small group of college-educated blind people. During its infant stage, its membership was open only to blind college graduates, but soon, the organization welcomed everyone and the word "Graduates" was dropped. As a result, the organization was renamed as the NFB in 1972 (J.L. Kaul, personal interview, February 14, 2005; A.K. Mittal, personal interview, May 16, 2005; B.V. Reddy, personal interview, July 31, 2005; H. Shah, personal interview, March 24, 2005). "The deletion of the word 'graduate' was made to enhance its scope of membership" (J.L. Kaul, February 14, 2005). However, real change in the nature of the movement took place in 1978 when the new leadership, relying on the new membership, took charge after a split between the old and the newly emerging leadership of NFB. This led to a widening of the scope of the demands raised by NFB as a part of its struggle and the adoption of new methods of advocacy. The movement then acquired a radical character in the post-1978 period.

Tensions and Disappointments Within the Movement

During the formative years of NFB in the early part of 1970s, the first generation of leadership adopted a very mild approach toward advocacy. Other than a major protest in 1973, in most of the cases, the federation had confined itself to the use of mild methods of advocacy through correspondence and often kept itself busy in pleasing the leaders of service agencies such as NAB and looking for jobs for the relatively less qualified blind people in the private sector with the help of a placement officer. The emerging educated group, the bulk of the membership of which came from these three schools discussed in this chapter, was dissatisfied with this approach, but the leadership failed to sense the change in the air owing to its indifference toward the needs of the newly educated group of blind activists and a movement built up against it. The approach of mild methods of advocacy adopted by the first generation of leadership in early 1970s failed to yield any positive results in securing suitable government jobs for the newly educated blind, which frustrated them, and that created a need for a radical change in the leadership resulting into the split of 1978.

 The major source of conflict between the younger members of NFB and the first generation of leadership by the later part of the 1970s was on the issue of pressuring the government for implementing the 3% quota in employment for the blind promised by the central government under the Executive Order of 1977 (Mani, 1988, pp. 183–185). Under this Executive Order (a form of legislation), quota system was introduced for the first time and 3% of lower level jobs were reserved for the blind in India in the central government offices. The first generation of leadership was reluctant to fight with the officials in power to get the provision for this quota implemented as taking up such issues and lauching a vigorous struggle against the government could have led to the cancellation of grants for service delivery projects. The expectations of the group of newly educated unemployed blind from the government had highly increased due to the existence of the provision for this quota in employment. Consequently, a prochange wave started in the federation. This wave acquired the form of "anti-Kaul" questioning and opposing the leadership of the federation by Jawar Lal Kaul, the founding leader of the NFB, who remained a unquestionable leader until 1976.

Since the election for the leadership of NFB held in Jaipur, Rajasthan in 1976, a lopsided contest took place between Kaul and Shivjatan Thakur who was incidentally a student of the Model School (J. Bhargav, personal interview, May 17, 2005; Luthra, 2005; H. Shah, personal interview, March 24, 2005). Thakur was representing the group led by Santosh Kumar Rungta, the emerging new leader of NFB having a wide support base among the younger members of the federation. The struggle for leadership of NFB reached its peak in the ensuing election of 1978 at Kanpur, Uttar Pradesh, when Rungta himself contested elections against Kaul for the position of secretary general, the most powerful position in the organization. As a result of massive support of the younger members of NFB, Rungta won the elections. The students of all the above-mentioned three schools formed the core group that organized itself to use their influence to make victory of the new leadership of NFB possible in the proper count of heads. But anticipating his own defeat, Kaul used his influence to get the election cancelled before the results of voting were officially announced.

This was the first time in the history of the federation that the then reigning leadership sensed failure and used antidemocratic means in the name of insecure future of the federation and got the election cancelled. This is a weakness in any organization in which democracy is not properly institutionalized and leadership is not ready to accept inevitable change. The federation saw a black age in which conflict over leadership between the two leaders continued and ultimately resulted in the resignation of Kaul as it was difficult for two horses of different tempers to pull the cart. For all practical purposes, Rungta started heading the organization. A mobilization of almost two years enabled Santosh Kumar Rungta to take control of the power in a real sense.

After the leadership imbroglio was settled in 1979, the new office bearers started using pressure tactics to get their demands implemented (S.K. Rungta, personal interview, April 4, 2005). In contrast with the approach of the previous leadership, which was focused on absorbing blind workers into petty jobs in the private sector, the emphasis of the movement shifted to jobs in government sector on the basis of the promises made by the government by declaring the policy of 3% quota in the central government jobs in the year 1977. This led to a widening of the scope of the demands raised by the NFB as a part of its struggle and the adoption of new methods of advocacy. The advocacy activities under the new leadership of Rungta resulted in a sustained movement based on the methods of rallies, picketing, courting arrest, and so on. The demand charter given by the new leadership also included the demand for a special law for the blind that will cover problems such as employment, education, and other rehabilitation facilities.

1980: A major turning point

The foremost action taken in the history of wide-based national level movement was a rally on the occasion of the World Disabled Day, the third Sunday of March, 1980. It was stopped by the police, who lathi charged (beat with bamboo sticks) the rally participants. This event proved to be a watershed in the history of the advocacy movement of the blind, as it was widely covered nationally and internationally by the media. and even the houses of parliament echoed with demands of the opposition political parties to institute an inquiry into the matter. This issue was covered by the press with various headlines such as "Procession of blind lathi charged" (*Lokvani*, March 17, 1980), "Criticism of lathi charge on blind everywhere" (*Jansatta*, March 17, 1980), "All Round Condemnation of lathi charge: Inquiry Judge Named, S.H.O Suspended" (*The Indian Express*: March 17, 1980), "Brutal congress administration lathi charges the blind" (*The Patriot*: March 18, 1980). It was this event that determined the future trend as the issues of the blind began to be discussed in the corridors of power. This also gave a feeling to the then leadership that the methods of rallies and courting arrests were the easier and populist ways of pressuring the government for various demands of the blind.

It was not the first ever-organized rally of the blind in Delhi per se. Organizations such as the NBYA and the National Students Organization of the Blind used to organize rallies and pickets over issues relating to local problems in Delhi. Prior to the rally of March 16, 1980 on the occasion of the World Disabled Day, the NBYA organized a rally in November 1978, and approximately 100 people courted arrests (B.P. Yadav, personal interview, April 17, 2005).

The difference between both the rallies was in the insistence at the 1980 rally on meeting the prime minister and in choosing the day of rally. In the case of the rally organized by the NBYA, it was an expression of protest in front of the parliament, but the participants in the rally organized by the NFB demanded to see the prime minister on the occasion of the World Disabled Day with the goal of asking the government to pass a comprehensive legislation ensuring the rights of the disabled, particularly, the blind. But it was the lathi charge that brought the latter rally into limelight and changed the focus from the demands for the implementation of quotas for the blind in jobs and the need of for legislation, to the brutal lathi charge on the innocent blind. It was an emotional outburst and perhaps the most suitable one to the print and audiovisual mass media and even to the politicians. It needs to be emphasized that the activists who took part in both the rallies mostly comprised the alumni of these three schools (R.K. Sarin, January 30, 2005; B.P. Yadav, April, 2005).

It is unfortunate for those affected that, for more than five months after the incident, the government claimed to have kept itself busy in trying to find out the culprits responsible for the lathi charge on March 16 through a judicial inquiry. This gave the government sufficient excuse to put aside the genuine demands raised by the new leadership of the movement, which prompted the NFB to organize a fast unto death from August 1 to 5, 1980. Though not with the same fervor, this step was covered by various newspapers under headlines such as "Rungta's Condition Deteriorates" (*The Hindustan Times*: August 4, 1980), "Two more Blind Joined Fast" (*The Patriot*: August 4, 1980), "Ray of Hope for the Blind" (*The Statesman*: August 6, 1980). During these five days, of those who participated in the hunger strike, 60% were from these three schools (Sarin, personal interview, January 30, 2005). This movement was organized under the leadership of S.K. Rungta, an alumnus of the Model School.

The fast unto death is a legacy of Mahatma Gandhi (Gandhi, 1927) and has been used by various leaders, but in the case of a scattered minority such as the blind, it could not promote sympathy as had the lathi charge. The use of the hunger strike method did not prove to be a grand success except that it extracted a promise of fulfillment of the demands presented to the government as a part of this movement before the end of the year. However, use of this method introduced a new technique in the advocacy movement of the blind to pressure the government.

1981: The International Year for the Disabled Persons (IYDP)

This year started with a twenty-one day (January 1–21, 1981) movement led by the NFB (Sarin, personal interview, January 30, 2005). Apart from picketing and a token hunger strike (chain fast), courting arrests in front of the prime minister's residence became a daily activity as a part of the struggle. The movement was then called off as a result of the intervention of Mr. N.D. Tiwari, the then Union labor minister as he was known to the new leadership of NFB since late 1970s when some of the activists of NFB were in the Lucknow jail in the state of Uttar Pradesh. He and his colleagues in Uttar Pradesh were arrested in 1979 for their participation in the protest against the arrest of Mrs. Indira Gandhi (the former prime minister of India) during the regime of Janta government.

> Since some of us were also arrested due to indulgence in the advocacy movement of blind in the State of Uttar Pradesh and put in the Lucknow jail at the same time, we developed friendly relations with the other inmates like N.D. Tiwari who was a senior political leader during the regime of Mrs. Indira Gandhi. Tiwari used to call us "comrades" because of sharing of our time together in the jail. He promised us that our demands would be materialized within that year, but we were highly cheated as no follow up action was taken up in regard to our demands once the movement was called off based on the assurance from him. (V.P.S. Yadav, March 25, 2005)

Though the movement was called off on January 21, 1981 (Sarin, personal interview, January 30, 2005) without any substantial accomplishment in terms of any productive results, the indirect outcome of this movement was that it brought closer the blind community members who were dotted over the country in a scattered manner. This time too, the bulk of the participating activists in this movement came from the three schools discussed in this chapter. Though there were a number of populist programs by the government in the name of the IYDP, the movement of twenty-one days also set the pace of the government terms of thinking on the lines of implementing the quota in jobs and identification of jobs for this purpose. However, the representatives of the NBYA who supported this movement wholeheartedly separated themselves from NFB calling this movement "a great failure as its leaders could not find a satisfactory excuse to call off this movement and, thereby, it ditched the blind" (B.P. Yadav, April 17, 2005).

Analysis of the movement of January, 1981 reveals that both the schools situated in Delhi, the Andha Mahavidyalaya (located at Punchkuian Road) and the Government Boys Secondary School (located at Kingsway Camp), were used to provide shelter to the participants. The majority of the participants were from the colleges, but more than 95% (Sarin, personal communication, March 3, 2006) of the participants were the high school graduates or currents students of the residential schools for the blind. Most of them belonged to these three schools.

National Blind Youth Association

In addition to the movement carried out by NFB in the early 1980s, the NBYA was another strong advocacy organization that carried out different kinds of advocacy activities from time to time. As mentioned above, during the 1980s, some differences arose over calling off the movement of 1981 between the leadership of NBYA and NFB. It was the NBYA that organized picketing for a day on December 31, 1981, in front of the Ministry of Labor (B.P. Yadav, personal interview, April 17, 2005). In addition, a 158-daylong movement was organized from March to August, 1984 (B.P. Yadav, personal interview, April 17, 2005) with use of a variety of movement tactics. Yet as can happen with prolonged movements, it could not yield results proportionate to the effort put in. This movement also faded away with the hunger strike, but it could pave the way for the formulation of policy on scholarships that would be reviewed every three years, for blind students pursuing their education beyond high school. As pointed out earlier, leader of NBYA, Dr. Bharat Prasad Yadav, was an alumnus of Andha Mahavidyalaya and most of its activists were from the Government Senior Secondary School for the Blind Boys and the Hostel for College-Going Blind Students. Some similar movements led by the NBYA and NFB continued, but they were stopped for a longer period when a promise was made in the year 1987 to hold examinations by the Staff Selection Commission to launch a special recruitment drive to fill up the quota of jobs promised under the Executive Order of 1977 (Mani, 1988, pp. 183–185).

1995: Legislation

NFB kept a dialogue with the government going and kept itself busy pressuring the government with the twin agenda of the demand for the implementation of the Executive Order of 1977 and enactment of a comprehensive disability legislation ensuring the rights of the disabled, particularly the blind. For this purpose, NFB carried on with the movement utilizing various pressure tactics such as picketing, demonstration, rallies, and token or indefinite hunger strikes (with the exception of the movement of 1973). The NBYA's movement in the late 1970s and 1980s was more focused on the fulfillment of the demands for accommodations at the higher education level and the filling-up of the quota in jobs. Ultimately, the disability law titled, The Persons with Disabilities (Equal opportunities, Protection of Rights and Full Participation) Act (1995), was brought in the parliament during its dying hours and passed in November 1995 (Bhambhani, 2004, pp. 40–42). For some, this act was "a door to heaven" (Abidi, 1995 cited in Bhambhani, 2004) and for others, a chance to approach the judiciary in case of its nonimplementation (S.K. Rungta, personal interview,

April 4, 2005). However, it is important to point out that in the absence of participation of active beneficiaries in the process of drafting of the act, this act remains nothing more than an ethical statement.

CONCLUSION

Before concluding, it is important to mention that the participation of blind women in the advocacy movement in India has been very marginal. Bye and large, India is a male-dominant country (Ghai, 2003; Hans & Patri, 2003), so it is not surprising that the advocacy movement of blind in India, has remained for the most part dominated by blind men and there has been a very limited participation of women in the movement. There are a few schools for the blind girls in India including that in Delhi, but the exposure of these girls outside their schools is always very limited and hence, their participation in the movement has also been almost negligible (A. Mohit, June 19, 2005). Even in coeducation schools including the Government Model School in Dehradun, the participation of blind girls in the advocacy-related activities has been much marginalized (R.K. Sarin, January 30, 2005).

In conclusion, it can be said that the advocacy movement of the blind was started mainly with the establishment of the NFB, which was highly influenced and inspired by the philosophy of self-advocacy propagated by the NFB in the United States since 1940. At the infant stage, the NFB in India relied upon correspondence and casual pressure tactics to achieve its target. During this period, they were content with employment in the private sector with jobs such as packing, assembling, lathe machine operation and so on. However, with the advent of a newly educated group whose expectations were higher, the new generation of leadership changed the dimension of the movement by adopting pressure tactics in the form of rallies, picketing, demonstration, and so on.

According to the activists and the leadership, in most cases, the strength of the movement was derived from the participation of activists from the three schools discussed in this chapter. The involvement of these schools became possible due to the fact that such institutions provide a concentration of a large number of blind people. This also enabled the participants from distant areas to obtain shelter during the movement. The teachers of these schools also played a vital role, as the majority of them were blind. Moreover, it is the geographical affinity that made it possible for the residents of these schools to find the high officials within ready reach and influence them through various means. These schools remained the focal point for the higher studies of blind students in northern India. The students who joined these schools also influenced others with their new ideas that they imbibed from their environment.

REFERENCES

All round condemnation of lathi charge: Inquiry judge named, S.H.O suspended. (1980, March 18). *Patriot*, p. 5.
Abidi, J. (2004)."No Pity." *Health for the Millions* (November–December 1995) In Bhambhani, M. *From charity to self-advocacy: The emergence of disability rights*. Unpublished master's thesis, University of Illinois at Chicago.
Baquer, A. (1994). *Disabled, disablement, disablism*. New Delhi, India: VHAI.
Baquer, A., & Sharma, A. (1997). *Disability: Challenges vs. responses*. New Delhi, India: Concerned Action Now.
Barnartt, S., & Scotch, R. (2001). *Disability protests: Contentious politics 1970–1999*. Washington, DC: Gallaudet University.
Bhambhani, M. (2004). *From charity to self-advocacy: The emergence of disability rights movement in India*. Unpublished master's thesis, University of Illinois at Chicago.
Blind children revolt. (1967, March 25). *Doon Darpan*, p. A12.
Brutal congress administration lathi charges the blind. (March 17, 1980). *Lokvani*, p. 27.
Campbell, J., & Oliver, M. (1996). *Disability politics: Understanding our past, changing our future*. London, New York: Routledge.
Charlton, J.I. (1998). *Nothing about us without us: Disability, oppression and Empowerment*. Berkeley: University of California Press.
Chaturvedi, T.N. (Ed.). (1981). *Administration for the disabled:Policy and organizational issues*. New Delhi: Indian Institute of Public Administration.
Criticism of lathi charge on blind everywhere. (1980, March 17). *Jansatta*, pp. 2, 6.
Davis, L.J. (2002). *Bending over backwards: Disability, dismodernism, and other difficult positions*. New York, London: New York University press.
Gandhi, M.K. (1927). *An autobiography: The story of my experiments with truth*. Ahmedabad, India: Navajivan Publishing House.
Ghai, A. (2003). *Embodied form: Issues of disabled women*. New Delhi, India: Shakti Publications.
Hans, A., & Patri, A. (Eds.). (2003). *Women, disability, and identity*. New Delhi, India: Sage Publications.
Jernigan, K. (1999). *The master, the mission, the movement*. Retrieved on November 15, 2005 from http://www.nfb.org/books/books1/kjbook.htm. Baltimore MD: NFB.
Kitchlu, T.N. (Ed.). (1991). *A century of blind welfare in India*. Delhi, India: Penman Publishers.
Linton, S. (1998). *Claiming disability: Knowledge and identity*. New York: New York University Press.
Mani, D.R. (1988). *The physically handicapped in India: Policy and programmes*. Delhi, India: Ashish Publishing House.
Matson, F. (1990). *Walking alone and marching together*. Baltimore, MD: NFB.
Oliver, M. (1990). *The politics of disablement*. London: Macmillan Press.
Oliver, M. (1996). *Understanding disability: From theory to practice*. New York: Palgrave.
Pandey, R.S., & Advani, L. (1995). *Perspectives on disability and rehabilitation*. Delhi, India: Vikas Publishing House.
Procession of blind lathi charged. (1980, March 17). *Indian Express*, p. 1.
Ray of hope for the blind. (1980, August 6). *Statesman*, p. 2.
Rudolph, R.I., & Rudolph, S.H. (1987). *In pursuit of Lakshmi: The political economy of the Indian state*. London, England: University of Chicago Press.
Rungta's condition deteriorates. (1980, August 4). *Hindustan Times*, p. 1.

Russell, M. (1998). *Beyond ramps: Disability at the end of the social contract.* Monroe, ME: Common Courage Press.

Sanyal, S.C., & Giri, P.K. (1984). *Education and employment of the blind.* Narendrapur, India: South Asian Publishers/UNESCO.

Scotch, R.K. (1984). *From good will to civil rights: Transforming federal disability policy.* Philadelphia, PA: Temple University Press.

Shapiro, J.P. (1993). *No pity: People with disabilities forging a new Civil Rights Movement.* New York: Times Books (Random House).

Two more blind joined fast. (1980, August 4). *Patriot*, p. 2.

Vanaik, A. (1990). *The painful transition: Bourgeois democracy in India.* New York: Verso.

CHAPTER THIRTEEN

Politics, Inclusion, AND Disabled Children: The Colombian Context

MARISOL MORENO ANGARITA AND SUSAN L. GABEL

The Republic of Colombia is a small country of 42,889 million people (DANE, 2005) situated in northern South America on the North Pacific coast bordering the Caribbean Sea between Ecuador and Panama. As does much of South America, it faces significant environmental issues—deforestation, soil and water quality damage, urban air pollution and so on—that are not only difficult to address but that affect the country's ability to funnel resources into education and other social support systems. In addition to environmental dilemmas, Colombia struggles to meet its economic challenges. Unemployment is high and 64% of the population is below the poverty line, yet 93% of the adult population is literate, indicating a degree of success within the educational system (World Bank, 2006).

Bogotá, the capital and the locale of this study, is in the center of the country and is Colombia's largest city with almost 8 million inhabitants. It faces most of the challenges of any large urban center, including the difficulties of managing an educational system in a densely populated city, and attempts to meet the educational needs of the wealthy, the middle class, and the poorest squatters living in the poorest areas of the city.

The aim of this chapter is to describe the current situation for inclusion in Bogotá and to situate it within its legislative context. We address three things in this chapter: the current legislative priorities, the social and educational stalemates that remain unresponsive to legislative priorities, and recommendations for the future.

In this chapter we use the terms inclusion to refer to the participation of disabled children in public education whether or not it is segregated education. We use integration and mainstreaming to refer to situations in which disabled children are in general education schools regardless of whether they are in general education classrooms. This is consistent with its usage in Colombia.

DISABILITY IN COLOMBIA: LEGISLATIVE ADVANCES, PRACTICAL STALEMATES

Although disability is an integral part of our world and a fundamental aspect of the human condition, Colombians have yet to fully understand it as such. Throughout the history of Colombia, disabled people have lived through periods where they have been hidden from society, shamed, rejected, and discriminated against. Disabled people in Colombia experience deep social, political, and ethical displacement. Even today, disability is very rarely a topic of public debate within the broader Colombian society, even though it has been in other countries (Abberley, 1987; Batavia, 2001; Cuervo, 2005; Dejong, Palsbo, Beatty, Jones, et. al., 2002; Lollar, 2002; Longmore, 2001). The study of disability's social contexts within academia is just beginning (Moreno, 2005).

Colombian Constitution and Education Law 115

Colombia has been aware of the international disability rights movement for some time. During the last few decades, various policies have been developed around civil rights, some of which have been influenced by the international context and multilateral organizations such as Rehabilitation International, the Pan American Health Organization, and the World Health Organization (WHO). In light of the international sociopolitical climate's influence on governmental approaches to disability, it is important to consider how this influence plays out in Colombian society, particularly as society is reflected in educational institutions (Moreno, 2003). The 1990s were particularly important years for disability rights legislation in Colombia. For example, the right to education for all children is enshrined in the Colombian Constitution (Republic of Colombia, 1991). The inclusion of disabled children into public education has been legislated since 1994, under Law 115 (Congreso de la República de Colombia, 1994) that establishes nondiscrimination on the basis of impairment in any public or private educational institution, including postsecondary institutions. However, Law 115 has always been applied intermittently, according to a variety of factors including local school preferences, available resources, and resource allocation decisions. While the human rights community has long pushed for an inclusive education model to be implemented, Colombian educational institutions have not always cooperated. Paradoxically, while all children are thought to have the right to education and there is a push for universal education for all school-age children, the conditions to ensure this right do not exist (Azula, 2005; Díaz y Fernández, 2005). For example Law 115 remains an unfunded mandate that leaves local schools to decide whether they have the resources needed to educate disabled students. Many of the sectors involved have made considerable efforts to change this situation but there are many roadblocks against change, including lack of information, misinformation, bureaucracy, inaccessible buildings, and the persistent problem of resources.

In addition to the Colombian Constitution of 1991 and Education Law 115 in 1994, Law 100 in 1993 (Congress of Colombia, 1993), established a pluralistic public health approach with a slogan of "Health for Everyone." Law 324 (Congress of Colombia, 1996) guarantees that the State will provide economic, logistic, and infrastructural means to assure that the deaf community has access to local and nationwide television to provide a wide reach to the community's programs, culture, and interests. This was important for the deaf community since without this law, deaf people did not have the access to public information services needed to remain informed citizens. Law 361 of 1997 (Congress of Colombia, 1997), The Act for People with Disability establishes "mechanisms ... for the social integration of disabled people" and places emphasis on the fundamental rights of disabled people.

The constitution established the legal framework for the rights of disabled people, as well as the obligations of the state and society in general toward this population. In articles 13, 47, 54, and 68 these obligations are expressed as care, protection, support, and social integration for disabled people. In addition, a series of fundamental social, economic, and cultural rights are defined—which owing to their universal nature automatically include disabled people (articles 25, 48, 49, 52, 67 and 70).

Subsequent Legislative Developments

There have been subsequent developments related to the constitutional mandate, including Decree 2082 (Presidencia de la República de Colombia, 1992) regulating how education must be provided to people with impairments or those with exceptional talents. State responsibilities and obligations are identified throughout all levels and institutions, ostensibly to assure that disabled people can achieve complete social integration (Consejería Presidencial para la Política Social, 2002). For this reason, education, rehabilitation, employment, integration, social welfare, and access are legislative priorities even if they have not trickled down to be the priorities of practitioners (Cuervo, Trujillo, & de Villate, 1998).

In May 2001, Law 762 (Congress of the Republic of Colombia, 2001) was passed, approving the Inter-American Convention for the Elimination of All Forms of Discrimination against Persons with Disabilities, which had been adopted in Guatemala City on 7 June 1999. Its goal is to "prevent and eliminate all forms of discrimination against people with disabilities and promote their full integration into society" (Convención Interamericana, 1999, 7). This law calls for states to adopt legislative, social, educational, labor, and any other relevant measures that allow them to fulfill the objectives proposed by the convention.

More recently, the CONPES 80 document of 26 July 2004 (CONPES, 2004) approved the public policy on disability and made commitments for its implementation, as part of the National Development Plan (NDP) 2002–2006, entitled, "Towards a Community State" (Velez, 2003). This document proposes strategies for policy development with the participation of state institutions, various governing bodies, civil society, and private citizens. This public policy is concentrated around three components: prevention of impairment and promotion of public health, access to rehabilitation, and provision of employment and social support networks modeled on World Bank recommendations, particularly the United Nations Convention on the Rights of Persons with Disabilities (2006).

This effort has certainly led to significant advances in the legislative field, including more concern about educational, health, as well as social and labor needs of the disabled population. However, there has been insufficient implementation. Consequently, the anticipated outcomes have not been achieved (Parra, 2005). The NDP has been monitored by the National Consultative Committee on Disability and Civil Society, a group formed from alliances between organizations of and for disabled people. The committee's final evaluation reads as a warning. It describes carelessness during regulatory processes, disintegration among the different sectors while responding to the population's needs, dispersed efforts, scarce resources, lack of information within the disabled population about their rights, insufficient training for those responsible for implementing the processes, low impact, insufficient information in decision-making processes, and the inoperative state of the Consultative Committee on Disability deriving from state negligence (Dissnett, 2003a, 2003b, 2003c, 2004).

Lack of Cohesive Networks

While it is true that there are enough existing regulations to indicate governmental support of educational inclusion, there are no available resources for enactment. The situation is even more critical due to the lack of coordination between the health, education, and social welfare sectors, none of which have begun to work efficiently together as a team, with goals, plans, and medium or long-term projects related to social inclusion. The rights of children and their families—to healthcare, education, social inclusion, and social welfare—are seriously affected by this lack of cohesion at the national, regional, and city levels. Even though the District and Local Councils on Disability have made some progress in terms of social organization and participation, the results are yet to be seen, given the magnitude of the problem (Cedeño, 2001; *Secretaría Distrital de Salud de Bogotá*, 2001, 2004a, 2004b, 2005; Càrdenas, 2003).

Inclusion for Disabled Students

In a recent study financed by the district secretary for education, Flórez and Moreno (2006) found that the main obstacle to the social development of school-age children is the lack of coordination between the health, education, and social welfare services. Education Law 115 demands the inclusion of these young people in mainstream education. Yet disabled children have not received the services due to them for a number of reasons. Of primary concern is that disabled children are not attending mainstream schools and if they did attend, the schools are not equipped for their needs. (Mejía Royet, 2003, 2004, 2005).

Barriers to inclusion

Colombian researchers have identified the barriers to inclusion. These include bureaucratic roadblocks and confusing red tape, lack of teacher preparation for integration, poor understanding of learning difficulties and strategies for teaching, and inaccessible physical environments in schools (Díaz, 2002; Flórez & Moreno, 2006). Yet the Colombian government has not acted on their recommendations. This lack of governmental attention to the recommendations by researchers could be explained by a number of professional, social, cultural, and economic factors. First, there are no integrated networks within the state structure to deal with the population's needs. As a result, each individual family has to negotiate its way unaided through the considerable bureaucratic processes involved—including applications, examinations, and consultancies. This leads to untimely or insufficient results that are unlikely to improve quality of life for the student or the family. These kinds of bureaucratic barriers have been persistently reported in international studies of other developing countries (Beazley & Moore, 1995; Fain, 1998; Hurst, 1999a, 1999b; Jeffrey, 1999; Kastan, 2000; Majumder & Cuervo, 2003).

Second, when a family is successful in gaining access to a mainstream school, attendance at the school presents another challenge owing to lack of sufficient teacher preparation, even ten years after the constitution promoted integration (Flórez &

Moreno, 2006). The Network of Teachers for Integration (REDMAIN, 2005) in Bogotá, has highlighted serious concerns about the obstacles against social integration. On the one hand, there is insufficient training available for teachers to be able to confront the pedagogical challenges involved in teaching children with autism, mental disability, deafness, blindness, multiple disabilities, emotional problems, or mental disorders. On the other hand, there is insufficient support for families to deal with the demands of a disabled student, amid contexts of abandonment, poverty, abuse, neglect, and ignorance. When these problems are added to the challenges mentioned earlier, the entire community is unprepared for the process.

Third, it is important to highlight that learning difficulties are not recognized as learning disabilities nor have learning disabilities been addressed in educational policy. This has prevented children with significant learning difficulties from obtaining any kind of specialist support. This often leaves many children to struggle without the child, family, or school understanding what can be done about it.

Fourth, physical barriers often impede access to the very buildings in which education, health, and welfare services are located. Even if physically disabled children are able to gain permission to attend mainstream schools, it is unlikely that they would be able to get into the buildings.

Demographics of inclusion in Bogotá

Demographic data vary depending on which source is used. To make sense of the conflicting data sources, it is necessary to deduce what is most likely the case based on numerous sources. The 1993 census indicated that the number of disabled people in the country was 593,618 (DANE, 2003). This would have been 1.8% of the population, a figure vastly less than the 12% estimated by the WHO. WHO estimates bring the 1993 total to 5,280,000 (WHO, n.d.) and yet until recently, governmental policy was driven by the 1993 DANE figures, creating a situation in which the need for resources was greatly underestimated. The 2005 census (DANE, 2005) moved figures a little closer to WHO estimates by indicating that 2% to 6% of the population is disabled. This lack of reliable data has had drastic consequences for disabled children of school age because for many years their participation in school has been overestimated.

Colombian officials rest on the above confusing figures that show that educational coverage has risen in recent years. However, those figures ignore the plight of disabled school-age children. Ten years after the passage of Law 115, levels of attendance vary significantly throughout the educational life span of disabled students and decline markedly as disabled children age (see Table 13.1).

Table 13.1. Percentage of disabled children attending school by age group (national).

Age group	Percentage attending	Percentage not attending
3–4 years	63.6	38.4
4–9 years	67.5	32.5
10–14 years	39.1	60.9
15–19 years	14.0	86.0
20–24 years	19.3	80.7

Source: DANE (2006).

The Center for International Rehabilitation (CIR) (2007) figures are most discouraging and call into question the DANE figures in Table 13.1.

> Of 11,781,161 students in the Colombian educational system, 38,000 are students with some kind of disability. Conservative estimates suggest that 450,000 children with disabilities may be excluded from the educational system. (CIR, 2007, Section 5.2)

In contrast to the figures for disabled children, the World Bank (2007) estimates that 98.5% of the Colombians complete primary education and that the school life expectancy averages 13.1 years, which is the equivalent of a middle school education in the United States (World Bank, 2007). It is unclear whether the World Bank data include disabled children but it seems unlikely considering the data from other sources.

The data on the type of schools attended by disabled children are as confusing as the data on population size. However, Flórez and Moreno (2006) argue that the case of Bogotá is representative of the national situation. Their research indicates that there are 8 million inhabitants in the city, 350,000 disabled people (approximately 5.5% of city population), 2,700 state schools, 58 mainstream schools, and 3,500 children (approximately 1% of disabled people) who attend these schools. Yet the departmental health secretary and the Javeriana Unviersity (2001) estimate that across the country 30,000 disabled children attend elementary schools and 8,000 attend high schools. Since Bogotà is by far the largest city in the country, one would expect to find more than 3,500 disabled children attending school in the city and one would definitely expect to find more than 1% of disabled people to be children.

In addition to the questions that arise from the poor statistical data and low percentage of disabled children attending any kind of school, several other core questions stand out. To what extent are disabled children in school in inclusive or segregated settings? The Departmental Health secretary and Javeriana

University (2001) figures indicate that 80% of disabled children attending school are in inclusive settings and 20% are in segregated classrooms in regular schools. This does not cohere with what Florez and Moreno, (2006) found at all. Are these conflicting data part of the conversation in social policy planning; does the government even recognize that there are disparate data sets? Meanwhile, the National Education Ministry has made advances in the design of regulations for educational integration (District Council on Disability, 2004), the Local Committee on Disability has progressed on the subject (National Ministry of Education, 2002; Bogotá Health Secretary, 2004) and the *Saldarriaga Concha* Foundation is developing a project around these issues (*Saldarriaga Concha* Foundation, 2005). These combined plans are based on concern for public welfare including fights against hunger, poverty, and exclusion from society.

CONCLUSION

This chapter emphasizes the political context within which inclusion must be understood in Colombia. As a society, Colombia needs to deeply analyze the disconnect between its constitutional values and legislative commitments on one hand and the practical world of schooling from which disabled children are excluded in surprising numbers, on the other hand. Policymakers proclaim that they are following recommendations set by the World Bank's promotion of educational inclusion for all. Yet they seem to ignore or minimize the conditions under which public policy is found to be inadequate. What was meant to be a great leap forward in favor of students with special educational needs—Law 115 in particular—has become a severe example of the lack of preparation and lack of recognition of the complexities of large scale educational reform, particularly when that reform is based on insufficient data. The situation in Bogotá demonstrates that Colombia has a great deal of work to do to align educational policy, practice, and resource allocation with legislative edicts.

REFERENCES

Abberley, P. (1987). The concept of oppression and the development of a social theory of disability. *Disability, Handicap and Society, 2* (1), 5–19.

Azula, W. (2005). Perspectivas para las personas en situación de discapacidad. In C. Cuervo, C. (Ed.), *Discapacidad e inclusión social: reflexiones desde la Universidad Nacional de Colombia,* pp. 49–60. Maestría en Discapacidad e Inclusión Social. Bogotá: Colombia.

Batavia, A. I. (2001). The new paternalism: Portraying people with disabilities as an oppressed minority. *Journal of Disability Policy Studies, 12* (2), 107.

Beazley, S. and Moore, M. (1995). *Deaf children, their families and professionals.* London: David Fulton.
Bogotà Health Secretary. (2004). Sistematizaciòn de la experiencia de la rehabilitación basada en la comunidad. Organizaciòn Panamericana de la Salud. Bogotá: Colombia.
Cárdenas, S. (2003). Fundación Saldarriaga Concha: 30 años apoyando a los que ayudan. *Fundamentos., Edición Especial.*
Cedeño, F. (2001). *Lineamientos para la integración educativa en Bogotá.* Bogotá, Secretaría de Educación Distrital.
Center for International Rehabilitation. (2007). Colombia: 2004 IDRM Country Report. Cited on IDEAnet and retrieved June 30, 2007 from http://www.ideanet.org/content.cfm?id=5359.
Congress of the Republic of Columbia. (1993). Law 100. Por la cual se crea el sistema de seguridad social integreal y se dictan otras disposiciones. Bogotá, Colombia.
Congress of the Republic of Colombia. (1994). Law 115 on General Education. Bogotá, Colombia.
Congress of the Republic of Colombia. (1994). Law 115. Bogotá, Colombia.
Congress of the Republic of Colombia. (1996). Law 324. Por la cual se crean algunas normas a favor de la población sorda. Bogotá, Colombia.
Congress of the Republic of Colombia. (1997). Law 361. Bogotá, Colombia.
Congress of the Republic of Colombia. (1997). Law 361. Establishment of mechanisms of social integration for people with disabilities. Bogotà, Colombia.
Congress of the Republic of Colombia. (2001). Law 762. Bogotá: Colombia.
CONPES. (2004). Consejo Nacional de Política Económica y Social República de Colombia. Departamento Nacional de Planeación. Política Pública Nacional de Discapacidad. Bogotá: Colombia.
Consejería Presidencial para la Política Social. (2002). Proyecto piloto para la construcción de la política Pública en Discapacidad. Corporación Andina de Fomento. Bogotá: Colombia.
Convención Interamericana. (1999). Convención Interamericana para la Eliminación de todas las Formas de Discriminación contra las Personas con Discapacidad. Guatemala.
Cuervo, C. (Ed.). (2005). *Discapacidad e inclusión social: reflexiones desde la Universidad Nacional de Colombia.* Maestría en Discapacidad e Inclusión Social. Bogotá: Colombia.
Cuervo, C., Trujillo, A., & de Villate, Martha. (1998). *Factores que determinan el impacto de los servicios de rehabilitación fisioterapéutica, ocupacional y fonoaudiológica en las instituciones de la Secretaría Distrital de Salud de Santa Fe de Bogotá. Informe final.* Bogotá: Secretaría Distrital de Salud. Universidad Nacional de Colombia.
DANE. (2003). Departamento Nacional de Estadísticas. Censo Nacional. DANE. *Propuesta para la captación de información sobre discapacidad.* Encuentro interinstitucional. Censos de población y vivienda 2003. Población con discapacidad. Bogotá, Colombia.
DANE. (2005). Departamento Administrativo Nacional de estadistica. Censo 2005. Bogotá, Colombia.
DANE. (2006). *Estudio de registro y caracterización de la población discapacitada en Bogotá, D.C. Informe de avance.* Bogotá, Colombia.
DeJong, G., Palsbo, S. E., Beatty, P. W., Jones, G. C., Kroll, T., & Neri, M. T. (2002). The organization and financing of health services for persons with disabilities. *Milbank Quarterly, 80* (2), 261.
Departmental Health Secretary and Javeriana University. (2001). Prevalencia de discapacidad en el valle del Cauca [Disability Prevalence in the Cauca Valley].
Díaz, O. C. (2002). Lineamientos curriculares para la atención a personas en situación de Discapacidad. Ministerio de Educación Nacional. Documento de trabajo. Bogotá, Colombia.
Díaz, O. C., y Fernández, A. (2005). Problematización sobre las concepciones vigentes en la educación de las personas en situación de discapacidad. In Cuervo y otros.(Ed.), *Discapacidad e inclusión*

social: reflexiones desde la Universidad Nacional de Colombia. Bogotá, Maestría en Discapacidad e Inclusión Social.
Dissnett. (2003a). *Boletín electrónico.* Issue 915.
Dissnett. (2003b). *Boletín electrónico.* Issue 927.
Dissnett. (2003c). *Boletín electrónico.* Issue 944.
Dissnett. (2004). *Boletín electrónico.* Issue 950.
District Council on Disability. (2004). Agreement 137. Establishment of a district system for integrating people with disabilities in Bogotà. Bogotà, Colombia.
Fain, G. S. (1998). Special education: Justice, tolerance, and beneficence as duty. *Journal of Education, 180* (2), 41.
Flórez, R., & Moreno, M. (2006). *Currículo flexible: Adecuaciones curriculares para estudiantes en situación de discapacidad.* En: Aprender desde la Diferencia. Bogotá, Editorial Magisterio. Secretaría de Educación Distrital.
Hurst, A. (1999a). Deaf and disabled or deafness disabled? Towards a human rights perspective. *Disability & Society, 14* (1), 146.
Hurst, A. (1999b). The Dearing report and students with disabilities and learning difficulties. *Disability & Society, 14* (1), 65.
Jeffrey, K. (1999). Incentives for the identification and treatment of children with disabilities: The supplemental security income program. *Journal of Publics Economics, 73* (2), 187–216.
Kastan, J. (2000). School-based mental health program development: A case study of interorganizational collaboration. *Journal of Health Politics, Policy and Law, 25* (5), 845–864.
Lollar, D. J. (2002). Public health and disability: Emerging opportunities. *Public Health Reports, 117* (2), 131.
Longmore, P. (2001). *The new disability history. American perspectives.* Chicago: New York University Press.
Majumder, R., y Cuervo, C. (2003). In M. Moreno (Ed.), *Inclusión social de las personas con discapacidad: realidades, reflexiones y retos.* Bogotá. Instituto del Desempeño Humano y la Discapacidad-Maestría en Discapacidad e Inclusión Social, Universidad Nacional de Colombia.
Mejía Royet, H. (2003). Conferencia sobre Inclusiòn Social de las personas con discapacidad. Retos, experiencias y realidades. Universidad Nacional de Colombia. Instituto del Desempeño Humano y la discapacidad. Bogotà, Colombia.
Mejía Royet, H. (2004). Foro Pensar la Discapacidad. Consejo Nacional de Planeación. Bogotá, Colombia.
Mejía Royet, H. (2005). Encuentro de evaluación de la política pública en discapacidad. Ministerio de la protección Social. Bogotá, Colombia.
Moreno, M. (2003). *Universidad accesible* (Documento inédito). Bogotá. Instituto del Desempeño Humano y la Discapacidad. Facultad de Medicina. Universidad Nacional de Colombia. Bogotà, Colombia.
Moreno, M. (2005). Medios y discapacidad. *In Cuervo y otros.* (Ed.), *Discapacidad e inclusión social: reflexiones desde la Universidad Nacional de Colombia.* Bogotá. Maestría en Discapacidad e Inclusión Social. Universidad Nacional de Colombia.
National Ministry of Education. (2002). Concepción de la atención educativa de las personas con discapacidad. Documento de trabajo. Bogotá: Colombia.
Parra, O. (2005). Perspectivas respecto al derecho de la discapacidad en Colombia. Foro sobre Medios de Comunicación e Inclusión Social. Universidad de la Sabana-Ministerio de Comunicaciones.
Presidencia de la República de Colombia. (1992). Decree 2082. Bogotá, Colombia.
REDMAIN. (2005). Red de Maestros integradores de Bogotà. Bogotà, Colombia.

Republic of Colombia. (1991). *Constitution of the Republic of Colombia.* Bogotà: Secretary General, National Assembly. Retrieved June 2, 2007 from http://pdba.georgetown.edu/constitutions/colombia/colombia.html.

Saldarriaga Concha Foundation. (2005). *Estudio nacional de necesidades, oferta y demanda de servicios de rehabilitación. Colombia. Informe final. Primera Parte.* Bogotá, Fundación Saldarriaga Concha.

Secretaría de Salud Distrital. (2001). *Lineamientos para una política en discapacidad. Comité Intersectorial del Componente de Prevención y Promoción Habilitación-Rehabilitación.* Bogotá, Secretaría Distrital de Salud.

Secretaría de Salud Distrital. (2004a). *Lineamientos de atención en salud para la población discapacitada.* Bogotá, Secretaría Distrital de Salud.

Secretaría de Salud Distrital. (2004b). *Política para la atención a la población en situación de discapacidad. Documento.* Bogotá, Secretaría de Salud Distrital.

Secretaría de Salud Distrital. (2005). *Política pública en salud, niñez e infancia. Plan de Desarrollo Bogotá sin Indiferencia.* Bogotá, Secretaría de Salud Distrital.

United Nations. (2006). Convention on the rights of persons with disabilities. Retrieved June 19, 2007 from http://www.un.org/disabilities/convention/conventionfull.shtml.

Velez, A. U. (2003). Departamento Nacional de Planeación. (2003). Plan Nacional de Desarrollo 2002–2006. Hacia un estado comunitario. Bogotá, Colombia.

World Bank. (2006). Colombia at a glance. Retrieved June 2, 2007 from http://devdata.worldbank.org/AAG/col_aag.pdf.

World Bank. (2007). Summary education profile: Colombia. Retrieved June 2, 2007 from http://devdata.worldbank.org/edstats/SummaryEducationProfiles/CountryData/GetShowData.asp?sCtry=COL,Colombia.

World Health Organization. (n.d.). Resultado de la revision de deversos documentos sobre Prevalencia de la discapacidad elaborados por los paises, 1997–2000. [Revised results of the prevalence of disabilities by country 1997–2000], Retrieved from http://www.ops.org.ni/opsnic/tematicas/rehabilita/resumen_americas. htm#cifras_discapacidad.

CHAPTER FOURTEEN

Inclusive Education AND School Choice: Democratic Rights IN A Devolved System

LIZ GORDON AND MISSY MORTON

In New Zealand, the policies and practices that provide for the inclusion of students with disabilities have developed concomitantly with the framework of a devolved, competitive, and managerialist system of individual school choice and local governance (Cochran-Smith, 2005). Central policies and practices supporting inclusion are channelled through each school in complex and contradictory ways. The desire for inclusion, based on social justice and group democracy, is constantly at odds with the promotion of individual rights, competition, and the best learning environment for each child.

John Goodlad (2005) argues that public schooling has at least four enduring purposes:

1. Preparing students to be active, involved participants in democracy;
2. Preparing students to have access to knowledge and critical thinking within the disciplines;
3. Preparing students to lead rich and rewarding personal lives, and to be responsible and responsive community members; and
4. Preparing students to assume their highest possible place in the economy. (Goodlad, 2005, p. xviii).

One of the most enduring criticisms of public schools is that certain groups, people of colour, people with disabilities, poor and working-class children, for example, have been excluded from democratic education ideals (Ball & Gewirtz, 1996; Bauknight, 1998; Pearce & Gordon, 2005; Slee, 2001). Indeed, O'Hanlon puts the issue baldly: "[S]chooling never was intended to educate the majority of pupils" (O'Hanlon, 2003, p. 9).

The failure of "universal education" to effectively educate all citizens opened the door for the emergence of alternative models of schooling. For the past fifteen to twenty years, many nations have implemented aspects of a school reform agenda, which has its genesis in neoliberal economics. Key tenets of neoliberal economics include education being seen as a personal gain (rather than a public good). Education is thus a commodity in the market place, to be bought and sold. The education system is seen as but one form of delivery of this product. There is a concomitant focus on inputs (including direct and indirect costs), outputs (such as student achievement data and qualifications), and accountability (Gordon, 2003). These characteristics potentially stand in stark contrast to the aims described by Goodlad (2005). Further, the basis of the neoliberal reforms has been a significant rejection of public education:

> According to conservatives, the main problem with public schools is that they are public—they are managed by government bureaucracies and staffed by unionised, tenured and largely unaccountable teachers. (Carnoy, 1995, p. 29).

In practice, however, the radical agenda for change advocated by neoliberal critics, such as across-the-board voucher schemes or the abandonment of public provision in favour of priviatisation (Friedman, 1962), has not been fully realised. Instead, reforms based on elements of "school choice" have been adopted in many countries, in a variety of forms. Such models claim to "fix" the problems of ineffective public schooling systems through a variety of mechanisms. Martin Carnoy (1998) outlines five neoliberal claims that, he says, require careful scrutiny:

> The first is that school choice increases the total welfare of families who send their children to school. The second is that social costs from increasing choice through privatising public education are minimal. The third is that privately managed education is inherently more effective and cost-effective in producing learning. The fourth is that public schools competing for pupils with private and other public schools will become more effective. And the fifth is that a privatised and competitive education system is more likely to improve social mobility for the children of low-income families. (Carnoy, 1998, p. 310)

At the heart of the school choice movement is the notion that the mechanism of choice will allow parents to get the kind of education they desire for their children, forcing schools either to improve their services or suffer failure (Boyd, 2002; Goldhaber & Eide, 2002). On the face of it, this mechanism has a lot to offer families with disabled children. The promise of choice is that disadvantaged groups, in particular, are provided with the leverage to effect quality services for their children. However, there is now widespread evidence that school choice systems do not provide a measurable overall improvement in school achievement (Lauder et al., 1994; Lubienski, 2003). Evidence on the effectiveness for specific groups, such as children with disabilities, is equivocal (Estes, 2004; Goldhaber & Eide, 2002).

This chapter explores school choice in New Zealand, but with reference to international research and policy. The key question is: Does the policy of school choice offer improved educational opportunities for children with disabilities? In particular, do such systems foster inclusive education (Kearney & Kane, 2006)? While apparently a simple question, there are numerous difficulties in providing an effective answer. The difficulties that will be explored here include policy as rhetoric, who is making choices and, what we have called "slippage."

THE POLICY OF SCHOOL CHOICE IN NEW ZEALAND

Before the 1984 political reforms in New Zealand, responsibility for most of the administration of schools was held centrally in the New Zealand Department of Education. The department employed school inspectors, who had responsibility for inspecting primary and secondary teachers in their classrooms and grading them. The inspectors also had subject responsibilities, including organising (but not necessarily providing) professional development for teachers. The twelve Regional Boards of Education were elected once in three years, and were responsible for the administration of the primary school system, including managing budgets, maintenance, resources, and the appointment of teaching staff and principals. Secondary schools each had their own elected boards of governors with responsibility for managing budgets, maintenance, resources, and the appointment of teaching staff and principals (Rentoul & Rosanowski, 2000).

Keith Ballard describes clearly how post-1984 political reform in New Zealand brought about a more unequal, unfair, and unjust society, the values most opposed to inclusion (Ballard, 2003). Key elements of successive neoliberal governments were cuts in services, tax cuts, the privatisation of services, a shift from universal to targeted entitlements, a competitive environment, and the promotion of individual choice.

The major reform of the schooling system took place in 1989 and was enshrined in the Education Act of that year (New Zealand Education Act, 1989).

Key elements included a devolution of governance and responsibility for running schools to the level of the individual school, the removal of or reduction in intermediary (regional and support) services and a shift in central government from direct control to "steering at a distance" (Gordon, 2003; Kearney & Kane, 2006; Wills, 2006). Whereas secondary schools had already had at least some experience of local management, for primary schools, this shift was more significant.

While, under the new system, schools had significant freedoms devolved to them, from the beginning, these were mitigated both by the legislative framework (e.g., all children were entitled to enrol at their local school at the age of six, and to attend school until they were fifteen) and also by a range of other requirements. This is summarised by Wylie (2003)

> Each school is governed by its own board of trustees, which includes 5 parent representatives elected by the school's current parents, the principal, a staff representative elected by school staff, and a student representative in secondary schools. The board of trustees appoints and employs the school principal and school staff, though in most schools the principal is the effective employer. Schools' government funding is largely based on student roll numbers, with weightings for socioeconomic disadvantage, remoteness, and small size. Teaching staff numbers are decided by student roll numbers, with central government covering actual staff salaries. Schools operate within a national framework of administrative and curriculum guidelines, must supply annual audited accounts, and are inspected by the Education Review Office (ERO) every 3 years, or more often if the reviews identify areas in need of attention. (p. 1)

For example, the National Education Guidelines required schools to analyse barriers to learning and seek ways to overcome these. School charters were required to be developed, and an early concern of schools was that 80% of the content, including a requirement for the school to seek equitable outcomes for all learners, was pre-written by the Ministry of Education (Codd & Gordon, 1991). New Zealand has had a national curriculum for many years, and the rewritten framework in 1993 required schools to identify and respond to the educational needs of all children (Millar & Morton, 2007; Mitchell, 1999).

However, this appearance of inclusiveness was not accompanied by any attempt to require schools to develop robust frameworks to achieve it. The new "audit and review" framework that replaced school inspections operated primarily as a checklist approach to compliance with legal requirements to create mission statements, departmental policies and manuals. This had no real engagement with school philosophy, or inclusive practice, and was based on a particular form of managerialist philosophy (Thrupp & Smith, 1999). This approach focussed on ensuring that schools delivered the curriculum properly, met their contractual requirements to the state, had good financial systems in place, and developed and implemented school policies as required. It did not, and could not, measure the pursuit of inclusive practices in schools or post-school, the development of students as good citizens within a democratic community, or the goals of equity. The policy-practice gap, mentioned frequently in the literature (Mittler, 2002; Reynolds, 2001; Timmons, 2002; Vlachou, 2004), was further widened by the devolution project. The purposes of education identified by Goodlad (2005) and described above were also made that much less attainable.

The devolved system forced schools to compete with one another for students. While, under the old system, students largely went to their local school (in theory at least), in the new system parents were encouraged to "choose" the school that they considered best for their child. This led to a rush of enrolments in schools in high socio-economic areas, as parents fought to enrol children in schools based on their social aspirations for their child (Copeland et al., 2002). Throughout most of the 1990s, schools with full rolls were allowed to select students on any basis they chose, subject to anti-discriminatory legislation such as the Human Rights Act (1993, 2001) and the Bill of Rights Act (1990). These acts spelled out education as one of the areas of public life to which unlawful grounds of discrimination applied. They specified personal characteristics, including disability, as prohibited grounds of discrimination. Unfortunately, no one checked the grounds on which schools turned down enrolments (Pearce & Gordon, 2005). Other schools were required to enrol all children who arrived at the gate, subject only to the "special services and facilities" clause of the Human Rights Act: "whose disability is such that that person requires special services or facilities that in the circumstances cannot reasonably be made available" (s60, Human Rights Act, 1993).

There was also the problem of what Booth refers to (in the English context) as "policy as rhetoric," where intent and appearances fail to match practice, and where there are insufficient or inadequate strategies and resources to implement policy:

> The sheer number of initiatives and the different principles on which they are based make it difficult for staff in schools and colleges to become familiar with them all, let alone put them into practice. If they have serious intent, policies have to be linked to clear implementation strategies. (Booth, 2003, p. 35)

If this is true of England, with its regional governance systems, then it is much more so in a context in which each individual school must work it out for themselves.

The 1989 policy had the appearance of fostering community values, innovation, and responsiveness. Under the new model, parents were the population from which school governors were elected, providing (in theory at least) a powerful link between parental wishes and school governance. The intention of this was that local needs could be met. However, the overriding values of the new system were not responsiveness to communities but competition for students, as "choice" provided a mandate for parents to shop around for the "best" school for their children, and schools scampered to position themselves in the marketplace. At the secondary level, schools did this by being able to show higher academic achievement by their students as demonstrated through published "league tables" recording the performance of students on national examinations. The ability to attend the "high performing" schools was dependent on living in the correct school zone and thus being eligible to enrol. The desirable primary schools were those that were also in that catchment area, and thus "contributed" to the "high-performing" secondary school.

THE POLITICAL RHETORIC OF INCLUSION AND THE REALITY

The first wave of reform (Mitchell, 1999) in the special education sector occurred concurrently with the devolution of school governance to individual schools in 1989. This had quite contradictory effects on people with disabilities. For this first time there was a guarantee of full inclusion in state schools, inserted into the legislation as follows:

> .... people who have special educational needs (whether because of disability or otherwise) have the same rights to enrol and receive education at state schools as people who do not. (s. 8, New Zealand Education Act, 1989)

But the reforms also included a significant element of privatisation of the public Special Education Service (SES), forcing schools to "purchase" special services as they were needed, from funds previously held by central government to funds devolved to the individual school. However, the privatisation plan proved unworkable and the SES remained for years as a stand-alone public entity, albeit significantly underfunded (Mitchell, 1999). In effect, the reforms while promising inclusion distanced schools from the means to achieve it.

The second wave of reform occurred in the mid-1990s (Wills, 2006), at the height of the period of free market policy fervour in education (Pearce & Gordon, 2005). This was the policy known as Special Education 2000. This policy reaffirmed the legislative requirement that children with disabilities belonged in every classroom in every school in New Zealand (Kearney & Kane, 2006). On the other hand, the system of devolved funding paid on an individual basis emphasised an exclusive model predicated on the identification of students as having high "needs":

> There was a clash between the mechanisms that targeted funding to a reduced number of individual students with special educational needs and the philosophy that expected all students to be educated inclusively in the regular classroom with the same national curriculum as all other students. (Kearney & Kane, 2006, p. 202)

Wills argues that while the manifest intention of policymakers was to ensure that education for people with disabilities would take place in all schools, at a deeper level the intention was quite different: "to introduce the new public management approaches of the reforms in education into special education" (2006, p. 192).

Thus the reform path of special education towards an inclusive system contained a policy paradox: that while the rhetoric of policy from the level of central government increased, its implementation became more problematic, due to the overriding exigencies of a competitive schooling system. The reasons for choice and competition not tending bring about good choices for people with disabilities are explored in the next section. But, before tackling this issue, we want to examine evidence from New Zealand and overseas about the effects of school choice systems on educational opportunities for people with disabilities.

Children with disabilities have the same rights to school choice as any other children, but there is emerging research evidence that these children may be less welcome than others in schools of choice (Estes, 2003, 2004). In the major evaluation of Special Education 2000, parents reported a strong sense of frustration that they were unable to access schools, classrooms, and resources that would allow their disabled children to receive a high quality inclusive education (Bourke et al., 1999). Despite the rhetoric of partnership, many parents felt as unwelcome as their disabled children.

A further element of the Special Education 2000 policy encouraged schools to develop inclusive practices. Dedicated funding was no longer to be given to schools to fund special units (i.e., separate classrooms or group of classrooms for only children with identified special education needs); funding would now be tagged to individual students who had been "verified" as having high or very high needs in relation to accessing the curriculum (i.e., the funding was not linked to a particular diagnosis or impairment. See Bourke et al., 1999). Schools could still have such units, but they would need to be resourced by individual entitlements. The result of this policy was that a number of special units were closed. This had adverse effects, particularly in the cities where competition between schools created specific market conditions. Unfortunately, some schools that had shed their units then sought to exclude students with disabilities, arguing that they no longer had facilities to deal with them.

This eventually lead to a judicial review in the High Court, *Daniels v. Attorney General* (Court of Appeal, 2003), which focused on the question of whether it was the responsibility of the state to provide facilities to meet "special educational needs" (Wills, 2006). While apparently a case about the provision of special units, in fact it was about the legal responsibility of the state to ensure that disabled children had a quality place, however provided. The Court of Appeal upheld the notion that, despite devolution to the school level, the state as a whole retained a responsibility, and, as Justice Baragwanath later commented, the Court of Appeal,

> ... confirmed this (High) Court's decision that the former Minister of Education acted unlawfully when he purported to disestablish special units in 1998. (2, New Zealand Law Review, p. 632)

The *Daniels* case also has, potentially, a much wider application in regard to issues of the provision of appropriate education in a devolved system. What it forced, in this instance, was an agreement that the Ministry of Education would review special education provision to ensure that appropriate services were available to all students with special needs in their own region. These regional reports, which required consultation with communities and schools, were released at the end of 2004, and have ongoing implications for the design and shaping of special education provision and support. In principle, this planned approach provides the basis for a move to further inclusion, which is government policy: "a world class inclusive education system" (Kearney & Kane, 2006). How it plays out in practice remains to be seen. However, the shape of the system of school choice acts as a continuing barrier to meeting the goal of full inclusion for children with disabilities. Research both within New Zealand and internationally demonstrates that the ways in which school choice works are not the same for everyone, as it enhances choice for some and reduces choice for others (Ball & Vincent, 1998; Gordon, 2003; Gordon & Whitty, 1997; Lauder et al., 1994; Pearce & Gordon, 2005; Reay, 1996; Reay & Ball, 1997, 1998). Patterns and reasons for choice are explored in the next section.

WHAT IS CHOSEN IN SCHOOL CHOICE?

School choice is a policy that allows parents to select a school place for their child, rather than some regional or national agency directing the child to go to a particular school. However, after years of school choice systems operating internationally, it is clear that it is not as simple as this. In school choice systems, some schools become full very quickly and others are undersubscribed. In country after country, it has been the observation of research that school choice is determined primarily on the basis of the social characteristics of the area and school composition, including social economic status and ethnicity, rather than on any rational assessment of the educational quality or offerings of individual schools (Morton & Gordon, 2006).

This applies equally in New Zealand (Gordon & Whitty, 1997; Lauder et al., 1994) as in other countries. In the United Kingdom, there has been significant work that demonstrates that school choices tend to be made on the basis of social networks, such as race and class (Ball & Vincent, 1998; Reay & Ball, 1997, 1998), and that certain groups consider themselves "excluded" from the discourse of choice (Reay, 1996).

In the United States, similar processes have been demonstrated. In one study (Holme, 2002), wealthy parents revealed that they sold homes in one area and bought them in another simply on the advice of their social networks about what schools are best for their children. Remarkably, in many cases these transactions were completed without ever visiting either the rejected schools, nor the ones into which access was being bought.

There has been little work on where disabled families "fit" in the social hierarchy. There are some contextual issues that may provide clues, however. The first is that there is evidence that, under conditions of choice and competition, schools tend to take on a traditional, conservative look. School uniforms are introduced, there is an increase in suspensions and expulsions, and schools aim for all the trappings of institutions of high academic achievement and serious learning (Whitty, Power, & Halpin, 1997). While one of the main goals of choice reforms is to foster innovative and responsive schools, there is little evidence that this goal has been achieved (Lubienski, 2003).

This has profound implications for inclusion. There is significant evidence that the dominant middle class, who to a great extent determine school reputation, have an insatiable desire for an increased academic curriculum and ever higher levels of "achievement" for their children (Davies, 2004; Davies, Aurini, & Quirke, 2002).

Such desires can come into direct conflict with the impulse of other middle-class parents to seek democratic participation in normal life for their disabled child. Inclusion, a democratic impulse that is about building communities, may have little place in the purposeful classroom of today, especially as children get older. In our recent research (Morton & Gordon, 2006), we have recorded both "tirades" against inclusion, which may be characterised as a selfish desire on the part of unrealistic parents, and the concern expressed by some teachers that inclusion does not belong in the "academic" secondary school classroom.

There is some evidence, from the United States at least, that students with disabilities are participating in school choice (Lange & Ysseldyke, 1998), although probably to a lesser extent that their peers elsewhere (Estes, 2003). Participation is not the same thing as inclusion, of course. Lange and Ysseldyke's paper appears to indicate that the reason for participation in choice programmes by students with disabilities is to access special programmes, rather than inclusive classrooms. More research is needed into what kinds of choices are offered to disabled children and their families, and the extent to which inclusion is fostered or hindered by policies of choice.

"SLIPPAGE" AND INCLUSION

> The policy-makers appeared to have given insufficient attention to the work required to re-align the thinking of communities and schools toward students with special educational needs so their inclusive education would be a commonly desired goal. (Wills, 2006, p. 191)

Despite a state and ministerial responsibility to provide education for children with special educational needs on the same basis as others, as upheld by the courts of New Zealand in *Daniels*, it is far from clear that systems of school choice actually foster inclusion at the (devolved) level of practice. From a policy perspective, it is devolution itself that is the culprit here. While it may be the responsibility of schools to implement government policy, what happens when that policy is unclear, vaguely worded, unachievable within resources, philosophically misaligned with the goals and desires of school governors, or where there is no proper accountability.

All these reasons may be given as to why the inclusive classroom is not the standard in New Zealand schools. Our own research (Morton & Gordon, 2006) has focused on how new teachers are prepared to provide inclusive classrooms for children with disabilities. We found that the discourses of inclusion permeated all teacher education courses in New Zealand. However, the practice did not always meet the rhetoric. Inclusive education courses may or may not be compulsory, might be scheduled against core courses, and in some shorter courses, especially for secondary teachers, may be completely absent. Teaching and course standards issued by the New Zealand Teachers Council refer not to "inclusion" as a professional standard but only to a requirement to meet the needs of "diverse" populations, with little or no direction over how that is to be achieved.

We refer to this bundle of problems as *slippage*. In a devolved schooling system, and one in which it will be difficult for the democratic and inclusive classroom to flourish, there appears to be no clear direction, and little evidence of leadership, to ensure that the national policy of inclusion is actually implemented in schools. This is not to say that there are no schools that practice inclusion. There are many, and they are sustained by the vision and skills of principals and teachers. Unfortunately, as currently structured in New Zealand, inclusion has to be won, classroom by classroom, school by school. Once won, it can also be lost again, if a dedicated teacher leaves or other circumstances change. From a policy perspective, then, inclusion is slippery and difficult, even when it can be recognised, defined, and implemented. Too often

> [t]he theoretical and pragmatic imprecisions of this thing we, and it is a very broad we, call inclusive education has permitted all manner of thinking, discourse and activity to pass itself off as inclusive. (Slee, 2006, p. 111)

The problem of slippage is not insurmountable. There could be a national policy of inclusive classrooms, requiring schools to offer quality, safe, inclusive education to all children, including those with disabilities. Such a policy would empower parents, who, anecdotally, are often discouraged from enrolling their child at particular schools because "school X down the road has really good facilities for children like her and we have none." Every school might be required to show in its annual plans how it is moving towards becoming a fully inclusive school, and, if it is not, why not. High quality professional development that provides all teachers with expertise, skills, and enthusiasm to construct and run inclusive classrooms would also make a difference. Teachers might be asked to demonstrate their inclusive skills to hold and renew their certificate of practice. It is not impossible to construct a really inclusive system from the policy upwards, but few if any countries have managed to do it yet.

CONCLUSION: INCLUSION AND SCHOOL CHOICE

We began this chapter with a list of attributes of schooling taken from Goodlad (2005). Two of these goals related to the acquisition of knowledge and preparing for the economic future. The other two were about fostering democracy and becoming good citizens. A school choice system tends to heavily distort these goals, underemphasising the democratic and overplaying academic achievement. School choice may, over time, concentrate "like" communities, of colour, religion, class, and taste into the same schools, creating bastions of similar kinds of persons and probably promoting social intolerance and unrest between them. This is disastrous news for the families of people with disabilities, who have fought against the constraints of ableism for many years, and who now look to the democratic and inclusive classroom to guarantee their citizenship rights into the future.

Research findings on school choice do not provide good news for the supporters of inclusion. Choices are not free, but are constrained by a battery of social factors. People generally choose schools on the basis of the social characteristics of the children attending the school, and there is no evidence that, for most parents, "disability" is a valued social quality. Indeed, a perception that inclusive classrooms hamper learning, for which we found some evidence in our research, may negatively affect the choices of people with disabilities, or force them into units with other "similar" people.

Even in a system as devolved as New Zealand's, in which each school is run by its own governing body, national policy goals can affect what goes on in schools. We noted that there is a national policy of inclusion in this country. However, it is nowhere defined precisely what that means, nor how it should be implemented (Kearney & Kane, 2006). There is a problem with implementation, too, in that the philosophy of devolution essentially requires the government to set goals and standards, but requires schools alone to determine how these should be achieved.

Even within a policy framework of inclusion, then, it is evident that the inclusive classroom and school has not flourished. Teachers often do not know how to "do" inclusion, and parents of non-disabled children are suspicious of it. Parents of children with disabilities are left to wonder how to achieve inclusion, and why it seems so unattainable (Morton & Gordon, 2006).

There is no evidence that policies of school choice have "worked" any more than non-choice systems worked, to bring policies of inclusion into effect in New Zealand schools, or other countries with similar policies. While school choice appears to be a policy about inclusion, about parents being empowered to choose what they want, the sum of choices favours certain privileged and dominant groups over others. The power hierarchies of schooling have not changed under choice policies, and children with disabilities remain, as they have always been, far down the list in terms of getting their needs met.

But it does not have to be like this. Schools in New Zealand are now expected to plan annually to meet the needs of their students, and to report the following year on how they achieved these goals. The government could insert into the reporting process a mandatory section on students with disabilities and the fostering of inclusive classrooms. Parents who believe their children's needs are not being met could use the planning and reporting process to push for change. A mechanism already exists for at least the beginning of a more robust implementation of the inclusion policy. The mechanism exists, but does the will?

REFERENCES

Ball, S. J., & Gewirtz, S. (1996). Education markets, school competition, and parental choice in the U.K.: A report of research findings. *International Journal of Educational Reform, 5* (2), 152–158.

Ball, S. J., & Vincent, C. (1998). "I heard it on the grapevine": "Hot" knowledge and school choice. *British Journal of Sociology of Education, 19* (3), 377–400.

Ballard, K. (2003). The analysis of context: Some thoughts on teacher education, culture, colonisation and inequality. In T. Booth, K. Nes & M. Stromstad (Eds.), *Developing inclusive teacher education* (pp. 59–78). London: RoutledgeFalmer.

Bauknight, S. H. (1998). The search for constitutional school choice. *Journal of Law and Education, 27* (4), 525–550.

Booth, T. (2003). Views from the institution: Overcoming barriers to inclusive teacher education. In T. Booth, K. Nes & M. Stromstad (Eds.), *Developing inclusive teacher education* (pp. 33–59). London: RoutledgeFalmer.

Bourke, R., Bevan-Brown, J., Bevan-Brown, W., Carroll-Lind, J., Chapman, J., Cullen, J., et al. (1999). *Special Education 2000: Monitoring and evaluation of the implementation of the policy.* Wellington, New Zealand: Ministry of Education.

Boyd, W. L. (2002). Market forces, globalization and values in public education. *Education Canada, 42* (3), 12–15.

Carnoy, M. (1995). Is school privatization the answer? Data from other countries help burst the voucher bubble. *American Educator, 19,* 29–30.

Carnoy, M. (1998). National voucher plans in Chile and Sweden: Did privatization reforms make for better education? *Comparative Education Review, 42* (3), 309–337.

Cochran-Smith, M. (2005). The new teacher education: For better or for worse? *Educational Researcher, 34* (7), 3–17.

Codd, J., & Gordon, L. (1991). School charters: The contractualist state and education policy. *New Zealand Journal of Educational Studies, 26* (1), 21–34.

Copeland, S. R., Hughes, C., Agran, M., Wehmeyer, M. L., & Fowler, S. E. (2002). An intervention package to support high school students with mental retardation in general education classrooms. *American Journal on Mental Retardation, 107* (1), 32–45.

Daniels v Attorney General. (Court of Appeal, 2003)

Davies, S. (2004). School choice by default? Understanding the demand for private tutoring in Canada. *American Journal of Education, 110* (3), 233.

Davies, S., Aurini, J., & Quirke, L. (2002). New markets for private education in Canada. *Education Canada, 42* (3), 36–38.

Estes, M. B. (2003). Zero reject and school choice: Students with disabilities in Texas' charter schools. *Leadership and Policy in Schools, 2* (3), 213–235.

Estes, M. B. (2004). Choice for all? Charter schools and students with special needs. *Journal of Special Education, 37* (4), 257–267.

Friedman, M. (1962). *Capitalism and freedom.* Chicago: University of Chicago Press.

Goldhaber, D. D., & Eide, E. R. (2002). What do we know (and need to know) about the impact of school choice reforms on disadvantaged students? *Harvard Educational Review, 72* (2), 157–176.

Goodlad, J. (2005). Foreword. In N. Michelli & D. Keiser (Eds.), *Teacher education for democracy and social justice.* New York: Routledge.

Gordon, L. (2003). School choice and the social market in New Zealand: Educational reform in an era of increasing inequality. *International Studies in Sociology of Education, 13* (1), 17–34.

Gordon, L., & Whitty, G. (1997). Giving the "hidden hand" a helping hand?: The rhetoric and reality of neoliberal education reform in England and New Zealand. *Comparative Education, 33* (3), 453–467.

Helme, J. J. (2002). Buying homes, buying schools: School choice and the social construction of school quality. *Harvard Educational Review, 72* (2), 177–205.

Kearney, A., & Kane, R. (2006). Inclusive education policy in New Zealand: Reality or ruse. *International Journal of Inclusive Education, 10* (2–3), 201–219.

Lange, C. M., & Ysseldyke, J. E. (1998). School choice policies and practices for students with disabilities. *Exceptional Children, 64* (2), 255–270.

Lauder, H., Hughes, D., Waslander, S., Thrupp, M., McGlinn, J., Newton, S., & Dupius, A. (1994). *The creation of market competition in New Zealand: An empirical analysis of a New Zealand secondary school market 1990–1993.* Wellington, New Zealand: Ministry of Education.

Lubienski, C. (2003). Innovation in education markets: Theory and evidence on the impact of competition and choice in charter schools. *American Educational Research Journal, 40* (2), 395–443.

Millar, R. & Morton, M. (2007). Bridging two worlds: Special education and curriculum policy. *International Journal of Inclusive Education, 11* (2), 163–176.

Mitchell, D. (1999). Special education in New Zealand: A decade of change. *New Zealand Journal of Educational Studies, 34* (1), 199–210.

Mittler, P. (2002). Educating pupils with intellectual disabilities in England: Thirty years on. *International Journal of Disability, Development and Education, 49* (2), 145–160.

Morton, M., & Gordon, L. (2006). In the public good? Preparing teachers to be inclusive educators. Report of a New Zealand research project, *AERA*: San Francisco.

New Zealand Bill of Rights Act. (1990).

New Zealand Education Act. (1989).

New Zealand Human Rights Act. (1993).

New Zealand Human Rights Amendment Act. (2001).

O'Hanlon, C. (2003). *Education inclusion as action research*. Maidenhead, UK: Open University Press.

Pearce, D., & Gordon, L. (2005). In the zone: New Zealand's legislation for a system of school choice and its effects. *London Review of Education, 3* (2), 145–147.

Reay, D. (1996). Contextualising choice: Social power and parental involvement. *British Educational Research Journal, 22* (5), 581–596.

Reay, D., & Ball, S. J. (1997). "Spoilt for choice": The working classes and educational markets. *Oxford Review of Education, 23* (1), 89–101.

Reay, D., & Ball, S. J. (1998). "Making their minds up": Family dynamics of school choice. *British Educational Research Journal, 24* (4), 431–448.

Rentoul, J., & Rosanowski, J., with Dempster, N., Fisher, D., Hosking, N., Hunter, R., Pugh, G., & Walford, G. (2000). *The effects of school governance, ownership, organisation and management on educational outcomes*. Strategic Research Initiative Literature review 4, from Christchurch College of Education. Wellington: Ministry of Education.

Reynolds, M. (2001). Education for inclusion, teacher education and the teacher training agency standards. *Journal of In-service Education, 27* (3), 465–476.

Slee, R. (2001). "Inclusion in practice": Does practice make perfect? *Educational Review, 53* (2), 113–123.

Slee, R. (2006). Limits to and possibilities for educational reform. *International Journal of Inclusive Education, 10* (2–3), 109–119.

Thrupp, M., & Smith, R. (1999). A decade of ERO. *New Zealand Journal of Educational Studies, 34* (1), 186–198.

Timmons, V. (2002). International perspectives on inclusion: Concluding thoughts. *Exceptionality Education Canada, 12* (2–3), 187–192.

Vlachou, A. (2004). Education and inclusive policy-making: Implications for research and practice. *International Journal of Inclusive Education, 8* (1), 3–21.

Whitty, G., Power, S., & Halpin, D. (1997). *Devolution and choice in education: The school, the state and the market*. Buckingham, UK: Open University Press.

Wills, R. (2006). Special Education 2000: A New Zealand experiment. *International Journal of Inclusive Education, 10* (2–3), 189–199.

Wylie, C., & Mitchell, L. (2003). *Sustaining school development in a decentralised system: Lessons from New Zealand*. Paper presented at the International Congress for School Effectiveness and Improvement, 5–8 January 2003, Sydney.

CHAPTER FIFTEEN

Private Troubles or Public Issues? The Social Construction of "the Disabled Baby" in the Context of Social Policy and Social and Technological Changes

DÓRA S. BJARNASON

INTRODUCTION

The purpose of this chapter is to describe, explore, and interpret how a difference in the family gets constructed as a social status at (or before) birth or at the discovery of impairment within the sociocultural and social policy context of Iceland, a wealthy, Western modern society. Recent and important changes in Icelandic social policy related to disabled people and their families are described and discussed. These changes set the stage for the interpretation of disability within the society and provide parameters for available choices of action.

The chapter addresses three broad questions; first, how is the social construction of a child (or fetus) transformed into a social construction of the disabled child? In order to unravel and discuss plausible answers, the chapter explores the parents' and potential parents' perspectives on learning that "all is not well" with their child, and the perspectives of the professionals who as part of their work have the power of diagnosis and labeling. Second, how does the new knowledge and technology related to neonatal services, including prenatal diagnosis of impaired fetuses, impact the way in which parents and professionals negotiate the social construction of the disabled baby or "the nonviable damaged fetus"? Thus, how does the process of interpretation and reinterpretation that occurs within the parent-professional negotiation impact the prospects and choices open to the disabled child and the family? Third, how does the social construction of the disabled child or fetus and the subsequent negotiation process connect to broader social issues such as culture and relevant social processes and changes in social policy in Iceland? By applying C. Wright Mills (1959) thoughts on the sociological imagination I will try to understand the connection between what he calls "private troubles and public issues" related to the social construction of the disabled child within my society.

The theoretical perspective applied here is social constructionism (Schwandt, 2001). Social constructionism is about how meanings get constructed in social context (Berger & Luckman, 1967; Gergen, 1994; see also Ferguson 2003). It draws upon symbolic interactionism (Mead, 1937; Blumer, 1969) and fundamental to symbolic interactionism is the view that we as people construct our own and each other's identities through our everyday encounters with each other in social interactions via language and other symbols. The social constructionist position, as I understand it, focuses on social processes, intersubjectivity, and interaction; for me, it also means that human criteria for identifying action or events are highly circumscribed by culture, history, and the social context. Social constructionism implies that we take a critical stance toward our taken-for-granted ways of understanding ourselves and the world, and that the terms and forms by which we achieve such understanding are social artifacts, products of historically and culturally situated interchange amongst people (Berger & Luckman, 1967; Gergen, 1994). From this theoretical stance, "disability" is a socially constructed phenomenon, idealist product of interactions and relationships, embedded within society and its history, and generated from its culture, norms, and values (Ferguson & Ferguson, 1995). "Disability" is here taken to be constructed, embodied, and embedded in Icelandic society and culture. As Gergen (1994) reminds us, social constructionism argues that because we negotiate understandings, and because these understandings can take a wide variety of forms, we can talk of many social constructions of the world. Each different construction brings with it a different kind of action. Particular forms of knowledge in any culture are thus seen to be social artifacts. Thus, in this chapter, I treat current medical "knowledge," clinical practice, gene technology, and prenatal health services as social artifacts based on cultural, national, and international social constructions.

The chapter also draws upon a postmodernist framework, a radically interdisciplinary theoretical approach that rejects conventional styles of academic discourse and endorses heterogeneity, difference, fragmentation, and indeterminacy (Crook, 2001). The approach indicates that all knowledge is produced through discourse, all knowledge is constructed, contested, incessantly perspectival and polyphonic, and inextricably bound up with power. Further, knowledge in the postmodern sense is seen as dependent on sociocultural contexts, unacknowledged values, tacit discourses, and interpretive traditions, and it recognizes the significance of language, discourse, and power in any knowledge claim (Denzin, 1996a; Ferguson & Ferguson, 1995). In the late twentieth century, postmodernism, with its departure from fundamental social transformation of modern societies, was seen to be set up as a fundamental challenge to interactionist theories; but it has also cross-fertilized these and many other theoretical perspectives including feminist theories, neo-Marxist theories, post-structuralism, cultural studies, disability scholarship, and others. Thus, it forms a backdrop for the social constructionist approach (Denzin, 1996b) as used in this research.

From the postmodernistic framework this chapter invokes, for example, the concept "the medical gaze," a concept that Foucault (1973) developed in his book *The birth of the Clinic*. The concept helps capture the power vested in the medical profession derived from the complex strategic situation doctors and other health workers gain with their training in the institution of the clinic (the teaching hospital with all its tradition, culture, and forms).

The research method is qualitative (Bogdan & Taylor, 1992; Wolcott, 1995). Data sources stem from two of my research projects and from documentary analysis of official documents. The first source of data comes from an extensive research project concerning the social construction of young disabled adulthood (Bjarnason, 2003b, 2004). That research explored the experiences and perspectives of thirty-six young adults (age sixteen to twenty-four), their parents, friends, and teachers. All the young people were born in the 1970s and early 1980s, before ultrasound and other prenatal tests were made available to all pregnant women in Iceland. I draw on data sources from interviews with parents of the young adults. Those parents are here called "the older parents." The second source of data is from research in progress. These consist of interviews with one or both parents of ten disabled children born after 1995, and with key medical staff involved in prenatal care, ultrasound and other tests, and guidance to prospective parents whose fetuses were diagnosed with atypical conditions such as trisomy 21 (Down syndrome), trisomy 18 (Edward's syndrome) and 13 (Patau's syndrome), spinal bifida, significant brain, heart or lung malformation, and a missing limb or vital organ. Parents forming this group will be referred to as "the younger parents" or "parents of the choice generation" because couples of that generation may have to choose before the birth whether to abort their impaired fetus.

BACKGROUND

Iceland is a large island on the North Atlantic Ridge, with a population of 300, 000 and a highly prosperous and modern Nordic society. Iceland can be described as a liberal democratic society with a strong welfare state (Ólafsson, 1999). The Icelandic welfare state, modeled on relevant Nordic law and ideas, developed gradually from the 1930s but with a temporary setback in the 1990s (Herbertsson, 2005). Globalization, new technologies, and neoliberalism with their economic, political, and cultural implications have dramatically impacted on the Icelandic economy and society particularly in late 1980s and 1990s, thus transforming ordinary lives. Iceland used to be relatively homogeneous both with regard to its population and average family incomes. It is safe to say that there was neither extreme poverty nor significant wealth in Iceland during most of the latter half of the twentieth century, and that people of foreign origin—people of a different ethnic, cultural, or religious—were a rare sight. In 1994 Iceland, with Norway and Liechtenstein, signed a treaty with the European Economic Community (EEC) common market, which in effect opened up the internal European finance and labor markets and forced the Icelandic state to adopt its legal framework rules and regulations from Brussels (http://secretariat.efta.int/Web/EuropeanEconomicArea/EEAAgreement). This and the fact that Iceland signed the Schengen agreement, an agreement between fourteen European countries from 1985 that opened up a free movement of people within the Schengen zone (http://www.mfa.is/), changed in 2001 both economic opportunities and the sociocultural composition of the population. Since the late 1990s the country has experienced a sharp economic boom largely driven by public and private investments (e.g., in new hydro-electrical power plants for new foreign-owned aluminum plants). The boom resulted in an acute labor shortage and the influx of foreign workers. Consequently, the population has become significantly more heterogeneous both economically and socioculturally. The changing socioeconomic landscape in Iceland, full employment for both men and women, and general access to information (e.g., on the Internet) has affected the composition, lifestyles, and expectations of Icelandic families including families with disabled children. Young families generally expect a decent standard of living, adequate state and communal services such as good public schools, largely free health and welfare services, and good work prospects.

Social policy is here taken to mean *both* the principles that the state and local governments have defined governance as action that is directed to improve or support the lives of a given segment of its population seen to be in need of supports, *and* the systems and practices involved in such actions.

Going by Titmuss (1974), this implies actions about *ends* and about *means* to the defined ends. He writes, "[T]he concept policy is only meaningful if we (i.e., the actions of government in expressing the general will of the people) believe that we can affect change" (23–24).

Further, Titmuss (1974) reminds us that to understand (social) policy and distinguish between ends (what we think we want) and the means (how to get there), we have to see it in the context of a particular set of circumstances, a given society and culture, and a more or less specified period of social history.

Prenatal Services

Ultrasound technology was introduced in 1975, and by 1986 all pregnant women in Iceland had the option of having free prenatal ultrasound in the 18th and 19th week of pregnancy. According to two Norwegian medical doctors Getz and Kirkengen:

> The scope of prenatal ultrasound screening has undergone significant changes since it was introduced in the 1980's. Its original goal was to reduce obstetric risk by enhancing safety for mother and child, correcting gestational age, locating placenta, and diagnosing twin pregnancies. As imaging technology developed and societal expectations changed, there has been an increasing focus on fetal diagnosis, namely disclosure of structural abnormalities in the unborn child. (in Getz, 2006, 214)

Ultrasound is fast becoming an integral part of every family's pregnancy. Couples attend together and sometimes they bring older children, close friends, or relatives to witness what for most is a joyful event. Pictures of the fetus can be bought from the hospital staff, and are sometimes proudly presented to family, friends, and relatives. By 2004 approximately 99% of all pregnant women in Iceland made use of the ultrasound in the eighteenth and nineteenth week as a part of prenatal medical care. That year approximately 2% of the pregnant women who used the ultrasound technology were estimated to carry fetuses with unusual differences. Infrequent structural differences such as missing brain (anencephaly), open abdomen (gastroschisis) but also more subtle structural differences such as cleft lip are detected in fetuses in the second trimester of pregnancy; however, attempts to screen for fetuses with chromosomal differences, in particular Down syndrome, have proved less reliable at that time. Genetic conditions are diagnosed via the identification of so called anatomical soft markers. The term "soft marker" is defined by medical experts as:

> [S]tructural changes detected at ultrasound scan which may be transient and in themselves have little or no pathological significance, but are thought to be more commonly found in fetuses with congenial abnormalities, particularly karyotypic [chromosomal characteristics] abnormalities. (Bricker et al., quoted in Getz, 2006, 214)

Soft markers that can be detected by the second trimester ultrasound scan include choroid plexus cysts (CPCs), renal pelvic dilatation, echogenic foci in the fetal heart or fetal gut, short limbs, and nuchal thickening. Most soft markers are associated with Down syndrome. However, even when two soft markers are identified, the likelihood of parents having a child with, for example, Down syndrome is unclear and statistically f. ex. 1:100. Invasive diagnostic tests (chorionic villus biopsy or amniocentesis) are generally offered to the pregnant woman when the possibility of her having a child with Down syndrome is 1:300 or higher. The invasive tests carry a risk of fetal loss by 1:100. If the chromosomal difference is confirmed by invasive tests, Getz and Kirkengen point out, "then the 'therapeutic' options are to have an abortion or prepare for the arrival of the child" (Getz & Kirkengen, 2003, 55).

In 2004 approximately 80% of all pregnant women in Iceland also went for an earlier ultrasound in eleventh to fourteenth week of pregnancy. The early ultrasound is available at a small price. When impairment is suspected a subsequent battery of tests (e.g., blood tests and maternal serum tests) is carried out (Landsspítali University Hospital).

Ultrasound screening in the first trimester of pregnancy is explicitly promoted as screening for Down syndrome. Early ultrasound screening enables the detection of 75%–80% of fetuses with Down syndrome. The probability of detecting fetal chromosome difference (e.g., Down syndrome) can be enhanced, throughout the gestation period, by combining the ultrasound technique with the invasive maternal serum tests. But because the test results are always based on statistical probabilities, the loss of a fetus through the invasive tests cannot be ruled out.

The Abortion Law

The current legislation on abortion from 1975 permits abortion for either medical or social reasons or both. According to the law, abortions should be carried out early in pregnancy, preferably no later than the twelfth week. After sixteen weeks of pregnancy abortions are only permitted on medical grounds, but if the fetus is found to be impaired, then abortions can be carried out up in to the twenty-first week. Most abortions are permitted for social reasons. Abortions owing to detected infrequent genetic or potential birth variation are classified under medical reasons, but the exact number of such abortions is not available for the late twentieth and early twenty-first centuries. However reliable figures are available for the year 2003. That year the number of births in Iceland was 3,317, abortions totaled to 951; 37 women through ultrasound were found with impaired fetuses owing to "genetic or other defects," and of those 26 chose to have their baby despite the prognoses, but 11 women chose abortion (Landsspítali-University Hospital).

Rights and Restrictions

Since the 1980s people with disabilities have gradually become more visible in Icelandic society. The disability movement and disability activists have grown in strength and managed to impact public discourse and public policy. Two large advocacy associations, The Organization of Disabled in Iceland (*Öryrkjabandalag Íslands*), and The National Federation for People with Learning Disability (*Þroskahjálp*) have representatives in most national and local government committees that draft legal bills and formal rules that concern the affairs of people labeled as disabled. Both associations also initiate public policy by applying all means available to them in a democratic society; from drawing the attention of the media to problems within the legislation or practice that affect the lives of people with disabilities, to calling public meetings and protests, or consulting with relevant government ministers. In 2000, The Organization of Disabled in Iceland took the state to the High Court and won their case—an action that improved significantly the disability pension for disabled people.

A special legislative framework aimed at supporting disabled people has gradually been established. The first such legislation, "the Law on the Affaires of the Intellectually disabled," was passed by the Icelandic Parliament in 1979. The aim of the law was to ensure that people with intellectual disability enjoy as normal a life as possible within our society and to secure a relevant administrative framework to provide them and in case of children, their families with necessary support and services. In 1984 the legislation was replaced by a similar legislation that included all people with disabilities except for people labeled with mental retardation who were also later included under the law. The current legislation is "the Law on the Affaires of the Disabled" (1992). This law is intended to support disabled people, including disabled children and youth and their families and secure their right to support, relevant services, and full inclusion in society. Public education is free or largely free and open to all learners from preschool throughout upper-secondary school. The education legislation from the 1990s prescribes inclusive education. According to the law, this means that all children have access to their local regular compulsory schools and that the schools should educate each and every child effectively and according to their needs. The National Curriculum from 1999, which has statutory status, states:

> ... regular compulsory schools must accept all children irrespective of their ability or disability. This applies to disabled children, non disabled, exceptionally intelligent, intellectually impaired and all children in between... The compulsory school is obliged to provide all children with an effective quality education. (The National Curriculum/*Aðalnámskrá grunnskóla, alm. hluti* 1999, 14)

Similar clauses are in the preschool and upper-secondary school legislation. However the legislation also states that parents of disabled children can choose between regular school and special school or special education facilities within regular schools. The main legislative goals draw on ideas of equality, equal access, and the equalizing of opportunities. Iceland signed the Salamanca Declaration in 1994. Less than 0.4% of the compulsory school population (aged 6–16) attend special education schools and about 1% attend private schools; all other school-aged children attend their home school through integration or inclusion programs (Statistics Iceland, 2004, 2005).

THE SOCIAL CONSTRUCTION OF THE DISABLED BABY

Families of Disabled Children

In an article Tim Booth (1978) noted how the clinical perspective on intellectual impairment does not help or explain how such people are valued and treated in their everyday life. He used case histories drawn from forty-six families of intellectually disabled children to map the unfolding of the ideas of professionals, parents, and their social networks of difference in the family, and traced how these gradually changed the child's status from a normal to a disabled baby. According to Booth's analysis, the social construction of a difference is created and shaped by the social meaning imputed by the diagnosis. He focused on four stages in the process of framing such difference as a disability; First, *"the arousal of suspicion"* within the family, because of conceptions of irregularities in child development and behavior. Second, *"the prevarication"* stage when professional's response is characterized by their being dismissive of the babies' impairment, but appreciative of the parents' worries, and uninformative. Thus they put the parents under a great strain of uncertainty, sometimes for an extended period of time. Third, *"the growth of conviction,"* when the negotiation between the parents and the doctors resulted in the parents learning that all is "not right" with their child, and they are persuaded to make judgments about their child's fate, framed in the terms of medicine, and finally *"the labeling"* when the *"the degradation"* of the child is completed with the diagnosis. At that point in time, parents and doctors arrive at a consensus about the reality of the child's condition, which results in establishing the status of impairment and disability. Booth (1978) concludes:

> From this point onwards it is left up to the parents to build the social meaning of mental handicap by making the link between the diagnosis of sub-normality and the social world of every day life … (and that the link is forged in the cause of parents efforts to reinstate the child into the family in a role which is compatible with the limitations imposed by his handicap and to establish predictable relationships with him based on their first hand experiences in practical affairs of his personal strength and weaknesses. (206)

Even though the language is dated, Booth, by applying labeling theories of deviance and stigmatization (Goffman, 1963), provided an insight into the construction of disability as a child's master status.

Before the prenatal ultrasound procedure, or when the fetal difference is overlooked, the process of labeling starts when parents or sometimes other family members or friends begin to suspect that something is "not right with a child." This captures the experiences of many of the older parents, the parents of the young adults I interviewed in the 1990s. For some of these older parents, the time of *"the arousal of suspicion"* occurred at the birth or it could be drawn out for weeks, months, or even years.

The next step, *"the prevarication"* stage, was to take the child to a doctor, who might or might not identify the impairment right away. If the doctor agreed with the parents, he or she usually referred the child to *Kjarvalshús*, the first National Assessment Centre in Iceland, where their child would more often than not be placed on a waiting list, before being admitted for assessment. Some parents felt that they were not taken seriously by the doctor; they were sent home or on to other inappropriate medical specialists. In such cases *the stage of prevarication* could be drawn out and be very painful to the family. Parents in that situation felt that they were not listened to, or that their and their child's time was being wasted.

Once the child has been accepted for evaluation and eventual diagnosis at the National Assessment Centre, the third stage *"the growth of conviction"* took over. It takes usually six to eight weeks for a child to be assessed by a team of different professionals including medical doctors, psychologists, and therapists of various kinds. By the end of that period, parents are given the results of a comprehensive battery of tests and observations (including medical, psychological, physiotherapy, as well as speech and language tests). They are then given the label of the child's disability and advice on their rights and how and from where to get support. In a few instances, the local pediatrician and other local experts carry out the negotiations with parents, and finally provide the label and suggest supports. The fourth stage *"the labeling"* is accomplished with the degradation of the child into the disabled child.

However, how families interpret the meaning of this process must be contextualized. The meaning is defined within the family interaction patterns, family rhythms and routines, activities and attitudes, and the relationship between the family, its social network and professionals, within the larger cultural interpretations of impairment and disability. The meaning that families give to the impairment is not uniform. Such contextualization depends upon the perspectives of different families, the power balance between the professionals and the parents, the professional portrayals of parental reactions that have roots in the professionals' formal expertise and practice (Ferguson, 2001). All these ingredients go into the paradigms that the parents and the professionals must negotiate to reach the new construct, that of the disabled child and how to deal with the new situation of the family and the child, different visions of a future, and a new decisions to be made to ensure that future.

Our Child Given by God or Fate

Having a child with disabilities is described in various ways by parents and in the research literature (Bjarnason, 2002, 2003b; Ferguson, 2001; Ferguson & Ash, 1989; Kirkebæk et al., 1994; Turnbull & Turnbull, 1997). Many, but not all parents describe their first revelation "that something is not right" as a fundamental shock with life-changing consequences. I have interviewed scores of parents of disabled children and youth from all walks in life who remembered that experience in almost graphic detail. Thirty parents (forty-four individuals) of young disabled adults were interviewed for the research mentioned above and published in a book (Bjarnason, 2004). Those data form the basis of the stories told "the older parents," that is, those parents who had the child "God" or "fate" gave them. Each story is unique but there are similar themes that run through most of them. For example, a mother of an eighteen-year-old girl with significant impairment described her experience so:

> As soon as they gave her to me I saw that something was the matter. I said it aloud. They all heard me and the delivery room grew instantly quiet … It hit like thunder … it was just awful. The child was not normal … it was a crisis.

A mother of a twenty-four-year-old woman with intellectual impairment said: "I do not remember what the doctor said, I just felt that my daughter had died and now we had to figure out what to do with this syndrome."

Ásta and Andri, the parents of two children, both born in the late 1970s with a life-threatening dystrophy, realized that something was not quite right with their elder son's movements. In the first two years of his life they took him from one doctor to another in search of help, but without success. In the meantime they had another child born with the same diagnosis. Finally when they got the correct diagnosis, more damage had been done to the body of their elder son owing to a wrong treatment. The parents reacted to the diagnosis with disbelief. The mother, Ása said:

> I do not remember much from the first weeks after … Mother helped and family and friends. Still, I remember that we were completely worn out. We decided to take a good holiday. Jón [the older son] was in a cast, but that was no problem. We had a good car and we put him on the back seat. We went to our summer resort in the mountains … I have beautiful memories from this time … But what I remember is this deep sorrow gnawing at me … or may be it was not sorrow, the sorrow had not manifested itself yet. The sorrow did of course not come immediately, and they had not yet diagnosed Páll [the younger son] … The kids were so happy … and this was some how … this cannot be true. A kind of denial for a time … It was in a way not so hard.

A year later after they had the diagnosis of their younger son, the shock hit them. Ása said:

> It was the darkest time of the year. Then I just … my greatest wish was that we would all die some how. I thought it would be good to crash with a plane, so we did not have to endure what was ahead … it would have been good to have somebody, some professional service that could have explained … at first I thought I was getting insane … I simply did not want to live … there was nothing but a pitch-dark night, nothing to smile about and nothing to look forward to.

And she explained that it was the heaviest blow they had ever had when it dawned on them that there was nothing to be done. The only thing they could do was to give the boys a quality life as long as possible.

These parents learned to support each other. They realized that, at the beginning that they grieved most intensely at different times and that that probably saved their marriage. "One could be stronger while the other weakened for a while." They said that they had gone through some difficult times in their marriage, but learned to cooperate, laugh together, and to divide the workload and time.

Many parents ask "why us," "how could this happen to us," but there are also parents who accept the difference almost immediately with words like "why not us?" It is not uncommon for parents to grieve when they learn that their child is not perfect and that its difference may affect its life in the society that is not geared for including disabled people. Most parents grow to love their child, and they get used to their child's difference. Their child is their child and the difference is part of who he or she is.

All the parents of disabled children who did not know in advance that their child might be born with an impairment experienced a painful period of the degradation of their child, which gradually or rapidly constructed it into "a disabled child." The actual label was often felt as a relief from uncertainty and opened up a new era of sorrow, but also of learning and for the most part coping with a new and taxing situation as a part of their everyday family life. When the label was finally in place, the Othering process (Brantlinger & Ross-Campbell, 2001) took different forms depending on what choices the parents made from available generic or special services and what supports they were able to enlist for themselves and their families (Bjarnason, 2002). However, all these parents shared the feeling that their disabled child was first and foremost their child, impaired by an act of "God" or "fate." The child and its special needs was viewed by the families as their "private troubles" (see Mills, 1959). Thus it was seen to be up to the family to carve out rhythms and routines of family life. To do this, enlisting professional help and other support that the family found necessary, creating supports that were missing, or adapting to available professional as well as formal and informal services, all these were seen as important.

THE CHOICE GENERATION—YOUNGER PARENTS

The younger parents had their impaired children in the new era of knowledge, technology, and new generally available prenatal services including the opening up of the ultrasound scanning to all pregnant women. When the ultrasound and the subsequent battery of tests showed significant fetal difference, the potential parent(s) faced the difficult choice of whether to terminate the pregnancy. On the other hand, couples who had done everything that the medical experts had advised, but still had a child with impairment, faced a different dilemma. Their child was born impaired, despite "a clean bill of health" from the experts.

This section is based on interviews with ten parents, six couples, and four single mothers. The data were collected in 2004–2006 and were a part of a research in process. For all the young parents the birth of their disabled child occurred in a different social context from that of the older parents "more natural" or traditional experiences.

Some of the younger parents who had prenatal screening indicated that the fetus was abnormal, decided to have their disabled child even against professional advice. Others did so with the full support of the professionals, and still others did not know in advance that the fetus was damaged. Either the mother had not gone to prenatal screening, or she had done so and been told that everything was in order, but subsequently gave birth to a disabled child.

Ólafur and Sólveig, the parents of Vera, a daughter with a genetic impairment born in the late 1990s described how they experienced the prenatal services and the birth. This story is unique to these parents' experiences. However, even though other such parents' stories were not quite so filled with demeaning details, this account represents some of the themes they reported. The mother, Sólveig, explained that her pregnancy was normal until some bleeding occurred in the sixteenth week. Then she had her first prenatal screening and the couple was assured that everything was fine. Then in the nineteenth week they went again for screening. They had not planned to go, but did so in the end. Sólveig described their experience thus:

> This is a kind of family meeting, people come out with pictures and there is lots of excitement and joy. So we went like everybody else, very excited … All of a sudden the atmosphere changed. A woman came in and started talking to the others.

The parents were sent out of the room and had no idea what was coming, not even when they were told to wait for the doctor, and have another ultrasound done. Then the obstetrician came and they realized that something was not right with their unborn baby's brain. Sólveig said:

> When I got home it seemed to me that more or less all the baby's brain was missing … You don't listen properly, maybe they do not tell you clearly enough, or may be you cannot comprehend what you are being told. I remember the medical staff looking at books with pictures. I just lay there kind of numb … they [said] … can it be this or that?… leafing through, comparing pictures, getting out some more books, trying to figure this one out… I was lying there and he [my husband] was sitting by me on a chair. It was as if we were nothing. Then they sent us home. We went home, and decided to have the child, impairment or not. This was our child.

As we talked, I probed further wondering why they made the choice. Sólveig paused for a minute and then replied: "I don't really know. This was always our child … it was as if the medics were silly, I saw them as a bit stupid. We knew that this was our child, never mind what they said about it." Sólveig was in her nineteenth week of pregnancy and had stopped working. She was over thirty, and they were ready for a child. And, she pointed out:

> The doctors did not mention the word child. All they talked about was "a picture," "the brain," "the fetus"… Nobody mentioned a child until we went later for information to a pediatrician … he used the word child.

I asked her what advice they got from the doctors, and she said that they did not give specific advice, but she thought that they expected her to have an abortion. When the parents returned to the hospital two days later, they refused more tests because they feared that they would harm their unborn baby. A doctor asked if they were going to have the child. Sólveig said:

> I answered, yes, and he said; Do you know what this costs, do you know what this means, and do you know anyone who is disabled? He went on and on … in a nervous blabber. I tried to explain that we knew disabled people, and that we had made our decision. Then someone got our obstetrician. He came directly from an operation, with blood on his coat. He heard our story and said; Yes, sometimes this happens, that we discover such things. We will try and do all we can for you for the rest of your pregnancy. He supported us and respected our decision.

Ólafur remembered the birth clearly. He said:

> Her water broke in the early evening. I took her to the hospital, but we were asked if we would mind if the birth was delayed so that some people could be there. We did not refuse, we did not know [that the doctors at the teaching hospital wanted a number of students and experts to attend the birth] … Then, the next morning when we went into the delivery room, it was lined with people … It was as if they expected a monster. I did not know what to say. Then the obstetrician entered. He looked around, obviously angry, and told everyone not directly involved to get out. That was a big relief … Then our daughter was born and looked beautiful, nothing like the children in the pictures …

These parents described their young daughter, with great love and pride. At age six, Vera could read and could not wait to start school. She had suffered a life-threatening illness, and been in and out of hospitals for almost four years, but got through that with excellent medical help. Life was again good to the small family. Yet, the mother said that if she got into the same situation once more she could not say beforehand what they would decide (i.e., have a second child with impairment or not) These quotes were given to health professionals I interviewed and they were asked to comment on them. Some of their comments are referred to below in the section on professionals.

The context in which this data is anchored begs a lot of questions. Why had the parents envisaged their unborn child as a child, but the professionals saw only a brain or an impaired fetus? Did the fact that the parents knew some people with disabilities who enjoyed their lives make a difference to their decision? How can one explain the different perspectives of various medical staff? Why did the couple have to witness the consultation of medical books, and why did they feel that they were treated like objects? Further, why did they not get adequate counseling, why was the delivery delayed, and why was the delivery room filled with people? Many more questions come to mind, but I argue that these data reflect contraries in peoples' perspectives, and that the individual/medical model, held inappropriately, caused the hurt and the clumsiness that the data lay bare. For Sólveig and Ólafur, their pregnancy was turned into a time of anxiety and fear for the future of their unborn child, and worries about whether they could cope as parents and as a couple. The actual birth was turned into an undignified episode, a theater with a clinical lesson for the potential onlookers, and a deeply humiliating event for the parents. Things such as prenatal counseling are said to have been improved but these prospective parents' feelings of despair, dilemma, and being rushed remains one major theme arising from this data.

Ólafur and Sólveig, who knew in advance that they were going to have a baby with impairment, reported that their pregnancy was a difficult time. Margrét, a mother who had gone through a fertility treatment and was expecting twins, knew in advance that one of them was most likely be significantly impaired but that the other was not impaired had to make a difficult decision along with her husband. Aborting one fetus would destroy the other. Because the couple was unlikely to be able to conceive again, they decided to go through with their pregnancy. Those parents praised the medical services and supports they received throughout from the diagnosis onward. When their one child was borne with multiple disabilities and significant health problems, the doctor and other health staff guided them through the maze of both health and social services, ensured that they got whatever special service and financial support available, and kept in contact with the family for years. Margrét described the doctor as "a true friend and a wonderful man. He supports us even now—and he has saved our family. I do not know what we would have done without him."

The younger parents did not speak with one voice about their and their child's predicament during the prenatal period. But all the parents interviewed said that in retrospect they could not imagine their families without their impaired child, but many acknowledged that they would make use of prenatal screening and possibly choose not to have a second impaired baby.

The younger parents had in common a tendency to look at special services and professional and financial support from the state as a right. This holds true whether or not they choose inclusive or segregated service settings for their disabled child. This may be partly explained by changes in social policy and the fact that that specialized services are more readily available now than they were twenty years ago. The parents who chose to have their baby despite its fetal difference saw their choice as inevitable for them and stated that given such a choice, society was also responsible for the provision of support for the child and its family. I also interviewed parents who believed that they had "done everything according to the book"; obeyed their doctors, had the ultrasound, gotten "a clear bill of health" for their prospective baby, only to have a disabled child. These parents certainly expressed their love and care for their child as did the other parents in this research, but they were the most likely to see their child's impairment and disability as a public issue as well as a private trouble.

PROFESSIONALS

The Icelandic medical profession is highly trained and medical doctors enjoy a high social status. Most work long hours and try to do their very best for their patients; they are also aware of broader public health issues and of their own hospitals' reputation backed by official public health statistics. Doctors are able to make use of the hegemony invested in their profession to influence their patients' choices beyond choices directly related to their patients' medical conditions. Professional medical work contains many a priori assumptions and prejudices about normality and full human existence. From the individual/ medical model's perspective, impairment is inevitably a serious harm and a significant infringement on the autonomy of the future child (Shakespeare, 1999) and a costly public health problem. Thus prospective mothers (and their partners) are often encouraged by medical practitioners, to have their pregnancy terminated when prenatal ultrasound and a subsequent battery of tests indicate certain genetic deviations such as Down's syndrome, Fragile X syndrome, Huntington's disease, and others for which there are no effective treatments or cures available. But the perspective also encourages scientists and medical practitioners involved with prenatal screening or the screening of babies, to search for ways in which to alleviate possible pain and suffering by preventive treatment or symptom management trough the use of drugs, other preventive methods and gene therapy such as in the case of Cystic fibrosis, Phenylketonuria (PKU), and others (Ward, 2001). Doctors and other medical experts are also trained to be concerned with disability as a public health issue that needs to be minimized as much as possible. Furthermore, the fact that Iceland has good public health records including one of the lowest neonatal and child mortality rates in the world may also impact the medical perspective.

Medical staff, trained to alleviate suffering and prevent harm, tend to favor screening and the termination of pregnancy when the fetus is found to be impaired. Prospective parents are more than likely to share this view owing to the widespread acceptance of the medical perspective. Such prospective parents are likely to take upon themselves the suffering of abortion to save their future child and the family from suffering, stress, and harm, and to prevent the unborn fetus the loss of future opportunities. This is more likely if the information given to prospective parents, and the verbal or nonverbal attitudes of the professionals support such decisions, and when society does not provide sufficient and necessary support for impaired children, adults, and their families (see Bogdan, Brown & Foster, 1982).

Voices of the Medical Experts

Medical experts related to an ultrasound unit, three doctors, two nurses and two midwifes were given a transcript of the part of the interviews with Ólafur and Sólveig, the expecting parents quoted above, who experienced a room filled with people at the birth of their child. After reading the extracts carefully, one health worker commented that she had heard such stories before. She believed that these parents had already formed a picture of their baby in their minds before its birth. When I probed further, she explained that she thought that when something unexpected that did not fit that picture was detected, the parents' reaction was to paint the staff "in dark colors" because "it is well known that the bringers of bad tidings are often portrayed like that."

Another health worker commented on the episode where the father talked about the number of people who expected to attend the birth of his daughter:

> You can expect up to 10 to 12 specialists to be present at a birth if it likely to become complex and difficult. That is how it is. But it seems to me that the example you are giving me could be 10 to 12 years old ... We try not to do this like that [referring to the ultrasound episode]—but sometimes we have to compare notes.

A midwife commented further and said:

> It is extremely uncomfortable and difficult for people when they are told that something may not be OK—You lie there full of anticipation, you want to see, and to ask questions. But the staff working the ultrasound instrument neither can nor will answer. We need time to figure out what this is, time to understand that this cannot be dealt with in an ordinary way ... This story does not necessarily imply that the medical staff particularly wanted this woman to have an abortion ... It seems as if this particular woman experienced all this in an especially negative way, may be because in her mind and that of her husbands the fetus was 100% "their baby." When we then say something that does not fit their understanding, then everything we try can be seen as negative ... up until the doctor with the blood on his coat, came and said: "Yes, yes, I am your friend, I stand by you ..."

It is interesting that the staff interviewed on the one hand stated that the prenatal services had been greatly improved, and that the story reflected in the transcripts must be an old one. At the same time the staff interviewed, all justified the work methods used and reflected in the data extracts. It was an uncomfortable part of their work to give a few expecting parents devastating news. I was also told by a medical expert in charge of the ultrasound screening and subsequent tests, that the counseling of expecting parents whose fetus was found to be unusual had improved. Procedures for whom, how, where, when and how much to tell had been clarified in recent years and leaflets and other written information had been made available to both staff and the parents-to-be. Thus the doctor was convinced that the information given to such expectant parents was objective. But research suggests that there is no such thing as an unbiased counseling (Kerr & Shakespeare, 2002). People providing others with information and counseling are affected by their own perspectives. The medical model perspective on disability and the concern with broader public health issues as well as personal experiences and beliefs are bound to shape the experts point of view, and affect both "the telling" and the counseling.

The Negotiation Process

Health workers interviewed explained that when ultrasound and the subsequent battery of tests showed "fetal abnormalities," it is up to the potential parents to make the decisions. "This is their fetus," explained one health worker. "We give them all the relevant information about the facts." However, she added: "we present the information differently to different people." She said that the medical professionals at the prenatal services apply the following considerations when deciding how to present the facts about the fetal impairment to potential parents:

- The prognosis regarding the fetus's health if born;
- The child's potential intellectual development;
- The socioeconomic situation of the prospective parents;
- An estimation of the potential parents' psychological/emotional strength;
- An estimation of the strength of the marriage or relationship of the couple;
- An estimation of the possibility of a quality of life for the potential child if born.

Clearly only the first of these considerations is related to the scientific knowledge-based disease model and the skills of medical professionals. Even here the meaning of the term "health" may be problematic. All the others are outside their particular professional sphere, and based on their social and educational backgrounds, their experiences, their will to help and heal, and their concerns with disability as a public health issue. The doctors are examining the individual unborn child, but they may also see public health issues to be sorted out. They are socialized to view parents-to-be and the unborn impaired child as patients, thus objectifying them. Foucault's (1963) term *the medical gaze* is helpful here. It implies the power the medical professionals gain over their patients when they denote the often-dehumanizing method of separating the patients' body from the person in diagnosis and treatment. This term captures some of the broader social issues involved, that reify the impaired fetuses as "a social artifact" and how that is communicated to parents-to-be who themselves are placed under the gaze as patients.

No systematic data are gathered by the medical experts to evaluate, for example, the potential parents' emotional strength or the strength of their marriage or relationship. The hegemony of the profession is both strong and persuasive to potential parents without knowledge in medical science. Furthermore the potential parents do not know about the considerations referred to above. They do not know that such value judgments are used by the professionals to "slant the facts" when giving them the bad news, and they have not yet seen their baby except as a blurred blob on a screen.

In the light of this, the negotiation process between the potential parents and the professionals has to be uneven and based on subjective speculation and perspectives on the meaning of disability. These perspectives are, on the one hand, embedded in our Nordic culture and society that has a strong belief that intelligence, personal independence, and self-sufficiency matter greatly to every individual and that each life has a purpose and value (see for example *Hávamál*, a poem from *ca*. 800). On the other hand, we have the medical perspective that disability is an abnormality harmful to individuals, families, and a public health problem.

Sometimes parents and professionals agree on a course of action. Potential parents and health professionals are in an agreement when the prognosis suggests that the baby, if born, is unlikely to live much beyond the birth or likely to suffer great and prolonged pain. In such events potential parents and the professionals I interviewed were likely to agree on an abortion. They were also in an agreement to see the birth through, where the fetal impairment was seen to be minor or reparable, for example, if the baby was likely to be born with a cleft lip. Other instances were much more tricky to negotiate. Where a medical professional might think an abortion would be appropriate, as for example when the child would be born with significant intellectual impairment and/or irreparable physical abnormalities, the expectant parent(s) thought of their fetus first and foremost as *their child* and objected to an abortion, as in the example above. Parents of the choice generation who chose to have *their child*, despite a negative prognosis, were aware of rights and public services for disabled children and their families in Iceland. These parents expected to have social support options that the older parents could not expect. Thus the social conditions surrounding the younger parents may have influenced their decisions.

As Kerr and Shakespeare remind us, despite the powerful cultural and social forces "that undermine people's autonomy, and which prevent individuals and families from exercising informed choices in the antenatal scenario" (Kerr & Shakespeare, 2002, 6), the professionals felt that they should at all times try to give expectant parents "correct and appropriate information." One of the key players on the ultrasound team said: "The problem is a fact and the professionals try to ..." and then she listed:

- Gain time (certain things need to be looked at more than once).
- Consult with colleagues.
- Contact the doctor that the woman or the couple trust the most.
- Try not to hurt.
- Present the information in such a way as to try and affect the decision in favor or against an abort.
- Direct the woman or the couple, when possible and appropriate, to available support. Such support can, for example, be The Association of Parents of Children with Down syndrome, a clergyman, a deacon, or a social worker.

Recent research shows however that there is no such thing as a nondirective counseling (Kerr & Shakespeare, 2002, 120–141). The professionals have the power of diagnosis and the belief that they are acting professionally and providing "correct and appropriate information" about a given fact. It takes determination and courage to oppose their professional advice, advice that will affect the future of the family and the unborn child. Only parent(s) who apparently had developed a clear vision of their fetus as *their child* and who longed for a son or daughter found that courage. In one instance the expecting parents, who had tried to conceive for a long time, had to choose between aborting twins, only one of which was found to be impaired.

The families I interviewed who had done everything the prenatal services advised but who still had a baby with impairment, were disappointed with what one father jokingly called "the damaged good." These parents loved and cared for their child and were proud of her. However, there was a sense of: "what if?" and "but," and "whose responsibility?" in their narratives.

CONCLUSION

The chapter demonstrates that there is a marked difference between the traditional birth and subsequent labeling of a disabled child, as experienced by the older parents and the experiences of the parents of the choice generation. The former had to accept the hand fate or God dealt them as best they could. When these parents gave birth to a child with impairment, the principles (the laws and statutory regulations) of our social policy affecting the lives of disabled people and their families were either brand-new or unclear. Further, the systems and practices involved in providing necessary and adequate formal support were in their infancy or nonexistent. The social construction of their disabled child mostly occurred gradually within the negotiation process between the parents/family, the professionals, and the families' larger social network, after the birth of the child. On the other hand, the parents of the choice generation gave birth to their impaired children in an area when the principles of the relevant social policy had been made much clearer both with regard to rights and special support needs of disabled people and the families of disabled children and youth. However the systems and practices involved still leave much to be desired. They are fragmented, underfinanced, and manned by professionals such as health workers, teachers, social workers, and others—sometimes unqualified persons—who have bought into the medical model as if it was the only perspective.

Different from the older parents, the parents of the choice generation, often experienced challenging dilemmas *before* their child could be born, or they faced an unexpected impairment despite having followed the rules and believing that all was well. The way people make choices or deal with dilemmas is situated in their personal histories, their experiences, knowledge, and perspectives that are embedded within their societies and culture. Personally, I do support women's and their partner's right to choose. But the politicians who create and shape social policy should be crystal clear about the principals of equity for all disabled people and their families to full active participation in society and all its institutions, and the policy should ensure necessary and sufficient support to that end—financial, institutional, and ideological. Furthermore, the teachers at educational institutions such as the university, the teaching hospital, and other relevant educational establishments need to rethink the education of professional experts who are likely serve parents of disabled people (from before birth to adulthood). Social policy must not only spell out clearly the principals of full human rights for all it citizens, but also provide and sustain adequate, inclusive, and individualized support systems for disabled people from birth onward, and for the special needs of family members of disabled children and youth.

General knowledge of adequate support in the event of impairment in the family and the probability of a different but good life is necessary if we want to enable couples to exercise real choices to continue or terminate pregnancy in cases where significant genetic or developmental conditions are diagnosed. The professional experts providing information need to understand that there are many possible outcomes from giving birth to and rearing a disabled child. The experts should also be sensitized to possible discrepancies between their interests as members of their professional communities and the interests of the parents and their disabled child. The choice rests with the parents. All choices are situated in social contexts, and we have the duty to ensure that those contexts are supportive of both possible decisions in the widest possible sense. That goes also for women's (and their partners') right to choose prenatal screening and tests, obtain full and adequate information if impairment is a significant characteristics of the fetus, and to terminate pregnancy if they believe that this is the best option for the potential child and the family. But I do worry about the sociocultural context in which choices are made and the lack of coherence within the Icelandic social policy and practice in this context. Are the medical professionals and the prenatal counselors helping the parents, adequately informed by the social model perspective as well as the medical knowledge, or are they locked within the more common medical model? The answer to that question may decide who is going to get born and who is not.

Disability is neither measles nor a syndrome. Disability has more to do with how individuals and society relate to people with impairment, their families, and close friends. The prenatal screening technologies are available and will be refined and used. However, prospective parents should be given a broad picture, including information from families with similarly impaired children and from disabled adults, and then be supported in their own choice. Different parents will then make different choices.

Disabled people form an integral part of all human society. The quality of life and the human rights of disabled people are not just their private troubles, but important public issues. The important question is, how can we build a more flexible and accepting society that includes, supports and values different or disabled people?

REFERENCES

Berger, P.L. & Luckman, T. (1967). *The social construction of reality: A treatise in the sociology of knowledge*. London: Penguin.

Bjarnason, D.S. (2002). New voices in Iceland: Parents and adult children: Juggling supports and choices in time and space. *Disability & Society, 17* (3), 307–326.

Bjarnason, D.S. (2003a). School inclusion in Iceland: The cloak of invisibility. In B.T. Peck (Ed.), *Education: Emerging goals in a new millennium*. New York: Nova Science.

Bjarnason, D.S. (2003b). The social construction of adulthood with a difference in Iceland. In J. Allan (Ed). *Inclusion, participation and democracy: What is the purpose?* (pp 83–104). London Kluwer Academic Publishers.

Bjarnason, D.S. (2004). *New Voices from Iceland: Disability and young adulthood.* New York: Nova Science.
Blumer, H. (1969). *Symbolic interactionism: Perspective and method.* Engelwood Cliffs, NJ: Prentice Hall.
Bogdan, R. & Taylor, S.J. (1992). *Qualitative research for education: An introduction to theory and methods.* Boston, MA: Allyn & Bacon.
Bogdan, R., Brown, M.A. & Foster, S.B. (1982). Be honest not cruel: Staff/parent communication on a neonatal unit. *Human Organization, 41,* 6–16.
Booth, T. (1978). From a normal baby to handicapped child: Unravelling the idea of subnormality in families of mentally handicapped children. *Sociology, 12,* 203–221.
Brantlinger, E.A. & Ross-Campbell, Zaline (2001). Trends in disproportionate representation: Implications for multicultural education. In C.A. Utley & F.E. Obiakor (Eds.), *Special education, multicultural education, and school reform.* Springfield, IL: Charles C. Thomas.
Corker, M. & Tom, S. (2002). Mapping the terrain. In M. Corker & T. Shakespeare (Eds.), *Disability/postmodernity* (pp. 1–17). London: Continuum.
Crook, S. (2001). Social theory and the postmodern. In G. Ritzer & B. Smart (Eds.), *Handbook of Social theory* (pp. 308–323). London: Sage Publications.
Denzin, N. (1996a). Sociology at the end of the century. *Sociological Quarterly* 37, 743–752.
Denzin, N. (1996b). Prophetic pragmatism and the post modern: A comment on Maines. *Symbolic interaction,* 19, 341–356.
Directorate of Health [Landlæknisembættið]. Retrieved on July 7, 2006 from Directorate of health Web site [Landlæknisembættið]: http://landlaeknir.is
EFTA homepage (http://secretariat.efta.int/Web/EuropeanEconomicArea/EEAagreement). Retrieved on August 9, 2006.
Ferguson, P.M. (2001). Mapping the family: Disability studies and the exploration of parental responses to disability. In G.L. Albreckt, K.D. Seelman & M. Bury. *Handbook of disability studies,* pp. 373–395. Thousand Oaks, CA: Sage Publications.
Ferguson, P.M. (2003). Winks, blinks, squints and twitches: Looking at culture and disability through my son's left eye. In P. Devlieger, F. Rusch & D. Pfeiffer (Eds.), *Rethinking disability: The emergence of new definitions, concepts and communities* (pp. 131–147). Philadelphia, PA: Grean/Coronet Books.
Ferguson, D.L. & Ferguson, P.M. (1995). The interpretivist view of special education and disability: The value of telling stories. In T.M. Skrtic (Ed.), *Disability and democracy: Reconstructing special education for postmodernity* pp. (104–122). New York: Teachers College Press.
Ferguson, P.M. & Ash, A. (1989). Lessons from life: Personal and parental perspectives on school, childhood and disability. In D.P. Biklen, D.L. Ferguson & A. Ford (Eds.), *Schooling and disability: Eighty-eight yearbook of the National Society for the Study of Education: Vol. II,* pp. 10140. Chicago: National Society for the Study of Education.
Foucault, M. (1963/1975). *The birth of the clinic: An archeology of medical perception.* New York: Vintage.
Gergen, K.J. (1997/1994). *Realities and relationships. Soundings in social construction.* Cambridge, MA: Harvard University Press.
Getz, L. (2006). *Sustainable and responsible preventive medicine: Conceptualising ethical dilemmas arising from clinical implementation of advancing medical technology.* Trondheim, Norway: NTNU Innovation and Creativity.
Getz, L. & Kirkengen, A.L. (2003). Ultrasound screening in pregnancy: Advancing technology, soft markers for fetal chromosomal aberrations, and unacknowledged ethical dilemmas. *Social Science & Medicine,* 56, 2045–2057.

Goffman, E. (1963). *Stigma: Notes on the management of spoiled identity.* Engelwood Cliffs, NJ: Prentice Hall.

Hávamál. (e. The Words of The High) (ca. AD 800) Retrieved July 10, 2006, from Virtually *Virtual Iceland* Web site: http://www.isholf.is/gardarj/havamal.htm

Herbertsson, T. (2005). Fjölgun öryrkja á Íslandi: Orskakir og afleiðingar.Retreieved on July 7, 2006 from Ministry of Health in Iceland Web site [Heilbrigðisráðuneytið]: http://www.heilbrigdisraduneyti.is/media/Skyrslur/Fjolgun_oryrkja_-_orsakir_og_afleidingar.pdf

The High Court of Iceland [Hæstiréttur Íslands]. (2000). *High Court case no. 125/2000.* Retrieved on July 7, 2006 from High Court of Iceland Web site [Hæstiréttur Íslands]: http://www.haestirettur.is/

The Icelandic Ministry of Foreign Affaires Homepage (http://www.mfa.is/) Retrieved on July 18, 2006.

Kerr, A. & Shakespeare, T. (2002). *Genetic politics from eugenics to genome.* Cheltenham, UK: New Clarion Press.

Kirkebæk, B., Clausen, H., Storm, K. & Dyssegaard, B. (1994). *Skröbelig kontakt: For tidligt födte born og deres samspil med omgivelserne.* Köbenhavn, Dansk psykologisk Forlag.

Landsspítali University Hospital [Landsspítali- háskólasjúkrahús.]. Retrieved on July 13, 2006 from Landsspítali University Hospital Web site [Landsspítali –háskólasjúkrahús]: http://www4.landspitali.is/

Law on the Affairs of the Disabled [Lög um málefni fatlaðra] (1992).

Law on Assistance of the Mentally Retarded [Lög um aðstoð við þroskahefta] (1974).

Mead, G.H. (1934). *Mind, self and society.* Chicago: University of Chicago Press.

Mills, C.W. (1959). *The sociological imagination.* New York: Oxford University Press.

The National Curriculum [Aðalnámsskrá Grunnskóla] (1999). Reykjavík: Ministry of Education [Menntamálaráðuneytið].

Ólafsson, S. 1999. *Íslenska leiðin: almannatryggingar og velferð í fjölþjóðlegum samanburði,* Reykjavík, Háskólaútgáfan.

The Salamanca Statement and Framework of Action on Special Need Education. (1994). Paris: UNESCO.

Schwandt, T. (2001). *Dictionary of qualitative inquiry.* 2nd edition. London: Sage Publications Inc.

Shakespeare, T. (1999). Losing the plot? Medical and activist discourses of contemporary genetics and disability. *Sociology of Health and Illness, 21* (5), 669–688.

Shakespeare, T. (2001). Introduction. In Ward, L., (Ed.), *Considered choices? The new genetics, prenatal testing and people with learning disabilities.* Worcestershire, UK: British Institute of Learning Disabilities.

Statistics Iceland [Hagstofa Íslands] *Statistics 2004–2005.* Retrieved on July 12, 2006 from Statistics Iceland [Hagstofa Íslands] Web site: http://www.statice.is/

Titmuss, R.M. (1974). *Social Policy: An Introduction.* B.A. Smith & K. Titmuss (Eds.). London: Allen & Unwin.

Turnbull, A.P. & Turnbull, H.R. (1997). *Families, professionals and exceptionality: A special partnership.* Upper Saddle River, NJ: Merrill.

Ward, L. (2001). *Considered choices? The new genetics, prenatal testing and people with learning disabilities.* Worcestershire, UK: British Institute of Learning Disabilities.

Wolcott, H.F. (1995). *The art of fieldwork.* Walnut Creek, CA: AltaMira Press.

CHAPTER SIXTEEN

Czech Republic: Empowerment OF d/Deaf Community THROUGH Education (1945–2006)

JITKA SINECKA

INTRODUCTION

This chapter introduces the state of Czech d/Deaf education before and after 1989. It was in 1989 that the communist regime ended in the country. It examines the prohibition of Sign language in education during communist rule and its impact on people with hearing impairments and d/Deaf people. The second part of this chapter discusses the emerging empowerment of the Czech d/Deaf community through education and Sign language in the last decade in the historical, political, and social context. In conclusion, personal accounts and narratives of parents and d/Deaf young people illustrate the history and current state of d/Deaf education as well as the oppression of the Czech d/Deaf community in the past. Although the focus of this chapter is the Czech d/Deaf movement, there have been many characteristics and milestones shared internationally, such as debates over oralism or Sign, debates about the use of cochlear implants, or exclusion/inclusion in education.

In this chapter, I argue that while integration of d/Deaf children and young people into mainstream regular schools for hearing students has increased after 1989, there are still obstacles to successful educational integration of d/Deaf children. Education and the usage of Sign language can also contribute to the empowerment of d/Deaf community that experienced a rebirth after 1989.

Although more and more hearing teachers are educated in special programs to teach the d/Deaf and are aware of the importance of Sign language in d/Deaf education, it has not yet become a common practice in spite of the existence of Sign Language Act of 1998.

The deprivation for more than forty-five years of a full, natural language has created a gap that is hard to bridge. The barrier can be overcome with the arrival of new d/Deaf and/or hearing teachers who will be able to use Sign language, with the full implementation of the Sign Language Act that would enable integration of more d/Deaf children and students into regular schools, and with changing assumptions about the potential of d/Deaf people both in hearing and d/Deaf communities.

HISTORICAL, SOCIAL, AND CULTURAL CONTEXT

The Czech Republic is a relatively small country with ten million people. There are no exact statistical data on the total number of people with disabilities in the country, yet there have been many attempts to count different groups of people with disabilities, either for census or various ministries and their benefits. There are disparities among these data and the number of specific groups of people with disabilities due to varying definitions of what it means to be a person with a disability in different laws and policy sectors. For example, the "Report on the Situation of the Disabled" submitted to the Government of the Czech Republic in 1992 (Governmental Board for People with Disabilities, 1992) estimates that there are approximately 300,000 hearing impaired persons, and 15,000 persons profoundly d/Deaf. Hruby presents slightly lower estimates of the number of d/Deaf people: 10,000 d/Deaf and 250,000 hard of hearing people (Hruby, 1998). He notes that the majority of the hard of hearing individuals are elderly and thus they are not Sign language users. The number of d/Deaf people in relation to the whole population is not an exception to European or world average; 1% of all citizens.

The milestone in the Czech disability history is the year 1989. Earlier, the country was part of a communist block under the Soviet influence; after 1989, the democracy and civil society were established. The communists allowed only one centralized disability organization to exist ("Syndicate of Invalids") and other groups of people with disabilities were clustered together under this umbrella organization. People with disabilities did not literally exist during the communist Czechoslovakia and were hidden in institutions, special schools, sheltered workshops, or their families. Deaf people were also oppressed. The only d/Deaf people's organization existed under the umbrella of "invalids." Sign language was not officially recognized and d/Deaf culture was diminishing because of its ignorance and nonrecognition by the governing party (Hruby, 1999). D/deaf people were experiencing similar situations not only in other countries of Central and Eastern Europe, but also in Germany, Great Britain, United States and many other countries, where exclusion models in schools and public life were common.

After the 1989 "Velvet Revolution" and the fall of communism, the politics, economy, and civil society faced the new challenge of democracy and capitalism. Integration of d/Deaf people into dominant society and inclusion in regular schools, workplace, or life activities became modern and powerful concepts in disability studies and activism internationally (Buchanan, 2002; Lane & Grodin, 1997; Priestley, 2001). Nowadays, there are several nonprofit organizations of and for the d/Deaf, hard of hearing, and hearing people that offer d/Deaf people an opportunity to come together. There are also parental or self-advocacy groups, all advocating and lobbying for various d/Deaf issues. They publish magazines; provide interpreting services, social and legal counseling, psychology advisory; and organize social and cultural events, leisure activities, and so on.

DEAFNESS AND EDUCATION (1945–1989)

Historically, d/Deaf children received special education in separate d/Deaf schools in many countries (Buchanan, 2002). In the communist Czechoslovakia, from 1945 to 1989, children were educated in special schools for d/Deaf that were further divided into categories depending on the hearing loss: there were schools for d/Deaf, pupils with residual hearing, and the hard of hearing. It was also claimed that children with minimal hearing loss were the most intelligent, so the quality of education was highest and most demanding at their schools compared with schools for d/Deaf. This pattern has continued to the present. The curriculum was developed alternatively to the mainstream education due to the perceived slow progress in learning and speech difficulties that was a result of aural teaching and the teaching of hearing teachers who had knowledge of sign language. Power and Leigh argue (as quoted at Marschark and Spencer, 2003) that "historically, specialized curricula, particularly at the upper school levels, focused on vocational (typically industrial) rather than on academic objectives" (p.42) with an emphasis on language and speech production. They also talk about so-called hidden curriculum that "refers to the unplanned learning outcomes associated with learners' exposure to particular attitudes, actions, and ideas" (p. 41). Given the fact that d/Deaf people were also referred to as "dumb" in Czech language and viewed as "intellectually weak" (Lane, 1993, p. 279) as speech relates to thinking, there was even a wider gap between claimed curriculum and the reality.

The prevailing teaching method was oralism claiming to teach children to speak and lip-read; the teachers were hearing teachers. This created a gap and lack of informal communication between pupils and teachers. Oralism became a dominant ideology in d/Deaf education worldwide after the Milan congress of teachers and specialists in 1880. Lane argues that the real intent of the ideology of oralism was to remove Sign languages and d/Deaf teachers from the education system, so that the system could be placed entirely in non-d/Deaf hands (Ladd, Gulliver and Batterbury, 2003; Lane, 1984). While teachers encouraged children to speak and lip-read, Sign language "survived" among d/Deaf people, in their families, and communities. However, local and generational differences existed and still exist among individuals.

There were no high schools for d/Deaf students in the country with the exception of two schools ("gymnasium" in Jecna and textile high school in Brno), and the job-training chances were very limited—men were usually trained as locksmiths, women as seamstresses. These two areas encompass around 80% of qualified and educated d/Deaf people (Hruby, 1999). Since there are no statistics from that period, this number is supported by personal experiences of d/Deaf people and this pattern was confirmed by interview results of more than 100 d/Deaf adults (Sinecka, 2000). Besides, d/Deaf people could receive vocational training as house painters, bakers, and carpenters, or they worked as cleaners and housekeepers. Sign language was prohibited in education. The personal accounts of d/Deaf young people confirm that children used to be punished when they tried to sign in schools (Baynton, 1996; Gregory, Bishop and Sheldon, 1995; Sacks, 1990; Sinecka, 2004). Oralism, limited choice of schooling, and the ban on Sign language were not limited to Czechoslovakian borders, but were happening in other countries in the world, such as Austria, Germany, Great Britain, or United States (Marschark and Spencer, 2003). However, the language still "survived" among people, and d/Deaf children of d/Deaf parents helped to spread Sign language in classrooms, among children coming from hearing families.

1989–2006

After 1989, we can truly talk about a renaissance of Czech Sign language. Sign language structure and grammar were researched, new dictionaries were published, Sign language courses and study programs for d/Deaf students were established; d/Deaf people were involved in analyzing the language and disseminating it among d/Deaf and hearing people.[1] With the deaf young people getting increasingly educated, schools started hiring d/Deaf assistants and sometimes even d/Deaf teachers in schools for d/Deaf. The most significant achievement of the d/Deaf community was the approval of Sign Language Act No. 155 in 1998, which recognized Sign language as a minority language that has a full potential for valuable communication and has an independent status from Czech language. The law also stated that d/Deaf children and students were guaranteed the opportunity to be educated in Sign language both in special and mainstream schools.

After 1989, some d/Deaf schools emphasized so-called total communication; some focused on bilingualism and some others remained oral. Although Sign language was used more often in classrooms, the usage was still not sufficient to cover the needs of d/Deaf students and to be in compliance with the Sign Language Act. Consequently, the implementation regulations of this act limited the amount of free interpreting hours for forty per month per child, which is in no way enough. Also, school curriculum for d/Deaf pupils is still rather simplified when compared with regular schools and divided over more years (*"Special Schools,"* 2006). Thus, d/Deaf children's school attendance is ten to eleven years comparing to nine years of "normal" students; d/Deaf children who are mainstreamed in regular classrooms at a later age usually encounter problems with "advanced" curriculum.

INTEGRATION OF D/DEAF STUDENTS

Before 1989, there was no mention of integration of children with disabilities in the existing school system and legislation. The Ordinance of the Ministry of Education, the Youths and Sport No. 291 of 1991 on Elementary Schools allows for a possibility, but not an obligation, to integrate children with sensory, learning, or physical disabilities into regular classrooms. Both parents and the principal of a particular school must agree with the integration of the child (in some cases, even parents of potential classmates must agree with integrating child into the classroom). Special Pedagogical Centres were established by a ministerial regulation in 1991 with the purpose of providing children and their parents with help, advice, and support in the process of school and social integration. In the 1991 Ordinance, the Ministry also introduced a plan for individual integration similar to the U.S. Individualized Education Plan (IEP). The ministry also agreed to be responsible for the financial support for every child with a disability in a class and took over the cost of necessary classroom equipment. Today, local authorities and districts manage the system after the public administration reform in 2004.

According to a study by Jaroslav Hruby (1998), approximately 40% of d/Deaf children were integrated into regular kindergarten with other hearing pupils in 1997. In 1997, 34% of d/Deaf children attended regular elementary schools; 2.1% were in special schools for hearing children with educational problems; 24.5% of d/Deaf children attended schools for d/Deaf, and 39.4% went to schools for hard of hearing children where those gifted d/Deaf children able to speak and lip-read were sent by their parents or teachers from d/Deaf schools to access advanced curricula. Approximately 20% of d/Deaf students were integrated into high schools for hearing students. Although this number does not seem too optimistic, there has been some positive development when compared to limited choice of secondary school education during communism.

D/deaf students now have an opportunity to pursue a university diploma. Three study programs exist specifically to accommodate the needs of d/Deaf students. These are "Special Education" study programs at several Schools of Education around the country, "Dramatic Education" at Janacek Academy of Music and Dramatic Arts in Brno, and "Czech Language and Communication" at the Faculty of Philosophy at the Charles University. The last is the only academic institution in the Czech Republic where there are Sign language interpreters available during all classes. Based on my research, I estimate that the entire number of d/Deaf students at university level is approximately thirty to forty.

Studies show (Hruby, 1998) that integrated children were somewhat exceptional: their hearing loss enabled them to communicate orally, they did not use Czech Sign language, they could speak comprehensively, and many of them acquired cochlear implants.[2]

EMPOWERMENT OF THE DEAF COMMUNITY

The Czech d/Deaf community unquestionably has been experiencing a different environment after the fall of communism. The growing awareness and self-confidence of d/Deaf persons currently results from increased educational opportunities, recognition of the Czech Sign language by law, in politics, education, and academia, and the reemergence of the d/Deaf community. Another factor that positively contributed to empowerment of d/Deaf people was the technological revolution and an increased access to information. Many new devices such as special phone equipment called TTY, Internet access, and electronic communication enable d/Deaf people to overcome the isolation and to access and share information to the extent they never could before.

Education is one of the areas that can have an impact on the identity and self-confidence of young people. With regard to education, d/Deaf children have increased choices of schools and programs at various levels today. They also get access to higher education that they never had during the communist regime. There are higher academic demands on children in d/Deaf schools, and more and more students are integrated into regular schools with hearing children. All these factors contribute to emergence of a new generation of d/Deaf persons, who are educated in programs of their choice by using Sign language, are proud that they are d/Deaf, and form the new d/Deaf elite (Gregory, Bishop and Sheldon, 1995; Sinecka, 2004).

EMPOWERMENT BARRIERS IN EDUCATION

Yet, there are still barriers and challenges to be overcome: The requirements for d/Deaf children are still reduced at some schools and the special d/Deaf school's curriculum is still simplified. The majority of teachers in d/Deaf schools are hearing and although they have an opportunity to attend Sign language classes for their professional enhancement, many of them do not take it as they are not required to use Sign language in their classes. Many of them prefer oral methods as I have witnessed during my research and numerous onsite visits of the traditional three d/Deaf schools in Prague (Sinecka, 2002). The inability of both general and special education teachers in schools to sign also creates a gap between them and their students who use sign language to communicate among themselves both in out of classrooms. Moreover, owing to the lack of Sign language interpreters and the inability of schools to pay for them (this issue remains unresolved even after the recent Sign Language Act of 1998), there are insufficient services in place for d/Deaf students to facilitate communication and the schooling process.

There is a lack of the d/Deaf elite and role models who would have a larger impact on d/Deaf children and on the development of self-understanding and self-recognition as d/Deaf individuals. There is also lack of images of d/Deaf professionals in the media that would empower the d/Deaf community and create positive patterns to follow. Hurst argues (1995) that one of the lessons learned from European Union countries and their disability organizations is that "disabled people must take a leading role in their own empowerment process" (p. 534) Clearly, d/Deaf people have not yet fully accepted the leading role in the Czech Republic. Only recently, for the first time, d/Deaf individuals were elected as presidents of two main nonprofit organizations for the d/Deaf in the Czech Republic. The third organization in the country is still run by hearing people. Hearing society is often viewed as superior due to the access to information and power structures, which creates internal barriers for emergence of d/Deaf identity and movement.

There is also the unresolved implementation of the Sign Language Act of 1998. Although the law provides for interpreting services at schools, it has not yet been made clear who will pay for such service and how many hours of schooling will be covered. The latest version of the implementation regulation launched by the Ministry of Social Affairs stated that only around forty hours of interpreting per month are guaranteed by state (Sign Language Act of 1998, www.msmt.cz).

It makes up a week of classes. This speaks to the communication gap between d/Deaf students in regular schools and their hearing peers and teachers unless the latter show an effort to learn Sign language. Organizations for d/Deaf, advocates, and self-advocates protested against the limited hours, but the issue is yet to be resolved.

EDUCATIONAL EXPERIENCES: NARRATIVES OF D/DEAF YOUNG PEOPLE AND THEIR FAMILIES

The second part of this chapter is based on qualitative research and in-depth interviews conducted with five families, both hearing and d/Deaf, with d/Deaf young people in Prague, the Czech Republic during 2002–2003 (Sinecka, 2004). In this research, comparative perspectives of d/Deaf young people, their parents, grandparents, and siblings were sought on various issues, such as discovering the child's d/Deafness, family reactions to it, upbringing of the child, communication within and outside the family, schooling and educational experiences, employment, independence, friendships and partnerships, or identity. This research was enriched by critical analysis of articles on education and deafness, d/Deaf identity, the state of disability policy in Central and Eastern European countries, newspaper articles on d/Deaf education in Czech Republic, or analysis of organizations for d/Deaf and hard of hearing people in the Czech Republic.

"If you Sign, he Won't Speak": Education and Oralism

Many families with d/Deaf children have raised their sons and daughters during the dominant ideology of oralism in the 1970s and 1980s. They were advised by doctors and "professionals" such as speech therapists, audiologists, or special education teachers not to use Sign language; otherwise—they were too often told—the child will never learn to speak. From today's point of view, this is perceived by all researched families as a mistake based on their contemporary experience with Sign language. The opinion that the usage of Sign language will stop the development of speech in the early age has been proved an untrue assumption in many studies (Bradacova, 1998; Gregory, Bishop and Sheldon, 1995; Marschark and Spencer, 2003).

A hearing mother of three deaf children experienced the largest deficits of oral communication. She was advised by "experts" to speak and not to sign. Paradoxically, she devoted extensive time to practicing speech and lip-reading with the oldest son, whose spoken skills are very limited today. On the other hand, the youngest daughter, who received the least of oral and speech therapy training (after parents realized the failure of oralism) and learned sign language from her siblings, now speaks most comprehensively and also has acquired a foreign language. The mother reflects on the past:

> *I was persuaded that oralism was good, but now I see that it was not. It is not entirely true that if a child learns to sign, he or she will never learn to speak. Our third child has never learned to speak so artificially in front of a mirror as the other two, and her speech is very comprehensible. She learned everything from her siblings and at school.*

Deaf parents were also challenged by the prevailing oral paradigm and were forced to speak to their children if they could, or pass the education and upbringing to the hearing family members, which was the case of both d/Deaf families in the research.

A d/Deaf mother says that she did not sign with her son until he was seven when he came back from school and signed her a story he learned from his classmates. She realized how fast he could acquire signs and develop communication skills compared with his struggle with oral communication. She says:

> When he was at the first grade, I started to sign with him, because till then, I was waiting for him to start speaking. But he did not; he just looked at me and around. He understood me when I talked to him loudly, but did not respond. I wondered how fast he picked up sign language. I was surprised how easily kids understand things in sign language and wondered why the professionals did not tell us.

The decision where the child goes to school was also influenced by the professionals' advice—a child was assigned to a school based on the severity of the child's hearing loss. There were three special schools in Prague at that time, one for deaf students, one for children with residual hearing, and one for hard of hearing pupils. A hearing mother of one family says:

> We put him to this school because the doctor told us to do so. We did not have any choice, we just followed their advice.

Doctors have been traditionally looking for ways of curing illnesses and fix disabilities. Susan Wendell argues (1996) that "scientific, Western medicine has both the cognitive and the social authority to describe our bodies to ourselves and others" (p. 117), owing to the language barriers (the terminology) or the knowledge gap. Thus, doctors wanted to fix the child's deafness by speaking to the child and teaching the child how to lip-read.

> Another mother recalls the limited choice of schools. She says: *My son has always asked me: Why should I, when I have all A grades, have a choice of 4 study programs that are locksmith, dressmaker, baker and one more? I was desperate and did not know what to reply.*

As the curriculum was limited in the d/Deaf and residual hearing schools, gifted d/Deaf children could exceptionally enter the school for hard of hearing pupils. This happened in one of the families, and the girl, although deaf, was educated orally and learned to speak. The grandmother of the family explains:

> We struggled to get her to Jecna elementary school (the school for hard of hearing). We tried twice as for the first time our daughter was not in a good mood and did not like the principal who interviewed us and tried to play with her. In Jecna elementary school children were educated orally, but our daughter had no problems to lip-read or speak. We wanted her to go there as the curriculum was more advanced. People said back then that Holeckova (the other school for d/Deaf children) was the final stop at the educational journey.

A d/Deaf girl of d/Deaf parents who used Sign language since her childhood remembers the hard time she had in a classroom with predominantly speaking teachers:

> Everything was just repeated again and again and explained as long as kids got it. Everything was so primitive and I wanted to learn more. I wanted to learn how to write a correct Czech sentence but we spent so much time on repeating the same things again and again. If only Sign language had been used, children would have understood everything easier and quicker.

Higher Education

All the d/Deaf young people in this study attended high schools after 1989 at the time when Sign language was rediscovered, and when interpreters started to be available for d/Deaf people. Thus if we compare elementary with high or university education, we find that the deaf young people's memories of high schools and/or college are positive because of to the extended communication in Sign. A d/Deaf girl says:

> I was so happy when I was admitted to the university program. It was perfect—the way they lecture and translate everything into Sign language, it was great. We also had a really good subjects and I have learned a lot during the first year.

When evaluating their schooling experience, d/Deaf young people liked the high school period the most, when compared to the elementary and middle schools. They mostly concluded that the reason was the nonusage of Sign language at the lower school levels. Susan Gregory, who interviewed more than 100 families with d/Deaf children, came up with similar conclusions. She writes that d/Deaf young people reflect on the elementary school period as a time when they were confused and did not fully benefit from the educational process. On the other hand, they showed more understanding of their environment and surrounding in high school classes, and their identity and self-understanding as d/Deaf persons have increased during this period (Gregory, Bishop and Sheldon, 1995).

CONCLUSIONS

Importance of Sign Language

Based on the personal accounts and memories of d/Deaf people and their families, it has been shown that using Sign language during early childhood, in families and at schools for d/Deaf children is of crucial importance (Baynton, 1996; Marschark and Spencer, 2003; Sacks, 1990). The interviewed parents struggled with oralism and could not find an efficient communication tool. They talked and their children tried to lip-read. Children in hearing families noted feelings of frustration and loneliness. d/Deaf young people suffered from prohibition of Sign language in their schooling, and felt deprived growing up in hearing families where they often missed the context of events or conversations. Later on, in their adolescence years, all interviewed d/Deaf people found their self-confidence in Sign language communication and through the discovery of a sense of community among those who identify with d/Deaf culture. Nevertheless, communication in hearing families remained oral and is viewed as established status quo, although some parents recognize the importance of Sign language for their children.

So why is Sign language so important? Acquiring any language in early childhood is essential to developing a second language, and literacy in this language—for the majority of d/Deaf people, the second language is the spoken and written language (Marschark and Spencer, 2003; Gregory, Bishop and Sheldon, 1995). It has been shown that the knowledge of Sign language gives d/Deaf children the opportunity to learn the second language easier by having the roots they can build the other language on and from.

Identification: Deaf as Disabled, Deaf versus Deaf

Some Deaf people consider themselves a language or cultural minority rather than a disability group (Marschark and Spencer, 2003). Although deafness is not perceived as a disability by the majority of d/Deaf adults, and some d/Deaf people consider deafness not to be diversity rather than disability, in the past and in the present, d/Deaf people have been classified as disabled for the purpose of education, social benefits, rehabilitation, accessibility and accommodations, or employment. Lane (1993) suggests that deaf[3] people are living in a deaf community with its own language (American Sign Language [ASL]) and culture is within a cultural frame in which to be deaf is not to be disabled; quite the contrary, it is an asset in deaf culture to be deaf in behavior, values, knowledge, and fluency in ASL. Tucker argues on the contrary that d/Deaf culture is basically a concept developed by a minority of d/Deaf people and their hearing advocates (Tucker, 1993). She questions d/Deaf culture by saying that d/Deaf culture does not fall within the usual realm of "culture," does not have, for example, d/Deaf songs, dances, foods, modes of dress, and so on and that it is a group that chooses to isolate itself from mainstream society (Tucker, 1998). To challenge Tucker's opinion, culture does not need to comprise all areas of life, and, for example, d/Deaf songs and dances do exist (in Czech Republic, for example Ticha Hudba), related to interpretation of music in Sign language. Clearly, what is understood by d/Deaf culture differs at d/Deaf and hearing people perspectives, and "deafness is constructed differently in Deaf cultures then it is in hearing cultures" (Lane, 1995, p. 179).

Some authors argue (Lane, 1995) that the "association with disability has been damaging for Deaf people as it provides policy makers and 'specialists' with an excuse to focus on individuals and their perceived 'impairment' rather than recognizing the intrinsic cultural value of Deaf communities and supporting and protecting their languages" (p. 184). The disability-deficiency model also fails to understand the unique linguistic and cultural community, which frames the lives of d/Deaf people. Lane (1993) further states that d/Deaf people "oppose the medicalization of deafness and challenge the persuasive infirmity model based on special education, special practices at home or wearing of technological stigmata such as electronic devices." Ladd, Gulliver and Batterbury argue (2003, p. 287) that d/Deaf communities have experienced "a savage form of linguistic oppression which has sought to replace their languages but which has also, often, deprived Deaf communities of access and literacy, access to education, to knowledge about shared collective history and culture" (p. 19).

To understand the current claims of d/Deaf community, we have to consider the oppression in the past, history of special education, stigma of being "deaf and dumb" and medicalization of deafness. Czech d/Deaf people also experienced "a savage form of linguistic oppression" during the communist past of the country and in some cases, children are still denied Sign language communication in d/Deaf and regular schools today owing to the inability of hearing teachers to learn the language and the reluctance of principals to hire d/Deaf teachers and fire those who have been in the school for twenty or more years unable to sign (Sinecka, 2002).

After 1989, there were examples and practices from other countries, especially from the United States and Western Europe influencing the reemergence and emancipation of the Czech d/Deaf community. A discussion on writing d/Deaf with lowercase or capital D has developed recently (in mid-1990s) and there are more and more Czech d/Deaf people, especially among young ones, who use the capital letter and identify themselves with d/Deaf culture. The issue of writing and referring to yourself as Deaf versus deaf is related to the sense belonging to a d/Deaf culture (capital D is a signifier of d/Deaf identity that includes language identity (Sign language), social identity (sense of belonging, acceptance by the group—clubs, disability rights movement), and identification with the d/Deaf world and community. The identification with the d/Deaf world is based on shared experiences such as attending schools for d/Deaf, work experience, being outsiders in the hearing world, communication barriers, disability rights movement such as the Deaf President Now movement in 1998, Sign language recognition, minority experience of "difference," and/or oppression (Bat-Chava, 2000, Higgins, 1980).

In my opinion, in spite of the unique history and characteristics of d/Deafness and Deaf movement as language minority (Lane, 1993), d/Deaf people are perceived as disabled by the dominant hearing society. If the disability rights movement wants to achieve a change in societal attitudes and awareness of disability, all people with disabilities should stand united as they share similar experiences and histories. Today, there is no national umbrella organization of people with disabilities in the Czech Republic bringing together representatives and advocates from different disability groups that could represent their broader political and social interests, bringing public attention to disability issues and raising awareness of the challenges they face in dominant society. Based on the construction of d/Deafness as disability, d/Deaf people receive many services that help them integrate into dominant society. They cannot leave in a vacuum, isolated from of the hearing world.

NOTES

1. Sign language research centers are affiliated to universities and their programs for d/Deaf students. Examples include the Charles University in Prague or Palacky University in Olomouc. An independent National Institute on Disability is also engaged in researching the language and preparing dictionaries.
2. Cochlear implants were developed in 1980s and tested first on adults and later on children and babies with whom better results were achieved. Cochlear implantation became a widespread medical intervention sought by especially hearing parents of d/Deaf babies and children trying to find a cure to fix their children's deafness. The cochlear implants research area is primarily presented from the medical point of view, as the implantation is a surgical procedure of an electronic device, and very rarely from cultural and social view of d/Deaf people who consider d/Deafness not to be a disability but rather diversity, and who are proud members of deaf community and culture (Lane 1993; Tucker 1998). The d/Deaf community has tended to view cochlear implants

as another means for "regulating, and, ultimately, eliminating deaf culture, language and community" (Lane 1993, p. 287). However, as a documentary *Sound and Fury* shows (2000), the d/Deaf community is divided between those who believe that cochlear implants endanger deaf culture, Sign language and community, and those who realize how d/Deaf people are isolated in hearing world and wish their children had an easier access to larger society. The issue remains controversial, as some d/Deaf activists and hearing advocates argue, mainly because infants and children are not able to decide on such serious intervention to their life orientation and health, they "cannot give informed consent, and their parents, usually unfamiliar with deaf culture or the deaf community, are unaware of the potential their children have as culturally deaf individuals" (Lane 1993, p. 272).
3. Harlan Lane always uses the term "deaf" referring to both groups, medically and culturally Deaf people.

REFERENCES

Bat-Chava, Jael. (2000). Diversity of Deaf Identities. *American Annals of the Deaf*, 155 (5), 420–428.

Baynton, Douglas C. (1996). *Forbidden Signs: American Culture and the Campaign Against Sign Language*. Chicago: University of Chicago Press.

Bradacova, Zdena. (1998). *Zkusenosti rodicu (Parent's Experiences)*. Praha, FRPSP.

Buchanan, Robert M. (2002). *Illusions of Equality: Deaf Americans in School and Factory 1850–1950*. Washington DC: Gallaudet University Press.

Governmental Board for People with Disabilities. (1992). *The Report on the Situation of the Disabled*. Available online at http://www.vvzpo.cz (March 30, 2005).

Gregory, S., Bishop, J., and Sheldon, L. (1995). *Deaf Young People and Their Families*. Cambridge, UK: Cambridge University Press.

Higgins, Paul. (1980). *OutsidersIn a Hearing World: A Sociology of Deafness*. London: Sage Publications.

Hruby, Jaroslav. (1998). How Many Deaf People There Are in the Country? (Kolik je u nás sluchove postizenych?). *Speciální pedagogika*, 2, 5–21.

Hruby, Jaroslav. (1999). *Velky ilustrovany pruvodce neslysících a nedoslychavych po jejich vlastním osudu*. Praha: Septima.

Hurst, Rachel. (1995). Choice and Empowerment—Lessons from Europe. *Disability & Society*, 10, (4), 529–534.

Ladd, Paddy, Gulliver, Mike, and Batterbury, Sarah. (2003). Reassessing Minority Language Empowerment from a Deaf perspective: The other 32 Languages. Online at <http://www.aber.ac.uk/~merwww/general/papers/mercSym_03-04-08/Ladd,%20Gulliver,%20Batterbury%20paper,%2009.04.031.doc> (October 25, 2005).

Lane, Harlan. (1984). *When the Mind Hears: A History of the Deaf*. New York: Random House.

Lane, Harlan. (1993). Cochlear Implants: Their Cultural and Historical Meaning. In Cleve, John V. van (Ed.) *Deaf History Unveiled: Interpretations from the New Scholarship* (pp. 272–291). Washington DC: Gallaudet University Press.

Lane, Harlan. (1995). Construction of Deafness. *Disability & Society*, 10 (2), 171–189.

Lane, Harlan and Grodin, Michael. (1997). Ethical Issues in Cochlear Implant Surgery: An Exploration into Disease, Disability, and the Best Interests of the Child. *Kennedy Institute of Ethics Journal*, 7 (3), 231–251.

Marschark, Mark and Spencer, Patricia E. (2003). *Oxford Handbook of Deaf Studies, Language, and Education.* Oxford: Oxford University Press.

Priestley, Mark. (2001). Introduction: The Global Context of Disability. In Priestley, M. (Ed.), *Disability and the Life Course: Global Perspectives* (pp. 3–14). Cambridge: Cambridge University Press.

Sacks, Oliver. (1990). *Seeing Voices. A Journey Into the World of the Deaf.* New York: HarperCollins Publishers.

Sinecka, Jitka. (2000). *People With Disabilities: The Community of Deaf – Limits of Integration.* Bachelor's Thesis (*Zdravotne postizené skupiny – komunita neslysících: limity integrace.* Bakalárská práce). Praha: Faculty of Humanities, Charles University.

———. (2002). *Analysis of the Current Situation in Deaf Children Education in Elementary, Middle and High Schools in the Capital of the CR, Prague. (Analyza stávající situace ve vzdelávání neslysících na materskych, základních, stredních a vysokych skolách v hlavním meste Praze.)* A course paper. Praha: Faculty of Social Sciences, Charles University.

———. (2004). *Deaf Young People and their Families, Family and its Deaf Child. (Rodina a jeji neslysici dite, neslysici mladi liede a jejich rodiny).* Master's Thesis. Prague: Faculty of Social Sciences, Charles University.

"*Special Schools.*" Ministry of Education, the Youth and Sport. Online at <http://www.msmt.cz> (March 4, 2006).

Tucker, Bonnie Poitras. (1998). The Auditory-Verbal Approach: The Voices of Experience, Education: The Teaching Perspective, Cochlear Implants and Deaf Culture. In Jefferson (Ed.), *Cochlear Implants: A Handbook* (pp. 93–46, 147–170, 171–193). North Carolina and London: McFarland.

Wendell, Susan. (1996). *The Rejected Body. Feminist Philosophical Reflections on Disability.* London, New York: Routledge.

Video:

Sound and Fury. The Communication Wars of the Deaf. (2000). Directed by Josh Aronson.

CHAPTER SEVENTEEN

Reframing Global Education FROM A Disability Rights Movement Perspective

SUSAN PETERS, KIMBERLY WOLBERS, AND LISA DIMLING

INTRODUCTION

We live in a world that has become increasingly globalized as we enter the twenty-first century. Globalization is a multifaceted phemonenon with multiple dimensions—economic, technological, and political. Stromquist (2002) argues that these dimensions "spill into culture and affect in all-encompassing ways the kinds of knowledge that are created, assigned merit, and distributed" (p. 3). Because this knowledge is central to the creation of new identities, "globalization assigns a special role to education, creating a terrain subject to substantial conflict and contradiction" (p. 16). Current trends in education emphasize international economic competition and participation of all society's members in a global marketplace. Global advances in technological and scientific development have provided unprecedented opportunities that have been transported into homes and schools around the world. These opportunities have contributed substantially to "economic, social, scientific and cultural development and to the ability of people to create communities where diversity is valued … But these same advances have also led to a growing polarisation between societies sufficiently affluent and educated … and those who, through poverty, ignorance and discrimination are denied such benefits" (Shaeffer, Dykstra, Irvine, Pigozzi, & Torres, 2003, p. 2). Disabled people are among those who have been largely excluded from all these changes and development and forgotten. They are often viewed as a burden, and their education as a matter of charity rather than rights.

In the 1960s and 1970s, education worldwide was driven by social justice objectives such as providing greater equality of opportunity, especially to those who had traditionally been underrepresented participants in education. This view of education, as a democratic conception, intended to "equal out the playing fields" by making education accessible to a diverse body of youth and adults.

However, in the past two decades, education has been driven by the human capital paradigm whereby education connotes continuous work-related training and skill development to meet the needs of economic productivity and to emphasize the global marketplace in modern societies (Schuller, Schuetze, & Istance, 2002). These current trends have been made apparent by international corporations and organizations such as the Organization for Economic Co-operation and Development and the European Union (Papadopoulos, 2002).[1] From this view, employability becomes the ultimate objective. Viewing education through an economic lens has shifted attention away from community building to educating a competent workforce with work-related skills.

While there is some rationale and purpose for why education has concentrated heavily on direct utility of knowledge and skills in recent years, the field must not lose sight of original social objectives. In addition to social objectives, current thinking about education has begun to incorporate a humanistic or cultural paradigm in the discourse. A humanistic or cultural paradigm acknowledges that learning may have intrinsic value to a person that leads to feelings of personal fulfillment or satisfaction with one's achievement (Barrow & Keeney, 2001). Learning can lead to empowerment, self-realization, and development of a personal identity— areas of importance for all learners, but particularly for those with disabilities. Contemporary discourses from this perspective often center on "nurturing the personhood" and valuing student choice and needs. This way of thinking is greatly concerned with developing the identity of a person as a cultural participant.

A more balanced view of education in a globalized world can provide flexible opportunities for education of people with disabilities that include active participation in society, promotion of quality life-experiences, and assistance for achieving life goals. Because each approach to education (i.e., economic/human capital, social justice, humanism/cultural paradigm) has something to contribute to an emerging globalized world, we suggest using these paradigms to develop a framework based on the experiences of the Disability Rights Movements (DRM) that incorporates all three. The proposed DRM framework also builds on UNESCO's four pillars of learning (United Nations Educational, Scientific and Cultural

Organization [UNESCO, 1996]). In 1996, the International Commission on Education for the 21st Century reported to UNESCO with a powerful plea to view education in a broader context. The report, *Learning: The Treasure Within* (Delors, 1996), argued that education throughout life is based on four pillars:

1. learning to know: to master the instruments of knowledge
2. learning to be: to develop one's personal identity and to be able to act critically and with autonomy and responsibility
3. learning to do: to gain occupational skills
4. learning to live together: to work toward common objectives, to respect diversity, and to actively participate in all that society has to offer.

Each leg of the triangle in Figure 17.1 corresponds with a particular paradigm, which, when combined with UNESCO's four pillars of learning, can result in multifaceted and holistic, lifelong learning experiences. The cultural portion of the framework, relates to "learning to be" outcomes, the economic portion aligns with "learning to do," and the social component correlates with "learning to live together." These all come together in the center: learning to know.

While the DRM builds on these paradigms and four pillars of learning, the proposed integrated framework for global education uses the disability experience as its platform for developing a model with wider application. In the next section, the disability experience is described as the basis for this wider application.

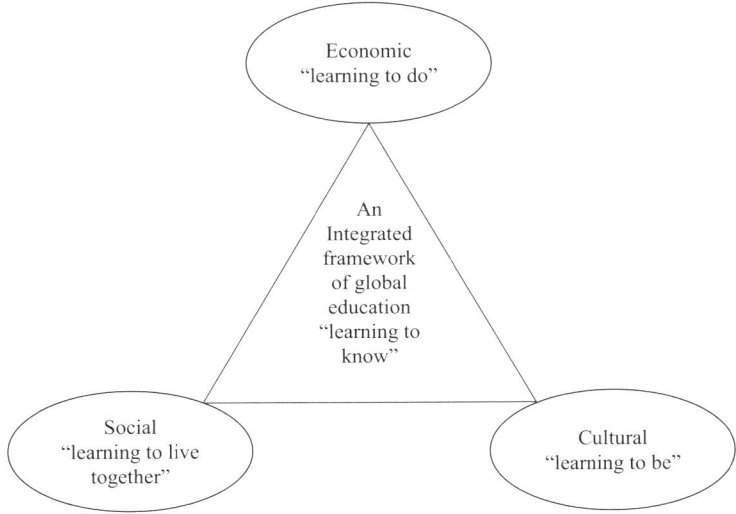

Figure 17. 1. An integrated and balanced DRM framework for global education.

A RADICAL MINORITY PERSPECTIVE: TOWARD A NEW CRITICAL MODEL OF GLOBAL EDUCATION

Historical and social trends in the international movement for social justice of disabled people provide a specific lens through which current notions of global education might be reconstructed. We argue that this lens and its concepts could be applied to *all* learners. In this section we discuss these trends to provide a context for a model that integrates these trends in the subsequent sections.

Historical and social context

A recent report by the Special Rapporteur on Human Rights and Disability found that at least one in ten persons in the majority of countries has a physical, mental, or sensory impairment. Because these persons reside within families, it is estimated that at least 25% of the entire world population is affected by the presence of disability. Of the 500 million disabled people worldwide, 120–150 million are children. Eighty percent reside in developing countries. Further, there is every indication that this number is growing due to global conditions of increasing poverty, armed conflict, child labor practices, violence and abuse, and HIV/AIDS. For example, International Labour Organization (ILO) reports that of the 250 million children working, more than two-thirds (69%) are affected by injury or illness. Almost a third of all people living with HIV/AIDS are 15–24 years of age, or 10 million children and youth—2.2 million in sub-Saharan Africa (Lansdown, 2001, p. 9). In developing countries, 50% of all disabilities are acquired before the age of fifteen. Estimates of the percentage of disabled children and youth who attend school in developing countries range from less than 1% (Salamanca Framework for Action, ¶10) to 5% (Habibi, 1999, p. 2). Once in school, this 1–5% are often segregated from their peers and not provided an education equal to that of their peers. Further, incidence of disability increases with age, so that the total population of learners may reach as many as 600–800 million by the year 2015.

Largely excluded from societal opportunities and equal rights afforded to nondisabled citizens of nation states, disabled people have found solidarity and community through banding together. DRM born from this banding together, have fought for equal rights in all that society has to offer. Their presence at macrolevels of societies began to be felt as early as the 1970s and 1980s, especially in the United States and in England. Today, DRM umbrella organizations such as Disabled Peoples' International and the International Disability Alliance, enjoy international membership of more than eighty countries representing the North, South, East, and West.

One of the priority target areas of disability rights movements is education. To mark the International Year of Disabled Persons in 1981 (later transformed to a decade), the Sundberg Declaration in Malaga, Spain forecasted what was to become an organized effort by international groups of disabled people to put their education on the international agenda (The World Conference on Actions and Strategies for Education, Prevention and Integration, 1981). The concept of education promulgated by these groups corresponds with an emancipation or social justice paradigm of global education. Encapsulated in Articles 3 and 4 of the Sundberg Declaration, disabled people "must be given the opportunities to utilize their creative, artistic and intellectual potential to the full" for their own benefit as well as the community (Article 3). Further, educational programs must be conceived and implemented "within a global framework of lifelong education" (Article 4).

In 1994, the SalamancaStatement—developed at the World Conference on Special Needs Education in Salamanca, Spain—reaffirmed the right to education of every individual, and proclaimed that all learners should have access to schools as welcoming communities that combat discrimination and build an inclusive society. With the adoption of Education For All 2000, endorsed virtually worldwide, 152 member countries must show progress toward including those who have traditionally been excluded from education—disabled people, a significant group among them.

Building on an integrated and balanced framework for global education

Exclusion from schools and formal education has led disabled people to take charge of their own learning. As a radically marginalized sector of society, individuals with disabilities have found solidarity and community to fight for their right to education, through a process of conscientization and identity politics. These processes and politics emanating from community building might serve as a model for future directions in education for a globalized world.

The following paragraphs describe three key principles of a disability rights movement that can then be applied to a reconceptualization of education writ large.

 # 1. The principle of conscientization and community building

First, in the context of disability rights movements, identity politics has been defined as an

> ethic of care that is responsive to and incorporates the diverse characteristics of individuals as agents of change and resistance within an active economic-political agenda negotiated through cultural process of educational praxis. (Peters & Chimedza, 2000, p. 250)

This emphasis on conscientization through educational praxis constitutes education for liberation *from* oppression and *for* transformation through reflection and action. Whether coming together in sanghams in India, or Independent Living Centers in the United States, or sports clubs in Zimbabwe, disabled people have taken on education as a political project for liberation. The process of community building through which they have achieved their education for critical consciousness, includes several steps.

In the first step, through institutionalization and exclusion, disabled people form bonds of togetherness through which they raise their awareness of oppression. Second, informal groups form the basis of socialization in which positive identities develop. In the third step, an interconnectedness develops and members begin to organize, with a concomitant expansion of group membership. This expansion leads to an increased political awareness and a deepening conscientization of oppression in which political identities develop. In the last step, empowered by positive identity—both political and personal—members work to transform oppression in society.

This political and personal project constitutes a key breakthrough in understanding global education as both a philosophy and as a practice. Disability and the strategies developed by disability rights movements offer a way to rethink education that breaks with current thinking in both the social justice and human capital paradigms (Schuetz, 2004, March).

2. The principle of recognition

The second major notion involved in global education from a disability perspective emphasizes *a recognition paradigm*, rather than a *distributive paradigm*. Currently, mainstream social justice approaches to education tend toward concepts of life interest, exploitation, and redistribution. That is, the focus is on injustice for marginalized groups that is rooted in political/economic structures. Social justice models thus tend toward transforming structures, organizations, or governments to allow access, equity, and quality education for all learners. By contrast, the *recognition paradigm* central to disability focuses instead on issues of identity, difference, and culture. Injustice, from this perspective is not rooted so much in political/economic structures, but in cultural disrespect. Disability recognition aims to transform cultural respect within a broad redistributive framework. In essence, the disability recognition principle stands "for the right to communicate, participate, and assert self-determined social identities" (Christensen & Rizvi, 1996, p. 92).

Essentially, disabled people have come together across and within cultural groups to form communities of praxis with the goal of not only educating themselves, but also of educating the educators. In support of this principle, Paulo Freire has said that "education is by nature social, historical, and political" (Shor, 1987, p. 211). At its heart, conscientization and the recognition paradigm involved in disability communities of praxis recognize this nature.

#3. The principle of critical literacy

The final major principle central to a disability approach to global education is critical literacy. As a manifestation of educational praxis from a disability perspective, critical literacy becomes a principle essential to the application of global education. From the recognition paradigm within which disability rights movements operate, literacy is viewed as much more than functional or basic skills. Critical literacy, as used in disability rights movements, refers to "the means marginalized individuals and groups have to communicate their experiences and interests in public discourse" (Rioux, Zubrow, Bunch, & Miller, 2004, p. 31). Thus, critical literacy "does not measure skills people have in reading ... but implications of literacy and societal communication systems in relation to their own ways of communicating" (ibid., p. 101). This notion of critical literacy crosses all subjects and disciplines, not merely reading (see Peters & Chimedza, 2000, for greater specification of these principles).

A PROPOSED CRITICAL MODEL OF GLOBAL EDUCATION

Use of these three DRM principles—(1) conscientization and community building; (2) recognition; and (3) critical literacy—provides a model of global education that departs from previous approaches in at least two important ways:

1. Education becomes a political project that incorporates the idea of communities of learners that is broader than individual learners per se.
2. Education requires more than structural transformation of institutions. It also entails transforming values and beliefs of educators as well as broader cultural practices and beliefs.

An integrated approach to global education, as reconstructed by a disability perspective, balances DRM elements with human capital, social capital, and cultural respect factors. An adaptation of UNESCO's four pillars of education (UNESCO, 2004) that incorporates the principles of disability perspective provides a useful framework for explicating these combined components.

Pillar #1. Learning to do (human capital through educational praxis)

Defined as developing personal initiative, interpersonal skills, and new forms of personal competence combined with personal dynamism and good problem-solving, decision-making as well as innovative and team skills.

Pillar #2. Learning to live together (social capital through community building)

Defined as instilling an awareness of the similarities and interdependence of all people, understanding and respecting multiple points of view, developing a spirit of empathy, and recognizing the rights of others.

Pillar #3. Learning to be (cultural respect through recognition)

Defined as a person's complete development—mind and body, intelligence, sensitivity, aesthetic appreciation, and spirituality. Persons develop their own independent critical way of thinking and judgment so that they can make up their own minds on the best courses of action in the different circumstances of their lives.

Pillar #4. Learning to know (conscientization through reflection and action)

Defined as people learning to understand the world around them, at least as much as is necessary for them to lead their lives with some dignity, develop their occupational skills, and communicate with other people.

Multiple and critical *Domains of influence* in this model include home, work, and community—the primary sites where authentic learning takes place. All ways of learning (i.e., learning to do, learning to be, learning to know, learning to live together) should occur across work, community, and home and school settings.

The *Tools* for implementing the processes are language and literacy, but redefined as critical literacy. These tools are the vertical and horizontal linkages between processes inherent in the four pillars, and spheres of influence. For instance, "learning to know" constitutes conscientization, or an awareness of oppression, and possibilities for transformation (educational praxis). Critical literacy is a tool for developing conscientization that affords marginalized individuals and groups a means to communicate their experiences and interests to public discourse.

In addition to conscientization, there are other learner *Outcomes* with application of this model. Social capital as an outcome is defined as access to and participation in community networks for quality of life. Cultural capital as an outcome involves positive self-identity, self-worth, and participation in the cultural life of communities. Economic capital outcomes mean the ability to generate income in support of the basic necessities of life:food, and shelter.

By incorporating the experience of a radical minority into an integrated framework of global education, a model based on the DRM framework and principles constructs an approach that is uniquely responsive to a diverse body of learners, especially to those who have been traditionally disenfranchised and silenced. Because of the critically reflective and transformative nature of this model, we hereafter refer to it as the Critical Model of Global Education. The components of the Critical Model (i.e., inputs, tools, domains of influence, and outcomes) can be viewed in Figure 17.2.

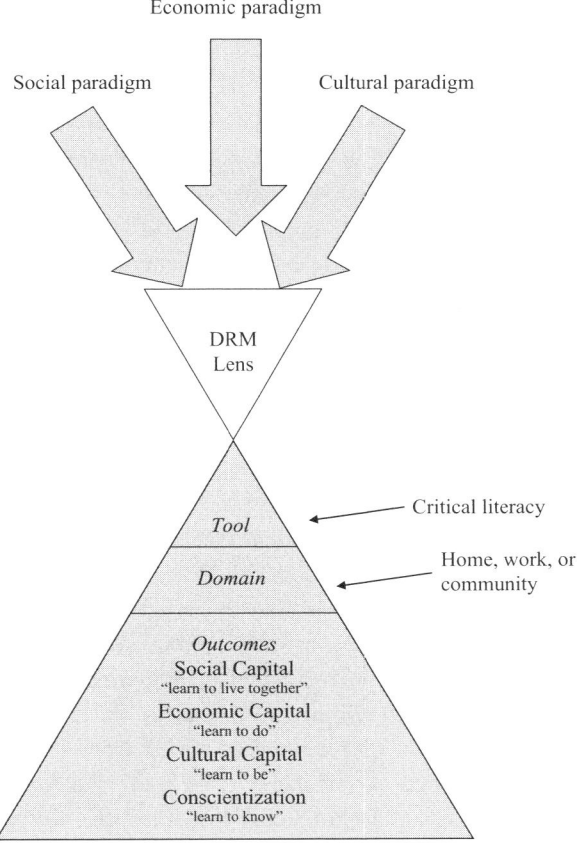

Figure 17. 2. The critical model of global education: Applying a DRM lens to an integrated framework.

In essence, the Critical Model constructs education as reality-based, emphasizing self-determination and cultural respect, while at the same time stressing the interconnectedness between individuals and communities. This model directly addresses a *current paradox* in thinking about global education: How to promote individual autonomy and self-determination, while at the same time address the necessity of living together within a structured society.

APPLICATION OF THE CRITICAL MODEL: DEAF LEARNERS IN THE UNITED STATES

While global education encompasses much more than schools, we focus partly on schools as an opportunity to increase chances for *lifelong* learning, not only for children and youth with disabilities, but for all children and youth. We argue that dispositions toward learning should be planted and cultivated during early years of mandatory schooling, in order for these dispositions to continue throughout their life span.

Using this Critical Model specifically in relation to the schooling and experience of the Deaf[2] in the United States as a radically marginalized sector of society—even within the disability community—we strive to illuminate its practical potentials, and at the same time provide a provocative glimpse of its usefulness in reframing general conceptions of education that may be applicable across different sectors globally. Keeping in mind that Deaf individuals have the commonality of hearing loss but, at the same time, make up a very heterogeneous group in terms of race/ethnicity, gender, and level of hearing loss, we broadly articulate aspects of learner development as they apply to the four outcomes in the model.

Development of economic capital (learning to do)

Across the United States, the nation's system educates more than 40,000 deaf and hard of hearing students annually (Gallaudet Research Institute, 2003). Among these students, those between the ages of fourteen and twenty-one who are required to receive transition services include more than 14,000. Yet, many deaf and hard of hearing students in this age range are not achieving at grade level in reading, writing, and mathematics. In fact, deaf children tend to plateau during this period, making only one year of gain in literacy over a ten year-period from age twelve to twenty-one (Yoshinaga-Itano, Snyder, & Mayberry, 1996). At the time of high school graduation, the median reading level of a deaf student in the United States is commensurate with the fourth grade (Gallaudet Research Institute, 2003). Researchers in the field are perplexed that the reading achievement of deaf high school graduates over the past fifty years (Yoshinaga-Itano & Snyder, 1985) remains stagnant despite intervention and educational, and technological efforts (Kelly, 2003a, 2003b).

A new category of deaf students, in recent years, has been identified by several state vocational rehabilitation counselors; approximately 2,000 students are now labeled "low-functioning deaf" because of their reading and math skills below the second grade level (Bowe, 2003; Dew, 1999). Unsurprisingly, many deaf students do not feel prepared for a work environment, nor do they have the life skills necessary for successful independent living (Garay, 2003). Bullis, Bull, Johnson, and Peters (1995) noted that three to four years after high school, deaf students in the United States had lower rates of work attendance, spent less time at their jobs, earned lower wages, worked slightly more hours, and had had fewer close friendships than their hearing counterparts. Basic academic skills such as reading, writing, and mathematics among deaf and hard of hearing individuals are paramount for successful postsecondary, economic capital outcomes. The attainment of these skills is crucial, not only for occupational life, but for independent living and community participation as well.

Development of social capital (learning to live together)

In the late 1990s and early 2000s, amendments to U.S. federal law IDEA (Individuals with Disabilities Education Act) have increased participation of deaf students in the regular education classroom and curriculum, and reflect the increasing view that diversity is a valued entity. Specifically, there have been greater attempts at breaking down the linguistic barriers inherent in students, evidenced by the exponential increase of hearing students desiring to learn American Sign Language (ASL). Increasingly, educational institutions are acknowledging ASL as a foreign language and are hiring ASL teachers at all levels including primary, secondary, and postsecondary (Rosen, 2005). In addition, growing numbers of general education teachers are learning basic signs and incorporating them into their daily routines or lessons. The mere everyday exposure to deaf individuals, interpreters, and teachers in the classroom who sign has enabled some hearing children to informally pick up conversational elements and vocabulary of ASL. Likewise, deaf individuals have also gained practice in using communication skills with hearing individuals—writing notes, gesture, mime, body language, and conversational sign language are among them.

Whereas the above examples are the successful attempts at community building among diverse individuals, critical barriers to living together, such as access to conversation, still remain. The rising numbers of deaf students who are placed in general education classrooms, for example, has resulted in demands for interpreter accommodations that are difficult to meet: the current needs far outweigh the supply of trained educational interpreters. Thus, some have resorted to hiring signers with minimal sign language experience and education, which, as a result, impedes fluent communication between diverse individuals. Finally, the social needs of deaf learners (i.e., language and communication development, interpersonal skills, turn taking) are sometimes overlooked in a largely diverse body of students. This lack of social opportunities and communication mediation is a structural barrier that stands in the way of deaf children's access to education and social capital outcomes.

Development of cultural capital (learning to be)

At the heart of Deaf culture is a social community rich with language, expression, and shared understanding. Not only is language a way to communicate ideas, but it is also a sure route to cultural participation—for many deaf people, a necessary component of their self-identity. Traditional methods of education have focused heavily on assimilating the Deaf (Lane, 1992) into a hearing society and workforce. Yet, such an approach fails to recognize that a Deaf community with a natural and complete language of its own also exists in the world. The deaf child, for instance, who is fully integrated in his/her home district and not exposed to the larger deaf community and its language is stripped of an opportunity to identify as a bilingual and bicultural deaf person. "Learning to be" a deaf person in the world can either be a prideful or shameful experience and can have lifelong effects.

In recent decades, Total Communication[3] as the predominant language system for the Deaf used in U.S. schools has undergone drastic alterations just as the human capital paradigm has redefined global education initiatives. Educators have changed from viewing Total Communication as a philosophy of interaction to defining it as a method of communication. The method now most always employs the use of simultaneous speech and sign, called "simcom" (ibid.; Woodward & Allen, 1987, 1988). Since ASL and English abide by very different syntactical and grammatical principles, persons using simcom must reconfigure sign language into an English-based version that is compatible with and can be used simultaneously with spoken English. Thus, when Total Communication is adopted as a method instead of as a philosophy, ASL is thrust aside in favor of an English-only agenda. By subscribing to such an agenda, ASL, the language of the deaf community, is excluded from the schooling practices of deaf children and its educational importance is devalued.

It is time to move away from this narrow conception of Total Communication and toward a philosophy of communication that gives equal status to ASL in the schools. Whereas the use of ASL has its instructional and educational advantages

(Stewart, 1990; Wilbur, 2000), here we emphasize the affordances in terms of cultural capital. Deaf students are given the opportunity to identity with the language of the deaf at a young age instead of being unaware of these opportunities until adulthood. Being knowledgeable of the language used in the deaf community opens opportunities for group membership and cultural affiliation, which can be prideful and empowering. Furthermore, such identification can impact students' self-esteem and personal satisfaction when they may otherwise feel isolated. An approach that gives value to ASL in the classroom (see Stewart, 2004) and allows students the option of Deaf community membership is essential to "learning to be."

Conscientization (learning to know)

In March of 1988, the principles of conscientization and community building to transform oppression in society were well illustrated by the deaf community. The world's only university for Deaf and hard of hearing students, Gallaudet University, in Washington, DC, set the stage for Deaf students to rise up and protest against the university's decision to elect a hearing president. Despite support and advocacy for the university's first Deaf president from the Deaf community, students, and faculty, the board of trustees chose to elect the only hearing candidate out of the three finalists. What followed during the week in March was a collective effort on the part of students, faculty, and staff coming together to boycott classes, attend rallies, and speeches, and lend their support for a "Deaf President Now." Student protesters presented the board of trustees a list of demands requiring that both the new president Elizabeth Zinser, and the Board Chair Jane Spilman resign, as well as increasing the percentage of Deaf members on the board of trustees to at least 51%, and no punishment against the protesters (Gallaudet University, 1998a, 1998b, 1998d).

Throughout the week, the national media covered the protest and featured members of the Deaf community, the student body president, and the current president of Gallaudet (Elizabeth Zinser) on radio and television shows discussing the protest and the student's need for a deaf president. After an emotional week of protests and support for the "Deaf President Now," all of the student's demands were met and the university's first deaf president, Dr. I. King Jordan was elected. This movement by the deaf students at Gallaudet University provides support for the elements of conscientization and community building to overcome oppression and transform society. Gallaudet's web site states this well: "at some point, however, the oppressed decide they have had enough; they realize that their circumstances will only change if they take matters into their own hands; they protest" (Gallaudet University, 1997, 1998c).

CRITICAL LITERACY AS A TOOL

In 1996, a group of educators known as the New London Group met in New London, New Hampshire, to discuss the changing face of literacy education and new demands of literacy in a global society. The New London Group agreed that new instructional methods were called for and that they should draw on life world experience, social context, shared meaning making, and the development of a metalanguage. An approach to literacy instruction that incorporates critical literacy as an essential tool would address the global education needs of Deaf students for empowerment, self-determination, and the development of the individual self.

The following is an example of critical literacy as a tool for global education that took place in Dimling's (third author) classroom with a member of the Deaf community.

> My 6th grade class was new to our middle school and had not learned in elementary school how to use a Teletype (TTY) for phone conversations. A TTY is a portable typewriter connected to a phone by a special adaptor. Deaf people can make and receive calls using this special phone. This year, we had a deaf education practicum student who was part of our class for several days a week during the entire year. Mary, who was deaf, was delighted to share her knowledge and experience with our class, and what a great opportunity for literacy instruction, as well as skills that deaf students would need every day of their life in terms of work, social, and community participation! We observed Mary using her TTY, and she demonstrated to the students how to make calls. We made our own calls. We called her at home, called businesses for different services, and used the relay service. Mary also shared TTY etiquette and the right abbreviations with the class as well as stories of how she taught her own deaf children to use the TTY. To further our learning, we continued to make calls. One such call was to our local library to inquire about a book. The library advertised in the phonebook that they had a TTY phone, and so we called. Unfortunately, no one was able to help us. Unable to find the TTY phone, they stated that it belonged to the "deaf woman" on the 3rd floor. In light of this problem, we wrote a letter of complaint to the library regarding their lack of accessibility and basic understanding of the TTY they had in their possession. This example was clearly embedded in a social context with a member of the deaf community, and engaged multi-literacy components. Mary also shared with us some of her lifelong learning strategies, when she recently purchased a new pager with a TTY component and talked about her learning to use the device.

Deaf children and adults not only use visual language as a mode of expression, but take part in essential critical literacy exchanges such as the use of TTYs, e-mail, and social learning. Dimling's sixth-grade class experience illustrates a balanced integrated framework for education that focuses on the multiple Critical Model environments of home, work, and community. It also supports the community aspirations of Deaf students for a rich literacy environment in which they will thrive and succeed. In addition, critical literacy, as a tool of global education, has far-reaching implications for the education of deaf students, as well as other students. This approach calls for building skills in critical literacy through community partners that will allow students to become successful members of their home and family life, community life, and work life, as well as taking part in education that will provide a smooth transition into a life of learning and skill building. Without this approach, Deaf students may not acquire global education dispositions or increase their life chances.

However, this integrated approach does not come without its challenges and commitments. For example, educational reform scholars such as Fullan (1991) note that change is multidimensional, interactive, and requires acceptance at all levels. For successful implementation, several simultaneous goals are necessary:

1. Obtaining proficiency in critical literacy skills.
2. Strengthening the Deaf community and culture in relation to critical literacy.
3. Creating a balance of critical literacy education in all sectors: home, family, work, and community.

Several other factors are also needed in the change process proposed in this example of education for Deaf students. These factors include active and purposeful leadership on the part of members of the Deaf community, supportive professional work environments, positive learning opportunities, continuous improvement, parent involvement, and improved record keeping, among others (ibid.). However, with a strong commitment, the challenges may be overcome and education can truly benefit deaf students.

CONCLUSION: APPLICATIONS AND IMPLICATIONS OF THE CRITICAL MODEL

The Critical Model for global education, with its integrated DRM framework, reveals a move away from positioning the individual as subject, to positioning communities as subject. We live in an interdependent world, in which individualism "may be eroding the 'social glue' that is essential not only for individual and social development, but also for economic development" (OECD, 2001, p. 39).

Global education, as a community project, calls for reinforcement of the social justice function of schools. Recent projects such as the European OECS Schooling for Tomorrow Program have proposed a similar emphasis, however the focus in projects such as these is on "learning organizations" (p. 64) and "learning cities." By contrast, the Critical Model's conception of learning communities rests on recognition and cultural respect beginning at the individual level, but is then cultivated through communities of educational praxis, that is, groups of learners who are both educators and students at the same time. It is only through community building and cultural respect, that economic objectives of the model can be achieved.

The Critical Model of global education through community building, conscientization, critical literacy, and cultural recognition requires several key changes. First, the purpose of schools would need to be defined more broadly than preparation for the world of work, but as preparation for living in *community*. Second, a strong knowledge agenda must be developed and linked to liberation pedagogy as well as the core notion of *critical literacy*. Third, a liberation pedagogy of teaching and learning must be cultivated that supports the core notion of *conscientization* for personal/community identity within public discourse. That is, personal experiences in community should provide the telescope for scrutinizing education policies and for accountability to individual difference. Without a political consciousness that is simultaneously personal and communal, individuals have no influential or sustainable defense against oppression. Finally, a focus on positive identity, and learner as active participant is essential. The current banking model of learning whereby students are viewed as empty repositories who must learn rules of conformity and unscrutinized values, has no place in education for a globalized world. When people find a sense of place through positive personal identity and political identity within community, it allows those who have been marginalized (such as our example of the Deaf students at Gallaudet University) to engage in a transformative project to reconstruct public attitudes toward difference that are manifested in school and society. This transformative project constitutes the core principle of *cultural recognition and is an essential prerequisite to economic transformation.*

Ultimately, the Critical Model with its integrated DRM framework, whether exercised through formal schooling, or outside of schools, provides opportunities for multiple and self-identities of *all* learners to emerge from various cultures and social classes and to engage targets of liberation: worldwide poverty, economic deprivation, detrimental public policies ,and social attitudes—as well as the institutions deriving from these attitudes and policies.

NOTES

1. In this chapter, we define paradigm as particular assumptions about the world, often linked to particular communities of researchers (e.g., humanists, structuralists, functionalists). We view a theory as a body of knowledge emerging from a paradigm that is used to guide research and to organize investigations and communications. A theory is often associated with subjective or

objective dimensions of reality. We define a model as a clarifying and organizing set of practices or tools for testing or deconstructing theories. A model is typically constructed using multiple theories and can be useful within both subjective and objective theoretical frameworks. A framework is used in this paper to mean an organizing schema for a model.
2. In this case, "deaf" is intentionally capitalized to indicate a subpopulation of persons with hearing loss who are culturally and linguistically affiliated with the prideful and collectively empowered, Deaf community.
3. Total communication, constructed by Roy Holcomb in the late 1960s, was a philosophy, not a method, of communicating with deaf children. Total communication was initially created to be responsive to students' needs as opposed to the rigid oral-only method of the time. It involved using one or more methods of communication such as American Sign Language, English-based signing, voice, written expression, gesturing, facial expressions, fingerspelling, or auditory techniques. "The original expectation of (total communication) was for teachers to use the communication method(s) most appropriate for a particular child at a particular stage of development" (Hawkins & Brawner, 1997).

REFERENCES

Barrow, R. & Keeney, P. (2001). Lifelong learning and personal fulfillment. In D. Aspin, J. Chapman, M. Hatton, & Y. Sawano (Eds.), *International handbook of lifelong learning, part one* (pp. 53–60). London: Kluwer Academic Publishers.

Bowe, F. G. (2003). Transition for deaf-and-hard-of-hearing students: A blueprint for change. *Journal of Deaf Studies and Deaf Education, 8* (4), 485–493.

Bullis, M., Bull, B., Johnson, B., & Peters, D. (1995). The school-to-community transition experience of hearing adults and young adults who are deaf. *Journal of Special Education, 28* (4), 405–423.

Christensen, C. & Rizvi, F. (1996). *Disability and the dilemmas of education and justice*. Buckingham: Open University Press.

Delors, J. (1996). *Learning: The treasure within*. Paris: UNESCO.

Dew, D. W. (Ed.). (1999). *Serving individuals who are low-functioning deaf.* Twenty-fifth Institute on Rehabilitation Issues. Washigton DC: George Washington University, Regional Rehabilitation Continuing Education Program.

Fullan, M. (1991). *The new meaning of educational change*. New York: Teachers College Press.

Gallaudet Research Institute. (2003, October 30). *Literacy and deaf students*. Retrieved August 17, 2005, from http://gri.gallaudet.edu/Literacy/index.html

Gallaudet University. (1997). *The roots of unrest*. Retrieved October 12, 2005, from http://pr.gallaudet.edu/dpn/issues/HISTORY/newhistory4.html

Gallaudet University. (1998a). *Day 1: Sunday March 6*. Retrieved October 12, 2005, from http://pr.gallaudet.edu/dpn/issues/THEWEEK/sunmar6.html

Gallaudet University. (1998b). *Day 2: Monday March 7*. Retrieved October 12, 2005, from http://pr.gallaudet.edu/dpn/issues/THEWEEK/monmar7.html

Gallaudet University. (1998c). *Day 4: Wednesday March 7*. Retrieved October 12, 2005, from http://pr.gallaudet.edu/dpn/issues/THEWEEK/wedmar9.htm

Gallaudet University. (1998d). *Introduction*. Retrieved October 12, 2005, from http://pr.gallaudet.edu/dpn/issues/HISTORY/newhistory.html

Garay, S. V. (2003). Listening to the voices of deaf students: Essential transition issues. *Teaching Exceptional Children, 35* (4), 44–48.
Habibi, G. (1999). UNICEF & children with disabilities, *Education Update, 2* (4), 2.
Hawkins, L. & Brawner, J. (1997). *Educating children who are deaf or hard of hearing: Total communication* (Report No. EDO-EC-97-6). Reston, VA: ERIC Clearinghouse on Disabilities and Gifted Education (ERIC Document Reproduction Service No. ED414677).
Kelly, L. P. (2003a). Considerations for designing practices for deaf readers. *Journal of Deaf Studies and Deaf Education, 8,* 171–185.
Kelly, L. P. (2003b). The importance of processing automaticity and temporary storage capacity to the differences in comprehension between skilled and less skilled college-age deaf readers. *Journal of Deaf Studies and Deaf Education, 8,* 230–249.
Lane, H. (1992). *The mask of benevolence.* New York: Alfred A. Knopf, inc.
Lansdown, G. (2001). *It is our world too! A report on the lives of disabled children.* London: Disability Awareness in Action.
OECD. (2001). *Schooling for tomorrow: What schools for the future?* Paris: Organization for Economic Cooperation and Development.
Papadopoulos, G. (2002). Policies for lifelong learning: An overview of international trends. *Learning throughout life: Challenges for the twenty-first century* (pp. 37–62). Paris: UNESCO.
Peters, S. & Chimedza, R. (2000). Conscientization and the cultural politics of education: A radical minority perspective. *Comparative Education Review, 44* (3), 245–271.
Rioux, M., Zubrow, E., Bunch, M., & W. Miller (2004). *Geography of literacy and disability in Canada.* Toronto: Canadian Abilities Foundation.
Rosen, R. (2005, May). *An unintended consequence of IDEA: Mainstreaming of ASL and the American deaf community and culture in education.* Paper presented at the meeting of the Disabilities in Education Conference, New York.
Schuetze, H. G. (2004, March). *Four models of lifelong learning.* Paper presented at the annual meeting of the Comparative International Education Society Conference, Salt Lake City, Utah.
Schuller, T., Schuetze, H. G., & Istance, D. (2002). From recurrent education to the knowledge society: An introduction. In D. Instance, H.G. Schuetze, & T. Schuller (Eds.), *International perspectives on lifelong learning* (pp. 1–21). Philadelphia: Open University Press.
Shaeffer, S., Dykstra, A., Irvine, J., Pigozzi, M., & R. M. Torres (2003). *The global agenda for children: Learning for the 21st century.* New York: UNICEF.
Shor, I. (1987). *Freire for the classroom: A sourcebook for liberatory teaching.* Portsmouth: Boynton/Cook Publishers.
Stewart, D. (1990). Rationale and strategies for American Sign Language intervention. *American Annals of the Deaf, 135,* 205–210.
Stewart, D. (2004). *Instructional and practical communication: ASL and English-based signing in the classroom.* Unpublished manuscript, Michigan State University.
Stromquist, N. (2002). *Education in a globalized world.* New York: Rowman & Littlefield.
United Nations Educational, Scientific and Cultural Organization. (2004). *The four pillars of education.* Retrieved September 7, 2004, from http://www.unesco.org/delors/fourpil.htm
Wilbur, R. B. (2000). The use of ASL to support the development of English and literacy. *Journal of Deaf Studies and Deaf Education, 5* (1), 81–104.
Woodward, J. & Allen, T. (1987). Classroom use of ASL by teachers. *Sign Language Studies, 54,* 1–10.
Woodward, J. & Allen, T. (1988). Classroom use of artificial sign systems by teachers. *Sign Language Studies, 61,* 405–418.

The World Conference on Actions and Strategies for Education, Prevention and Integration (1981, November 2–7). *Sundberg Declaration*. Retrieved August 4, 2006 from http://www.unesco.org/education/nfsunesco/pdf/SUNDBE_E.PDF

Yoshinaga-Itano, C. & Snyder, L. (1985). Form and meaning in the written language of hearing-impaired children. *Volta Review, 87* (5), 75–90.

Yoshinaga-Itano, C., Snyder, L.S., & Mayberry, R. (1996). How deaf and normally hearing students convey meaning within and between written sentences. *Volta Review, 98* (1), 9–38.

CHAPTER EIGHTEEN

A Model FOR Policy Activism

SUSAN L. GABEL

CALL TO POLITICAL ACTION

In what was prescient and now seems imperative, five years ago Len Barton (2001) wrote that "there is now an urgency about the need for further attention being given to the development of a political analysis which is inspired by a desire for transformative change and that constitutes hope at the center of the struggles for inclusivity" (3). To achieve this, he argues against "piecemeal or minimalist approaches" to political analyses. Rather, he adds that a "theory of political action" is needed "which also involves the generation of tactics or strategies for its implementation" (ibid.). In considering whether or not a social movement is positioned for strategic political action, Barton asks two questions.

1. Has the social movement identified the "vacuum, the gaps that are not being addressed and what impact these have on the specific group to be targeted?"
2. Has the social movement amassed the "energy and resources which mobilize people for collective action?" (4)

For the purposes of this chapter I assume that disability studies is part of the broader Disability Rights Movement (DRM) and that disability studies in education (DSE) play an important role in the struggle. In this chapter I respond to Barton's call by outlining a model for policy activism, or strategic action to influence policy for the purpose of achieving equity and other sociopolitical goals. I associate policy activism with conscientization (Freire, 1970), or the coming to full awareness of and engagement with the ways in which policy shapes and reflects to us the world in which we live and the ways in which members of social movements can act to change the world through policy work and toward the goal of a just society. Policy does not exist in an epistemological or value-free vacuum. On the contrary, policy and its associated practices and procedures are tangible evidence of values systems within political structures and processes. Therefore, praxis can be exercised toward policy, as it can be exercised toward practice, research, and theorizing. All activity related to debating or shaping policy is understood here as policy work, a general term under which policy activism can be subsumed; and those individuals engaged in policy work (generally) or policy activism (specifically) are referred to as policy workers. I use the term policy to refer to positions on and delineations of practice outlined in official texts and intended for implementation. Of course there are other policy forms; for example, policy can be informal (i.e., not delineated in official texts but procedures denoted and enacted by practitioners), but this chapter focuses on official policy, as will become clear later.

I believe that the model I propose speaks to the concern underlying Barton's sense of urgency in that it speaks to a gap in the disability studies literature in education in the United States (US)—policy studies—and does so by proposing a framework within which political action can be planned, initiated, and evaluated. Throughout the chapter I use U.S. educational policy as a touchstone, although I believe that this model for policy activism could be useful in other national contexts in which public debate influences policy decisions.

To begin, in the next section I demonstrate the convocation of events that mark the early twenty-first century in the United States as ripe for educational policy activism. After that I proceed to two technical sections—the Model parts 1 and 2—in which I lay out the framework for the Model. These technicalities provide necessary background information for the next section—the Model in action. My conclusion indicates that hope exists in the expansion of the DSE repertoire of policy work and policy research methods, particularly those that speak persuasively to the general public and policy elites (i.e., politicos who wield the purse strings, pass laws, and influence federal, state, and local educational policy and practice.)

THE TIMING OF IT ALL

John Kingdon (2003) has described the critical nature of timing in policy work and in a later section—the Model, Part I—I reiterate this. Kingdon argues that policy windows—the convergence of factors that make it likely that a policy will be enacted—open for short periods of time and can do so unexpectedly. This makes it imperative that policy workers are prepared, organized, and ready with solutions to problems if they are to be influential at all. Carol Weiss (1991) also notes the importance of timing when she identifies how to recognize the moments during which argumentation can be most influential:

1. "when conflict is high … where different sides have staked out their positions, [when] each is seeking justification to strengthen its own case,"
2. in legislatures, where "argumentation is the prevailing mode, and research that supports argumentation will be welcome," and
3. "after decisions have been made," when implementation is of concern and continued argumentation solidifies support for the policy change (Section 3, ¶6).

Using Weiss's three points as a way to assess whether the policy climate in the United States is ripe for the success of argumentation, I propose that criteria #1 (conflict is high) and #3 (decisions have been made) are applicable to the policy contexts within which disabled students are educated in the United States. Although criteria #2 is important I do not include it in this section because disability studies scholars have not, to my knowledge, been engaged with legislatures in the United States in relation to educational policy.

Criterion #1: Conflict is High

Weiss's first criterion for determining whether the time is right for argumentation or debate is when conflict is high. In what follows I provide an all too brief overview of the depth and breadth of the conflicts to which Deborah Gallagher (2006) speaks when she points out that conflict, at least in terms of epistemology, is both high and sustained in relation to U.S. special education.

> Over the past 20 or so years, the philosophical debates in special education have reached the status of what might be described as a pitched battle where those on each side appear to suspect the other of dubious motives and distorted values. (Gallagher, 2006, 91)

Gallagher's time frame suggests a reference to Lous Heshusius's (1989) classic article in the *Journal of Learning Disabilities* articulating her critique of the epistemological foundations of special education. Using the metaphor of the Newtonian mechanistic paradigm, Heshusius argues that in the epistemological paradigm of special education, "all complexity is … broken down into components; translated into practice" leading to, "for instance, task analysis and isolated skill training" (404). Heshusius proposes a new paradigm, a holistic one that emphasizes situated meaning and authenticity. Her metaphor suggests that mechanistic practices remain locked in a distant past without regard for contemporary breakthroughs, much like the early critics of Einstein who did not recognize the significance of his work's challenge to Newtonian physics.

While Heshusius refers in part to the late 1980s flurry of activity around the definition of learning disability, she also addresses the more basic issue of the epistemological foundations of special education. In addition, she argues that the experts of the time were confusing "theory" with "paradigm" and subsequently were "creating an illusion of fundamental change" (407), when in fact there had been no change. This illusion of change more recently has been identified by Roger Slee and Julie Allan (2001) in reference to the paradoxical appropriation of the term "inclusive education" by traditionalists in special education, or those whom Ellen Brantlinger (1997) identifies as individuals who support "traditional educational structures and research methods" (430).

In the last decade epistemological debates in the United States have been particularly tense with a resurgent debate beginning in the late 1990s (e.g., Danforth, 1997; Gallagher, 1998) early 2000s (Sasso, 2001). In his 2001 article, Gary Sasso claims that some scholars critical of traditionalism in special education "spin incongruous theories" that "rush hell-bent to a form of reasoning that disregards truth, genuine inquiry, and intellectual integrity" (179). His attack takes aim at postmodernism, associating it with oppression and "giving up on children" (188). In his article, Sasso's primary concern is with those special educators who question the status quo, particularly Gallagher (1998), Danforth (1997), and Doug Biklen and Judith Duchan (1994). Most recently, the journal *Exceptionality* has published a series of articles in response/rejoinder format in which James Kauffman and Gary Sasso (2006a, 2006b) and Deborah Gallagher (2006) represent contrasting positions in the debates. For their part, Kauffman and Sasso early on argue that "in some cases," and here they are referring to significant epistemological differences, "there is no common ground except the scorched earth of extremists who insist that their view is always and absolutely correct and will entertain no qualifiers" (2006a, 67). Again, postmodernism is to blame for the extremism and it is painted in such broad brush strokes as to encompass critical theory, hermeneutics, and general interpretivism (2006b). Gallagher's (2006) response to Kauffman and Sasso is met in their rejoinder (Kauffman & Sasso, 2006b) with claims that "she puts forward postmodern foppery" (109), associating her with a postmodernism that "give[s] license to demagogues of the extreme left and the extreme right, to fundamentalists and oppressors who define the truth according to their particular orthodoxy regardless of any evidence to the contrary" (111). Claims about fundamentalists and extremism are quite incendiary in light of the current world political climate but they demonstrate the passions that have been brought to such debates.

Criterion #3: Decisions Have Been Made

Weiss's third criterion for determining whether the time is right for argumentation and debate is when policy decisions have been made. With the recent reauthorization of the Individuals with Disabilities Education Improvement Act (IDEIA, formerly IDEA) (U.S. Congress, 2004), one can say that decisions have been made. Interestingly, not only have decisions been made about the IDEIAs content, policy, and funding, but those decisions have produced a document in which the conflicts described previously are reflected in the policy's text. Those conflicts are represented in the IDEIA by the simultaneous presence of two antithetical ethos: (1) the medical model of disability's ethos of identification of deficits and clinical intervention (Ferguson, 2002; Hehir, 2005; Rauscher & McClintock, 1996) and (2) universal design's (UD) ethos of removing barriers to create access for all (Campbell, 2004; Hackman & Rauscher, 2004; Johnson, 2004; McGuire, Scott, & Shaw, 2006; Mino, 2004; Ouelett, 2004; Pliner & Johnson, 2004; Scott, McGuire, & Shaw, 2003). UD is addressed in more detail in other chapters in this book (Burgstahler & Cory, 2007; Marshall, 2007) but briefly, it is a conceptual tool that comes from the ethical principle of universal access. UD was first conceived over thirty years ago by an architect who was a wheelchair user who proposed that physical environments should be "designed to meet the needs of the broadly diverse individuals who access spaces" (McGuire et al., 167; also see Wilkoff & Abed, 1994). As the idea evolved, it has come to be defined by the Center for Universal Design at North Carolina State University (NCSU) as

> the design of *products* and environments to be usable by all people to the greatest extent possible without the need for adaptation or specialized design. (Center for Universal Design, 2006, ¶1, emphasis added)

The IDEIA (US Department of Education, 2004) explicates UD as important for:

1. Technology: Section 674 supports "research, development, and dissemination of technology with universal design features, so that technology is accessible to the broadest range of individuals with disabilities without further modification or adaptation" (p. 118, Stat. 2793; see also Stat. 2797). "Technology with universal design principles" is required "to maximize accessibility to the general education curriculum for children with disabilities" (p. 118, Stat. 2668).

2. General education curriculum: Section 674 requires research centers that "examine and incorporate universal design concepts in the development of standards, assessments, curricula, and instructional methods ..." (p. 118, Stat 2800).
3. State policy: "The state educational agency shall, to the extent feasible, use universal design principles in developing and administering any assessments" (p. 118, Stat. 2688).

Given UD's consistency with a disability rights position on inclusive education and the broader DRM's goal of an inclusive society, one might expect to see resistance to UD. Yet, in the text of the *Federal Register* (U.S. Department of Education, 2006) containing the final announcement of the authorization of the IDEIA, UD is mentioned twenty times. The purpose of this issue of the *Register* is to delineate the final policy decisions and summarize the content of the discussions in public hearings around the country in the months prior to the congressional vote on reauthorization. The text indicates support with no comments or discussion to suggest resistance to including UD in the legislation. In contrast, this issue of the *Register* also contains comments on the more widely known Response to Intervention (RTI) (Fuchs, 2003; Gresham, 2005; Marston, 2005) strategy that indicate some debate on its value and effectiveness. While this report could represent actual public comments and discussions or, conversely, could be the result of congressional authorial decisions, or both, it is remarkable that given the radical nature of UD's ethos of access, the *Register* reports no resistance to it. It remains unclear whether those involved in the reauthorization process recognized the conflicts between UD and the medical model, or if there was an awareness but it was ignored for political expediency. Regardless, such tensions are common in policy and the IDEIA is no exception.

The government has invested millions of dollars into UD research and dissemination projects, which is further evidence that things have been decided at the federal level. Here I mention a few examples. The National Endowment for the Arts (NEA) currently has an open grant competition that seeks proposals for projects that "will create greater public awareness of and demand for universal design environments, by educating designers, consumers, educators ... and others on this important design process" (NEA, nd, Section 5). The Georgia Institute of Technology (GIT) has recently completed a five-year grant to study "the practical use of print and web resources by stakeholders" to document "the continued lack of universally designed products available on the market, despite recent legislation that was intended to boost developments in this area" (GIT, ¶1). The DO-IT program at the University of Washington has received large grants from the U.S. Department of Education, Office of

Postsecondary Education to disseminate information about UD (Burgstahler, 2005). NCSU has received multiple grants from the National Institute on Disability and Rehabilitation Research (NIDRR) to study and disseminate information (NCSU, 2006).

Several states have also recognized the need for and benefits of UD and as the IDEIA is implemented, it is likely that more states will do so. For example, in February 2006, the State of Michigan Board of Education approved the State's educational technology plan in which UD holds a key spot (State of Michigan, 2006). The State's board of education strategic plan for 2005–2010 (Michigan State Board of Education, n.d.) objective #1—"improve all students' achievement in all academic areas especially in English language arts and mathematics" (5)—identifies UD as one strategy for accomplishing this goal in the following way.

> Identify and disseminate resources for universal design for instruction to meet the needs of diverse learners who are at risk for targeted achievement standards. (6)

Kentucky's Department of Education Web site also contains pages on UD related to technology (Commonwealth of Kentucky, 2006). Even the Illinois Alternate Assessment Writing Frameworks Priorities Grades 6–8 (ISBE, 2006) requires the use of UD principles when designing alternative assessments.

UD has not gone unnoticed in relation to K-12 education in the United States. The president's Commission on Excellence in Special Education (U.S. Department of Education, 2002) recommended the use of UD in general *and* special education instruction. The commission specifically stated that "all measures used to assess accountability and educational progress be developed according to principles of universal design" (U.S. Department of Education, 2002, Section 2, ¶ 24).

MODEL FOR POLICY ACTIVISM: PART 1

In the previous section, I use UD as an example of policy decisions that have been made at the federal level. The example of the IDEIA demonstrates the paradoxes that can be found in policy during what Weiss (1991) refers to as times of high conflict. In this case, the ethos of UD stands in contrast to the ethos of the medical model, yet both are established in the IDEIA. Later I return to the UD example to describe ways in which DSE can engage in policy activism. In this section I provide the first part of a model for policy activism. Weiss refers to policy activism as "stirring the policy pot," which puts the policy worker in the middle of the policy process, or what John Kingdon (2003) calls the "policy primeval soup" (116), where ideas float around disconnected from problems or solutions.

(Weiss uses the term policy advocacy but I have adapted it for this chapter.) It is in this milieu that paradoxes emerge, as in the present example of UD and the IDEIA. In an elaboration of his metaphor, Kingdon writes that ideas

> become prominent and then fade. There is a long process of "softening up" … ideas confront one another and combine with one another in various ways. The "soup" changes not only through the appearance of … new elements, but even more by the recombination of previously existing elements. The [ideas] that last, as in a natural selection system, meet some criteria. (116–117)

In the case of the IDEIA, one might conclude that there is an ever so slight fading of medical model interventions and an emergence of attention to UD. In that relationship we see what Kingdon refers to as a confrontation of ideas, something Deborah Stone (2002) has identified as a fairly typical policy paradox.

The idea selection process, which leads to the development of new policy, depends on what Kingdon refers to as an open policy window, or that moment at which problems and potential solutions (or alternatives) convene with the political ripeness that creates opportunities for the policy worker to intervene, offer solutions, and influence change. With UD established in the IDEIA, remaining policy questions include: Will UD, as an idea, gain the attention and support of practitioners? When will state and local policy incorporate UD and how will it be incorporated? Can UD be demonstrated to improve educational outcomes, including access to a rigorous curriculum and the desegregation of disabled students? If enacted, will UD affect the disproportionality problem and if so, how? These four questions represent points through which DSE can enter into relationships and activities that constitute policy activism.

Policy Streams

As previously explained, Kingdon's is a policy model in which the primeval soup gives rise to three policy streams that run simultaneously and in parallel: (1) problems, (2) solutions or alternatives, (3) and politics (Figure 18.1). Policy workers are active in all three streams. In the *problems stream*, they work toward identifying and defining problems or refining problems that have been identified by others. Kingdon purports that unless something is viewed as a problem, it will not receive the attention of politicians or the public. Therefore, the problem stream is a critical one, and it is the job of the policy worker concerned about particular problems to make them visible and to define and delineate them in ways that are persuasive for others. Here, Weiss's notion of argumentation is useful. Policy activists can frame the problem in ways that give like-minded individuals, or those with the potential for like-mindedness, the opportunities to debate and

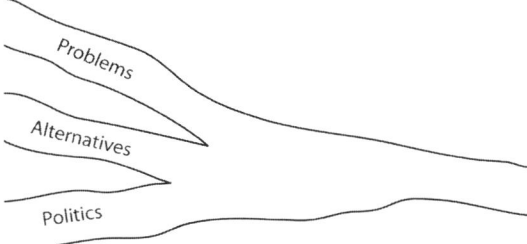

Figure 18.1. Policy Streams.

understand the problem and talk about it with others. Since policy activism is likely to occur during times of high conflict, these opportunities are useful for creating a climate of deliberation in which participants can become invested in and committed to the ideas and their practical consequences.

Kingdon's view of problems is an emancipatory one for those representing a minority epistemology (e.g., DSE) in that in this view, problems are the results of public debate and strongly influenced by policy workers using persuasive conversations and research data as evidence. Remembering that argumentation is most successful in a climate of intense conflict or disagreement—the contemporary epistemological debates, for example—and when decisions have already been made and it is time for implementation, serves to keep the players focused on outcomes they hope to achieve. To succeed in this stream, the minority view needs arguments and research data more so, perhaps, than do those representing the majority view. Fortunately, sound arguments exist and research data are available to us through, for example, the work done by the Harvard Civil Rights Project (HCRP, n.d.; Losen & Orfield, 2002), that has documented the racial inequities in special education. Now that UD is built into federal and state policy, DSE can build on that strength by

1. studying whether and how implementation is taking place;
2. identifying and arguing persuasively about problems of implementation.

In the *solutions* or *alternatives stream*, policy workers are actively creating solutions and remaining ready to combine them with problems when the time is right. Kingdon has argued that streams flow simultaneously and problems and solutions are not necessarily connected until a policy window opens. In other words, the solutions emerging from this stream may not be directly related to problems clarified and argued by policy workers in the problem stream until much later. Using the example of UD, whether or not specific problems of implementation have been identified, it can be predicted that there will be problems and it is possible to predict what some of them will be, for example: resistance to change, fear of "watering down" the curriculum, systemic incapacity, ineffective or insufficient staff development, fading from view, or the loss of public attention (a fairly typical policy problem). In this stream, then, policy activists do not wait for evidence of problems, though evidence is like icing on the cake. Rather, they imagine solutions for possible problems and devise ways of arguing persuasively for their solutions. In the second part of the model I present a framework for understanding how to gather public support for solutions as the need arises.

The third stream, the *political*, is composed of policy elites (e.g., legislators and their aides) as well as the political climate in which they operate. Thus, the community at large operates within the political stream. While the goal of elected public office may not be relevant to most policy activists, the goal of visibility in the public sphere can and should be held in view. Some achievable activities include publication of newspaper opinion pieces, publication in journals for educational practitioners and administrators, working directly with teachers' unions on accessibility issues, and lobbying state and federal legislators.

The counterintuitive aspect of Kingdon's model is in his claim that solutions are not matched with problems until a policy window opens and all three streams unite. Rather than a linear model that flows from problem to political action to solution, the streams represent a fluid and somewhat unpredictable model. When all three streams converge—the political atmosphere is just right, problems are clearly defined, and solutions are available and acceptable—consensus may emerge and policy may be shaped. This makes it imperative that we in DSE are ready with solutions and that we are visible enough to be called upon for our ideas. Moving some of our activities into the public sphere will help to create that visibility. Kingdon's model suggests that policy happens through processes much like survival of the fittest. In this case, the fittest is the policy that emerges as a result of the combination of policy streams, the policy that has been crafted through the most persuasive argumentation with solid supporting evidence at the right political moment and attached to a problem well defined and communicated has the best chance of success.

DISCOURSE COALITIONS: MODEL PART 2

In the previous section, I describe a model for understanding policy work as crossing several policy streams, or interstream policy activism. In this section, I describe the second part of the model, or what can be considered intrastream policy activism. While the tangible outcomes of policy are important, Weiss

(1990) has stated that a more essential aspect entails argumentation, Maarten Hajer and Hendrik Wagenaar (2003) and Deborah Stone (2002) emphasize the more dialogical process of deliberation, and Frank Fischer (2003) suggests "public enlightenment" (12). Weiss (1991) indicates that policy activism can be useful for democratic decision making if it increases the visibility of policy issues and influences decision making by providing alternatives. To be successful in its effort to build discourse coalitions, activism must be persuasive to a wide range of stakeholders but particularly to those individuals and groups who agree with the activist agenda or who can be persuaded through deliberative means. Policy activism speaks directly to supporters or likely supporters of the policy position, increasing their confidence by providing what Weiss calls "talking points" and Fischer (2003) refers to as story lines. Both serve several purposes: (1) they are co-constructed by discourse coalition members, (2) they offer ways of communicating shared meanings to potential discourse coalition members, and (3) they provide ways of talking to those not in the coalition who might be persuaded to join the coalition. This increases the range of the policy discussion to include those who share or might share the policy goals but who, without the coalition's story lines, would be less likely to participate in the policy discussion.

The impact on democratic social life is the key, as Fischer emphasizes when he notes that, "[b]asic to the politics of policymaking, then, must be an understanding of the discursive struggle to create and control systems of shared social meanings" (13). This struggle, according to Hajer (1993), can be understood as a process of forming discourse coalitions, or the "ensemble of a set of story lines, the actors that utters [*sic*] these story lines, and the practices that conform to these story lines organiz[ed] around a discourse" (47). Story lines can be depicted as large, permeable circles (Figure 18.2). The actors and practices that conform to these story lines are smaller circles that enter and exit the larger circles to combine and recombine, according to Kingdon's metaphor. Discourse coalitions form when actors and practices merge with a story line, representing an agreement about what is a matter of shared concern. Fischer (2003) describes story lines as "narrative beliefs" that "symbolically condense the facts and values basic to a belief system" and that "reflect the

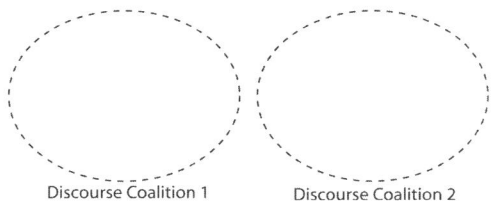

Figure 18.2. Discourse Coaliations.

concerns of core beliefs rather than the beliefs themselves" (102). For example, a discourse coalition in the problems stream of policy activism would:

> provide the tools with which problems are constructed. Discourses at the same time form the context in which phenomena are understood and thus predetermines the *definition of the problem*. (Hajer, 1993, 45–46, emphasis added)

Finally, while these story lines "can be empirically examined … their meaning and role in change is qualitative in nature and has to be interpreted in the specific contexts of action" (ibid.). Discourse coalition members "share a particular way of thinking about and discussing … issues" that cannot necessarily be "nailed down empirically" and "different ways of talking" or competing story lines emerge when different discourse coalitions talk about the issue (Fischer, 2003, 107). Competing story lines may be found to engage in an "argumentative struggle" (ibid.) reminiscent of the last twenty years of epistemological debate in the United States.

Discourse coalitions and the notion of narrative story lines fit well with Kingdon's model of policy streams. Within each stream multiple story lines form and actors and practices merge with story lines and move between story lines, eventually linking to form larger, stronger, and more diverse discourse coalitions that encourage shared meanings and practices and that exercise greater influence on the public (Figure 18.3). The emphasis on narrative reflects the deliberation necessary to "create and control systems of shared meanings" and suggests that the construction of narrative story lines is a fluid, dynamic process.

THE MODEL IN ACTION

I have outlined a two-part model for policy activism that includes (1) policy streams that serve to clarify where policy activism strategies need to be directed and (2) discourse coalitions that can operate in any stream and that offer story

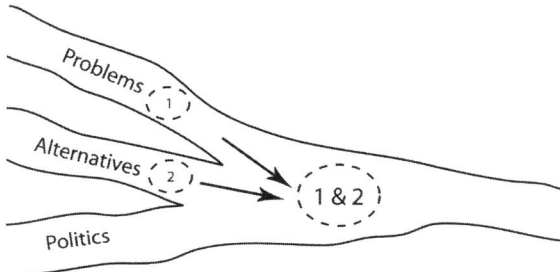

Figure 18.3. Model for Policy Activism.

lines for building community support for policy ideas and policy activism. In this section I pull together the two parts of the policy activism model—policy streams and discourse coalitions—using UD and the IDEIA as an example of the model in action. First, however, I lay out a current IDEIA story line that falls within problems stream of this model. This represents a typical story line within the DSE literature.

Problems Stream, Story Line #1

Scholars of DSE have been active in the problems stream, perhaps owing to the conflicts between disability studies perspectives on the social conditions of schooling and the policy influences on those conditions, particularly as they relate to labeling, stigma, segregation, and inequitable educational opportunities. Bernadette Baker (2002) notes that "categories of disability are part of policy language, and public schools are compelled to engage in identification and counting if they wish to receive funding" (689). She calls this a "bureaucratic imperative" (ibid.) adhering schools, teachers, and families to a system that doles out money only when they cooperate with its policies, which, according to Baker, results in a "hunt for disability," or a search for students who might be eligible for special education ostensibly to assure sufficient funding but also because categorization is just what schools do. Believed by some to be necessary and perhaps even beneficial to struggling students, Baker argues that "[labeling] a child is currently a provocative and unsettled question in public schools and families, even in school districts that have followed federal and state mandates and guidelines for special education provision" (ibid.).

For schools, the legitimate definition of what it means to be disabled and what to do about disability is clearly delineated in the IDEIA. Gregg Beratan's (2006) deconstruction of the then IDEA suggests an inherent institutional ableism, or "discriminatory structures and practices, as well as uninterrogated beliefs about disability deeply ingrained within educational systems" (¶5). Though IDEIA and its predecessors are widely acclaimed as civil rights legislation, Beratan demonstrates that "the meanings of disability embedded within IDEA actively construct disabled students' marginalized positioning within schools" (Section 4, ¶1). As a route toward funding support services for struggling students, Beratan implies, the IDEA actually offers incentives to label students, thereby increasing the likelihood that students with "unwanted difference" (Peters, Johnstone, & Ferguson, 2005) will be stigmatized. These two critiques—Baker's deconstruction of eugenic educational structures and processes and Beratan's deconstruction of the IDEA's racist and ableist consequences—identify several problems with federal policy and serve as good examples of what DSE can contribute to the problems stream.

Alternatives Stream, Story Line #2

Deconstructing the medical model's applications in the IDEIA is an important activity for a social movement that values an inclusive society. Such critiques and coalition building must continue in parallel with what I frame here, which is to construct and tell an additional story that builds an alternative system of shared meanings and takes advantage of the ideological tension in the current IDEIA. Narratives can operate in all three streams, but in this section I emphasize work in the alternatives stream. I previously argued that UD is an alternative consistent with disability studies frameworks and the goals of the DRM. I also have indicated that the current narrative about the IDEIA in U.S. disability studies tends to be positioned in the problem stream. In the alternatives stream, the problems with the IDEIA are accepted but not the focus. Instead, the narrative gathers support around the ethos, uses, and benefits of UD as an alternative that already has federal and state support and that offers "hope at the center of the struggle for inclusivity" (Barton, 2001, 3). Furthermore, I concentrate on the accumulation of quantitative data because this form of persuasion has been neglected by DSE. This may seem to conflict with Fischer's (2003) claim that discourse coalition members "share a particular way of thinking about and discussing … issues" that cannot necessarily be "nailed down empirically" (107); however Fischer is not purporting that *empirical evidence* is never part of the discourse coalition conversation. Rather, he is indicating that *empiricism* is not the narrative of discourse coalitions because these coalitions are, by definition, composed of diverse actors and practices creating narratives about shared concerns and a discourse of concern is not an empiricist discourse.

Next I offer ideas for building discourse coalitions (1) between DSE researchers and schools or districts, and (2) between DSE researchers and institutions of higher education. First, it is important to build a discourse coalition with a school or district that makes a commitment to UD principles and implementation in which quantitative and qualitative data can indicate whether implementation of UD principles is effective in decreasing segregated special education services, increasing access to the general education curriculum, and increasing access to higher education. This could be measured quantitatively by analyzing the percentage of students with individualized education plans (IEPs) who over time: (1) utilize each service delivery option, (2) receive all academic subjects in the general education classroom and are graded by the general education teacher, and at the secondary level, pass college preparatory courses, (3) graduate with a high school diploma, and (4) finally, continue on to college competitive employment. As Thomas Hehir (2002) has indicated, the obsession with impairments or deficits and their remediation has distracted schools from providing the rigorous academic curriculum most disabled students need and deserve. It seems possible that dedication to the principles of UD and the refocusing of efforts and resources on the above four indicators could result in a de-emphasis on remediation. Of course, these data would have to be analyzed to tease out factors such as race, gender, and class to the extent that this is possible and to compare pre-and post-UD implementation.

Perhaps equally important would be what is done with these data once they have been collected. If the key to building the discourse coalition is the "discursive struggle to create and control systems of shared meanings" (Fischer, 2003, 13), then how can these data be translated into "different ways of talking" (ibid., 107) that speak to potential discourse coalition members? How can policy activists strategically build discourse coalitions that increase the visibility, acceptance, and application of UD, thereby decreasing focus on the aspects of the IDEIA that serve to exclude students from full access?

Second, while the IDEIA has no jurisdiction over institutions of higher education, its consequences reach into postsecondary education, and therefore discourse coalitions are needed at this level as well. D. Kim Reid and Michelle Knight (2006) and Carla O'Connor and Sonia Fernandez (2006) describe the historical relationship between overrepresentation of African American students in K-12 special education and underrepresentation of African American students in higher or postsecondary education. While some statistics are available to indicate whether disabled and African American students are gaining access to higher education, "the statistics do not reveal how access … is based on the intersection of race, class, and disability and the inadequate services provided to labeled students in high school" (Reid & Knight, 2006, 20). For example, Reid and Knight note that while "students labeled LD [learning disabled] who attend college has increased from 16% to 40% of the college students with disabilities in the past 12 years," they also note that "this statistic represents a White, upper-middle-class increase in post-secondary attendance" (ibid). At the higher education level, then, there could be an initial focus on three indicators of success in an institution that makes a commitment to UD: (1) admission, (2) retention, and (3) graduation rates of disabled students with close attention to race, class, and disability status both as they intersect and as they are disaggregated. These are important indicators of more than just education levels. They also indicate the likelihood of disabled adults being employed and living above the poverty line. The 2000 census data (U.S. Census Bureau, 2003) indicates that for the age group 16–64, only 51.4% of disabled women and 67.3% of disabled men are employed.[1] This means that 32.7–48.6 disabled adults are unemployed (depending on gender), most of whom, therefore, require support from entitlement programs (i.e., food stamps, social security disability, etc.). The importance of the connection between educational equity in K-12 schools, access to a college education, competitive employment, and the politics and policies of education becomes very clear when viewed this way.

Again, how can policy activists use these data to create a shared system of meaning with members of a discourse coalition? Better yet, who are the potential discourse coalition members, how can they be reached and organized? These are some of the challenges facing policy activism and recall Barton's (2001) second question about whether a social movement is positioned for strategic political action: has it amassed the "energy and resources which mobilize people for collective action?" (4) Regarding U.S. DSE, this question has yet to be answered in the affirmative.

My recommendations in this section do not preclude the collection of qualitative data or narrative descriptions of UD in action, nor am I attempting to ignore the importance of building discourse coalitions and working in policy streams with individual teachers, teacher educators, members of the community, or advocacy organizations. Qualitative studies would be very useful for building the narratives of discourse coalitions. Rather, my intent with the examples I have used is to encourage two things that DSE in the United States tends to avoid: (1) the recognition of the material reality of the policy stream, in which the policy elites who hold the purse strings are persuaded by hard data, and (2) larger-scale studies that can provide broad-based evidence of the ways in which UD can affect equity in education.

For UD to avoid fading from view it must maintain story lines and discourse coalitions that are consistently persuasive to those working in all three streams as well as the general public. Therefore, one must not forget how and where research findings are reported. Here, too, DSE researchers can be savvy about reporting mechanisms and can be sure to publish for the general public as well as for other academicians. Harriet McBryde Johnson (2003a, 2003b, 2004, 2006a, 2006b) is a good example to follow. Though not an academician, she is a disabled woman and an attorney and to date, she has published five pieces in the *New York Times*, a venue with an audience likely to be persuaded by the arguments from DSE.

HOPE AT THE CENTER

Returning to Barton's two questions about the strength of social movements, has DSE identified the vacuum or gaps in the existing research? Many gaps have been identified in the last few years, and some of those are represented in this *Reader*. UD, for example, has been gaining in visibility thanks to numerous researchers and scholars, many of whom do not identify with disability studies. It would seem that frameworks for thinking about and providing access for all can never get enough attention. Second, to the question of whether we have mobilized enough resources for action, I propose that indeed, in education there is enough of a mobilization for a beginning, that UD gives the field something to rally around that is hopeful and now needs the nurture of discourse coalitions to assure its full implementation and to prevent its fading away. Furthermore, UD gives the policy activist something to offer as a solution to practitioners who are so often searching for solutions.

To be ratified in official policy, UD has not needed ideological consistency with the grand narrative of the IDEIA. Instead, UD has emerged from a policy stream—probably the alternatives stream—situated both within and in parallel to what seems to be an antithetical IDEIA discourse. I propose that it is the responsibility of DSE to engage in strategic actions that build momentum for UD in an attempt to create a widespread and public "system of shared social meanings" (Fischer, 2003, 13) rising out of the value of access for all. There are several ways to do this: (1) create demonstration projects and disseminate information about UD, (2) form active partnerships with those researchers who are already working on UD, (3) gather empirical data on the effectiveness of UD in addressing disability discrimination and racism (e.g., school dropout or pushout, low graduation rates), and (4) intentionally build discourse coalitions in local communities to study and respond to specific, community-based problems or to offer community-based solutions. These discourse coalitions can also make connections with discourse coalitions in other communities, building a rippling support system. The more vigorously we do this, by following Barton's advice and doing so in a systematic fashion, the more likely we are to encourage the continued evolution of an ethos of access for all.

By using one or more of these strategies, we take up what Weiss (1990) refers to as public deliberation, Fischer (2003) frames as public enlightenment, and Barton (2001) offers as "hope at the center of struggles for inclusivity" (3). We can go public with some good news for a change, even if that good news is buried in the IDEIA. While I do not suggest that UD is the magic potion that will eliminate the structural violence of ableism, I see it as offering a glimmer of hope that is long overdue. Building on that hope, I have offered a model for policy activism that provides a framework for political action in which the struggle for inclusivity includes policy activism that whenever possible should be persuasive to policy elites as well as the general public. To this end, policy activism places the field of DSE and its proponents within policy streams and in conversations with allies who share our concerns about an inclusive society—many general and special education teachers or administrators, disabled students and their families, disabled adults in the community, local community members, and even local or state politicians. This model for policy activism provides the conceptual tools with which to achieve a degree of policy conscientization toward planning and engaging in praxis by not only defining problems but also offering solutions, creating coalitions, and constructing narratives of hope.

NOTE

1. These data do not include institutionalized disabled people. If they are included, the unemployment percentage is higher.

REFERENCES

Baker, B. (2002). The hunt for disability: The new eugenics and the normalization of school children. *Teachers College Record*, 104 (4), 553–703.

Barton, L. (2001). Disability, struggle and the politics of hope. In L. Barton (Ed.), *Disability Politics and the Struggle for Change*, pp. 1–10. New York: David Fulton Publishing.

Beratan, G. (2006). Institutionalizing ableism: Ableism, racism, and IDEA 2004. *Disability Studies Quarterly*, 26 (2). Retrieved March 28, 2006 from http://www.dsq-sds.org/current_issue.html.

Biklen, D., & Duchan, J. F. (1994). "I am intelligent": The social construction of mental retardation. *Journal of the Association for Persons with Severe Handicaps*, 19, 173–184.

Brantlinger, E. (1997). Using ideology: Cases of nonrecognition of the politics of research and practice in special education. *Review of Educational Research*, 67 (4), 425–459.

Burgstahler, S. (2005). Universal design of instruction: Definition, principles, and examples. Retrieved September 29, 2006 from http://www-world.cac.washington.edu/doit/Brochures/Academics/instruction.html.

Burgstahler, S., & Cory, R. (2007). Moving in from the margins: From accommodation to universal design. In S. L. Gabel & S. Danforth (Eds.), *Disability and the politics of education: An international reader*. New York: Peter Lang.

Campbell, D. M. (2004). Assistive technology and universal instructional design: A postsecondary perspective. *Equity and Excellence in Education*, 37, 167–173.

Center for Universal Design. (1997). The principles of universal design. Retrieved September 18, 2006 from http://www.design.ncsu.edu/cud/about_ud/udprinciplestext.htm.

Commonwealth of Kentucky. (2006). Pathway to achievement: Universal design for learning. Retrieved September 29, 2006 from http://www.education.ky.gov/KDE/Instructional+Resources/Curriculum+Documents+and+Resources/Universal+Design+for+Learning/default.htm.

Danforth, S. (1997). On what basis hope? Modern progress and postmodern possibilities. *Mental Retardation*, 35, 93–106.

Ferguson, P. (2002). Notes toward a history of hopelessness: Disability and the places of therapeutic failure. *Disability, Culture and Education*, 1 (1), 27–40.

Fischer, F. (2003). *Reframing public policy: Discursive politics and deliberative practices*. Oxford: Oxford University Press.

Freire, P. (1970). *Pedagogy of the oppressed*. New York: Continuum.

Fuchs, L. S. (2003). Assessing intervention responsiveness: Conceptual and technical issues. *Learning Disabilities Research and Practice*, 18 (3), 172–186.

Gallagher, D. J. (1998). The scientific knowledge base of special education: Do we know what we think we know? *Exceptional Children*, 64 (4), 93–502.

———. (2006). If not absolute objectivity, then what? A reply to Kauffman and Sasso. *Exceptionality*, 14 (2), 91–107.

Georgia Institute of Technology. (n.d.). Our mission. Retrieved October 20, 2006 from http://www.ittatc.org/about/mission.php.

Gresham, F. M. (2005). Response to intervention: An alternative means of identifying students as emotionally disturbed. *Education and Treatment of Children*, 28 (4), 328–344.

Hackman, H. W., & Rauscher, L. (2004). A pathway to access for all: Exploring the connections between universal instructional design and social justice education. *Equity and Excellence in Education*, 37, 114–123.

Hajer, M. (1993). Discourse coalitions and the institutionalization of practice: The case of acid rain in Great Britain. In F. Fischer & J. Forester (Eds.), *The argumentative turn in policy analysis and planning*, pp. 43–67. London: Durham.

Hajer, M., & Wagenaar, H. (Eds.). (2003). *Deliberative policy analysis: Understanding governance in the network society*. Cambridge: Cambridge University Press.

Harvard Civil Rights Project (HCRP). (n.d.). Special education. Retrieved October 20, 2006 from http://www.civilrightsproject.harvard.edu/research/specialed/specialed_gen.php.

Hehir, T. (2002). Eliminating ableism in education. *Harvard Educational Review*, 72 (1). Retrieved October 20, 2006 from http://gseweb.harvard.edu/~hepg/hehir.htm.

———. (2005). *New directions in special education: Eliminating ableism in policy and practice*. Cambridge, MA: Harvard University Press.

Heshusius, L. (1989). The Newtonian mechanistic paradigm, special education, and contours of alternatives: An overview. *Journal of Learning Disabilities*, 2 (7), 403–415.

Illinois State Board of Education. (2006). The Illinois alternate assessment writing frameworks priorities grades 6–8. Retrieved September 29, 2006 from http://www.isbe.state.il.us/assessment/pdfs/writing_priorities_6–8.pdf#search=%22%22ISBE%22%20%22universal%20design%22%22.

Johnson, J. R. (2004). Universal instructional design and critical (communication) pedagogy: Strategies for voice, inclusion, and social justice/change. *Equity and Excellence in Education*, 37, 145–153.

Kauffman, J. M., & Sasso, G. M. (2006a). Toward ending cultural and cognitive relativism in special education. *Exceptionality*, 14 (2), 65–90.

———. (2006b). Certainty, doubt, and the reduction of uncertainty. *Exceptionality*, 14 (2), 109–120.

Kingdon, J. W. (2003). *Agendas, alternatives, and public policies*. New York: Longman.

Losen, D., & Orfield, G. (2002). *Racial inequity in special education*. Cambridge, MA: Harvard University Press.

Marshall, K. (2007). The reasonable adjustments duty for higher education in England and Wales. In S. L. Gabel & S. Danforth (Eds.), *Disability studies in education: An international reader*. New York: Peter Lang.

Marston, D. (2005). Tiers of intervention in responsiveness to intervention: Prevention outcomes and learning disabilities identification patterns. *Journal of Learning Disabilities*, 38 (6), 539–544.

McBryde Johnson, H. (2003a). Disability gulag. *New York Times*, November 23. Retrieved December 26, 2006 from http://query.nytimes.com/gst/fullpage.html.

———. (2003b). Unspeakable conversations. *New York Times*, February 16. Retrieved December 26, 2006 from http://query.nytimes.com/gst/fullpage.html.

McBryde Johnson, H. (2004). The way we live now: 5-30-04; Stairway to justice. *New York Times*, May 30. Retrieved December 26, 2006 from http://query.nytimes.com/gst/fullpage.html.

———. (2006a) Wheelchair unbound. *New York Times*, April 23. Retrieved December 26, 2006 from http://www.nytimes.com/2006/04/23/magazine/23lives.html.

McBryde Johnson, H. (2006b). Alas for Tiny Tim, he became a Christmas cliché. *New York Times*, December 25. Retrieved December 26, 2006, from http://www.nytimes.com/2006/12/25/opinion/25johnson.html.

McGuire, J. M., Scott, S. S., & Shaw, S. F. (2006). Universal design and its applications in educational environments. *Remedial and Special Education,* 27 (3), 166–175.

Michigan State Board of Education. (n.d.). Strategic Plan 2005–2010. Retrieved September 29, 2006 from http://www.michigan.gov/documents/MDE_2005_Strategic_Plan_129469_7.pdf.

Mino, J. J. (2004). Planning for inclusion: Using universal instructional design to create a learner-centered community college classroom. *Equity and Excellence in Education,* 37, 154–160.

National Endowment for the Arts. (n.d.). Universal design leadership project. Retrieved September 29, 2006 from http://www.grants.gov/search/search.do?oppId=10744&mode=VIEW.

North Carolina State University. (2006). About the center: Center history. Retrieved September 29, 2006 from http://www.design.ncsu.edu/cud/about_us/ushistory.htm.

O'Connor, C., & Fernandez, Sonia DeLuca. (2006). Race, class, and disproportionality: Reevaluating the relationship between poverty and special education placement. *Educational Researcher,* 35 (6), 6–11.

Ouelett, M. L. (2004). Faculty development and universal instructional design. *Equity and Excellence in Education,* 37, 135–144.

Peters, S., Johnstone, C., & Ferguson, P. (2005). Disability rights in an education model for evaluating inclusive education. *International Journal of Inclusive Education,* 9 (1), 1–22.

Pliner, S. M., & Johnson, J. R. (2004). Historical, theoretical, and foundational principles of universal instructional design in higher education. *Equity and Excellence in Education,* 37, 105–113.

Rauscher, L. & McClintock, J. (1996). Ablesim and curriculum design. In M. Adams, L. A. Bell & P. Griffen (Eds.), *Teaching for diversity and social justice,* pp. 198–231. New York: Routledge.

Reid, D. K., & Knight, M.G. (2006). Disability justifies exclusion of minority students: A critical history grounded in disability studies. *Educational Researcher,* 35 (6), 18–23.

Sasso, G. M. (2001). The retreat from inquiry and knowledge in special education. *Journal of Special Education,* 34 (4), 178–193.

Scott, S. S., McGuire, J. M., & Shaw, S. F. (2003). Universal design for instruction: A new paradigm for adult instruction in postsecondary education. *Remedial and Special Education,* 24 (6), 369–379.

Slee, R., & Allan, J. (2001). Excluding the included: A reconsideration of inclusive education. *International Studies in Sociology of Education,* 11 (2), 173–191.

State of Michigan. (2006). Leading educational transformation for today's global society. Lansing, MI: State of Michigan. Retrieved September 29, 2006 from http://www.michigan.gov/documents/Item_U_151905_7.pdf.

Stone, D. (2002). *Policy paradox: The art of political decision making.* (3rd Edition). New York: W. W. Norton.

US Census Bureau. (2003). Disability Status: 2000. Census Brief. Retrieved December 26, 2006 from http://www.census.gov/prod/2003pubs/c2kbr-17.pdf.

US Congress. (2002). *President's commission on excellence in special education report: A new era: Revitalizing special education for children and their families.* Washington, DC: Author.

———. (2004). *Individuals with disability educational improvement act.* Washington, DC: Author.

———. (2006). *Federal Register 71* (156). Retrieved December 26, 2006 from http://www.ed.gov/legislation/FedRegister/finrule/2006-3/081406a.pdf.

Weiss, C. H. (1991). Policy research as advocacy: Pro and con. *Knowledge and Policy,* 4 (1/2), 37–56.

———. (1990). Policy research: Data, ideas, or arguments? In Wagner, P., Weiss, C. H., Wittrock, B., & Wollmann, H. (Eds.), *Social sciences and modern states,* pp. 307–332. Cambridge: Cambridge University Press.

Wilkoff, W. L., & Abed, L. W. (1994). *Practicing universal design: An interpretation of the ADA*. New York: Van Nostrand Reinhold.

Section III
Theorizing Disability

In her deconstruction of a fourth grader's response to the question of how she is doing in school, Tanya Titchkosky (chapter 19) offers the first of the theoretical packages unwrapped by authors in this section. The child's response, "I got trouble with my reading," discloses what she has internalized about the purposes of schooling, the relationship between the school's assumptions about competence and disability, and the ways in which children like this girl and others "trouble" education. In fact, a fitting theme for the first chapters in this section might be "Troubling Disability." For example, Anna Hickey-Moody (chapter 20) critiques the social constructionist position that intellectual disability is "*solely* discursively constructed [and] can entail an assumption that human bodies and human societies are two discrete and somewhat contained fields". She finds this position untethered to lived experience, a position that ignores the flesh and bones of embodiment. Recalling the young girl who "has trouble" with her reading, can one honestly ask: Is she is experiencing only a mental state? Is her body involved at all—in tensed muscles, tears of frustration, faltering voice when reading aloud, nauseating anxiety? Further troubling the educational tendency to euphemize and simplify, Valerie Harwood and Nici Humphrey (chapter 21) argue that discourses of exceptionality (e.g., the ideal, and the norm) need to be unpacked to the end that the "spectrum," or "normal distribution" (i.e., bell curve), no longer seems a given and instead is viewed as a curiosity. Their references to the Australian Government's discourse of "national interest" in "every child's gifts and talents" causes one to wonder what happens to those students "who got trouble with their reading."

Of course, students who have trouble—with reading or, as discussed in the next chapter, with "acting out"—disturb the order of things and can become viewed as problems. Scot Danforth (chapter 22) exposes this in his analysis of the subconscious use of metaphor as a means of constructing disability. In Danforth's analysis, everyday phrases reveal the insidious bottom line: "*Keep your cool. Cool heads prevail. He's such a hothead. Blow off some steam. He blew his top.*" Behaviorism is complicit in the use of metaphor, argues Danforth, but his most damaging allegation is aimed at the racist use of the emotional/behavioral disorder label used in US public schools. Rod Michalko (chapter 23) wraps up the trouble of problems (or the problem of trouble) by arguing, as do the previous authors to one extent or another, that "categories such as gender and disability" simplify things to the extent that "in one quick move, the trouble of the body is swept away." Michalko's reference to W. E. B. DuBois (1903/1989), an important civil rights leader in the United States, tells all: "How does it feel to be a problem?" asks DuBois (1). Michalko's answer hits hard:

> There is no point asking whether or not difference is a problem since this is unquestionable and it is thus impossible to ask … it is this impossibility that makes being a problem such a strange experience.

How are problems solved, particularly when the problems are people? The next chapters offer historic answers to this question and can be summarized in two words: cure (i.e., eliminate) and care. First, Phil Smith (chapter 24) maps out the "cartography" of a "(pseudo-)scientific movement called eugenics" that is more accurately described as "a complex set of cultural ideologies" that have outlined the boundaries of "normative terrains." In so doing, Smith implies that the "cure" is the elimination of "normal" concomitant with the constitution of difference. "The work of eugenics involves a kind of disappearance act," writes Smith.

> Those inscribed as Normal cannot (must not) see themselves as such…if they see their own image, the Normals see themselves only hazily—forgetting that the fashioning of Difference also fashions themselves.

Once constituted, difference itself requires cure, which Bernadette Baker (2002) aptly frames within the "new eugenics" of schools' "hunt for disability." Annemieke van Drenth (chapter 25) probes the second solution historically aimed at problem people, which she labels "regimes of care" that depend on "caring power," a kind of repressive humanitarianism utilizing technologies of professionalization that "[favor] rational, scientific insights over religious confessions. … [and] the objectivization of individuals." Her chapter is reminiscent of Phil Ferguson's (2002) exposition on therapeutic failure, which actually addresses both the cure and care impulse toward problem people. What happens when therapeutic cures fail, asks Ferguson? They are "cared for" since efforts to cure them have proven hopeless.

> Those with the most challenging behaviors, or the most dependent on technology, or with the most profound cognitive disabilities would be left behind, once again burdened with the social responsibility for keeping their chronicity to themselves and their setting. (35)

The final three chapters explore the theoretical intersections of Disability Studies with other fields of inquiry and here, too, we find trouble. David Connor (chapter 26) traces the "overlapping lenses" of Disability Studies and Critical Race Studies. Although he finds some important conjectures (i.e., shared concern for activism or interdisciplinarity), there are also absent spaces into which tension is inserted. For example, Disability Studies has been criticized for racial and ethnic homogeneity and Critical Race Theory has tended to ignore disability. The absences and their resulting tensions weaken both fields for many reasons, one of which at this time is the fact that disability in the United States has been used as a pawn in institutionalized racism.

Daniel Goodley and Rebecca Lawthom (chapter 27) take a different turn, examining the uses of psychology for Disability Studies and vice versa. Given the history of the "deep suspicion" of psychology by Disability Studies, this is a brave tact. Goodley and Lawthom accept that "psychology appears to be obsessed with difference (usually referred to as deviance) in forms which are both real and statistical," but they succeed in comparing the tensions within the field of psychology to those in special education. In other words, both fields have what the authors call "unhappy bedfellows" who are inside agitators. "To situate psychology as a bounded discipline engaged with enforcing normalcy," they write, "does a disservice to the dynamic nature of knowledge disciplines and paradigm shifts."

Finally, Kathryn Young and Emily Mintz (chapter 28) compare Disability Studies and Special Education perspectives on difference, dependency, and stigma. They see Disability Studies as offering special education a socially situated understanding of disability and although they do not explicitly advocate dismantling special education, the "radical minority perspective" (Peters et al., chapter 17) of Disability Studies undermines the basic assumptions of special education as outlined by Young and Mintz.

In all, these chapters offer fresh new lenses for theorizing disability. Together, they point to some of the most important theoretical work being done in Disability Studies in Education. However, these chapters do not give us a sense of the theorizing that is occurring in Asia, Africa, or South America; this is unfortunate, given the rich possibilities those theorists could offer. Although this section did not receive any proposals from outside Europe, North America, or Australia, it is imperative that future editors determine how to solicit such manuscripts.

Other authors in this volume address themes or topics related to theorizing disability: Graham and Slee (chapter 6), Azzopardi (chapter 7), Van Hove, Roets, Mortier, De Schauwer, Leroy, and Broekaert (chapter 8), and Bjarnason (chapter 15).

REFERENCES

Baker, B. (2002). The hunt for disability: The new eugenics and the normalization of school children. *Teachers College Record,* 104, 663–703.

DuBois, W. E. B. (1903/1989). *The souls of Black folk.* New York: Bantam.

Ferguson, P. (2002). Notes toward a history of hopelessness: Disability and the places of therapeutic failure. *Disability, Culture, and Education,* 1(1), 27–40.

CHAPTER NINETEEN

"I Got Trouble WITH My Reading": An Emerging Literacy

TANYA TITCHKOSKY

---

one of my most powerful assumptions about being literate is my confidence about what I *needn't* read.

—(MARGARET MEEK, 1991, 5)[1]

INTRODUCTION

Beyond recognizing letters and signs, sounding them out, putting together the sentences, how might we read what it means to become a reader? How might we imagine the social significance of "reader" as something more than the result of individual skill acquisitions or ability, something at least equal in weight and substance to the issue of reading troubles? Asking such a question can begin to reveal the social significance of the current proliferation of reading disabilities, or learning difficulties, occurring in Western cultures.

In this chapter, I will unpack interpretations of disability as represented by common professional ways of talking about children's reading troubles in Western(ized) worlds. In addressing education as a context overflowing with forms of trouble accompanied by daily professional practices that use a kind of "literacy of trouble," I aim to start to uncover the social meaning that surrounds "reading disabilities" today. One specific concern of my chapter is that the expert deployment of a new literacy of trouble is a complex set of community relations still in need of theorizing. Since my analysis makes use of interpretive methods of social inquiry committed to a disability studies perspective, this chapter also demonstrates the incisive power of addressing talk and conduct as a force that socially organizes our everyday conceptions of disability.

THE IRONY OF READING

There are obviously many material and technical matters involved in learning to read and write. Those becoming literate need access to, among other things, teachers; space and time appropriate for such focused work; the absence of overwhelming distractions such as too much hunger or too much anger; as well as reading materials that address the particular kinds of bodies, minds, senses, and ages of readers who are always situated in a complicated nexus of social differences, including being raced, classed, and gendered in various ways. However, what is not so obvious is the social fact that literacy is a community matter.

Reading is not only an activity that intersects with the politics of identity, since reading forms identities intersecting with all aspects of community life in Western(ized) worlds. Communities make decisions regarding the material necessities surrounding reading and such ongoing decisions are connected to how people notice, frame, and respond to reading issues. This means that learning to read always occurs in the midst of others who "are" readers, such as, educational boards, educators, and teacher's aids; family, friends, or classmates; office workers, store keepers, and neighbors; or the more abstract, *literate society*.

In fact, "literate" is one way we have to characterize contemporary Western cultures. We become literate, then, in the midst of literacy. We say that we live in literate times; or that ours is a knowledge-based economy reliant on the sort of competencies that accompany literacy. It is even said that this is The Information Age. In this text mediated, computer-generated world of print. the meaning of becoming and being literate does hold extraordinary significance. In such a context, "reader" is a poignantly provocative issue for contemplating how we make up the meaning of people. Following Paulo Freire's insistence (1983, 9) on the importance of understanding the complex act of reading through our own existential experience of it, we can uncover such meanings. Among countries committed to a fully bureaucratized capitalist system, there has been little work on the social meaning of competent or good reading; there is even less work on those readers dedicated to the diagnosis (reading) of others for their reading troubles. Some have suggested, "Identities influence our readings of texts, our social and moral views ..." (Hill, Teuton, and Werner, 2003). However, one of the most ordinary and common ways of attending to reading is for some readers to notice and diagnose illiteracy and reading troubles thereby treating, even constituting, specific troubled readers.

When you consider the poor reader, inadequate reading skills, functionally illiterate, learning disabled, reading difficulties, reading disabilities, writing or expression problems, learning differences, and literacy incompetencies, we realize that in the realm of reading, there are innumerable ways that communities have to connect troubles and individuals together. Professionals addressing such troubles have attended to good reading skills or even to the practices pursued by competent readers. It is, however, conventionally assumed that reading troubles are located in individuals who are subject to either/or rankings of literacy, continuums of skill evaluation, or inventories of miscues and mistakes, all of which lead to the generation of strong or weak, abled, or disabled readers.

Dividing people into different sorts of literacy groups on the basis of who is having trouble with what is a key feature of contemporary educational practice. But, Margaret Meek (1991, 9, 11) suggests there is more going on:

> The great divide in literacy is not between those who can read and write and those who have not yet learned how to. It is between those who have discovered what kinds of literacy society values and how to demonstrate their competences in ways that earn recognition … most of what we have to discover about literacy is embedded in the social practices for which we use it and in the ways which, if we are not careful, we may use it to divide rather than to unite us.

Some forms of literacy are valued; are regarded as necessary; even treated as natural. Some forms of literacy can be used every day to perform powerful practices of sorting, dividing, and ordering of all kinds of matter, such as, numbers, money, things and, of course, people. The practical power of literacy helps to make sense of seemingly contradictory experiences surrounding everyday ways that people pay attention to literacy. For example, one evening of watching the news, I am told of a successful professional, white hockey coach who is coming out as functionally illiterate by selling his book about his life. In the same newscast, I watch a story showing rhythmically rhyming literate streetwise children, many who are people of color or poor. The news reports on how these children, just pictured as poetically playing with word and world, are "crowding" segregated special education classes and "can't read." The hockey coach possessed some way of reading the ice, reading the players, and reading literate culture so as to not demonstrate that he could not read print. The coach aided by his privileged social differences, shaped interaction in such a way that his competencies are noted. The "streetwise kids" are described as students who "can't read" even though they are shown on TV *literally* making up rhymes of the names of the streets. Reading the ice hockey rink and rhyming the streets receive different forms of recognition. Depictions of illiterate authors selling books and literate children regarded as troublesomely crowding special education classrooms certainly serve as a vivid depiction of the complex social fact that literacy is embedded in the daily practices of its use. Clearly, one way that we use literacy is as a method to demarcate those who have not been able to demonstrate a recognizable or valued competency in relation to reading. That people are demarcated as having reading trouble may have far more to teach us about what a community values than it does about individual skill acquisition.

While demonstrating valued competencies is an essential practice of daily life, it is also the context where people draw the dividing lines not also between average and superior performance, but also between reading competence and reading difficulty. With regard to dividing practices in educational contexts, Charlotte Davies (1998, 105) says that:

> Persons having learning difficulties that can be attributed to known organic causes are fairly evenly distributed across social classes and ethnic divisions. But the remainder, the vast majority of people with learning difficulties, are disproportionately present in the lower socio-economic classes and in certain ethnic groups.

Richard Jenkins' (1998, 17) work speaks of dividing practices as well:

> … well-documented and continuing predisposition in Europe and North America [is] to label as incompetent or intellectually disabled disproportionately more black or Asian people than white Europeans.

The "over-representation of minority and socially disadvantaged students in the category of disability" (Green and Kostogriz, 2002, 107) can be understood as a part of the sorting, dividing, and ordering power of literacy (see, also, Ferri and Connor, 2006, 4–5). Just as Judith Shklar (1990) reminds us that the line between "misfortune and injustice" should not be taken as a given; so too the lines between difficulty, disability, and diagnosis should not be taken as a given, since these demarcations are charged with the complex politics of time and place. There are, then, good reasons to study how learning disabilities appear in learning environments so as to uncover the variable normative cultural orders that constitute (in)competency (e.g., Gabel, 2005; Jenkins, 1998; Peters, 2005; Titchkosky 2003, 2005, 2007). The uses to which literacy can be put, including the ordering of space, time and people, serves as a salient source of power in the formation of where we find ourselves and what or who legitimizes our activities.

However, in a historical context characterized as literate, the meaning of "reader," especially the reader who is charged with the task of reading others for their learning troubles, receives far less attention than does the presumed quantifiable, and thus measurable, individual (in)ability to read. While literacy can be used to make other persons into special cases in need of diagnosis and remedy, it is also possible to use literacy to make our own identity as "reader" barely noticeable. The weight of literate times can seem featherlight for the full-fledged literate person, so much so that "reader" hardly appears as an identity category even though literacy serves as a form of access to most of whatever culture deems valuable. The irony is palpable; while the contemporary literate person is positioned to use his or her reading ability so as to dis-attend to the activity and meaning of reading for himself or her self, the person may use this same positioning to attend to others. The luxury of this self-forgetfulness is not accessible to anyone who has an uncomfortable relationship with these literate times. In the 1980s, it was commonly held that 10% of the population had learning disabilities (Adams, 1985, 37); this rate is now commonly held to be 20% or higher (Gunning, 2006; Winzer, 2005)—this is a noteworthy group of uncomfortable people not afforded the luxury of forgetfulness.

The basic task before us now is to explore this ironic power of reading so as to reveal how reading difficulties and disabilities might best be understood. How do forms of attention that are given to reading control how we, as Rod Michalko (chapter 23) suggests in this volume, imagine trouble. The ways that we imagine trouble are part of how we organize relations between community and its various members. I turn now to texts on reading problems as a way to develop a sense of how we might continue to address reading as a community issue instead of as only an individual one. I seek to uncover the significance of the social act of demarcating readers who have trouble by imaging reading as more than individual skill acquisition. What sort of valued social competencies are involved in discovering that the other has reading troubles? Might this literacy of trouble be acknowledged as bearing the same sort of weight and influence as does the trouble deemed to belong to individual readers?

"I GOT TROUBLE WITH MY READING"

Programs and texts on reading typically say something about what reading troubles *are* as well as how educational professionals and others can recognize and respond to them. Indeed, texts about learners usually hold the "definition" of trouble as itself a major dilemma facing educators. For example, Margaret Winzer (2005, 7) begins her book, *Children with Exceptionalities*, by stressing, "Even today, the entire area of disability is characterized by conceptual chaos. Children who are exceptional are constantly being reconceptualized, reconsidered, and renamed." Lamenting on this definitional disorder, as well as seeking to solve it are readily apparent in almost all mainstream texts on reading difficulties (see e.g., Brown and McGreevy, 1994, 3; Farrell, 2003; Rasinski and Padak, 1996, 3; Soler, Wearmouth, and Reid, 2002; Winzer, 2005). Such texts also provide various responses to such definitional disorders. Sometimes authors turn to legal definitions; or medical definitions; or deploy some unique redefinition, such as renaming disability "exceptionality," "special needs," "(dis)Ability," and so on.

Instead of reviewing this definitional disorder further, I want to analyze how any attempt to define reading difficulty is constituted by (and helps to constitute) a sense of what reading is, of what literacy means. From a historical framework, Karin Nelson and Bengt Sandin's (2005, 191) work suggests that the development of general participation in schooling has been simultaneously accompanied by the development of differing scholarly definitions of reading and writing problems. Put differently, "To understand what counts as (dis)ability means, then, to address what counts as literacy as well as what counts as (in)competence" (Green and Kostogriz, 2002, 107). In order to pursue this sort of understanding, I will provide an example of one way of defining reading troubles and analyze its constitutive powers in detail.

In his *Assessing and Correcting Reading and Writing Difficulties*, Thomas Gunning (2006, 2) writes:

> There are many ways of defining reading difficulty, but the most telling definition was uttered by Awilda, a fourth-grader in a large urban school. When asked how school was going, she replied, "I got trouble with my reading."

Given that school is a complex arena of social life, its goings-on are also dynamically diverse and so school can be experienced in any number of ways. Someone asks a student how school was going; a fourth-grade student, Awilda, responds. Having no difficulty reading the interactional demands of the question/answer sequence, Awilda says, "I got trouble with my reading." We do not know how Awilda decided to provide this answer and not some other. We know little about how the question came to be posed to her or even who asked it since Gunning says "when asked," but does not say who did the asking. We know even less about what sort of actual experience Awilda formulates as trouble with reading. We also do not know Awilda's relation to the need to understand her particular reading experience, even though her words are being used to develop a definition of reading difficulty in general. After describing the supports in Awilda's life that make her "lack of reading ability" all the more noticeable and anomalous, Awilda figures in the text again only as a question "How many Awildas are there?" (Gunning, 2006, 5). While we know so little, Gunning's assurance that "I got trouble with my reading" certainly tells us much. Let us explore this.

"When asked how school was going, she replied, 'I got trouble with my reading.'" This story begins by showing us that at least for this fourth-grade student there is a close connection between going to school and reading. At the intersection of the place of school and the practice of learning to read, we are told the story of how to conceive of reading as a difficulty or a disability. The story tells us that reading is to be conceived of as a certain something that belongs to individuals, since Awilda has "trouble with *my* reading" [italics my own]. While school is the place where Awilda experiences herself as having troubles, this context is not regarded as the source of trouble. In this "telling definition," reading troubles are being read as belonging to the individual who happens to be going to that school. In the face of all the various ways that reading difficulties can be defined, what is telling about "I got trouble with my reading" is that it makes the educational enterprise's general definitional disorder into a clearly personal trouble. This process is best understood, not as blaming the victim, but instead as framing the problem by governing how we do and do not bring attention to reading. Awilda's personal trouble has become a solution to educators' general struggle with the idea that there are many ways to define reading difficulties. Using Awilda's words as a solution to the problem of having many different definitions accomplishes the taken-for-granted understanding that whatever the trouble might be, it is in individual students and not in communities that are actively working to imagine, diagnose, and treat trouble while also teaching students to read.

Margaret Meek (1991, 13) reminds us that, "Literacy has two beginnings: one, in the world, the other, in each person who learns to read and write." Gunning's articulation of reading trouble begins to tell us a story of how to forget one of these beginnings, namely, that reading begins in the world. Insofar as Awilda's words are a most telling definition, they suggest that in the face of reading troubles, it is possible to move directly from reading context (school) to individual reader *as if* there is little need to attend to the continuous connection between the two. We are being told by Gunning that the form of trouble that amounts to reading difficulties or disabilities is the one where the reader is able to locate their reading trouble within a self. As the narrative attributed to Awilda suggests, reading is a possession that we can worry about insofar as it reflects our subjectivity, even as it is also an ability that we struggle to express. Therefore, as a reader, I read my reading and I may comprehend that I have trouble. Having trouble with reading can, however, make one subject to being deciphered and addressed by reading experts and, then, a reader can come to be recognized as learning disabled.

"I got trouble with my reading" is itself a complicated form of literacy, that is, Awilda has displayed a complex way of reading herself. It requires Awilda to block out the context: the community of readers within which her problems are located, deciphered, and experienced. (Interestingly, Gunning reads in the same complex way,

as does Awilda.) This story of becoming a troubled reader suggests the blocking of contemplation on that which cannot easily be subsumed under the self in the act of reading, for example, the influence of a large urban school, as this is composed in relation to issues of race, class and gender. Awilda's words represent the competent accomplishment of a complicated form of literacy. She has no trouble moving from school to self, using "my" to describe her reading, and she does not refer to other readers, such as teachers or classmates, among whom reading actually takes place. Thus, my reading is troubled, and it is so, insofar as I can imagine some others whose reading is not; still the problem with reading is mine and not theirs, it is in me and not in them.

Gunning recommends the legitimacy of this version of reading trouble by suggesting that Awilda is definitively exemplary in her move from school to self, from dynamic social context to an evaluation of individual deficit or inability. Blocking the context of how our worlds make and locate reading difficulties, Awilda'a story, Awilda and Gunning's story really, shows us how we transform people who "have" a problem, into people who are problems, into problem people, namely, a population of learners about whom today many textbooks are written. Thus, "How many Awildas are there? ... Based on National Assessment and other data, it is estimated that up to 25 percent of the [US] population has some difficulty with reading." (Gunning, 2006, 5) Finally, what is so telling about this story of defining reading difficulties is that it shows the complicated set of interactional moves readers need to make to recognize the self as troubled. I can read (activity) that I've got trouble with my reading (identity). We can orient to these interactional interpretive moves or ignore them, but we cannot escape them, since this is part of what it means to live in "literate times" among communities of readers.

The narrative, "When asked how school was going, she replied, 'I got trouble with my reading,'" does not only tell us that the appearance of reading disabilities requires the radical individualization of reading experience, but it also tells us that in the face of the individual troubled reader we are meeting a personal relation to a common doing. School is a place where we may learn and do reading; a place where we read and become readers; a place where through doing reading some become readers and others become readers with reading difficulties. The student "with" reading difficulty or disability is, paradoxically, positioned as one who serves as a scene where activity and identity come to conscious attention. The troubled reader can serve as just such a scene of attention for others, or for one's self, or for both.

Another aspect of this narrative of trouble is that it is made to function as a "telling definition" for professionals dealing with reading difficulties and disabilities. Awilda's words, after all, appear in a book addressed to those who are interested in "assessing and correcting" reading and writing difficulties and not addressed to those undergoing these troubles, not addressed to Awilda for example. The definition does not so much orient to the actual experience of reading as it upholds lack of ability or deficiency as the defining experience of reading difficulties.

Every reader exists at the intersection of doing reading while being some sort of reader, but only some people need, desire, or are forced to attend this intersection. Not every sort of reader can so poignantly bring to the fore the social character of reading. For example, the unquestionably "competent" reader is one who is enabled to escape from having to pay attention to the split; the "expert" on reading is one who can bring this sort of attention to bear on others while not making it show up at all on one's self. The troubled reader, of course, exists in between the competent reader and the expert reader. It is between these types that Awilda can come to the experience that "I got trouble with my reading," since she recognizes herself as unlike those readers who do not have trouble and unlike those others who take interest in how she is doing.

Like Awilda, we too are now attending to the meaning of reading trouble, as this is made to appear in relation to other readers and in relation to the ways in which we commonly make sense of trouble and reading. Perhaps, again like Awilda, we can take up a space between competency and expertise. Resisting the merely competent reading or expert solution, seeking reading competence, we can now reflect on the social significance of reading difficulties and disabilities. To this end, I pursue a reflection that has something to reveal about the normative ordering of reading under contemporary conditions.

A NEW LITERACY

Those who have trouble with reading are not alone. Among people who claim expertise in the field of reading troubles, there appears to be a growing consensus that there is an expanding population of readers with difficulties. For example,

> In our current educational climate a particular concern is the shockingly large percentage of students who are unable to demonstrate proficiency in text comprehension. For example, 68% of fourth graders were at or below "Basic" level on the reading assessment of the National Assessment of Educational Progress ... These results have created a sense of urgency in our search for answers to the questions of how best to assess students' reading comprehension ... Assessments are a means of taking stock. (Carlisle and Rice, 2004, 521)

Some have argued that the international "literacy crisis" is a manufactured issue serving a variety of competing economic and social ends (see, e.g., Nelson and Sandin, 2005; Welch and Freebody, 2002). Part of any manufacturing process, regardless of its genesis, is its consequence. Today there is, for example, a proliferation of students believed to be, or are counted among those having trouble. There is also a proliferation in the various ways educational systems, including experts and educators define, study, and address such trouble. In the midst of this perceived crisis, there are calls for more extensive or involved assessments. For example,

> Reading professionals face a real challenge in determining just what it is about a particular student that is undermining comprehension; that is, at present, there is no standard assessment regimen. Assessment should be thorough, in order to assess as many reading weaknesses and strengths as possible … Be ready to accept the possibility that students who cannot comprehend have a variety of problems. (Duke, Pressley, and Hilden, 2004, 515)

It is widely acknowledged among educational professionals that there are not standard definitions of, nor comprehensive assessment regimes for, reading difficulties and disabilities. Yet, there is a consensus that the number of people who have reading trouble is growing. In this fascinating milieu of proliferating troubles, multiple testing regimens, and several suggested solutions, the number of professionals tackling such problems is also proliferating. What are some of the consequences that flow from the fact that along with the professional management of reading difficulties and disabilities, there are a growing number of ways to have a problem and thus to become a problem reader?

As Beth Ferri and David Connor (2006, 129) suggest, educational settings are "places where students are socialized into certain ways of being and thinking." Schooling practices teach us more than skills; they teach different ways to embody, live with, and identify ourselves in relation to skills sets. Individuals are, for example, schooled to read for their personal learning difficulties. This expert discourse on reading, schools its readers (i.e., us) to understand any personal difficulty as part of a large and expanding population in need of comprehensive assessment and remedy. Such schooling entails a unique form of reading that urgently aims to search for "answers to the questions of how best to assess students' reading comprehension." The question as to how best to assess students typically excludes the question as to why the proliferation of reading troubles is being located in individual students in the first place.

The formation of reading trouble does not begin nor end with the diagnosis of an individual student with reading difficulties. Instead, from a sociological perspective, "… any initial formulation of what the trouble 'really is' is conditional upon the subsequent effects of the attempted remedy" (Emerson and Messinger, 1977, 123). Those schooling practices that surround the making of people into readers, as well as the remedies suggested for those who are failing to undergo this transformation satisfactorily, need analysis. Determining "just what it is about a particular student that is undermining comprehension" or asking "how best to assess students" about this growing trouble highlights for some a lack of standards or a lack of universal mechanisms of assessment. However, from a more sociological perspective, we can also come to understand "lack" as part of a productive force. All the described lacks and limitations make an appearance today through the unexamined but powerful presence of our collective conceptions of reading. Reading is imagined as an individual ability in need of special individualized assessment and instruction; that is, part of the solution seems to be to school more people able to read for reading troubles. Lack of a unified definition, missing a singular assessment, as well as a basic belief in a growing lack of ability, make present or signify a new way of reading reading. This consistent, albeit anxious, methodology of lament regarding all that this not well or not present in the realm of reading signifies that we are now facing a new literacy—the literacy of reading troubles.

An ability to read reading troubles is a powerful form of literacy since it sorts, divides, and schools people not only as to how to imagine trouble but also how to recognize, who embodies it. Such a form of reading is also an act of individualization. In neoliberal times, the ability to individualize is a skill used, required, and often praised by people situated in bureaucratic structures. As Zygmunt Bauman (2000, 30–38) argues, "individuality" has become the key task of current times, and it requires people to believe and act as if all problems and all solutions can be located in the individual, a kind of enforced "individuality as fate." The power to individualize the normative daily order of literacy (a form of embodiment that is expected seemingly everywhere) makes this new literacy of reading reading troubles particularly powerful (see Titchkosky, 2007).

Perhaps there are more lessons to be gleaned from this new literacy other than its obvious participation in the individualization of troubles. James Heap (1991, 111), attending to what seems like we need not read, or the unnoticed, suggests that "Each type of reading theory, whether bottom-up, top-down, or interactive, formulates a version of the value, the Good … which reading serves." The hypothesis that there is a growing population of troubled readers is another type of reading theory that comes with its own version of the value or good of reading. We, the growing number of experts, teachers, parents, and new readers, are learning how to read for reading troubles which begs the question what are reading troubles good for? What value do reading difficulties and disabilities serve? What good do reading troubles serve?

There is a host of utilitarian or even crass answers to the question regarding what reading troubles are good for. For example, reading difficulties and disabilities are the material by-product of the Special Education industry that provides jobs for thousands of people in the form of training, teaching, and research that may also entail the production and distribution of programs, grants, thesis topics, texts, and so on. As one of the founders of disability studies, Irving Zola (1977, 66), reminds us, so long as it is possible to "live, and live well off the suffering" and differences of others, the individualization and medicalization of everyday life will continue unabated, with reward for some at the expense of many. But even understanding reading as part of the ongoing expansion of the medicalization of everyday life begs further questions. How is the meaning of reading being constructed within and by such a community of readers? What else might reading troubles be good for?

To read reading troubles is to come face to face with the existential character of reading itself—it is to have, if only for a moment, an experience of reading as both a way of being and a way of doing delivered to us as question: How might we relate to this? Perhaps this experience of the dual character of reading as a question of *relationality* is startling, so that we typically miscue and think that the question of reading belongs only to the problem reader. If the brakes can be put on the act of individualizing what is essential to reading itself and if the brakes could also be put on the production, commoditization, and distribution of trouble, perhaps something new could arise. We could then ask: How might I, my community, or this educational context relate to the fact that reading is both a way of being and a way of doing which we seem collectively interested in attending to, only when faced with the "troubled" reader? Such questioning demands that we do more than evaluate the quality of the material resources of the educational environment. Such questioning demands that we reflect on how we read others for their reading troubles.

Typically, the scene of the performance of reading reading already devalues or disowns the question of our collective relation to reading by locating trouble only in individuals. When we do not recognize our common fate as having to develop a relation to reading as something that we are and something that we do, we shore up barriers between different readers and reading communities thereby using literacy to divide. Surely it is possible to develop a more oriented or self-reflective relation to this scene? The "shocking" scene of a growing number of students with reading difficulties and disabilities might be the very place where we can begin to acknowledge our connection to the split character of reading. In this way, we could make the experience a featherlight reading competency subject to reflection. Recognizing the literacy of reading for trouble is a good occasion to reflect on how communities make up the meaning of persons, and perhaps do it differently.

CONCLUSION

We have a new literacy—reading for reading troubles. While a new grammar has been established for forming the meaning of people, not all people are being called upon equally to learn the actual workings of the grammar of this new literacy even though they may expertly deploy it. Acknowledging this social fact enables the possibility of studying this new literacy's grammar, its rules of constitution, as well as the power of its ordered and ordering logic. Such a critical move entails a commitment to encouraging all people, especially expert readers, to read *their* reading of the reading of others.

Reading *how* we read for reading troubles means bringing to consciousness a new form of literacy, how we access this literacy, as well as its actual everyday practical uses. The demand to attend to reading troubles does not belong only to those with reading difficulties and disabilities, since reading troubles belong to the perceiver as well as to the perceived. Collective forms of literacy can come under scrutiny at least equal in weight and significance to the scrutiny individual readers undergo. Through such critical scrutiny, we may discover that solutions to perceived problems may be as problematic as the shocking number of people regarded as a problem.

One aspect of the grammar of this literacy-of-trouble involves the specific ways individuals are understood as socially related to each other. The identification of reading disabilities by those who themselves have no identified difficulties with reading signifies the social fact that learning to read happens in the midst of some imagined community of readers. Paying attention to this new literacy allows for a new reading, that is, reading for how cultural texts on reading troubles narrate our literate communities and their membership requirements.

This sort of rereading of reading trouble grants access to a powerful irony. Reading is everywhere while the identity "reader" remains rather unnoticed. This irony doubles back on itself; we read about reading without reading this reading of others and we do this without having to reread ourselves as readers surrounded by imagined communities of other readers. The irony grows; becoming a reading subject, in contemporary times, is the privilege of not needing to consider what it means to be a reading subject while noticing those who have failed to be identified as reading subjects. The one in possession of the unquestioned identity as reader is the one who questions and frames the significance, placement, and treatment of the other—the troubled-reader. Through this process we constitute the meaning of persons with reading difficulties or disabilities. Operating within the confines of this grammar of reading troubles, reading continues to be individualized without consideration for what it means to live in a community that reads others in the ways that we do.

Disability studies offer the opportunity to "equalize attention"; it can teach us how to read our readings and thus to attend to the interpretations of those of us who are regarded as inscribed with embodied limitations and inadequacies. Learning to attend to those who read others for their reading troubles is not a flippant desire, since I recommend this as one keenly aware that how we formulate reading is also how we find ourselves belonging and not belonging in the world. My world is literate, I am dyslexic; I can only be dyslexic in a literate world; it is in me and I am in it. This is to suggest that we might bring together, and bring to consciousness, our words about one another and the worlds from which our words spring. As Paulo Freire (1983, 10) puts it:

> … this movement from the world to the word and from the word to the world is always present … In a way, however, we can go further, and say that reading the word is not preceded merely by reading the world, but by a certain form of writing it or re-writing it, that is, of transforming it by means of conscious practical work.

Reading differences are not only a way of reading, they are also a way of rewriting; they are the conscious practical work of people and are achieved at particular times and in specific places. It is in this light that Susan Peters (2005, 158) suggests that "the process of becoming learning disabled is, in fact, a political act." Thus, it matters to consider how we might no longer enable the possibility of regarding the very character of our literate times as disconnected from the formation of people with reading difficulties and disabilities. We might critically rewrite the stories of literacy problems so as to reveal the sort of world or community of readers that gives rise to "putting the word out" that I, you, or so many others have difficulty. One way to reveal the connection between word and world, as well as between forms of writing and types of readers, is to critically investigate the way we already read and write about those conceived of as marginal to reading and writing. This chapter represents the beginning of an inquiry into how accounts of reading difficulties can be read differently so as to reveal what they might teach us about the meaning of reading as a fully social phenomenon.

NOTES

1. I would like to thank the editors, Susan Gabel and Scot Danforth, for provoking me to read what I had not attended to in my work, namely, the "literacy of trouble."

REFERENCES

Adams, Mary Louise (1985). If they could see it we'd get more help: A Women's Experience with Dyslexia. In Pat Israel & Frances Rooney, *Resources for Feminist Research: Women and Disability*, 14 (1) 37–39.

Baker, Carolyn D., and Allan Luke (Eds.), (1991) *Towards a Critical Sociology of Reading Pedagogy: Papers of the XII World Congress on Reading,* pp. 103–129. Amsterdam, Netherlands: John Benjamins Publishing.

Bauman, Zygmunt. (2000). *Liquid Modernity*. Malden, MA: Blackwell Publishing.
Brown, Sandra and William McGreevy. (1994). *Experiencing Reading*. Dubaque, IW: Kendall/Hunt Publishing Company.
Carlisle, Joanne F. and Melinda S. Rice. (2004). Assessment of Reading Comprehension. In C. Addison Stone, Elkaine R. Silliman, Barbara J. Ehren and Kenn Apel (Eds.), *Handbook of Language and Literacy: Development and Disorders*, pp. 521–540. New York: Guilford Press.
Davies, Charlotte. (1998). Constructing Other Selves: (In)Competences and the Category of Learning Difficulties. In Richard Jenkins (Ed.), *Questions of Competence: Culture, Classification and Intellectual Disability*, pp. 102–124. Cambridge: Cambridge University Press.
Duke, Nell K., Michael Pressley and Katherine Hilden. (2004). Difficulties with Reading Comprehension. In C. Addison Stone, Elkaine R. Silliman, Barbara J. Ehren and Kenn Apel (Eds.), *Handbook of Language and Literacy: Development and Disorders*, pp. 501–520. New York: Guilford Press.
Emerson, Robert M. and Seldon L. Messinger. (1977). The Micro-Politics of Trouble. *Social Problems*, 25 (2): 121–134.
Farrell, Michael. (2003). *Understanding Special Educational Needs: A Guide for Student Teachers*. London: Routledge Falmer.
Ferri, Beth and David Connor. (2006). *Reading Resistance: Discourses of Exclusion in Desegregation and Inclusion Debates*. New York: Peter Lang.
Freire, Paulo. (1983). The Importance of the Act of Reading. *Journal of Education*, 165 (1): 5–11.
Gabel, Susan L. (Ed.). (2005). *Disability Studies in Education: Readings in Theory and Method*. New York: Peter Lang.
Green, Bill and Alex Kostogriz. (2002). Learning Difficulties and the New Literacy Studies: A Socially-critical Perspective. In Janet Soler, Janice Wearmouth and Gavin Reid (Eds.), *Contextualizing Difficulties in Literacy Development: Exploring Politics, Culture, Ethnicity and Ethics*, pp. 102–114. London: Routledge Falmer.
Gunning, Thomas G. (2006). *Assessing and Correcting Reading and Writing Difficulties*. 3rd Edition. Boston, MA: Pearson.
Heap, James. (1991). A Situated Perspective on What Counts as Reading. In Carolyn D. Hill, Roberta, Sean Tueton and Craig Werner. (2003, October 9–11). Reading Identity–Literature, Pedagogy, and Social Thought at *Working Conference: The Future of Minority Studies National Research Project*. Madison: University of Wisconsin.
Jenkins, Richard (Ed.). (1998). Culture, Classification and (In)Competence. In *Questions of Competence: Culture, Classification and Intellectual Disability*, pp. 1–24. Cambridge: Cambridge University Press.
Meek, Margaret. (1991). *On Being Literate*. New Hampshire, England: Heinemann.
Nelson, Karin Zeiterqvist and Bengt Sandin. (2005). The Politics of Reading and Writing Problems: Changing Definitions in Swedish Schooling During the Twentieth Century. *History of Education*, 24 (2): 189–205.
Peters, Susan. (2005). Transforming Literacy Instruction: Unpacking the Pedagogy of Privledge. In Susan L. Gabel (Ed.), *Disability Studies in Education: Readings in Theory and Method*, pp. 155–172. New York: Peter Lang.
Rasinski, Timothy and Nancy Padak. (1996). *Effective Reading Strategies: Teaching Children Who Find Reading Difficult*. 2nd Edition. Columbus, OH: Merrill, Prentice Hall.
Shklar, Judith N. (1990). *The Faces of Injustice*. New Haven, CT: Yale University Press.
Slee, Roger. (2004). Meaning in the Service of Power. In Linda Ware (Ed.), *Ideology and the Politics of (In)Exclusion*, pp. 46–60. New York: Peter Lang.

Soler, Janet, Wearmouth, Janice and Reid, Gavien (eds.). (2002). *Contextulaizing Difficulties in Literacy Development: Exploring Politics, Culture, Ethnicity and Ethics*. New York: Routledge Falmer.

Titchkosky, Tanya. (2003). *Disability, Self and Society*. Toronto, Canada: University of Toronto Press.

———. (2005). Disability in the News: A Reconsideration of Reading. *Disability and Society,* 20 (6) October: 653–666.

———. (2007). *Reading and Writing Disability Differently: The Textured Life of Embodiment*. Toronto, Canada: University of Toronto Press.

Welch, Anthony and Peter Freebody. (2002). Explanations of the Current International Literacy Crises. In Janet Soler, Janice Wearmouth and Gavin Reid (Eds.), *Contextualizing Difficulties in Literacy Development: Exploring Politics, Culture, Ethnicity and Ethics,* pp. 61–72. London: Routledge Falmer.

Winzer, Margaret. (2005). *Children with Exceptionalities in Canadian Classrooms*. Toronto: Pearson.

Zola, Irving K. (1977). Healthism and Disabling Medicalization. In Ivan Illich, Irving Zola, John McKnight, Jonathan Caplan and Harley Shaiken (Eds.), *Disabling Professions,* pp. 41–68. London: Marion Bayars Publishers.

CHAPTER TWENTY

Deleuze, Guattari, AND THE Boundaries OF Intellectual Disability

ANNA C. HICKEY-MOODY

In this chapter I outline some ways in which Deleuze's scholarship, and his joint work with Guattari, offer strategies for moving beyond extant boundaries of intellectual disability. I argue that the formation of intellectual disability, and the methods via which this notion is employed in discourses of inclusive education, form a medicalized conceptual and physical synthesis. Taking up Deleuze's writing on sensation (1990a, 2003) and Deleuze and Guattari's collaborative political philosophy (1983, 1987, 1996), I suggest a fracture and redesign of medicalized mappings of intellectual disability in which bodies and beliefs are stitched together. This act of reconceptualization is then positioned in relation to discourses of inclusive education. The theoretical developments put forward inform studies in inclusive education and special education and will be of interest for educational theoreticians looking for new frames of reference.

My contention that the formation of intellectual disability is a particular, medicalized form of conceptual and physical synthesis can be considered in relation to the following quotations. The first of these, taken from the work of Deleuze (1990a, p. 143) posits processes of knowledge formation as affective events: they shape the bodies that they simultaneously imagine. The second of these quotations, taken from the work of Slee (2001, p. 169), locates specific processes of knowledge production within discourses of disability. Slee associates specific ideological formations with discourses of disability. I consider knowledges of intellectual disability as a subsidiary of such discourses. Beginning with Deleuze, these passages read as follows:

> … divinatory interpretation [or the production of meaning] consists of the relation between pure event (not yet actualized) and the depth of bodies, the corporeal actions and passions whence it results. We can state precisely how this interpretation proceeds: it is always a question of cutting into the thickness, of carving out surfaces, of orienting them, of increasing and multiplying them in order to follow out the tracing of lines and of incisions inscribed on them." (Deleuze 1990a, p. 143)

The bodies to which Deleuze refers are social formations, composed of various corporealities, institutional and material forms, and bodies of knowledge. The above quote illustrates Deleuze's belief that possibility and limits, within a given range of potentiality, are inscribed into bodies via the knowledges through which they are known. Slee's work can be taken up to apply this theory about the power of knowledge formation to discourses of disability. Slee highlights the limits, as well as the accommodations, that discourses of disability afford. He states:

> The formation of disability, and thereby its ideological representations, suggests and simultaneously restricts a range of possibilities … It is with the creation and denial of possibility that I am concerned. (2001, p. 169)

The "formation of disability" to which Slee (2001, p. 169) refers in the latter of the quotations above is a specific act of "cutting into the thickness [of bodies], of carving out surfaces, of orienting them" (Deleuze 1990a, p. 143). In such formations, surfaces of bodies and beliefs are created in acts of divination that can deny numerous possibilities. Through embodied relations, sensory exchange and the craft of dance theater, it is possible to fracture and redesign mappings of disability in which bodies and beliefs are sutured together.

In developing this argument, I contrast the opportunities afforded by performance texts and performative methods of thought to "majoritarian" (Deleuze & Guattari, 1983, 1987, 1996) discourses of the social construction of intellectual disability. I claim a separate space for my theorization from that in which discourses of the social construction of intellectual disability are accorded power. In so doing, I argue that the work of theorists who consider the social construction of intellectual disability is productive, yet often bound to specific limits within thought. Such limits can be restrictive, while at the same time, they offer a political context in—and from—which to speak.

I reference the work of Adelaide-based Restless Dance Company (2000, 2001, 2002) as a site of inquiry and a source of knowledge production (Hickey-Moody 2000, 2001, 2002). Restless is critically regarded as Australia's leading youth dance company inspired by cultures of disability. It remains one of a select number of companies operating in the field of integrated dance in Australia. The Restless performance ensemble is composed of young dancers with and without intellectual disability. Building relationships between the affective surfaces of Restless Dance performance texts and Deleuze's philosophy, I fold some specificities of embodied differences into thought. I look to create what Deleuze (1988a, p. 71) articulates as a Spinozist, joyful or useful union "which so disposes the body that it can be affected [and act] in a greater number of ways" (Deleuze 1988a, 71) [author's square parentheses]. Such an active conception of bodily relations, and of thought, can be conceived as performative. It is performative in that it constitutes a philosophical dialogue via a reciprocal mode of engagement that allows empirical encounters to affect the worldview being acted out.[1] Deleuze and Guattari refer to such a performative dialogue of knowledge production as "mapping" (1987, pp. 5–25). They argue for the importance of making "maps" rather than "tracings."

NEW KNOWLEDGES AND OPEN SYSTEMS

In opposition to fluid, open "map" knowledge, a "tracing" is a closed knowledge system. "Tracing" is representative knowledge; it is a reproduction of power relations and blockages that unfold in a discourse or social space. "Mapping" creates new lines of movement. It prompts creative relations between social bodies. While "tracing" is a fixed representation, "mapping" is flexible, malleable, and open to change. Its outcome is unknowable. Deleuze and Guattari (1987, p. 13) explain these two contrasted yet complimentary conceptions of thought via their contention that "What distinguishes the map from the tracing is that it is entirely oriented toward experimentation in contact with the real." They explain this further, noting,

> … it is inaccurate to say that a tracing reproduces a map. It is instead like a photograph or X ray that begins by selecting or isolating, by artificial means such as colourations or other restrictive procedures, what it intends to reproduce. The imitator always creates the model, and attracts it. The tracing has already translated the map into an image; it has already transformed the rhizome into roots and radicles. (1987, p. 13)

The "map," or map knowledge, is flexible and responsive. While tracings are important in the respect that they can be used to communicate social problematics, mappings facilitate change.

"Tracing" is what Deleuze and Guattari (1983, 1987, 1996) call an "overcoding." This is a representational knowledge that outlines an existing social or institutional body in a way that accords a particular sense to it. Tracings are necessary. They outline given power relationships or establish a particular status quo between lived social fields and bodies of scholarly knowledge. Yet Deleuze and Guattari (1987) are adamant that the broader ecology of knowledge production always includes mapping as well as tracing, even if the map is not always acknowledged in scholarly discourses. They prompt us to connect map knowledge and tracing knowledge through what they call a "rhizome": an open system of conceptual arrangement that connects "line[s] of deterritorialization," processes of "veritable becoming" that merge "the good and the bad" (1987, p. 10).

This chapter can be conceived as a rhizome. Breakaway lines of conceptual development that investigate some histories and contemporary performances of the limits of studies of the social construction of intellectual disability, consistently tie back into my core arguments. These arguments are, first, that intellectual disability is a medicalized discursive formation that is composed of particular modes of relating to people with intellectual disability. Second, the discursive formation of "intellectual disability," while continually being remade through socialized medical practices, can be reconfigured through sensory knowledges. Deleuze (1990a, 2003) conceives sensory knowledges as planes of sensation. Integrated dance theater texts, such as those devised and performed in the work of Restless (2000, 2001, 2002), articulate the force of bodies with intellectual disability via economies of kinesthetic relation. The modes of engagement put forward here differ profoundly from those established within medical discourses of intellectual disability. For discussion of such medical texts, see the work of Merton (1968), Miller (1996), Osburn (1998), Wolfensberger (1975, 1982, 1989, 1991, 2001). For further discussion of the limits of medical discourses of medical knowledge see Williams and Calnan (1996).

As a creative performance of Deleuze and Guattari's rhizome (1987, p. 10), my interdisciplinary work in this chapter fosters multiplicities and change: "Write, form a rhizome, increase your territory by deterritorialization, extend the line of flight to the point where it becomes an abstract machine" (Deleuze & Guattari 1987, p. 11). As an experiment with, and performance of, such a philosophy of knowledge production, this chapter moves towards appropriating and reconfiguring limits of the "abstract machine" (Deleuze & Guattari 1983, 1987) of studies of the social construction of intellectual disability.

Tracing the Intellectually Disabled Body

The broad term "disability" establishes specific boundaries of bodily capacities. While the names "disability" and "intellectual disability" have been developed within medical discourses to support medical practices, social or sociological academic discourses need not reproduce the methods of thought pioneered for scientific purposes. Indeed, the problematic of the "intellectually disabled" body within discourses of the social construction of intellectual disability is, I argue, a tired legacy of medical models of thought. As Dewsbury et al. (2004, p. 156) contend,

> ... development for disabled people faces ... problems in that, as Williams (1996) argues, there is no neutral, "untainted," language with which to begin the process of discussion. The language categories we use influence both the definition and "solution" of the problem.

As this quote makes plain, the question of how bodies with intellectual disability can be thought in positive and productive ways is a problematic that is largely posed by language. Arguably, this problematic is constructed by dominant modes of discursive representation, more than by people with intellectual disabilities, inasmuch as bodies can be separated from the discursive formations that fold in to partially constitute them. Medical models of intellectual disability (which developed the term) and theories of the social construction of intellectual disability are frameworks of socially embedded knowledge production.

Medical models of disability are largely concerned with comparative analyses of individual's bodies (see DIRC 2001, DSSSA 2004, Ruhi, et al., 2001), within which the term "disabled" is offered as a limited understanding of difference. Here, knowledge propositions utilized within medical discourses are translated into epistemological claims. This is because the effects of medical discourses are, in part, social and sociological applications of knowledges constructed within medical discursive limits.

The social constructivist model of intellectual disability (Wolfensberger 1975, 1982, 1989, 1991, 2001) was developed as a framework through which to understand physical and epistemological differences as social constructions, which are layered upon embodied experiences. The conceptual structure underlying the social construction model is also evident in the work of scholars in the broader field of studies of social constructivism. As a school of thought, the work of theorists of social constructivism and the social construction of disability build upon the early conceptual foundations laid by the antipsychiatry movement of the 1960s. The scholarly position that evolved from this movement is that presenting otherness, such as "disability" (or practices of social "othering") as a construction might emancipate individuals from an understanding of embodied personal failure. By mobilizing and augmenting this theoretical framework, contemporary disability studies scholars (Albrecht 2002, Oliver 1983, 1989, 1990a, 1990b) present disability as being constructed by the state or reconstructed through social interactions, rather than embodied by the individual.

An example of thinking about otherness as being constructed by the state and reconstructed through social interactions, rather than embodied by the individual, can be found in the work of Edgar (2002). Edgar summarizes Goffman's (1956,

1959, 1961, 1963) earlier, foundation building approach to conceptualizing practices of social "othering" by suggesting that

> Goffman ... was concerned with the ways in which encounters are managed, and the skills that actors bring to encounters. These skills are those required not only to present ourselves to others, but also to maintain the coherence and meaningfulness of the encounter ... physical or other abnormalities may be used to disrupt a person's presentation of his or her self, and thereby exclude them from full participation in society (Edgar 2002, p. 86).

This quote offers a clear example of early thought around the ways in which individuals, individual experiences, and individuals' senses of self, can be seen to be constructed through social interactions. As a model for thinking about social interaction and the social construction of embodied subjectivity, a social constructivist model of disability was taken up in scholarly methods for thinking about intellectual disability after being developed in the profoundly influential work of Oliver (1983, 1990a). While Oliver's project (1983, 1990a) is concerned with the politics of thinking about disability rather than with intellectual disability specifically, he offers a notable, benchmark example of attempts at thinking beyond boundaries of earlier social constructivist thought concerned with social othering.

In arguing for a social model of disability, Oliver (1983, 1990a) both extends and augments the work of earlier theorists of social constructivism and the social construction of disability. An illustration of the method of thought advocated in much of Oliver's work can be found in his suggestion (1983, p. 23) that

> This new paradigm [a social model of disability] involves nothing more or less fundamental than a switch away from focusing on the physical limitations of particular individuals to the way the physical and social environments impose limitations upon certain groups or categories of people ... [a]djustment within the social model, then, is a problem for society, not for disabled individuals.

> Oliver's social model of disability, outlined briefly in the quote above, has been profoundly influential in the field of studies of the social construction of disability. Conceptual developments in relation to Oliver's work and ensuing debates looking to retheorize corporeality in relation to a social model of disability warrant a book-length study in themselves. This is not the focus of my work here and for my purposes in this chapter, I merely canvass the line of thought emerging from these debates that is most pertinent to my concerns.

Scholars such as Dewsbury et al. (2004), Galvin (2003), McHenry (1999), and Riddell and Wilson (2001) have employed notably different methodologies[2] to construct arguments that are based on a common concern. This shared contention—to think "disability" (and for my purposes here, intellectual disability) as *solely* discursively constructed—can entail an assumption that human bodies and human societies are two discrete and somewhat contained fields.

Thinking through the binary conceptual fields of human bodies (individuals) and human societies, discourses of the social construction of disability can privilege society as the more powerful entity that "writes" the nature of bodies. For example, Dewsbury et al. (2004, p. 156) argue that "… the 'social model' recognizes … many different philosophical positions, which have been described as involving a tension between realism and constructionism." The theoretical leaning toward this constructionism mentioned by Dewsbury et al. (2004, p. 156) can limit views of corporeal agency of the disabled subject within studies of the social construction of disability.

By subscribing to a theoretical understanding of bodies as socially constructed, individuals' experiences of embodiment can be overlooked (Price & Shildrick 2002, Thompson 1997a, 1997b, Wendell 1997). Authors who subscribe to the constructivist model of intellectual disability risk failing to mediate conflicting discourses surrounding theories of "intellectual disability" and individuals' embodied experiences of intellectual disability. More importantly, space is not provided in which to retheorize the power structures that are already performed by the term "intellectual disability," as the social construction of bodies with intellectual disability begins with the name "intellectual disability."

Feminist discussions of the nature/nurture debate have clearly illustrated that the boundaries between "nature" and "culture," or social construction and embodiment, are inherently problematic. Indeed, it seems that "[w]hatever else we say about conceptions of the body, it is clear that how we conceptualize the body forms and limits the meaning of the body in culture in various ways" (Gatens 1996, p. 49). Embodied experiences and the ways we think about, and refer to, bodies need to be understood as constituting valid and powerful sites of knowledge production. This consideration allows embodied experiences and the ways bodies are thought about and referred to, to constitute sites of contestation, surrounding, interleaving, disrupting, and reworking ideas of intellectual disability and the corresponding ideas of self-worth and academic capital that are encompassed by the term.

MAPPING THE UNTHOUGHT: FROM THE MEDICAL TO THE SOCIAL

An undertheorized notion of the body as a socially inscriptive surface can be traced from critiques of the medical model conducted in the antipsychiatry movement through to parallel arguments in the field of studies of the social construction of disability. The mid- to late 1980s saw the rise of Disability Studies as a multifocal discipline grounded in the premise that "disability is above all a form of institutional discrimination and social exclusion, rather than a product of physical difference between individuals" (Centre for Disability Studies 2002). Generally referred to as the social model, discussed above, the conceptual framework of studies of the social construction of disability continues to challenge the veritable pathology of writing the body as silent: a vessel inscribed by social discourses and largely devoid of agency. As Thompson (1997a, 1997b) and Wendell (1997) have cautioned, if theoreticians are not careful, power can be accorded to the politics of "disability" constructed within sociological academic discourses, and disabled individuals may not necessarily be conceptualized as playing an active role in the constitution of these discourses. If dialogic space is not created, tracings write over maps.

While the body no longer remains the totally silenced party within studies of the social construction of disability, this field of research is yet to fully engage an active understanding of corporeality. For example, Freund's (2001) "Bodies, Disability and Spaces: The Social Model and Disabling Spatial Organizations" challenges, but does not entirely turn away from static conceptualizations of the body. While Freund's work is a very valuable contribution to studies that mobilize disabled embodiment to develop critical perspectives on disability, there remain some methods of scholarly expression in his work that can be seen as resurfacings of dominant divisions between corporeality and subjectivity. For example, he (Freund 2001, p. 691) contends that his research goal is to develop theorized relationships between "embodied agency, psychosomatic capacities and society"; however he (2001, p. 701) also suggests that:

> [t]he sociology of the body and health and illness have focused on the narratives of those who have a chronic illness or disability with the goal of capturing aspects of their experiences, including embodiment experiences.

This statement implicitly suggests that a person's experiences might be disembodied (i.e. somehow might not include "embodiment experiences"). Such a suggestion points toward the difficulties of bringing a comprehensive acknowledgment of the body into disability theory. Ideally, the very thought of "disability theory" would be acknowledged as a product of embodied experience, as the imaginings of a collection of bodies who seek to extend the metaphysical aspects of their material, or substantial, selves.

As a method of thought and a mode of practice, social constructivism finds a stronghold in the field of education. Much academic work concerned with intellectual disability and education is grounded in ideas of inclusive educational practices. In contexts such as schools and academic discourses of educational research, "inclusion" can be a useful word because it reflects a sentiment of resistance to market-driven ideas of egalitarianism and practices that are developed to support these ideals. This is largely the line of argument that Barton and Slee (1999) pursue in their article, "Competition, selection and inclusive education: some observations." I briefly discuss this article here, arguing that the boundaries of thought constructed in relation to intellectual disability need to be reassessed. Barton and Slee, both leaders in the field of inclusive education, begin by outlining the rhetoric that they work to counter, namely that of market-driven educational policies that encourage competition between individual educational institutions.

Developing productive methods for working with people who do not respond to academically competitive environments entails, they argue, the inception and performance of a philosophy of resistance to conservative, egalitarian social terms. This process must begin with methods of thought:

> It is important therefore to resist compartmentalized thinking, and seriously to endeavor to make connections between these different factors [social and moral terms—and the interpersonal relations that inform and constitute these terms]. This is both an urgent and demanding task (ibid., 9, p. 4).

In sympathy with my broader concerns about thinking through the social construction of intellectual disability, Barton and Slee (ibid.) highlight the importance of moving away from terms grounded in binary power relations. Arguing against ideas of "right" and "wrong," "ability" and "disability," "inclusion" and "exclusion," Barton and Slee (ibid.) suggest that the methods of thought these ideas perform limit possibilities for recognizing an often diverse range of practically positive (although not economically assessable) educational outcomes. In constructing this argument, they draw upon the work of Rose (1995) who suggests:

> ... if we determine success primarily in terms of test score, then we ignore the social, moral and aesthetic dimensions of teaching and learning—and, as well, we'll miss those substantial intellectual achievements that aren't easily quantifiable. (Rose 1995, pp. 2–3 in Barton & Slee 1999, p. 9)

However, Barton and Slee (ibid.) also contend that the practical realities of inclusive education are not as exciting as the theoretical ideals outlined in the quote above. As Slee (2001) later argues, discourses of "inclusion" within mainstream educational practices have become a system of othering, a system that will only be dissolved through developing new methods for thinking about identity and embodied difference. The process of dissolving this system of othering must begin with methods of thought.

Frameworks for educational practice that are grounded in ideals of "competition and selection" (Barton & Slee 1999) operate through preestablished ideals of success that are contextually specific to Western economies of academic and social capital (Bourdieu & Wacquant 1992, Riddell & Wilson 2001). Furthermore, educational policies of "competition and selection" (Barton & Slee 1999) inadvertently employ an understanding of embodied worth that is contingent upon the singular student's academic performance. Within the conceptual framework imposed by discourses of competition and selection (ibid.), those who do not achieve academic excellence can only be known as a living intellectual/economic deficit. There are no conceptual tools available for thinking otherwise. Thus, methods of thought become translated into systems of educational winners and losers. Economies developed by certain kinds of bodies, support and value these [intellectually able] bodies and devalue difference [intellectual disability]. Once again, the body and embodied knowledge are marginalized through a cerebral model of subjectivity. As Barton and Slee (ibid., p. 11) suggest, "[t]he struggle for inclusion entails the serious effort to remove all forms of oppression …"

Such "forms of oppression" (Barton & Slee 1999, p. 11) must be understood as conceptual as well as social and practical. "Intelligence" can be a disabling idea when employed in contexts such as schools, where academic performance effectively becomes a marker of bodily worth. As Barton and Slee (1999, p. 11) suggest, school cultures that are developed to support educational policies of "competitive individualism, selection and credential achievement" (Barton & Slee 1999, p. 6) not only advocate the practice of viewing academic achievement as a marker of bodily worth but also reconstruct a limited idea of knowledge and an associated cerebral model of subjectivity that does not accord agency to the flesh:

> Conceptions of "ability" and "failure" have and continue to be constituted in and by the practices of schooling. They are part of a regulatory discourse involving power and control on the part of professional and government agencies (Slee 1995). In this context, concepts such as "special educational needs" are to be viewed as a euphemism for failure (Barton 1986). (Barton & Slee 1999, p. 7)

The observation that "special educational needs" (Barton & Slee 1999, p. 7) can be a "euphemism for failure" illustrates the ways in which theoretical problematics affect lived experiences when they are performed through social and cultural practices. The idea of inclusive education and perhaps more importantly, the practice of inclusive education, are reflective of broader egalitarian ideals and a Cartesian idea of knowledge (Descartes 1968a, 1968b, 2003) that accords value to bodies in light of their academic capacity. Of particular concern to me is the fact that discourses of inclusive education do not provide the conceptual tools for thinking outside of binary divides such as ability/disability.

EXCLUSIVE "INCLUSION"?

A clear example of the often restrictive nature of the idea of "inclusion" can be found in Biklen's (2000) article "Constructing inclusion: lessons from critical, disability narratives." Biklen employs the term "inclusion" in relation to an apparently binary divide between "disability voices" (2000, p. 337) and an unnamed "other." The conceptual framework of Biklen's research leads him to re-create the binary divide he critiques. This is the same binary in thought through which the practice of othering occurs. For example, Biklen's argument surrounding "constructing inclusion" is contingent on his assumption that people without intellectual disability "presume that their ideas about the actions of the person with a disability or about events and activities in the classroom accurately reflect how the person with a disability experiences them" (2000, p. 338). Biklen does not allow for the possibility that people without intellectual disability may not have a homogenous reaction of presuming they know what a person with intellectual disability is experiencing.

Biklen performs an egalitarian understanding of bodies akin to that presented by educational policies of competition and selection. Biklen (2000) imagines a homogenous population of "normate" (Thompson 1997a) people who share the same limited presumptions about people with intellectual disability. This "normate" (Thompson 1997) population is a construction of thought. The problem thus lies in the fact that Biklen (2000) does not directly discuss his methods of thought, nor does he refer to the "normate" population as a construction of thought. Rather, he assumes a population divided clearly between a "disabled" minority and a "normate" (Thompson 1997) majority. Biklen continues this inadvertent performance of egalitarianism through comments such as, "the dominant culture's non-disabled lens" (2000, p. 338), which suggests that there is a single, all-seeing culture from which a person might be excluded.

Biklen's (2000) binary construction of "normates" (Thompson 1997a) and "others" conceptually mirrors the discourses of "competition and selection" that Barton and Slee (1999) so avidly critique. In so doing, it offers a specific example of some ways in which thinking within a framework of the social construction of intellectual disability can lead to limited (in this case, binary) conceptions of the "intellectually disabled" body. Such discourses reiterate a narrow conceptual foundation of egalitarianism, within which bodies are largely valued for their capacity to produce thought. Hence the central importance of the term "inclusion" again becomes specific to very conservative conceptual foundations, within which practices of "inclusion" can be seen as a limited performance of resistance. As Barton and Slee (1999) contend and Slee (2001, p. 175) later reaffirms, we must consider whose interests it serves to view bodies as either productive machines with academic capacity or economic burdens "containing" intellectual deficit. While the immediate answer to this question is "the needs of the international market place" (Barton & Slee 1999, p. 6), such basic equations between educational achievement and market value have failed to provide structural support for thinking otherwise:

> It is now becoming increasingly clear that problems of inequalities of an economic, social, and civic nature are more prominent than in any other postwar period. Recognizing the centrality of structural issues in relation to the entrenched nature of poverty and inequality, Walker and Walker (1997, p. 8) maintain that explanations that focus on individualistic factors are totally inadequate and misleading in terms of the deep structural issues that need to be engaged with. (ibid., p. 6)

To engage with "deep, structural issues" (ibid., p. 6), issues of social concern, we must first think "the social" and "the body" through a method that dissolves egalitarian ideals and binary conceptual foundations. Reconceptualization must begin at a microlevel by working outside models of thought that perform "othering." The "tracing" of social construction needs to be brought together with the "map" of lived bodies.

In adopting this theoretical proposition, I contend that limited readings of people with intellectual disability that have been established within discourses of the social construction of intellectual disability are not always re-created through performance texts. As Goodley and Moore (2002) and Kueppers (2003) have argued, performance texts afford opportunities for working with people with intellectual disability who are not entirely constrained by the preestablished value systems that can accompany language.

In contrast to limits of thought established within academic discourses, methods of practice employed to construct performance texts can be quite specific to the bodies in question. Within methods of practice employed to compose integrated dance theater, bodywork is material as well as conceptual. Theorizing such methods of practice leads me to methods of thought employed by Deleuze (1990a, p. 28) in which

> Sense is never only one of the two terms of the duality which contrasts things and propositions, substantives and verbs, denotations and expressions; it is also a frontier, the cutting edge, or the articulation of the difference between the two terms, since it has at its disposal an impenetrability which is its own and within which it is reflected.

Deleuze further advocates the empirical significance of sense in moving beyond dualistic models of thought, arguing that: "... sense must be developed for its own sake ..." (1990a, p. 28). In addition, the work of Guattari with Deleuze

(1983, 1987, 1996), offers a means of constructing expansive, productive, and performative readings of bodies. Thinking through Deleuzo-Guattarian (1983, 1987, 1996) ideas opens up detailed methods for considering the socially affective or modulating capacities of performance texts.

In the next section of this chapter, I employ the concept of "becoming" (Deleuze & Guattari 1987, 1996) to offer an alternative understanding of bodies and embodied work, to the undertheorized body implied by the term "intellectual disability." Just as the rhizome brings together the tracing and the map, the concept of becoming (Deleuze & Guattari 1987, 1996) dissolves the hierarchical, dualistic power base (grounded in a knowledge/matter distinction) that discourses of intellectual disability assume. "Becoming" offers a method of thought that provides opportunities for theorizing bodies outside the privileging of thought. It entails thinking, or striving to think, form on its own terms, establishing evaluative schemas in relation to matter, rather than imposing preexisting, transcendent models of evaluation. The concept of "becoming" (Deleuze & Guattari 1987, 1996) offers a method for thinking about difference that is positive and productive because it reads bodies in relation to their contextual positioning and the actions they undertake. In exploring the concept of becoming as a performative method of thinking through difference, I contrast the opportunities afforded by these methods of thinking difference to physical spaces and theoretical trajectories in which a preestablished construction of "intellectual disability" is played out.

BECOMING BODIES

The body becoming is known through what it can "do," and what it actualizes. There is no equation with lack performed. I now discuss the possibilities afforded by performance texts as an alternative to the practices of inclusion discussed above and to the limits of thought determined by studies of the social construction of disability. Drawing on the work of Spinoza (1996, 2001) and Deleuze's earlier readings of Spinoza (1988a, 1990b), Deleuze and Guattari (1983, 1987, 1996) argue that matter, or substance, has an intrinsic worth that cannot be judged in relation to thought, or other modifications (expressions) of substance. Thought is a product of matter, and has an intrinsic value of its own. The value of thought is qualitatively different from the value of matter; the two entities "operate on different planes" (Deleuze & Guattari 1996, pp. 41, 53, 125–26, 211–12, 177–84). Differences in kind between modes of substance are not comparable, because modifications of substance are composed of different parts of the world. Everything is difference: a million varied articulations of difference. When taking up this framework as a method of thought, understandings of cultures, identities, and bodies must begin with minutiae: tiny particles of difference that share the same plane of composition:

> Substantial or essential forms have been critiqued in many different ways. Spinoza's approach is radical: arrive at elements that no longer have either form or function, that are abstract in this sense even though they are perfectly real. They are distinguished solely by movement and rest, slowness and speed. They are not atoms, in other words, finite elements still endowed with form. Nor are they indefinitely divisible. They are infinitely small, ultimate parts of an actual infinity, laid out on the same plane of consistency or composition. (Deleuze & Guattari 1987, p. 254)

Although the Spinozist (1996, 2001) concept Deleuze and Guattari employ in this excerpt is abstract in nature, like all kinds of thought, it can have a direct impact on people's worldviews, and the practices that evolve from these views. The educational discourses discussed earlier in this chapter offer an excellent example of the limits of perspectives that fail to reflexively acknowledge structural models in thought, such as binary conceptual frameworks. These structures, or limits of thought, can be both enabling and disabling depending on how they position materialities, how they are conceived, and whether or not they are viewed as conceptual tools.

MOVING "INTELLECTUAL DISABILITY": A CARTOGRAPHY OF FREEDOM

In contrast to models of thought mobilized in much work on the social construction of intellectual disability, Spinoza's (1996, 2001) concept of substance, deployed by Deleuze (1990a, 2003) and Deleuze and Guattari (1987, 1996) in their concept of becoming, offers a nonhierarchical ontology and perspective on thought. Deleuze and Guattari's (1987, pp. 41, 43, 52, 252–54) discussion of substance as that which is distinguished by "movement and rest, slowness and speed … (longitude)" (1987, p. 254) lays a broad conceptual framework within which a body and its capacities are always determined in relation to corporeal context. Context forms the latitude, or accessible power, that defines what the longitude, or consolidated matter can perform. Movement (longitude) is immeasurable and can be known only through what it does. A body's movements are both internal and external, in that bodies—individuals, institutions, nation states—have capacitates for self-regulation. This self-regulation exists in relation to external forces that act upon bodies. A force produced by art—a work of integrated dance theater or an image—can inform, or be folded into, individual processes. Movement is the ongoing process of becoming by which bodies continuously evolve in relation to greater and lesser bodies.

This model for thinking the body-becoming performs Spinoza's (1996, 2001) method for thinking about the material and the metaphysical as equally valuable. This method dissolves the privileging of academic knowledge or thought over matter. Spinoza (1996, 2001) calls for matter to be judged in material terms, and thought on terms inherent within thought. Thus, the practical and social implications of Spinoza's (1996, 2001) philosophy are considerable. For example, Slee (2001, p. 169) argues that new methods of thought offer discourses of inclusive education the tools for reconsidering binary systems of conceptualization. He states:

> At the centre of this discussion [of inclusive education] is an invitation for us to explore our own knowledge of disability and disablement and to examine the implications of the kinds of beliefs we hold … we do need to examine the way in which the uses and abuses of language frame meanings that disable and exclude.

Taking up this call to reassess the metaphysical—or prediscursive—suppositions being performed in language, Deleuze (1990a, 1990b, 2003) and Deleuze and Guattari's (1987, 1996) mobilization of Spinoza (1996, 2001) is a method for reworking "uses and abuses" (Slee 2001, p. 169) of language. Theorizing the body-becoming in performance texts allows us to develop new knowledges of disability and disablement. Language and thought, both of which express and act upon bodies, need to come from the bodies themselves. Language and thought need to articulate particular aspects of bodies' capacities, rather than speaking to preexisting, institutionalized structures in thought. Relationships with institutionalized structures in thought will continue to develop and be mediated in response to emergent grammars of self and new thoughts. This interdisciplinary cross-fertilization points toward the utility of what Slee (2001, p. 174) terms "cross cultural dialogues" or perhaps, the interdisciplinary dialogues that Deleuze and Guattari (1987, p. 174) suggest might "invite us to think otherwise."

NOTES

1. Butler's (1993, pp. x–xi) writings on the performative nature of discourse are instructive. Her example in the excerpt below develops an argument relating to the discursive construction of sex and the performative nature of gender. The logic applied here can be productively considered in relation to the discursive formation of intellectual disability:

   "To claim that … materiality … is constructed through a ritualized repetition of norms is hardly a self-evident claim. Indeed, our customary notions of "construction" seem to get in the way of understanding such a claim. … why is it that what is constructed in understood as an artificial and dispensable character? What are we to make of constructions without which we would not be able to think, to live, to make sense at all, those which have acquired for us a kind of necessity?"

2. Dewsbury, Clarke, Randall, Rouncefield & Sommerville (2004) develop what they call an "anti-social model of disability" through ethnographic research, with a view to informing the development of assistive technologies for people with disabilities. Galvin (2003) rethinks disability culture in relation to the politics of studies of the social construction of disability. McHenry (1999) mobilizes the body as an analytical lens through which to rethink disability and Riddell and Wilson (2001) apply Bourdieu's notions of bonding and bridging cultural capital to a longitudinal study of the lives of people with intellectual disability.

REFERENCES

Albrecht, G.L. (2002). American Pragmatism, Sociology and the development of Disability Studies. In Barnes, C. Oliver, M. & Barton, L. (Eds.), *Disability Studies Today*, pp. 18–37. Cambridge: Polity.
Barton, L. (1986). The politics of special educational needs. *Disability, Handicap & Society*, 1, 273–290.
Barton, L. & Slee, R. (1999). Competition, selection & inclusive education: some observations. *International Journal of Inclusive Education*, 3 (1), 3–12.
Biklen, D. (2000). Constructing inclusion: Lessons from critical, disability narratives. *International Journal of Inclusive Education*, 4 (4), 337–353.
Bourdieu, P. & Wacquant, L. (1992). *An invitation to reflexive sociology*. Cambridge: Polity Press.
Butler, J. (1993). *Bodies that Matter.* New York: Routledge.
Centre for Disability Studies. (2002). *What is Disability Studies?* Online URL: http//www.leeds.ac.uk/disability-studies/what.htm retrieved February 21, 2005.
Deleuze, G. (1988a). *Spinoza: Practical Philosophy.* San Francisco: City Light Books.
Deleuze, G. (1990a). *The Logic of Sense.* New York: Columbia University Press.
Deleuze, G. (1990b). *Expressionism in Philosophy: Spinoza.* New York: Zone Books.
Deleuze, G. (2003). *Francis Bacon: The logic of sensation.* Minneapolis: University of Minnesota Press.
Deleuze, G. & Guattari, F. (1983). *Anti—Oedipus, Capitalism & Schizophrenia.* Minneapolis: University of Minnesota Press.
Deleuze, G. & Guattari, F. (1987). *A Thousand Plateaus: Capitalism & Schizophrenia.* Minneapolis: University of Minnesota Press.
Deleuze, G. & Guattari, F. (1996). *What is Philosophy?* London: Verso Publishers.
Descartes, R. (1968a). *Discourse on Method.* F. E. Sutcliffe (Trans.), pp. 27–94. London: Penguin Books.
Descartes, R. (1968b). *The Meditations.* In F.E Sutcliffe (Trans.), pp. 95–169. London: Penguin Books.
Descartes, R. (2003). *The Principles of Philosophy.* Online URL: http://www.philosophyclassics.com/etexts/770/12462/ retrieved September 22, 2003.
Dewsbury, G. Clarke, K. Randall, D. Rouncefield, M. & Sommerville, I. (2004). The Anti-Social Model of Disability. *Disability & Society*, 19 (2), 159–169.
DIRC: South Australian Disability Information & Resource Centre. Online URL: http://www.dircsa.org.au/ retrieved November 13, 2001.
Down Syndrome Society of South Australia. Online URL http://www.downssa.asn.au/ retrieved May 10, 2004.
Edgar, A. (2002). Goffman. In Edgar, A. & Sedgwick, P. (Eds.), *Cultural Theory: The Key Thinkers* pp. 85–86. London: Routledge.
Freund, P. (2001). Bodies, Disability & Spaces: The social model & disabling spatial organizations. *Disability & Society*, 16 (5), 689–706.

Galvin, R. (2003). The Paradox of Disability Culture: The need to combine versus the imperative to let go. *Disability & Society,* 18 (5), 675–690.
Gatens, M. (1996). *Imaginary Bodies: Ethics, Corporeality & Power.* London: Routledge.
Goffman, I. (1956). Embarrassment & Social Organization. *American Journal of Sociology,* 62, 264–271.
Goffman, I. (1959). *Presentation of Self in Everyday Life.* Harmondsworth, London: Penguin.
Goffman, I. (1961). *Asylums: Essays on the Social Situation of Mental Patients & Other Inmates.* Victoria, Australia: Penguin Books.
Goffman, I. (1963). *Stigma: Notes on the Management of Spoiled Identity.* New York: Prentice Hall.
Goodley, D. & Moore, M. (2002). *Arts against Disability: The Performing Arts of People with Learning Difficulties.* Plymouth, MA: BILD.
Hickey-Moody, A.C. (2000). *Precious #2* tour remount, *Ethnographic Research Journal.* Australian Dance Theatre, Adelaide & Paralympics Arts Festival tour, Sydney.
Hickey-Moody, A.C. (2001). *Proximal, Ethnographic Research Journal.* World Dance Centre, Adelaide & North Adelaide Community Centre, North Adelaide & Opera Studio, Netley.
Hickey-Moody, A.C. (2002). *In the Blood, Ethnographic Research Journal.* Deaf Society Hall, Queen's Theatre, Adelaide.
Kueppers, P. (2003). *Disability & Contemporary Performance: Bodies on the Edge.* USA: Routledge.
McHenry, L. (1999). Thinking Through the Body: Moving Beyond the Social Construction of Disability. Masters Thesis, School of Information & Communication Studies, University of South Australia, Adelaide.
Merton, T. (1968). *Mankind in the Unmaking: The Anthropology of Mongolism.* Sydney: Bloxham & Chambers.
Miller, E. (1996). Idiocy in the Nineteenth Century. *History of Psychiatry,* 7 (3), 361–373.
Oliver, M. (1983). *Social Work with Disabled People.* Basingstoke: Macmillan.
Oliver, M. (1989). Disability & Dependency: A Creation of Industrial Societies? In L. Barton (Ed.), *Disability & Dependency,* pp. 6–23. London: Falmer Press.
Oliver, M. (1990a). *On the Politics of Disablement.* London: Macmillan.
Oliver, M. (1990b). The Individual & Social Models of Disability. Paper presented at joint workshop of *Living Options Group* & the *Research Unit of the Royal College of Physicians* on july 23,1990.
Osburn, J. (1998). An Overview of Social Role Valorization Theory. *International Social Role Valorisation Journal,* 3 (1), 7–12
Price, J. & Shildrick, M. (2002). Bodies Together: Touch, Ethics & Disability. In M. Corker & T. Shakespeare (Eds.), *Disability/Postmodernity: Embodying Disability Theory,* pp. 62–75. London: Continuum.
Restless Dance Company. (2000). *Precious* (remount). Directed by I. Voorendt; Paralympics Arts Festival tour, Seymour Theatre Centre, Sydney, October 15–20.
Restless Dance Company. (2001). *Proximal.* Directed by I. Voorendt. State Opera Studio, Netley, SA, October 23–26.
Restless Dance Company. (2002). *In the Blood.* Directed by I. Voorendt, Assistant Direction A. Hickey-Moody & P. Channels, Queen's Theatre, Adelaide, May 8–11.
Riddell, S. & Wilson, A. (2001). Gender, Social Capital & Lifelong Learning for People with Learning Difficulties. *International Studies in Sociology of Education,* 11 (1), 3–23.
Rose, M. (1995). *Possible Lives: The Promise of Public Education in America.* New York: Penguin.
Ruhi, Tukun, Karabulut, Bayazit & Bokesoy. (2001). A Down syndrome case with karotype of 46, XY, rec(21)dup(21q)inv(21)(p11q22) derived from paternal pericentric inversion of chromosome 21. *Clinical Genetics,* 59, 368–370.

Slee, R. (2001). Social Justice & the Changing Directions in Educational Research: The Case of Inclusive Education. *International Journal of Inclusive Education*, 5 (2–3), 167–177.

South Australian Disability Information & Resource Centre. (DIRC). Online URL: http://www.dircsa.org.au/pub/docs/factdown.txt retrieved November 13, 2001.

Spinoza, B. (1996). *Theologico-Political Treatise: A Political Discourse.* Online URL: http://csf.colorado.edu/forums/longwaves/98/oct98/1203.html retrieved July 17, 2002.

Spinoza, B. (2001). *Ethics.* England: Wadsworth.

Thompson, R.G. (1997a). *Extraordinary Bodies Figuring Physical Disability in American Culture & Literature.* New York: Columbia University Press.

Thompson, R.G. (1997b). Feminist Theory, the Body & the Disabled Figure. In L Davis. (Ed.), *The Disability Studies Reader*, pp. 279–312. London: Routledge.

Wendell, S. (1997). Towards a Feminist Theory of Disability. In L Davis. (Ed.), *The Disability Studies Reader*, pp. 279–292. London: Routledge.

Williams, S. & Calnan, M. (1996). The "Limits" of Medicalisation?: Modern Medicine & the Lay Populace in "Late" Modernity. *Social Science & Medicine*, 42 (12), 1610–1620.

Wolfensberger, W. (1975). *The Origin & Nature of Our Institutional Models Human.* Syracuse: Policy Press.

Wolfensberger, W. (1982). Eulogy for a Mentally Retarded Jester. *Mental Retardation*, 20 (6), 269–270.

Wolfensberger, W. (1989). Human Service Policies: The Rhetoric Versus the Reality. In L. Barton (Ed.), *Disability & Dependency*, pp. 23–41. London: Falmer Press.

Wolfensberger, W. (1991). *A Brief Introduction to Social Role Valorisation as a High-Order Concept for Structuring Human Services.* Syracuse, NY: Training Institute for Human Service Planning, Leadership & Change Agentry.

Wolfensberger, W. (2001). The story of the "Cruickshank chairs" at Syracuse University: A Contribution to the History of the Brain Injury Construct. *Mental Retardation*, 39 (6), 472–481.

CHAPTER TWENTY-ONE

Taking Exception: Discourses OF Exceptionality AND THE Invocation OF THE "Ideal"

VALERIE HARWOOD AND NICI HUMPHRY

> It has taken a long time for the condition of being positioned as "disabled" to be conceptualized as an oppression, rather than an unproblematic description of the characteristics and functionings of the bodies of some individuals. Even today in the subdiscipline with which I am most familiar, political philosophy, a relatively abstract notion of having a disability still appears in writings concerning justice, desert and responsibility, as the paradigm of the sort of disadvantage people might suffer that is simply a matter of bad luck. (Young, 2002, xii)

> The less able discover their finitude in a limited space of knowledge, life, production and language which constitutes them as second-class citizens and traverses them without residuum. (Krisjansen & Lapins, 2001, 65)

The statement by Iris Marion Young reminds us of the ways in which education, and particularly special education, all too often configure "an unproblematic description of the characteristics and functionings of the bodies of some individuals." The second quote brings this observation into sharp relief. In their remarks on "second-class citizens," Krisjansen and Lapins are referring to a consequence of expanding notions of "giftedness" and the emergence of "gifted pedagogy." In this paper we wish to take up this issue, namely, we want to consider what we consider to be a consequence of exceptionality discourses: the positing of a sharp dichotomy between an ideal student (the exceptional student) and a second-class student (the nonexceptional). Specifically, we maintain there is need to critically interrogate the discourses of exceptionality in terms of the productions of new notions of the "ideal student."

"Exceptionality" is often used to refer to educational discourses that seek to categorize and identify remarkable kinds of students. This literature encompasses discussion of programs and strategies that help or hinder the education of the exceptional child (Diezmann & Watters, 1997; Diezmann, Watters, & Fox, 2001; Freeman, 2000; Ireson & Hallam, 1999), literature regarding the special social and emotional needs of the exceptional (Hebert & Kent, 2000; Plucker & Stocking, 2001), and literature that canvasses problems arising in regard to exceptionality and inclusive education (Blanksby, 1999; Diezmann & Watters, 1997). These discourses can also include discussion of children and young people who are above and beyond the so-called norm of "gifted and talented." For example, in New South Wales (NSW) Australia, the Department of Education and Training (DET) uses the term "exceptional" in relation to the minority group of "exceptionally gifted" (DET, 2004, 11). Associated with such conceptualizations we can find discussion of issues pertaining to questions of "what is exceptional" (Baum, Olenchak, & Owen, 1998; Lovecky, 1994; Robinson, Zigler, & Gallagher, 2000). In addition, discourses of "exceptionality" can also invoke a different conceptualization where the term can be joined in special education discourses that identify children and young people in terms of "exceptional disability" (Grover, 2003). Such "exceptionally disabled" children are considered in the reverse sense of "beyond," that is, they seem to be depicted as below "the norm" of the "most" disabled.

For the purpose of this chapter, we treat discourses of exceptionality in terms of the range of education literature that pertains to notions of giftedness, and terms of the wider discourses that speak to notions of the outstanding student. In relation to the education literature, it is clear that the notion of the gifted or exceptional child is couched upon some type of marker that signifies them as more "exceptional" or more "gifted" than their peers. This leaves, as disability scholars have noted, the question of the remains, that is, how notions of exceptionality or giftedness simultaneously demark a nonexceptional and nongifted child (Krisjansen & Lapins, 2001). The seeming expansion of what constitutes "giftedness" is also an essential point to ponder. As Krisjansen and Lapins argue in relation to schooling in South Australia, notions of giftedness have expanded considerably from once being defined in terms of "IQ," to being thought of more broadly. They cite a description by the South Australian Department of Education and Children's Services (DECS, 1995):

> … a gifted child or student will possess, to an outstanding degree, demonstrated ability or potential in one or more of the following areas: general intelligence, specific

academic areas, visual and performing arts, psychomotor ability, leadership, creative thinking, interpersonal and intrapersonal skills. (DECS, 1995, 1996, cited in Krisjansen & Lapins, 2001, 54)

The notion of "outstanding degree" is echoed by Cigman who states in her proposed "criteria for giftedness" that "The first and primary criterion is exceptionally high achievement in at least one significant area of learning" (2006, 206). Such achievement is marked against a notion of "norm," a point saliently clear in the following statement by Robinson, Zigler and Gallagher: "Individuals who are mentally retarded or gifted share the burden of deviance from the norm, in both a developmental and a statistical sense" (2000, 1413). Whilst the notion of juxtaposing the "sharing (of) a burden" with the "mentally retarded" seems remarkable and not the least problematic, we can see again this fundamental emphasis on differing to a "norm."

Key to these discourses of exceptionality then is an assumption of variation from a norm in a fashion that "excels" it. However, to focus on these discourses as pertaining strictly to "outstanding" is to miss, what we contend to be, a subtle point. That is, these discourses of exceptionality have the potential to do much more than etch new "truths" regarding what is and is not outstanding. What they threaten is to mark out new forms of "ideal" student. In this chapter we critically consider the discourses of exceptionality and ask how constitutions of an "ideal" student invoke constitutions of the nonideal. How may we understand the constitution of the "ideal student" in early twenty-first century education in Australia (and arguably, in countries such as the United Kingdom, Canada, and the United States similarly influenced by notions of giftedness), and what are the implications for the work of critical disability studies?

FOUCAULDIAN PROBLEMATIZATION: CONCEIVING AN EXCEPTIONAL PROBLEM

The importance of conceptualizing discourses of exceptionality as a potential issue is a key tenet of our discussion. In so doing, we are not mounting an argument based on empirical data that invokes "proof" of the issue with discourses of exceptionality. Rather, we are mounting a theoretical argument that is based on the contention that these discourses need to be problematized. Following Foucault, we draw on two points of problematization, namely, first a focus on how something becomes an issue or problem, and second, on the task of problematization as a process (Harwood & Rasmussen, 2004).

Starting with the second point, we want to suggest that, in relation to discourses of exceptionality, it is important to invoke the task of problematization as process.[1] Referring to psychology and sexual identities, Harwood and Rasmussen write:

> (P)roblematisation can be understood as a specific process of analysing how a problem such as "sexual identity" is constructed. In so doing, it does not seek to "find" or represent "sexual identity" as an essentialised object. In this way problematisation can be used to analyse the discourses involved in the "problem of sexual identity" (including those that essentialise it) that are deployed in clinical conceptualisations. (2004, 405)

Working with this idea, we draw on "problematization as a process" as a means to analyze how discourses of exceptionality may be involved in the constitution of essentialized notions of the "ideal" student.

In relation to the first point, problematization can be drawn on to pose the question "how and why certain things (behaviour, phenomena, processes) became a problem" (Foucault, 2001, 171). For example, Foucault poses the question, "How and why were very different things in the world gathered together, characterized, analysed, and treated as, for example, "mental illness?" What are the elements, which are relevant for a given Problematization (ibid.). This provokes us to ask, paraphrasing Foucault, how notions of exceptionality may configure the "nonexceptional."

In this chapter we consider notions of "exceptionality" in two ways. The first refers to how exceptionality is frequently discussed in the range of literature pertaining to special practices for the "gifted" or "more able" student, notions that are tied to assumptions of categorical difference. The second relates to the ways in which discourses of exceptionality are not focused on categories of difference, but rather, configure new notions of the ideal student. This second way of speaking of the exceptional is subtle and warrants careful scrutiny. Here the "exceptional student" is posited as above and beyond the "normal student." Significantly, this is articulated in a manner that configures a new formation of "ideal" student. Our attention was first drawn to this notion of "ideal" via a description in *The Inquiry into the Provision of Public Education in NSW* (Vinson, 2002). This report included what we deem to be a troubling way of speaking about children and young people in the NSW public school system. In its introductory pages the report contains a list of the "Assets of the Public Education System" (ibid., iii–vii). This brief outline discusses a range of "assets," beginning with "Exceptional Students" and "Acceptance of the Full Range of Students" (iii). What caught our attention was the way in which this list of "assets" delineates two distinct groups of young people: the "exceptional" and the "full range." Students could attain a place in the "exceptional" student group based on meeting the criteria of "exceptional student." The consequence of not attaining "exceptionality" is that they are classified in the second group of students known as the "full range." Most noticeably, these two groupings are portrayed in very different ways, and perhaps most obviously (and most alarmingly) the "full range" student emerges as the antithesis of the "exceptional" student. In short, we have an "ideal" student, and consequently, the specter of the "nonideal" student.

DISCOURSES OF EXCEPTION:
THE HIGH CALIBER AND INSIGHTFUL

Portrayals of the exceptional student are marked by a language depicting them in "positive" ways. One of the striking features of this discourse of exceptionality is the way descriptions relating to "giftedness" are somewhat similar to the descriptions of students in promotional literature from certain schools (especially private schools). Here we want to put forward the tentative suggestion that these similarities need to be given pause. In locating this as point, our task of problematization is to find ways to name the "ideal" as an issue or problem.

According to the description in *The Inquiry into the Provision of Public Education in NSW* (ibid.) exceptional students are characterized by what *they can do* and what *they can achieve*. This "exceptional" student is "high caliber," "insightful," "articulate," and they have powers of reasoning, social awareness, initiative, and professionalism. Likewise exceptional discourses may also posit "gifted" students as being "wise," as demonstrated by "Wise Ones" a "… gifted education program for deep and complex thinkers" that is run at Brighton Primary School in Victoria, Australia (2006). Similar language is deployed by the NSW DET on their information page on "Gifted and Talented" students:

> *Gifted students* are those whose *potential* is distinctly above average in one or more of the following domains of human ability: intellectual, creative, social and physical … *Talented* students are those whose skills are distinctly above average in one or more areas of human *performance* … Students with exceptional abilities can also accelerate their progression in single subjects or whole grades … Exceptional students may also be allowed to start school before the normal enrolment age. (2006, emphasis in original)

Descriptions of exceptionality are similarly apparent in the literature describing the "exceptional school" or "elite" school (and consequently, the exceptional student produced by such schools). Here we propose it is instructive to consider examples of such descriptions taken from two exclusive schools, Eton College in England and Presbyterian Ladies' College (PLC) in Sydney, Australia. The former is selected for discussion as an exemplar of a famous elite boys school, the latter is an example of an Australian girls school that promotes itself as attracting a diverse range of pupils.

In the report *Inspection of Eton College* by the Independent Schools Council (2004), students at this exceptional school are reported to "reach the highest level of attainment" possible, that they make "good use of the opportunities provided," that they "undertake their own investigations," and that are able to "undertake their own lines of enquiry." They also achieve "personal success in [a] range of accomplishments" (Independent Schools Council, 2004, 10). These are eager learners who, in lessons, show keenness, originality, and "edge of their seat involvement," and they concentrate well and have high levels of attendance and are punctual (Independent Schools Council, 2004). In these descriptions we can see how the exceptional school is predicated on ideals of the exceptional student.

Whilst an elite school, Eton is also portrayed as encouraging the less privileged "gifted" student. For example, as Beck writes, "[i]n order to emphasize academic merit over financial means, Eton College currently provides financial support to a quarter of the student body in order to help gifted students receive a high-quality education regardless of parental income" (2006).

PLC, Sydney is a "non-selective school for girls" (2006a) and that states it "… offers a broad academic curriculum to students from a diverse range of backgrounds" (2006b, 1). Alongside these comments, discourses of exceptionality are apparent in the ways in which its students are characterized. For instance, a PLC student is one who will excel at her studies, who will gain "the essential qualities of leadership, personal grooming, trust, sharing, responsibility and the importance of community"; this student embraces diversity, respects difference, is tolerant, and reaches her "full potential academically, socially and personally" (Presbyterian Ladies' College, 2006d). The school also offers the "Excelsior Programme for Gifted and Talented Students." In this program,

> Students from Years 7 to 10, who have been identified as gifted and talented, may enter the Excelsior classes for English, Mathematics and Science. This programme modifies the curriculum for more able students to allow time for enrichment and extension. Its content is rigorous and beyond the scope of mainstream classroom work. (Presbyterian Ladies' College, 2006e)

In addition to this program, PLC operates an Extension Centre for students. This center is described as "one of the longest running continuous enrichment programmes for gifted and talented children in Australia" where "superior intellectual potential and academic achievement are highly regarded" (Presbyterian Ladies' College, 2006c). The value of catering to the exceptional student is palpable in the following:

> All children do better when they feel they belong somewhere and are recognised as individuals. By valuing their ideas and feelings, we nurture their sense of self-esteem,

when these needs are met. We hope participating in the Extension Centre programme gives students a sense of mastery by associating with their intellectual peers. (Presbyterian Ladies' College, 2006c)

Here there is a distinctive emphasis on, the value of the exceptional student. We propose that these ways of speaking about young people have significant implications in terms of positing an "ideal" (and consequently, invoking notions of the "nonideal" student). Such descriptions, we suggest, paint a picture of an ideal student, one that arguably, attends the ideal school. For the sake of this argument we have deliberately selected two high-profile exemplars of elite schools. Whilst we acknowledge the limitations of this small selection, we do maintain that consideration of the discourses of exceptionality in such cases is thought-provoking. Specifically the discourses drawn on by these privileged schools draws attention to some of the alarming ways in which a similar language is exploited in relation discourses of giftedness. It is not that we are suggesting that the discourses used by elite schools and those drawn on to describe the "gifted" are analogous, but rather, that *their potential effects* in terms of positing notions of the ideal student need to be interrogated. This leads us to a second focus of our critique: the "spectrum," which is we suggest, a conceptual apparatus that supports the "ideal" student to be constituted.

THE EXCEPTIONAL SPECTRUM AND THE CONSTITUTION OF THE "IDEAL STUDENT"

> If we look at the normal distribution of ability within a classroom, we see that although there is a bulge of "average" students, there are also those at both ends of the spectrum. (Palmerston District Primary School, 2006b)

Depictions of "spectrum" are not an uncommon means for depicting students in schools, and indeed, are devices that are almost certainly required, in one form or another, to demarcate differences such as "exceptionality." Such representation is illustrated in the above quote taken from the website of a primary school in Canberra, Australia. In these and in most other cases, the spectrum refers to a linear, ordered placement of particular levels that are ranked from one extreme to another. These levels are determined by some type of observation or testing of individuals, for example IQ testing, scales of personal attributes or levels of creativity, the results of which are compared to a predefined "norm" (Crowe, 2000; Monk, 2000; Robinson, Zigler, & Gallagher, 2000). On diagrams such as the one below, those students included in exceptionality discourses would appear at the upper end of the spectrum.

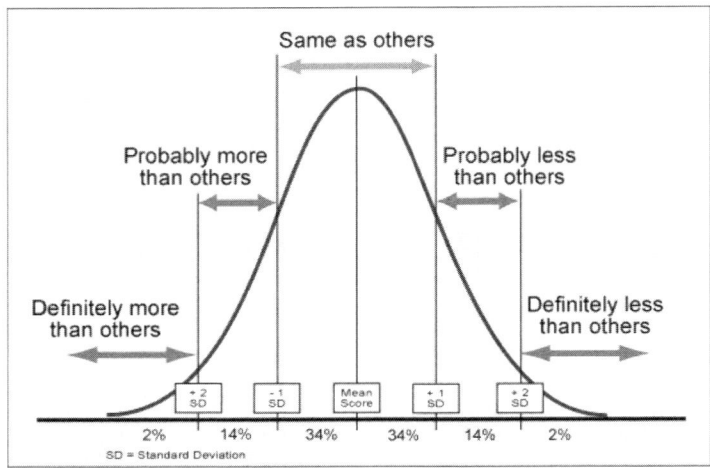

Source: www. fontys.nl

The application of the spectrum, and the location of the exceptional on it are made abundantly clear on the Palmerston District Primary School Web site. Alongside the above diagram, the statement is made: "If we examine the range of IQ of any randomly sampled population, it would show that about 15% could be described as 'gifted'" (Palmerston District Primary School, 2006a).

Established within the rationalities of scientific and mathematical regimes, the notion of spectrum has been drawn on in areas including autism (Prior et al., 1998); reading ability and dyslexia (Paulson & Henry, 2002; Stanovich, 1991); ADHD and other learning difficulties (Shaywitz, Fletcher, & Shaywitz, 1995) and exceptionality (Renzulli, 2002) as well as medical identifications such as physical function (Novacheck, Stout, & Tervo, 2000) and vision (Pesudovs & Coster, 1998). The notion of spectrum can also be invoked in relation to concepts such as a "continuum of services" applied in providing for disability (Neilson, 2002).

In these "spectrums," measured numerical spacings are drawn on to supposedly demark categorizations of ability—and these are marked in relation to a "norm." For instance, when Robinson, Zigler, and Gallagher (2000) applied the spectrum to the concept of mental retardation and giftedness, these two depictions of intelligence were located at two opposite ends of the "spectrum." With its two "ends," the spectrum can be imagined as having a set position (usually the midpoint) that is considered the "average." Levels of ability are thus positioned at either side of this point. The salient point we wish to emphasize is that critiques in disability studies need in our view, to revisit this notion of "norm." More exactly, we want to caution we need to be wary of an insidious form of "norm," the "ideal" that is constituted via discourses of exceptionality. In this configuration, the "ideal" would be located at the upper end of the "spectrum," that is, it would be juxtaposed alongside the exceptional and the gifted. An implication of this is that the "ideal" reconfigures the "average student," that is, the average student is now, quite simply, the "nonideal."

An alarming consequence of this "ideal" is the effects on the nonideal (or nonexceptional student). If we follow our line of reasoning, this means that the average student is not "ideal"; these are what are categorized in Vinson as the "full range" of students. Amongst the terms applied to the "full range" student are phrases such as "varying degrees of ability"; "limited means"; "limited educational sophistication"; "students with challenging behaviours"; "rejection by non-government schools"; "integration of students with disabilities" (Vinson, 2002, iii). Indeed exceptional students are depicted in terms of celebration and congratulations and by what they can do and what they have achieved. By contrast, the "full range" (or "nonexceptional") student is spoken of in terms of challenge, rejection, bad behavior, management, numbers, money and the amount of commitment they necessitate. In short, nonexceptional or nonideal students are branded by what was being *done for* them as opposed to what they *can do* or can achieve.

Extending this argument, we suggest it is important to consider how discourses of exceptionality invoke a normalization of the ideal student. As Baker (2002, 676) describes, normalizing practices can be understood as a type of "quality control" which is, she argues, citing Aberdeen (2000) "attemp(t) to prove the inferiority of others." The normalizing practices linked with this new ideal, are couched on a sense of "duty," a duty to educate the "full range" student to their (lesser) potential. This way of thinking, we maintain, immediately siphons off and isolates the "full range" of students from the "exceptional" ideal.

It is cogent to draw on a point from Price and Shildrick's argument regarding the influence of the "ideal" of "able-bodied." As they state, "Within disability, this is clearly seen in the actions of medical staff as they encourage disabled people to achieve ways of being, of moving, that in the name of rehabilitation approximate more closely to the bodily actions and practices of 'able-bodied' people …" (Price & Shildrick, 2002, 67). These authors then cite a poignant piece by Mary Duffy,

> "bionic" limbs arrive when i am five years old.
> They are big heavy hooks
> powered by gas cylinders
> (1994, 25, cited in ibid., 67)

Whilst acknowledging the distinctions, there are, we suggest similar practices at work here: practices that function based on notions of the "ideal." In the example above, the notion of "able-bodied" functions as an "ideal" that sanctions "big heavy hooks" to be affixed to a little five-year-old girl's arms. This point is provocative, for mustn't we ask, what "technologies of remediation" may be applied to the so-called non-ideal student? What does it mean to put in place additional measures to cater and give confidence to the gifted—and what does it mean to "manage" the rest? As Krisjansen and Lapins ask with reference to additional measures to encourage gifted students, "… why wouldn't everyone require this?" (2001, 56).

CONCLUSION

> The Australian Government believes that all Australian children should have the opportunity to maximise their educational potential and that it is in the *national interest that every child's gifts and talents* should be nurtured and allowed to flourish. The Australian Government seeks to work co-operatively with school education authorities throughout Australia to achieve this shared aspiration. (Department of Education Science & Training, 2006, emphasis added)

The above statement is taken from the opening paragraphs on the Australian Federal Department of Education Science and Training webpage on gifted and talented education. Although it could be interpreted at face value, that is, that it is addressing "all children," we suggest it is imperative to consider a more disturbing possibility. If exceptionality discourses have effects that constitute new forms of the ideal student, we must ask, what are the implications for the displacement of notions of the "average student" with the new notion of the "ideal student"? This ideal student resides at the upper reaches of the spectrum of students. In this privileged place, it marks the position of a new normativity of the *ideal* student—and by consequence, the nonideal. In the above quote, we can see how the ideal student can become coalesced with the Australian national interest. Reified in this way, the "ideal student" becomes a source of educational aspiration, a focus for futures. The question must be asked, what does that mean for the rest? Discourses of exceptionality have the potential to inadvertently or deliberately, produce what Graham (2006) has termed, the "incidental other." What looms large as an upshot of this attention to exceptionality is that new forms of "ideal" hold the promise of constituting ever-burgeoning numbers of incidental others. Just one consequence of this is the ever-increasing disparity in the provision of education to the "ideal" and the "non ideal."

Returning to the quote that opened this chapter, Young commented on the issue of disability "… as the paradigm of the sort of disadvantage people might suffer that is simply a matter of bad luck" (2002, xii). Our critique of the discourses of exceptionality comes from our concern with a somewhat similar practice that risks the shrugging of shoulders when we are presented with these new notions of the "norm" and the non-normal student. To paraphrase Young, a paradigm of normality is emerging where to be gifted is ideal, and to be nongifted is, is just a matter of bad luck.

NOTE

1. Harwood and Rasmussen explain, "This point is explicated in Rabinow's statement that Foucault 'defines his object of analysis (and also his task)' as problematisation (1997: xxxvi). This point is also made by O'Leary who states, 'Problematization is, therefore, both the subject matter of Foucault's history *and* the contemporary project of Foucault's critique' (2002: 117, emphasis in original). Thus problematisation can identify a process whereby (and especially historically) something becomes a problem, and can also refer to the name of a *task*, the *task of problematisation*" (2004: 401).

REFERENCES

Aberdeen, L. (2000). Australian scientific research, "Aboriginal blood," and the racial imaginary. In M. Crotty, J. Germoc, & G. Rodwell (Eds.), *"A race for place": Eugenics, Darwinism, and social thought and practice in Australia* (pp. 112–112). Newcastle, Australia: University of Newcastle Press.

Baker, B. (2002). The hunt for disability: The new eugenics and the normalization of school children. *Teachers College Record, 104*(4), 663–704.

Baum, S., Olenchak, F. R., & Owen, S. V. (1998). *Gifted students with attention deficits: Fact and/or fiction? Or can we see the forest for the trees?* Retrieved 01/05/2006, from www.sengifted.org.

Beck, K. (2006, 25 April). *Headmaster of Eton College Tony Little visits IUB and gives a talk on tradition and modern concepts in education.* Retrieved 22/05/2006, from http://www.iu-bremen.de/news/iubnews/09325/.

Blanksby, D. C. (1999). Not quite Eureka: Perceptions of a trial of cluster groupings as a model for addressing the diverse range of student abilities at a junior secondary school. *Educational Studies, 25*(1), 79–88.

Brighton Primary School. (2006). *Intervention programs.* Retrieved 23/05/2006, from http://www.brighton.vic.edu.au/cms/details.asp?NewsID=118.

Cigman, R. (2006). The gifted child: A conceptual enquiry. *Oxford Review of Education, 32*(2), 197–212.

Crowe, M. (2000). Constructing normality: A discourse analysis of the DSM-IV. *Journal of Psychiatric and Mental Health Nursing, 7*, 69–77.

Department for Education and Children's Services. (1995). *Policy statement: Gifted children and students.* Adelaide: DECS.

———. (1996). *Policy statement: Gifted children and students.* Adelaide: DECS.

Department of Education Science & Training. (2006). *Gifted and talented education.* Retrieved 23/05/006, from http://www.dest.gov.au/sectors/school_education/policy_initiatives_reviews/key_issues/student_learning/gifted_talented.htm.

Diezmann, C. M. & Watters, J. J. (1997). Bright but bored: Optimising the environment for gifted children. *Australian Journal of Early Childhood, 22*(2), 17–21.

Diezmann, C. M., Watters, J. J., & Fox, K. (2001). Early entry to school in Australia: Rhetoric, research and reality. *Australasian Journal for Gifted Education, 10*(2), 5–18.

Duffy, M. (1994). Making choices. In L. Keith (Ed.), *Mustn't grumble: Writing by disabled women*. London: Women's Press.

Foucault, M. (2001). Concluding remarks. In J. Pearson (Ed.), *Fearless speech* (pp. 167–173). Los Angeles: Semiotext(e).

Freeman, J. (2000). Families: The essential context for gifts and talents. In F. J. M. K. A. Heller, R. Stemberg, & R. Subotnik (Eds.), *International handbook of research and development of giftedness and talent* (pp. 573–585). Oxford: Pergamon Press.

Graham, L. (2006). Caught in the net: A Foucaultian interrogation of the incidental effects of limited notions of inclusion. *International Journal of Inclusive Education, 10*(1), 3–25.

Grover, S. (2003). When special needs categories for exceptional student overlap mental health diagnoses: The Canadian experience and its charter implications. *Education and the Law, 15*(1), 47–57.

Harwood, V. & Rasmussen, M. L. (2004). Problematising gender and sexual identities in psychological discourse. In D. Riggs & G. Walker (Eds.), *Gay and lesbian psychology: Australasian perspectives* (pp. 413–437). Perth: Brightfire Press.

Hebert, T. P. & Kent, R. (2000). *Nurturing social and emotional development in gifted teenagers through young adult literature*. Retrieved 01/05/2006, from http://www.sengifted.org/articles_counseling/HebertKent_NurturingDevelopmentYoungAdultLiterature.shtml.

Independent Schools Council. (2004). *Inspection of Eton College*. Retrieved 07/02/2006, from http://www.etoncollege.com/eton.asp?di=2206.

Ireson, J. & Hallam, S. (1999). Raising standards: Is ability grouping the answer? *Oxford Review of Education, 25*(3), 344–358.

Krisjansen, I. & Lapins, B. (2001). Gifted education in South Australia: The emerging student aristocracy. *Discourse: Studies in the Cultural Politics of Education, 22*(1), 49–66.

Lovecky, D. V. (1994). *Exceptionally gifted children: Different minds?* Retrieved 01/05/2006, from http://www.sengifted.org/articles_learningLovecky_ExceptionallyGiftedChildrenDifferentMinds.shtml.

Monk, D. (2000). Theorising education law and childhood: Constructing the ideal pupil. *British Journal of the Sociology of Education, 21*(3), 355–370.

Neilson, M. E. (2002). Gifted students with learning disabilities: Recommendations for identification and programming. *Exceptionality, 10*(2), 93–111.

NSW Department of Education and Training. (2004). *Policy implementation strategies for the education of gifted and talented students*. Sydney: NSW Department of Education and Training Curriculum K-12 Directorate.

———. (2006). *Gifted and talented education*. Retrieved 23/05/2006, from http://www.schools.nsw.edu.au/learning/yrk12focusareas/gifteded/index.php.

Novacheck, T. F., Stout, J., & Tervo, R. (2000) Reliability and validity of the Gillette functional assessment questionnaire as an outcome measure in children with walking disabilities. *Journal of Pediatric Orthopaedics, 20*(1), 75–81.

O'Leary, T. (2002). *Foucault and the art of ethics*. London: Continuum.

Palmerston District Primary School. (2006a, 21 February). *Gifted and talented*. Retrieved 22/05/2006, from http://www.palmdps.act.edu.au/info_docs/gifted_talented.htm.

———. (2006b, 21 February). *Student support*. Retrieved 22/05/2006, from http://www.palmdps.act.edu.au/info_docs/student_support.htm#d.s.t.a.

Paulson, P. J. & Henry, J. (2002). Does the degrees of reading power assessment reflect the reading process? An eye-movement examination: The modified cloze procedure demands an interruption of normal reading processes. *Journal of Adolescent and Adult Literacy, 26*(3), 234–244.

Pesudovs, K. & Coster, D. J. (1998). An instrument for assessment of subjective visual disability in cataract patients. *British Journal of Opthamology, 82*, 617–624.

Plucker, J. A. & Stocking, V. B. (2001). Looking outside and inside: Self-concept development of gifted adolescents. *Exceptional Children, 67*(4), 535–548.

Presbyterian Ladies' College. (2006a). *About*. Retrieved 28/04/2006, from http://www.plc.nsw.edu.au/public2/about_plc.asp.

———. (2006b). *Business regulations*. Sydney: Presbyterian Ladies' College, Sydney.

———. (2006c). *Extension centre*. Retrieved 28/04/2006, from http://www.plc.nsw.edu.au/public2/about_the_centre.asp.

———. (2006d). *Presbyterian Ladies' College: Information and application*. Retrieved 28/04/2006, from http://www.plc.nsw.edu.au/public2/prospectus.asp.

———. (2006e). *Specialities—Gifted and talented*. Retrieved 24/05/2006, from http://www.plc.nsw.edu.au/public2/specialities_gifted_and_talented.asp.

Price, J. & Shildrick, M. (2002). Bodies together: Touch, ethics and disability. In M. Corker & T. Shakespeare (Eds.), *Disability/postmodernity: Embodying disability theory* (pp. 62–75). London: Continuum.

Prior, M., Eisenmajer, R., Leekam, S., Wing, L., Gould, J., Ong, B. et al. (1998). Are there subgroups within the autistic spectrum? A cluster analysis of a group of children with autistic spectrum disorders. *The Journal of Child Psychology and Psychiatry and Allied Disciplines, 39*(6), 893–902.

Rabinow, P. (1997). Introduction: The history of systems of thought. In P. Rabinow (Ed.), *Ethics: Subjectivity and truth* (Vol. 1, pp. XI–XLIII). New York: New York Press.

Renzulli, J. S. E. (2002). Emerging conceptions of giftedness: Building a bridge to a new century. *Exceptionality*. 10(2), 67–75.

Robinson, N. M., Zigler, E., & Gallagher, J. J. (2000). Two tails of the normal curve: Similarities and differences in the study of mental retardation and giftedness. *American Psychologist, 55*(12), 1413–1424.

Shaywitz, B. A., Fletcher, J. M., & Shaywitz, S. E. (1995). Defining and classifying learning disabilities and attention-deficit/hyperactivity disorder. *Journal of Child Neurology, 10*(1), S50–57.

Stanovich, K. E. (1991). Discrepancy definitions of reading disability: Has intelligence led us astray? *Reading Research Quarterly, 26*(1), 7–29.

Vinson, T. (2002). *Inquiry into the provision of public education in NSW—First report*. NSW Teachers Federation and Federation of P&C Associations of NSW.

Young, I. M. (2002). Foreword. In M. Corker & T. Shakespeare (Eds.), *Disability/postmodernity: Embodying disability theory* (pp. xii–xiv). London: Continuum.

CHAPTER TWENTY-TWO

Using Metaphors to Research the Cultural and Ideological Construction of Disability

SCOT DANFORTH

The field of disability studies has long held a deep concern for the ways that depictions of disability further propagate cultural tales of misery, tragedy, and incompetence. Zola (1985) issued an early critique of how various forms of public media describe disabled persons, thereby rendering complex experiences of living with a disability as stereotyped characters defined by essential dysfunction. From Zola's early critique of popular media discourse, the field of disability studies has developed into numerous strands of scholarship that utilize spoken and written language as a point of entrée into cultural interpretation and critique. Scholars carefully track how words and phrases, casually used, propel disability constructs, allocating meaning, value, and social position in relation to a variety of economic and social backdrops. Through an interpretive analysis of language use, researchers burrow into the active social processes that give culture and identity, social structure and individuality, complexity, richness, and depth.

While Zola set a progressive political tone that has continued through decades of the critical analysis of language and culture, his approach to language itself is quickly becoming outdated in interpretive and post-structural academic circles. Reflecting a common objectivist tradition of linguistic analysis, Zola posited metaphor as a form of nonliterality, a harmful brand of creative falsification that plagued efforts to render accurate (read: positive) portrayals of disabled persons. This chapter embraces Zola's critical politics, engaging language as a cultural site of contestation over the meaning of disability and the political positioning of disabled persons, while replacing his view of language with a theory of metaphor that draws from scholarship in the interdisciplinary field of cognitive linguistics (Lakoff, 1987; Lakoff & Johnson, 1980, 1999; Leary, 1994; Ortony, 1993; Radman, 1995). That scholarship blurs the boundaries between literal and figurative language while holding that metaphor, as a mode of everyday cognition and language use, is vital to the cultural construction of meaning.

The purpose of this chapter is to explore ways that disability studies researchers can utilize a cognitive linguistic orientation to metaphor as an interpretive approach to the examination of the cultural meaning(s) of disability(ies) in educational activity. A wide variety of social and political meanings are constructed in and through disability. These meanings stir within the many lived contexts where human interaction, thought, and language use occurs, including the professional activity of educators. The analysis of metaphors within cognition and language is one way to illuminate and interrogate the social meanings of disabilities that are produced within cultural activity (Danforth & Naraian, 2007; Schmitt, 2005).

This exploration of metaphor interpretation will include an example drawn from a recent work (Danforth, 2007) in which I track the dominant metaphors that populate one disability category in the American public school, the emotional/behavioral disorder (EBD). This brief intellectual history of the metaphors of EBD in professional discourse will provide a stepping-off point for an ideological analysis (e.g., Thompson, 1984, 1990) of the construct. Specifically, that analysis asks, how do the central meanings of EBD as cast within the dominant professional metaphors operate to sustain unequal power relations based on social class and race in American schools? Through this exploration of cultural meaning, disability, and inequality within the public schools, this chapter presents one approach to the critical interpretive use of metaphor in disability studies research.

CULTURE AND METAPHOR

There seem to be two diametrically opposed theories about the relationship between metaphor and culture depending on whether one views metaphors as constituent components that actually build culture, as strands within humanity's self-spun "webs of significance" (Geertz, 1973, p. 5), or one theorizes metaphors as symbolic tools that derive from and demonstrate an underlying culture. Cognitive anthropologists (e.g., Quinn, 1991; Quinn & Holland, 1987) tend to view culture as the bottom-level explanatory category. These researchers often describe metaphors as surface features or demonstrative illustrations of the foundational cultural model that people carry and use in their daily lives. On the other hand, cognitive linguists (e.g., Lakoff & Johnson, 1980, 1999) tend to posit metaphors as the structure and substance of much of the cognitive dimension of cultural understanding.

For the purposes of this chapter, I will sidestep the controversy and draw equally from both theoretical camps, thereby articulating a range of notions about the depths of culture and metaphor that are ripe for the investigation of disability studies scholars. Our starting point for this effort is the idea of a cultural model, a concept with strong implications for research on the social meanings of disabilities within schooling and the work of educational professionals. According to Quinn and Holland (p. 4, italics in original),

> *Cultural models* are presupposed, taken-for-granted models of the world that are shared widely (although not necessarily to the exclusion of other, alternative models) by members of a society and that play an enormous role in their understanding of that world and their behavior in it.

These models provide conceptual orientation to the experiential world such that members of a social group may think, communicate, and act in socially acceptable and/or understandable ways.

D'Andrade (1987, p. 112) defines a cultural model as "a cognitive schema that is intersubjectively shared by a social group." That cognitive intersubjectivity has multiple dimensions. It is both implicit and obvious to group members, so plain-as-the-nose-on-your-face that it neither provokes meta-awareness (e.g., I realize I am using a cultural model.) nor requires any explicit explanation. The model is taken by the users as not an orientation to reality but as part and parcel of reality itself.

Further, the intersubjectivity of the cultural model is assumed by group members across numerous layers of mutually reassuring social interaction.

> A schema is *intersubjectively shared* when everybody in the group knows the schema, and everybody knows that everyone else knows the schema, and everybody knows that everyone knows that everyone knows the schema…. (Ibid., p. 113, italics in original)

For example, if an automobile driver in a Western country pulls up to an intersection and sees a green light, that driver will casually drive through that intersection despite the presence of cars on the crossing street. The driver not only knows what the green light means, he or she also knows that the other drivers know what the red light facing them means. Moreover, all drivers at the intersection not only know the meaning of the red and green lights, they also know that all the other drivers know this. These various levels of assumption do not require deep reflection and analysis on any driver's part. In an instant, all is assumed, and the feet either hit the brakes or the gas pedals according to the shared knowledge.

Certainly, although a cultural model is shared across a social group, it is important to note that such sharing is not nomothetic and complete, not static and deterministic. It is a work in progress, subject to various interpretations, and it is inevitably laced with holes, gaps, tensions, and spaces for alternatives. Disability studies scholars are interested in both the regularity of cultural understandings, the tendencies toward unconscious, unquestioned modes of thought about disability that often linger with oppressive weight, and the opportunities for the development and proliferation of alternative models offering new possibilities for disabled persons.

Wolpe (1994) has applied the cultural model concept to the work of professionals such as educators. A cultural model of a profession includes the active framework of language, practices, and beliefs that guide what professionals think, say, and do. Through common standards of preparation, regulated paths of entry into a profession, the circumscription of practice based on a scientific expertise, and the coordination of intent and action by professional associations, a profession such as teaching is based on a shared set of ideas and purposes. A profession's cultural model

> is dominated by the profession's ideology, but also includes its unique combination of myths, research findings, prophecies, techniques, organizational forms, standard political affiliations, and so on. (Ibid., 1136)

The centerpiece of a profession's cultural model is a shared ideology, a systematic conceptual constellation that simultaneously privileges some ideas and practices while—devaluing others, a way of thinking and acting within professional activity that seeks a monopoly through the systematic rejection of alternative concepts (Zito, 1983).

It is evident that schemas of thought employed about various actors within schooling, including professional educators, are central to the ideological construal of disability, to the social interpretation of disability, and to the active intentions and purposes of educators in their work. What remains to be examined, at this point, is how analyses of the use of metaphors within professional discourse–within thought, language, and action (e.g., Gee, 1990)—offer educational researchers opportunities for insight into the lived interpretation and utilization of disability in schooling activities and contexts.

METAPHOR AND COGNITIVE LINGUISTICS

The field of cognitive linguistics (e.g., Lakoff, 1987; Lakoff & Johnson, 1980, 1999; Leary, 1994; Ortony, 1993; Radman, 1995) finds metaphor at the center of human thought, action, and interaction. Earlier theories of metaphor, drawing from an objectivist orientation, dichotomized literal and figurative linguistic forms. The former were viewed as the literal, accurate stuff of science, the terms and phrases that represented physical and social activity without distortion. The latter were assumed to be unnecessary creative flourishes, rhetorical window-dressing that simultaneously yielded imprecision and novelty, inaccuracy and decoration.

The turning point in the development of a theory of metaphor in the field was Max Black's (1962, 1993) *interaction theory of metaphor*. Black theorized that meaning is cross-mapped from a source domain to a target domain through semantic interaction. For example, in the metaphor *man is a wolf*, the target domain *man* is enhanced with meanings (aggression, savageness, cold-heartedness, etc.) drawn from a cultural repertoire of meaning about source, *wolf*. To a lesser degree, the source domain *wolf* adopts new meanings from the semantic association with the target. The meanings of the target domain and the source domain within a metaphor *interact*, and the commonplace cultural meanings of each subject are projected on the other.

Cognitive linguists generally hold that everyday notions of any degree of abstraction frequently involve the active yet unconscious use of metaphors in their cognitive construction. An abstract area of thought and experience is cognitively represented through the appropriation of features and structures of a more concrete or embodied domain. For example, time is built cognitively and linguistically through spatial metaphors of distance and travel (Boroditsky, 2000; Lakoff & Johnson, 1980). Lakoff and Johnson (1999, p. 52) call this the *time is motion* metaphor. Events in time are understood as occurring in spatial relationship to the body as the body moves along a path or line. The future is viewed as lying in front of me, and the past is construed as residing behind me. In the two versions of this bodily travel metaphor, I either move myself forward along this timeline (I move through time), or else the timeline itself moves like a conveyor belt while I stand still (time moves past me). In either version of the metaphor, we use common expressions such as "We put the past behind us," or "My birthday is coming up soon" to render abstract time as a concrete, physical entity experienced in relation to the body.

The most basic building blocks of cognitive understanding, according Lakoff and Johnson (1999, p. 46), are called *primary metaphors*; simple conceptual mappings that play common roles in everyday explanations of human activity.

More complex metaphors are derived from a fund of primary metaphors. Of the many primary metaphors that Lakoff and Johnson (ibid., p. 50) list, two examples should suffice: "Happy is Up" and "Affection is Warmth." "Happy is Up" takes many common forms: *I'm feeling down today. Don't let it get you down. My head's in the clouds. I'm walking on air.* This metaphor maps vertical directional axes (up-down) onto the general topic of human mood, allowing for indexical calibrations ranging from the "heights" of happiness to the "depths" of sadness.

"Affection is Warmth" is demonstrated in many commonplace statements: *He turned a cold shoulder. She is cold as ice. He gave me a warm greeting. She is a warm, caring person.* This metaphor distills descriptions of human love, relationship, and interaction through a bimodal (hot-cold) grid of temperature. Both these primary metaphors provide not only a basis for the linguistic expression of abstract, vague human experiences, but they also supply a simplified grammar that gives definition and conceptual structure to emotions and social activity that would otherwise lack semantic structure. In each case, the dichotomous grammar is limiting and instructive of human experience. Just as high and low occur in opposition, so too the emotions of happiness and sadness are represented as distinct and opposing. Likewise, just as hot and cold cannot co-occur, social intimacy and detachment are drawn as clear and disconsonant counterexperiences. These primary metaphors supply semantic structure and meaning to otherwise ambiguous life activities by furnishing concrete frames of cognitive reference.

METAPHORS OF EBD IN AMERICAN SCHOOLS

> Because theory, scientific or otherwise, moves mainly by analogy, a "seeing-as" comprehension of the less intelligible by the more (the earth is a magnet, the heart is a pump, light is a wave, the brain is a computer, and space is a balloon), when its course shifts, the conceits in which it expresses itself shift with it. (Geertz, 1983, p. 22)

In this section, I will provide an example of a metaphorical analysis of professional discourse in American education. This analysis of the two primary metaphors that structure and comprise the EBD construct is an abridged version of a longer analysis found in Danforth (2007). In the United States, the two main theories of EBD have been derived from psychodynamic and behavior psychology. Arguably, the psychodynamic theory has lost popularity in recent decades as the behavioral understanding has ascended in the professional literature. As a discursive and cultural phenomenon in the public schools, EBD is currently a hybrid notion drawn from both theoretical traditions and utilizes the driving metaphors of each psychological theory.

PSYCHODYNAMIC THEORY: EMOTIONAL DISTURBANCE

After World War II, psychodynamic clinicians indebted to Freud and his followers developed the childhood *emotional disturbance* construct in psychiatric hospitals, treatment centers, and child guidance clinics (Richards & Simsarian, 1952; Reid & Hagan, 1952). Clinical concepts of therapeutic treatment were imported into educational settings such as special schools and classrooms (Berkowitz & Rothman, 1960; Bower, 1960; Lavietes, 1962).

Emotional disturbance, as crafted by psychodynamic theory, formulates causal connections between deep emotions and surface behaviors. The main dynamic interpretation holds that "human activity rests on the emotions" (Schumacher, 1948, p. 113) or, as summed up by prominent psychodynamic special educators Wood and Long (1991, p. 37): "Feelings trigger behavior." Internal emotions are viewed as the causal source of external, observable behaviors. The disturbance of emotion, although viewed in the deviant behavior of the individual, is said to truly reside within affective depths within.

Three central metaphors drive the psychodynamic notion of emotional disturbance:

1. *Mind as Container* (Gibbs, 1992; Lakoff & Johnson, 1980, 1999)—An entity called the mind is said to "hold" specific capacities, substances, and activities. There is space inside the mind, and there are locations outside of the mind.

In everyday talk, we say, *My mind can only hold so much. That's what I had in mind. His thoughts turned inward. It's in the back of my mind.*

2. *Emotion as Diseases of the Mind* (Averill, 1994)—The mind contains emotions. Dangerous, unregulated emotions, and confused emotions constitute illnesses of the mind that are demonstrated in deviant behaviors.

In everyday talk, we say, *She was sickened by love. She was crazy with jealousy. He was insane with rage* (ibid.).

3. *Emotion as Psychic Energy* (ibid.)—Emotion is energy in the mind that is translated into both healthy and unhealthy behavioral demonstrations.

In everyday talk, we say, *He was driven by fear. She was bursting with joy. He blew his stack* (ibid.).

Emotional disturbance has been typically represented as a profound unsettling and damaging of the emotions, whether the source is a traumatic event in the past or a biological dysfunction. Disturbance of emotion, of energy, in the mind is then distilled and made evident as socially problematic behaviors.

A well-known version of emotional disturbance is the case of the Acting-Out Child. Professionals have rendered many complete analytic descriptions of this particular type of emotionally disturbed child and the dynamic process of acting out (Abt & Weissman, 1976; Newman, 1956). "Acting out" remains a phrase often used today as an everyday description of unwanted or negative behavior.

In the dynamic process of acting out, as depicted in the three emotional disturbance metaphors, internal emotions are converted into external actions. Psychic energy becomes physical energy that is released as overt behaviors. The translation of energy from emotion to behavior is said to be mostly unconscious, occurring without much awareness or control. In the case of emotional disturbance, these overt behaviors are socially unacceptable or deviant.

The primary metaphor in Acting Out is a specific version of the *Emotion as Psychic Energy* metaphor called *Anger as Heated Fluid* (Gibbs, 1992). In this metaphor, Anger is a fluid that becomes dangerous if allowed to overheat. We use this metaphor in our everyday speech when we say, *Keep your cool. Cool heads prevail. He's such a hothead. Blow off some steam. He blew his top.*

Anger as Heated Fluid includes the following components:

1. Anger is Heated Fluid Contained in the Mind
2. Anger Can Be Controlled By Keeping It Cool
3. Overheated Anger Bursts Out of the Mind (Leaves the Container)
4. Overheated Anger Propels the Body Into Aggressive Behavior

The acting out child is victimized by his own overboiling anger. On the surface is observable behavior that might be aggressive or disruptive. Beneath the surface, the metaphor builds a psychodynamic explanation that explains how and why the behavior occurred using terms that laypersons and professional can easily relate to.

BEHAVIORAL DISORDER

Beginning in the late 1960s, special education researchers began adopting and adapting B. F. Skinner's behavioral theory to provide a "more objective" description of deviant behavior (Brown, 1972; Patterson, 1965; Philips, 1968; Whelan, 1966). In an effort to become more scientific (more positivistic), researchers dropped the quite obviously and admittedly metaphorical psychodynamic construct in favor of a Skinnerian construct called a behavioral disorder. This shift, by avoiding any mention of unobservable and unquantifiable operations of the mind, seemingly escaped metaphor to create a more literal, objective understanding of the disorder.

Skinner viewed metaphor as a nonliteral nonobjective linguistic form that had no part in a proper science. Yet he still fashioned his behavioral science from metaphor. Leaning heavily on the Darwinian evolutionary work of philosopher Ernst Mach, Skinner borrowed and utilized Darwin's concept of natural selection in the development of behavioral technology (Montuschi, 1995; Tonneau & Sokolowski, 2000; Smith, 1986, 1994). In Darwin's theory, nature picks the species traits and therefore the best varieties of species to reproduce and to survive based on adaptation to the environment. Nature is the master selector. Skinner posited the processes of "selection by consequences" and "selection by contingencies of reinforcement" (Skinner, 1981, p. 501) by substituting *behaviors* (segments of individualized, mini-activity) for *species traits* and the *environment* for *nature*. According to Skinner's conditioning, an anthropomorphized yet superior force called the environment *selects* human behaviors. This occurs through various forms of reinforcement that increase the exhibition of a particular behavior that is highly adapted to the environment. This process of behavior selection process is the path of human adaptation to the environment.

Skinner built his behavioral selection on the theoretical back of Darwin's natural selection, but what is the metaphor (or metaphors) at the crux of Darwin's theory? And how does that play out in Skinner's behaviorism and the behavioral disorder construct? Montuschi has traced Darwin's natural selection to an underlying *cosmic breeder* metaphor. She quotes Darwin:

> But if every plant or animal was to vary, and if a being infinitely more sagacious than man (not an omniscient creator) during thousands and thousands of years were to select all the variations which tended towards certain ends, etc. (as quoted in Montuschi, 1995, p. 315)

Species adaptation is a natural process that depends on the random occurrence of traits, leading to the ultimate ascendancy of species modifications that are specifically tuned to the goal of survival.

The *cosmic breeder* metaphor includes the following components:

1. Nature is the Agent of Causation.
2. Animals are Passive Recipients of Natural Causation.
3. Nature Modifies Animal Species through Selection of Traits.
4. Animal Species are Adapted to the Environment through Trait Selection.
5. Adaptation to the Environment Makes Species More Able to Survive.

In his writings on behaviorism, Skinner repeatedly describes operant conditioning in evolutionary terms, as a "process (that) supplements natural selection" (Skinner, 1974, p. 46; also see 1978, 1981, 1989). To Skinner, natural selection and operant conditioning are operationally similar processes that cooperate to produce improved biological efficiency and effectiveness. His *behavioral selection* version of the *cosmic breeder* metaphor places the environment in the selection role. The environment is a set of cues and reinforcers that interact with human responses, a process by which the environment actively selects more adaptive individual behaviors for continuation and less adaptive behaviors for cessation.

> Operant conditioning solves the problem more or less as natural selection solved a similar problem in evolutionary theory. As accidental traits, arising from mutations, are selected by their contribution to survival, so accidental variations in behavior are selected by their reinforcing consequences. (Skinner, 1974, p. 114)

The variables of contingency select specific behaviors to accrue as improved repertoires in a manner virtually synonymous with the way natural selection induces evolutionary change within a species through an accumulation of selection effects.

The one difference between Skinner's selection by consequences and Darwin's species evolution is the necessity of targeted human intervention in behavioral selection. The historical selection of more efficient and effective behaviors by the environment is flawed, requiring some "explicit design" (ibid., p. 205) of reinforcement contingencies by humans. In deviant persons who fail to adapt to the selecting environment, the behavioral selection process should be refined and guided through the human application of behavioral technology to maladaptive behaviors.

Skinner's *behavioral selection* metaphor includes the following features:

1. Environment is the Agent of Causation.
2. Humans are Recipients of Environmental Causation.
3. Environment Modifies Humans through Selection of Behaviors.
4. Humans are Adapted to the Environment through Behavior Selection.
5. Adaptation to the Environment Makes Humans More Able to Survive.

The behavioral formulation of EBD, the behavioral disorder, intentionally lacks a specific articulation of what the disorder is or how the disorder operates. Skinner's antitheory emphasis has been accepted by special education researchers. The goal has been to utilize Skinner's program of behavioral selection by design to change problematic behavior of schoolchildren without theorizing a deep psychology of individual disorder or deviance causation (CCBD, 1985).

The attempt by behavioral special educators to escape theory in defining EBD was unsuccessful. Skinner's selection by consequences and it Darwinian roots inform our understanding of the behavioral version of EBD. The behavioral disorder concept accepts that public schools students who appear to be deviant to school-based authority figures are simply in need of the label and a program of designed behavior modification. Adult authority figures in schools are assumed to be fair, relatively unbiased, qualified monitors of social norms of behavior. The effort of professionals is better spent on scientific procedures of behavior modification than questioning the social norms of a group or culture (Kauffman, Bantz, & McCullough, 2002).

The behavioral version of EBD involves the premise that the public school environment provides a combination of reinforcers designed (either well or poorly depending on the school) to select normative behaviors. This environment, to some extent, selects behaviors to promote individual adaptation to the moral codes of the social group. When that process of behavioral selection fails, as it does in the case of students labeled EBD, the behavior of a students remains deviant. Professional activities of "explicit design" (Skinner, 1974, p. 205) are required to further the adaptation of the deviants to the social norms. The intensive utilization of behavior modification processes will produce the desired adaptation. Students considered EBD require intensive adaptation technologies in separate schools and classrooms (Kauffman, Bantz, & McCullough, 2002).

EBD AS IDEOLOGY

Thompson's (1990, p. 7, italics in original) concept of ideology as p. 7 "*meaning in the service of power,*" is a unique combination of linguistic brevity, intellectual depth, and moral challenge. For disability researchers, Thompson's guidance on finding and understanding ideology at work within cultural activity makes us to interrogate the everyday utilization of disability concepts in the public schools. Our focus is not the age-old worry about whether the discourses of disability actually used within mundane schooling activities are accurate but how they contribute to disparities of power, of human valuing, of access, of participation. For the specific purposes of the EBD metaphors example, how are social benefits of schooling distributed based on the ways that educators construe EBD via the dominant metaphors?

In the American public schools, the EBD special education label is disproportionately applied to African American males and males from economically poor families (Danforth, 2000; Wagner, 1995). One analysis of a large national data set found that "students with disabilities in general and those with SED (serious emotional disturbance) were significantly more likely than students as a whole to be male, African American, and to experience a constellation of factors associated with economic disadvantage (Wagner, 1995, p. 95). In my own experience working in an EBD-segregated school in Florida, I can recall my first day of work when the school principal told me, "This is really a school for poor kids." Clearly, race, gender, and social class are central features to the practical constitution of EBD in the American public schools.

Both the psychodynamic and the behavioral metaphors of EBD contribute to this political arrangement by staving off meaningful social analyses of behavioral nonconformity. The psychodynamic metaphors of emotional disturbance paint pictures of internal flows of energy within the interiority of the individual mind and body. The heated activity behind the problematic behavior takes place within the psychic arena of the individual's mind. The social arenas of the classroom, the school, the neighborhood, and the broader society enter the analysis only as politically neutered influences on the internal energy states of the disturbed mind. Psychodynamic metaphors of energy and heat, while providing no useful conceptual orientation to the cultural politics of EBD, actively deter social analyses by framing the problem as wholly individual.

While the psychodynamic formulation of emotional disturbance simply omits opportunities for social and political interpretation, the behavioral metaphors of environmental selection provide an archconservative political program that actively seeks behavioral homogeneity under the authority of dominant cultural forces. The environment is essentialized as a single, homologous selector of moral action. Given the incredibly diverse range of activities, contexts, and social norms within a given society, and given the evident tensions, conflicts, and battles over complex moral questions of right action, it is hard to name a singular, consistent, unproblematic environment that selects best behaviors. Yet Skinner (1981, p. 503) describes that environment as consisting simply of the "prevailing contingencies of reinforcement," the current batch of stimuli and reinforcers that dominate within the cultural setting. How did that set of contingencies come to "prevail" over other possibilities? What are the practical outcomes—benefits and detriments to specific groups and individuals in society—of that set of contingencies? How do those contingencies contribute to or fail to contribute to a democratic way of life that values equality, freedom, and justice? The behavioral metaphor leaves these and more political questions unaddressed to develop a program yielding submission to the dominant cultural mores and forces of the historical moment. Deviant persons are subject to adaptation to the social order that prevails.

The EBD metaphors produced by the psychodynamic and the behavior theories place problematic individuals into opposition with a morally absolute society, revealing those individuals as defective and requiring alteration, given the clear prescriptions of a transcendent social complex. As the psychodynamic metaphors represent the thermodynamics of a dangerous interiority, a space ready to explode and wreak havoc on the safety of the social world, the behavioral metaphors exalt dominant social norms as the imperative solution. The combination achieves an effect of occluding the social nature of individualized problems. Difficulties and conflicts that happen in actual social interactions are distilled as occurring in specific individuals. By occluding the social nature of interpersonal and intergroup conflicts in schools, the metaphors produce an imaginary and essentialized social arena to which students deemed problematic must conform through acts of adaptation and self-control. The imaginary social arena is projected off screen, beyond the scope of any analysis or theorizing, thereby squelching any possible examination of how factors such as class, race, and gender influence the social production and use of EBD labels.

CONCLUSION: METAPHORS AND DISABILITY RESEARCH

The chapter has given a brief overview and a single example of what metaphor analysis using cognitive linguistics offers to research in the field of disability studies in education. The intent here has in no way been to produce a total account of research approaches in cultural anthropology, cognitive science, or ideological studies. From the single example of the EBD metaphors informing research and practice, I hope that readers are propelled to pursue further investigations of how human ideas feed and play out in the social structures and processes that generate disability as cultural meaning. The play of ideas, the activities of their composition, alteration, utilization, and resistance, and the production specifically of disability constructs and narratives, are very much the investigatory terrain of disability studies. The play of social benefits and statuses—the allocation of power—is central to our analyses of ideas in action. Our research focii in sifting and sorting these cultural and ideological grounds are the sense and nonsense that humans make of disability as humans make disability. Metaphors, as important features and processes in the social constellation of cultural signification, offer useful access to the cultural making of disability.

In Zola's original essay on the negative metaphors of disability in the public media, he augmented his critical analysis with advice for future disability studies scholarship. He argues that the traditional American values that have been miscast toward the cause of oppression can be recast for the cause of liberation. The goal for scholars is to find and generate the cultural images that create opportunities for disabled persons.

> Only collective action will do that (change negative images of disability). And by that action—of monitoring, correcting, organizing, and protesting—we will inevitably create new images. (p. 15)

I believe that we can take Zola's advice to the letter. Research can monitor the metaphors and images of disability that are employed in the public schools, offering corrective guidance in situations when the opportunities for disabled students to learn, interact, and participate are restricted or diminished. Disability studies research can contribute to the social change activities of organizing and protesting by providing narratives, images, analyses, and new metaphors that support cultural resistance.

REFERENCES

Abt, L. E. & Weissman, S. L. (eds.) (1976) *Acting out; theoretical and clinical aspects.* New York: Grune and Stratton.

Averill, J. R. (1994) Inner feelings, works of the flesh, the beast within, diseases of the mind, driving force, and putting on the show: Six metaphors of emotions and their theoretical extensions (pp. 104–132). In D. E. Leary (ed.) *Metaphors in the history of psychology.* New York: Cambridge University Press.

Berkowitz, P. H. & Rothman, E. P. (1960) *The disturbed child: Recognition and psychoeducational therapy in the classroom.* Oxford, England: New York University Press.

Black, M. (1962) *Models and metaphors.* Ithaca, NY: Cornell University Press.

Black, M. (1993) More about metaphor (pp. 19–41). In A. Ortony (ed.) *Metaphor and thought.* Cambridge: Cambridge University Press.

Boroditsky, L. (2000) Metaphoric structuring: Understanding time through spatial metaphors. *Cognition, 75,* 1–28.

Bower, E. M. (1960) *Early identification of emotionally handicapped children in school.* Springfield, IL: Charles C. Thomas.

Brown, D. G. (1972) Behavior modification with children. *Mental Hygiene, 56, 1,* 22–30.

Council for Children with Behavioral Disorders (CCBD). (1985) Position paper on substituting "behaviorally disordered" for "seriously emotionally disturbed" as a descriptor term for children and youth handicapped by behavior. *Behavioral Disorders, 10, 3,* 167–174.

D'Andrade, R. G. (1987) A folk model of the mind. In D. Holland and N. Quinn (eds.) *Cultural models in language and thoughts.* Cambridge: Cambridge University Press.

Danforth, S. (2000) Resistance theories: Exploring the politics of oppositional behavior. *Multiple Voices for Ethnically Diverse Learners, 4, 1,* 13–29.

Danforth, S. (2007) Disability as metaphor: Examining the conceptual framing of emotional behavioral disorder in American public education. *Educational Studies, 42, 1,* 8027.

Danforth, S. & Naraian, K. (2007) Use of the machine metaphor within autism research. *Journal of Developmental and Physical Disabilities, 19,* 273–290.

Gee, J. P. (1990) *Social linguistics and literacies: Ideology in discourses.* New York: Falmer Press.

Geertz, C. (1973) *The interpretation of cultures.* New York: Basic Books.

Geertz, C. (1983) *Local knowledge: Further essays in interpretive anthropology.* New York: Basic Books.

Gibbs, R. W. (1992) Categorization and metaphor understanding. *Psychological Review, 99, 3,* 572–577.

Kauffman, J. M., Bantz, J., & McCullough, J. (2002) Separate and better: A special public school class for students with emotional and behavioral disorders. *Exceptionality, 10, 3,* 149–170.

Lakoff, G. (1987) *Women, fire, and dangerous things: What categories reveal about the mind.* Chicago: University of Chicago Press

Lakoff, G. & Johnson, M. (1980) *Metaphors we live by.* Chicago: University of Chicago Press.

Lakoff, G. & Johnson, M. (1999) *Philosophy in the flesh: The embodied mind and its challenge to Western thought.* New York: Basic Books.

Lavietes, R. (1962) The teacher's role in the education of the emotionally disturbed child. *American Journal of Orthopsychiatry, 32, 5,* 854–862.

Leary, D. E. (ed.) (1994) *Metaphors in the history of psychology.* New York: Cambridge University Press.

Montuschi, E. (1995) What is wrong with talking of metaphors in science? (pp. 309–238). In Zdravko Radman (ed.) *From a metaphorical point of view: A multidisciplinary approach to the cognitive content of metaphor.* New York: de Gruyter.

Newman, R. (1956) The acting-out boy. *Exceptional Children, 22,* 186–190, 204–206, 215–216.

Ortony, A. (ed.) (1993) *Metaphor and thought.* New York: Cambridge University Press.

Patterson, G. R. (1965) An application of conditioning techniques to the control of a hyperactive child (pp. 370–375). In L. P. Ullmann & L. Krasner (eds.) *Case studies in behavior modification.* New York: Holt, Rinehart and Winston.

Philips, E. I. (1968) Achievement place: Token reinforcement procedures in a home style rehabilitation setting for predelinquent boys. *Journal of Applied Behavior Analysis, 1,* 213–223.

Quinn, N. & Holland, D. (1987) *Cultural models of language and thought.* New York: Cambridge University Press.

Quinn, N. (1991). The Cultural Basis of Metaphor. In ed. J. W. Fernandez *Beyond metaphor: the theory of tropes in anthropology,* Stanford, CA: Stanford University Press.

Radman, Z. (1995) *From a metaphorical point of view: A multidisciplinary approach to the cognitive content of metaphor.* New York: de Gruyter.

Reid, J. H. & Hagan, H. R. (1952) *Residential treatment of emotionally disturbed children: A descriptive study.* Oxford, England: Child Welfare League of America.

Richards, S. S. & Simsarian, F. P. (1952) A report from a school for emotionally disturbed children. *Mental Hygiene, 34,* 611–619.

Schmitt, R. (2005) Systematic metaphor analysis as a method of qualitative research. *The Qualitative Report, 10, 2,* 358–394.

Schumacher, H. S. (1948) Mental and emotional disturbance in adolescence. *Journal of Child Psychiatry, 1,* 113.

Skinner, B. F. (1974) *About behaviorism.* New York: Alfred A. Knopf.

Skinner, B. F. (1978) *Reflections on behaviorism and society.* Englewood Cliffs, NJ: Prentice-Hall.

Skinner, B. F. (1981) Selection by consequences. *Science, 213, 4507,* 501.

Skinner, B. F. (1989) *Recent issues in the analysis of behavior.* Columbus, OH: Merrill.

Smith, L. D. (1986) *Behaviorism and logical positivism: A reassessment of the alliance.* Stanford, CA: Stanford University Press.

Smith, L. D. (1994) Metaphors of knowledge and behavior in the behaviorist tradition (pp. 239–266). In D. E. Leary (ed.) *Metaphors in the history of psychology.* New York: Cambridge University Press.

Thompson, J. B. (1984) *Studies in the theory of ideology.* Berkeley, CA: University of California Press.

Thompson, J. B. (1990) *Ideology and modern culture.* Stanford, CA: Stanford University Press.

Tonneau, F. & Sokolowski, M. B. C. (2000) Pitfalls of behavioral selectionism (pp. 155–180). In F. Tonneau & N. S. Thompson (eds.) *Perspectives in ethology, 13, Evolution, Culture, and Behavior.* New York: Kluwer Academic/Plenum Publishers.

Wagner, M. M. (1995) Outcomes for youths with serious emotional disturbance in secondary school and early adulthood. *Critical Issues for Children and Youths, 5, 2,* 90–111.

Whelan, R. (1966) The relevance of behavior modification approaches for teachers of emotional disturbed children (pp. 35–78). In P. Knoblock (ed.) *Intervention approaches in educating emotionally disturbed children.* Syracuse, NY: Syracuse University Press.

Wolpe, P. R. (1994) The dynamics of heresy in a profession. *Social Science & Medicine, 39, 9,* 1133–1148.

Wood, M. M. & Long, N. J. (1991) *Life space intervention: Talking with children and youth in crisis.* Austin, Texas: Pro-Ed.

Zito, G. V. (1983) Toward a sociology of heresy. *Sociological Analysis, 44, 2,* 123–130.

Zola, I. K. (1985) Depictions of disability—metaphors, message, and medium: A research and political agenda. *The Social Science Journal, 22, 4,* 5–17.

CHAPTER TWENTY-THREE

Double Trouble: Disability AND Disability Studies IN Education

ROD MICHALKO

INTRODUCTION

Disability has been in our classrooms for decades now and so has the sense of disability as trouble. Trouble entered the classroom as disability did and it entered, not merely with disability, but with(in) it. It is almost superfluous to say that disability brings trouble or a problem since disability is conventionally conceived of as trouble and as a problem. The trouble is that disability presents a problem in and to the classroom insofar as education is oriented to and by an implicit (and sometimes explicit) conception of "normalcy" and is thus oriented to an implicit sense of the trouble of "abnormality." Disability is thus oriented to and by nondisabled versions of teaching and learning. Disability troubles the sensibility of "normalcy" and the problem becomes that of, as Tanya Titchkosky (2003) suggests, determining what to do with disability when it shows up, unexpectedly as it does.

The solution to this problem has most often been for the education system to fit disability into the classroom by "normalizing" it and conceiving of disabled students, following "people-first language," as students first and disabled second. A variety of programmatics were generated to complete this "normalizing" process—programmatics such as integration, mainstreaming, and, most recently, inclusion. And yet, the trouble of disability persists. As much as education wants to understand disability as "normal" and disabled students as "just students," that troublesome thing remains—how to teach disabled students. Many disabled students require different and more resources, different teaching methodologies, different technologies—and all this difference is experienced, ironically enough, in the face of the "sameness" ideology of "students are students," disabled or not.

As a way to address this trouble of difference while maintaining the ideology of sameness, again, an interesting irony, the education system introduced "special education." The difference of disability was now understood as a "special difference" requiring "special" educational attention. As did previous attempts at mainstreaming, special education treated disability as a technical problem in need of technical solutions. Find the right technologies and inclusion, and the problem is solved. The "right" technology was, of course, centered on adaptation—find adaptive classroom technology and, most especially, "help" disabled students to adapt to the "regular classroom." But, as it turns out, the problem is not solved. And if this wasn't enough, and just as special education began to establish itself in the classroom, enter Disability Studies—yet another trouble. The trouble of Disability Studies is that it made problematic not only the idea of special education but of education itself (e.g., see Gabel, 2005). Trouble was deflected from disability to education, a troubling, if not ironic, turn of events. Now, double trouble—the trouble of disability and the trouble of Disability Studies. Disabled students do show up in our classrooms and this "showing up" is the showing up of trouble, a social process that Disability Studies suggests may have more to teach us about the inherently troublesome character of the classroom than it does about the troublesome character of disability.

This chapter interrogates the double trouble faced by education with the unexpected appearance of disability and Disability Studies. I examine the experience of "being a problem" and make use of the work of W.E.B. DuBois (1989 [1903], 1) in his reflections of the "black experience" over one hundred years ago and his premise that "…being a problem is a strange experience…" I will explicate the strangeness of this experience in relation to disability. I also examine educational conceptions of disability that implicitly and explicitly govern the activity of teaching and learning. I examine the "educational fact" that disabled students' difference should not make a difference in order to develop a more fertile sense of the troubling character of both disability and Disability Studies. I follow Judith Butler's (1990) recommendation that trouble is inevitable and our task becomes how best to live with and in it. My interest is not to produce an exegesis of Butler's work, but to make use of how she introduces her work on troubling gender. My interest, then, is in introducing Butler's notion of trouble into my interrogation of the double trouble of disability and Disability Studies in relation to education. Thus I turn now to her sense of trouble.

BUTLER'S TROUBLE

In the preface to her *Gender Trouble,* Judith Butler (1990, vii) writes, "hence, I concluded that trouble is inevitable and the task, however best to make it, what best way to be in it." How do we develop a strong relation to trouble in the face of its inevitability? In relation to gender, Butler's essential question is "What best way to trouble the gender categories that support gender hierarchies and compulsory heterosexuality"? Butler continues, "serious as the medicalization of women's bodies is, the term is also laughable, and laughter in the face of serious categories is indispensable for feminism." This medicalization or naturalization of a body, any body, is also laughable. The serious categories of natural, normal, and abnormal in relation to disability, for example, are laughable categories in so far as they are presented and used as unambiguous and as themselves seriously natural. This, too, is laughable.

There is a certain tone of resignation and compliance in Butler's words; trouble is inevitable, we must resign ourselves to this; we must comply with this inevitability by making the best of trouble when it occurs. What Butler makes of trouble and the best way she recommends living in it is to understand trouble instrumentally. Trouble is inevitable, so make the best of it. At the same time, Butler wants to use the idea of trouble to interrogate gender, to trouble gender. This can be said of disability as well insofar as we can use the idea of trouble to trouble conventional conceptions of disability and the compulsory hierarchy of nondisability (McRuer, 2002, 88–99). This suggests that inasmuch as we are gendered and insofar as some of us are disabled, trouble is inevitable and will occur in the life of these two identity categories. Recall that Butler says that the medicalization of the woman's body is serious but laughable. The invocation of serious categories is laughable. But, is it merely medicalization that is laughable or is it the invocation of identity categories such as gender and disability that is laughable? Categories such as gender, disability, nondisablility, normal, abnormal, and natural are all very serious but also laughable.

If trouble *is* (exists), so *is* the body and so *is* the trouble of embodiment. The ambiguity in relation to understanding the nature of body is a serious trouble requiring serious solutions. The trouble of the body is put to one side by depicting it in unambiguous categories such as gender and disability. Moreover, the trouble of the body in general is swept away with the invocation of the category "normal" subsumed under the abstraction of the "natural." In one quick move, the trouble of the body is swept away. The inevitability of the ambiguity of the body (its trouble) is lived with best by saying that the natural body is the normal body and all other bodies are not. This serious move cannot be taken seriously, it is laughable. The serious move of "naturalization" runs from trouble as fast as its natural legs will carry it. It foolishly holds the clarity of the body in its natural hands, refusing to let go and refusing to let ambiguity and trouble enter the life of the body. It is laughable to think that the natural formulation of the body thinks so highly of itself.

Butler (1990, viii) says that, "the binary of sex, gender, and the body—can be shown as productions that create the effects of the natural, the original, and the inevitable." This suggests that genealogy, as a form of inquiry, is necessary in order to interrogate the serious categories surrounding gender. Genealogy is not so much interested in uncovering the original sense of sexuality or disability as it is in understanding these categories as sociopolitical and as discourses that spring from and support some sociopolitical imperative (Foucault, 1965, 1979, 1980). Thus, these serious categories find their basis in institutions. The task of genealogy is to decenter these institutions so as to uncover their *generation* (performance) rather than their *genesis* (origin).

This instability and trouble suggests that disability too is a relational term and, like Butler in her work on gender, I would suggest that categories such as disability and nondisability must be interrogated as such. Butler suggests that a radical critique of gender as identity would generate a new politics. An inquiry that does not proceed on the basis of a common identity or a search for it would produce a radical relation both to gender and identity. This can also be said of disability.

Butler (1990, 1) invokes Simone de Beauvoir: "one is not born a woman, but rather becomes one." Julia Kristeva (ibid., 1) says, "strictly speaking, 'women' cannot be said to exist." These sentiments are similar to Robert Scott's (1969, 111) stipulation that "blind men [*sic*] are not born, they are made." There is a sense here that the categories of gender and disability are socially constructed and are not steeped in some notion of the natural. If women cannot be said to exist, then neither can disabled people exist. Yet, these categories seriously exist. They do so in Beauvoir's sense of the "situation" and not in the strictly thing-like sense of the biological notion of the natural. If an inquiry proceeds with the paradox that gender and disability both exist and do not exist simultaneously, we can begin to uncover the ideas of both making an existence and living in it. In other words, how do we make disability exist? What is the social and political significance of the need for and the promotion of such an existence? What and whose existence turns on the existence of disability? Special education as well as Disability Studies are surely two endeavors that rely upon the existence of disability. Both of these endeavors suggest that disability is a troublesome thing. For special education, the trouble of disability generates the need for remedial educational practices while, for Disability Studies, the trouble of disability generates the need to understand disability as the trouble that troubles normalcy. Remedial educational practices are not restricted to special education since education in general with its requirements of producing an "educated population" and excluding dangerous and troublesome students and pedagogies provides the grounds for special education in the first place.

Butler (1990, 1–2) says, "…the qualification for being a subject must first be met before representation can be extended." For both special education and Disability Studies, then, the subject "disability" must first be established before it can be represented as requiring remedy or as troubling normalcy. Thus, special education and Disability Studies first of all produce the subject that they then come to represent. Special education discourse first constitutes disability as requiring remedy and then represents it as such. Disability Studies does the same in relation to its notion of disability as troubling normalcy. These practices, then, produce what they claim to merely represent.

Special education generates the subject of disability as originating in some biomedical impairment resulting in trouble and awaiting the representation of requiring remedy. Disability Studies, in contrast, generates the subject of disability as resulting in the trouble of oppression and awaiting the representation of troubling the oppressor, normalcy. The trouble-of-disability troubles both special education and Disability Studies. But, since special education relies upon its constitution of the subject of disability as individual biomedical trouble, Disability Studies, in its constitution of the subject of disability as troubling normalcy, troubles special education. This "double trouble" contributes to the production of disability experience as a strange one. Wherever disability appears, in a person, in a classroom, in Disability Studies analysis, it appears as trouble in one form or another. Any dominant collective sense of disability oriented to and by some often implicit sense of normalcy can do nothing other than "see" disability as trouble and be troubled by disability. Very often, disabled people experience life as trouble, for example, the trouble of gaining access to the built environment while using a wheelchair, the trouble our disabilities sometimes seem to "cause" nondisabled others, and this trouble seems to weld disability to the sense of being a problem. This welding takes place in the midst of others, disabled and nondisabled others, and takes place in a social realm where the idea of "problem" automatically evokes the need for a solution. It is indeed a strange experience to be the embodiment of a problem in need of a solution. I now turn to the work of W.E.B. DuBois as a way to begin to understand this "strangeness," where difference figures as a problem in need of a solution.

DUBOIS' STRANGER

In his seminal work *Souls of Black Folk* at the turn of the last century, W.E.B. DuBois develops a deeper understanding of the problem-of-difference, as it relates to race. The idea of "soul," as DuBois uses it, develops the sense that there is something critical about "being black" even though it is couched in the orientation of problem. Race and disability are not differences in need of a solution or remedy in the way that a broken arm or a malfunctioning computer is. Race and disability are problems more in the existential sense of "being a problem" and of problematizing a being-in-the-world in the midst of the dichotomic experiences of black/white and disabled/nondisabled. The experience of "being a problem" is further complicated by the knowledge that we are also seen by the other (white, nondisabled) as experiencing a problem. Being a problem is an experience whose genesis is found in the process of othering where the white and nondisabled orientations socially define nonwhite and disabled people as individuals whose soul or agency is what is lacking. More than whiteness and more than able-bodiedness, then, are lacking; what is lacking is some sense of an essential humanity, a humanity that signifies people as subjectively agentive, as having a soul.

It is this idea of experiencing a problem that often fascinates the nondisabled other. This fascination often compels the nondisabled other to ask about this experience of being a problem. Just as often, however, this compulsion to ask is linguistically framed by some comment about the disability—"Without my glasses, I can't see a thing," "There was this kid in my high school who was blind and he seemed to be okay." DuBois (1989 [1903], 1) faces the same sort of situation. He writes, "…to the real question, 'How does it feel to be a problem?' I answer seldom a word. And yet, being a problem is a strange experience…" Difference is a problem that entices a question—How does it feel to be a problem? This question is tacitly posed by those who are different and by those who are not; in the former instance, it is asked of the self, while in the latter it is asked of others. And yet, as DuBois tells us, seldom a word is uttered in response to this "real question."

It is not only the experience of being a problem that is strange, so too is the "real question" since it is experienced as though it cannot be asked and yet it lingers. The appearance of difference is an embodied experience, a lived experience, and it is lived by some one. From the point of view of nondifference, difference is a problem. There is no question(ing) about this. The problem of difference is not a "real question" since there is no question about it. For DuBois, the real question is—How does it feel to be a problem? This question presupposes the idea of problem—we can only ask how it feels to be a problem when being a problem is presupposed as an existential fact beyond question. There is no point asking whether or not difference is a problem since this is unquestionable and it is thus impossible to ask such a question. And it is this impossibility that makes being a problem such a strange experience.

Problems do come up from time to time and we look for solutions and sometimes even solve the problem. This is not a strange experience since it is the experience of everyone. Ordinary problems come up for disabled people and black people as they do for everyone else. But, disabled people and black people are not everyone else. We may have problems, like everyone else, but, unlike everyone else, we *ourselves are* a problem. We ask of one another—How does it feel to have this or that problem? "How does it feel to be a problem?" however, is a question we ask only of certain others. The "real question" of difference is the difference between "having a problem" and "being a problem."

Part of the experience of being a problem is that others have "a problem with it." We are a problem for others and as David Mitchell (2002, 15) reminds us, "Nearly every culture, views disability as a problem in need of a solution ... ." What is to be done with the problems of disability and race? There is no question that disability and race are problems—the only question: how to resolve them? History has been witness to a variety of solutions to the problem of disability and race, solutions such as colonization, enslavement for "black folk," genocide, institutionalization, assimilation, remedial education, special education, rehabilitation, genetic engineering for both "black and disabled folk."

There are many solutions to the experience of having a problem but not to the experience of being a problem. Unlike having a problem *with* difference, being a problem *of* difference requires working out the strangeness of that experience, including the strangeness of the experience of others seeking out and employing solutions to their experience of having a problem with difference. Being a problem is indeed a strange experience particularly in the face of that experience being removed, remedied, and solved. While, from the point of view of the dominant group, difference is still understood as a problem in need of a solution, nondifference does not quite understand what the problem of difference is except that it is different insofar as it is not the norm. The idea of the norm generates normal problems in need of a solution. The idea of the abnormal generates problems too, but problems "for the norm" thus requiring solutions that will keep the norm normal.

How is this normal-problem-solution paradigm represented to difference and experienced by it? Once again, the words of DuBois (4):

> The Negro is a sort of seventh son, born with a veil, and gifted with second-sight in this American world,—a world which yields him no true self-consciousness, but only lets him see himself through the revelation of the other world. It is a peculiar sensation, this double-consciousness, this sense of always looking at one's self through the eyes of others, of measuring one's soul by the tape of a world that looks on in amused contempt and pity. One ever feels his two-ness ...

While DuBois is speaking about the "life of the Negro" in America over a hundred years ago, his work is revelatory for the development of an understanding of the "life of disabled people" in contemporary Western culture. Disabled people, for example, are also born with a veil whether the birth of their disability is at their actual birth (congenital) or born at a different period during their life (adventitious).

Disability itself is a sort of veil—one that hides the soul of impairment from both the impaired person and from the world by drawing the veil of disability, a veil spun from the threads of the quintessential veil, the concept of the norm. From the moment impairment is born, it is transformed into disability since impairment (or any sensibility of biology) makes an appearance only within social structures of interpretation, only within society. Human biology, whether normal or abnormal, is not self-evident even though it is posited as such. What is self-evident is that we are embodied beings and we sensually and materially make an appearance in the world and appear to one another in this way. Human biology is a human (social) phenomenon and not a biological one, it is what we make of our embodied experience. It is the veil of the norm that hides the social interpretive processes that work to produce the abstractions of the "natural body," of the "normal body," and of the "body-gone-wrong," the disabled body. The concept of disability covers over the other (nondisability) world's refusal to unveil the norm, thus exposing its commitment to the constant and continuous social production of homogenous embodiment. The significance of DuBois double consciousness comes to the fore here—the strength of marginality is that it is a standpoint that is socially positioned to "see" the center and to act as a mirror reflecting the center to itself (see, e.g., hooks, 1990; Smith, 1999).

The commitment to homogenous embodiment is a tacit one insofar as we unreflexively "see" the human body as the concrete manifestation of being human and of humanity. To be human is to be physically embodied in a human body and, to this extent, we are all the same. Even though human biology has its sense of individual variation, this variation is subsumed under the concept of the norm. Any difference that falls outside of a concept of normal difference is relegated to the margins of humanity at best and to the region of nonhuman at worst. Both of these social locations are troublesome to the norm and they reflexively represent solutions to the troublesome character of difference. Socially locating difference on the margins of humanity simultaneously troubles the norm and is a solution to this trouble.

The acquisition of an impairment—whether at birth or during one's life—locates one on the margins of the normal and average body. This marginalizing process represents the societal response to impairment and, for some, is the genesis of disability (Oliver, 1996). The impaired body is disabled by society's failure to respond to it in a way that does not produce marginality and discrimination. The social processes of the birth of disability are veiled by the norms conception of human embodiment. Biology, with its concept of the normal human body, including normal variation, is one way of inserting bodies (people) into the world and of making them matter; following Butler (1993, 32), disability is thus simultaneously made to materialize and to mean. Even though all types of bodies are veiled, in DuBois sense, by the concept of the norm, the disabled body is made use of by the concept of the norm to veil any sense that the human body is indeed a social construction and not merely a strictly biological matter. It is impossible for the biological version of normal body to subsume the disabled body under its umbrella of normalcy without closing and thus making ineffectual that very same umbrella. The social processes and practices of marginalizing and normalizing of which I spoke earlier are invoked by normalcy and placed on the disabled body as a way to veil the social construction of the norm.

Most disabled people, as Irving Zola (1993) tells us, come from nondisabled families and grow up and live in social contexts governed by the biomedical version of the human body. We are told, in a variety of ways, that we are the same as everyone else and yet we experience ourselves as different and we experience ourselves as a problem. The world goes through all sorts of trouble for us, unless it's too much trouble, by installing wheelchair ramps, developing rehabilitation and special education programs, and goes through the trouble, which turns out to be no trouble at all, of developing prevention of disability programs, organizing telethons to raise money for medical research so that disability (we) can be cured or at least so that disability (we) will not happen to others. All of these practices have the biomedical orientation to the body and are all involved in defining disability and telling disabled people who and what we are.

The world of the normals (ibid.), "…yields [disabled people] no true self-consciousness, but only lets [them] see [themselves] through the revelation of the other world" (DuBois, 1989[1903], 4). What the world of the normals reveals to the disabled person about him/herself is the mirror upon which disabled people "see" their image, the image created and revealed to them by the world of the normals. As DuBois says, "…the sense of always looking at one's self through the eyes of others" is a peculiar sensation. We look at ourselves through the image created of us by the world of the normals and yet we have the peculiar sensation that we are something else. As does DuBois' "Negro," disabled people experience that peculiar sensation of double-consciousness—"one ever feels his twoness"—and yet, as DuBois says, it is difficult to resist looking at one's self through the eyes of others and "measuring one's soul by the tape of a world that looks on in amused contempt and pity." The nondisabled world looks at disability with contempt, amused as it is, insofar as disability reminds the world of the fragility of the human body and even, as Lennard Davis (1997, 2) says, of death itself. And yet, the world looks at disabled people with pity. It pities those of us who move through the world without seeing, without hearing, in a wheelchair, and so on.

DuBois is right, this is a sort of amused contempt and pity but it is also amusing. The world knows that no one would choose to be disabled and, in this sense, disabled people should be pitied. But, it is difficult for the world to pity those who choose disability, for example, to pity those who suggest disabled people have rights and who suggest that disability is a legitimate way of being-in-the-world. It is difficult to pity those disabled people who do not mourn and grieve the loss of the original appearance where such an appearance is interpreted as the right of everyone to have a normal body. The amused contempt and pity with which the world of the normals looks at disability is itself truly amusing.

Still, the feeling of two-ness persists. Disabled people can exist nowhere else than in the world of the normals. There is nowhere else we belong albeit if on the margins. And yet, this belongingness is tempered by the tension that comes from the strange experience of being a problem and thus of not belonging. But, if not in the world of the normals, where do disabled people belong? Disabled people do feel their humanity and personhood and yet do not feel part of "normal" humanity and personhood. We do strive to be part of the world and to "fit in" and to do the things that everyone else does even if we do these things differently. And yet, we are not ordinary. Indeed, disabled people are trouble to the ordinary. Many disabled people do not do ordinary things in ordinary ways and this too is trouble for the ordinary world.

It is, however, tempting for disabled people to act in as ordinary a way as possible. As Rosemary Garland Thomson (1996, xvii) points out, the cultural assumptions of the normal are both compelling and seductive:

> Pressures to deny, ignore, normalize, and remain silent about one's own disability are both compelling and seductive in a social order intolerant of deviations from the bodily standards enforced by a quotidian matrix of economic, social, and political forces.

We (disabled people) are often seduced to act and even to feel as if we belong in the world of the normals and, equally important, we are often compelled by the desire to belong. But, such conditions of belonging, as DuBois reminds us, do not yield a sense of true self-consciousness. Such a belonging leaves us with a peculiar and precocious sense of double-consciousness—we ever feel our two-ness. I want to turn now to education and how it addresses difference and the idea of two-ness.

TO LAUGH OR NOT TO LAUGH

Like all social institutions, education is committed to some notion of the "normal" and expresses this commitment in its desire to "normalize" students (Ferri and Connor, 2006, 128). Within the idea of the normal and average person, resides the notion that we are all limited, that we are all disabled. This sentiment is captured nicely in the following:

> I'm fat, I'm thin, I'm short, I'm tall
> I'm deaf, I'm blind, hey, aren't we all

—(ROGERS, SESKIN, AND ALLEN SHABLIN, 2002)

These are lines from a song that accompanies a book on difference and diversity titled *Don't Laugh at Me* (Seskin, 2000 [a creation of Peter Yarrow of Peter, Paul, and Mary fame]) written for elementary school–going children as part of an inclusive education program. As is readily noticeable in these lines, the book emphasizes sameness. Although we are different from one another and our differences are cogent and negatively so, this cogency is superseded and thus erased by our sameness. This suggests that the ideal body is the interchangeable one (Davis, 2002, 105). The only response to difference this book imagines is negative, in particular, laughing at those who are different.

"I'm deaf, I'm blind, hey, aren't we all" suggests, albeit tacitly, that there is something wrong with all of us and so we shouldn't laugh at bodily differences that, at first blush, do not appear as average difference. Any bodily difference that falls at either extreme of the bell-curve is a difference that is erased by invoking the contemporary method of saming, namely, we are all like everyone else.

Yet, that we are all like everyone else, while serving to erase difference, does not necessarily produce interchangeability. You may be blind, but you are not blind like me and my blindness is not like yours. Our eyes (bodies) are definitely not interchangeable. The idea that we are all blind or all deaf—even those who are neither—fails to imagine a life of blindness or deafness as anything other than negative. It posits the new frightening identity as that which resides beyond sameness, the ineffable and untheorized unsame person.

The inability to imagine the life of disability as nothing other than negative stems from the ubiquitous cultural representation of disability as a problem in need of a solution. It is virtually impossible to think of disability without simultaneously thinking of problem and of solution (Michalko, 2002). The utilitarian and pragmatic sensibility of contemporary society serves to linguistically pair the ideas of problem and solution since this contemporary sensibility cannot imagine the good of a problem let alone "the good problem." This lack of imagination cannot create the cultural adage—a solution in need of a problem. The book *Don't Laugh at Me*, for example, treats all nonaverage differences as problems in need of solutions. It isolates the problem of nonaverage difference as that of laughing and recommends the solution that we are all different and thus all the same, making laughing an inappropriate response. This solution may or may not solve the problem of laughing at difference. Despite the rhetorical character of this solution, however, it does not solve the problem of difference insofar as it never raises it in the first place. *Don't Laugh at Me* never problematizes difference or disability. It merely submits to the dominant cultural representation of difference and disability as problems, problems of laughter, problems of whatever. The solution recommended by *Don't Laugh at Me* is itself in need of a problem. Problematizing this solution would begin the work of uncovering the sense of difference and disability that is being socially generated by the solution. Not problematizing the conventional problem/solution dichotomy of disability and ending up with the admonition "Don't laugh at me" is itself seriously laughable.

The conception of the problem of disability as one of locating it within the social or of how to teach disabled students is not restricted to books written for children. This problem of saming disability is ubiquitous in our education system. Consider the following examples from books written for teachers that address "special needs" students:

> When serving children with special needs, professionals must view them as members of their society, community, and family. (Poon-McBrayer and Ming-gon, 2002, 9–10)

When early childhood practitioners contemplate having a child with special needs in their class, they may wonder:

- I've never worked with a child in a wheelchair before. Where do I begin?
- I don't have a degree in special education. How can I help a child in my class who has a condition called Turner Syndrome?
- I'm worried. What if Sam has a seizure in school? What should I do? (Kostelnik, Onaga, Rohde, and Whiren, 2002, ix)

Or, consider this definition of inclusive education:

> Being in an ordinary school with other students, following the same curriculum all the time, in the same classrooms, with the full acceptance of all, and in a way which makes the students feel no different from other students. (Bailey [1998] quoted in Farrell, 2003, 27).

The admonition given by Poon-McBrayer is as interesting for what is does not say as it is for what it does. She does say that professionals must view children with special needs as members of collectives—as members of families, of communities, and as members of society. Even though she does not say this directly, Poon-McBrayer must conceive of the possibility of viewing children with special needs as isolated from collective life. On the surface, it seems very unlikely, if not impossible, for professionals to conceive of children with special needs in this way. What, then, is the impetus for telling professionals to view children with special needs as children who belong to families, communities, and society?

It is not necessary for Poon-McBrayer to remind us that all children, especially nondisabled ones, must be viewed as members of collective life. This reminder directs our attention to a certain category of child, one with special needs. Professionals are asked to remember that, like all children, special needs children, too, are members of society, of communities, and of families. This reminder acts to admonish professionals to be mindful that all children, even those with special needs, are the same insofar as they are all members of collective life. Even though "collective life" may be expressed in heterogeneous forms, it is still homogeneous insofar as one version of being the same is that we are all members of a variety of collectives.

Kostelnik exemplifies the societal conception of disability (of special needs children) as a problem. Early childhood practitioners contemplate the presence of a special needs child in their class, and when they do so, they wonder and they worry. But, the wondering of these practitioners is limited to the contemplation of trouble; they are not used to wheelchair users; they are not educated to know what to do with a Turner Syndrome child; they do not know what to do with a child who has a seizure. This restricted view of contemplation conceives of "special needs" children as children with "special troubles." These "special troubles" are not the "ordinary troubles" that all children bring with them into the classroom. They are extraordinary troubles and these troubles require extraordinary solutions such as a degree in special education. Thus, the provision of early childhood education amounts to wondering how to deal with the trouble that enters the classroom with "special needs" children. Of course, it is not teachers per se that generate this sort of wondering, it is teachers as representatives of an unimaginative culture in relation to disability that marks the genesis of such wondering.

Bailey brings the problem of disability back to saming as the solution. Being in an ordinary school with other students, presumably ordinary ones, in ordinary classrooms with ordinary curriculum, makes "different students" feel no different from their ordinary counterparts. This is Bailey's version of inclusive education. For inclusion to work, though, Bailey requires the "full acceptance of all," the acceptance of all who are not different. Bailey's version of the successful inclusionary program occurs when no one feels different, when everyone is the same. The goal here is to address difference by erasing it. Difference, of course, can only be erased abstractly. Thus, the goal of saming difference is to socially achieve it as difference that does not make a difference (Michalko, 2002).

CONCLUSION

I have attempted to show that disability presents itself as trouble to education and that this trouble is conceived of as in need of a solution. Various programmatics, such as special education, inclusion and others, have been posited as solutions to the trouble of disability. I have suggested that Disability Studies, too, troubles education. Education has advanced similar solutions to the trouble of Disability Studies as it has to the trouble of disability.

The trouble that Disability Studies presents to education, and to all of us, is the trouble to problematize disability as an essential part of the human condition. Disability is not merely something to be educated about, thereby contributing to the solution to the trouble of disability. It is not merely a condition that some of us have and to which we must adjust. Nor is disability something that needs to be deemphasized in favor of privileging the sameness of personhood. Disability studies recommends that we, including educators, are parts that make up the whole of what we call disability. In this sense, disability is a teacher. It disrupts our conventional views of the "normal body," of what it means to educate and be educated, and of what it means to be human. Thus, the trouble of disability, when reconceived as the "disruption of teaching," can become the rich and fertile ground from which we can cultivate the desire to understand ourselves as those who live in the midst of others and to understand that we live with difference that makes a difference.

NOTE

I would like to thank Katie Aubrecht who has discussed aspects of the work of W. E. B. DuBois with me. I am also grateful to Erin Hynes for bringing the children's book, *Don't Laugh at Me*, to my attention.

REFERENCES

Butler, Judith. (1990). *Gender Trouble: Feminism and the Subversion of Identity*. New York: Routledge.
———. (1993). *Bodies That Matter: On the Discursive Limits of "Sex."* New York: Routledge.
Davis, Lennard J. (1997). *The Disability Studies Reader*. New York: Routledge.
———. (2002) "Bodies of Difference: Politics, Disability, and Representation." In Sharon Snyder, Brenda Jo Brueggemann, and Rosemarie Garland-Thomson (Eds.), *Disability Studies: Enabling the Humanities*. New York: Modern Language Association of America. 100–108.
DuBois, W.E.B. (1989 [1903]). *The Souls of Black Folk*. New York: Bantam.
Farrell, Michael. (2003). *Understanding Special Educational Needs: A Guide for Student Teachers*. London: RoutledgeFalmer.
Ferri, Beth and David Connor. (2006). *Reading Resistance: Discourses of Exclusion in Desegregation and Inclusion Debates*. New York: Peter Lang.
Foucault, Michel. (1965). *Madness and Civilization: A History of Insanity in the Age of Reason*. New York: Vintage Books.

Foucault, Michel. (1979). *Discipline and Punish: The Birth of the Prison*. Trans. Alan Sheridan. New York: Vintage Books.
———. (1980). *The History of Sexuality: Volume I: An Introduction*. New York: Vintage Books.
Gabel, Susan L. (Ed.). (2005). *Disability Studies in Education: Readings in Theory and Method*. New York: Peter Lang.
hooks, bell (1990). "Marginality as Site of Resistance." In Russel Ferguson, Martha Gevner, Trinh T. Minh-ha, and Cornel West (Eds.), *Out There: Marginalization and Contemporary Cultures*. New York: New Museum of Contemporary Art and Cambridge, MA: MIT Press. 341–345.
Kostelnik, Marjorie J., Esther Onaga, Barbara Rohde, and Alice Whiren. (2002). *Children with Special Needs: Lessons for Early Childhood Professionals*. New York: Teachers College.
McRuer, Robert. (2002). "Compulsory Able-Bodiedness and Queer/Disabled Existence." In Sharon L. Snyder, Brenda Jo Brueggemann, and Rosemarie Garland Thomson (Eds.), *Disability Studies: Enabling the Humanities*. New York: Modern Language Association. 88–99.
Michalko, Rod. (2002). *The Difference That Disability Makes*. Philadelphia: Temple University Press.
Mitchell, David T. (2002). "Narrative Prosthesis and the Materiality of Metaphor." In Sharon L. Snyder, Brenda Jo Brueggemann, and Rosemarie Garland Thomson (Eds.), *Disability Studies: Enabling the Humanities*. New York: Modern Language Association. 15–30.
Oliver, Michael. (1996). *Understanding Disability: From Theory to Practice*. New York: St. Martin's Press.
Poon-McBrayer, Kim Fong, and Ming-gon John Lian. (2002). *Special Needs Education: Children with Exceptionalities*. Hong Kong: Chinese University Press.
Rogers, Fred, Steve Seskin, and Allen Shablin. (2002). *Don't Laugh at Me*. Berkeley: Tricycle Press.
Seskin, Steve and Allen Shamblin. (2002). Don't Laugh at Me. Berkley: Tricycle Press.
Smith, Dorothy E. (1999). *Writing the Social: Critique, Theory, and Investigations*. Toronto: University of Toronto Press.
Thomson, Rosemarie Garland (Ed.). (1996). *Freakery: Cultural Spectacles of Extraordinary Body*. New York: New York University Press.
Titchkosky, Tanya. (2003). *Disability, Self and Society*. Toronto: University of Toronto Press.
Scott, Robert A. (1969). *The Making of Blind Men: A Study of Adult Socialization*. New Jersey: Transaction Books.
Zola, Irving Kenneth. (1993) "Self, Identity and the Naming Question: Reflections on the Language of Disability." *Social Science and Medicine, 36*(2), 167–173.

CHAPTER TWENTY-FOUR

Cartographies OF Eugenics AND Special Education: A History OF THE (Ab)normal

PHIL SMITH

"We live in a world of norms."

—(Davis, 1995, p. 23)

Eugenics is the normative outcome of social cartographic processes of industrialization and modernization that began in late nineteenth-and early twentieth-century America. While most mainstream social historians—and most of early twenty-first-century Western intelligentsia—place the pinnacle of eugenicist influence at a point shortly before the middle of the twentieth century, this is not the case. It is very much alive and well today, although transformed in ways that would not be recognized by its progenitors, and often invisible and forgotten by other scholars. Eugenics, whether framed as it was in early modernist terms, or as it can now be in terms of human genomic science, genetic technology, (special) education practice, and in the general ideological underpinnings of modernist Western culture, is essentially racist, classist, sexist, and ableist[1] (Baker, 2002). It was portrayed as

> ... the science of the genetic improvement of the human race ... used to establish race and class distinctions as "natural" and incontrovertible. The dominance of the upper class was mandated by their superior genetic heritage; the poor remained in poverty because of their degenerate genes. (Block, Balcazar, & Keys, 2002, p. 34)

It is a technology designed to segregate the normative hegemonic class from abnormative groups through hidden and iatrogenic processes of pathologizing diagnosis (Snyder & Mitchell, 2002). These processes rely on the powerful modernist tool of scientific forgetting. This kind of forgetting is active, and its work is "… to make the boundaries and demarcations of the dominant culture invisible …" (Norquay, 1999, p. 2).

This, then, is a (brief) history of normality, a history that begins with eugenics. I argue here that what Western social cartographers understand and portray as a (pseudo-) scientific movement called eugenics, whose influence on modernism ended in the middle of the twentieth century, is more precisely a complex set of cultural ideologies (Block et al., 2002; Winfield, 2004). These ideologies created social constructions of difference, ability, and normality, all in the service of neoliberal capitalism, and whose influence continues today. The result of this influence has been the outlining of social landscapes inhabited by those with the demonym[2] Normal. Others, lacking the social cachet of such a demonym, have been placed in social and physical ghettos outside of normative terrains, not merely at the margins of cultural maps, but off the page of socially textualized cartographies.

This is a standpoint history that reflects a particular subjectivity, a particular ideological standpoint. I am a bricoleur, with training and interest in the humanities, broadly defined, including rhetorics, literature, the arts, criticism, and media. In addition, I draw from the discourses of cultural, women's, race, whiteness, normal, and disability studies, all of which define themselves (if at times only partially) as cross-, trans-, multi-, and inter-disciplinary (e.g., Foucault, 1965; Giroux, 1997; Gomez-Pena, 1997; Hehir, 2002; Lather & Smithies, 1997; McLaren & Torres, 1999; Thomson, 1997). I also borrow from the disciplines of history, sociology, anthropology, psychology, and geography, using their metaphors, at times without their discoursed permission. As well, I am a white, male professional teaching special education at a midsized university in midwestern United States and live as much of my time as I can in north country of northeastern United States, where I count among my best friends those who come from working rural poor and lower middle-class backgrounds. I also describe myself as a person with a disability, and a parent of a child with a disability.

I define myself as both critical theorist and postmodernist—positions that are sometimes, intriguingly, at odds with each other (a foolish consistency, said one of my New England U.S. forebears, is the hobgoblin of little minds). By critical theory, I mean a complex critique of social and cultural power structures, whose objectives are "… to empower the powerless and transform existing social inequalities and injustices" (McLaren, 1989, p. 160). A dialectical approach, critical theory assumes "that men and women are essentially unfree and inhabit a world rife with contradictions and asymmetries of power and privilege" (ibid., p. 166). Following on the work of Horkheimer, Fromm, Marcuse, Adorno, Gadamer, and Habermas of the Frankfurt school, modern critical theorists such as Giroux, Apple, Kozol, McLaren, and Freire have opened up new terrains looking at race, gender, and class (Giroux, 1997; McLaren, 1989). Unfortunately, disability has been often left out of this exploration.

Critical theory and postmodernism are frequently seen as being at odds (Giroux, 2004; Smith, 2004). Like other of my colleagues, however, I seek to find a way out of such a binaric trap, "... to avoid the modern/postmodern divide that suggests that we can do either culture or economics but that we cannot do both" (Giroux, 2004, p. 32).

From this critical theory perspective, then, I understand that the set of cultural practices, social institutions, and ideological processes that we in the early part of the twenty-first century have come to call eugenics continues to create taxonomies of human difference that serve the needs of a Western, neoliberal, capitalist culture. This culture is increasingly reliant on technology, industry, and modernity to create wealth for the benefit of some, while ensuring that working and serving classes are happy with the course of their lives, and anxious to fill them by consuming an ever-growing diversity of goods and services constructed as "necessary" (ibid.). The most important work undertaken by eugenics is not the creation of disability and difference, although those are outcomes that are instrumental, the ones most obvious to modernist history, and the ones given most attention by historians and disability studies scholars. Instead (or in addition), eugenics essentially creates the Normal, a cultural landscape outlined in order to support the hegemony of its inhabitants, a liberalist bourgeois class of white, able-bodied and—able-minded men.[3] The borders of normative landscapes are at once clearly marked, closely guarded, and created in such a way as to make both the boundaries and their inhabitants invisible to themselves. Those who do not reside within these normative landscapes, described through the use of increasingly sophisticated cultural mapping tools, are deported to the marginalia of deviating terrains.

EUGENICS: BUT IS IT SCIENCE?

> ... scientific-sounding arguments often serve as rationalizations for doing harm to the most vulnerable elements of society. (Groce & Marks, 2000, p. 821)

The word eugenics was born in 1883, created by the cousin of Charles Darwin, Francis Galton, in 1883. Galton was influenced not only by the work of his more famous cousin, but by the social climate and mores of Victorian England in which he lived. Galton theorized, rather simply, that biological notions of heredity could be applied to humans, and that the tools of Mendelian genetics and Darwinian evolution could be used to transform and improve the human pedigree (Baker, 2002; Pelias & Markward, 2001).

As a good Victorian scholar, Galton searched for a label for this new ideology (though he understood and described it as a science) in the classics. The word eugenics comes from the Greek (via Latin and Middle English). The prefix "eu" means good. "Gen" has the meaning of the word "born," or of "producing." Together, then, the word means well-born, or well-bred (Morris, 1975).

Eugenicists developed increasingly complex taxonomic tools, tools that had the effect of sorting Normal from Different.[4] They began with sorting tools that relied on scopic analysis and measurement, including phrenology and craniometry (Baines & Stanley, 2004). Over time, they developed statistical tools that enabled them to analyze and "measure" intelligence, in spite of the fact that "the 'intelligence' that the IQ test is supposed to test and has never been defined in precise scientific terms and there is no evidence from cognitive neuroscience to indicate that it can be" (White, 2000, p. 33). Because statistical analysis relies on numbering, it was felt to be more objective and scientific (Gould, 1996; Tyner, 1999). It is clear that early eugenicists sought to rely on scientific rhetoric and discourse to legitimize a project that would otherwise now (but not then) be thought of as racist and colonialist (ibid.). Most importantly perhaps, they relied on the use of numbers, believing that "… everything in the universe operated under quantifiable laws and demonstrable order" (Baines & Stanley, 2004, p. 13). Supported by the likes of Teddy Roosevelt, John D. Rockefeller, Alexander Graham Bell, Luther Burbank, Margaret Sanger, W.E.B. Du Bois, Winston Churchill, George Bernard Shaw, Aldous Huxley, Calvin Coolidge, and Oliver Wendell Holmes, among a host of others, the early eugenics movement had tremendous cultural cachet (Berson & Cruz, 2001; Gray, 1999; Quinn, 2003).

The horrible results of eugenicist science, during the first part of the twentiethcentury, are well known. Galton's ideas were captured most profoundly in the United States, where scientists began to put them into practice, sterilizing tens of thousands of those who were deemed unfit—typically people with disabilities, from "low" or "working" classes, and from groups understood to be racial minorities (although the understanding of what constituted a racial minority then is different from what it is now; persons from Ireland or southern Europe, for example, would be classed as raced groups then). Well over 100,000 people, most with disabilities, were sterilized in the United States (Ridley, 2000; Kealey, 2002).

Eugenics was also widely taken up in Europe, particularly in Nazi Germany, which used the strength of its scientifically founded discourse as a rationale for cleansing the Aryan race. The Nazis applauded and learned from the work they found in the thought and practice of U.S. eugenicists, who reciprocated their admiration (Quinn, 2003). Although both early U.S. and Nazi approaches to eugenicism were deeply rooted in racism, they drew much of the rationale for their practice from the financial impact of disability on their respective societies (Sofair & Kaldjian, 2000). Drawing on the power of medical epistemologies as a rationale and method for sorting, the Nazis killed hundreds of thousands of people with disabilities, using their bodies as a proving ground for the technical expertise they needed to murder millions of Jews, Gypsies, and other social groups they believed were polluting human breeding stock (Mostert, 2002). They went on to sterilize several hundred thousand more people with disabilities, as well. The process for determining whether a person should be sterilized was quite simple: "… an individual was arraigned for being stupid before a panel of three judges, two of whom were doctors, one a lawyer. If found stupid, the individual was compulsorily sterilized" (Kealey, 2002, p. 114). The program for killing people with disabilities was called the T-4 project, named after the address of the office from which it was administered, Tiergartenstrasse 4.

When outcry from a (very) few clerics made overt murder and sterilization of people with disabilities politically inexpedient, Nazi German physicians developed more covert methods of extermination. For example, institutionalized children were kept in extremely cold living conditions until they developed pneumonia and died of "natural" causes (Gould, 1996; Groce & Marks, 2000).

Among other groups, the Nazis essentially wiped out a generation of European Deaf persons, disrupting their development of Deaf culture. In both the United States and in Germany, racism fueled social cries to ensure that white breeding stock remained pure (Pelias & Markward, 2001). While Nazi Germany was where widespread genocide was enacted on the bodies of people with disabilities, respected professionals in the United States called for euthanizing them during the 1930s and 1940s (Quinn, 2003).

The impact of eugenics did not end with the genocide of people with disabilities in Europe. For example, following World War II, when Nazis were put on trial for war crimes, those accused of killing people with disabilities were not given the same kind of treatment as others—their convictions were much more lenient, and acquittal rates were much higher (Siegel, 2005).

Beyond the world of disability studies, however, the history of this disability Holocaust—one that occurred on both sides of the Atlantic—is little remembered. It is a Shoah (a Hebrew word that translates as "whirlwind" and is used to describe the Jewish Holocaust) that is rarely thought about or discussed by the general public. It has been forgotten, literally—an extraordinary act of genocide that is virtually unknown except by those concerned specifically with disability issues. Few Holocaust memorials around the world mention the T-4 program, or its impact on people with disabilities. Following the war, people with disabilities were not recognized as persons who were persecuted by the Nazis, and they received no restitution.

From our position at the beginning of the twenty-first century, some progressive disability studies scholars perceive early eugenics

> ... as constructing and privileging certain kinds of whiteness over certain kinds of color, certain kinds of masculinity over certain kinds of femininity, certain kinds of ability over certain kinds of "corporeally anomalous" body-minds, and tolerating only narrow versions of heteronormativity and religious devotion ... (Baker, 2002, p. 665)

These scholars assert that the ideology of eugenics did not end, as many would have it, with the Nazi Holocaust but continued and even flourished throughout the balance of the twentieth and into the beginning of the twenty-first centuries (ibid.; Snyder & Mitchell, 2002).

Historians have generally asserted that eugenics died after World War II, principally because they saw it as a set of discrete practices and taxonomic technologies. What they fail(ed) to recognize is that eugenics—like ableism and racism—is not (just) how or what people do to sort, sterilize, or kill others. Eugenics is, like all scientific disciplines, at its root an ideology or, more properly, a set of ideologies (Smith, 1999a). This set of ideologies, tied closely to ableism and racism, is dynamic, reflecting larger sociocultural changes and linked closely to the heart of capitalism (Smith, 2004).

In a paper foreshadowing the trajectory of my own writing and thinking, Snyder and Mitchell (2002) argued that "... eugenicists effectively surrendered medical objectivity in order to make judgments about human mutation ... medical science abandoned the project of faithfully describing the body ..." (p. 80). The eugenicists did not surrender their objectivity. Instead they used the objectivity assumed to be inherent in medical scientific discourse to bolster their assertions about human difference. Objectivity is an artifact of modernist science, a ventriloquizing ideology masquerading as Truth assertions in order (in this and many other cases in modernist, Western culture) to serve the needs of neoliberalist capitalism (Smith, 2004). Eugenicist scientists could not (and cannot) see the inherently ideological nature of their work, one of the paradoxes of ideology pointed out by Althusser (1994 [1971]).

Nor did eugenicists give up on descriptions of the body (or the mind). Rather, they believed their work advanced those descriptions, through the use of the new field of statistics, also developed by eugenicists (Davis, 1995; Gould, 1996; Russell, 1998). Creating a new science of modernism, eugenicists believed that the essential trajectory of culture was toward increasing knowledge, sophistication, and Truth (Danforth, 1997). They were certain that any rational being, understanding the new genetics of the day, would have to come to the same conclusions that they had: that given that some people were, by race, sex, and class genetically inferior, then the right thing to do in order to continue to move Western culture forward was to eliminate those who were proven—rationally and scientifically—inferior and deviant.

EUGENICS: A FORGETTING

The work of eugenics is, ultimately, to ensure that the borders of hegemonic, normative, cultural landscapes are tightly guarded. Its job is to sort those who are Different out of the crowd, letting only those who are Normal remain. In doing so, eugenics creates both disability (Different) and the hegemony (Normal). The borders that are created are fashioned from a particular kind of mirror—to the inhabitants of the Land of Normal, there are no borders, only a reflection of themselves. The borders become invisible.

So the work of eugenics involves a kind of disappearance act—those inscribed as Normal cannot (must not) see themselves as such. It's as if the mirrored borders are like the one-way interrogation-room mirrors in all those cop-show TV programs—looking through them, the inhabitants of the Land of Normal see the Different on the other side, the ones being interrogated always declaring their innocence. If they see their own image, the Normals see themselves only hazily—forgetting that the fashioning of Difference also fashions themselves.

This kind of forgetting is involved in the creation of the Normal identity. It is a forgotten identity—an active process—that is created through the sorting of Difference. This process is similar to that used in the creation of Whiteness—in the process of creating racial identity, Whiteness is also outlined, but only through elimination (Smith, 2004). In the same way that Whites forget that they, too, are "colored," so too do Normals forget that they are Differenced: "what is not worth remembering is often constructed as 'normal'" (Norquay, 1999, p. 3).

Like the creation of Color, the creation of Difference is scopic, a visual work, both actual and metaphoric. Difference is perceived—seen. The contribution of eugenics is in creating a mode of perception that relies on and draws from the power given to the metaphors and discourse of science. The discourse most commonly drawn on by eugenics is statistics because it is a discourse that was theorized as being truly objective and neutral, both values held in high esteem in the ideology of science.

But what was—and is—actively forgotten about the discourse of statistics is that, like all discourses, it is essentially metaphoric. Metaphors are "linguistic tropes" (Cahoone, 1996, p. 16)—they are language elements that stand in for other ideas, numbers, or words. They provide a means for the author to communicate to his or her audience an idea through analogy, by relating it to an idea with which they are more familiar (Drabble, 1985; Holman, 1972; Richardson, 1994). The danger of all metaphors—the danger of statistics—is that they become reified over time, and that the makers and readers of metaphors lose the relationship between the tenor and its vehicle (Holman, 1972).

In the case of statistics, numbers are not people (just as words are not the perceived world). Numbers can only refer to other numbers (just as words can only refer to other words)—statistics is a metaphored language of numbers (one of many, I suspect). Metaphors are inherently value laden; so too are statistics. Like metaphors, statistics are "… always value constituting—making sense in a particular way, privileging one ordering of the 'facts' over others" (Richardson, 1994, p. 520). When eugenicists thought that they were describing real qualities through statistical analysis, they were describing the values that they had inscribed on those statistics—values that were, and are, inherently racist, sexist, ableist, colonialist, and (insert here any in the long line of isms that belong). What disability studies scholars are learning to do is to unpack the metaphors—to figure out what they mean, to explicate them (Smith, 2001a, 2001b, in press).

Positivist science had a huge impact on eugenics, and, in essence, eugenicists created much of the statistical underpinnings of what is commonly taken as science by policymakers and the public in the early twenty-first century. Even when special educators try to unpack the implications of eugenics for people with disabilities, they continue to rely on the understanding of science created by eugenics:

> … it is only by careful attention to canons of converging and replicable experimental evidence over time that we have any hope of rooting out pseudoscience, thereby improving the lives of persons of disabilities by the most effective and efficient means. (Mostert, 2002, p. 166)

I think another line of logic must be followed: to avoid falling into epistemological traps created by and supportive of eugenics, it is essential to explore understandings of science that are outside positivist and modernist approaches.[5]

EUGENICS AND CAPITALISM

What is implicit in a progressive understanding of eugenics is an element that is often unstated by mainstream historians and scholars. That is, eugenics was not then—nor is it not now—in its current incarnation as genomics and genetics—merely a set of practices, techniques, or strategies for changing the future of humanity. Rather, eugenics is an ideology, or set of ideologies inherent in capitalism and modernism. While modernism (one particular epistemology for understanding the universe) and capitalism (one particular system of political economy) should not be conflated, they share common ideologies founded in nineteenth-, twentieth-, and twenty-first-century Western culture (Smith, 2004). And where goes a capitalist, positivist, modernist epistemology, so goes eugenics. The development of IQ testing was demonstrably tied to the creation and implementation of industrialist ideology (Masear, 2004). Eugenics—and so capitalism and modernism—is inherently racist and colonialist.

Historians of disability typically note the convergence of the beginning of industrialization in the middle and latter parts of the nineteenth century, and the increasing recognition of disability as a social group. This convergence is often framed as an unfortunate and unintended consequence of ongoing social change, that the "… demands of an increasingly more complex society created by … urbanization and industrialization worked against those with limited intellectual skills and social competence" (Beirne-Smith, Ittenbach, & Patton, 2002, p. 10). Certain needs of industrialist capitalism—class stratification, commodity development, and a surplus of workers—are met by the increasing delineation of deviation through eugenicist science.

EUGENICISM AND COMMODIFICATION

Eugenics is closely tied to the pathologizing practices of diagnostic, modernist medicine (Snyder & Mitchell, 2002). When medicine can not be curative, or rehabilitative, it becomes eliminative—and this was an important feature of Nazi medicine and the medical practices of early twentieth century physicians in the United States, from whom the Nazis learned so much.

But at its heart, eugenics is a science of sorting and differentiation—it creates highly structured taxonomic cultural apparati. Early eugenicists developed powerful statistical tools to discriminate between groups of body and mind difference—in effect, sub-speciating humans. In addition to meeting other capitalist goals, eugenics created bodies and minds as commodities to be cured, rehabilitated, or eliminated. This has spawned what can only be described as a huge disability service-provision industry. This industry, powerfully iatrogenic in its work, brings in billions of dollars annually to the U.S. economy alone. Special education is one example of how a social institution has been commodified in what is becoming increasingly the industry of education (Aichroth et al., 2002; Smith, 1999b, 2001a, 2003).

Eugenicism and surplus workers

Perhaps eugenics' most important utility to capitalism is the creation of a set of surplus workers, ones willing to engage in functions that are otherwise abhorrent to the mainstream (Hahn, 1987). It has become almost a cliché in the disability service provision industry of supported employment that people with developmental and psychiatric disabilities, when they are employed at all, are engaged principally in work that is called the "3 F's:" Food, Filth, and Flowers (Baron & Salzer, 2002). And it is clear that most people with developmental disabilities are unemployed (Yamaki & Fujiura, 2002).

Eugenicism and class stratification

Through these sorting and differencing technologies, class stratification becomes increasingly pronounced. Wealth and social power is increasingly in the hands of fewer individuals and globalizing corporations, whose hegemonic borders are fenced by the razor-wired practices of colonialist, racist modernism. Capitalism creates a "… reality that disabled people's lives are … bounded by oppressive social and economic conditions that are … difficult to transcend" (Erevelles, 2001, pp. 93–94). Eugenic practices have and continue to accentuate stratification and to benefit those in dominating, hegemonic class positions: "IQ test scores correlate with education, income, and socioeconomic status, but these are anything but independent variables; they are criteria for one another. The people the test favors are important to the management of a complexly organized society; they tend to get paid well and have prestige" (White, 2000, p. 40).

IS EUGENICS DEAD?

> It's easy to speak of eugenics as something that is past, done with: by treating eugenics as a movement that flourished principally between 1880 and 1930, we tend, albeit unwittingly, to borrow history's comforting shroud, pushing our analyses back to the safety of the distant past (M. Smith, 2005, p. 896).

But it is not done with and is not dead (Furney, Glesne, Kervick, Pillai, & Smith, 1998; Gould, 2002; Kealey, 2002; Smith, 1999b, 2004, 2005). Over 400 book-length works on the subject were written in the last decade of the twentieth century alone (Glad, 2002); almost the same number were written in the first five years of the twenty-first century (Glad, 2005). Some of this writing has had a powerful impact on twenty-first-century culture, both popular and academic, and been printed by reputable publishing houses; among the most important of these works include writing by Herrnstein and Murray (1996), Jensen (1998), and Lynn (2001).

The discourse of those who wrote and researched in the eugenicist tradition at the end of the twentieth and beginning of the twenty-first century continues to reflect an ideology that can be described only as racist (see, e.g., Glad, 2005; Gottfredson, 1994, 2004, 2005a, 2005b, 2005c; Pearson, 1991, 1995; Rushton, 1997, 2001, 2002; Rushton & Jensen, 2005a, 2005b; Whitney, 1995). They argue that only one of the twenty-nine Western countries who enacted laws favoring eugenicist practices in the first half of the twentieth century slid down the slippery slope toward a Holocaust, implying that such practices were not inherently bad (Whitney, 1999). They continue to assert that there are economic benefits to eugenic programs, noting that the elimination of people with disabilities would have social cost benefits—a claim made without using the term "useless eaters" prevalent in Nazi eugenicist propaganda fifty years previously (Miller, 1997).

The intersection of what is commonly understood as mainstream science and eugenicist thinking is still present. The Cold Spring Harbor lab, perhaps the most important laboratory for early eugenicist work, is still in existence, and

> … has long been directed by James Watson, the co-discoverer of the structure of DNA, who also directed the Human Genome Project. Cold Spring Harbor may have dropped the term "eugenics" from its title but it is still playing the same game as when it was founded nearly a century ago. … (Kealey, 2002, p. 115)

Watson has clearly espoused a eugenicist approach in his own work (Watson & Berry, 2003). The heritage of eugenics continues to live on in current medical practice:

> The legacy of treatment models developed by eugenicists in the early 1900s (such as segregation from the opposite sex and sterilization) is still apparent in practices, such as genetic counseling, which encourage the abortion of fetuses with disabilities like Down Syndrome. (Block et al., 2002, p. 35)

And some report that covert and overt sterilization programs have continued in various parts of the world through the 1990s and beyond (Berson & Cruz, 2001; Brady, 2001).

NORMALITY

The idea of the Normal did not really come into being until the nineteenth century, when it was created by the science of eugenics and statistical analysis (Davis, 1995; Russell, 1998). Positivist, modernist science—of which eugenics is one example, and perhaps the most positivist of modern sciences—relies heavily on binary structures in understanding and representing the world. This presentation of the world in polar opposites creates what might be called "… binarism … part of an ideology of containment and a politics of power and fear" (Davis, 1995, p. 4). The expression of this ideology becomes most pronounced when only side of the binary is described. For example, in eugenicist terms, disability and deficiency are outlined in clear and explicit terms, leaving the Normal to be forgotten, only discovered through inference. This description of Difference is one that Thomson (1996) calls enfreakment, which "… emerges from cultural rituals that stylize, silence, differentiate, and distance …" (p. 10). The Normal is left out of these enfreaking cultural practices, reinforcing the dominance of its landscape over the cultural terrain.

Processes of enfreakment—of differentiation—are scopic. While Different minds are described through statistical analysis,

> the body is the primary vehicle through which prevailing economic and political institutions inscribe the self…The body is the most personalized form of politics; all power is, ultimately, power over the body. (Warf, 2004, p. 46)

By asserting power over the enfreaked Different bodies/minds of people with disabilities, the power of forgotten Normal cultural terrains is enhanced, ensured, and supported, even while (or especially because they are) hidden from both Normal and Different view.

In effect, eugenics created (and creates) commodified and reified deviation through taxonomic sorting practices. By naming those understood to be Different, eugenics created not just Difference but also stereotyped and reified understandings of that Difference. Eugenics also creates and supports an invisible and forgotten category of Normal, one that supports hegemonic capitalist and modernist social structures. Words used to clarify and label deviation take on metaphoric meanings beyond the simple letters inscribed on social texts (Smith, 2004, 2005).

Eugenicist thinking and understanding of people and their place in the world is pervasive in U.S. culture. Its ideological and scientific legacy continues to play important roles in economics, politics, and biology, and in the commonsense structure of daily American life. Historians, critical theorists, and disability studies scholars must devote increased attention to explicating the role that eugenics has played in late modernism, and the role that it continues to play in postmillennial neoliberal capitalism (Doyle, 2004).

NOTES

1. I define ableism, as I have elsewhere, "… as the belief in the natural physical and mental superiority of nondisabled people and the prejudice and discriminatory behavior that arise as a result of this belief" (Groch, 1998, p. 151). It is ideological and based in discrimination and oppression (Smith, 2004). Other, earlier cultural workers have called it handicapism, comparing it to racism

and sexism (Bogdan & Biklen, 1977). When I refer to ableism, I mean both so-called able-mindedness and able-bodiedness.
2. Demonym is a term borrowed from the field of geography that describes the inhabitants of a particular land, country, or locale.
3. I do not include women here, as they do not substantially benefit, in the same way that people of color do not benefit, as a result of white ableist male privilege.
4. Although they thought they were applying procedures from the natural sciences to the exploration of humans, a critical theory analysis would assert that they were rather blindly serving the needs of a capitalist, industrialist economy.
5. In a response to an article with significant racist and eugenicist biases in a major psychology journal in 2005, one author argues that the danger of such an approach will create "public-policy implications may come to be ideologically driven rather than data driven" (Sternberg, 2005). I would note that all science, positivist or otherwise, and all public policy, however it created, is driven by ideology, inescapably (Smith, 1999).

REFERENCES

Aichroth, S., Carpenter, J., Daniels, K., Grassette, P., Kelly, D., Murray, A., Rice, J., Rivard, B., Smith, C., Smith, P., and Topper, K. (2002). Creating a new system of supports: The Vermont self-determination project. *Rural Special Education Quarterly, 21*(2), 16–28.

Althusser, L. (1994) [1965, 1971]. Selected texts. In T. Eagleton (Ed.) *Ideology* (pp. 87–111). New York: Longman Publishing.

Baker, B. (2002). The hunt for disability: The new eugenics and the normalization of school children. *Teachers College Record, 104*, 663–703.

Baron, R., and Salzer, M. (2002). Accounting for unemployment among people with mental illness. *Behavioral Sciences and the Law, 20*, 585–599.

Beirne-Smith, M., Ittenbach, R., and Patton, J. (2002). *Mental retardation* (6th ed.). Columbus, OH: Merrill Prentice Hall.

Berson, M., and Cruz, B. (2001). Eugenics past and present. *Social Education, 65*, 300.

Block, P., Balcazar, F., and Keys, C. (2002). Race, poverty and disability: Three strikes and you're out! Or are you? *Social Policy, 33*, 34–38.

Bogdan, R., and Biklen, D. (1977). Handicapism. *Social Policy, 7*, 14–19.

Brady, S. (2001). Sterilization of girls and women with intellectual disabilities: Past and present justifications. *Violence against Women, 7*, 432–461.

Cahoone, L. (1996). Introduction. In L. Cahoone (Ed.) *From modernism to postmodernism: An anthology* (pp. 1–23). Cambridge, MA: Blackwell Publishers.

Danforth, S. (1997). On what basis hope? Modern progress and postmodern possibilities. *Mental Retardation, 35*, 93–106.

Davis, L. (1995). *Enforcing normalcy: Disability, deafness, and the body*. New York: Verso.

Doyle, L. (2004). The long arm of eugenics. *American Literary History, 16*, 520–535.

Drabble, M. (Ed.) (1985). *The Oxford companion to English literature* (5th ed.). New York: Oxford University Press.

Erevelles, N. (2001). In search of the disabled subject. In J. Wilson and C. Lewieki-Wilson (Eds.) *Embodied rhetorics: Disability in language and culture* (pp. 92–111). Carbondale, IL: Southern Illinois University Press.

Foucault, M. (1965). *Madness and civilization: A history of insanity in the age of reason.* Trans. Richard Howard. New York: Vintage Books.
Furney, K., Glesne, C., Kervick, C., Pillai, M., and Smith, P. (November 1998). The social construction of disability: A scripted conversation. Annual Meeting of American Educational Studies Association, Philadelphia, PA.
Giroux, H. A. (1997). *Pedagogy and the politics of hope.* Boulder, CO: Harper-Collins Publishers.
———. (2004). Critical pedagogy and the postmodern/modern divide: Towards a pedagogy of democratization. *Teacher Education Quarterly, 31,* 31–47.
Glad, J. (2002). Some recent books on eugenics. *Mankind Quarterly, 42,* 263–266.
———. (2005). *Future human evolution: Eugenics in the twenty-first century.* Schuykill Haven, PA: Hermitage Press.
Gomez-Pena, Guillermo. (1997). *The new world border: Prophecies, poems & loqueras for the end of the century.* San Francisco: City Lights.
Gottfredson, L. (1994). Egalitarian fiction and collective fraud. *Society, 31*(3), 53–60.
———. (2004). Intelligence: Is it the epidemiologists' elusive "fundamental cause" of social class inequalities in health? *Journal of Personality and Social Psychology, 86,* 174–199.
———. (2005a). Implications of cognitive differences for schooling within diverse societies. In C. Frisby and C. Reynolds (Eds.) *Comprehensive handbook of multicultural school psychology* (pp. 517–554). New York: Wiley.
———. (2005b). What if the hereditarian hypothesis is true? *Psychology, Public Policy, and Law, 11,* 311–319.
———. (2005c). Supressing intelligence research: Hurting those we intend to help. In R. Wright and N. Cummings (Eds.) *Destructive trends in mental health: The well-intentioned path to harm* (pp. 155–186). New York: Routledge.
Gould, S. (1996). *The mismeasure of man.* New York: W.W. Norton.
———. (2002). Carrie Buck's daughter. *Natural History, 111*(6), 12–17.
Gray, P. (1999). Cursed by eugenics. *Time, 153*(1), 84.
Groce, N., and Marks, J. (2000). The Great Ape Project and disability rights: Ominous undercurrents of eugenics in action. *American Anthropologist, 102,* 919–822.
Groch, S. (1998). Pathways to protest: The making of oppositional consciousness by people with disabilities. *Dissertation Abstracts International, 59* (12), 4533A. (University Microfilms No. 9913804).
Hahn, H. (1987). Advertising the acceptably employable image: Disability and capitalism. *Policy Studies Journal, 15*(3), 551–570.
Hehir, T. (2002). Eliminating ableism in education. *Harvard Educational Review, 72,* 1–32.
Herrnstein, R., and Murray, C. (1996). *The bell curve: Intelligence and class structure in American life.* New York: Simon and Schuster.
Holman, C. (1972). *A handbook to literature* (3rd ed.). Indianapolis, IN: Odyssey Press.
Jensen, R. (1998). *The g factor: The science of mental ability.* Westport, CT: Praeger Publishers.
Kealey, T. (2002). A black student's primer on the history of eugenics. *The Journal of Blacks in Higher Education, 34,* 114–115.
Lather, P., and Smithies, C. (1997). *Troubling the angels: Women living with HIV/AIDS.* Boulder, CO: Westview Press.
Lynn, R. (2001). *Eugenics: A Reassessment.* New York: Praeger Press.
McLaren, P. (1989). *Life in schools: An introduction to critical pedagogy in the foundations of education.* New York: Longman.

McLaren, P., and Torres, R. (1999). Racism and multicultural education: Rethinking "race" and "whiteness" in late capitalism. In S. May (Ed.) *Critical multiculturalism: Rethinking multicultural and antiracist education* (pp. 42–76). Philadelphia, PA: Falmer Press.

Miller, E. (1997). Eugenics: Economics for the long run. *Research in Biopolitics, 5*, 391–416.

Morris, W. (1975). *American heritage dictionary of English language.* New York: American Heritage Publishing and Houghton Mifflin Co.

Mostert, M. (2002). Useless eaters: Disability as genocidal marker in Nazi Germany. *Journal of Special Education, 36*, 155–168.

Norquay, N. (1999). Identity and forgetting. *Oral History Review, 26*(1), 1–12.

Pearson, R. (1991). *Race, intelligence, and bias in academe.* Washington, DC: Scott-Townsend Publishers.

———. (1995). The concept of heredity in the history of Western culture, part 1. *The Mankind Quarterly, 35*, 229–265.

Pelias, M., and Markward, N. (2001). The human genome in the public view: Genetics, geneticists, and eugenics. *St. Thomas Law Review, 13*, 827–849.

Quinn, P. (2003). Race cleansing in America. *American Heritage, 54*(1), 34–44.

Richardson, L. (1994). Writing: A method of inquiry. In N. Denzin and Y. Lincoln (Eds.) *Handbook of qualitative research* (pp. 516–529). Thousand Oaks, CA: Sage Publications.

Ridley, M. (2000). The new eugenics. *National Review, 52*(14), 34–36.

Rushton, J. (1997). *Race, evolution, and behavior.* New Brunswick, NJ: Transaction Publishers.

———. (2001). Black-white differences on the g-factor in South Africa: A "Jensen effect" on the Wechsler Intelligence Scale for Children, Revised. *Personality and Individual Differences, 31*, 1227–1232.

———. (2002). Jensen effects and African/Coloured/Indian/White differences on Raven's Standard Progressive Matrices in South Africa. *Personality and Individual Differences, 33*, 1279–1284.

Rushton, J., and Jensen, A. (2005a). Thirty years of research on race differences in cognitive ability. *Psychology, Public Policy, and Law, 11*, 235–294.

———. (2005b). Wanted: More race realism, less moralistic fallacy. *Psychology, Public Policy, and Law, 11*, 328–336.

Russell, M. (1998). *Beyond ramps: Disability at the end of the social contract.* Monroe, Maine: Common Courage Press.

Siegel, J. (2005). Nazi killers of mentally ill lightly sentenced. *Jerusalem Post.* Retrieved September 21, 2005 from http://www.jpost.com/servlet/Satellite?pagename=JPost/JPArticle/ShowFull&cid=1126924529675

Smith, M. (2005). Finding deficiency: On eugenics, economics, and certainty. *American Journal of Economics and Sociology, 64*, 887–900.

Smith, P. (1999a). (1999). Ideology, politics, and science in understanding developmental disabilities. *Mental Retardation, 37*, 71–72.

———. (1999b). Drawing new maps: A radical cartography of developmental disabilities. *Review of Educational Research, 69*(2), 117–144.

———. (2001a). MAN.i.f.e.s.t.o.: A Poetics of D(EVIL) op (MENTAL) Dis (ABILITY). *Taboo: The Journal of Education and Culture, 5*(1), 27–36.

———. (2001b). Inquiry cantos: A poetics of developmental disability. *Mental Retardation, 39*, 379–390.

———. (2003). Self-determination and independent support brokerage: Creating innovative second-level supports. *Mental Retardation, 41*, 294–298.

Smith, P. (2004). Whiteness, normal theory, and disability studies. *Disability Studies Quarterly, 24* (2), n.p.

———. (2005). Off the map: A critical geography of intellectual disabilities. *Health and Place, 11,* 87–92.

———. (2007). (in press). Split---ting the r o c k of {speci [ES]al} e.ducat.ion: FLOWers of lang[ue]age in >DIS<ability studies. In S. Danforth and S. Gabel (Eds.), *Vital questions in disability studies in education* (pp. 31–58). New York: Peter Lang.

Snyder, S., and Mitchell, D. (2002). Out of the ashes of eugenics: Diagnostic regimes in the United States and the making of a disability minority. *Patterns of Prejudice, 36,* 79–103.

Sofair, A., and Kaldjian, L. (2000). Eugenic sterilization and a qualified Nazi analogy: The United States and Germany, 1930–1945. *Annals of Internal Medicine, 132,* 312–319.

Sternberg, R. (2005). There are no public-policy implications: A reply to Rushton and Jensen (2005). *Psychology, Public Policy, and Law, 11,* 295–301.

Thomson, R. (1996). Introduction: From wonder to error—A genealogy of freak discourse in modernity. In R. Thomson (Ed.) *Freakery: Cultural spectacles of the extraordinary body* (pp. 1–10). New York: New York University Press.

———. (1997). *Extraordinary Bodies: Figuring Physical Disability in American Culture and Literature.* New York: Columbia University Press.

Tyner, J. (1999). The geopolitics of eugenics and the exclusion of Philippine immigrants from the United States. *The Geographical Review, 89,* 54–73.

Warf, B. (2004). Advancing human geography at the *commencement du siecle. The Professional Geography, 56,* 44–52.

Watson, J., and Berry, A. (2003). *DNA: The Secret of Life.* New York: Random House.

White, S. (2000). Conceptual foundations of IQ testing. *Psychology, Public Policy, and Law, 6,* 33–43.

Whitney, G. (1995). Ideology and censorship in behavior genetics. *The Mankind Quarterly, 35,* 327–342.

———. (1999). Reproduction technology for a new eugenics. *The Mankind Quarterly, 40,* 179–192.

Winfield, A. (2004). Eugenics and education: Implications of ideology, memory, and history for education in the United States. *Disability Abstracts International, 65*(01A), 93.

Yamaki, K., and Fujiura, G. (2002). Employment and income status of adults with developmental disabilities living in the community. *Mental Retardation, 40,* 132–141.

CHAPTER TWENTY-FIVE

Caring Power AND Disabled Children: THE Rise OF THE Educational Élan IN Europe, IN Particular IN Belgium AND THE Netherlands

ANNEMIEKE VAN DRENTH

La grande famille indéfinie et confuse des "anormaux," dont la peur hantera la fin du XIXe siècle, ne marque pas simplement une phase d'incertitude ou un épisode un peu malheureux dan l'histoire de la psychopathologie ; elle a été formée en corrélation avec tout un ensemble d'institutions de contrôle, toute une série de mécanismes de surveillance et de distribution; et lorsqu'elle aura été presque entièrement recouverte par la catégorie de la "dégénérescence," elle donnera lieu à des élaborations théoriques dérisoires, mais á des effects durement réels. Michel Foucault, Les Anormaux, *Dits et écrits* (1975), 822.

The human psyche itself has become a possible domain for systematic government in the pursuit of socio-political ends. Educate, cure, reform, punish—these are old imperatives no doubt. But the new vocabularies provided by the sciences of the psyche enable the aspirations of government to be articulated in terms of the knowledgeable management of the depths of the human soul. Nikolas Rose, *Governing the Soul* (1990), 7.

INTRODUCTION

Historians in the field of disability and special education such as Scheerenberger (1983) and Winzer (1993) have described a transformation that took place in the late eighteenth and the early nineteenth centuries. Gradually, disabled people were perceived as human beings and therefore as individuals whose well-being was an issue of concern. The traditional treatment of disabled individuals, which had often been characterized by an astounding level of cruelty, now changed with the introduction of new regimes of care and education. Philosophers, physicians, and educators constructed new images of the mentally ill and their troubled minds, and of the disabled and their impairments. From the turn of the eighteenth century onward, a new perspective came into existence, contesting the animal-like status that had so often been inflicted on so-called insane and disabled people in the past. Despite comparing these individuals with animals, Benjamin Rush (1745–1813), for example, a physician and pioneer worker with the so-called insane, stated that the insights based on "the eye of the man who possesses his reason" would improve the treatment of these people (Lightner, 1999, 10). His rationalistic humanitarianism opposed the prevailing idea among physicians in the eighteenth century that "insane people could be dealt with only by animal force" (Winzer, 1993, 60).

This new perception of individuals who were taken into custody in asylums and hospitals at the end of the eighteenth century was accompanied by new interventions. Early European psychiatrists such as Philippe Pinel (1745–1826), physician at Paris mental hospitals Salpétrière (for women) and Bicêtre (for men), and William Tuke (1732–1822), founder of the York Retreat for the Insane in England, affirmed the human identity of the insane by introducing "moral treatment" into institutions. These early psychiatrists adhered to a system of humane vigilance aimed at eliminating extreme physical abuse and treating individuals with basic kindness and understanding (Deutsch, 1946; Grob, 1973; Tomes, 1984). Moreover, they ceased to see the causes of madness and mental illness as primarily grounded in the nature of the inmates. Rather, the social environment experienced by the insane individuals was recognized as causing the psychological disturbance and mental illness. Consequently, gentle treatment in a caring environment was considered to be important in order to cure and comfort the disturbed minds and bodies of the inmates (Scheerenberger, 1983, 45–47; Winzer, 1993, 62–64). For instance, Samuel Gridley Howe (1801–1876), head of the New England (or Perkins) Asylum for the Blind founded in 1832 and later also involved in the education of so-called feeble-minded children, stipulated the principle of "humanity" by developing a more caring approach. Thus, by 1858, Howe's basic claim was that "we must care for idiots, not because we expect them to be productive, but because we are obligated to serve the weak" (quoted in Trent, 1994, 30).

This chapter will consider the transformation from an attitude predominantly characterized by a violent and neglectful approach into one that emphasized care and the possible development of the psyche. This transformation also went hand in hand with the rise of professionalism. Central to the understanding of this process is a theoretical perspective that assumes a close connection between knowledge and power and aims at contextualizing agency, policies, and structures concerning disability by examining their historical origins (see, for example, Carter Park & Radford, 1999). This perspective is derived from the work of French philosopher and historian Michel Foucault, who also stimulated reflections on the domain of disability studies and its history (Armstrong, 2002; Tremain, 2005; Oliphant, 2006). Furthermore, this approach is influenced by the work of scholars stipulating social constructionism while attending to problems of contingency and subjectivity in historical research (Higgins, 1992; Trent, 1994; 1998; Hacking, 1999; Jackson, 2000; Rapley, 2004).

CARING POWER

In "Capitalism and the Origins of Humanitarian Sensibility," Thomas Haskell (1985, 360) defined the emergence of a new wave of humanitarianism from the second half of the eighteenth century as a "sustained, collective pattern of behavior in which substantial numbers of people regularly act[ed] to alleviate the suffering of strangers." What is distinctive about this definition is the fact that the new humanitarian sensibility instigated collective ways of behaving that actually took the form of (reform) movements. These movements were recognizing the sufferings of "strangers," not only acknowledging their status as human individuals but also stipulating their significance as others, despite their "otherness." After 1750, not only in North America, but in many Western Europe countries as well, reform movements sprang up aimed at the improvement of the well-being of groups of individuals, varying from poor people and slaves to prisoners to insane and disabled people. This wave of humanitarianism was much indebted to Enlightenment ideas about equality of men (and woman) and the human responsibility to take care of others—that is, of individuals outside the private circle of the home and the family.

Advocates of these new reform movements, for example, for abolishing slavery, were often motivated by religious convictions. Along with the late 1720s Great Awakening in North America, the emergence of a spirit of religious independence was kindled among certain religious groups in addition to a renewed individual piety (Trattner, 1989). The Quakers, for example, became famous for their religiously inspired activities of social reform (Jorns, 1931; Leach, 2006). Other religious groups within the tradition of evangelical Protestantism, however, also encompassed this new drive to go out into the world and to do works of social reform in order to accomplish the salvation of all human beings in the face of God. As we pointed out in *The Rise of Caring Power* (van Drenth & De Haan, 1999), the care for others developed within the new humanitarian movements was not without any power. Indeed, this care embodied a new type of power that we termed "caring power."

Power is often mainly regarded in a repressive dimension. As we learned from Michel Foucault's work on asylums and prisons, this one-dimensional perspective of power is not always the most fruitful for examining modern strategies toward the incarcerated and the insane (Foucault, 1963, 1975). Rather, as Foucault proposed, the view should be directed toward power as a productive force, considering its exercise "the way in which certain actions may structure the field of other possible actions." Power can thus be seen as a social force that "incites, … induces, … seduces …; in the extreme it constrains or forbids absolutely; it is nevertheless always a way of acting upon an acting subject or acting subjects by virtue of their acting or being capable of action" (Foucault, 1982, 220–221).

From this perspective, if we consider the new wave of humanitarianism that unfurled during the eighteenth century, the activities and discourses of reformers within humanitarianism closely correspond to what Foucault has identified as "pastoral power." According to Foucault (1982, 214), this type of power originated within medieval Christianity, assuring individuals' salvation in the next world. Primarily exercised by the (male) clergy, pastoral power did not just command but also operated through the willingness "to sacrifice for the life and salvation of the flock," in caring for each individual "during his [*sic!*] entire life." Essential to the exercise of pastoral power was the knowledge of what went on inside people's minds and souls, of their innermost secrets, in Foucault's words, of "the truth of the individual himself." Traditionally, confessions had formed the basic strategy of gaining knowledge about the individual soul and the evils of personal life.

The new type of pastoral power, which we identified as an early form of caring power, emerged toward the end of the eighteenth and in the nineteenth century. Gradually, this power became effective through the strategy of gaining insight into the "truth" about the lives and souls of individuals. Caring power, however, favored rational, scientific insights over religious confessions. The development of a new knowledge of man legitimized a process of objectivization of individuals, a process that had started with the interventions of secular shepherds exercising their worldly power based on kindness and commitment. Hence, a growing army of health workers, policemen, psychologists, and educators directed their interventions toward specific categories of individuals in order to improve their well-being in this world. Moreover, they claimed that this would improve society in general as well (van Drenth & De Haan, 1999, 14–16).

The transformation from pastoral into caring power was a gradual process that involved a double secularization. Firstly, the religious aim of salvation in heaven was replaced by the goal of improving the well-being of individuals in the here and now (and thereby the constitution of society as a whole). Secondly, instead of clergymen and nuns, it was lay persons and in particular secular professionals, both men and women, who became the prime agents of power. Through caring power, they engaged in the lives of "others," with the presumption that their care would serve the well-being of those who were taken care of. In contrast to repression, violence, and cruelty, which characterized repressive power regimes, the agents of caring power worked through persuasion and seduction, based on their knowledge of the "true" state of individuals' minds and bodies. In doing so, they actually evoked the development of a self in the individual taken into custody or care. The importance given to care and education in the rise of caring power underlined the "self" as a central aspect in every human life and accepted the "otherness" of specific children who were recognized as "different" and in need of assistance.

Individuals with physical and mental impairments also came under the scope of caring power. In contrast to being neglected, violated, or exposed to the public gaze (Bogdan, 1988; Garland Thomson, 1996), "abnormal" individuals were gradually perceived as "special" human beings, who, notwithstanding their impairments and mental problems, had their own individuality. Moreover, an increasing belief in their potential capacities enhanced the idea that these capacities also had to be developed through treatment and instruction. Consequently, professionally trained caretakers became responsible for the diagnosis, treatment, and possible cure of the disabled and the insane. This lead to the development of "true knowledge" about the state of mind of these "others" and of children who were regarded as different. They could no longer simply be ignored or just accepted because of their "otherness." The increase in "expertise" resulted in a fast process of professionalization that in turn stimulated new forms of treatment and care. Naturally, this process also influenced the identity of the caretaker. Through practicing caring power that, like other power relations, is always reciprocal, the identity of the caretaker came under scrutiny. The increasing professionalization meant that questions were raised about who was or was not suitable to do the work of caring and instruction. Various advocacy groups disputed issues about how care should be provided to disabled and insane individuals and by whom. The different answers, however, all concerned the identity of the caretaker as a proper professional. This encouraged a "cult of professionalism" that, according to Bledstein, "liberated the creativity of the self, thereby encouraging the ego to explore the world and discover knowledge" (1976, x–xi). Nevertheless, at the same time, "professional expertise compelled people to believe the voices of authority unquestioningly." The professional dimension defined "the unique quality of a subject" and "a total coherent system of necessary knowledge within a precise territory" (Bledstein, 1976, 88).

EDUCATIONAL ÉLAN AND SENSORY IMPAIRED CHILDREN

As in Europe, the first schools for the disabled in the United States focused particularly on the instruction and education of children and youngsters with visual, hearing, and speech impairments. In 1817, the advocacy of a wealthy father on behalf of his deaf daughter stimulated and enabled Thomas Hopkins Gallaudet (1787–1851) to open the Connecticut Asylum for the Education and Instruction of Deaf and Dumb Persons (from 1819 known as the American Asylum at Hartford). In the years to follow, various other institutions for the hearing and speech impaired were established, for example, the New York Institution for the Deaf and Dumb in 1818, founded by John Stafford, chaplain of the Human and Criminal Institutions of New York City. In 1829, John Fischer, who as a medical student in Paris, had become acquainted with the education of the blind and initiated the first school for the blind in the United States. The New England (or Perkins) Asylum for the Blind was founded in 1832, headed by Samuel Gridley Howe. A year earlier, John D. Rush had established the New York School for the Blind. Other schools for the blind also came into existence in the next decade (Winzer, 1993; Osgood, 2000).

These first institutions and schools were characterized by the strong religious and humanitarian motives of their founders. In the wake of the general quest for common schooling during the nineteenth century led by reformers such as Horace Mann (1796–1859), appeals for education of children with impairments also increased. According to Winzer (1993, 92), Mann added his "evangelical models" to the European imperatives of education that were, however, increasingly based on salvation as "a matter of happiness in this world as much as of peace in the next." A second characteristic of the early initiatives within the field of special education is the involvement of family and of a number of specific families that advocated, established, and managed schools and asylums. Mostly in cooperation with parents of disabled children, the founders of institutions, both educators and physicians, and their family members determined the early developments within the field (Winzer, 1993, 123; Safford & Safford, 1996). For several decades, various members of the Gallaudet family, for instance, were engaged in activities to accommodate and instruct the deaf. Thomas Gallaudet married one of his deaf pupils and together they had eight children of whom two sons also became involved in deaf education. Both these characteristics were in keeping with the increasingly accepted idea that institutions for the disabled had to resemble a family, even if they were merely custodial, which was ultimately still considered to be the ideal situation for raising and morally educating dependent individuals. As Safford and Safford noted: "Building of character and inculcation of piety had lost none of their importance, but Gallaudet believed these goals better accomplished through gentle nurture than preachment and punishment" (1996, 63).

In Europe, attention to individual children with a visual, speech, or hearing impairment had a long tradition. Schools for these children, however, only appeared in the second half of the eighteenth century. As D.G. Pritchard noted in his *Education and the Handicapped 1760–1960* (1963, 25): "The strongest impetus to the provision of education sprang, however, from religious convictions," while "the salvation of the individual" was the "great concern." In combination with a developing "humanitarianism," institutions for the deaf, the deaf-mute, and the blind came into existence in many countries in Europe. Inspired by the work of French and German predecessors such as Charles Michel de L'Epée (1712–1789), Valentin Haüy (1745–1822), and Samuel Heinicke (1727–1790), institutions aimed at the education of the deaf and the blind originated in Belgium and the Netherlands. The first institutions for the blind were initiated in Amsterdam in 1808 and in Brussels in 1834, whereas children and youngsters with hearing or speech impairments received their first educational institutes in Groningen (the Netherlands), in 1790; and in Luik, in 1819, and in Gent, in 1820 (both in Belgium). In the Dutch context, Protestants were in charge of the first institutions; while in Belgium, Catholic religious orders established the first schools for children with these types of impairment (Taylor & Taylor, 1960; Desmet, 1969).

In the Netherlands, Henri Daniel Guyot (1753–1828), a minister of the Walloon Protestant Church, initiated the first institution for children with hearing impairments in Groningen in 1790 (Rietveld-Van Wingerden, 2003). Inspired by the work of L'Epée in Paris, Guyot started to educate these children in order to raise them as good citizens. The institution was expanded with boarding facilities in 1819 for boys and in 1822 for girls. The explicit aim of providing the children with safe and happy surroundings was the starting point for the development of a deaf culture in which the hearing-impaired child "loses his depressions, dullness, sadness and shyness, and will be glad and cheerful among his companions, playing and conversing with them" (quoted in Rietveld-Van Wingerden, 2003, 406). Next to learning sign language and speech training, the Reverend Guyot, assisted by his sons Charles and Rembt Tobie Guyot, taught his pupils arithmetic, geography, and history, as well as practical skills such as shoemaking, tailoring, printing, and carpentry for boys and household work for girls, in particular, the skills needed to work as a servant. Last but not least, religion was present as a domain of education. "Education will help them to understand their duties, to elevate their soul above the animal and to become conscious of the ultimate goal of human existence: the knowledge of the Supreme Being and the honouring of God as a creator and benefactor" (quoted in Rietveld-Van Wingerden, 2003, 407–408). The foundation of a Catholic Institution for children with hearing impairments in 1840 in Sint-Michiels-Gestel and a school for these children in 1853 in Rotterdam stirred up a controversy concerning the oral or the manual method used in language education. The orientation toward oralism in the Rotterdam school, managed by the Jewish teacher David Hirsch (1813–1895), was connected to the idea that deaf children would profit from living at home or with a foster family, as this would guarantee a certain degree of social integration. New institutions, for instance those founded in Voorburg, near The Hague, in 1892, and in Amsterdam, in 1910, used the oral method as well.

The educational élan toward children with sensory handicaps that developed during the nineteenth century in Belgium and the Netherlands was driven not only by the conviction that an impairment could be overcome through proper education. A whole process of individual and psychological development was also at stake as a pedagogical endeavor, and not only in terms of religious goals. Based on research into the case of the Belgian deaf-blind girl Anne Timmerman (1816–1859), Hellinckx and Verstraete (2004) have cast light on how early scientific interest in the development of sensory impaired children such as Anne stimulated pedagogical experiments. The Catholic clergymen Charles-Louis Carton (1802–1863) took Anne into care in his institute for the deaf-blind at Brugge in 1837, the same year that Samuel Gridley Howe accommodated Laura Bridgman (1829–1889), the famous deaf-blind girl, in his Perkins Institution. The daily care for both girls was actually in the hands of women (van Drenth, 2003). In the Belgium case, the nuns of the Congregation of the Sisters of the Childhood of Maria at Spermalie, an order established by Carton in order to support him in his pedagogical tasks, took care of Anne. In cooperation with the nuns, whose "female instinct" to penetrate the soul of children was praised by Carton, an integral pedagogical approach was developed for the girl, including clinical attention for her behavioral problems and eating disorder. When Howe visited Brugge in 1843, he compared the developments of Anne with those of his own pupil Laura and was not impressed by the results. He assumed this may have been caused by the fact that Anne's treatment had started rather late, at the age of 21 (Hellinckx & Verstraete, 2004, 50). Laura's treatment had begun at the age of five, when she was still very sensitive to treatment and guidance in developing her senses and her cognitive and emotional capacities (Freeberg, 2001). According to Hellinckx and Verstraete (2004), the fact that Howe's accounts of the individual and psychological development of his pupil were far more detailed than those of Carton is why the case of Laura Bridgman achieved such fame, which was also later true for the case of Helen Keller (Lash, 1997). In comparison, the case of Anne Timmerman and her treatment by Carton was relatively unknown.

BETWEEN CURE AND CARE: THE "FEEBLE" MIND

Before 1820, people with mental retardation and physical impairments, youngsters as well as adults, mostly lived among the general population (Hordern & Smith, 1998). The then-existing orphanage asylums were aimed at accommodating children whose parents had died or who had abandoned them. These institutions rarely admitted physically and mentally disabled children as their inmates (Trattner, 1989; Trent, 1994). As long as they were not abandoned by their family—which might put them in almshouses or punish them for crimes and deviance, so that they ended up in prisons and jails—asylums did not take care of them, even though they were more or less dependent (Rothman, 1990). Only the most dependent—and amongst them only those who were considered "worthy" of receiving any support or care—were provided with any real assistance, either in their own homes or in the homes of caregivers (Trent, 1994, 10).

By the mid-nineteenth century in the United States, care for the disabled, the mentally ill or retarded, and the physically impaired was most frequently provided for members of well-to-do families, who could afford to send their loved ones to private residential schools and institutions. Consequently, the regime of caring power had to include instruction and education in addition to basic care in terms of food, clothing, hygiene, and some emotional attention. In these times of social expansion and immigration, however, productivity became an increasingly important factor that corresponded with practicing caring power as the new strategy for governing dependent individuals. The conditions in the 1840s and 1850s created social expectations as well as social problems, and both influenced the development of special education in its mission to create productive and useful individuals (Winzer, 1993; Trent, 1994). Moreover, parents and educators developed a strong belief in the capacities of at least some of the disabled individuals who, until then, had mostly been considered to be incapable of learning anything of importance. Finally, influences from Europe opened the door for education as an important aspect in the treatment of disabled individuals as well as the so-called feebleminded.

The best example of these developments is the work of Edouard Séguin (1812–1880), who, born and educated in France, immigrated to the United States in 1850. Séguin was firmly convinced that a lack of "will," rather than human nature, caused problems in the mind, and consequently also in the physical and mental abilities of disabled individuals (1846; 1866). As far as feeblemirded or "idiot" individuals were concerned, an undeveloped will and the dormancy of senses provided the main explanation for their instinctual and often awkward behavior. The way to instigate change and to break through the atrophy of the senses was to stimulate the will of the person by forcing the individual to use his or her senses and muscles again, and to engage in activities of the body and the mind. To overcome the principal impediment to learning, the "negative will," exercising had to stimulate and excite the disabled, always drawing on their desire for enjoyment and the longing to be in the company of others. Thus, Séguin's strategy consisted of a planned seduction of disabled individuals in order to stimulate them physically and mentally. His intention was to engage them in instruction through sensory experiences and human interaction, rather than to punish them through restricting their confrontational behavior (Scheerenberger, 1983; Winzer, 1993; Trent, 1994; Osgood, 2000).

The Massachusetts School for Idiotic and Feeble-Minded Children, the first American institution for developing children with mental retardation, opened in 1850, headed again by Samuel Gridley Howe. In the early 1850s, several others followed suit and by 1890 fourteen states had institutions for these children (Winzer, 1993; Osgood, 2000). From the 1850s onward, the superintendents started to call pupils "inmates" and progressively described their problems in terms of medical categories rather than in terms of educational goals. Furthermore, questions concerning the curability and chronicity of the symptoms of the disabled swiftly gained importance, which was also in order to legitimize the political pressure on the state to invest money in the development of large institutions (Ferguson, 1994). As Trent (1994, 36) has pointed out, "the medicalizing of idiocy completed the constructing of a place for idiocy." Institutions for children diagnosed with having a "feeble mind" steadily demonstrated a greater resemblance to lunatic asylums than to common schools. Even before the foundation of the Association of Medical Officers of American Institutions for Idiotic and Feeble-Minded Persons in 1876, superintendents were expected to be physicians. They had often become managers of institutions with hospital facilities—managers who regarded their inmates as being in need of medical care rather than education. Ironically, Edouard Séguin, the French father of the education-inspired regime of care for disabled people, became the first president of the Association of Medical Officers, despite his profound skepticism about the medical and custodial approach that increasingly governed the care of the feebleminded (Trent 1994, 58).

In Europe, the educational élan aimed at children with a mental handicap had started earlier than it did in the United States, instigated by the work of people such as the French physician Jean-Marc-Gaspard Itard (1774–1838) and the German Karl Wilhem Saegert (1809–1879), director of the Royal Institute for the Deaf and Dumb in Berlin. Both were involved in diagnosing young children of whom the opinion was that they could not be educated—Itard with the famous "wild boy of Ayveron" and Saegert with a deaf-mute child. These children brought the men to the conviction that, instead of casting these problematic children off, they had to be raised and educated "normally." As Verstraete (2005) pointed out, in nineteenth-century Europe, the rise of the educational élan was, paradoxically enough, enhanced by physicians who favored the theory of phrenology, which focused on the brain rather than on the soul or the psyche. In particular, the second generation of phrenologists, such as Jacques Etienne Belhomme (1800–1880), Félix Voisin (1794–1872), and Louis Delasiauve (1804–1893), built a bridge between care and cure that was synthesized in the idea of "phrenological educability." According to Verstraete (2005, 134), by the strategies of "classification, observation and registration through the construction of scientifically structured norms," a form of Foucauldian "biopower," these phrenologists bridged the gap between (in)curability and educability. They thus enhanced the conceptions of the feeble mind by emphasizing notions of "individuality," "normalcy," and "efficiency" and stimulated the expansion of special education.

In the Netherlands, the first autonomous institution for children with mental problems came into being in the1850s (Weijers, 2000). In Belgium, this happened much later, in the 1880s. In contrast to the Netherlands, where the Protestants were the pioneers, in Belgium, it was Catholics who initiated the first institution for children with mental problems. In 1886, an asylum for girls was opened in Lokeren (Belgium). Here, nuns of the Order of the Sisters of the Love of Jesus and Maria were in charge. As early as 1855 in the Netherlands, the Dutch reverend Cornelis Elisa van Koetsveld established the first autonomous institution. In 1857, this "School for Idiots" became an institution with boarding facilities for children who could not live at home. Although the pastoral regime of educating children with an explicit religious goal was still important, van Koetsveld's general aim was "to physically, cognitively and morally educate those children who, because of their deficient or retarded mental capacities, were unfit for normal, even lower, education in school" (quoted in van Drenth, 2005b, 161). Van Koetsveld bridged the gap between cure and care by following the work of Saegert and Séguin and developing his own approach of "cure by education." During the second half of the nineteenth century, he and his increasingly female staff developed a gendered professionalism based on the first scientific theories on children with a so-called feeble mind. This early professionalism, however, did not continue after the turn of the century. As both Dekker (1996) and Weijers and Tonkens (1999) have shown, an emphasis on religious and philanthropic approaches, on the one hand, and ideas of (medical) incurability, on the other, curbed the optimism of the possibilities of educating children with a mental handicap, in particular a more severe one. Nevertheless, in Belgium, a more optimistic view on the possibilities to educate mentally retarded children remained in tact (De Wilde, 1992).

After the turn of the century, the Belgian scientist Ovide Decroly (1871–1932), specialized in neurology and psychiatry, researched into the domain of child studies and new education. Thus, he also stimulated professionalism within the institutions and organizations for special education where he practiced his "medico-pedagogical approach" (Van Gorp, Depaepe, & Simon, 2004; Van Gorp, 2005). In the Netherlands, the establishment of the first so-called Paedological Institutes in the 1930s gave important impetus for further scientific research into the subject of children with a "feeble mind." Here, child studies and new education likewise formed the main sources of inspiration. Systematic reflection on "normalcy" and "otherness" consequently enhanced the process of professionalization in the treatment of children with mental problems, especially in the domain of the training requirements for teachers working in special education.

POWER AND EXPERTISE

Central to my understanding of the nineteenth-century history of special education and care for disabled individuals is the process of professionalization. Like other agents in the embryonic state of their profession, educators and physicians involved in establishing schools and institutions for special education began to emphasize the importance of a specific body of knowledge. This knowledge was, on the one hand, based on their experiences with new treatments of individuals with mental and physical impairments. On the other hand, insights into these treatments were due to contact with professionals abroad, in which French, English, and German philosophers, educators, and reformers were leading the field. Early medical insights into the functioning of the human mind and the nature of mental illness had instigated a process of categorization of individuals along the lines of physiological and mental characteristics. In the interaction between "true" knowledge and practice, new professionals, physicians, as well as educators invented new strategies to cure, train, instruct, and educate gradually more specifically defined groups of disabled individuals.

Thus, theory and practice contributed to the emergence of a professional identity amongst physicians and teachers involved in the educational activities within asylums and institutions and in schools for disabled individuals. The development of a specific body of knowledge, valued as expertise, stimulated the process of differentiating amongst individuals in need of care and treatment. New possibilities were opened to further diagnose and categorize children and adults with specific impairments and mental problems, thereby underscoring the power of the professionals to intervene in the lives of these individuals. Moreover, the process of professionalization was advanced when various professional organizations began to emerge within the field during the second half of the nineteenth century.

This ongoing process of constructing and reconstructing an adequate professional identity was neither one-dimensional nor uncontested. The history of special education in nineteenth-century Europe and the United Stated is undoubtedly a history showing an increasingly more caring attitude toward special individuals. This is not to say that the rise of caring power had no custodial or paternalistic consequences for impaired and disabled adults and children, who became institutionalized and objectified through the interventions of the agents of caring power. The field of special education is full of histories that define and classify individuals according to specific concepts and along specific lines. These not only mark the individual development of those who are subjected to these procedures but also open up the possibilities for them to become agents within their own realities. "Instead of accepting these professionally ascribed identities as 'truth,'" Rapley noted in *The Social Construction of Intellectual Disability* (2004, 20), "we wish to discover where and when, how and why, identities such as these are relevant to persons themselves, then we must look at the doing of interactional business, and be prepared to encounter both collaborative identity production and also struggles, in interaction, over the relevance—or otherwise—of the candidate identities that professionals proffer to their interlocutors." Caring power was not and is not always "productive" in the sense that it can resolve every problem that disabled people face in everyday life. It is "productive," however, in the sense that it shows both experts and those subjected to their care and cure to be inevitably part of their time and culture and of the specific regimes of knowledge. Examining the productive aspect of power may, as Foucault stated, enable the historian as an intellectual to "change something in the mind of people" (in Martin, 1988, 10). Thus, the path may be opened "to live everyday life as an everyday thing, with and in the presence of special, specific human beings who are our disabled equals" (Stiker, 1999, 11).

Providing an analysis of what happened to the "self" of individuals seduced or forced by the power of care is beyond the scope of this chapter. The construction of identity and experiences of the disabled could and should, however, be an important theme on the agenda for future research. Fears and seemingly self-evident convictions about "normal man" have to be faced and transformed—for example, by research conducted at the intersection of gender and disability—and related to the historical context of social class and ethnicity. This is also the objective of the so-called new disability history (Longmore & Unmansky, 2001), which may, as Kudlick (2003) formulated, show us "why we need another 'other.'"

NOTE

I thank my Belgium colleague Pieter Verstraete for his support and comments. The basic research for this chapter was done at the Institute for Research on Women at Rutgers University (State University of New Jersey, United States) and supported by a grant of the Netherlands Organisation for Scientific Research (NWO).

REFERENCES

Armstrong, F. (2002). The Historical Development of Special Education: Humanitarian Rationality or "Wild Profusion of Entangled Events"? *History of Education, 31,* 437–456.

Bledstein, B. J. (1976). *The Culture of Professionalism. The Middle Class and the Development of Higher Education in America* (New York: Norton & Company).

Bogdan, R. (1988). *Freak Show: Presenting Human Oddities for Amusement and Profit* (Chicago: Chicago University Press).

Carter Park, Deborah, and Radford, John (1999). Rhetoric and Place in the "Mental Deficiency" Asylum, pp. 70–97. In R. Butler and H. Parr (Eds.). *Mind and Body Spaces. Geographies of Illness, Impairment and Disability* (London and New York: Routledge).

Dekker, J.H. (1996). An Educational Regime: Medical Doctors, Schoolmasters, Jurists and the Education of Retarded and Deprived Children in the Netherlands around 1990. *History of Education, 25,* 255–268.

Desmet, E. (1969). *De pedagogische bekommernis voor de doven in België in de periode 1820–1880* (Leuven: KU Leuven).

Deutsch, A. (1946, first ed. 1937). *The Mentally Ill in America. A History of Their Care and Treatment from the Colonial Times,* third ed. (New York: Columbia University Press).

De Wilde, P. (1992). Eugenetisch pessimisme en pedagogisch optimisme bij J. Demoor. Case-study naar het geneeskundig denken over abnormaliteit eind negentiende—begin twintigste eeuw. *Pedagogisch Tijdschrift, 17,* 349–369.

Ferguson, P.M. (1994). *Abandoned to Their Fate. Social Policy and Practice toward Severely Retarded People in America, 1820–1920* (Philadelphia: Temple University Press).

Foucault, M. (1963). *Naissance de la clinique. Une archéologie du regard médicale* (Paris: Presses Universitaires de France).

———. (1975). *Surveillir et punir. Naissance de la prison* (Paris: Gallimard).
———. (1982). Afterword: The Subject and Power. In Hubert L. Dreyfus and Paul Rabinow, *Michel Foucault. Beyond Structuralism and Hermeneutics. With an Afterword by Michel Foucault* (Chicago: University of Chicago), pp. 208–226.
———. (1994). Dits et écrits 1954–1988. II 1970–1975 (Paris: Gallimard).
Freeberg, E. (2001). *The Education of Laura Bridgman. First Deaf and Blind Person to Learn Language* (Cambridge, MA: Harvard University Press).
Garland Thomson, R. (Ed.) (1996). *Freakery. Cultural Spectacles of the Extraordinary Body* (New York: New York University Press).
Grob, G.N. (1973). *Mental Institutions in America. Social Policy to 1875* (New York: The Free Press).
Hacking, I. (1999). *The Social Construction of What?* (Cambridge, MA /London: Harvard University Press).
Haskell, T.L. (1985). Capitalism and the Origins of the Humanitarian Sensibility. *American Historical Review*, 90, 339–361 and 547–566.
Hellinckx, W., and Verstraete, P. (2004). Een vergeten casus uit de geschiedenis van de doofblinden: de (ortho)pedagogische aanpak van Anne Timmerman (1816–1859) door Charles-Louis Carton (1802–1863), pp. 36–58. In Rietveld-Van Wingerden, M., D'hoker, M., van Drenth, A., Groenendijk, L., and Bakker, N. (Eds.). *Zorgenkinderen in beeld. Facetten van de orthopedagogische praktijk in Nederland en België in de negentiende en twintigste eeuw* (Assen: Van Gorcum).
Higgins, P.C. (1992). *Making Disability. Exploring the Social Formation of Human Variation* (Springfield/Illinois: Charles C. Thomas Publisher).
Hordern, P., and Smith, R. (Eds.) (1998). *Locus of Care: Families, Communities, Institution and the Provision of Welfare since Antiquity* (London: Routledge).
Jackson, M. (2000). *The Borderline of Imbecility. Medicine, Society and the Fabrication of the Feeble Mind in Late Victorian England* (Manchester & New York: Manchester University Press).
Jorns, A. (1931). *The Quakers as Pioneers in Social Work* (New York: The Macmillan Company).
Kudlick, C.J. (2003). Review Essay. Disability History: Why We Need Another "Other." *American Historical Review*, 108, 763–793.
Lash, J.P. (1997). *Helen and Teacher. The Story of Helen Keller and Anne Sullivan Macy* (Reading MA: Addison-Wesley Publishing Company).
Leach, C. (2006). Religion and Rationality: Quaker Women and Science Education. *History of Education*, 35, 69–90.
Lightner, D.L. (1999). *Asylum, Prison, and Poorhouse. The Writings and Reform Work of Dorothea Dix in Illinois* (Carbondale: Southern Illinois University Press).
Longmore, P.K., and Umansky, L. (2001). *The New Disability History: American Perspectives* (New York/London: New York University Press).
Martin, R. (1988), Truth, Power, Self: An Interview with Michel Foucault, October 25, 1985. In L.H. Martin, H. Gutman, and P.H. Hutton (Eds.). *Technologies of the Self: A Seminar with Michel Foucault* (London: Tavistock, 1988).
Oliphant, J. (2006). Empowerment and Debilitation in the Educational Experience of the Blind in Nineteenth-Century England and Scotland. *History of Education*, 35, 47–68.
Osgood, R.L. (2000). *For "Children Who Vary from the Normal Type." Special Education in Boston, 1838–1930* (Washington D.C.: Gallaudet University Press).
Pritchard, D.G. (1963). *Education and the Handicapped 1760–1960* (London: Routledge & Kegan Paul).

Rapley, M. (2004). *The Social Construction of Intellectual Disability* (Cambridge, UK: Cambridge University Press).
Rietveld-Van Wingerden, M. (2003). Educating the Deaf in The Netherlands: A Methodological Controversy in Historical Perspective. *History of Education*, 32, 401–416.
Rose, N. (1990). *Governing the Soul. The Shaping of the Private Self* (London/New York: Routledge).
Safford, P.L., and Safford, E.J. (1996). *A History of Childhood and Disability* (New York & London: Teachers College Columbia University).
Scheerenberger, R.C. (1983). *A History of Mental Retardation* (Baltimore: Paul H. Brookes Publishing Co.).
Séguin, E. (1846). *Traitement Moral. Hygiène et education des idiots et des autres enfants arriérés ou retardés dans leur développement, agrités de moevement involuntaires, débiles, muets non-sourd, bègues, etc.* (Paris: Ballllière).
———. (1971, first edition 1866). *Idiocy and Its Treatment by the Physiological Method* (New York: Kelley).
Stiker, H-J. (1999). *A History of Disability,* translated by W. Sayers (first published 1982 as *Corps infirmes et sociétés*). Ann Arbor: University of Michigan.
Taylor, W.W., and Wagner-Taylor (1960). *Special Education of Physically Handicapped Children in Western Europe* (New York: International Society for the Welfare of Cripples).
Tomes, N. (1984). *A Generous Confidence. Thomas Story Kirkbide and the Art of Asylum-keeping, 1840–1883* (Cambridge etc: Cambridge University Press).
Trattner, W. I. (1989, first ed. 1974). *From the Poor Law to Welfare State. A History of Social Welfare in America,* fourth ed. (New York & London: The Free Press).
Tremain, S. (2005). *Foucault and the Government of Disability* (Ann Arbor: University of Michigan Press).
Trent, J.W. (1994). *Inventing the Feeble Mind. A History of Mental Retardation in the United States* (Berkeley etc: University of California Press).
———. (1998). Defectives at the World's Fair. Constructing Disability in 1904. *Remedial and Special Education, 19,* 201–211.
van Drenth, A. (2003). "Tender Sympathy and Scrupulous Fidelity": Gender and Professionalism in the History of Deaf Education in the United States. *International Journal of Disability, Development and Education, 50,* 367–383.
———. (2005a). Doctors, Philanthropists and Teachers as "True" Ventriloquists? Introduction to a Special Issue on the History of Special Education. *History of Education, 34,* 107–117.
———. (2005b). Van Koetsveld and his "School for Idiots" in The Hague (1855–1920). Gender and the History of Special Education in the Netherlands. *History of Education, 34,* 151–169.
van Drenth, A., and De Haan, F. (1999). *The Rise of Caring Power. Elizabeth Fry and Josephine Butler in Britain and the Netherlands* (Amsterdam: Amsterdam University Press).
Van Gorp, A. (2005). From Special Education to New Education: The Biological, Psychological, and Sociological Foundations of Ovide Decroly's Educational Work (1871–1932). *History of Education, 34,* 135–149.
Van Gorp, A., Depaepe, M., and Simon, F. (2004). Backing the Actor as Agent in Discipline Formation: An Example of the "Secondary Disciplinarisation" of the Educational Sciences, Based on the Networks of Ovide Decroly (1901–1931). *Paedagogica Historica, 40,* 591–616.
Verstraete, P. (2005). The Taming of Disability: Phrenology and Bio-power on the Road to the Destruction of Otherness in France (1800–60). *History of Education, 34,* 119–134.
Weijers, I. (2000). Educational Initiatives in Mental Retardation in Nineteenth-Century Holland, *History of Education Quarterly, 40,* 460–476.

Weijers, I., and Tonkens, E. (1999). Christianisation of the Soul. Religious Traditions in the Care of People with Learning Disabilities in the Netherlands in the Nineteenth Century. *Social History of Medicine, 12,* 351–369.

Winzer, M. (1993). *The History of Special Education. From Isolation to Integration* (Washington D.C.: Gallaudet University Press).

CHAPTER TWENTY-SIX

Not So Strange Bedfellows: The Promise OF Disability Studies AND Critical Race Theory

DAVID J. CONNOR

INTRODUCTION

In this chapter I call attention to what I see as a great potential for Disability Studies (DS) and Critical Race Theory (CRT) to be utilized simultaneously in researching how the concepts of disability and race operate in American society, offering more nuanced understandings of each phenomenon. I begin by briefly outlining the tenets of DS and CRT, allowing the similarities to become evident. This is followed by an extensive look at the broad concepts of disability and race, illuminating similarities and differences. By revealing resonances and parallelisms of being "othered" as contrasted against able-bodied Whites, similarities experienced by people with disabilities and people of color can be highlighted (However, while doing this, I also caution against essentializing experience or assuming interchangeability between these two very distinct markers of identity). Once multiple connections have been made, the value of using both disciplines together can be evidenced. For example, one such possibility is the contemplation of the overrepresentation of students of color in segregated special education classes. I argue that DS and CRT can serve to educate and strengthen each other through addressing ableist and racist assumptions within each discipline, often difficult to see or act upon. Finally, possibilities for the simultaneous use of both disciplines are suggested.

BRIEF BACKGROUND AND CHARACTERISTICS OF DISABILITY STUDIES

Disability Studies have emerged within many fields of inquiry over the past thirty years. Linton (1998) describes DS as "…an organized critique on the constricted, inadequate, and inaccurate conceptualizations of disability that have dominated academic inquiry. Above all, the critique includes a challenge to the notion that disability is primarily a medical category" (p. 2). Indeed, the pervasive medicalization of disability helps account for the nondisabled's obsession with prevention and cure that, according to Wendell (2001), focuses "…public attention on the medical model, which leads us to ignore the social conditions that are causing or increasing disability among people with impairments" (p. 31). In contrast, instead of perceiving disabilities primarily as medicalized deficits (physical, sensory, emotional, or intellectual), scholars within the field of DS view them as natural human differences categorized as "disabilities" by a society reticent to reorganize through the removal of barriers and restrictions (Fleischer & Zames, 2001; Russell, 1998). The focus with DS, therefore, shifts "problematic" disabled bodies onto social structures and cultural practices. As reframed by Oliver, the issue becomes: "… disability is something wrong with society" (1996, p. 129).

Proponents of the social model, ideologically located in a framework of social change akin to the Civil Rights movement pioneered by African Americans in the 1950s, conceptualize disability in a radically different manner than that of the dominant medical paradigm. As Longmore (2003) points out, "… social scientists studying the disability experience have increasingly turned to a minority group model, defining 'disability' not as fated and 'inevitable' condition, but as a socially constructed identity and role triggered by a stigmatized biological trait" (p. 37). Thus, DS seeks to challenge widely held beliefs that manifest themselves in restrictive social structures, networks, and institutions.

One of the core issues in DS is the celebration of disability beyond the framework of oppression, emphasizing the *value* of people with disabilities. Living with embodied differences gives rise to different ways of knowing and understanding particularized through the experience of disability (Handler, 1999; Kleege, 1999; Mairs, 1996; Garland-Thomson, 2001). Another core issue in DS is the reclamation of previously subjugated knowledge(s), accomplished by foregrounding the voices of people with disabilities in contemporary society, and tracing the experiences of people with disabilities throughout history. Yet another core issue in

DS is its unabashed challenge to traditional conceptualizations of "normal" and "deviations from the norm" through to highlighting social conventions that *enable* some people while disabling others. In redefining disability through the active dismantling of normalcy, scholars in DS challenge the presumed hegemony of the non-disabled; the labelers are questioned by those they have labeled.

One important issue in DS is that disability is often portrayed in terms of *advantages*, reinforced by people who state they do not want to change or be "cured" as their disability is integral to who they are and how they have come to understand themselves and the world (Mooney & Cole, 2000; O'Connor, 2001; Piziali, 2001). Another important aspect of DS is that many people with disabilities—be they scholars, research participants, or both—call upon their own personal understandings and speak from a position that allows them to be unequivocally heard. This inversion of power allows people with disabilities a central position from which to addressing self-selected issues, interests, and concerns "… as defined by disabled people and as they relate to social exclusion and oppression" (Gabel, 2005, p. 17).

BRIEF BACKGROUND AND CHARACTERISTICS OF CRITICAL RACE THEORY

Critical Race Theory originated within, and focused on, the black experience in America, and subsequently grew to incorporate critical perspectives of Latinos (Delgado & Stefanicic, 2001; Solorzano & Yosso, 2001), Asian Americans (Chae, 2005; Teranishi, 2002), Native Americans (Snipp, 1998) and European Americans (Marx, 2004; Marx & Pennington, 2003). Described as "interdisciplinary and eclectic" by Tate (1997), the roots of CRT lie in "the development of African-American thought in the post-civil rights era: the 1970s to the present" (p. 206). Six major tenets of CRT were developed by Matsuda et al. (1993), and are outlined as follows: CRT (1) recognizes that racism is endemic to American life; (2) expresses skepticism toward dominant legal claims of neutrality, objectivity, color blindness,[1] and meritocracy; (3) challenges ahistoricism and insists on a contextual/historical analysis of the law … [and a presumption that] racism has contributed to all contemporary manifestations of groups advantage and disadvantage along racial lines …; (4) insists on the recognition of the experiential knowledge of people of color and our communities of origin in analyzing law and society; (5) is interdisciplinary; and (6) works toward the end of eliminating racial oppression as part of the broader goal of ending all forms of oppression.

Vital to CRT is "the importance of examining the social construction of race through the law" (Tate, 1997, p. 218). Because legal discourse is viewed as the foundation of CRT, much of the scholarship has attempted to "analyze legal ideology and discourse as a mechanism that functions to re-create and legitimate social structures in the United States" (p. 206). In contrast to the formal, sanctified, and officially legitimated hegemony of legal discourses, CRT foregrounds narratives, stories, and perspectives *from* people of color. Paraphrasing Delgado's (1990) notion of validating situated knowledge, Tate explains, "[p]eople of color in our society speak from experience framed by racism. This framework gives their stories a common structure warranting the term voice ... social reality is constructed by the creation and exchange of stories about individual situations" (p. 210).

Delgado (1989) posits four reasons for the cultivation of legal analysis and scholarship that incorporate the experiences of people of color: (1) reality is socially constructed; (2) stories are a powerful means for destroying and changing mind sets; (3) stories have a community-building function; and (4) stories provide members of out-groups mental self-preservation. Delgado's work, often positioned within a specific extension of CRT developed by Latino(a)s and widely known as LatCrit studies. According to Delgado-Bernal (2002), LatCrit "elucidates Latinas/Latinos' multidimensional identities and can address the intersectionality of racism, sexism, classism, and other forms of oppression" (p. 108). Delgado-Bernal elaborates upon this important point by calling attention to the "intersectionality of subordination," asserting "…one's identity is not based on the social construction of race but rather is multidimensional and intersects with various experiences" (p. 118). Solorzano and Yosso (2002) agree, reemphasizing the need to trouble the notion of singular categories such as race *or* class *or* gender, explaining:

> We argue that it is crucial to focus on the intersections of oppression because storytelling is racialized, gendered, and classed and these stories affect racialized, gendered, and classed communities. This means that when examining the experiences of students of color, a class-based theory or even a class-gendered theory is insufficient. Methodologies that dismiss or decenter racism and its intersections with other forms of subordination omit and distort the experiences of those whose lives are daily affected by racism. (p. 27)

In brief, scholars within CRT raise the important issue of intersectionality, and how each marker of identity impacts upon, and shapes, the experience of the others.

OVERLAPPING LENSES

DS and CRT appear to have many commonalities. As disciplines, they have evolved within the same time period, and reflect a level of compatibility. Scholars of CRT, like those in DS, desire "both academic and social activist goals" (Tate, 1997, p. 198). Scholars in CRT seek to eliminate racial oppression "as part of the larger goal of eradicating all forms of oppression," similar to the emancipatory stance of scholars within DS. Tate describes CRT as "interdisciplinary and eclectic by nature," (1997, p. 233), and the same can be said for DS (Corker & Shakespeare, 2002; Linton, 1998). These disciplines share recognition of, but not subscription to, the legal construction of race or disability. In addition, they both seek to challenge existing practices in schools and societies that marginalize individuals based on a socially-constructed "characteristic;" both privilege voices of marginalized groups to be heard from historically subjugated positions; and, both challenge dominant practices—upheld by traditional paradigms—that have positioned them as inferior.

Conversely, there exist potential tensions between these lenses. For example, DS has been criticized for not being racially and ethnically diverse (Bell, 2006). In a similar manner CRT scholars do not mention disability issues along with gender and class, when talking of eradicating oppressions (Solorzano & Yosso, 2002). Furthermore, while the high incidence of students of color special education has been acknowledged over time by scholars in CRT (Ladson-Billings & Henry, 1990) the concept of disability per se is not sufficiently problematized. Indeed it could be argued that while DS is attempting to cultivate sensitivity to the politics of race, CRT does not appear to have opened up to the politics of disability. In addition, both disciplines have different locations (that not necessarily compatible) as their starting points. DS is primarily positioned within a sociocultural framework, whereas CRT is largely situated within legal frameworks. However, DS does include legal studies and legal scholars (Krieger, 2003), and CRT often extends into the sociocultural domain (Delgado-Gaitan, 1994). All in all, these tensions may actually serve to interanimate each discipline, for example, the racism within DS and the ableism within CRT require each discipline to face and reflect upon complicity in oppression while negotiating being oppressed, and foregrounds the need to consider intersectional understandings of knowledge, such as individuals who are people of color and have a disability. How might their knowledge inform both disciplines?

RACING DISABILITY, DISABLING RACE

Because such an overlap between DS and CRT exists, I thought it would be interesting to stop and reflect upon why—as disciplines—they appear somewhat compatible. As previously stated, my intention is not to draw simple analogies between race and disability, thereby erroneously essentializing such experiences.

My purpose, rather, is to illuminate points of connection that resonate with one another. In doings so, I believe that the premise of DS and the tenets of CRT are revealed to be built upon, in part, philosophical, theoretical, social, and political foundations: philosophical in their premise of believing in equality; theoretical in foregrounding the imperative of equality; social in their demands for equal access to resources, education, employment; and political in their understanding of how power operates to inhibit or nurture equality. On the other hand, the two disciplines are noticeably divided in the foundation of experience, both groups having undergone different histories in American life.

As such, it can be argued that while their platforms are constituted from similar ideological foundations, distinct experiences of oppression based on ability or race cannot be readily interchanged, and differences may even be exacerbated through non-recognition of privilege held by each group (Whiteness by most people with disabilities, and able-bodiedness by most people of color), unless—as mentioned—individuals stand at these particular intersections of race and disability.

The tangled histories of disability and race in the public imagination

The relationship between race and disability in the United States is lengthy, complex, and beyond the scope of this chapter. However, in this section I will draw attention to several areas that illuminate connections and intersections between disability and race. To begin, since official history has primarily been documented and (re)presented from a Northwest European-American point of view, individuals outside of this category have long been cast as "other" than White. Nonwhites have traditionally been assigned an inferior status when compared to Whites (Hall, 2000; hooks, 1994; Loewen, 1996). All "other" peoples of African, Native-American, Arabic, Asian, Australian, and Latino ancestry—as well as Southern and Eastern Europeans—were deemed less cognitively developed than their "pure" white counterparts (Gould, 1996). It is interesting to note that what is now conceived as White is a relatively recent invention, a status originally denied people of Italian and Irish origin in particular (Haney-Lopez, 1996). Furthermore, Blacks in particular were assigned a position in the *lowest* strata of racial hierarchy within the scientific worlds of the 18th and 19th centuries, viewed by the establishment as a different species altogether. Thus, as Gould pointedly notes, "…the identification of blacks as a separate and unequal species had obvious appeal as an argument for slavery" (p. 101).

In *The White Man's Burden*, Kipling (1899/1998) describes the populace subject to colonialism as "…new-caught sullen people, half-devil and half-child," conjuring images of dour, fiendish pagans, limited by their perpetually infantilized state (p. 57). In contrast, the pious, mature, and fully responsible White colonizers bore the burden (viewed as a charitable obligation) to "take care" of nonwhites, saving them from their own ineptitude. Alleged intellectual and physical idiosyncrasies of the "Black race" were frequently discussed in mid 19th century medical journals, and used to justify slavery (Baynton, 2004). As Baynton points out, because of assumed inabilities, "…their inherent physical and mental weaknesses, [meant Blacks] were prone to become *disabled* [my italics] under conditions of freedom and equality" (p. 3). In addition, offspring resulting from "miscegenous" intercourse were viewed as "monstrous," "abnormal," "degenerate," often "lacking intellectual endowments," and usually subject to "inherent physical weaknesses." Interestingly, all of these words and phrases have been historically used to describe individuals with disabilities (p. 2).

The curiosity of (largely) European and European-American imagination toward the assumed peculiarities and idiosyncrasies of Africans and their descendents can be encapsulated in the story of Saartje Baartman, known as the "Hotentot Venus." Exhibited in England and France during the early 19th century, Baartman served as spectacle for public consumption, in many ways strikingly similar to the story of John Merrick, or "The Elephant Man." Like Merrick, Baartman was scrutinized and measured in every detail by scientists awed by embodied human difference, yet duly pathologized for falling outside existing classificatory systems (Hall, 2000). Over a century later, Ota Benga, a "pygmy" man from the Congo Free State was brought to the United States, billed as a cannibal, and confined to permanent exhibit in a monkey cage at the Bronx Zoo (Adams, 2001). A common historic connection, therefore, is that "animality" ascribed to "uncivilized" or non-white "foreign" people, has also traditionally been attributed to people with disabilities (Garland-Thomson, 1996).

Another cultural sphere in which race and disability often overlapped or merged was the popular world of sideshows. For a small price, the "deviant" body was paraded for the world to see. Coexisting with people of short stature, limbless performers, obese women, and conjoined twins, ethnographic "freaks" from far-flung "exotic" places like Melanesia, the Philippines, and Africa, created and reinforced notions of "others" (Trent, 1998). As public spectacles, such individuals served to allow the public to see what they themselves were *not*. Blurring the lines between disability, intelligence, animality, and race, the "freaks" simultaneously served to buttress widespread notions of racial and able-bodied superiority.

While the "low class" spectacle of the sideshow continued to influence the public imagination throughout the 1920s and 1930s, European and American universities became entranced by the possibilities of eugenics. The "scientific" work that purposefully and pervasively upheld the "natural" superiority of white cognitive ability over all other races stressed the widest gap among races could be found between White and Black intellectual capacity (Selden, 1999). During this era, Selden notes the forced sterilization procedures on American "imbeciles" resulted in hundreds of black women losing their ability to bear children, a significantly higher percentage than their similarly designated White counterparts (p. 44).

Finally, stereotyped "savage," "primitive," and "incomplete" portrayals of Blacks have pervaded all aspects of American culture throughout history, evidenced in the canon of mainstream literature and film. Traditional representations of uneducated slaves such as Tom in *Uncle Tom's Cabin* (Beecher-Stowe, 1853/1998) and Jim in *Huckleberry Finn* (Twain, 1885/2001) foreshadowed tragic Tom Robinson in *To Kill a Mockingbird* (Lee, 1960/1982) and even perhaps bumbling, murderous Bigger Thomas in *Native Son* (Wright, 1940/1992). When contemplated simultaneously, the characters coalesce into an image of a male with little intelligence, positioned (and contained) in a hostile world that views him as slow/stupid, inevitably a danger to himself and others. It can be argued that, even today, popular movies such as *The Green Mile* (Darabont, 1999) and *Radio* (Gains et al., 2003) subtly fuel stereotypic association between African Americans males and mental retardation. Unfortunately, not only is this connection alive and well in the public imagination, but it is manifest, as recent research indicates, in the world of special education in which in which African Americans are three times as likely to received the label of mental retardation and twice as likely to be labeled emotionally disturbed in comparison to Whites (Parrish, 2002).

Positioned as inferior

People with disabilities and people of color have historically been positioned not only as inferior to nondisabled, White counterparts, but they have also been portrayed as not quite "whole." The legal precedent that slaves were considered three-fifths human epitomizes what West (1993) refers to when commenting, "… white America has been historically weak-willed in ensuring racial justice and has continued to resist fully accepting the humanity of blacks" (p. 3). Throughout history, people with disabilities, too, have been perceived as having a *deficiency*, viewed as incomplete beings and duly stigmatized because of their corporeal differences (Stiker, 1999).

Stigmatization results from inequitable positions between the definer and the defined. Garland-Thomson (1997) observes that "…stigma is an interactive social process in which particular human traits are deemed not only different, but deviant," further noting, "It is a form of social comparison apparently found in all societies, though the specific characteristics singled out vary across cultures and history" (p. 31). People come to understand their positionality as their location within existing systems of power. Goffman describes how one "cripple" pointed out that "[people] expect you to know your place" (1963, p. 120), calling to mind cultural mores imposed upon Blacks by Whites such as physical separation of public facilities and infantilization of status through common use of "boy" and "girl" thereby effectively denying adulthood. As recipients of stigmatization, both people with disabilities and Black people have generally been cast as inadequate in their comparison to nondisabled, White counterparts.

Minority status and the privilege of majority groups

The act of self-defining as a minority group is, in and of itself, an exertion of power. It is a claim that delineates the difference between radically different lived experiences of the majority group. Just as Delgado and Stefanicic (2001) assert, in terms of race, minority status "…brings with it a presumed competence to speak about race and racism" (p. 9). In terms of disability, it also brings legitimacy to speaking about ableism experienced by people with disabilities. Traditional research has historically medicalized and pathologized disability and therefore contributed to ableism. Foucault (1977) calls attention to "the indignity of speaking for others" (p. 209), yet research about disability has been executed largely by nondisabled people who then make profoundly life-shaping decisions for people with disabilities. There is undoubtedly cause for people with disabilities to mistrust traditional research methodologies and deficit-based conceptual frameworks of disability. As Oliver (1992) explains, "[d]isabled people have come to see research as a violation of their experience, as irrelevant to their needs and as failing to improve their material circumstances and quality of life" (p. 105). Similarly, Delpit points out that "…people of color are, in general, skeptical of research as a determiner of our fates. Academic research has, after all, found us genetically inferior, culturally deprived, and verbally deficient" (1995, p. 47).

DS and CRT believe that research that does not take into consideration issues of disability and race, respectively, reinforces current inequities operant within the status quo. The institution of special education (perhaps more honestly called "education for the 'disabled'") has grown to be so powerful because, in the words of Carrier (1986), "[it] attains legitimacy by basing itself on what are taken to be the objective sciences of medicine and psychology" (p. 11). Such disciplines purport to be neutral, and in doing so obfuscate their own location within historical, cultural, and social contexts. To counter this, both DS and CRT support the privileging of voices that have traditionally been excluded, and respect for the knowledge they bring. As Delpit (1995) contends, "We must keep the perspective that people are experts on their own lives" (p. 47). Thus, counter-narratives challenge hegemonic knowledge and understandings, providing epistemological insights unknown to majority groups.

Empowerment, activism, and social change

With new and self-legitimized knowledge comes an increased sense of empowerment. Scholars in CRT cull from the concept of Edward Said's *antithetical knowledge*, encouraging "… the development of counter accounts of social reality by subversive and subaltern element of the reigning order" (Crenshaw et al., 1995, p. xiii). By creating and institutionalizing the disciplines of CRT and DS, previously marginalized people are now able to self-preserve their community's knowledge. Furthermore, such knowledge often serves as an academic springboard to social activism that can take many forms, including challenging stereotypical portrayals of disability and race in the media, applying pressure to local schools for increased integration into the "mainstream," and facing widespread attitudinal barriers.

Restrictive tropes of racial stereotypes in the media identified by Blacks, both blatant (overrepresentation of criminals) and subtle (you cannot be educated *and* get the girl) distort and misrepresent their experiences; likewise, some Latinos see neither accurate nor respectful representations of themselves in mainstream media (Connor, in press). In a similar manner, Morris (1991) reflects upon

> The general culture invalidates me both by ignoring me and by its particular representations of disability. Disabled people are missing from mainstream culture. When we do appear, it is in specialized forms—from charity telethons to plays about an individual struck down by tragedy—which impose the non-disabled world's definition on us and our experience. (p. 85)

Critiquing inaccurate representations of disability (Garland-Thomson, 2001; Linton, 1998; Safran, 1998) and race (Crenshaw, 1993; Hall, 2000; West, 1993) "talk back" to dominant assumptions that serve to ignore the daily realities of people with disabilities and people of color in dehumanizing ways.

In another example of activism, the inclusion movement has made significant changes in schooling experiences for both students with and without disabilities. Since the late 1980s, there has been a steady trend, often in the face of adversity, for students to shift from segregated to integrated education settings (Allan, 1999). However, one great irony is that many students with disabilities, when integrated into general education, remain in racially segregated environments (Losen & Orfield, 2002).

Arguably, directly addressing attitudinal barriers provides one of the most formidable challenges. Shakespeare (2004) claims that people with impairments are disabled, not only by material discrimination but also by prejudice, explaining, "[t]his prejudice is not just interpersonal, it is also implicit in cultural representation, in language and in socialization" (p. 296). In focusing on these issues, he raises questions about the formation of attitudes toward people with disabilities by the nondisabled, an area explored extensively in DS (Davis, 1995; Fleishner &

Zames, 2001; Garland-Thomson, 1996; Linton, 1998; Longmore & Umansky, 2001; Mitchell & Snyder, 2000; Russell, 1998). In a similar manner, CRT has focused upon addressing differentiated power dynamics between and among races, directly questioning the hegemony of Whites (Ladson-Billings & Tate, 1995; Marx, 2004; Tatum, 1993).

Caution, oppressions within: resisting replication of hierarchies

Both DS and CRT purport to be against all manifestations of oppression, yet one of the most difficult issues to acknowledge in liberatory movements is oppression within. Forms of intraoppression contradict the very foundations on which a movement stands. Hierarchies within DS and CRT exist, and by virtue of being hierarchies position some aspects of disability and race below others. For example, oftentimes invisible disabilities are not understood to be as serious or severe as visible ones. Similarly, in the hierarchy of race, stereotypic assumptions of Asian-Americans may paint them as not particularly oppressed (Teranishi, 2002). To give another example, darker skinned people may be subject to racism by others of lighter "Black" skin. These instances exemplify internalized oppression as each form of discrimination is based upon an *approximation of assumed normalcy*—with the unspoken idea of normalcy constituted as able-bodied whiteness.

The oppressed, therefore, because of values, perspectives, and beliefs, located in a network of interconnected systems that support constructions of identity according to ability, race, ethnicity, class, gender, age, sexual orientation, and so on are also, in turn, oppressors. Goffman points out that "…it should come as no surprise that in many cases he [*sic*] who is stigmatized in one regard nicely exhibits all the normal prejudices held toward those who are stigmatized in another" (1963, p. 138). The phenomena of one oppressive discourse eclipsing, and therefore ironically oppressing another, occurs with regularity both *within* and *between* DS and CRT. However, when researching and analyzing with an intersectional framework, that is, considering issues of disability, race, social class, gender, sexual orientation, age, and so on together, Crenshaw (1993) believe that we can see "ways in which the reformist politics of one discourse enforces subordinating aspects of another" (p. 114). Indeed, it does seem like we must always work against the tide of multiple forms of oppression, toward an ideal society in which equality and mutual respect are possible.

Identity and social constructions

DS and CRT both argue that markers of identity such as disability and race respectively are social constructs, inventions located within a certain time, place, and culture. As such, both concepts are seen as fluid and often highly contextual. Longmore (2003) succinctly explains, "[d]isability, then, is not a fixed thing. It is an elastic and dynamic social category. It is not an objective condition. It is a set of socially produced, highly mutable, historically evolving social identities and roles" (p. 239). Scholars within CRT believe that race should be conceptualized in the same way, holding that "…race and races are products of social thoughts and relations. Not objective, inherent, or fixed, they correspond to no biographical or genetic reality; rather, races are categories that society invents, manipulates, or retires when convenient" (Delgado & Stefanicic, 2001, p. 7). It is at the common ground of understanding "enforced" markers of identity as social constructions, that DS and CRT appear very similar. If "race" was substituted for "disability" in Longmore's explanation, and "disability" substituted for "race" in Delgado and Stefanic, each would still make sense.

Lawrence (1993) explains the process of how "racing" constitutes what it means to be raced, stating "The meaning of 'Black' or 'White' is derived through a history of acted-upon ideology. Moreover, the cultural meaning of race is promulgated through millions of ongoing contemporaneous speech/acts…The social construction of race is an ongoing process" (p. 62). Furthermore, because much of the speech, and many of the acts are what Solorzano (1998) terms "racial microagressions," they work against people of color feeling accepted and integrated into some social institutions and specific settings. In a similar manner, the connections between pervasive, ongoing discrimination experienced through "able-bodied microagressions," reveal people with disabilities are positioned in society, and their limited options in comparison to nondisabled counterparts.

DISABILITY STUDIES AND CRITICAL RACE THEORY: DIFFERENCES AND DISCREPANCIES

While arguing that there is much overlap between DS and CRT, some differences and discrepancies also exist. As previously mentioned, DS are primarily located within a sociocultural framework, while CRT and LatCrit theory are largely located within legal frameworks—thereby having different locations (that not necessarily compatible) as their starting points. While racism is a widely circulated term, used in everyday conversations, ableism is not. This is problematic on many fronts, as its lack of acceptance and use minimizes or ignores the value of the word to convey experiences of people with disabilities.

Perhaps most interesting in contemplating the connections between DS and CRT is that DS has been criticized as being predominantly informed by White and middle-class experience (Bell, 2006; Campbell & Oliver, 1996; Couser, 1997).

This has been evident in extensive discussions in the Society for Disabilities Studies listserv, giving rise to the 2005 annual conference being dedicated to issues of disability and race. While obviously well intended and a movement in the right direction, the event raised more questions than provided answers—and spurred a pre-conference summit in 2006 on disability and race. In a similar manner, CRT claims that by challenging racism, all other forms of oppression can be challenged. As Yosso (2002) writes, a Critical Race Curriculum, "…is unapologetically race *inter*centric, which means it centralizes race and racism while also focusing on the intersections of racism with other forms of subordination, based on gender, class, culture, language, immigration status, phenotype, sexual orientation, and accent" (p. 99). While "phenotype" denotes observable bodily differences in the appearance of an organism, it obscures the more familiar concept of "disability" and inadvertently suggests the inclusion of people with *visible* disabilities. However, the suggestion is ambiguous, and even if read optimistically, does not recognize *invisible* disabilities, which constitute the largest group. Given her passionate declaration desirous of being inclusive, it is unlikely that Yosso seeks to consciously omit people with disabilities. What she shows, however, is the failure of CRT to have disability on the radar screen, just as DS neglects to adequately incorporate issues of race.

On another note, most minority groups gather great strength in proclaiming pride in their embraced marker of identity. African Americans, for example, declared "Black is Beautiful," and homosexuals asserted affirmation, through saying they were "Glad to be Gay." In turn, while not in the form of a mantra, disability pride also exists in the form of "Crip Culture," inversing a stigmatized "trait" into badge of honor. Furthermore, disability *is* clearly celebrated by some as offering a distinct form of epistemological awareness. In Linton's monumental *Claiming Disability* (1998) and her compelling memoir *My Body Politic* (2006) she is persuasive in aligning disability with other major markers of identity and cultivating a hard earned pride from the countless and relentless "micro aggressions" of ableism. Many people have adopted a "minority group" model and self define as disabled and proud (Clare, 1999; Coughlin, 1997; Mooney & Cole, 2000; Weeber, 1999). However, the power of stigmatization in our society according to disability cannot be underestimated (Goffman, 1963), and while society accepts a person for being proud of who s/he is, disability per se is often viewed as a personal tragedy. Contemplating the stigmatization accorded disability, DS scholar Shakespeare has likened it to poverty in that oftentimes disability is perceived as something missing (2004, ¶3).

Another significant difference between DS and CRT is the "progress" of integration in public schooling. Since 1975, P.L. 142 The Education of All Handicapped Children Act (subsequently renamed Individuals with Disabilities

Education Act, in 1990) has ensured access to American schools for all students with disabilities. While many children and youth have greatly benefited, many others have been educated in settings segregated according to disability (Lipsky & Gardner, 1997). Nevertheless, Paul Longmore (2003), historian of disability, believes that "Perhaps the greatest progress toward the integration of people with disabilities has appeared in the U.S. public schools" (p. 26). In contrast, the ruling of *Brown v. Board of Education, Topeka, Kansas* in 2004 mandated desegregation in American schools, yet Bell (2004) has termed the ruling a "magnificent mirage" that obscures continued patterns segregation half a century later. Thus, perspectives on equal access to a quality public education differ drastically, yet still overlap in that excessive numbers of students of color as designated with disabilities (Losen & Orfield, 2002). This phenomenon of overrepresentation is exactly one example of why DS and CRT can work together, as both powerful disciplines are needed to frame and understand the complex, interconnected issues of disability and race.

OF MUTUAL INTEREST: RACIAL OVERREPRESENTATION IN SPECIAL EDUCATION

With the passage of PL 94-142 in the United States, students with disabilities gained access to an education. However, their placements were more likely to be with other students considered disabled than their nondisabled peers. Within the first decade of the law, Gartner and Lipsky (1987) noted that "Overall, 74 percent of special education students are in pull-out or separate programs" (p. 374). Even more troubling was that segregated classes in special education classes were populated by a disproportionate number of Black and Latino(a) students. This finding was been supported in a number of sources revealing city, state, and federal data (Artiles et al., 2002; Gartner & Lipsky, 1987; National Research Council, 2002).

On a national level, recent studies have show that Black males are over twice as likely as whites to be overidentified as mentally retarded in thirty-eight states, emotionally disturbed in twenty-nine states, and learning disabled in eight states (Parrish, 2002). In analyzing nationwide data, Parrish concludes, "…whites are generally only placed in more restrictive self-contained classes when they need intensive services. Minority students, however, may be more likely to be placed in the restrictive settings whether they require intensive services or not" (p. 26). Fierros and Conroy (2002) have noticed similar patterns, and conclude such overlabeling results in segregation, signifying "unwarranted isolation" from the mainstream (p. 40). The authors also conclude that urban settings are more likely to have restrictive environments for students labeled learning disabled (p. 61), and assert that their current research, along with previous studies (Conroy, 1999; Harry, 1992) suggests that "increased time in the regular education classroom is largely attributable to a special needs student's race" (p. 53).

Recent publications have directly confronted the issue of overrepresentation, reflected in telling titles such as *Racial Inequality in Special Education* (Losen & Orfield, 2002) and *Why Are So Many Minority Students in Special Education? Understanding Race & Disability in Schools* (Harry & Klingner, 2005). The nexus of disability and race has also been addressed in entire special education journals such as *Remedial and Special Education* (see Blanchett et al., 2005) as well as given significant space in publications such as the *Journal of African American History* (see Jordan, 2005).

Within these publications, many issues are highlighted and debated, including: the historical legacy of racism; the "invention" and growth of what are now commonplace disability labels (such as learning disabled, emotionally disturbed, speech and language, etc.); middle-class professional perceptions of working-class and poor children and families; second language acquisition; reliability of testing and evaluation instruments; the growth of bureaucracies; urban issues; interpretation of the law in terms of school and setting placements; overrepresentation of males; limited access to healthcare; and widespread institutionalized racism, both subtle and blatant, operant within personal and professional daily interchanges. From this list, it is clear that an intersectional approach using a lens constituted by DS and CRT is beneficial in order to analyze these tangled issues that often are not clearly delineated, and may in fact, bleed into each other.

USING CRT TO INFORM AND EXPAND DS

Several ideas originally developed within CRT offer new ways of looking at issues within DS. The first is the notion developed by Harris (1995) in terms of identity, "Whiteness became the quintessential property of personhood" (p. 278). She elaborates, while the law constructed whiteness as an objective fact, it is really "an ideological proposition imposed by subordination" (p. 281). Thus, those accorded "White" may be seen as proprietors of Whiteness, more valued in society, and with a corresponding sense of entitlement. In a similar manner, disability as defined in public law, can also been seen as the construction of able-bodiedness, of normalcy. As such, can it be said that Ability[2] be conceived as a quintessential property of personhood? What did it mean when people have historically applied for status of Whiteness (Haney-Lopez, 1996)? And, by extension, what does it mean when people apply for Ability status in contemporary times, such as the process of decertification in special education?

Another intriguing idea in CRT is what Bell terms "interest convergence" (1995, p. 20), namely, when those in power have the same interest as those in oppressed positions, *but* for self-motivated reasons—not a moral or ethical stance against subjugation. In one example, the author explains three trends that influenced the U.S. Governments motivation to racially integrate schools. The first trend was U.S. paranoia about communism in the early 1950s; it was seen as a palpable threat to American democracy and superpower influence. The second factor was the anger of Black citizens returning from war to indignity, degradation, and containment (the opposite of what Paul Robeson claimed could be found in the Soviet Union). The third factor was the promise of material gain; economic policymakers saw the "freeing" of the South to be a financially lucrative in terms of industrialization. Derek Bell (1995) articulates how the federal government's concerns converged with its Black citizens to forge much needed social change.

This explanation gives rise to understanding where and how power is manifest, and its conscious exertion to ensure the occurrence of a desired event. How might legal constructions of race from the U.S. Individuals with Disabilities Education Act (IDEA) be unpacked? What were the constellation of forces that gave birth the IDEA in the United States? What are "official" stories of how it came to be, and how do they contrast with unofficial accounts? While laws are passed, why are they not properly or even approximate being fully enforced, such as the Americans with Disabilities Act (Russell, 1998)? What were the convergence of interests that gave rise to civil legislation based on disabilities? Furthermore, how much of the legislation is predicated upon ableist assumptions about the "nature" of disability (see Beratan, 2006)?

In another example of CRT scholarship that speaks to potential use in DS, Dixon and Rousseau (2005) call attention to Richard Delgado's notion of students "Beyond love" (1995, p. 13). Delgado asserts:

> Blacks, especially, the black poor, have so few chances, so little interaction with majority society, that they might as well be exiles, outcasts, permanent black sheep who will never be permitted into the fold. Majority society has, in effect, written them off. (p. 49)

These sentiments can also be applied to citizens with disabilities, and in particular, poor children with disabilities. The very term, *beyond love* can also be stated as "unlovable." This sentiment is extremely disturbing, yet disturbingly persistent, seen in the systematic exclusion and marginalization of Black male students from U.S. schools (overrepresentation, high dropout rate, restrictive environments, etc.). Unfortunately, this phenomenon is often seen as a "predictable, albeit unfortunate, outcome of a reasonably fair system" (p. 134). In a similar manner, students with disabilities also experience widespread marginalization, appearing beyond the love (think: interactions/friendships/affiliation with) nondisabled peers in general education classes.

USING DS TO INFORM AND EXPAND CRT

In his research on college aspirations and experiences of Asian Pacific Americans, Teranishi (2002) points out how different the college experience can be for each subgroup—including Chinese, Filipinos, Hmongs, Cambodians, Laotians, and so forth. He calls attention to the stereotypic model "Asian American" student, yet points out the likelihood between various groups going to college, illustrating significant discrepancies. Students with disabilities can be found in all of the groups he mentions and, by extension, the college experiences influenced by race/ethnicity that he sought to understand are further compounded by disability. In addition, it is worth noting that while students with disabilities do attend colleges in the United States in increasing numbers, the "types" of disability vary significantly—and these differences also influence the (w)holistic experience of the student. As an aside, while the "passing" of people of color as White seems a phenomenon from bygone days, not disclosing one's status as disabled is tempting for individuals who are no longer openly declared disabled through everyday schooling practices, and want to make their own way in the world (Ferri et al., 2005). However, transitioning into the academic demands of college often leads students to enlist the supports services for students with disabilities as a last resort (Shayesti, 2006).

As part of CRT, Critical White Studies urge Whites to examine and reflect upon what being White means—what privileges it affords, what sense of entitlements, previously unexamined assumptions about nonWhites, and how the power that circulates among Whites is largely unacknowledged and yet is responsible for the maintenance of "how things are." Addressing Whiteness in teacher education includes focusing upon themes such as the neutrality of Whiteness and the markedness of color, as well as the association of color with deficits (Marx, 2004). In addition, the author advocates that White racism be challenged through honest words and feelings, drawing attention to overtly racist comments, challenging easy solutions, realizing "good" people are racist. In a similar manner, as an educator I have borrowed this approach from CRT, but instead of asking people to reflect upon their Whiteness, I have required them to think upon their Ability status in brief: what privileges it affords, what sense of entitlements, what unexamined assumptions about "the disabled," and how the power that circulates between Abled people is largely unacknowledged yet is responsible for maintaining inequities within the status quo. Like Marx, (2004) addressing ableism in teacher education focuses on themes such as the transparency of able-bodiedness through the labeling of disability, and the association of impairments with deficits. Similarly, authentic dialogue, challenging overtly ableist beliefs and comments, challenging easy solutions, realizing "good" people are ableist—also holds. By reflecting upon being Abled, what becomes apparent for able-bodied people of all "races" is that until now, they have had the privilege of *not* considering the taken for granted benefits being Abled affords them.

Another aspect of DS that CRT may benefit from is challenging the concept of normalcy. DS scholar Davis (1995) artfully deconstructs the very concept of normalcy, tracing its historical origins back to mid nineteenth century Europe and governmental desire to measure, quantify, and regulate bodies. Thus, the "normal" citizen—desired by the state, has been historically portrayed as White, able-bodied, and male while rarely being overtly identified as such (but clearly evident in choice of presidents). Every "other" manifestation of humanity is therefore measured *against* this constructed myth of normalcy, by definition out of reach for people who happen to be non-White and/or disabled and/or female. Therefore, instead of seeing race or ability (or gender etc.) as merely a different way of looking, thinking, or being, the difference is always perceived as a deficit. Indeed DS reveals that the formidable power of normalcy (generally equated with "mainstream" and "majority"), used to constitute the very infrastructure of the limited ways in which we view human diversity can actually be challenged, undermined, and reconstructed in more inclusive terms.

INTERANIMATION BETWEEN DS AND CRT

Both DS and CRT can, and often do, stand alone. However, as suggested, they can also work in conjunction with each to achieve syntheses that may be, in fact, more complex and revealing than either discipline in and of itself. In the following section, I encourage the use of an intersectional approach in research that contemplates the dynamic and very real interplay between disability and race (along with other markers of identity). In addition to this, I articulate several possibilities in which DS and CRT can interanimate each other. The concept of interanimation has been used by Mariage et al. (2004) in their speculations of how to increase the focus of social justice in the field of education. The authors believe that educational social justice "is made possible through the interanimation of ways of knowing that create dynamic tensions and challenge reliance on narrow views of what counts as legitimate knowledge" (p. 534). I believe that by using concepts and tools from each other's framework, DS and CRT can exchange critical guidance to each other in developing their mutual agendas of eradicating oppressions.

In favor of intersectionality

While most educational researchers have continued to investigate disability and race (or class or gender etc. for that matter), each is usually characterized as a discrete factor—or form of oppression—in determining a person's life experience. In contrast, intersectionality can be particularly useful when contemplating *multiple* forms of oppression. As a concept, it challenges restrictive notions of two-dimensional hierarchical ordering that often give way to prioritizations of oppression. By using the fluid framework of intersectionality, possibilities of knowing are expanded into a more three dimensional realm.

Anderson and Collins (1998) suggest the usefulness of conceiving intersectionality as operating within a matrix of domination. Such a framework "posits multiple, interlocking levels of domination that stem from societal configurations of race, class, and gender relations. This structural pattern affects individual consciousness, group interaction, and group access to institutional power and privileges" (p. 3). By simultaneously contemplating the discourses of disability, race, and class, researchers can explore the structural pattern(s) that have significantly affected the lived experiences of the group with whom they work.

In considering life at these intersections of disability and race, opportunities for analysis are broadened, pushing beyond "dualistic conceptions of identity and to discourage the current practice of balkanizing analytical categories in a kind of cultural and critical separatism in order to ensure legitimacy" (Garland-Thomson, 1997, p. 137). The meaning of intersectionality, according to Delgado and Stefancic, is "the examination of race, sex, class, national origin, and sexual orientation, and how their combination plays out in different settings" (2001, p. 51). Once again, *disability* must be added to their list of social categories that often serve to marginalize people.

Several scholars have argued that viewing oppressions in terms of a hierarchical ordering is over-simplistic and misleading because each oppression is inextricably woven with, and informed by, others. Barnes et al. (1999) note that "…simply adding on one form of oppression to another generates a false picture which does not help understand how, for example, disability is mediated through the experience of being black" (p. 90). As a Black woman with a disability, Hill (1994) explains "[I] cannot compartmentalize or separate aspects of my identity in this way. The collective experience of my race, disability, and gender are what shape and inform my life" (cited in Barnes et al., 1999, p. 90). Despite being portrayed as a form of "double" or "triple" jeopardy (Fierros & Conroy, 2002; Losen & Welner, 2002), Stuart (1992) conceptualizes multiple forms of discrimination as "simultaneous oppression" (cited in Barnes et al., 1999, p. 90).

In CRT, Crenshaw (1993) has focused upon the intersection of race and gender, explaining that "intersectionality is a core concept both provisional and illustrative…[because] our understanding of each category becomes more multi-dimensional" (p. 114–115). This point can be further illustrated by Begum et al. (1984) description of experiencing simultaneous discourses of race and disability, and the tensions that exist within an individual:

> Many of us will identify with different bits of our identity at different times. Different issues become important. Although none of them can you ever leave on the doorstep and say, 'It's irrelevant'…people say to me that black disabled people identify disability as the main issue, which worried me, because we really shouldn't be trying to get people to separate our identity. But the reality is that some of us, at different stages of our lives, are going to identify with different things as at that particular point being more pressing, perhaps (cited in Campbell & Oliver, 1996, p. 127).

If, as Finklestein claims, "…disabled people's control over their own lives and disability is not a single issue" (Campbell & Oliver, 1996, p. 64), it follows that if you are labeled disabled and "raced" (particularly as a person of color) each of these aspects influences the shaping and understanding of the others. Combined in lived human experience, they can never be entirely untangled. Together, they constitute "related products of the same social process and practices that shape bodies according to ideological structures" (Garland-Thomson, 1997, p. 136).

The examples above demonstrate that all discourses, including disability, race, ethnicity, and poverty, are *inseparable* and experienced simultaneously within each person. Experienced as interactive material and social forces, they create knowledge that, in turn, shapes the individual's (and influences collective) understanding of the world. By examining *embodiments* of multiple oppressions occurring simultaneously we can understand the effects of discourses, and challenge their hegemonic status. Thus, "It is impossible," write Campbell and Oliver, "…to confront one type of oppression without confronting them all and, of course, the cultural values that created and sustained them" (1996, p. 12).

> In her intersectional work on race and gender, Crenshaw (1993) explains:

> I conceive intersectionality as a provisional concept that links contemporary politics with postmodern theory. In examining the intersections of race and gender, I engage the dominant assumptions that these are essentially separate; by tracing the categories to their intersections, I hope to suggest a methodology that will ultimately disrupt the tendencies to see race and gender as exclusive or separable categories. (p. 114)

Intersectionality, therefore, requires the contemplation of ways in which numerous discourses together create multidimensional experiences, complicating notions of how people come to know, and understand their lives.

CONCLUSION

As evidenced throughout this chapter, both DS and CRT are multidimensional fields of study. Each is distinct, and when chosen and used appropriately, offer tools for framing, analyzing, and interpreting the important issues of disability and race. In addition, I have argued that using DS and CRT simultaneously opens up many hitherto unexplored possibilities. By doing so, attention has been called to illuminating ways in which parallels and connections between both can help each discipline interanimate one another in the service of making racism and ableism transparent in contexts where privileged eyes may be originally conditioned to see none. Intersectional scholarship using DS and CRT has recently begun to emerge, for example, see: Watts and Erevelles (2004) on school violence; Ferri and Connor (2006) on overrepresentation; Mitchell (2006) on "alternating" identities; and Erevelles (2006) on the history of race and disability in schooling. However, we must acknowledge that scholarly work in his direction is both nascent *and* fragile, warranting caution and clarity as it continues to grow. As Bell (2006) writes, "… it is essential to illuminate the fragile relationship between disability, race, and ethnicity in extant DS, arguing not so much for a sea change in this formulation, rather for a more definitive and accurate identification of the happening."

Finally, it has been called to attention that both *Vital Questions facing Disability Studies in Education* (Danforth & Gabel, 2007) and *CRT in Education* (Carbado, 2002) have not sufficiently developed curricula that challenges the tenacious hold of ableism and racism pervasive throughout school structures. Given the size and scope of the challenges, this is not entirely surprising. Yet, as allies critical of existing social arrangements, including widespread schooling practices, both disciplines offer each other and the academy at large entrée into new ways of ways of thinking, that in turn, motivate actions toward creating a more equitable and just society. Herein lies their promise.

NOTES

1. "Blindness" is often used as a metaphor synonymous with lack of understanding, and is an example of commonplace use of ableist language. Ableism embedded in language can be considered analogous to everyday subtleties of racism embedded within language such as "white lie" and "black hole," revealing unequal value-laden associations of color. I stop to pause at this simple example to note that CRT and DS overtly interrogate language use within themselves, but not sufficiently between each other.
2. In my use of the term Ability, I collapse the Cartesian dualism of body and mind—believing them to be inseparable. Able-bodiedness, therefore, includes able-mindedness.

REFERENCES

Adams, R. (2001). *Sideshow U.S.A.: Freaks and the American cultural imagination.* Chicago, IL: University of Chicago Press.

Anderson, M. L., & Collins, P. H. (1998). Introduction. In M. L. Anderson & P. H. Collins (Eds.), *Race, class, and gender: An anthology* (pp. 1–10). Belmont, CA: Wadsworth.

Artiles, A. J., Rueda, R., Salazar, J. J., & Higareda, I. (2002). English-language learner representation in special education in California urban school districts. In Losen & Orfield (2002), *Racial inequity in special education* (pp. 117–136). Cambridge, MA: Harvard Education Press.

Barnes, C., Mercer, G., & Shakespeare, T. (1999). *Exploring disability: A sociological introduction.* Malden, MA: Polity.

Baynton, D. (2004). Disability and citizenship (paper presented at the meeting of the Modern Language Association on Teaching Disability at the University Level, Atlanta, Georgia, March 5–7).

Beecher-Stowe, H. (1853/1998). *Uncle Tom's cabin.* New York: Bantam Classics.

Begum, N., Hill, M., & Stevens, S. (Eds.). (1994). *Reflections: Views of Black disabled people on their lives and community care.* London: Central Council for Education and Training in Social Work.

Bell, C. (2006). Personal communication.

Bell, C. (forthcoming). Introducing white disability studies: A modest proposal. In L. J. Davis (ed.) The Disability Studies Reader (2nd ed.). New York: Routledge.

Bell, D. A. (2004). *Silent covenants: Brown vs Board of Education and the unfulfilled hopes for racial reform.* New York: Oxford University Press.

Bell Jr., D. A. (1995). *Brown V. Board of Education* and the interest convergence dilemma. In K. Crenshaw, N. Gotanda, G. Peller, & K. Thomas (Eds.), *Critical race theory: The key writings that formed the movement* (pp. 20–28). New York: New Press.

Beratan, G. D. (2006). Institutionalizing inequity: Ableism, Racism, and IDEA 2004. *Disability Studies Quarterly,* March. http://www.dsq-sds.org/_articles_html/2006/spring/beratan.asp. Retrieved May 4, 2005.

Blanchett, W. J., Brantlinger, E., & Shealey, M. W. (2005). Brown 50 years later—exclusion, segregation, and inclusion: Guest editors' Introduction. *Remedial and Special Education,* 26(2), 66–69.

Campbell, J., & Oliver, M. (1996). *Disability politics: Understanding our past, changing our future.* New York: Routledge.

Carbado, D. W. (2002). Afterword: (E)Racing education. *Equity and Excellence in Education,* 35(2), 181–194.

Carrier, J. (1986). *Learning disability: Social class and the construction of inequality in American education.* New York: Greenwood.

Chae, H. S. (2005). Using critical Asian theory (AsianCrit) to explore Korean-origin, working-class/poor youths' experiences in high school. Unpublished manuscript.

Clare, E. (1999). *Exile & pride: Disability, queerness and liberation.* Cambridge, MA: South End.

Connor, D. J. (in press). Breaking containment: The power of narrative knowing—countering silences within traditional special education. *International Journal of Inclusive Education.*

Conroy, J. W. (1999). Connecticut's special education labeling and displacement practices: Analysis of the ISSIS data base. Unpublished report. Center for Outcome Analysis, Rosemont, PA.

Corker, M., & Shakespeare, T. (Eds.). (2002). *Disability/Postmodernity.* London: Continuum.

Coughlin, D. (1997). The person with a learning disability as minority group member. *Journal of Learning Disabilities,* 30(5), 572–575.

Couser, G. T. (1997). *Recovering bodies: Illness, disability, and life writing.* Madison, WI: University of Wisconsin Press.

Crenshaw, K. W. (1993). Beyond racism and mysogyny: Black feminism and 2 live crew. In Matsuda et al. (1993) (pp. 111–132).
Crenshaw, K. W., Gotanda, N., Peller, G., & Thomas, K. (Eds.). (1995). *Critical race theory: The key writings that formed the movement.* New York: New Press.
Danforth, S., & Gabel, S. L. (Eds.) (2007). *Vital Questions facing Disabilities Studies in education.* New York: Peter Lang.
Darabont, F. (Producer/Writer/Director) (1999). *The green mile* [motion picture]. United States: Time Warner Pictures.
Davis, L. J. (1995). *Enforcing normalcy: Disability, deafness and the body.* London: Verso.
Delgado, R. (1989). Storytelling for oppositionists and others: A plea for narrative. *Michigan Law Review, 87,* 2411–2441. Retrieved January 3, 2003, from Proquest database.
———. (1990). When a story is just a story: Does voice really matter? *Virginia Law Review, 76,* 95–111.
Delgado, R., & Stefancic, J. (2001). *Critical race theory; An introduction.* New York: New York University Press. Retrieved January 3, 2003, from Proquest database.
Delgado-Bernal, D. (2002). Critical race theory, Latino critical theory, and critical raced-gendered epistemologies: Recognizing students of color as holders and creators of knowledge. *Qualitative Inquiry,* 8(1), 105–126.
Delgado-Gaitan, C. (1994). *Consejos:* The power of cultural narratives. *Anthropology & Education Quarterly,* 25(3), 298–316.
Delpit, L. (1995). *Other people's children: Cultural conflict in the classroom.* New York: New Press.
Erevelles, N. (2006). How does it feel to be a problem? Race, disability, and exclusion in educational policy. In E. A. Brantlinger (Ed.), *Who benefits from special education? Remediating (fixing) other people's children* (pp. 77–99). Mahwah, NJ: Lawrence Erlbaum Associates.
Ferri, B. A., Connor, D., Solis, S., Valle, J., & Volpitta, D. (2005). Teachers with LD: Ongoing negotiations with discourses of disability. *Journal of Learning Disabilities,* 38(1), 62–78.
Ferri, B. A., & Connor, D. J. (2006). *Reading resistance: Discourses of exclusion in the desegregation and inclusion debates.* New York: Peter Lang.
Fierros, E. G., & Conroy, J. W. (2002). Double jeopardy: An exploration of restrictiveness and race in special education. In Losen & Orfield (2002) *Racial inequity in special education* (pp. 39–70).
Fleischer, D. Z., & Zames, F. (2001). *The disabilities rights movement: From charity to confrontation.* Philadelphia, PA: Temple University Press.
Foucault, M. (1977). Intellectuals and power. In D. F. Bouchard (Ed.), *Language, counter-memory, practice* (pp. 204–217). Ithaca, NY: Cornell University Press.
Gabel, S. L. (2005). Introduction: Disability studies in education. In S. L. Gabel (Ed.), *Disability studies in education: Readings in theory and method* (pp. 1–20). New York: Peter Lang.
Gains, H., Leibert, J., & Robbins, B. (Producers) (2003). *Radio* [motion picture]. United States: Columbia Pictures.
Garland-Thomson, R. (Ed.). (1996). *Freakery: Cultural spectacles of the extraordinary body.* New York: New York University.
———. (1997). *Extraordinary bodies.* New York: Columbia University Press.
———. (2001). Toward a feminist disability theory. Paper presented at the Gender and Disability, March 2–3, Rutgers University, New Jersey.
Gartner, A. & Lipsky, D. K. (1987). Beyond special education: Toward a quality system for all students. *Harvard Education Review,* 57(4), 367–395.
Goffman, E. (1963). *Stigma: Notes on the management of spoiled identity.* New York: Simon & Schuster.

Gould, S. J. (1996). *The mismeasure of man*. New York: W.W. Norton and Company.
Hall, S. (2000). The work of representation. In S. Hall (Ed.), *Representation: Cultural representations and signifying practices* (pp. 13–74). London: Sage.
Handler, L. (1999). *Twitch and shout: A touretter's tale*. New York: Plume.
Haney-Lopez, I. F. (1996). *White by law: The legal construction of race*. New York: New York University Press.
Harris, C. I. (1995). Whiteness as property. In N. G. K. Crenshaw, G. Peller, & K. Thomas (Ed.), *Critical race theory: The key writings that formed the movement* (pp. 276–291). New York: New Press.
Harry, B. (1992). *Cultural diversity, families, and the special education system: communication and empowerment*. New York: Teachers College Press (Eric Document Reproduction Service No. ED 343 967).
Harry, B., & Klingner, J. K. (2005). *Why are so many minority students in special education? Understanding Race & Disability in Schools*. New York: Teachers College Press.
Hill, M. (1994). They are not our brothers: The disability movement and the Black disability movement. In N. Begum, M. Hill & A. Stevens (Eds.), *Reflections*. London: Central Council for the Education and Training of Social Workers.
hooks, b. (1992). *Black looks: Race and representation*. Boston, MA: South End Press.
Jordan, K. A. (2005). Discourses of difference and the overrepresentation of black students in special education. *Journal of African American History, 90*(1–2), 128–149.
Kipling, R. (1899/1998). *Selected poems*. New York: Barnes and Noble.
Kleege, G. (1999). *Sight unseen*. New Haven, NJ: Yale University Press.
Krieger, L. H. (2003). *Backlash against the ADA*. Ann Arbor, MI: University of Michigan Press.
Ladson-Billings, G., & Henry, A. (1990). Blurring the borders: Voices of African liberatory pedagogy in the United States and Canada. *Journal of Education, 172*(2), 72–88.
Ladson-Billings, G., & Tate IV, W. F. (1995). Toward a critical race theory of education. *Teachers College Record, 97*(1), 47–68.
Lawrence, C. R. (1993). If he hollers let him go: Regulating racist speech on campus. In Matsuda et al. (1993) (pp. 53–88).
Lee, H. (1960/1982). *To kill a mockingbird*. New York: Warner Books.
Linton, S. (1998). *Claiming disability*. New York: New York University Press.
Lipsky, D. K., & Gartner, A. (1997). *Inclusion and school reform: Transforming America's classrooms*. Baltimore, MD: Paul H. Brookes.
Loewen, J. (1996). *Lies my teacher told me*. New York: Touchstone.
Longmore, P. K. (2003). *Why I burned my book and other essays on disability*. Philadelphia, PA: Temple University Press.
Longmore, P. K., & Umansky, L. (Ed.). (2001). *The new disability history: American perspectives*. New York: New York University Press.
Losen, D. J., & Orfield, G. (Eds.). (2002). *Racial inequality in special education*. Cambridge, MA: Harvard Education Press.
Losen, D. J., & Welner, K. G. (2002). Legal challenges to inappropriate and inadequate special education for minority children. In Losen & Orfield (2002) *Racial inequity in special education*, (pp. 167–194). Cambridge, MA: Harvard Education Press.
Mairs, N. (1996). *Waist-high in the world: A life among the nondisabled*. Boston, MA: Beacon.
Mariage, T. V., Paxton-Buursma, D. J., & Bouck, E. C. (2004). Interanimation: Repositioning possibilities in educational contexts. *Journal of Learning Disabilities, 37*(6), 534–549.
Marx, S. (2004). Regarding whiteness: Exploring and intervening in the effects of white racism in teacher education. *Equity and Excellence in Education, 37*(1), 31–43.

Matsuda, M. J., Lawrence, C. R., Delgado, R., & Crenshaw, K. W. (1993). *Words that wound: Critical race theory, assaultative speech, and the first amendment.* Boulder, CO: Westview Press.

Mitchell, D. D. (2006). Flashcard: Alternating between visible and invisible identities. *Equity & Excellence in Education, 39*(2), 154–165.

Mitchell, D. T., & Snyder, S. L. (2000). *Narrative Prosthesis: Disability and the Dependencies of Discourse.* Ann Arbor, MI: The University of Michigan Press.

Mooney, J., & Cole, D. (2000). *Learning outside the lines.* New York: Simon & Schuster.

Morris, J. (1991). *Pride against prejudice.* London: Women's Press.

National Research Council. (2002). *Minority students in special and gifted education.* Washington, DC: Author.

O'Connor, G. (2001). Bad. In P. Rodis, S. Garrod & M. L. Boscardin (Eds.), *Learning Disabilities & Life Stories* (pp. 62–72). Needham Heights, MA: Allyn & Bacon.

Oliver, M. (1992). Changing the social relations of research production? *Disability, Handicap and Society, 7*(2), 101–114.

———. (1996). Understanding the hegemony of disability. In M. Oliver (Ed.), *Understanding disability: From theory to practice* (pp. 126–144). New York: St. Martin's Press.

Parrish, T. (2002). Racial disparities in the identification, funding, and provision of special education. In Losen & Orfield (Eds.), *Racial in equality in special education.* (pp. 15–37). Cambridge, MA: Harvard Education Press.

Piziali, A. (2001). Revolution. In P. Rodis, S. Garrod, & M. L. Boscardin (Eds.), *Learning disabilities and life stories* (pp. 29–38). Needham Heights: Allyn & Bacon.

Russell, M. (1998). *Beyond ramps: Disability at the end of the social construct.* Monroe, ME: Common Courage.

Safran, S. P. (1998). The first century of disability portrayal in Film: An analysis of the literature. *Journal of Special Education,* 31(4), 467–479.

Selden, S. (1999). *Inheriting shame: The story of eugenics and racism in America.* New York: Teachers College Press.

Shakespeare, T. (2004, November 4). The economics of metaphysics. Message posted to disability-research@jiscmail.ac.uk.

Shayesti, S. (2006). Personal conversation.

Snipp, C. M. (1998). The first Americans: American Indians. In M. L. Anderson & P. H. Collins (Eds.), *Race, Class, and Gender* (pp. 357–364). Belmont, CA: Wadsworth.

Solorzano, D. G. (1998). Critical race theory, race and gender microaggressions, and the experience of Chicana and Chicano scholars. *International Journal of Qualitative Studies in Education,* 11(1), 121–136.

Solorzano, D. G., & Yosso, T. J. (2001). Critical race and LatCrit theory and method. *Qualitative Studies in Education,* 14(4), 471–495.

———. (2002). Critical race methodology: Counter-storytelling as an analytical framework for education research. *Qualitative Inquiry,* 8(1), 23–44.

Stiker, H. J. (1999). *A History of Disability.* Ann Arbor, MI: Love Publishing House.

Stuart, O. (1992). Race and disability: Just a double oppression? *Disability, Handicap and Society, 7*(2), 177–188.

Tate IV, W. F. (1997). Critical race theory and education: History, theory, and implications. *Review of Research in Education,* 22, 195–247.

Tatum, B. (1993). *Why are all the Black kids sitting together in the cafeteria?* (Revised edition). New York: Basic Books.

Teranishi, R. (2002). Asian Pacific Americans and critical race theory: An examination of school racial climate. *Equity and Excellence in Education*, 35(2), 144–154.

Trent, J. W. (1998). Defectives at the World's Fair: Constructing disability in 1904. *Remedial and Special Education*, 19(4), 201–211.

Twain, M. (1885/2001). *Huckleberry Finn*. New York: Barnes and Noble Classics Series.

Watts, I. E., & Erevelles, N. (2004). These deadly times: Reconceptualizing school violence by using critical race theory and disability studies. *American Education Research Journal*, 41(2), 271–299.

Weeber, J. E. (1999). What could I know of racism? *Journal of Counseling & Development*, 77, 20–23.

Wendell, S. (2001). Unhealthy disabled: Treating chronic illnesses as disabilities. *Hypatia*, 16(4), 17–33.

West, C. (1993). *Race matters*. Boston, MA: Beacon.

Wright, R. (1940/1992). *Native son*. Harper Collins: New York.

Yosso, T. J. (2002). Toward a critical race curriculum. *Equity and Excellence in Education*, 35(2), 93–107.

CHAPTER TWENTY-SEVEN

Disability Studies AND Psychology: Emancipatory Opportunities

DAN GOODLEY AND REBECCA LAWTHOM

INTRODUCTION: A PSYCHOLOGY TO EMBRACE?

This chapter brings together our dual interests: as activists engaged with the politics of disability and researchers interested in the use of psychological theories. These interests are not easily partnered. British approaches to disability studies have tended to emphasise a social model of disability. This model has been variously interpreted as an epistemology (Goodley, 2001), a hammer to use on a disabling world (Oliver, 1999), and a socio-political attitude which understands and challenges the materialist bases of disablement and exclusion (Abberley, 1987; Barnes and Mercer, 1997, 2003, 1991). The model is often viewed as something owned by the disabled people's movement (Hasler, 1993) and has been, understandably, guarded by activists from the "intellectual masturbation" of academics (Swain, 2006). Meanwhile, debates reign about the model's adaptability to include issues associated with the "realities" of impairment (Shakespeare and Watson, 2001; Thomas, 1999; Watson, 2002), mental health (Wilson and Beresford, 2002), and learning difficulties/ intellectual impairment (Chappell, 1998; Chappell, Goodley, and Lawthom, 2001; Goodley, 2001). The place of theorising with—or against—the social model of disability is highly contested (Albrecht et al., 2001; Barton, 2001; Barnes and Mercer, 1997, 2003; Barnes et al., 1999, 2002).[1] Our suggestion to make connections with psychology opens up a number of further contestations.

Popular versions of psychology assume that psychologists are perpetually engaged in the therapeutic counselling of another's problems. In our current psychoanalytic culture (Parker, 1999), psychology appears to feed into a climate of "trauma" television, of Oprah-esque proportions; where senses are dulled and the trivial reified, promoting a naval-gazing and confessional culture (Lasch's notion of the "narcissistic self"). Simultaneously, while psychology-as-analysis is dismissed as trivialising nonsense, it is also treated with deep suspicion. Psychology appears to be obsessed with difference (usually referred to as deviance) in forms which are both real and statistical. This invariably leads to a focus on that which stands out from the norm. Hence, displaying anger in the car is now a psychological label that requires the intervention of suitably qualified experts. Naughty kids are now kids caught up in a psychopathology of challenging behaviour, emotional/behavioural difficulties, autism and attention deficit hyperactivity disorder (Billington, 2000; Timimi, 2005). When disability (or other associated labels) is raised in the training of psychologists then it tends to be considered in terms of individual biological factors (Olkin and Pledger, 2003) and labelled as a syndrome (Tobbell and Lawthom, 2005). Such a focus is allied to the advent of the psy-complex (Rose, 1989); the institutionalisation of psychological interventions into people's lives. This clearly raises anxieties. These concerns are particularly acute for people with impairments. Disabled people have extensive and intensive experience of the intrusions of professionals such as psychologists whose major aim of intruding appears to be one of enforcing normalcy (Oliver, 1996), knowing that the norm is shifting over time. Psychology is to be distrusted because it is:

- Individualistic—the scientific study of mind and behaviour;
- Bourgeois—ideas of the majority (and ruling) are exercised over the minority (http://www.fireflysun.com/);
- Apolitical—changing individuals rather than society (Masson, 1988);
- Professional-led—experts over the lay;
- Pseudo-scientific—an emphasis on science and a poor version of it at that (Popper, 1997);
- Normalising—concerned with individuals adjusting to their impairment;
- Oppressive—disabled people are mere subjects of psychology's individualising practices.

However, even a brief immersion in the labyrinth of psychology reveals a complex community of often unhappy bedfellows, so much so that *psychologies* may be a more apt disciplinary label. There are many psychological perspectives and theories spanning: cognitive, behavioural, child, psychoanalytic, humanistic, existential, social, cultural, political, social constructionist, feminist, critical, critical race, postmodern, discursive, forensic, spiritual, developmental, narrative and community psychologies, to name but a few. There are numerous practitioner roles which can confer professional status including, educational, clinical, organisational, criminologist, child, counselling and therapist and others which do not (e.g., community psychology [CP]). Furthermore, like all viable social scientific disciplines, debates rage about epistemology, ontology, theory, methodology, method, analysis, ethics, application and political potency. To situate psychology as a bounded discipline engaged with enforcing normalcy does a disservice to the dynamic nature of knowledge disciplines and paradigm shifts. Psychology is but a collection of many different communities, each with their like-minded members, constituting a myriad of psychological paradigms (Kuhn, 1965). Although many theories and practitioners are involved in the disability industry and implicated in particular, perhaps oppressive, ways of working with disabled people, as with any loosely related collection of community members, discord and debate reign (Lawthom, 2004). The history of psychology is peppered by radical collectives and individuals challenging the (disabling) status quo. In terms of what be of use to the development of an emancipatory disability studies, we can point to four key paradigmatic battles—if not exactly paradigm shifts—where the status and role of psychological knowledge and practice have been thrown open to debate and critique. It is within these locations that we view possibilities for developing further emancipatory theories and practices in relation to disability: moving on but with the radical stance of a social model of disability. Our premise is not to dismiss the social, cultural, political, historical and economic conditions of disability. Far from it, we are concerned with drawing upon emerging psychological debates—from potentially radical quarters—that allow us to further expose the conditions of exclusion and promote forms of practice on the part of practitioners, allies, community members that work alongside the radical aims of the disabled people's movement. Our aims are well articulated by Henry Giroux (2003, p. 9)

> at best, theories of resistance are useful as highly nuanced theoretical tools for understanding and intervening within structures of power as they define diverse contexts across a range of institutional and ideological formations … Theories of resistance become useful when they provide concrete ways in which to articulate knowledge to practical effects, mediated by the imperatives of social justice, and uphold forms of education capable of expanding the meaning of critical citizenship and the relations of democratic public life.

We now turn to some of these nuanced tools—resources so often ignored in mainstream psychological circles.

(1) Critical Psychology: Critical Foundations

Our first encounter with psychology begins with what has been termed *critical psychology*. Recent global developments in critical psychology have recast versions of psychological practice and theory in ways that, we feel, are amenable to the politics of disability. Researchers and activists associated with this community share an interest in challenging the tacit assumption that psychology is a progressive and enabling practice. Fox and Prilleltensky (1997) argue that psychology's traditional practices and norms hinder social justice, to the detriment of individuals and communities in general and to oppressed groups in particular. The task for critical psychologists is to confront the practices of psychology that sustain oppression, promote a politicised and aware psychology, work alongside users and survivors of psychology and link into wider social justice agendas as ethically responsible psychologists. The 1970's "crisis" in social psychology saw a major shift in thinking about how psychology should go about its business. Parker (1989) suggests that a key crisis emerged in social psychology just as ethnomethodologists and interpretivists challenged the dominating forces of positivism. While there are traditions of qualitative research to be found in (social) psychology (e.g., Allport, 1947), the "crisis" refers to the increasing dissatisfaction with psychological functionalism: a mistaken view of atomistic beings in socio-political vacuums.

Even now, psychological forums abound with debates about the psychology's relationship to science and positivism; the role of qualitative versus quantitative methodologies in accessing the social world; the place of subjectivity and objectivity in research and the place of partisanship in psychology. Overall, these debates have resulted in a rise of more meaning-oriented theoretical persuasions, often with political orientations and affiliations. It is no surprise that feminist psychologists were some of the most vociferous opponents of "malestream" positivistic approaches to psychology (e.g., Ussher, 1991). Sadly, disability studies never really got represented in these early interventions, as the UK disability movement was still relatively in its infancy in the 1970s. However, as we look back now, the challenges that were posed to over-ride (ruling) dominating knowledge are clear evidence of the discipline's willingness to be opened up and radicalised.

Crucially, the crisis provided a space for alternative theorising. Critical psychology shares much with the social model of disability and other sociological views of disability across the globe (e.g., Linton, 1998; Traustadottir, 2004). Each are reactions to hegemonic constructions of subjectivity, the disabled body, the labelled child, the medicalisation of distress, the segregation of groups of people, the construction of a human services industry that diagnoses, assesses and treats individuals rather than changing cultural and environmental forms of alienation and marginalisation. Similarly, each is a model that invites activists, theorists and practitioners to develop their criticality and worth. They share attitudes and persuasions that encourage members to form communities of practice engaged with social change (Fox, 1985; 1993). Consequently, critical psychology has allowed for the growing recognition of the potency of critical theories associated with feminisms, critical race, queer and (though neglected) disability studies (Fox and Prilleltensky, 1997). These resources can be used to recognise and resist the often elusive psychological elements of disablement. A critical persuasion supports disabled activists and researchers in their attempts to unpick the structural, institutional and relational bases of the social and educational exclusion of people with impairments. We add (social) psychological flesh to the materialist bones of disability studies. We also demand critical interventions on the part of related practitioners. Hence, psychological knowledge is utilised to understand *and* challenge the psychological experiences of exclusion. Psychological theories of subjectivity can be drawn upon to display the consequences of, for example, nuanced education (Murray, 2006; Todd, 2006), pathologising gerontology practice (Priestley, 2005) and fears within marginalised communities (Kagan et al., 2000), that subtly but nonetheless significantly exclude young and old disabled people. Yet, where there is critique there is also hope. Alternatives are offered in education and beyond.

Malestream forms of psychological knowledge have faced some of their stiffest tests from theories associated with psychoanalysis, community and discursive psychology. These three not necessarily inclusive nor bounded theoretical resources share the aim of critical psychology: to contest some of psychology's given truth claims. In essence, they provide not only critical psychological theories but pose major challenges to the mainstream practices of the discipline of psychology. We offer these alternative theories as entry points into radicalising psychologies that make alliances with a politics of disability and offer transdisciplinary interventions.

(2) Psychoanalysis: Psycho-Emotional Spaces and Disabled Subjectivities

We turn now to psychoanalysis as a resource that can be used to understand oppression whilst also offering spaces for resistance. Such a move might seem perverse. The counselling room is perhaps the first scenario that critics think of when documenting the oppressive horrors of psychological practice. Pop-Freudian understandings, publicised incidents of therapeutic abuse and controversies such as false-memory syndrome have all contributed to a damning view of psychoanalysis as a therapeutic model which is profoundly alienating. Yet, psychoanalysis is, in some respects, "the repressed other of psychology" (Billington, 2006;

Burman, 1994), at least in Anglo-American circles. Sustained attempts by "scientific psychology" to shut away psychoanalytic understandings of subjectivity ironically make it so appealing. Psychoanalysis is a powerful narrative about the self. While it is maybe too powerful in some contexts, most notoriously in authoritarian therapeutic communities, the emphasis on subjectivity as a socio-cultural artefact affords opportunities for theorising disablement and impairment. There is a long history of radical psychoanalysis, most notably evident in the pre-Second World War work of the Frankfurt school. Scholars associated with the Institute of Social Research, Frankfurt, Germany, include Theodor W. Adorno, Herbert Marcuse, Max Horkheimer and Jurgen Habermas (see Frosch, 1999). These writers shared the aim of bringing together the work of Marx and Freud, in order to promote radical social theory. Kovel's (1988) analysis is a more modern attempt to bring back the work of the Frankfurt school work alongside a celebration of spirituality and human worth.

Utilising psychoanalytic perspectives in disability research does not automatically imply a pathological turn to the inner troubles of the psyche. Psychoanalytic theory can be viewed as a description rather than a prescription of the ways in which social-cultural knowledge impacts upon our consciousness (Mitchell, 1974). The work of Marks (1999), whose bridging work between disability studies and psychoanalysis was so innovative, has to date been largely ignored. This work appeals to the sensibilities of the Frankfurt school and critical theorists (see Frosh, 1999; Parker, 1997) as it understands subjectivity as being constructed in social and cultural formations (see also Marks, 2002). This is a significant point for three reasons. First, previous uses of psychoanalysis on the subjectivities of disabled people have tended to emphasise subjectivities associated with the "tragedy" of living with impairment (Sinason, 1992). In short, they have emphasised pathological subjectivities. Second, and in contrast, a turn to the social nature of subjectivity repositions disabled people as experts and analysts of disability and impairment. In other words, psychoanalysis supports the view that disabled people's experiences of living with and challenging oppression creates subjectivities which have the potential to occupy a privileged or at least powerful position in relation to developing disability studies (see Barnes and Mercer, 1997; Oliver, 1996). Third, psychoanalytic encounters with subjectivity allow possibilities for interrogating the relational, psycho-emotional aspects of exclusion and resistance: private, hidden aspects of disability/impairment that are often ignored by legislative and campaigning emphases on the public aspects of disablement.

Three recent pieces of shed light on some of these considerations. Firstly, Tregaskis and Goodley (2006) account for their experiences as non-disabled/disabled researchers in profoundly personal, implicitly therapeutic and potentially vulnerable ways. They attempt to scrutinise some of the more hidden words, emotions, feelings and thoughts of developing a working relationship between disabled and non-disabled researchers. They write:

> We have found that many other disabled researchers do not recognize their own personal ontological position as being key to the development of disability studies' understanding of disabling practices. We wonder if this is because of the still troubling role of auto/biography in social research (Goodley et al., 2004), or because disabled people's views are still seen as inferior to those of "informed professionals," or because of the ongoing debate within disability studies about the wisdom or otherwise of airing what are perceived as "private troubles" within public settings (Finkelstein, 1996; Thomas, 1999). However, we are not saying that a disabled researcher has to offer personal disclosure just because they happen to be disabled people and doing disability research. Yet, we do find it intriguing that so many disabled researchers we know have not explicitly drawn upon their own personal biographies in developing their research agendas—biographies, by the way, that non-disabled researchers spend many a year trying to authentically access through disability research. (Goodley et al., 2004 from Tregaskis and Goodley, 2005, pp. 367–368)

Psychoanalytic orientations encourage the (safe) articulation of personal experience by (non)disabled people in relation to analyses of disability and modes of research practice. By doing so, the subjectivities of disabled people are celebrated and augmented. These accounts invoke the complex relationships between social, relational, psychological, and emotional realms. Disclosure is also carefully handled and its consequences monitored.

Secondly, and similarly, Reeve's work (2004) forefronts the psycho-emotional dimensions of disability. Recasting psycho-emotional disablism as profoundly social rather than individualised allows a particular psychology of disability to emerge. Using narrative interviews of disabled people within "landscapes of exclusion" (Kitchin, 1998), Reeves demonstrates how structural dimensions of disability are compounded by psycho-emotional dimensions of disability. Interaction, reactions and relationships with others are the very ingredients that demarcate us as social beings. For disabled people, however, "scripts" of everyday engagement are often ignored in favour of "othering" responses on the part of others associated with avoidance, fear, help or curiosity. The staring, invalidating gaze of society (Reeve, 2002) impacts upon emotional well being and threatens to internalise oppression. Discourses around euthanasia, medical intervention, genetic counselling and bioethics signal clear indicators of disabled people's worth. Psycho-emotional disablism operates at both conscious and unconscious levels. "Emotion work" as a response may need unpacking. Using psychoanalytical lens, psycho-emotional dimensions of disability need to be seen as pervasive and cumulative justifiable emotional responses to marginalisation and exclusion. Thirdly, Billington's (e.g., 2000; 2006) reflections as a critical educational psychologist, draw upon the work of writers such as Lacan in order to think again about how we speak of children; how we work with children; how we write about them; how we understand "them" and "ourselves." This interface of schooling, psychology and disability remains a key area of interrogation. Here consciousness is recognised as an entity created in powerful registers of language: to the extent that "therapy" might involve a deconstruction of such registers. This has clear links with the demands of disability studies and inclusive education scholars for the destabilisation of normalising ideologies of disabling society.

A critical psychoanalytic approach promotes reflexivity of all. At the very least this resource allows for recognition of ambivalent feelings and views—projections, introjections and assimilations—that can affect our analytic frames of reference in terms of how we conduct our research; conceptualise the social constructs of "impairment" and "disability" and understand the people we work with. We are reminded that our intellectual and personal creativities are so often stifled by the excessive repression of a capitalist, disabling society. Instead, following Mitchell (1974), we need to take seriously our subjectivities which describe rather than prescribe disabling societies. Psychoanalysis—the "othered" relation in psychology—provides a useful forum in which to understand emotional work across personal and institutional settings. Examples cited above highlight the ways in which psychoanalytical understandings can recover the personal/political arenas of disability studies.

(3) Community Psychology: Modelling Theory and Practice

Our next resource moves us from the interiority/exteriority of subjectivity to the individual/community of relationships. Alliances between CP and disability have been increasingly articulated (Lawthom and Goodley, 2005; Goodley and Lawthom, 2005b; Kagan et al., 2005). Kagan and Burton (2005) suggest that disability studies and CP share a vision of eradicating marginalisation. CP has a growing presence in the United Kingdom (www.compsy.org.uk) and whilst a conclusive definition is not possible here, certain features allow a consensus to emerge:

- A focus on context—the wider features of lived experience (culture, politics, history) rather than an emphasis on the individual;
- A commitment to social transformation and an agenda for change in order to promote well being;
- Practices that are multi-level and work within systems and communities alongside people in their own environments.

Central to the vision and practice is a set of underpinning values which are politicised. Values here such as diversity and respect are inevitably linked to a wider social justice agenda (adapted from Rappaport, 1977, Heller et al., 1984, Orford, 1992; Duffy and Wong, 1997, Levine and Perkins, 1997; Kagan, 2002). Crucial to most conceptions of CP is the idea of working alongside the primary source of knowing and instrument of research: "the self-directing person within a community of inquiry" (Reason and Heron, 1995, p. 123). The view of psychology promoted by CP is inherently political. It considers psychology as a liberatory space (Martin-Baró, Aron, and Corne, 1994; Kagan, 2002), in which researchers, who are armed with theoretical and practical knowledge of the social and interpersonal world, aim to work alongside communities towards positive social change. Psychology is up for grabs: particularly by those communities whose psychologies have been pathologised and alienated by labour markets, poor housing, welfare dependency and material poverty. We should not confuse an engagement with the community with atheoretical practice. An agenda for change is also an engagement with theory and critical praxis promotes deep conversations with theory (Lynn, 2004). If we take, for example, CP's engagement with "mental distress" then it is possible to view this as a journey through a variety of epistemological/theoretical destinations: a journey compatible with the travelling disability studies researcher (see Goodley and Lawthom, 2005a). This journey might be encapsulated like so:

Following Burrell and Morgan (1979) model of epistemology (Figure 27.1), we can understand these four epistemological positions—how we may come to know "mental distress" and the disabling world—in the following ways (adapted from Goodley and Lawthom, 2005a):

POSITION 1: A functionalist view of the world sees society as regulated and ordered, promotes objective measures of (dys)functional mental states and behaviours and, inevitably, views disabled people as adherents of a "sick role" (Barnes, 1997). There is little room for the community psychologist to maneavour in terms of conceptualising "mental distress" other than adopt a position associated with pathology.

POSITION 2: An interpretive stance understands the social world as an emergent social process, created by the individuals concerned and the sharing of subjective understandings and experiences. Crucial to this epistemology is the formation of disabling/enabling identities and attitudes between voluntaristic individuals in a coherent and regulated world (Ferguson et al., 1995). Here the community psychologist works alongside people—who are in some way identified in relation to mental distress—in order to gain understandings that are closely tied to lived realities and stories.

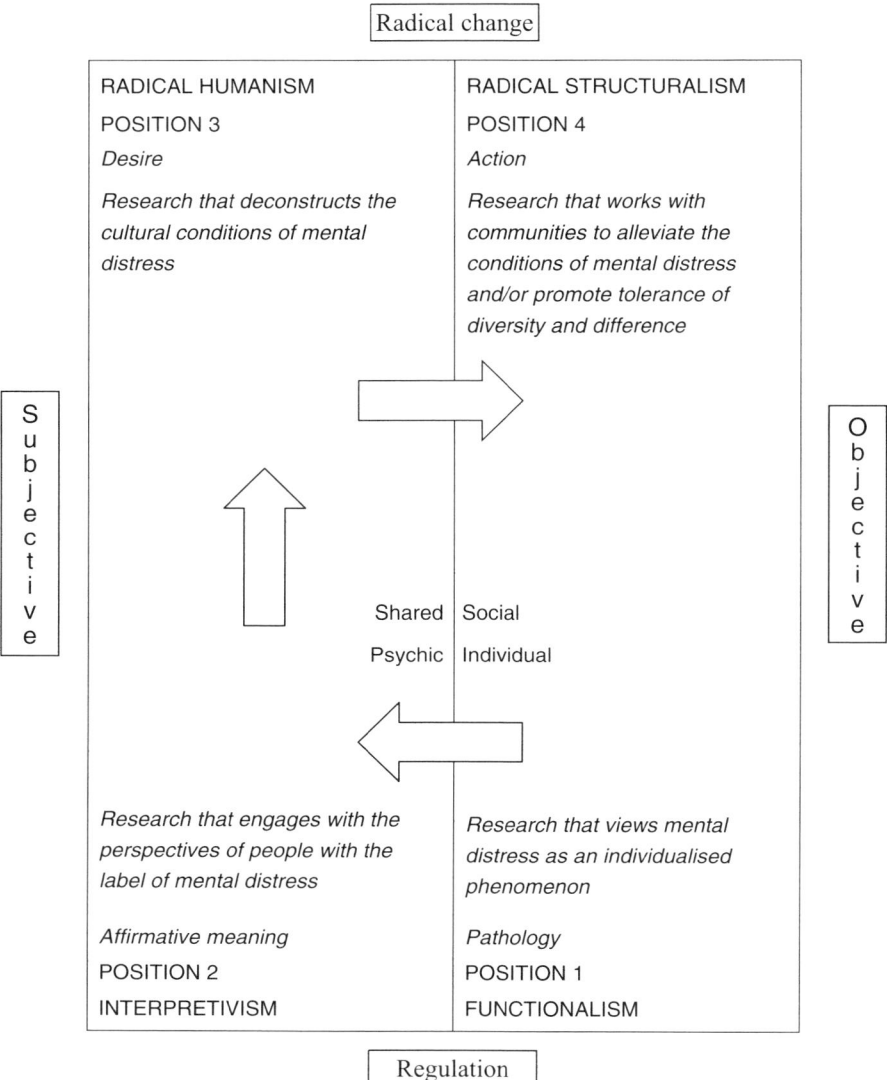

Figure 27.1. Adaptation of Burrell and Morgan's (1979) model of epistemological bases of paradigms.

POSITION 3: Radical humanism situates knowledge production in the often elusive shared subjective creation of dominant disability discourses, hegemonies and social meaning-making processes of wider society. Meanings are imprisoned within ideological processes and patterns of dominance but also produced by resistant counter-hegemonic cultural practices and emergent community identities (see for example Marks, 1999). Community psychologists are now engaged with wider cultural formations of mental distress—perhaps in ways that tap into the counter-hegemonic actions of new social movements associated with "mental distress."

POSITION 4: Finally, a radical structuralist epistemology understands the social world as constantly in conflict, whose structures can be objectively observed and in which certain social groupings are always at risk of alienation, oppression and false consciousness. This stance is acutely connected with emancipatory aims (Barnes, 1997; Oliver, 1990, 1996). The aims of the community psychologist are associated with socio-cultural and political change. Research is an emancipatory endeavour.

The journey described above is a well told story in CP: giving up the pathological tendencies of psychology in search of emancipatory change. Similarly, this travel story is popular in disability studies too and is articulated well by Priestley (1998) who considers the ways in which social theorising around disability in British disability studies has moved away from functionalism (of Parsons' sick role and psychological individualism) to radical structuralism (and the dialectical materialism of Marx, Engels and, to some extents, Gramsci). Following Scott-Hill (2002), CP research works with marginalized communities to think again about their own communities and themselves in ways that may promote self-emancipation over social exclusion. Such potentiality is particularly significant in view of disability studies debates which suggest that for some disabled people the social model lacks authenticity and relevance (Shakespeare and Watson, 2001). We would argue that social and cultural models of disability are visions of emancipation, and that research can allow opportunities for thinking through these ideas. Simultaneously, research needs to engage with long-held and entrenched views of "disability" and "impairment" which are at risk of governing people in ways that prevent them from seeing possibilities. Furthermore, there appears to be an argument here for making research—and the exercising of professional interventions—a more hands-on and humanistic venture. CP's journeys embrace a whole host of concerns by virtue of working with the community members to achieve the goals that they set out for themselves and their communities. In the very process of identifying these goals, key issues associated with identity, politics, community and emancipation were explored theoretically and practically. The move across the epistemologies has obvious parallels with Freire's (1970) concept of conscientization: cumulatively developing consciousness, but consciousness that is understood to have the power to transform reality. There are obviously clear linkages here with the areas of educational and school psychology; which we follow up later.

(4) Discursive Psychology: Deconstructing Disablement

The fourth psychological resource we want to identify is that of *social constructionism*. This persuasion has challenged the concept of the self as an embodied and unitary human subject and opened it up as a distributed self, dependent on different contexts and the meanings in those contexts at given times (e.g., Gergen, 1985; Nightingale and Cromby, 1999; Burr, 2003). The self is constructed phenomena through meaning-making, language and human practice. The very concept of personality, for example, is therefore ripped out of its usual embodied site and recast as a socio-cultural formation. Personalities are increasingly consumable entities of a society obsessed with identity. In contrast, the supposed undesirability of a disabled identity raises questions about what identities are deemed social valued. Discursive psychology furthers an engagement with constructions by positing that there can be no truth without language and the ideologies and institutions implicated in the production of language. The various forms of discursive psychology are beyond the remit of this chapter, though two classic texts capture at least some of this diversity (for more details see Nikander, 1995). Potter and Wetherell (1987) exemplify an approach to discursive psychology which is concerned with picking out the contradictions and variations of seemingly fixed entities such as attitudes. Their main thesis is that mainstream approaches to social psychology assume a stability of self that is actually far from the reality of everyday psychology. For Potter and Wetherell, self is always constituted by the language people use to account for self. Through the use of conversation analysis we can see how these very accounts reveal contradictions and complexities. The use of sophisticated conversational strategies and resources make a mockery of the fixed concept of the human psyche assumed by attitude tests and psychometric analyses. People do attitude through their talk and attitudes shift and change according to context and the conversational strategies that are used. Rapley's (2003) work exemplifies a conversational analysis approach which takes a purportedly real, organic and individualised phenomena such as "intellectual disability" and reveals how it is constituted by the talk about it. Parker's (2002) approach to discourse analysis is also concerned with providing a social account of subjectivity. His approach, though, leans more heavily on poststructuralist writers such as Michel Foucault and Jacques Derrida, whose aim is to deconstruct, subvert and account for societal discourses—what Lyotard (1974) terms grand narratives (see also Burman and Parker, 1993). Hence, in an associated text, Parker et al. (1995) unpick the ways in which psychopathological conditions are the product of normalising institutions and professional practice. Mental illness is not a condition that exists prior to the psychologist intervening—mental illness is a social creation of institutions within society that psychology has helped to construct.

Goodley and Rapley (2002) connect these different positions to discursive psychology. First, the conversation analysis approach, often associated with Potter and Wetherell (1987), is adopted to unpack the situated social construction of "acquiescence bias" and interactional "incompetence," which are usually seen as being inevitable *dispositional attributes* of people described as "intellectually disabled." In contrast, they suggest that—by making their linguistic construction explicit—these notions can be re-examined in ways that challenge traditional, modernist, reductionist thinking. Second, they draw upon poststructuralist methods of enquiry, specifically deconstruction (see Parker, 2002), to examine the taken-for-granted construction of "learning difficulties" as a naturalised impairment. The notions of "inscribing impairment" and "promoting independence" are examined. They suggest that poststructuralism adds to, rather than detracts from, the need for politicised social theory by providing a political and social vision of impairment in relation to "learning difficulties" (see also Goodley, 2001). Similarly, Tobbell and Lawthom (2005) use the communities of practice literature to explore how a label such as EBD (emotional and behavioural difficulties) works in educational practice. Rather then locating problems within the child (impairment specific) EBD is understood as being part of the distributed competencies and behaviours of a group of children that require whole class solutions. Todd (2007) argues that discursive psychology challenges "professional thought disorder." Only when professionals can see how discourses enable or hinder inclusion can alternative practices occur, leading professionals towards greater "political literacy" (see also Hughes and Paterson, 1997).

APPLICATIONS: TOWARD TRANS-DISCIPLINARY WORK IN EDUCATION

Throughout this chapter we have suggested that some radical parts of psychology, often under-represented in mainstream psychology, can be exploited by disability studies scholars and activists in this time of trans-disciplinary work in education. For now, we identify two challenges.

(1) Critical pedagogy: Recognise Disablement, Support Resistance

Our psychologies contribute to the big contradiction of disability studies: where there is oppression, there is also resistance. We are mindful of the ingrained institutionalised discrimination faced by disabled people. We must recognise that simply challenging psychological practice will not overturn the exclusion of disabled people. Yet, in making alliances between psychology and disability studies, we feel that some significant ideas and practices can be elicited which chip away at disablement. Questions are clearly raised about the values and affiliations of psychologists. The values of social justice, equality, respect, democracy, autonomy and justice seem most readily able to inform an alliance between disability studies and psychology (Kagan et al., 2005). The growth of the disability movement and the progress it has made has produced a significant corpus of expert knowledge. Psychological practice therefore needs to be a collaborative activity with this knowledge, disabled people and their communities. This reiterates a common practice now of psychological professionals working alongside voluntary groups. Revisioning forms of enabling psychological practice emerges only when community, activist and service settings are transcended together; when disabled people are fully collaborating in the services and practice that they are being offered; when disabled people are represented as psychologists and when the values of psychologists and disabled people are shared. Clearly, this has links with critical pedagogy (Gabel, 2002; Giroux, 2003; Holmes, 2002; McLaren and Leanord, 1999), where educators are encouraged to:

> reject forms of schooling that marginalize students who are poor, black and least advantaged. This points to the necessity for developing school practices that recognize how issues related to gender, class, race and sexual orientation can be used as a resource for learning rather than being contained in schools through a systemic pattern of exclusion, punishment and failure. (Giroux, 2003, 10)

From a shared awareness of contradictions can emerge productive possibilities.

(2) Promote a psychology of inclusion, develop an inclusive psychology

Barton (2004) advocates that as critical (educational) researchers we need to re/explore our key concepts; re/examine where we are theoretically; re/onsider our models of citizenship and ask what our educational (or in this case with disabled people then their training should reflect the state of knowledge about disability promoted by the discipline of disability studies in which such knowledge is synthesised and explicated. Psychological practice must engage with inclusion. Psychologists working in institutional, professional and community spaces should ask:

- What is my understanding of impairment and disability?
- Can my theoretical and professional knowledge help to challenge conditions of disablement?
- How do I understand inclusion and exclusion?
- What role do a play in the exclusion and inclusion of disabled people?
- How do I see disabled people—as active or tragic beings?

- Am I a hindrance or help to the furthering of inclusion?
- What is the aim of my work and how can it contribute to the aims of disability studies, the disability community and disabled people's movement?

Furthermore, we need to put disability in context (Olkin and Pledger, 2003). Disabled people do not constitute a homogeneous group and their lives intersect the relations of "race," class, sexuality and gender (see for examples, Davidson-Payne and Corbett, 1995; Morris, 1991; 1993; 1996; Shakespeare and Gillespie-Sells, 1996; Stuart, 1993; Sheldon, 1999; Stone, 1999; Thomas, 1999; Tremain, 1996; Vernon, 1996). Inclusion is not simply a buzz word for the disability industry. A psychology of inclusion should create a psychology that is amenable to diversity. Many psychological theories have been embraced throughout the history of counselling and therapy. The question to ask ourselves, then, is which theoretical/disciplinary positions promote a enabling understandings and practices for the betterment of disabled people? Olkin and Pledger's (2003) thinking is helpful here, in terms of unpicking the epistemological grounds of theory:

Paradigm 1 underpins much rehabilitative and mainstream psychological thinking about disability, while paradigm 2 is indicative of a disability studies perspective (Figure 27.2). Clegg asks whether a psychology of disability can graduate beyond the medical model—or paradigm 1—in a united, theoretically strong manner? The diversity of positions represented in this chapter suggest that unity is not the same as homogeneity of theory. Rather, we need to ask:

- Do out theories allow us to understand impairment as a part of personhood rather than being the essence of disabled people?
- Do our psychological theories allow us to unpack the social construction of disability?
- Do our theories support the principle of systematic study and elimination of disablement?

The psychologies we present in this chapter fit readily with aims of paradigm 2. Psychological theories of learning that readily embrace Vygotskian ideas (see Vygotsky, 1978) promote a very environmentally of learning; located understanding in line with the tenets of paradigm 2. Using Vygotsky's zones of proximal development we are drawn to the ways in which collaboration enhances potential. Too often educational systems are organised around individualised activities (such as tests, outcomes, assessment, statementing, etc.) where independence is stressed over interdependence. Vygotsky's theories allow us to consider how impairment is exploited by some educational professionals to justify not working collaborative and inclusively with disabled children. This pitches understanding of the disabled learner in her/his social cultural environment. In this sense, then, it is possible to

Paradigm 1	Paradigm 2
Is based on a medical model of disability	Is based on a social model or the new paradigm of disability
Is pathology oriented	Shifts to a systemic and societal perspective
Views differences due to disability [impairment] as deficits or developmental aberrations	Takes a lifespan approach
Is usually cross-sectional	Uses concept of "response" to disability as a fluid process
Sees people with disabilities [impairments] and their families as at high risk for difficulties	Promotes health and resilience
Focuses predominantly on intrapsychic, personal characteristics or intrapersonal variables	Values disability history and culture
Research on disabled people—which is more likely to be inpatient or treatment settings	Research with disabled people– Incorporates those being researched into the research process
Uses concept of "adjustment" or "adaptation" to disability	Sees the major problems of disability as social, political, economic, legal
Uses norms based on non-disabled/able-bodied individuals for comparison	Is grounded in the belief that those with impairments have been denied their civil rights
Is about, but rarely, disabled people	Is usually not just about, but by, disabled people
Perpetuates a we-they model	Seeks remedies in public policy, legislation, and systemic programmatic changes

Figure 27. 2. Two paradigms of disability thinking. *Source*: Adapted from Olkin and Pledger, 2003, p. 301

draw upon psychological theories that are in tune with a disability studies perspective. While what we know is limited, it is not negligible. The different theoretical psychological positions represented in this chapter bring with them, to varying extents, a vision of disability as (1) social, cultural, political; material, discursive and relational exclusion; and (2) a recognition of the resistance of disabled people.

CONCLUSIONS/STARTING POINTS

The field of disability studies has a long history of promoting research practices that work alongside and with disabled people (Barnes, 1997; Clough and

Barton, 1998; Oliver and Barnes, 1997; Special issue on disability research, 1992; Stone and Priestley, 1996; Zarb, 1992). The underpinning assumptions of the social model of disability have led to a number of core research issues, including:

- *Inclusion*—more and more disabled researchers involved in academia;
- *Accountability*—the disabled people's movement demands researchers and academics to be accountable to the experiences and aims of disabled people, reflected in the slogan "Nothing about us, without us";
- *Praxis*—theories of disability emerge from an engagement with the changing nature of disabled people's lives;
- *Dialectical*—research *draws* and *builds* upon the social model of disability;
- *Ontological knowledge*—disabled people understand the conditions of disablement and impairment;
- *Disablement rather than impairment*—disability research should engage with the material, social, cultural, relational and political conditions of disablement; and
- *Partisan*—research/ers are on the side of disabled people.

These issues are, of course, contestable and have provoked major debate in the field. Nevertheless, they remain for us key points of consideration when thinking through the relationship between disability and psychology. In so doing, we bring together disability studies and psychology from a particular stance. For us, disability studies comes first and psychology second. Our overarching concern is to explore how disability studies can benefit from a critical and not unproblematic engagement with psychology, rather than how psychology can colonise disability studies. Our aim is to examine the ways in which psychology can work in ways that contribute to the individual and collective empowerment of disabled people. Our focus is not on the normally rehabilitative association of psychology and disability but on the ways in which psychology can contribute to the radical social changes demanded by disability studies.

NOTE

We would like to thank Palgrave Macmillan Publishers for their kind permission to reproduce extracts from Introduction and discussion of Goodley and Lawthom (2005b).

1. The disability studies we describe in this chapter is mostly, though not exclusively, a British disability studies. There are clear points of divergence between different contextual (and conceptual) takes on disability studies, not least in the difference between what might broadly be called North American (e.g., Linton, 1998; Albrecht et al, 2001; Longman and Umansky, 2001), Nordic

disability research (e.g., Traustadottir, 2004, *Scandinavian Journal of Disability Research,* 2004) and British Disability Studies (e.g., Shakespeare, 1998; Oliver and Barnes, 1998; Barnes and Mercer, 2003; Barnes et al, 2002; Barnes et al, 2002; Corker and French, 1999; Thomas, 1999; Swain et al, 2003). When we talk about disability we are discussing people who have the ascribed identities of "disability." Such an identity term includes various people who have been historically situated in a whole myriad of impairment groupings including physical and sensory impairments, learning difficulties and people with mental health issues. As befits a British disability studies stance, however, we endeavour not to embrace impairment specific considerations—as have many charities and organisations *for* disabled people—but instead consider disabled people as a heterogeneous group, with many impairment labels who face a number of overlapping experiences of exclusion or disablement.

REFERENCES

Abberley, P. (1987). The Concept of Oppression and the Development of a Social Theory of Disability. *Disability, Handicap and Society,* 2, 1, pp. 5–21; reproduced in Barton, L. and Oliver, M. (1997). *Disability Studies: Past Present and Future.* Leeds, UK: Disability Press.

Albrecht, G., Seelman, and Bury, M. (2001). *Handbook of Disability Studies.* New York: Sage.

Allport, G. W. (1947). *The Use of Personal Documents in Psychological Science.* New York: Social Science Research Council.

———. (1997). Disability and the Myth of the Independent Researcher. In Shakespeare, T. (1997). Rules of Engagement: Changing Disability Research both in, Barton, L. and Oliver, M. (Eds). *Disability Studies: Past Present and Future.* Leeds: Disability Press.

Barnes, C. (2003). Disability studies: what's the point? Keynote paper presented at *Disability Studies: Theory, Policy and Practice Conference,* Lancaster, September.

Barnes, C. and Mercer, G. (1997). *Doing Disability Research.* Leeds, UK: Disability Press.

———. (2003). *Disability.* London: Polity.

Barnes, C., Mercer, G., and Shakespeare, T. (1999). *Exploring Disability: A Sociological Introduction.* Cambridge: Polity.

Barnes, C., Oliver, M., and Barton, L. (Eds.) (2002). *Disability Studies Today.* Cambridge: Polity.

Barton, L. (2001). (Ed) *Disability Politics and the Struggle for Change.* London: David Fulton.

———. (2004). Social Inclusion and Education: Issues and Questions. Paper presented at the ESRC seminar *Towards Inclusion: Social Inclusion and Education.* 19 July 2004, Institute of Education, London.

Billington, T. (2000) *Separating, Losing and Excluding Children: Narratives of Difference.* London: RoutledgeFalmer.

———. (2006). *Lacan, the "Turn to Language" and Professional Practices When Working with Children.* Paper presented to 1st seminar "Pedagogies and the Making of Futures" of the Pedagogies, Policy and Professionalism seminar series, School of Education, University of Sheffield.

Burman, E. (1994). *Deconstructing Developmental Psychology,* London: Routledge.

Burman, E. and Parker, I. (eds) (1993). *Discourse Analytic Research: Repertoires and readings of texts in action (co-edited with I. Parker),* London: Routledge.

Burr, V. (2003) *Social Constructionism.* London: Psychology Press.

Burrell, G. & Morgan, G. (1979) *Sociological paradigms and organisational analysis: elements of thesociology of corporate life.*London: Heinemann.

Campbell, J., and Oliver, M. (1996). *Disability Politics: Understanding our Past, Changing our future*. London: Routledge.
Chappell, A. L. (1998). Still out in the Cold: People with Learning Difficulties and the Social Model of Disability. In T. Shakespeare (ed.) *The Disability Reader: Social Science Perspectives*. London: Cassell.
Chappell, A., Goodley, D. and Lawthom, R. (2001). Making Connections: The Relevance of the Social Model of Disability for People with Learning Difficulties. *British Journal of Learning Disabilities, 29,2,* 45–50.
Clough, P. and Barton, L. (Ed.). (1998). *Articulating with Difficulty: Research Voices in Special Education*. London: Paul Chapman Ltd.
Corker, M. and French, S. (1999). *Disability Discourse*. Buckingham: Open University Press.
Davidson-Payne, C. and Corbett, J. (1995). A Double Coming Out: Gay Men with Learning Disabilities. *British Journal of Learning Disabilities, 23,* 147–151.
Duffy, K.G. and Wong, F.Y. (1997). *Community Psychology*. Boston, MA: Allyn Bacon.
Ferguson, P.M., Ferguson, D.L & Taylor, S.T. (eds). (1995). *Interpreting Disability*. New York: Teachers Press College.
Finkelstein, V. (1996) *Experience and Consciousness* [Internet]. Available from <http://www.leeds.ac.uk/disability-studies/archiveuk/finkelstein/expconsc.pdf> [Accessed 3 October 2003].
Fox, D. and Prilleltensky, I. (Eds). (1997). *Critical Psychology: An Introduction.* London: Sage.
Fox, D.R. (1985). Psychology, Ideology, Utopia, and the Commons. *American Psychologist, 40,* pp. 48–58.
———. (1993). Psychological Jurisprudence And Radical Social Change. *American Psychologist, 48,* pp. 234–241.
Freire, P. (1970). *Pedagogy of the Oppressed*. London: Penguin.
Frosch, S. (1999). *Politics of Psychoanalysis*. London: Palgrave.
Gabel, S. (2002). Some Conceptual Problems with Critical Pedagogy. *Curriculum Inquiry, 32, 2,* pp. 177–201.
Gergen, K.J. (1985). The Social Constructionist Movement in Modern Psychology. *American Psychologist,* 40: 266–275.
Giroux, H.A. (2003). Public Pedagogy and the Politics of Resistance: Notes on a Critical Theory of Educational Struggle. *Educational Philosophy and Theory, 35, 1,* pp. 5–16.
Goodley, D. (2001). 'Learning difficulties', the social model of disability and impairment: challenging epistemologies, *Disability & Society, 16, 2,* 207–231.
Goodley, D. and Lawthom, R. (Eds). (2005a). Journeys in Emancipatory Disability Research: Alliances between Community Psychology and Disability Studies. *Disability & Society, 20, 2,* 135–151.
Goodley, D. and Lawthom, R. (2005b). *Psychology and Disability: Critical Introductions and Reflections*. London: Palgrave Macmillan.
Goodley, D. A., Rapley, M. 2002. "Changing the Subject: Postmodernity and People with 'learning difficulties'" in: *M. Corker and T. Shakespeare (eds) Disability and Postmodernity*. Cassell.
Goodley, D. A., Lawthom, R., Clough, P., Moore, M. 2004. "Researching Life Stories Method, Theory and Analyses in a Biographical Age". Routledge Falmer.
Hasler, F. (1993) Developments in the disabled people's movement, in: J. Swain, V. Finkelstein, S. French & M. Oliver (Eds) *Disabling barriers—enabling environments* (London, Sage).
Heller, K., Price, R., Reinharz, S., Riger, S. and Wandersman, A. (1984) Psychology and Community Change, 2nd edn. Homewood, IL: Dorsey Press.
Holmes, C.A. (2002). Academics and Practitioners: Nurses as Intellectuals. *Nursing Inquiry, 9, 2,*. 73–83.

Hughes, B. and Paterson, K. (1997). The Social Model of Disability and the Disappearing Body: Toward a Sociology of Impairment. *Disability & Society*, 12, 2, 325–340.
Kagan, C. and Burton, M. (2005). 'Community psychological perspectives and work with people with learning difficulties', *Clinical Psychology*.
Kagan, C., Lawthom, R., Knowles, K. & Burton, M. (2000). Community activism, participation and social capital on a peripheral housing estate, paper presented at the *European Community Psychology Conference*, Bergen, Norway, September.
Kitchin, R. (1998). "Out of place", "knowing one's place": Space, power and the exclusion of disabled people, *Disability & Society*, 13,3, 343–356.
Kovel, J. (1988). *The Radical Spirit: Essays on Psychoanalysis and Society*. London: Free Association Books.
Kuhn, T. (1965). *The structure of scientific revolutions* (reprinted 1996). London: Routledge.
Lawthom, R. (2004). *Managing diversity: Narratives, paradigms and communities of practice*. Manchester Metropolitan University: Unpublished PhD thesis.
Lawthom, R. and Goodley, D. (2005). Community Psychology: Towards an empowering vision of disability. The Psychologist, 18 (7), 423–425.
Levine, M. and Perkins, D.V. (1997). Principles of Community Psychology: Perspectives and Applications. Oxford: Oxford University Press.
Linton, S. (1998). *Claiming Disability: Knowledge and Identity*. New York: New York University Press.
Longman, P. and Umansky, L. (Eds). (2001). *The New Disability History: American Perspectives (History of Disability)*. New York: New York University Press.
Lynn, M. (2004). Inserting the race into critical pedagogy: an analysis of race-based epistemologies. *The Journal of Educational Philosophy and Theory*, 37, 2, 153–165.
Marks, D. (1999) *Disability: Controversial debates and psychosocial perspective.*(London: Routledge.
———. (2002) Some concluding notes—healing the split between psyche and social: Constructions and experiences of disability. *Disability Studies Quarterly*, 22, 3, pp. 46–52.
Martin-Baró, I., Aron, A. and Corne, S. (1994). Writings for a Liberation Psychology. Belknap: Harvard University Press.
Masson, J. (1988). *Against Therapy: Emotional Tyranny and the Myth of Psychological Healing*. New York: Athenaeum.
McLaren, P. and Leanord, P. (1999) (Eds). *Paulo Friere: A critical encounter*. New York: Routledge.
Mitchell, J. (1974). *Psychoanalysis and Feminism. Freud, Reich, Laing and Women*, 1974, reissued as: *Psychoanalysis and Feminism: A Radical Reassessment of Freudian Psychoanalysis*, Basic Books 2000.
Morris, J. (1991). *Pride Against Prejudice: Transforming Attitudes to Disability*. London: Women's Press.
———. (1993). Gender and Disability. In J. Swain, V. Finkelstein, S. French, and M. Oliver (Ed.), *Disabling Barriers—Enabling Environments*. London: Sage.
———. (Ed.). (1996). *Encounters with Strangers*: *Feminism and Disability*. London: Women's Press.
Murray, P (2000). Disabled Children, Parents and Professionals: partnership on whose terms? *Disability & Society* 15,4, 683–698.
Nightingale, D.J. and Cromby, J., (Eds.). (1999). *Social constructionist psychology: A critical analysis of theory and practice*. Buckingham, UK: Open University Press (1999)
Nikander, P. (1995). The turn to the text: the critical potential of discursive social psychology. *Nordiske Upkast*, 2, pp. 3–15.
Oliver, M. (1990). *The politics of disablement* Basingstoke: Macmillan.

———. (1996). *Understanding disability: From theory to practice.* London: Macmillan.

———. (1999). Final accounts and the parasite people. In M. Corker, & S. French (Eds), *Disability and Discourse.* Buckingham: Open University Press.

Olkin, R. and Pledger, P. (2003). Can disability studies and psychology join hands? *American Psychologist, 58, 4,* 296–304.

Orford, J. (1992). *Community Psychology: Theory and Practice.* Chichester: John Wiley & Sons.

Parker, I. (1989). *The Crisis in Modern Social Psychology, and how to end it.* London and New York: Routledge.

———. (1997). *Psychoanalytic Culture: Psychoanalytic Discourse in Western Society.* London: Sage.

———. (1999). Deconstructing psychotherapy, in I. Parker (ed.), *Deconstructing Psychotherapy.* London: Sage.

———. (2002). *Critical Discursive Psychology.* London: Palgrave Macmillan.

Parker, I., Georgaca, E., Harper, D., McLaughlin, T., and Stowell Smith, M. (1995). *Deconstructing Psychopathology.* London: Sage.

Popper, K. (1977). *The Logic of Scientific Discovery.* London: Routledge.

Potter, J., Wetherell, M., (1987). *Discourse and Social Psychology: Beyond Attitudes and Behaviour.* London: Sage.

Priestley, M. (1998). Constructions and Creations: idealism, materialism and disability theory, *Disability & Society,* 13(1), 75–94.

———. (2005). Disability and old age: or why it isn't all in the mind. In D. Goodley and R. Lawthom (eds.) *Psychology and Disability: critical introductions and reflections,* Palgrave.

Rapley, M. (2003). *The Social Construction of Intellectual Disability.* Cambridge: Cambridge University Press.

Rappaport, J. (1977). *Community Psychology: Values, Research, and Action.* London: Holt, Rinehart and Winston.

Reason, P. and Heron, J. (1995). 'Co-operative inquiry'. In R. Harré, J. Smith and L. Van Langenhove (eds), *Rethinking Methods in Psychology.* London: Sage.

Reeve, D. (2002). Negotiating psycho-emotional dimensions of disability and their influence on identity constructions. *Disability & Society,* 17, 5, 493–508.

———. (2004) 'Psycho-emotional dimensions of disability and the social model'. In C. Barnes and G. Mercer (eds), *Implementing the Social Model of Disability: Theory and Research.* Leeds: Disability Press, pp. 83–100.

Rose, N. (1989). *Governing the Soul.* London: Routledge. *Scandinavian Journal of Disability Research. (2004).* 6, 1.

Scott-Hill, M. (2002). Policy, politics and the silencing of "voice". *Policy & Politics, 30, (3),* 397–409 (13)

Shakespeare, T. and Watson N. (2001). The Social Model of Disability: An outdated ideology? *Exploring Theories and Expanding Methodologies: Research in Social Science and Disability,* 2, 9–28.

Shakespeare, T. and Gillespie-Sells, K. (1996). *The Sexual Politics of Disability: Untold Desires.* London: Cassell.

Sheldon, A. (1999). Personal and Perplexing: feminist disability politics evaluated, *Disability & Society,* 14,5, 645–659.

Sinason, V. (1992). *Mental Handicap and the Human Condition.* London: Free Association Books.

Special issue on disability research. (1992). *Disability, Handicap and Society, 7, 2.*

Stanley, M. (1983). *Obedience to Authority: An Experimental View.* New York: Harper/Collins.

Stone, E. (Ed.). (1999). *Disability and Development: Learning from Action and Research on Disability in the Majority World.* Leeds: Disability Press.

Stone, E. and Priestley, M. (1996) Parasites, Pawns and Partners: Disability Research and the Role of Non-disabled Researchers. *British Journal of Sociology, 47, 4,* 699–716.

Stuart, O. (1993). Double Oppression: An Appropriate Starting Point? In J. Swain, V. Finkelstein, S. French, and M. Oliver (Eds.), *Disabling Barriers—Enabling Environments.* London: Sage.

Swain, J. (2006). Key Debates in Disability Studies, Paper presented to the Centre of Applied Disability Studies, New directions in applied disability studies seminar series, University of Sheffield, 5 April, Sheffield.

Swain, J., French, S., and Cameron, C. (2003). *Controversial Issues in a Disabling Society.* Buckingham, UK: Open University Press.

Thomas, C. (1999). *Female Forms: Experiencing and Understanding Disability.* Buckingham, UK: Open University Press.

Timimi, S. (2005). *Naughty Boys: Anti-Social Behaviour, ADHD and the Role of Culture.* London: Palgrave.

Todd, L. (2007). *Partnerships for Inclusive Education: A Critical Approach to Collaborative Working.* London: Routledge.

Traustadottir, R. (2004). Disability Studies: A Nordic Perspective. Keynote lecture, British Disability Studies Association Conference, Lancaster, UK, June, 2004.

Tregaskis, C. and Goodley, D.A. (2006). Disability Research with Non/Disabled People: Towards a relational methodology of research production. *International Journal of Social Research Methodology, 8, 5,* 364–374.

Tremain, S. (1996). (Ed.). *Pushing the Limits: Disabled Dykes produce Culture.* Canada: Women's Press.

Ussher, J. (1991). *Women's Madness: Misogyny on Mental Illness?* New York: Harvester Press.

Vernon, A. (1996). A Stranger in Many Camps: The Experience of Disabled Black and Ethnic Minority Women. In Morris, J. (Ed.). *Encounters with Strangers*: *Feminism and Disability* (pp. 48–68). London: Women's Press.

Vygotsky L. S., (1978). *Mind in Society,* Cambridge, MA: Harvard University Press.

Watson, N. (2002) Well, I know this is going to sound very strange to you, but I don't see myself as a disabled person: Identity and Disability. *Disability & Society,* 17, 5, 509–529.

Wilson, A. and Beresford, P. (2002.). Madness, Distress and Postmodernity: Putting the Record Straight. In Mairian Corker and Tom Shakespeare (eds). *Disability/Postmodernity.* London: Continuum, 143–158.

Zarb, G. (1992). On the Road to Damascus: First Steps Towards Changing the Relations of Disability Research. *Disability, Handicap & Society,* 7, 125–138.

CHAPTER TWENTY-EIGHT

A Comparison: Difference, Dependency, AND Stigmatization IN Special Education AND Disability Studies

KATHRYN YOUNG AND EMILY MINTZ

INTRODUCTION

Special education research in the United States struggles with its theoretical foundations. Historically its guiding concepts emerged from the discipline of psychology that relies on identifying individual deficits and developing individual solutions to academic, social, and behavioral problems in schools. Special education research offers short term solutions of individual adaptation to long term problems of educational inequality for students labeled "disabled" in schools. However, these solutions only partially address a pervasive need to fully integrate students with disabilities into schools. Disability studies provide an alternative lens to that of special education—one that shifts questions about educational inequality from the individual to that of society, from the child to schools and classroom structures.

Since the early days of American compulsory schooling in the late nineteenth century children identified as different were first excluded from schools and sent to institutions or poorhouses, then educated in separate schools, or separate classrooms within the same school, and increasingly, educated with their peers in general education settings (Winzer, 1993). Degrees of exclusion or inclusion often relate to ideas about what is determined as "best" for the labeled child, other children, teachers, and schools. Different actors have different views about what best looks like. The enduring debate of inclusion versus degrees of exclusion centers on how best to educate children with disabilities in American schools.

Special education and disabilities studies have different goals for the same students—special education works to remediate students so they may live independently in the future and disability studies explores societal constraints that keep students from accessing social and academic experiences now and in the future. Different analytic lenses lead to different causes, concerns, and solutions for these students and their accompanying disability labels. Special education seeks to remedy students' individual deficits so that they may become more like their peers socially and academically. Disability studies rejects notions of individual deficit. The field builds on social, economic, political (and educational) critiques of systematic treatment of disability in our nation and elsewhere. The history of exclusion and marginalization of people with disabilities in American society and schooling galvanized disabled people and their allies to form the Disability Rights Movement and the discipline of disability studies—both retheorize commonly held assumptions about individual difference, unpack the role of dependency in a variety of settings, and lay out theoretical considerations of stigmatization.

Contrasting disability studies with theoretical underpinnings of special education allows us to understand the tension between giving students the services they need, while not subscribing these same students to a future of social and economic dependence. Traditionally, special education theory does not embrace a sociopolitical analysis of the field; however, we feel it must reanalyze commonly held assumptions about disability in order to push past this stage in American education. Students with disabilities are more included in educational settings than they were ten or twenty years ago; they all have a right to education and do receive public education. We do not critique to say the gains are nonexistent; instead we critique to provide a vision of the next step in the evolution of creating schools where all students are valued and seen as having potential.

Until recently the applied fields such as special education have been left out of disability studies because they are disciplines that have traditionally relied on an individual pathology model of responding to disability (at its core, disability studies rejects the medical model as the foundation of an effective understanding of disability). However, as this chapter will argue, disability studies must inform special education research, policy, and practice in order to contribute to the development of an alternate framework to the traditional paradigms that largely inform special education. Disability studies offers an alternative theoretical lens that can perhaps more effectively help researchers and practitioners grapple with systemic challenges facing special education.

NORMALIZING STUDENT DIFFERENCE

The idea of "fixing" an individual with a disability (trying to minimize the evidence or appearance of disability so that an individual fits into socially prescribed standards) is referred to as "normalization." Normalization refers to the desire to improve humans so that deviations from the norm, on any given characteristic, diminish (Davis, 1997). The implications for education are large. Traditional special education is the service that helps children become more like their peers—more normal. Physical, cognitive, communication, social, emotional, or adaptive differences in the classroom setting quickly become physical, cognitive, communication, social, emotional, or adaptive deficits that need to be defined and fixed. Difference is often seen as a negative part of the child. James Kauffman, a special educator and teacher educator, writes, "In our view, students with disabilities do have specific shortcomings and do need the services of specially trained professionals to achieve their potential" (Kauffman et al. 2004, p. 613). He fears that if students and their "shortcomings" are not labeled, they will not receive individualized, appropriate services. Scholars in disability studies question the idea that a label is necessary for appropriate education. They interrogate educational structures that require an ever-growing list of student disability labels under the guise of providing these students with a quality education. They ask, "How can we rethink and remake educational systems that will provide more flexibility and educate more students effectively?"

Before the passage of PL 94–142, The Education for All Handicapped Children Act (EHA) in 1975, and subsequent reauthorization as Individuals with Disabilities Education Act (IDEA) students with disabilities were not guaranteed educational services in public schools. The passage of this law nationally created a provision for ensuring education for all students, created due process for students and their parents, and required that students receive their educational services in the least restrictive appropriate environment. However, these laws also codified differences within individual students as something to be identified and labeled. Common understanding at the time and still pervasive today in the United States is that if we can identify students who have learning needs in schools, we can provide them with educational services so that they have an equal opportunity at schooling. Another limitation of federal legislation is the "continuum of placement options," which legally protects the ability of school districts to sustain segregated and restrictive classroom settings for students with disabilities through its broad interpretation. Although these laws provide legal protection for students and their families, as well as force school districts to account for previously excluded students, they also more firmly establish disability labels as the means by which to provide an education for these students and continue to support the existence of separate educational settings.

Applying the concept of normalization to students with disabilities perpetuates the paradigm that disabilities can be fixed, as well as supports the continued segregation of these students until they have achieved normalcy. Disability studies posits that disability is created in the institutional practices found in schools and elsewhere, that it is socially constructed and that human variation is natural, not pathological. The educational system standardizes all students through the use of diagnostic tests and pathologizes difference (Davis, 1997). The concept of standardization, on the basis of the bell curve and "normal distribution," immediately identifies those at either end as deviant or extreme (ibid.). Students who lie in the upper end of this distribution are seen in American schools as "gifted." Students whose physical bodies, mode of communication, or learning differences fall at the lower end of this distribution are believed to deviate from the norm and are given the label "disabled." Questioning the normality of the "able" body and mind forces questions like, "When does difference count, under what conditions, in what ways, and for what reasons?" (Artiles, 1998, p. 32).

Some families prefer segregated classrooms for perceived safety or educational benefits for their children, or want their children to be more like peers in order to lessen potential social stigma; both these examples, however, perpetuate societal norms of difference as undesirable and locate the problem of disability within individual children. This is clearly understood in practices designed to "remediate" learning or behavioral disabilities away, or in the assumption that some students have disabilities that are too "severe" to gain anything from the general curriculum or school community. We acknowledge that these students receive a form of public education, however we would like to see them afforded the same opportunities and access to curricular content and pedagogical methods—equal to that of their nonlabeled peers.

Imagine a school where everyone has as much time to complete school work or take a test as they needed. In that school working slowly would not be a sign of a learning disability, it would be an option for all students to take enough time to complete their work without the added pressure of a deadline. If student disability were reframed as a social construct—that it exists because our classrooms, the curricula, and the instructional methods we use to teach them were inaccessible—it then becomes our responsibility, as educators, to make schools and classrooms accessible (instead of fixing something that inherently exists within students). This reconceptualization has been articulated as "organizational pathology" instead of "student pathology" (Sobsey, 1994; Ware, 2002). Redefining acceptable school practices to include as many students as possible reframes the theoretical and practical possibilities of students with disabilities in schools.

In addition, if teachers were engaged in reflective practices that taught them to question the moral consequences of segregating students with disabilities they would also question the "discovery" or identification of disability through scientific methods (Gallagher, 2004). Historically, a child is just a child in a classroom until the referral process begins. Once the child is referred for special education services, tested, and has received a label, s/he becomes the disability in the eyes of many teachers. This can be seen by calling students with disabilities in schools "special ed kids"—the label forms initial impressions for teachers before they ever know a child. Gallagher (2004) argues for a solution in which schools would not use "invidious" comparisons in order to achieve uniformity, but rather would support each student's dignity and humanity in the process of teaching and learning. Similarly, Minow (1997, p. 87) encourages us to "remember and remedy group-based harms, and encourage more avenues for individual self-invention." She takes individual perspectives as important but asks us not to forget group level consequences as well. Instead of normalizing student difference, schools could accept differences in children and seek ways to change school structures in order to maximize the potential of all students.

DEPENDENCY

Benevolence, or the desire to "help others less fortunate," has contributed to the development of a "culture of expertise," through which people with disabilities are often kept in a dependent role (Barton, 1998). Similar to other "helping professions," special education professional ideology incorporates notions of benevolence and power. The benevolent intentions of many special educators, combined with the power inequities that often arise when specialized knowledge is exercised, can lead to dependency by others and reduce the need for personal reflection. The culture of expertise also leads to professionals being required to depersonalize the disability from the child and being able to distance themselves from the moral implications of their work.

Pfeiffer et al. (2003) conducted a study on attitudes toward disability in the helping professions and summarized:

> ...many people in the helping professions are threatened if the sincerity of their actions in relation to people with disabilities is described as hollow and their actions are seen as not helpful. Part of their identity is being a person who is seen as working hard to help unfortunate persons, people with disabilities." (p. 133)

"Helping" typically occurs within existing programmatic options, such as offering an array of vocational experiences to a student based not on their individual interests or strengths, but on a preestablished list. Further, when children or parents reject these forms of helping, they are identified as "problems." Rossetti and

Tashie (2002) assert that most special education professionals do not recognize practices that label and segregate students as prejudice justified by paradigms of deficiency, but rather see these practices as "compassionate" and justify their work as help. In interview data collected by the first author, several teachers justified sending students out of the classroom for "special help" even though they had no idea what help would be provided for the children or if the help actually helped. They believed that it was in the child's best interest to receive instruction in a smaller, quieter setting. However studies on the quality of academic education in special education classrooms are inconclusive. It is unclear whether sending students out of the general education classroom supports their learning at all. Special educators (or other disability-related professionals, for that matter) do not have harmful intentions, despite the often, harmful results of the decisions they make for and about students with disabilities.

Questioning the role of the expert and the power given to someone in that role is important because reliance on "expert" knowledge creates dependency on the part of parents/families and students, as well by nonspecial education school professionals. This dependency often results in two consequences: (1) it reinforces that through experts' specialized knowledge, a student's disability can be fixed, and (2) in order to "fix" the disability, students may need to be moved to segregated, specialized placements that can better serve educational needs that lie outside accepted norms. In schools this means a system that not only separates students for academic instruction, but separates with the claim that separate can indeed be equal. The expert often does not have the lived experience of disability and operates from the belief that categories based on societal norms of normal and abnormal are correct, even though these categories shift over time and ideas about how to fix the "problem" of student disability do as well.

Mehan (1993) highlights the power of "helpful" special education "expertise," through his description of the special education referral process, identification of disability, and subsequent labeling of a child and removal from the classroom for services. His case study demonstrates how all participants in the referral process defer to the "expertise" of the school psychologist in identification of student difference (which becomes deficit, disorder, and then disability). Trusting the psychologist with a manila folder exists in contrast to valuing the opinion of people who have known the child better and longer than the psychologist. It also indicates the deference to (which, in turn, becomes dependency on) the specialized knowledge of special education professionals in deciding how to "treat" or "remediate" the now labeled student and where is the best location to do so. What began as a desire to help a child receive the education s/he needs resulted in the labeling and potential segregation of the now disabled student.

Helping professionals also try to separate the disability from the person with the disability in order to eliminate the need to consider potential moral consequences of expert decisions (Sobsey, 1994; Pfeiffer et al., 2003). According to Pfeiffer et al. (2003), if disability professionals can separate disability from the person then they do not need to view the disability as part of the person and can distance themselves from the effects of their interventions. Myths that legitimize and support methods of segregating individuals with disabilities "in their best interests" developed in part out of the culture of expertise that keeps people with disabilities in a dependent role. Other consequences, such as eugenics, sterilization, institutionalization, and school/community segregation have resulted from seemingly benevolent decisions about "what is in their (individuals with disabilities) best interest." As professionals we must interrogate the reasons people want to go into teaching (and other disability-related fields) to better understand the potential of and limitation to benevolent decision-making. The next section offers potential ways forward to account for and confront the creation and maintenance of dependency in schools.

Where is there room to respect the knowledge gained by expertise while critiquing the way expert knowledge is used on a day-to-day basis? Perhaps an answer can come from experts who are trying to see their role as one of guide or facilitator rather than all-knowing expert. Ware (2002) and Harry et al. (1999) both identify potential solutions to the power and dependency that result from professional benevolence. Ware simply urges teachers to be more fully conscious of the results of their actions. She cites MacIntyre's (1999) concept "suspicion of ourselves" as a starting point for reflective practice that examines the role of disability and dependence in teachers' lives and classrooms. MacIntyre's concept requires an examination of human vulnerability and dependency in order to explore "whose good is included in the common good." Through an understanding provided by MacIntyre, Ware urges special education professionals to acknowledge "…our complicity with past constructions of disability that have clearly limited our view of humanity" (2002, p. 145). Ware's ideas encourage the belief that, contrary to social norms that disability is undesirable and needs to be remediated or eradicated, difference (disability being one measure of this) is good (or at least neutral) and should be accepted as mind/body variation without negative consequences. Harry et al. (1999) argue that the goals of service provision should be informed by two principles: (1) cultural reciprocity, whereby professionals work in a collaborative manner with families, and (2) a sociocultural view of learning and development as a way to offset the traditional dominant paradigm found in the interactions between experts and the families and students using special education services.

Finally, emancipatory research that enlists the "insider" perspective of disability in schools, in order to inform and guide research questions and methods, is an additional approach to the problem of benevolence in traditional special education practices. The use of emancipatory research methods that explore students' own reactions to special education placement and to their disability identity should be explored and developed. These methods would begin to address the need for increased activism, agency, and autonomy in the experiences of students with disabilities (Brisenden 1998; Williams 2001; Ware 2002). Emancipatory approaches require critical self-reflection and awareness, including how we, as special education professionals, have contributed to the creation of "disabling" research practices through the theoretical foundations we rely on, the language we use, and the subsequent perceptions and expectations of students with disabilities (Barton, 1998; Barton and Armstrong, 2001). Leigh O'Brien (2006) gives examples of international educational terminology that shift perceptions and expectations of students: in Sweden they say children "in need of special support," the Welsch use "children having 'additional'" needs, and in Italy "children with special rights." Thinking through the theoretical foundations of these terms and perceptions held by students, their teachers, and their families, one can see how the culture behind chosen terminology matters; they can reinforce the status quo or push for a new understanding of students in schools.

The development of and use of power between individuals in the helping professions and people with disabilities comes from the professional ideology of benevolence described above. People with disabilities and their families are encouraged to rely on the knowledge and expertise of experts rather than knowledge gained through their own, lived (e.g., social/political) experience of disability. Societal reinforcement of expert knowledge as the only knowledge creates a cycle where expert and disabled person alike perpetuate the "mask of benevolence" (Lane, 1992). Research in disability studies works to unmask cycles of benevolent oppression found in schools and in special education.

STIGMATIZATION

Educational practices that categorize children with disabilities on the basis of their disability labels, and develop educational settings based on these categories are modeled on the belief that categorical education can best meet individualized learning needs. These practices are also based in the belief that students need to have a disability label in order to receive any specialized services or supports. There is debate in the field of special education about stigmatization (as evidenced through the assignment of disability labels and separate classrooms for these students) and its effects.

As special education currently exists in the United States a student cannot receive any individualized "special" services without also receiving a disability label. Skrtic and Sailor (1996) refer to these as "prescriptive labels," as a student's disability label often prescribes what individualized services are offered to him/her and dictates where these services are provided. They also note that these labels decrease access to "nondisabled" services (such as instruction in the general curriculum). Lipsky and Gartner (1997) identify that special education has indeed become a "place," instead of an array of services, as it was intended; students who become "disabled" students are typically removed from the general classroom in order to receive whatever services accompany their disability label. In this way, the special education services do, in fact, become the special education place—the classroom, speech room, or other separate settings within the school. Similarly, Zuna and Turnbull (2004) discuss the need for disability identification and labeling as a limitation of federal special education legislation. They state, "…the classification and labeling that categorize and stigmatize, sort, separate, and endure. These consequences, in essence, 'consume' their identity. They are no long just children. They are now, even with our polite, 'person-first' language, children with disabilities" (p. 211). These authors point not only to the stigmatization of these students, but also to the "sorting" and "separating" practices that accompany the ever-increasing list of disability labels in the United States.

Some researchers theorize that children are stigmatized by the label and the label might lead to worse outcomes than no label and no services would have (Connor, 2004; Danforth and Rhodes, 1997; Gartner and Lipsky, 1987). Other concerns relate to the effects of being labeled. When these children are rejected from the general education classroom, typically the rejection will result in stigmatization by the remaining students and the teacher (Brantlinger, 1997). Stigma in a school setting impacts both students' self esteem (Connor, 2004) and educational achievement (Steele, 1997). The effects of stigmatization extend beyond educational settings. Cumulative effects lead to disabled students becoming disabled adults with poor, if any, job prospects (often because of the lack of adequate educational experiences), as well as expectation by others that they will need "care" throughout their adult lives. Thus, disabled adults are thought of as "dependent" and are relegated to second class citizens. They are pitied or feared, have trouble in relationships and in gaining and maintaining employment (National Organization on Disability, 1994). Stigmatizing labels and their consequences, often first assigned in educational settings (because of a federal system that requires labeling to receive extra funding and services), follow students into adulthood. Nondisabled students, who learned to stigmatize others in childhood, carry that into adulthood as well—thus perpetuating a system of social and, by implication, economic and political inequality for people with disabilities.

Not all special educators agree with concerns about labeling leading to stigmatization (Kauffman et al., 2004). Some educators think the disability itself is stigmatizing. Kauffman et al., (ibid.) make a normative argument that disability does not create stigma. They point out that some children need services that other children do not. Labels, they say, afford students certain services (like physical or speech therapy) they would otherwise be unable to receive without labels (Fuchs et al., 1993; Kauffman, 2003). Their argument, however, stops there because they believe that labeling students is the only way to provide needed services. This is true as long as educational structures force services to be tied to disability labels and as long as difference, academic or otherwise, is equated with deficit.

Disability studies takes aim at issues of stigma and disability. The field theorizes that the label itself is often stigmatizing but can also be reclaimed as an affirmation of group identity. When the disability label stigmatizes, it creates an imbalance of power where students are segregated out of bureaucratic convenience and the desire of others to avoid them. Garland-Thomson (1997) says that stigmatization reinforces the dominant group's self-idealized identity as "normal" and "legitimate," so that the characteristics of less powerful groups can be perpetuated as inferior. These categories of "normal" and "abnormal," assert Ferguson et al. (1992), not only mark differences between groups of people, but also indicate characteristics that discredit an individual's moral fiber. A child who cannot sit still in school, one who shows external aggression, and even one who cannot run and play ball with other children becomes abnormal in the school setting and stigmatized. Though not apparent in current school structures, spaces for disabled students to congregate can also provide for "crip culture" to develop and for group identity to be formed. Traditional special education could argue that segregated spaces are good for students with disabilities so they can develop relationships with other students "like them." Disability studies researchers would question why assignment to these spaces is mandatory (not a choice). They would argue that these same students could form a student group based on their own, commonly created disability identity (versus that established by membership in an assigned classroom), through which they share experiences based on power imbalances and work to disrupt structural inequalities in schools.

Like benevolence, the relationship between stigmatization and disability brings up issues about the use of power. Power is not only exercised through the ability of nondisabled individuals to (consciously or, more likely, not) keep people with disabilities in stigmatized and inferior roles in society; it is also reinforced by the ability of categories to mark characteristics that discredit an individual's moral character (Ferguson et al., 1992). Social agencies and organizations such as schools further reinforce and support the socialization of the disability role. Sobsey (1994) describes the self-perpetuating cycle of the stigmatized disability role. First, is the belief that individuals with disabilities are differently (and thus, less) human than ourselves. This is followed by differential treatment justified by these beliefs, and the subsequent outcome of "atypical" behavior on the part of the individual with disabilities. Finally, nondisabled individuals observe the "atypical" behavior, which confirms their initial beliefs and begins the cycle again (p. 313). Thus, people with disabilities are "rewarded" for behavior that conforms to the disability role, while at the same time reinforces and confirms beliefs of nondisabled individuals (Ferguson et al., 1992; Sobsey, 1994).

Understanding more about stigmatization and its relationship to disability labels in schools might enable more reflective practitioners, but could also call into question the moral consequences of assigning these labels. Closer examination of stigmatization could also provide the impetus for a reconceptualization of both the general and special education systems. Applying redefinitions of disability and impairment to educational settings would require that school professionals look beyond both normative or standardized test scores and positivist concerns with universality and generalizability in order to create teaching and learning environments that are accessible to a wider range of students. One alternative to the current system of assigning disability labels would be to acknowledge student impairment, while at the same time addressing structural barriers in classrooms and schools that prohibit a wider range of students from accessing what schools have to offer all students.

CONCLUSION

Disability studies research questions much of what is assumed to be true in our society. It asks us to unpack assumptions about normalcy, benevolence and power, as well as stigmatization. It forces us to question attitudes and structural barriers that disabled people face daily but that are often invisible to nondisabled people. In education, the potential impact of disabilities studies research is enormous. It can help special education and schools of education develop a more complete understanding of students with disabilities, not just as individuals whose educational needs must receive attention, but also as members of a group in society who face unequal opportunities within and outside of schools. We know the United States has come a long way over the course of a century. A century ago it was acceptable not to educate children with disabilities. Now disabled students are in school buildings and receiving public education. The next step is to align the needs of the individual within a sociopolitical analysis of societal advancements and limitations so that when a teacher is asked, "Where do you see this student as an adult?" the answer for disabled students and nondisabled students will be similar.

As this chapter has attempted to demonstrate, the time is ripe for the development of an alternative theoretical framework that can inform the field of special education in order to incorporate new knowledge and understanding about disability into educational research and practice. This chapter offers the conclusion that the wide-ranging field of disability studies can and should provide an alternative theoretical frame for special education. Disability studies challenges the dominant theoretical and conceptual frameworks that have traditionally informed the field of special education. Further, disability studies offers alternatives to the positivistic underpinnings of the medical model (which identify disability as a problem in the individual for which interventions can be designed) in its examination of disabling environments and social and economic policies. This chapter has also attempted to identify some broad ways in which the perspective offered by disability studies can be applied to special education research and practice. Although disability studies theory suggests alternate practices to many of those currently in use, it remains up to researchers, communities of educators, and people with disabilities to identify and implement the suitable alternatives.

Disability studies seeks to do more than affirm differences as acceptable in individuals, more than celebrate one more cultural group's identity. It seeks to change social oppression into social equality for disabled people in order to have equivalent economic and political possibilities in society.

REFERENCES

Artiles, A. J. (1998). The dilemma of difference: Enriching the disproportionality discourse with theory and context. *Journal of Special Education*, 32(1), 32–36.

Barton, L. (1998). Sociology, disability studies and education: Some observations. In T. Shakespeare (Ed.), *The disability reader* (pp. 53–64). London: Cassell.

Barton, L. and Armstrong, F. (2001). Disability, education, and inclusion: Cross-cultural issues and dilemmas. In G. L. Albrecht, K. D. Sleeman, and M. Bury (Eds.), *Handbook of disability studies* (pp. 693–710). Thousand Oaks, CA: Sage.

Brantlinger, E. A. (1997). Using ideology: Cases of nonrecognition of the politics of research and practice in special education. *Review of Educational Research*, 67(4), 425–459.

Brisenden, S. (1998). Independent living and the medical model of disability. In T. Shakespeare. (Ed.), *The disability reader* (pp. 20–27). London: Cassell.

Connor, D. J. (2004). Infusing disability studies into "Mainstream" educational thought: One person's story. *Review of Disability Studies*, 1(1), 100–120.

Danforth, S. and Rhodes, W. C. (1997). Deconstructing disability—A philosophy for inclusion. *Remedial and Special Education*, 18(6), 357–366.

Davis, L. J. (1997). *The disability studies reader*. New York: Routledge.

Ferguson, P. M., Ferguson, D., and Taylor, S. J. (1992). *Interpreting disability: A qualitative reader*. New York: Teachers College Press.

Fuchs, D., Fuchs, L. S., and Fernstrom, P. (1993). A conservative approach to special education reform—Mainstreaming through transenvironmental programming and curriculum-based measurement. *American Educational Research Journal*, 30(1), 149–177.

Gallagher, D. J. (2004). The importance of constructivism and constructivist pedagogy for disability studies in education. *Disability Studies Quarterly*, 24(2), Retrieved September, 21, 2006, from http://www.dsq-sds.org/_articles_html/2004/spring/gallagher.asp.

Garland-Thomas, R. (1997). Integrating disability studies into the existing curriculum. In L. J. Davis (Ed.), *The disability studies reader* (pp. 295–306). New York: Routledge.

Gartner, A. and Lipsky, D. K. (1987). Beyond special education—Toward a quality system for all students. *Harvard Educational Review*, 57(4), 367–395.

Harry, B., Rueda, R., and Kalyanpur, M. (1999). Cultural reciprocity in sociocultural perspective: Adapting the normalization principle for family collaboration. *Exceptional Children*, 66(1), 123–136.

Kauffman, J. M. (2003). Reflections on the field. *Education and Treatment of Children*, 26(4), 325–329.

Kauffman, J. M., McGee, K., and Brigham, M. (2004). Enabling or disabling? Observations on changes in special education. *Phi Delta Kappan*, 85(8), 613.

Lane, H. (1992). The mask of benevolence: Disabling the deaf community. New York: Knopf.

Lipsky, D. K. and Gartner, A. (1997). *Inclusion and school reform: Transforming America's classrooms*. Baltimore, MD: P. H. Brookes Pub. Co.

MacIntyre, A. (1999). *Dependent rational animals: Why human beings need virtue*. Berkeley: Open Court Press.

Mehan, H. (1993). Beneath the skin and between the ears: A case study in the politics of representation. In Chaiklin, S. and Lave, J. (Eds.), *Understanding practice: Perspectives on activity and context* (pp. 241–268). New York: Cambridge University Press.

Minow, M. (1997). *Not only for myself: Identity, politics and the law*. New York: New York Press.

National Organization on Disability. (1994). Washington, DC: National Organization on Disability.

O'Brien. (2006). Being bent over backward: A mother and teacher educator challenges the positioning of her daughter with disabilities. *Disability Studies Quarterly*, 26(2). Retrived September 1, 2006, from http://www.dsqsds.org/_articles_html/2006/spring/obrien.asp.

Pfeiffer, D., Sam, A. A., Giunan, M., Ratliffe, K. T., Robinson, N. B., and Stodden, N. J. (2003). Attitudes towards disability in the helping professions. *Disability Studies Quarterly*, 23(2), 132–149.

Rossetti, Z. and Tashie, C. (2002). Outing the prejudice: Making the least dangerous assumption. *Newsletter of the Autism National Committee*.

Skrtic, T. M. and Sailor, W. (1996). Voice, collaboration, and inclusion. *Remedial and Special Education*, 17(3), 142–158.

Sobsey, D. (1994). *Violence and abuse in the lives of people with disabilities: The end of silent acceptance*. Baltimore, MD: Paul H. Brookes.

Steele, C. (1997). A threat in the air: How stereotypes shape intellectual identity and performance. *American Psychologist*, 52(6), 613–629.

Ware, L. (2002). A moral conversation on disability: Risking the personal in educational contexts. *Hypatia*, 17(3), 143–172.

Williams, G. (2001). Theorizing disability. In G. L. Albrecht, K. D. Sleeman and M. Bury (Eds.), *Handbook of disability studies* (pp. 123–144). Thousand Oaks, CA: Sage.

Winzer, M. (1993). *The history of special education: From isolation to integration*. Washington DC: Gallaudet University Press.

Zuna, N. and Turnbull, R. (2004). "Imagine all the people, sharing …" or a (not so) modest proposal made on the eve of IDEA reauthorization." *Research and Practice for Persons with Severe Disabilities*, 29(3), 210–213.

Section IV
Higher Education

The UN/UNESCO Task force on Higher Education (2000) has identified higher education as a key aspect of nation building in today's global economy or what the Task Force calls the "knowledge revolution" (Intro., Section 3). This knowledge revolution poses challenges for developing nations in particular, where a lack of adequate institutional resources and autonomy and limited numbers of qualified faculty constrain higher education development opportunities. These institutional challenges pose problems of a structural nature while students in these countries face their own problems including lack of resources, insufficient or minimal elementary and secondary education, and interference from regional conflicts.

Despite the roadblocks, and in light of the high stakes of globalization, the *World Declaration on Higher Education* (UNESCO, 1998) recognizes that "there is an unprecedented demand for and a great diversification in higher education as well as an increased awareness of its vital importance for sociocultural and economic development" (Preamble, 1). Between 1960 and 1995, worldwide student enrollment in higher education increased more than sixfold from 13 to 82 million while at the same time the gap between the richest and poorest countries widened (ibid., 2). These data indicate the timeliness of focus on higher education by the disability rights community.

According to Article Three of the *World Declaration*, higher education should provide equity of access and should involve a "seamless system starting with early childhood and primary education and continuing through life" (3.b.). Chapter 29, by Justin Powell, Kai Felkendorff, and Judith Hollenweger, on higher education in German-speaking countries (Germany, Switzerland, Austria), illustrates the importance of a "seamless system" and provides a good overview for the higher education issues explored in this section They note that in the countries they have studied, a traditional two-tiered system of higher education—university and vocational school—continues to exist with mixed consequences for disabled people. They document the low percentage of disabled people in higher education in these countries and link this to the influence of policy and tradition, particularly the absence or late emergence of policy that tends to the needs of disabled students.

Problems of access to higher education are limited not only to countries developing special education policy. For example, in the United States, where a "free appropriate public education" has been legislated for nearly 30 years, 11.3% of postsecondary undergraduates in 2003–2004 reported being disabled (US Department of Education, 2006); unfortunately, however, race plays a role in access (Reid and Knight, 2006). The vast majority of US disabled students in college are White and learning disabled (Henderson, 2001), yet Black students are overrepresented in elementary and secondary special education (Blanchett, 2006). This phenomenon is not unique to the United States; marginalized social groups are underrepresented in higher education worldwide. In India, caste plays a role in determining access to higher education (Government of India, 2004). The underrepresentation of indigenous people in higher education among New Zealand's Maori and Canada's Inuit is linked to overrepresentation in special education leading to inadequate preparation for higher education (e.g., Mattson and Caffrey, 2001). Underrepresentation of indigenous people also can be a factor of discrimination, cultural isolation, or fear of assimilation (Johnston, 2004; Ambler, 2005; Capozza, 2001). Yet regardless of the reason for inequity, accessible quality higher education is becoming more important for the economic security of both the individual as well as the nation and, consequently, more critical to the welfare of disabled people.

The phrase "equal access to higher education" should not be mistaken for equal opportunity to be admitted to higher education. Access also requires institutional support and transformed learning environments once disabled students begin their courses. Here, Kim Marshall (chapter 30) and Sheryl Burgstahler and Rebecca Cory (chapter 31) speak to the issues. Marshall analyses the troubling legal concept of "reasonable adjustments duty" found in British educational policy. This concept is similar to the requirement for "reasonable accommodation" in US policy. Marshall rightly critiques the medical model framework within which "reasonable adjustments" must be determined, but this criticism raises a paradox similar to the two-tiered postsecondary education system in German-speaking countries: reasonable adjustments solve some problems of inclusion while also creating problems of exclusion. Burgstahler and Cory follow with an answer to this dilemma in their overview of Universal Design applied to higher education. Their work at the University of Washington has yielded important strategies for creating accessible programs and curricula.

The last two chapters in this section address the Disability Studies content of the university curriculum. Levan Lim, Thana Thaver, and Kenneth Poon (chapter 32) describe their journey of adopting a Disability Studies perspective in Singapore's National Institute of Education where they prepare regular or mainstream educators. They have created a model that is not culturally dependent and their ideas could be useful for teacher educators in other countries. Finally, Christopher Johnstone, Alex Lubet, and Leonard Goldfine (chapter 33) provide a case study of attempts to create a Disability Studies program at a large research university in the United States. The case is an example of the tentative status of Disability Studies, the territorial disputes that arise in academia when it is introduced, the persistence of the medical model of disability, and the struggle for meaning. In this sense, the case they describe is representative of the situation facing Disability Studies on a number of fronts in addition to policy.

Other authors in this volume address themes or topics related to higher education including: Gabel and Chander (chapter 5) and Chander (chapter 12).

REFERENCES

Ambler, M. (2005). While globalizing their movement, tribal colleges import ideas. *Tribal College Journal*, 16(4). Retrieved on July 8, 2007 from https://tribalcollegejournal.org/themag/backissues/summer2005/sum05ambler.htm.

Blanchett, W. (2006). Disproportionate representation of African American students in special education: Acknowledging the role of White privilege and racism. *Educational Researcher*, 35(6). Retrieved on July 7, 2007 from http://www.aera.net/uploadedFiles/Publications/Journals/Educational_Researcher/3506/06ERv35n6_Blanchett.pdf.

Capozza, K. L. (2001). Canadian territory of Nunavut pushes to expand college offerings. Inuit educators face obstacles of distance and tradition. *Chronicle of Higher Education*, July 27. Retrieved on July 8, 2007 from http://chronicle.com/weekly/v47/i46/46a03801.htm.

Government of India (2004). *India: National report on the development of education*. The Indian education system at the beginning of the 21st century: An overview. Retrieved on July 1, 2007 from http://www.ibe.unesco.org/International/ICE47/english/Natreps/reports/india.pdf.

Henderson, C. (2001). *College freshmen with disabilities, 2001: A biennial statistical profile*. Washington, DC: American Council on Education.

Johnston, P. (2004). Maori in higher education: Examining indicators of success. Paper presented at the American Educational Research Association conference. San Diego, CA.

Mattson, L., and Caffrey, L. (2001). *Barriers to equal education for aboriginal learners: A review of the literature*. Vancouver: British Columbia Human Rights Commission.

Reid, D. K., and Knight, M. G. (2006). Disability justifies exclusion of disabled students: A critical history grounded in disability studies. *Educational Researcher*, 35(6). Retrieved on July 7, 2007 from http://www.aera.net/uploadedFiles/Publications/Journals/Educational_Researcher/3506/05ERv35n6_Reid.pdf.

UNESCO (1998). World declaration on higher education for the twenty-first century: Vision and action. Retrieved on July 8, 2007 from http://www.unesco.org/education/educprog/wche/declaration_eng.htm.

United Nations/UNESCO (2000). *Peril and promise: Higher education in developing countries.* New York: United Nations. Retrieved on July 8, 2007 from http://www.tfhe.net/.

US Department of Education, National Center for Education Statistics (2006). *Profile of Undergraduates in U.S. Postsecondary Education Institutions: 2003–04.* Washington, DC: US Department of Education.

CHAPTER TWENTY-NINE

Disability IN THE German, Swiss, AND Austrian Higher Education Systems

JUSTIN J.W. POWELL, KAI FELKENDORFF, AND
JUDITH HOLLENWEGER

INTRODUCTION: CROSS-NATIONAL STUDIES OF DISABILITY AND HIGHER EDUCATION

Disabled people's exclusion from higher education continues even as their participation in primary and secondary schooling has expanded considerably, especially over the postwar period. Successes in achieving education for all and inclusive education have not automatically translated into equal opportunities in later stages of an educational career, even if such developments have led to a larger population *eligible* for postsecondary education and training. Transitions pose a major challenge for students in low-status tracks, such as most sections of special education. Around the world, even those higher education institutions that aim to equalize access, provide services, and make necessary accommodations have not yet succeeded in completely eliminating discrimination because of ableist policies and practices.[1] Higher educational institutions have too long ignored the physical and attitudinal changes that they could make to reduce barriers that make studies difficult or impossible for students with disabilities.

Although education is an increasingly valued individual and public good, beyond minimal levels it has yet to be secured as a right for *all* citizens, even in self-proclaimed "information" or "education" societies (Peters, 2004). Access for specific disadvantaged groups, such as individuals with disabilities, along with immigrants, ethnic minorities, and those of lower social-class backgrounds, remains tenuous or has been ensured only at the bottom of stratified educational systems. The resulting low educational attainment levels negatively affect their employment opportunities and life chances. More generally, complex interactions between cultural, institutional, familial, economic, and political changes and their effects on young people—and the manner in which these programs and policies facilitate or impede their passages to adulthood—are just beginning to be understood (Settersten et al., 2005).

Although interest in higher education has grown among educational researchers in the German-speaking countries, the focus of educational and sociological research on the phenomenon of disability in education continues to be compulsory schooling and integration (more recently, inclusion). The knowledge base about previous pathways as well as higher education participation and experiences of disabled students in German-speaking countries remains limited. Despite the quantification and comparison of every aspect of schooling, cross-nationally comparable data on educational outcomes is almost completely lacking for students who receive additional educational resources to access school curricula, with the collection of outcome statistics to be emphasized in future data gathering activities (OECD, 2004b: 131). As educational systems become more inclusive and qualification rates among certain groups of disabled youth increase, we will need additional research on transitions to postsecondary education as well as further educational pathways. What contribution the emergent Disability Studies discourse in German-speaking countries will make to improve empirical research on disability in higher education is just beginning to be outlined.[2]

In this chapter, we will review recent research in the German-speaking countries, comparing these nationally and regionally variant systems, recent policy developments, and accessibility provisions. In these countries, segregated special education, extensive systems of vocational training (as a viable alternative to university education for most graduates of lower secondary education), and lack of accessibility in higher education pose considerable barriers to equality. Looking to three countries with differentiated postsecondary education systems, but with largely segregated provision of secondary education indicates the modest extent to which the goals of universal access to education and inclusive education have been achieved. In the meantime, however, we should not neglect those pioneers who have succeeded to enroll in postsecondary educational institutions after experiencing segregated secondary schooling. Narrative interviews with these current students with disabilities point to areas needing improvement (Hollenweger et al., 2005; Meister, 1998). Here, we combine information based on individuals' experiences in postsecondary education with available aggregate data on participation rates as well as representative surveys. This cross-national comparison identifies a variety of barriers whose elimination would facilitate disabled students' success in higher education. For the first time, a Swiss study presents a comprehensive picture of disability among Swiss institutions of higher education, combining surveys, case studies, and different forms of interviews with students as well as university and external counseling staff (Hollenweger et al., 2005). Relying on such decisive research projects, Disability Studies in education can provide recommendations for the reform of policies and practices.

TOWARD UNIVERSAL ACCESS? PATHWAYS AND BARRIERS TO HIGHER EDUCATION FOR YOUTH WITH DISABILITIES

Segregated schooling

The trend of participation in tertiary education is upward in all three countries, while access and accommodations for students with disabilities persist as areas in need of considerable further development. The most important limitation, found in all German-speaking countries despite recent reform efforts, is prevalent segregation of disabled children and youth. In Germany, ten separate types of special schools, differentiated on the basis of categories of educational support since 1994, continue to serve the vast majority of pupils classified as having special educational needs (Powell, 2006). School segregation is a major source of social inequality early in the life course and has cumulative negative effects on further educational participation among young adults with disabilities (Powell, 2003a). Because of highly selective primary and secondary schooling structures in all German-speaking countries, youth who were labeled early in school as "disabled" according to the relevant educational-administrative definitions of disability have historically been largely excluded from postsecondary education. In most states, curricular and credential requirements for postsecondary education (especially university study) could not, and indeed still cannot, be met while participating in special education programs. In Germany, only 48 of around 45,000 special school-leavers attained the certification necessary for university entrance in 2000, and 80 percent did not even receive the lowest qualified certificate (*Hauptschulabschluss*) (Krappmann et al., 2003: 773). By 2003, the number of special school-leavers holding a higher education entrance qualification had risen to 66 (KMK, 2005: 48).

Austria is the only country of the three that has a national law extending the right to school integration for pupils with special educational needs through the end of compulsory school age. This integration law has resulted in significantly rising integration rates since 1996, as more parents choose such settings for their children (Dujmovits, 2004). As segregation rates in Austria decline, larger cohorts of integrated or even inclusively educated schoolchildren with special educational needs have begun to reach college age. In Germany and Switzerland, by contrast, school integration has only been achieved in some states, with inclusive education often offered only in pilot projects with consulting educational researchers. But most German states (*Länder*) and Swiss cantons do not even guarantee an effective right to school integration, defined as attending a general school, despite the forceful demands of parents and disability activists. Recommendations passed by the German and Swiss Standing Conferences of Ministers of Education in the 1990s aimed to establish integrated schooling as a fully viable form of schooling for pupils deemed to have special educational needs. However, these recommendations, as well as some amendments to state or canton school laws, have not yet resulted in lower segregation rates. In fact, there is an ever-increasing proportion of pupils in mainstream schools diagnosed as having some form of special educational need. Rates of pupils attending segregated special schools during compulsory education in German-speaking countries are consistently among the highest in world (Powell, 2006). Paradoxically, the segregation rate of all children in compulsory education in Germany has risen to 4.8 percent in 2003, up from 4.3 percent in 1995, when influential recommendations concerning integrated schooling had just been issued by the ministries of education (KMK, 2005: 25). In Switzerland, 6.2 percent of all schoolchildren were taught either in special schools (funded by the national "invalidity insurance" scheme), or in special classes (mainly funded and managed by the cantons) in 2004. There are striking regional disparities with regard to segregation rates in special classes, varying from 0 to 7.2 percent between Swiss cantons. Furthermore, male and ethnic minority children and youth are overrepresented in Swiss special education, as they are in Germany (Powell & Wagner, 2002). Pupils whose special educational needs are diagnosed in primary or secondary school risk segregation and are highly unlikely to return to general education (Preuss-Lausitz, 2001). Their subsequent learning opportunities are often reduced, and the possibility of meeting curricular requirements for accessing postsecondary education is seriously limited.

Postsecondary education structures and access to higher education

The German-speaking (and influenced) countries have extensive systems of vocational training that provide attractive apprenticeship opportunities at the upper secondary level. Because these educational systems place emphasis on upper secondary schooling and well-developed vocational training, a consequently smaller group participates in tertiary education. Further, university education has traditionally been reserved for members of higher classes. Thus, vocational training plays a far more significant role in preparing young adults for employment than it does in other European countries, and this is especially true for those youth who participate in special education. German-speaking countries combine in-school and in-firm education and training (apprenticeships) in a so-called *dual system* to utilize the benefits of both teaching/learning settings, and vocational training institutions are an integral part of secondary school structures. Due to the traditional definitions of "disability" in educational systems and the early segregation of disabled and disadvantaged children into lower-status tracks, research concerning transitions of youth with disabilities to the labor market focuses almost exclusively on transitions through structures of upper secondary level vocational training (Felkendorff & Lischer, 2005).

However, students in Germany and Switzerland stay in secondary education longer (Figure 29. 1). Austria's students transition faster, with a smaller proportion than the Organisation for Economic Co-operation and Development (OECD) mean remaining in secondary education at age twenty. This comparison indicates that even within the German-speaking world, pathways from school to work are considerably differently structured: At age eighteen, Germany has 40 percent more students still in some form of secondary education than does Austria. At age twenty, a fifth of young adults in both Germany and Switzerland are still enrolled in public or private secondary schools. Societies differ in the pathways and support they provide youth transitioning from secondary to tertiary educa-

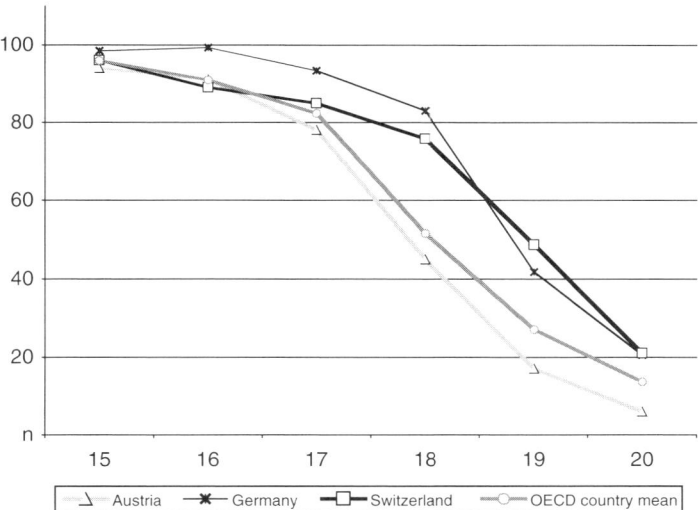

Figure 29.1. Exiting secondary education: Transitions at ages 15–20 (Net enrolment rates in secondary education, public and private institutions), 2002. *Source*: Authors' figure based on OECD 2004a: Indicator C1.3.

tion. Cross-national research suggests that regulated and vocation-oriented systems, such as those in the German-speaking countries, tend to lead to relatively smooth transitions to the labor market, reducing the risk of underemployment and unemployment for those with vocational training; however, these systems also tend to foreclose these individuals' access to higher education (Shavit & Müller, 1998). In other words, secondary school tracking systems and vocational education can play two contrary roles simultaneously—as a safety net for some, but as a mechanism of social exclusion for others.

Since most people in the younger cohorts hold vocational (or academic) qualifications in these countries and access to coveted apprenticeships increasingly requires qualified lower or even intermediate level secondary certificates, youth with disabilities face particular difficulties. Their chances at the next stage, such as into Germany's certificate-oriented and training-focused labor markets, will be considerably constrained for those who have not participated in the dual system. As Seibert (2005) has shown for ethnic minority youth, equalizing access to vocational training itself, rather than attempting integration at the stage of transition into labor markets, promises greater equality of opportunity. As in the United States, in Germany certain ethnic minority groups are disproportionately represented in special education and face higher risk of remaining less educated (Powell, 2006).

In most OECD countries, the proportion of low-skilled persons has decreased considerably over the last two decades, but the remaining, smaller group faces heightened stigmatization (Solga, 2005). Germany seems to be an exception in having an increasing percentage of less-educated persons in the 25–34 age-group, over the same time period in which more of that age-group in Switzerland and Austria were attaining upper secondary certificates, but this may be related to the unification of East and West Germany in 1990 (Table 29. 1). All three

TABLE 29. 1. Percentage of persons who hold less than upper secondary school qualifications, by age-group (1992, 2001).

Age-group	1992			2001		
	25–64	25–34	55–64	25–64	25–34	55–64
Germany	18	11	31	17	15	24
Switzerland	19	13	30	13	8	19
Austria	32	21	50	23	16	35
OECD avg.	45	35	62	36	26	51

Source: List & Schnabel, 2004: 12 (OECD data).

German-speaking countries are at least 10 percentage points below the OECD average, pointing to high educational standards and participation rates in these nations. The majority of students graduating from upper secondary level participated in programs that prepare for and provide access to tertiary education (OECD, 2005). Without such upper secondary qualifications, youth with disabilities will face higher unemployment rates (23) and compete in labor markets at a considerable disadvantage. In fact, not only is the estimated long-term effect on economic output of an additional year of education in the OECD between 3 and 6 percent, but analyses also indicate a causal relationship between higher educational attainment and better mental and physical health (27).

Thus, equality of opportunity for students with disabilities implies access to high expectations and learning opportunities throughout compulsory schooling as well as to college preparatory curricula in upper secondary education. Given the increased importance of holding educational certificates in all three societies, youth transitioning from school to higher education, vocational training, and employment need enhanced support to participate and attain qualifications. On the basis of a cross-national comparison, Wetzel (2002) outlined general requirements educational programs must fulfill to facilitate successful transitions of disabled youth: Explicit and stable, long-term institutional frameworks to ensure planning security; a regionally decentralized and individually personalized and flexible support system; intervention beginning before secondary school-leaving; and no division between more or less favored groups to avoid large effects of "creaming out" in the selection of participants.

Comparing the proportions of students completing first tertiary-level degrees (of their age-group), the German-speaking countries hover around 20 percent, considerably below Japan and the USA at around a third and Australia at nearly 50 percent (OECD, 2005: 13). Thus, tertiary education plays a less significant role in Germany, Switzerland, and Austria than in these other countries, which has to be taken into account when we discuss the participation of persons with disabilities in tertiary education.

STUDENTS WITH DISABILITIES IN HIGHER EDUCATION

Participation rates

Obtaining an adequate picture of the prevalence of "disability" or "special educational needs" among the relevant age-groups requires Disability Studies research to look beyond data generated by schools or welfare administrations and their sometimes contradictory, rarely compatible conceptions and measures of disability.

The quantity and quality of groups of youth and young adults with disabilities—measured with currently utilized sociological, legal, educational, or medical concepts of disability—need not be, and are empirically not identical (Felkendorff, 2003a; 2003b; Hollenweger et al., 2005; Powell, 2003b). For decades, German-speaking sociology has emphasized that disability and disablement, but also concepts like impairment and illness, can only be understood as shifting, contingent and highly value-laden sociopolitical constructs and practices (Cloerkes, 2003). Other disciplines, especially related to the medical, pedagogical, or legal professions, have generated and implemented a multitude of concepts of disability that shape social reality. Thus, social scientists have to take into consideration these concepts as social facts when undertaking empirical research before going beyond. Disability Studies calls on all these disciplines to problematize their understandings of "disability" and critically engage the complexity of disablement.

The most obvious evidence for the shortcomings of present definitions and statistics concerning disability in childhood and youth is the fact that young adults whose impairments or chronic illnesses were of little direct relevance for *schooling* structures have attained higher education entrance qualifications in large numbers in all three countries. It is solely this group's access to higher education that can account for the participation rates of disabled and chronically ill persons in higher education that we present here. Recent changes toward more inclusive education throughout Europe emphasize the need for data gathering efforts to explicitly analyze the current situation of disabled pupils (EADSNE, 2003). The rights and responsibilities of both persons with disabilities and institutions shift considerably from secondary to postsecondary education (OCR, 2005). In order to enhance reliability and validity, data collection efforts and analyses must attend to these differences.

In 2003, the proportion of students in German higher education self-reporting a disability reached 2.5 percent, but 10 percent of students reported living with chronic illness (BMBF, 2004; DSW, 2000). In Austria's national survey of 2002, 11.7 percent of all students defined themselves as "physically handicapped," varying from 6 percent to 16 percent by university. Of the Austrian national average of nearly 12 percent, 7.6 percent of all students reported having a serious chronic illness, and 4.1 percent reported having a disability (IHS, 2005: AT 4). In an earlier survey, 12 percent of students in Austria self-reported an "impairment." Over half of the students with an impairment indicated allergies or respiratory problems, one-fifth a chronic illness, 15 percent mentioned a mental impairment, 15 percent a visual impairment, nearly 10 percent a physical or mobility impairment, 6.9 percent other impairments, and 5.5 percent a hearing impairment; but a third mentioned multiple impairments—yet only 1 percent of all these individuals self-identified as "disabled" (Wroblewski & Unger, 2003). Comparing students with impairments and those without, the former are older, start their studies later and take longer to complete, switch their course of study and drop out more often, are more likely to live with their parents, and have higher costs related to their impairments (ibid.).

A survey of 16,554 university students carried out in Switzerland during the 2003/2004 academic year brought forth similar data: 2.2 percent of all students reported having a disability, but 10.5 percent reported chronic illnesses, with no significant differences between men and women(Hollenweger et al., 2005: 43). Nearly half of all students reporting chronic illness or disability indicated allergies or respiratory problems (45.7%), 21.5 percent an impairment of mobility functions, 13.9 percent chronic skin problems, 12.9 percent mental impairment, 12.6 percent impairments of inner organs, 5.2 percent a serious visual impairment, 4.9 percent chronic pain or difficulty sleeping, 4.6 percent a hearing impairment, 3.9 percent impairments of the central nervous system, 3.6 percent addiction problems, and 1 percent reported learning problems such as dyslexia. Multiple impairments are quite common: Four-fifths of all students reporting addiction, for example, also indicated another form of impairment (48). Interestingly, substantial differences in disability rates with regard to subject fields were found: while in theology, 21.9 percent of all students reported a disability or chronic illness, only 8.2 percent of students in economics did so (47). Prima facie, these rates appear to be rather high, compared to the data summarized in the European Union's "Eurostudent Report 2005" that as little as 1 percent of all students in Italy, Ireland, and Spain, or 3–4 percent in France, the Netherlands, and Latvia "feel impaired in their studies" (HIS, 2005: Figure 4). For the German-speaking countries, if we take into account national census, household panel or health survey data on the relevant age-groups, there seems to be no *under*representation of disabled people and those with chronic illnesses among the higher education student population. A valid and reliable matching of the available data, however, is not possible. National census or household panel data collection instruments like the German Socio-economic Panel Study, when gathering disability data, almost exclusively apply items that ask persons whether they hold a legal disability status. Process-generated statistics from national welfare schemes are even less reliable. Furthermore, the boundaries between the key concepts of "chronic illness" and "impairment" are far from clear, even highly contested (e.g., Barnartt & Altman, 2001 on disability measurement). In accordance with influential social science models of disability, most people self-reporting chronic illnesses in health surveys are counted as "disabled people" when they cannot participate fully in any significant domain of social life.

The legal classification processes of "disability" in the German-speaking countries still reflect the historic concept of "(work) invalidity." This is especially evident in the case of Switzerland, where the employment disability insurance system (*Invalidenversicherung,* IV) supports roughly 0.5 percent of all university students (Hollenweger et al., 2005: 19). Only a tiny minority of students self-reporting a disability in the Swiss survey had had themselves registered as "disabled persons" with the IV. For many people, especially those among the age-groups relevant to this chapter, undergoing the often humiliating diagnostic processes necessary to obtain legal disability status is either not recommendable (because of negative side effects, e.g., the obligation to declare oneself "disabled" or even "invalid" when applying for a job) or simply irrelevant. For many of the forms of support they need, personal eligibility is not based upon the status of being a person legally classified as having a disability. Still, many secondary school-leavers who succeed in attaining the necessary formal qualifications to enter tertiary education find higher education institutions that are thoroughly inaccessible. In fact, about half of all students with disabilities or chronic illnesses in German-speaking countries regard themselves as being disabled by conditions related to their course of study.

Policy frameworks

A major factor limiting change in disability and higher education in these three countries is that both education policies and disability policies consist of highly complex fields that are not easily unified. Cooperation among these policy fields has been further complicated by the fact that, in Switzerland and Germany, the responsibility for higher education institutions is divided between the federal government and highly autonomous constituent state governments, an exception being the two Swiss Federal Institutes of Technology (ETH). Both countries do not have single national agencies or ministries responsible for higher education. Interstate conferences and agreements regulate large parts of higher education policy. In Switzerland, however, a constitutional amendment that passed public referendum in May 2006 provides for a significant unification of standards and funding in higher education.

In Germany, the principle of cultural sovereignty *(Kultushoheit)* guarantees the sixteen German states (*Länder*) governance control over education and culture. Thus, higher education is the responsibility of the states. Germany's federal context structures institutional change and differentiation, which then proceeds mostly within rather than between the *Länder* (Mayer et al., in press). Yet the federal government did retain some areas of joint responsibility with the *Länder* through the periodically amended Higher Education Framework Act (*Hochschulrahmengesetz*). Its priorities are to plan education development, to promote research activities, to ensure that disabled students' disadvantages are compensated for, to construct higher education facilities and maintain infrastructure, and to reduce disparities in living conditions between the *Länder*, which differ considerably by size, economic conditions, and cultural diversity. Promoting the concerns of students with disabilities is considered in policy relating to social assistance, but is not treated independently (in contrast to gender equality, which is). Concerns about accessibility not only fall victim to this disregard, but also to a much larger problem of German federalism, characterized by conflicts of interest and policy preferences between the levels of government. Indeed, recent conflicts over education reform caused the failure of the very commission charged with considering constitutional change to reduce the serious problems associated with federalist (non-) decision-making (Scharpf, 2005). In 2005, a compromise concerning the reform of German federalism was reached. The forthcoming reform will reduce effective competencies of the federal government in the educational sector even further. Yet for disabled students, national legislation such as the Federal Education and Training Assistance Act (BAföG) that supplies financial support to all students and the specific national directives on disability equality remains crucial, especially those rules that stipulate that all institutions of higher education must improve access for students with disabilities (Federal Disability Equality Law, Social Code IX, 2002).

In Austria, higher education policy has traditionally been a domain of the federal government. A major reform that paved the way for institutional autonomy of Austrian universities was the University Organization Act of 1993, which shifted extensive decision-making powers from the Federal Ministry to individual universities. This change was to facilitate the introduction of management principles and service orientation "to achieve efficiency and quality enhancements" (BMBWK, 2006).

Only recently has federal disability equality legislation (*Behindertengleichstellungsgesetze*) come into effect in Germany, Switzerland, and Austria in 2002, 2004, and 2006, respectively. Public debates, disability movement pressure, and legislative processes led to the passage of disability equality bills on federal and, subsequently, on state levels. The passage of these detailed laws was enhanced by constitutional amendments made during the 1990s that explicitly forbid the negative discrimination of persons "because of their disability." However, as part of public law—like the constitutional amendments—the potential effect of disability equality acts in all three countries has thus far been limited to those arenas in which federal government has direct authority. Thus far, mostly physical and communication barriers as well as certain fields of social life, such as public buildings, public administration, and transport have been addressed. Since higher education institutions in German-speaking countries are mostly governed by public law, higher education may be one of the fields where such disability equality legislation could have significant impact. Even there, however, comprehensive and fast change cannot be expected to result directly from these laws, since extensive "transition periods" apply, especially in the field of public works construction. Thus, it remains unclear whether and how fast disability equality legislation can reduce even the most glaring barriers to and within higher education institutions for students with disabilities.

In private law, no comprehensive legislation concerning disability equality has come into effect until now. Presently, EU guidelines urging member states to implement antidiscrimination legislation into private law have led to some intense debates in Austria (Naue, 2006) and in Germany (Köbsell & Waldschmidt, 2006), where just days before the May 5 "European Protest Day for Disability Equality" finally a compromise was reached. Long-running debates concerning precise legal definitions of key terms like "disability" and "equal treatment" are intertwined with ideological debates about the state's right to interfere with decisions made by citizens and businesses. The compromise reached by the majority in Germany's federal parliament does not contain many of the key elements demanded by the disability rights movement, such as eliminating an exemption whereby insurance companies can refuse to insure persons with preexisting conditions. In Switzerland, which has the least interventionist welfare state model of the German-speaking countries and which is not a member of the European Union, legal projects like a comprehensive and effective antidiscrimination bill governing private law still do not have reasonable chances of passage.

Perhaps the most pressing problem in these countries' higher education systems is a lack of funding in general, with the degree of (under)funding varying between states, universities, and disciplines or courses of study. Whereas the numbers of beginning students and the number of graduates in Germany have doubled since the 1970s, the number of students has *quadrupled* (Mayer, 2003: 596), pointing to the need for fundamental reform, for more effective courses of study and better matching, and for renewed investment. The conditions at not a few universities in the German-speaking countries seriously constrain learning opportunities, such as when there are not enough chairs for students, subscriptions to journals are suspended, or when high student-faculty ratios render mentoring impossible. Symbolizing students' dissatisfaction with the original university and/or course of study in which they enrolled, approximately 15 percent of all German first-degree students transfer to another university before degree completion (DSW, 2002). College choices in Germany remain a blend of individual decision-making and administrative fiat without provision of much systematic information, guidance or counseling that help prepare youth for successful transitions from schools to universities. For example, the current lack of information on the new university programs has consequences: Despite the massively expanded supply of bachelor's degree programs, only one-quarter of incoming students in the Winter semester 2003/2004 even considered them as an option (Heine et al., 2005: 3). Students need more information, about courses of study and accessibility, prior to and during their studies. Such information is particularly important for potential students with disabilities as they organize diverse services to facilitate their access to the curriculum (in Germany, a good source is the guidebook published by the National Association of Student Affairs, *Studentenwerk*).

Types of institutions

In the German-speaking countries, most tertiary education institutions are publicly funded. These provide courses of study in a broad range of subjects, combine teaching and research, offer varying degrees of specialization (including technical, medical, theological, or arts foci), and have the exclusive right to award doctoral degrees. While some private universities have been established in recent years, many specialize on a limited range of subjects. Applied science institutions (*Fachhochschulen*), which may now grant B.A. and M.A. degrees instead of their traditional *Diplom*, represent the higher education sector expanding fastest in all three countries. Most of them have developed from precursor institutions of non-university tertiary or upper secondary education over the past few decades. They offer training in a growing variety of fields, combining applied research and comparatively extensive practical training. Besides these major types of institutions, some German states maintain colleges of advanced vocational studies (*Berufsakademien*) that offer courses of study that combine postsecondary-level teaching with an apprenticeship or training contract with a private or public employer. Some *Fachhochschulen* in these countries have started offering such dual courses as well. In Austria, several forms of separate professional colleges persist, whose courses of study in Germany and Switzerland have either been integrated into the *Fachhochschulen* or are still formally part of upper secondary level education, such as midwifery or paramedic training courses in Germany. Formal distinctions between all postsecondary institutions are breaking down with standardization in Europe.

    A most significant process of change affecting all institutions of higher education throughout Europe is the so-called Bologna process which aims to harmonize European higher education to enhance European education's attractiveness and competitiveness worldwide (Reinalda & Kulesza, 2005).[3] The introduction of consecutive bachelor's and master's degree courses and the formal accreditation of individual achievements through the "European Credit Transfer System" (ECTS) bring about major changes in higher education systems. Within a short period of time, differing by country, all traditional degrees and courses will be replaced by the new system, based more or less upon Anglo-American models of sequential college and university courses of study and degrees. The Bologna process aims to increase permeability between diverse types of institutions with traditional status differences as well as geographic mobility within Europe. This should provide perspective and motivation for many students who previously were confined to certain status tracks or regions. Furthermore, in assessing the status, prestige, or other features of "success" of tertiary institutions, its formal type will likely play a less significant role than it does currently as these institutions differentiate. Rankings of universities and fields, carried out by private or public agencies, are relatively new to German-speaking higher education, but they have become increasingly common, shaking up governments and university administrations as public discourse on higher education proliferates.

These developments are accompanied by a gradual shift of competencies from the respective state governments to universities, giving universities more financial and administrative autonomy and, to an increasing extent, competencies to autonomously select prospective students. In Austria, public universities became separate legal entities under public law in 2004. Other major recent changes include the 2001 introduction of tuition fees in Austria and in many German states and Swiss cantons. Whereas previously, tertiary education was a freely provided public good for a select group, the costs of higher education participation for all individuals are on the rise, and competition between universities and students is increasing throughout higher education. The consequences these developments may have for students with disabilities have yet to be fully analyzed. What is clear from the above analysis is that many of these institutions are engaged in fundamental change processes. Most of these institutions lacked the support provisions needed to level the playing field for students with disabilities. What effects increasingly structured and standardized but more expensive education will have on students with disabilities remains unclear, especially given the complex institutional arrangements that serve students with disabilities or chronic illnesses.

Provisions for students with disabilities

Higher education policy, welfare policy, health policy, and labor market policy (including various forms of counseling) form rigidly separated systems in the German-speaking countries, each maintaining its own agencies and local level offices. Many crucial services and supports for students with disabilities are neither related to student status nor provided by the higher education institutions themselves: Such key resources include personal assistance and care, income support and allowances, employment-related support in vocational training, therapy, personalized technical equipment, career services maintained by the states' employment agencies, and public transport.

Services disabled students may request are provided by an enormous variety of agencies and organizations inside and outside higher education institutions. Thus, extensive referral systems force disabled students to spend considerable amounts of time and energy on administrative issues in order to claim their rights. Bureaucratic hurdles pose one of the most difficult of all challenges that students with impairments and chronic illnesses face. It seems that instead of being treated first and foremost as students who also happen to have a disability, most disabled students are treated like disabled persons who happen to be students as well. Despite attempts to integrate counseling and services for disabled students, policies and administrative processes with regard to students with disabilities generally do not work in collaboration. Specialized on-campus services include library services for students with visual impairments (only at a few universities); voluntary peer counseling by local self-help associations, with availability varying between universities and by year of study, and psychotherapy. Detailed descriptions of the forms of support and assistance available to students with disabilities cannot be presented here (Felkendorff, 2003b: 133 for a selected overview concerning Germany; Hollenweger et al., 2005: 111–146, for detailed examination of students' experiences with these structures in Switzerland). However, under the legal frameworks available in all German-speaking countries, it is clearly the duty of higher education institutions and their funding bodies to reduce the extant barriers, to understand the challenges students face on a daily basis, and to assist when asked.

In an increasing number of universities in German-speaking countries, posts of "disability affairs representatives" have been created in recent decades. Similarly, in Switzerland, this process is ongoing. By contrast, in those Austrian universities in which representatives are available, these managers have the most far-reaching competencies. Depending on the funding available, the degree of professionalization, and the legal position of the representatives, their activities include providing orientation and information for prospective students; informing about aspects of financial, personal, technical assistance as well as modifications to examination procedures; and advising building experts on accessibility issues and facility management. In most cases, however, these posts are filled on a voluntary basis by members of the (academic) staff, and these representatives have limited rights and resources compared to the considerable legal and administrative powers of equal rights coordinators working to reduce gender inequality.

In Germany, Student Affairs Associations have local responsibility to reduce barriers, to supply counseling, support, and technical equipment, and to guide students with disabilities through the bureaucratic hurdles or refer them to other sources of assistance. Some of them maintain specialized full-time counseling services for students with disabilities. On the national level, only Germany has a specialized "Advice Center for Studies and Disability" (www.studentenwerke.de), which offers various kinds of information materials, training courses for students and representatives of disability affairs, coordination of local counseling institutions, and individual counseling. It also represents the interests of students with disabilities vis-à-vis governments, administrative bodies, and the public. Moreover, in both Germany and Austria, students with disabilities have formed nationwide special interest groups or formal associations (www.behinderung-und-studium.de). Helpful information is regularly collected by local and nationwide self-help associations, mainly on the Web. The regular editions of the handbook *Studies and Disability* (*Studium und Behinderung*, DSW, 2005), published by the German center mentioned above, are regarded as the key reference in the field of counseling for students and university applicants with disabilities in Germany. Such publications, however, often resemble a legal textbook crossed with an address book, indicating to readers that it requires some initiative to gather all the relevant information, support, and services necessary to gain full access to the myriad offerings in higher education.

Recent areas of improvement in general conditions of study common to the three German-speaking countries include reductions in required attendance (through distance learning), improvements in architectural access, renewed service provision in such areas as personal assistance, dictation and sign language interpretation services, and less bureaucratic inflexibility in dealing with study interruptions and modifications of examination regulations. Generally speaking, the rise of distance learning and new assistive technologies has lowered barriers to university studies for certain groups of disabled people.

Dimensions of persistent disablement

Summarizing the progress made in the last few decades, the Joint Commission on Higher Education Reform of Germany's largest state of North Rhine-Westphalia stated that very few higher education institutions had achieved the goals of integration of disabled students emphasized by the Standing Conference of Ministers of Education and Culture (KMK), the Conference of University Rectors (HRK), and the National Association of Student Affairs (DSW) since the early 1980s: adequate technical and building provisions; high quality counseling before, during, and after college studies; and laws amended to specifically include disability (NRW, 1999). Whereas the latter dimensions were addressed generally, and some physical barriers were removed in particular locations, typical special programs for disabled students, most of which are additional and segregating measures, remain unsatisfactory. German higher education institutions must still integrate their services in support of the education of *all* students.

In 2002, for the first time, not only did the national Austrian student survey ask about impairment, chronic illness, or disability, but it also had an additional questionnaire addressed to this group specifically. Wroblewski and Unger (2003) report that this group of students has, on average, less scholarship support, receives more aid from their families, and spends more of their monthly income on health-related products and services, but the main difficulties that this group reports are such issues as meeting performance standards, difficulties learning or working, and private problems such as insecurities and fears. Whereas students with chronic and mental illnesses were more likely to be disabled in their studies, over a third of students reporting some health issue reported that their impairment had no effect on their everyday life as a student (ibid.). The authors also indicate that health and financial difficulties, along with insufficient information and consultation in advance, together lead to significantly higher transfers and dropouts. Students with disabilities in Austria emphasize that, changes in the organization of courses of study, more understanding and awareness among teachers, enhanced financial support, improved guidance and counseling, as well as technical and communication assistance would help them complete their studies. The major problem areas in Austrian higher education for students with disabilities include limits on choice of courses of study and lack of understanding and flexibility among teachers and administration regarding completion of required courses, organizational issues such as overfilled seminars and physical barriers, as well as general lack of information (ibid.). Finally, the study also reports that especially students with mental illness exhibit an increased tendency to drop out and note difficulties in learning and exam situations in addition to interactions with lecturers.

Similar patterns were found in Switzerland. The aforementioned Swiss study shows that students with mental health problems, chronic pain, addiction, and learning difficulties are most likely to feel severely disabled during their studies (Hollenweger et al., 2005: 56). Perhaps surprisingly, however, the range of individually perceived degrees of disablement in this specific life domain is complete in all groups: One student with tetraplegia (spinal cord injury), for example, reported that his studies were hampered only slightly, whereas another student with tetraplegia reported being severely disabled by the context in which he pursues his studies. Both of them indicated a high overall quality of life and a good state of health. On the other hand, activity limitations that are typically regarded as being specific to "disabled persons" can also be found among large groups of students who indicated no disability or chronic illness (148–157). These findings represent further pieces of evidence supporting the hypothesis common in Disability Studies that models of disability that assume a causal link between impairment and disability fail to explain sometimes contraintuitive or contradictory empirical results reflecting the complex phenomenon of disablement as a process deriving from social interaction and movement within barrier-filled environments.

In the future, it seems plausible that many purely technical barriers will be removed. In addition, even in the German-speaking countries, bureaucracies may develop toward greater user-friendliness. Yet perhaps the most decisive and difficult-to-ameliorate mechanisms that have failed to reduce inequalities are those related to public or semipublic counseling, administrative, and teaching staff acting within ableist institutions. Hidden or implicit forms of disability disadvantage and discrimination in everyday, face-to-face interactions between disabled students and university staff are caused by deeply rooted ableist attitudes and misconceptions. Narrative interviews point to the fact that disabled students are confronted with manifold forms of ableism on every step of their higher education careers, from access procedures to final exams (Hollenweger et al., 2005; Jäger & Jussen, 2002; Meister, 1998). Expert interviews carried out with Swiss universities' counseling staff indicate an enormous lack of information even among specially trained staff. For example, more than two-thirds of the university representatives surveyed would generally not recommend deaf students to take up any course of study at their institution (Hollenweger et al., 2005: 163). The following narrative told by a female sports student with a visual impairment who, against the odds, successfully completed her studies, provides a graphic account of the process of overcoming attitudinal barriers in education:

> "One day it was snowing very heavily. My classmates were all standing on their snowboards like drunkards; were no longer able to ski downhill properly. It came as a surprise to them when I skied downhill as if the weather conditions didn't make any difference. Afterwards the skiing instructor, who had hitherto failed to be of any assistance to me, told me that he had finally realized that my ability to see was always limited to the impaired level of vision they had experienced in that stormy weather. From then on this skiing instructor admired my skills and my performance and he started to act in a more respectful way towards me, which was not of much use to me, however, since I was about to finish my studies anyway." *(translated from German by Susan Gürber)*

Furthermore, this study emphasizes that inequities in lower and upper secondary education hinder a large number of potential higher education students—not only in Switzerland—from attaining the necessary entry certificates (147). Analyses of the cross-national Trends in International Mathematics and Science Study (TIMSS) of pupils' math and science achievement demonstrate that unequal distributions of basic educational resources and failure to counterbalance the concentration of educational difficulties—such as low achievement, attainment, and dropout—among disadvantaged youth lowers a nation's overall educational performance and thus international standing (Baker et al., 2005). Neither nations nor localities or schools can afford to ignore those students having difficulties in schools and universities if they are to compete. The German-speaking countries' traditional emphasis on extensive and intensive vocational training has long mediated the disadvantage in terms of low educational attainments of disadvantaged youth; however, high unemployment rates and shifts in supply and demand for apprenticeships and other training opportunities threaten that international standing—especially as many countries increase the proportion of postsecondary level students.

PERSPECTIVES OF DISABILITY EQUALITY IN HIGHER EDUCATION

Summarizing an extensive comparison of disability policies in higher education, OECD researchers point out that

> *neglecting the mechanisms at play in universities and other higher education institutions would amount to making the disabled more vulnerable and increasing the discrimination against them. The gradual substitution of a participatory model involving everyone in every facet of economic, political and social life, for the more traditional integration model that seeks to adapt and normalise people with disabilities, requires that the disabled become increasingly skilled individuals who see themselves as stakeholders in their own future (Ebersold, 2002). Access to higher education means acquiring the knowledge and know-how to live in a society that views itself as a partnership of responsible, co-operative stakeholders with the ability to define and shape their own roles. This perspective puts the onus on individuals to build the world in which they live. (OECD, 2003: 9)*

Not only for the German-speaking countries, the mechanisms of exclusion operating both prior to tertiary level and within higher education institutions need to be further examined, but, above all, concrete reforms following the many research-based recommendations should be implemented more completely.

On the basis of more than sixty interviews with disabled students throughout Germany, Meister (1998: 145–147) synthesizes their general suggestions as follows: Societal change vis-à-vis disability (e.g., from an individual deficit to a social model) that extends the antidiscrimination principle in Germany's Constitution into everyday reality; professional counseling to assist in the individual process of finding and accepting her or his strengths and weaknesses that are a precondition for optimizing learning opportunities within tertiary education's requirements; preparation for this phase beginning early in school and in the family of origin. More specific recommendations were also put forth, including: The need for orientation programs, for specific guidance in selecting a course of study (not just those understood to be typical), and for continuing support; awareness-raising and continuing education of teachers in accessibility-related pedagogical techniques; clear statements regarding accommodations in testing situations; student service offices operating on some campuses should be established elsewhere to further equality of opportunity; technical aids could be offered for multiple campuses and requested on an ad hoc basis; and finally, universities should coordinate the financial transfers that individual students often have to fight for with multiple bureaucracies, waiting too long for their rightful claims to be processed, a key source of dropout (147–153).

Addressing many of these very concerns, the leaders of the German Association of Student Affairs in 2004 passed a "Resolution for Barrier-free Higher Education Institutions" (DSW, 2004) to require both federal and state governments as well as the higher education institutions and the student services providers to assist students with disabilities and chronic illnesses to achieve equal participatory rights by implementing the following key elements needed to achieve a barrier-free higher education system: (1) secure equality of opportunity in terms of access to courses of study, (2) set forth in law adequate accommodations to address individual disadvantage in study and testing situations, (3) build and expand existing barrier-free structures, (4) secure and develop financial supports, (5) maintain and extend professional information, consultation and service offerings during their studies and in the transition phases between school and higher education and career, and (6) design a framework for equalizing participation in higher education within Europe and internationally. Thus far, attempts to harmonize European higher education have focused on facilitating change and standardizing credits, certificates, and courses of study. Given the findings presented here about Austria, Switzerland, and Germany, issues of accessibility and inclusive education, from primary and secondary schooling onwards, must also be acknowledged and enter into these European deliberations. It is not necessary to find a common and agreed-upon definition of "disability" before reforming education systems, especially when the challenges disabled pupils and students face emphasize vast disparities between the rhetorical goals of equality and quality and the realities on college and university campuses of ableism and disadvantage.

NOTES

1. Ableism refers to discrimination against people with disabilities and favoring of people who are able-bodied based on the belief that disabled people are inferior. Hehir (2002) suggests that educational programs could counteract ableism by acknowledging disability within diversity programs, helping disabled students develop in ways most effective and efficient for them as individual learners, and promoting high standards as well as universal design. Universally designed campuses would be constructed to be usable by all potential students, to the greatest extent possible, without the need for adaptation (cf. Mace, 1997). Yet physical and communication barriers still hinder access at nearly all campuses in Germany, Switzerland, and Austria.

2. Whereas activists and advocates in the disability movement in the German-speaking countries have been active and published quite a few articles and books over the past few decades (for overview, e.g., Cloerkes, 2001; 2003), Disability Studies has only very recently emerged as a cohesive field of inquiry—with Germany witnessing a much faster and more diverse development of discourse than Austria and Switzerland, thus far (Köbsell & Waldschmidt, 2006). Recent DS contributions in those countries include Naue (2006) and Weisser & Renggli (2004). One major event with 500 participants from all German-speaking countries was a two-week series of conferences and workshops held in 2003 at the University of Bremen "Disability Studies in Germany: Re-thinking Disability" as part of the European Year of Disabled Persons (Hermes & Köbsell, 2003; Waldschmidt, 2003). A useful selection of DS literature in German can be found at http://www.disability-studies-deutschland.de/.
3. Given that by 2005, 40 countries have become involved in the Bologna process, it is no longer just a European program of standardizing higher education, but far more an international project. Key tenets of the Bologna Declaration (1999) include (1) an understandable and comparable system of academic grades, including the introduction of a supplement to educational certificates to facilitate cross-national transparency and recognition of qualifications), (2) a modular system based on two levels, the first (Bachelor) geared to labor markets of at least three years' duration and a second level (Master) that requires successful completion of the first level, (3) application of the European Credit Transfer System (already in use in the Socrates and Erasmus programs) to regulate accumulation and transfer of credits, (4) mobility of students, teachers and researchers, and (5) cooperation with regard to quality assurance. No less than to make the higher education systems in Europe converge toward a more transparent system was set as the aim of the process that ultimately should make European higher education more attractive worldwide.

REFERENCES

Baker, D., LeTendre, G. & Goesling, B. (2005) "Rich Land, Poor Schools," in: D. Baker and LeTendre, G. (Eds.) *National Differences, Global Similarities: World Culture and the Future of Schooling*, Stanford: Stanford University Press, 71–85.

Barnartt, S.N. & Altman, B.M. (2001). *Exploring Theories and Expanding Methodologies* (Research in Social Science and Disability, Vol. 2). Stamford, CT: JAI Press.

BMBF. (2004). *Die wirtschaftliche und soziale Lage der Studierenden in der Bundesrepublik Deutschland 2003. 17. Sozialerhebung des Deutschen Studentenwerks.* Berlin, Germany: Bundesministerium für Bildung und Forschung.

BMBWK. (2006). Higher Education in Austria—Reforms 2001. Vienna, Austria: Bundesministerium für Bildung, Wissenschaft und Kultur. Retrieved on March 15, 2006 from www.bmbwk.gv.at/universitaeten/pm/publ/Higher_Education_in_Aust6821.xml

Cloerkes, G. (2001). *Soziologie der Behinderten.* Heidelberg, Germany: Winter.

——— (Ed.). (2003). *Wie man behindert wird. Texte zur Konstruktion einer sozialen Rolle und zur Lebenssituation betroffener Menschen.* Heidelberg, Germany: Winter.

Cortina, K.S., Baumert, J., Leschinsky, A., Mayer, K.U. & Trommer, L. (Eds.) (2003). *Das Bildungswesen in der Bundesrepublik Deutschland. Strukturen und Entwicklungen im Überblick.* Reinbek: Rowohlt.

DSW. (2000). *Economic and Social Conditions of Student Life in Germany.* Berlin, Germany: Deutsches Studentenwerk. Retrieved on February 21, 2006 from www.his.de/Abt2/Foerderung/pdf/abt2/Soz16en.pdf

DSW. (2002). *16. Sozialerhebung des Deutschen Studentenwerks.* Berlin, Germany: Deutsches Studentenwerk.
———. (2004). *Beschluss für eine barrierefreie Hochschule.* Berlin, Germany: Deutsches Studentenwerk.
———. (2005). *Studium und Behinderung.* Berlin, Germany: Deutsches Studentenwerk.
Dujmovits, E. (2004). "Integrative oder 'besondere' Beschulung von Schülern mit sonderpädagogischem Förderbedarf? Landesbericht Österreich." In Becker, U. & Graser, A. (Eds.), *Perspektiven der schulischen Integration von Kindern mit Behinderung.* Baden-Baden, Germany: Nomos, 125–149.
EADSNE. (2003). *Special Education across Europe in 2003: Trends in Provision in 18 European Countries.* Middlefart, Denmark: European Agency for Development in Special Needs Education.
Ebersold, S. (2002). "Les enjeux et les défis de l'ambition participative." *Vie sociale* 2002/1.
Federal Disability Equality Law, Social Code IX (2002). "Behindertengleichstellungsgesetz vom 27. April 2002 (BGBl. I S. 1467, 1468), zuletzt geändert durch Artikel 262 der Verordnung vom 31. Oktober 2006 (BGBl. I S. 2407)"
Felkendorff, K. (2003a). "Ausweitung der Behinderungszone: Neuere Behinderungsbegriffe und ihre Folgen," in: Cloerkes, 2003: 25–52.
———. (2003b). "Disability and Higher Education in Germany," in: OECD, *Disability in Higher Education.* Paris: OECD, 109–148.
Felkendorff, K. & Lischer, E. (Eds.). (2005): *Barrierefreie Übergänge? Jugendliche mit Behinderungen und Lernschwierigkeiten zwischen Schule und Berufsleben.* Zurich, Switzerland: Pestalozzianum.
Hehir, T. (2002). "Eliminating Ableism in Education," *Harvard Educational Review* 72, 1, 1–32.
Heine, C., Spangenberg, H., Schreiber, J., & Sommer, D. (2005). *Studienanfänger in den Wintersemestern 2003/04 und 2004/05. Wege zum Studium, Studien- und Hochschulwahl, Situation bei Studienbeginn.* Hannover, Germany: Hochschul-Informations-System.
Hermes, G. & Köbsell, S. (2003). *Disability Studies in Deutschland—Behinderung neu denken! Dokumentation der Sommeruniversität Bremen 2003.* Kassel, Germany: bifos.
HIS. (2005). *Eurostudent Report. Social and Economic Conditions of Student Life in Europe: Synopsis of Indicators.* Hannover: Hochschul-Informations-System.
Hollenweger, J., Gürber, S., & Keck, A. (2005). *Menschen mit Behinderungen an Schweizer Hochschulen: Befunde und Empfehlungen.* Zurich, Switzerland: Rüegger.
IHS. (2005). *Eurostudent Report. Social and Economic Conditions of Student Life in Europe: National Profile Austria.* Vienna, Austria: Institut für Höhere Studien.
Jäger, M. & Jussen, H. (Eds.) (2002). *Förderung körper- und sinnesbehinderter Hochbegabter – Erkenntnisse und Notwendigkeiten.* Villingen-Schwenningen: Neckar-Verlag.
KMK. (2005). *Sonderpädagogische Förderung in Schulen 1994 bis 2003.* (Statistische Veröffentlichungen der Kultusministerkonferenz, Vol. 177). Bonn, Germany: Kultusministerkonferenz.
Köbsell, S. & Waldschmidt, A. (2006). "Disability Studies in Austria, Germany and Switzerland: Introduction." *Disability Studies Quarterly* 26, 2, 1–6.
Krappmann, L., Leschinsky, A., & Powell, J. J.W. (2003). "Kinder, die besonderer pädagogischer Förderung bedürfen," in: Cortina et al., 2003: 755–786.
List, J. & Schnabel, C. (2004). *Bildungsstagnation bei abnehmender Erwerbsbevölkerung—Bildungspolitische Herausforderungen durch Geringqualifizierte.* Universität Erlangen-Nürnberg: Lehrstuhl für Arbeitsmarkt- und Regionalpolitik.
Mace, R. (1997). "What Is Universal Design?" Retrieved on April 5, 2006 from http://design.ncsu.edu/cud/.
Mayer, K.U. (2003). "Das Hochschulwesen," in: Cortina et al., 2003: 581–624.

Mayer, K.U., Müller, W., & Pollak, R. (in press). "Institutional Change and Inequalities of Access in German Higher Education," in: Y. Shavit, R. Arum, A. Gamoran, & G. Menahem (Eds.), *Expansion, Differentiation and Stratification in Higher Education: A Comparative Study.* Tel Aviv, Israel: University of Tel Aviv.

Meister, J-J. (1998). *Studienverhalten, Studienbedingungen und Studienorganisation behinderter Studierender.* Munich, Germany: Bayerisches Staatsinstitut für Hochschulforschung und Hochschulplanung.

Naue, U. (2006). "Governing Disability in Austria: Reflections on a Changing Political Field." *Disability Studies Quarterly* 26, 2, n.p.

NRW. (1999). Universability for Disability: Studium von Behinderten und Studienreform an Hochschulen in NRW. Bochum: Gemeinsame Kommission für die Studienreform im Land Nordrhein-Westfalen.

OCR. (2005). *Students with Disabilities Preparing for Postsecondary Education: Know Your Rights and Responsibilities.* Washington, D.C.: U.S. Department of Education, Office for Civil Rights.

OECD. (2003). *Disability in Higher Education.* Paris, France: OECD.

———. (2004a). *Education at a Glance. OECD Indicators 2004.* Paris, France: OECD.

———. (2004b). *Equity in Education. Students with Disabilities, Learning Difficulties and Disadvantages.* Paris, France: OECD.

———. (2005). *Education at a Glance. OECD Indicators, Executive Summary.* Paris, France: OECD.

Peters, S.J. (2004). *Inclusive Education: An EFA Strategy for All Children.* Washington, DC: World Bank.

Powell, J.J.W. (2003a). "Constructing Disability and Social Inequality Early in the Life Course: The Case of Special Education in Germany and the United States." *Disability Studies Quarterly* 23, 2, 57–75.

———. (2003b): "Hochbegabt, behindert oder normal? Klassifikationssysteme des sonderpädagogischen Förderbedarfs in Deutschland und den Vereinigten Staaten," in: Cloerkes, 2003: 103–140.

———. (forthcoming). *Barriers to Inclusion: Special Education in the United States and Germany.* Boulder, CO: Paradigm.

Powell, J.J.W. & Wagner, S.J. (2002). "'Zur Entwicklung der Überrepräsentanz von Migrantenjugendlichen an Sonderschulen in der Bundesrepublik Deutschland seit 1991,' Gemeinsam Leben." *Zeitschrift für Integrative Erziehung* 10, 2, 66–71. Retrieved on September 22, 2007 from http://bidok.uibk.ac.at/library/powell-migranten.html.

Preuss-Lausitz, U. (2001). "Gemeinsamer Unterricht Behinderter und Nichtbehinderter, Ein Weg für Sonderpädagogik und allgemeine Schulpädagogik zu einer gemeinsamen integrativen Pädagogik." *Zeitschrift für Erziehungswissenschaft* 4, 2, 209–224.

Reinalda, B. & Kulesza, E. (2005). *The Bologna Process—Harmonizing Europe's Higher Education.* Opladen, Germany: Barbara Budrich.

Scharpf, F.W. (2005). "No Exit from the Joint Decision Trap? Can German Federalism Reform Itself?" MPIfG Working Paper 05/8. Cologne, Germany: Max Planck Institute for the Study of Societies.

Seibert, H. (2005). *Integration durch Ausbildung?* Berlin, Germany: Logos.

Settersten, R.A., Jr., Furstenberg, F.F., Jr., & Rumbaut, R.G. (Eds.). (2005). *On the Frontier of Adulthood: Theory, Research, and Public Policy.* Chicago, IL: University of Chicago Press.

Shavit, Y. & Müller, W. (Eds.). (1998). *From School to Work. A Comparative Study of Educational Qualifications and Occupational Destinations.* Oxford: Oxford University Press.

Solga, H. (2005). *Ohne Abschluss in die Bildungsgesellschaft.* Opladen: Barbara Budrich.

Waldschmidt, A. (Ed). (2003). *Kulturwissenschaftliche Perspektiven der Disability Studies. Tagungsdokumentation.* Kassel, Germany: bifos.

Weisser, J. & Renggli, C. (2004). *Disability Studies. Ein Lesebuch.* Luzern, Switzerland: Edition SZH.

Wetzel, G. (2002). Unterstützung für Jugendliche mit sonderpädagogischem Förderbedarf beim Übergang von der Schule ins Berufsleben: Österreich im internationalen Vergleich. Retrieved on December 21, 2003 from http://bidok.uibk.ac.at/library/wetzel-vergleich.html.

Wroblewski, A. & Unger, M. (2003). *Studierenden-Sozialerhebung 2002. Bericht zur sozialen Lage der Studierenden.* Vienna, Austria: Bundesministerium für Bildung, Wissenschaft und Kultur.

CHAPTER THIRTY

The Reasonable Adjustments Duty FOR Higher Education IN England AND Wales

KIM MARSHALL

INTRODUCTION

While the Disability Discrimination Act (DDA) (1995) gave rights to people with disabilities to be protected from discrimination with regard to employment and the provisions of goods, facilities and services, there were many lacunae in the Act. One of these areas of omission was that of education. It was believed by the government of the time that it would not be appropriate to apply the provisions of the DDA 1995 to education as "the Further and Higher Education Act 1992 (FHEA 1992) [had] established a comprehensive framework for meeting the requirements of students with disabilities" (Mackay 1995). Although the amendment of the FHEA 1992 by the DDA 1995 placed duties on the Higher Education Funding Councils for England and Wales (HEFCE/W) to "have regard to the requirements of disabled persons," (FHEA 1992, s 62(7A)), there was no legal obligation for higher education institutions (HEIs) to make provision for disabled students other than to produce a "disability statement" (FHEA 1992, s 5(7A)(a)). A "disability statement" is produced by every HEI and sets out the provision that the HEI makes for disabled students.

Financial support for students with disabilities was recognised in 1990 with the introduction of the Disabled Student's Allowance (DSA), an Act that introduced varying levels of financial support for some disabled students to assist with the direct costs incurred as a result of undertaking a course of study. The idea of introducing the DSA was to enable disabled students to attend university by providing non means tested assistance to pay for specialist equipment, for non-medical helpers or for travel costs. However, the formalisation of a policy of inclusion of disabled students was not pursued until the Quality Assurance Agency (QAA) produced its 24 precepts for students with disabilities as part of its Code of Practice (QAA 1999). Although the QAA Code sets a benchmark standard for institutions in the provision of adjustments for disabled students, it is not mandatory. Compliance with the QAA Code is a factor that is considered during institutional review. However, it is expressed in terms of "should consider," which is rather less than forceful in achieving access to the same educational opportunities for disabled students as their able bodied peers.

PART 4 DISABILITY DISCRIMINATION ACT 1995

It was not until 2002 that legal protection was finally given to disabled students who have declared their disabilities. There is evidence that many educational institutions were already attempting to implement strategies designed to meet the needs of all their students prior to this date (Riddell et al. 2004). Most institutions claimed to meet the base level provision set by HEFCE/W, which was minimal, but at that time it what could be said was that most of the provision 'for disabled students still remains largely the province of student support services' (p. 19).

The passing of the Special Education Needs and Disability Act 2001 (SENDA 2001) was a consequence of the Disability Rights Taskforce Review of disability provision. This became the new Part 4 of the DDA 1995.[1] This chapter will focus on the reasonable adjustments duty in relation to higher education (DDA 1995, s 28T(1)), which came into effect from September 1, 2002, but at the same time HEIs were also placed under a duty not to treat disabled people or students less favourably (DDA 1995, s 28S(1)). The reasonable adjustments duty was expanded by the introduction of the duty to provide auxiliary aids and services (DDA 1995, S 28T) from September 1, 2003 and the final duties to make adjustments to premises came into force as from September 1, 2005 (DDA 1995, s 28T). If a claim of discrimination is brought under DDA 1995 Part 4, then the parties may attempt conciliation via the Disability Rights Commission (DRC) Conciliation Service. If conciliation fails, then the claim will be heard in the county court. The remedies available include compensation, an injunction or a declaration of rights and or responsibilities.

THE EXPANSION OF HIGHER EDUCATION IN THE UNITED KINGDOM AND INCREASED PARTICIPATION BY STUDENTS WITH DISABILITIES

Higher education in the United Kingdom has undergone a dramatic expansion in recent years and this is mirrored by the increase in numbers of students who have declared a disability (see Table 30. 1). The figures are taken from the Higher Education Statistics Agency (HESA) and relate to admissions to all higher education courses for the years 1996–1997 to 2003–2004. There is a line between the academic years 1999–2000 and 2000–2001. At this point HESA changed its method of calculation. It is notable that in the year following the change that numbers of students who were not identified as disabled dropped by about 60 percent. This was also the point at which the QAA introduced its Code of Practice for students with disabilities so it is likely that institutions were making greater efforts to identify which students were disabled. The figures demonstrate a 27 percent rise in overall student numbers and a rise of 108 percent in disabled students. However, if specific categories of disabled students are selected then the percentage increase in participation is more dramatic. The numbers of students with dyslexia quadrupled, students with mental health difficulties trebled and the numbers of students with multiple disabilities increased nearly fivefold. Curiously, the proportions of wheelchair users/mobility impaired and those with unseen disabilities remained fairly static, but this is likely to be linked to the delayed introduction of the access provisions of Part 4 to September 2005. Some of this expansion can be explained by the overall increase in student numbers. There are simply more people at university and statistically a proportion of them will have a disability. It can be argued that much of the rest of the expansion in numbers of disabled students is due to the rights given by DDA 1995 Part 4. However, there are some caveats that need to be entered with regard to these numbers. First, the numbers of declared students are likely to be an underestimate of the numbers of students with disabilities in higher education. Some disabilities carry a stigma, such as mental health problems, HIV/AIDS or cancer, and students may decide that they do not wish to declare as it may prejudice their application to an institution or because they fear both staff and fellow students may treat them unjustly. In addition, some students may decide not to declare because they do not consider themselves to be 'disabled' within the terms of the legislation. Studies have shown that less than half of claimants under the employment provisions of the DDA considered themselves disabled and under a third were aware that they were covered by the DDA (Hurstfield et al., 2004). It is submitted that the proportions believing themselves to be disabled would be similar for students. Second, the number of students who have

Table 30.1. The total number of disabled HE students (all years of study and from all locations, e.g. UK domiciled and international) on UK HEI programmes (by impairment).

Year	Total number students	Total number students known to have a disability	Total number students with no known disability	Total number students where disability status not known/sought	The number of students with impairment/disability							
					Dyslexia	Blind/ Partially sighted	Deaf/ Hearing impairment	Wheelchair user/ Mobility difficulties	Personal care support	Mental health difficulties	An unseen disability (1)	Multiple disabilities	Other disability
1996-1997	1756180	58100	1500200	197875	10635	2325	3885	4730	115	1400	24665	2720	7620
1997-1998	1800065	66520	1605950	127595	13590	2505	4205	2795	145	1400	28000	6350	7530
1998-1999	1845755	72090	1681735	91930	16780	2505	4190	3100	160	1685	28515	6590	8570
1999-2000	1856335	77480	1649085	129765	21615	2685	4355	3295	190	2015	26835	7090	9400
2000-2001	1990625	86250	1825845	78530	27580	2885	5020	3830	225	2790	25975	7165	10775
2001-2002	2056075	98030	1933270	5477	35435	3160	5580	4380	280	3490	25295	8340	12075
2002-2003	2175115	110770	2010555	53795	43665	3320	5985	4870	295	4525	24590	9605	13920
2003-2004	2247440	121080	2076535	49825	49945	3405	6120	4930	260	5270	24340	11965	14840

Source: Higher Education Statistics Agency Limited (HESA).

declared a disability is about 5.5 percent of the total student population (HESA 2005). The number of people with disabilities in the United Kingdom is about 8.6 million (DRC 2006), which is about 20 percent of the population. However, this imbalance in proportions of people with disabilities within higher education compared to whose recognised as disabled as a percentage of the population is partly explained by the disabled student population being younger on average than the overall disabled population. However, research conducted by the DRC has shown that many young disabled people had low expectations with regard to employment and a substantial number had been discouraged from entering higher education by their teachers. (NOP survey 2002)

THE REASONABLE ADJUSTMENTS DUTY

In order to be covered by the reasonable adjustments duty, a student first has to show that they are disabled within the definition of the Act (DDA 1995 s 1(1)). Despite the amendments made to the definition by the DDA 2005 which have extended the scope of protection, the definition remains firmly based on the medical model of disability. This definition is perceived as complex and difficult to apply as there are four separate limbs to it. To prove that a student is disabled they must have (1) a physical or mental impairment that has an effect that is (2) substantial, (3) adverse and (4) long term (lasting or expected to last for at least a year) on his or her ability to carry out 'normal day to day activities'. There is little assistance offered within the Act to determine who is covered by the definition. Guidance in determining who is disabled under the Act has been given in the case of *Goodwin v. the Patent Office* (1999). Goodwin was the first case under the DDA in which a structured approach was set out to enable future courts and tribunals to analyse the claim. Further assistance is offered by the statutory "Guidance" issued by the Department of Work and Pensions and updated in 2006. Although the Guidance does not have any legal binding force, it is designed to assist in determining whether a person meets the definition of disability if there is any doubt. The Guidance gives many examples of what will and what will not be considered as sufficient to qualify as disabled under the DDA 1995. However, in 2006, in response to a Government request as part of the Discrimination Law Review, the DRC carried out a consultation to assist in revising the definition of disability used in the DDA. It is hoped that any revision will result in a move to a definition based on the social model of disability instead similar to that employed by the Australian Federal system, which results in the emphasis of any claims being placed on whether discrimination has occurred rather than proving eligibility to claim.

To comply with the reasonable adjustments duty a HEI should: take such steps as it is reasonable for it to have taken to ensure that

1. in relation to the arrangements it makes for determining admission to the institution, disabled persons are not placed at a substantial disadvantage in comparison with persons who are not disabled; and
2. in relation to student services provided for, or offered to, students by it, disabled students are not placed at a substantial disadvantage in comparison with students who are not disabled. (DDA 1995, s 28T (1) and (2)).

As can be seen from the wording of the section, the duty placed on HEIs to make reasonable adjustments is extensive and ill-defined. Apart from the reference to admissions, the only other reference is to 'student services'. 'Student services' are defined within the Act as 'any services that an institution provides or offers to provide wholly or mainly for students attending or undertaking courses' (DDA 1995 s 28R). More detailed guidance on what can constitute student services can be found in the 'Post 16 Code of Practice' (DRC 2002). The extensive list given in the guide is stated to be illustrative, not exhaustive. For example, in addition to teaching and teaching related activities at all levels, the Post 16 Code covers learning facilities and equipment, parking, accommodation, and careers services. Despite this list the provision of services to disabled students can still be perceived as the province of 'disability services,' by many employees of an HEI rather than the responsibility of all. Reviews of disability provision prior to 2006 tended to focus on teaching to the exclusion of all other services. With the forthcoming implementation of the Disability Equality Duty, the scope of reviews of disability provision should cover an entire institution.

Under Section 58 of the DDA 1995, an employer is liable for acts of their employees and agents. This means all staff should have received appropriate training on whether an adjustment needs to be made and what type of adjustment is reasonable. It is doubtful whether many institutions have provided this type of training for all staff. A majority of institutions will rely on the requirement for staff to undertake training on or sooner after appointment. However, unless an institution has moved to making equality training compulsory on a continuing professional development basis across all grades, the dependence on induction training may result in staff who have been in post for some time either not receiving or choosing not to attend training on compliance with Part 4 of the DDA. The suitability of the training for different grades of staff is a further issue with which many UK institutions have not fully engaged. For example, the University of Westminster attempts to meet its obligations in relation to diversity generally rather than tackle the specific issues raised by the DDA by asking, not requiring, staff to complete an on line test based on a short handbook (University of Westminster 2003). The test is pitched at a level that enables all staff to attempt it. However, this generalist approach means that some staff do fail to fully comprehend the extent of their responsibility under the DDA. Weedon and Fuller stated that 30 percent of lecturing staff were unsympathetic to the needs of disabled students (Weedon and Fuller 2004). These members of staff tend to see any problems as to be dealt with by a local disability officer, rather than disability as something that all staff should be equipped to respond to.

There are several consequences that arise from the reasonable adjustments duty. Given the space limitations of this chapter there are three issues which will be considered:

1. the anticipatory nature of the duty;
2. the problem of disclosure and confidentiality; and
3. the definition of 'reasonableness'.

The duty to make adjustments is anticipatory. It is owed to all students and disabled people, not simply to individuals. The corollary of this being that even if staff at an institution believed that there were no disabled students at that institution, systems and processes would still have to be evaluated to ensure that potentially discriminatory practices are removed. Many institutions have not carried out this process because of resource implications and preferred to take the option of dealing with issues as they arose. For example, the production of handouts in electronic form is a simple way of anticipating a reasonable adjustment. Lecture handouts could be easily converted into other formats, but some academics are resistant to the production of handouts on grounds of intellectual property or cite pedagogical reasons why they do not use handouts (anecdotal evidence given at post paper discussion at Socio-Legal Studies Association Conference in 2002). Institutions could arrange for dyslexic students to have needs assessments in order to make appropriate adjustments for them if it is unclear what type of provisions are required but many HEIs would not countenance this option owing to the costs involved. Feedback on assignments could be given in electronic format, which would benefit all students, as well as those with a visual impairment. However, resource and time constraints may militate against this simple adjustment. Further, many HEIs simply have not been sure exactly how extensive their reasonable adjustment duties are in regard to franchise operations both within the United Kingdom and abroad. The answer to this appears to be that it depends on the contractual arrangements between institutions. This has the potential for differential standards, which may also be affected by resourcing issues.

The duty to make reasonable adjustments is ongoing. Thus a review may be required after a change in the student's circumstances. If a further needs assessment has been carried out then the HEI is usually guided by the recommendations contained within it. However, following discussion with the student, it may be decided that a prior adjustment is no longer reasonable and alternative provision may be suggested. Careful negotiation between the two parties may be required in order to arrive at a mutually satisfactory solution.

The issue of disclosure from the student perspective has been touched on briefly above. The rule appears to be that an institution only owes duties to those students that are known to the institution to be disabled. However, this has to be balanced with the anticipatory nature of the reasonable adjustments duty. Students should be given opportunities to disclose but there are instances where disclosure would not be necessary, such as if the disability is visible. Disclosure can also produce difficulties with regard to when a student can be deemed to have disclosed. Advice given by Skill suggests that disclosure of a disability to an academic member of staff probably is sufficient for an institution to be deemed to 'know' of that disability (Skill 2002). The question of disclosure has to be balanced against the student's wish for confidentiality (DDA 1995, s 28T(3)–(5)). There are rights to confidentiality given under the Data Protection Act 1988, as well as under the DDA 1995. A student may decline to disclose or only wish to disclose to those who need to know owing to the nature of their disability, for example, students with HIV/Aids. There are limits placed on confidentiality by the demands of health and safety as certain conditions may require disclosure in order to ensure the student receives suitable medical treatment, for example, first aiders should be given information if any students have declared that they have epilepsy, so that the student concerned can be treated appropriately.

The wording of the duty under the DDA to make reasonable adjustments presents problems in that the institution is not allowed to 'substantially disadvantage' a student who has declared that they are disabled. This can have the consequence that an institution makes an adjustment in order to comply with the duty but the adjustment is not one that removes the adverse impact from the student. A standard response to an application for special exam arrangements tends to be the provision of extra time. This is done as it is a relative simple and, more usually, an administratively convenient response which can completely fail to meet the objective of being a 'reasonable' adjustment for a particular student as it may result in greater physical stress being placed on the student owing to reduced recovery time between assessment events. This defeats the adjustment. A frequent comment that has been made to the author by dyslexic students when discussing the 'reasonable adjustments' made for exams is that "it's not a question of extra time, it's a question of needing a different way of showing what I [the student] can do" (Final year LL.B student with declared disabilities at the University of Westminster 2006. The student graduated with first class honours but there was on average a 10–15 percent discrepancy in performance between modules with a heavy exam weighting and modules which were assessed by non-time constrained methods.)

The variety and diversity of assessment methods would suggest that HEIs should not have a problem with regard to successfully testing the particular skills that the selected assessment is intended to address. However, many institutions, predominantly the old universities, tend to rely on the usual suspects of essay and closed book examination (Weedon and Fuller 2004). Just a sample of the available assessment methods are written examination which can be seen, unseen or open book, vivas, presentations, reports, essays, dissertation, learning logs, learning journals, reflective commentaries, group work, poster presentation, on line assessment, portfolios or independent study modules. However, there is a noted and increasing problem with plagiarism in UK universities. To combat this, many academics have expressed their inclination to return to exam based assessments. This could adversely affect many disabled students, for example a student with mobility issues may be permitted extra time to take the exam but this extension of the exam will reduce the available recovery time following the exam and also cut down on revision time between assessments. However, this will be permissible under the academic standards defence.

The timely notification of assessment is a feature from which all students can benefit. Many institutions deal with this by issuing a module handbook (naturally available in a variety of formats!) at the start of the module which contains all the information that students need to complete the assessment required for the module. Flexibility in deadlines for submission of work has been frequently cited as a problem for many disabled students (Weedon and Fuller 2004). Many institutions have regulations that do not permit teaching staff to vary the date of submission because administrative processes are linked to set submission dates. However, the rise of the modular system has resulted in frequent 'log jams' of work at the end of semesters for many students and this may be a system which puts disabled students at a substantial disadvantage. Staggering of deadlines may help but there may not be the scope to move dates by more than a couple of days. Creativity in the type of assessment required may be a better way to assist students with disabilities (Freewood et al. 2005).

In determining whether an adjustment is reasonable or not there are a variety of factors that can be taken into account. Responsible bodies must have regard to relevant provisions of the Code of Practice (s 28T(2)). When it comes to deciding what are the reasonable steps that need to be taken to avoid placing a student at a substantial disadvantage, a comparator needs to found in order to determine the 'time, inconvenience, effort or discomfort entailed in comparison with other people or students' (DRC Code of Practice 2002 para 5.2). An example of substantial disadvantage given in the Code is of a "tutor in Zoology delivers one of his modules through a computer-based learning environment and awards marks for students' participation in online discussion. The system does not work with a visually impaired student's software." (DRC Code of Practice 2002 para 5.2F).

At present there are several grounds on which an institution may refuse to make an adjustment. The institution will not be expected to lower its academic standards or other prescribed standards. In determining academic standards for a course, core elements need to be identified. Outcomes and objectives should be designed in such a way as to build in scope for adjustments, rather than have to 'bolt on' the adjustments afterwards. However, there are many subject areas where the necessary competences are determined by an external professional body, for example, pharmacy, law, architecture. Any mandatory requirements for a programme must be objectively justified by the relevant professional organisation. (DDA 1995, s 14(D)). For example, most undergraduate courses include objectives related to the ability to communicate effectively via a variety of methods. Many institutions place a high reliance on the ability to communicate in writing. Weedon and Fuller (2004) have identified this as a potential problem for many disabled students, particularly those with dyslexia. They found that 50 percent of disabled students 'indicated that they had difficulties with literacy skills'. More worryingly, a large proportion of students (between 70 and 90 percent depending on the institution) claimed that they had no support with literacy. Further, some of the students who have received literacy support stated that the support that they did receive was not helpful (Weedon and Fuller 2004). This may be a cause for concern as there is a suggestion that students who may have academic strengths, but poor literacy skills could be excluded from higher education as they may fail to comply with required degree competences. However, there may also be a justified academic standards defence for an institution to require a given standard of literacy. This remains to be tested in case law.

In additional, a HEI should take into consideration the financial resources involved in making the adjustment. The size of the institution and its income are relevant in determining reasonableness. The larger the institution, the more likely it should invest in making the adjustment. However, the expansion of higher education has not been matched by a proportionate increase in funding. Institutions have been assisted by funding from HEFCE to initially support disabled students but this is a declining fund. Reasonableness in regard to finance will also be affected by the availability of grants or loans, the cost of making the adjustment and whether it is practical. For example, alternative methods of assessing students may be a cost-effective way of making an adjustment. Institutions should also take into account other aids or services available and whether the student is already using DSA to fund services but institutions have to ensure that they have set aside money to enable them to cover the costs generated by making adjustments for students who are disabled but who not qualify for DSA.

If confidentiality is a priority then this should be considered in making the adjustment (DDA 1995, s 28T(4)). A point of contention is that health and safety is a ground on which adjustments may be refused and it is feared that this could become a safety screen for institutions to evade their responsibilities. Finally the institution should consider the relevant interests of other people, which includes other students. For example, assessment on a group basis may prove problematic if a student has a disability that makes it difficult for them to fully participate in the preparation and research. The tutor should ensure that all involved are aware of any potential difficulties and it may be appropriate to arrange an alternative form of assessment that meets the required learning outcomes.

The final question to be considered is the definition of 'reasonableness'. As noted above the scope of the duty is very extensive and has been interpreted very broadly. What is reasonable is not always an easy notion to define. A tutor's conception of what is reasonable to provide and a student's perception of what they could reasonably require tend to be very different. For example, a tutor provides materials prior to a lecture by posting them to an accessible intranet site. A dyslexic student argues that the provision of 'materials' is not a reasonable adjustment. The student believes that they should have access to the tutor's personal lecture notes so as not to be substantially disadvantaged as the student is not able to take full notes, despite the provision of a mini disk recorder. The tutor refuses. It is likely the student's demand is not reasonable, but the tutor's provision of the materials will be (University of Westminster, second year student 2006). However, if the materials provided are PowerPoint slides, then there is an arguable case that the same material should be provided in a note style format. A report by Weedon and Fuller (2004) has stated that students described PowerPoint presentations and poorly presented handouts as of 'limited value.'

In making reasonable adjustments to delivery of courses, research has shown that this has proved more successful than anticipated (Riddell et al. 2004). Despite the requirement for lecturers in the United Kingdom to have an established research track record, a qualification in teaching is not generally regarded as essential. It is a minority of lecturing staff that do hold a formal qualification in teaching. However, the establishment of the Higher Education Academy (following on from the creation of the Institute of Teaching and Learning in Higher Education in 1999) in 2004 has lead to many institutions encouraging staff to become members, with a consequently increased focus on the process of teaching and good practice, including accommodating students with disabilities on higher education courses. These can range from simple adjustments such facing the front of the class to facilitate lip reading or explaining the content of overhead slides for a student with a visual impairment (Code of Practice 2002 para 5.2A). The provision of extra information in an appropriate format or additional preparation time may need to be considered in order to facilitate in class activities. This material should also be given to the student's support worker such as a signer, lip speaker or note taker (Teachability Project 2000).

Many staff in HEIs are willing to help students with disabilities but are hesitant as to how this can best be done. There is a tendency to rely on the information given to them either by the disability officer or whatever is available via the institution's records. The simplest way to establish how to best meet the needs of the student is to talk to the student. Unfortunately many students do not realise that they could approach their tutors and equally many tutors feel awkward about raising a subject that they (the tutor) could find embarrassing. The needs of students with different disabilities have to be met in different ways. Providing materials in a format suitable for a student who has British Sign Language as a first language may mean problems for the visually impaired student who uses screen-reader software in reading the same information. The level that the student is studying at may also make a difference in terms of the student's own understanding of what they need as support. It is recognised that most disabled students will develop their own coping strategies For example, an undergraduate student may have less confidence in asking for support because they may not be sure exactly what is expected of them on a degree course. In contrast, a postgraduate student will be able to build on their experiences to date as a student and be proactive in requesting support.

The course of study and the institution may also raise different issues as to the reasonableness of adjustments. The work carried out on the TRLP/ERSC study by Fuller et al. has demonstrated that that there is a distinct gap in practice between the "old" universities in the United Kingdom and the post-1992 institutions. The "new" universities appear to be much more willing to accommodate adjustments and staff in these institutions appear to be more supportive of their students (Weedon and Fuller 2004).

THE DISABILITY EQUALITY DUTY

With the passage of the DDA 2005, the responsibilities of universities towards their students and prospective students with disabilities have been further extended. This has been done by introducing the duty to promote DED in the public sector. The DED will come into force as from 4th December 2006. The

DED parallels the provisions introduced into the Race Relations Act 1976 in order to eliminate institutional discrimination. This duty has been introduced to endeavour to facilitate the participation of disabled people in public life and is a move towards the social model of disability by focusing on the policies of public authorities rather than the disability of the individual. However, this duty has the potential to be more far reaching in effecting changes in HEIs to promote access than the provisions of Part 4 have achieved to date. The Act is breaking new ground in the field of discrimination legislation in the United Kingdom as the duty to promote disability equality ranges into the territory of positive discrimination to ensure that there is compliance with the duty.

The DED is divided into two parts: the general duty and the specific duty. The general duty is outlined in Section 49A of the DDA and will affect all public authorities when carrying out their functions. From December 2006 all public authorities are required to have 'due regard' to eliminating discrimination that is stated to be unlawful under the DDA; to eliminate harassment of disabled persons; to promote equality of opportunity for disabled people; to positively discriminate in favour of disabled people; to promote 'positive attitudes' towards disabled people and to "need to encourage participation by disabled persons in public life."

The introduction of this duty has the potential to have the widest impact yet in terms of the number of disabled people that will be affected by the provisions. However, Section 49A is qualified by the use of the phrase 'having due regard.' The definition of 'due regard' given in the DRC Code of Practice on the DED is 'that authorities should give due weight to the need to promote disability equality in proportion to its relevance. It requires more than simply giving consideration to "disability equality" (DRC para 1.14). In addition, the Code states that "due regard" comprises two linked elements: proportionality and relevance (DRC para 2.34). Further, it is submitted that this is an anticipatory duty, which is being placed on all authorities. It is likely that the parts of Section 49 that will be the most important for HEIs are Subsection (c) the need to promote equality of opportunity between disabled persons and other persons and Subsection (d) the need to take steps to take account of disabled persons' disabilities, even where that involves treating disabled persons more favourably than other persons. Higher education is about extending opportunity. Moreover, the section reinforces the reasonable adjustments duties by encouraging institutions to go beyond offering simple parity of treatment and ensure that any adjustments that are made result in actual equality.

The second part of the DED is the "specific duty" set out in Section 49D.[2] Under this section the public authority has a duty to produce a 'Disability Equality Scheme'(DES). The scheme will have to set out how the authority intends to comply with the duties in Section 49 within a three year plan. One of the main outcomes of the DES is that many HEIs are by default carrying out disability mapping exercises and are taking the opportunity to review what provision is being made for students with disabilities. This review should be in depth and examine not only the overall institutional provision but what adjustments have been made by individual faculties as different faculties will be subject to different adjustments. Many institutions are complying with this part of the duty by carrying out Impact Assessments which evaluate current practice and suggest modifications for the future. A major problem of adapting provision for disabled students that will have to be remedied consequent to the introduction of the DED is that meeting the adjustments duties imposed by the DDA have, to date, tended to be treated by most HEIs as 'bolt-on' rather than 'built in' (DART 2006). Thus reasonable adjustments should become embedded into institutional provision following the drawing up of a DES. An important requirement in drawing up the DES is that disabled students must be involved with the production of the scheme. This should result in greater convergence between the expectations of students and the ability of HEIs to meet those expectations. The duty will be ongoing and HEIs will be expected to ensure that monitoring and compliance are maintained. The DRC is given the ability to issue compliance notices under Section 49E to ensure that disability equality is taken seriously. The DRC produced a basic DED guidance for HEIs in July 2006, and further information can be obtained from the Equality Challenge Unit Website where they have case studies from a number of HEIs who are tackling the DES.

CONCLUSIONS

As stated previously, the remedy for a student who claims that an institution has failed to make a reasonable adjustment is to first attempt to conciliate the claim and then to proceed to the county court if conciliation is unsuccessful. It is unclear whether to attribute the fact that no claim has, at the time of writing, been successful in court to the willingness of institutions to make adjustments or that those claims that been brought have been settled prior to hearing because no institution wishes to be the first to lose.

The progress that has been made in terms of improving access to higher education for disabled students can be simply demonstrated by reference to the statistics but an increase in numbers does not demonstrate whether those students are enjoying a comparable experience of higher education to their able bodied colleagues. The work of Fuller et al. will provide some guidance to the effectiveness of Part 4 when complete. However, the introduction of the reasonable adjustments duties has been shown by the limited research carried out to date (Riddell et al.

2004, Fuller et al. 2006) to have brought changes to many institutions to enable disabled students to participate more easily, if not always equally.

Despite the reasonable adjustments duty and the DED, there are still areas that an institution will not be able to control. The informal social networks that students develop in both socialising and studying provide huge amounts of support. These networks are not readily accessible to all disabled students. The nature of some disabilities, such as agoraphobia or schizophrenia, will still act as a segregating factor. The DED has fascinating potential with regard to changing not just the behaviour of staff, but the latent requirement that the behaviour of fellow students becomes more "disability friendly." There are examples given of adjustments being made by institutions but the actions of fellow students then negate that adjustment. For example, the use of recording devices in lectures being rendered useless because of the noise created by the other students (Weedon and Fuller 2004) or a student with mobility problems being unable to use a lift because able bodied students will not allow disabled students priority use of the lifts (witnessed by the author 2006). The DED requires that HEIs have due regard to the promotion of equality of opportunity for disabled students. This may have to become part of induction for all students.

With the campaigning of academics such as Alan Hurst (1993) in the 1990s, the lack of access for disabled students was brought onto the agenda. Gradually legislation has been put in place to underpin the support that should be offered to students with disabilities. This will be further reinforced by changes to the reasonable adjustments duty later in 2006. The combination of reasonable adjustments and the DED should enable more disabled students to attend university but a paradigm shift in attitudes and funding is still needed for equality of opportunity to become a reality.

NOTES

1. Many authors continue to refer to "SENDA" but this was simply the amending legislation. The correct citation is to the sections of Part 4 of the Disability Discrimination Act 1995.
2. Not all public authorities are subject to the specific duties but under the Disability Discrimination (Public Authorities) (Statutory Duties) Regulations 2005 SI2005/2901 it os stated that Higher Education institutions (HEIs) are included.

BIBLIOGRAPHY

Books

Doyle, B. (2005) *Disability Discrimination: Law and Practice* (5th ed.). Bristol, UK: Jordans.

Hurst, A. (1993) *Steps Towards Graduation: Access to Higher Education and People with Disabilities.* Aldershot, UK: Avebury Press.

McColgan, A. (2005) *Discrimination Law* (2nd ed.). Oxford: Hart.
Monaghan, K. (2005) *Blackstone's Guide to the Disability Discrimination Legislation.* Oxford: OUP.
Teachability: *Creating an Accessible Curriculum for Students with Disabilities.* (2000). Glasgow, UK: University of Strathclyde.

Cases

Goodwin v the Patent Office [1999] ICR 302.

Electronic Resources

DART (2006) *Disabilities Academic Research Tool*
Retrieved 5 May 2006 from
http://dart.lboro.ac.uk/dart-cgi/viewcase.pl?case_id=18.

Department of Work and Pensions (2006) *Guidance on matters to be taken into account in determining questions relating to the definition of disability*
Retrieved 28 April 2006 from
http://www.drc-gb.org/documents/Final_version_of_guidance_Feb06_as_submitted_to_DRC_16-03-06.doc.

Disability Discrimination Act 1995
Retrieved 13 April 2006 from
http://www.opsi.gov.uk/acts/acts1995/Ukpga_19950050_en_1.htm.

Disability Discrimination Act 2005
Retrieved 13 April 2006 from
http://www.opsi.gov.uk/acts/acts2005/20050013.htm.

Disability Rights Commission (2005) *The Duty to Promote Disability Equality: Statutory Code of Practice*
Retrieved 5 May 2006 from
http://www.drc-gb.org/businessandservices/docs/Code_19_10_mp_marked.proofed_CA.doc.

Disability Rights Commission (2002) *Code of Practice for Providers of Post 16 Education and Related Services*
Retrieved 19 April 2006 from
http://www.drc-gb.org/uploaded_files/documents/2008_187_DDA_Pt4_Code_of_Practice_for_Post_16_education.doc.

NOP Survey (2002) *Education for all: Getting in, getting on or getting nowhere?* A survey of 18–24 year olds conducted by NOP
Retrieved 14 August 2006 from
http://www.drc-gb.org/Docs/20_204_NOP%20and%20debate%20pr%20%20NOP%20summary%20-%204.12.2002.doc.

Disability Rights Commission (2006) *Test Your Eq*: Post 16 education checklist
Retrieved 14 August 2006 from
http://www.drc.org.uk/docs/DED_checklist_post_16_education.doc.

Freewood, M. with Cunliffe-Charlesworth, H. and Hewson, J. (2005) *Accessible Assessments*
Retrieved 6 May 2006 from
http://www.shu.ac.uk/services/lti/accessibleassessments/content/section_1/1.2.html#we.

Fuller. M. (2005) *Disabled and Non-disabled Students' Experiences of Teaching, Learning and Assessment: Similarities & Differences*
Retrieved 4 May 2006 from
http://www.glos.ac.uk/shareddata/dms/9FFFB1ECBCD42A039EC7FD1D5F4D34FE.doc.

Fuller, M., Bradley, A., Healey, M., Hurst, A., Oddy, G., Piggot, L. et al. (2006). *Enhancing the Quality and Outcomes of Disabled Students' Learning in Higher Education.*
Retrieved 4 May 2006 from
http://www.creid.ed.ac.uk/projects/qualityoutcomes.htm.

HESA statistics (2005)
Retrieved 19 April 2006 from
http://www.natdisteam.ac.uk/documents/8AllyrsAlllocnoTotal.doc.

Hurstfield, J., Meager, N., Aston, J., Davies, J., Mann, K., Mitchell, H et al. (2004) *Monitoring the Disability Discrimination Act (DDA) 1995 Phase 3*, DRC Research Report
Retrieved 14 August 2006 from
http://www.drc-gb.org/PDF/monitoring_dda.pdf.

Lord Mackay of Ardbrecknish, Hansard, 22 May 1995, Col 804
Retrieved 19 April 2006 from
http://www.publications.parliament.uk/pa/ld199495/ldhansrd/vo950522/text/50522-03.htm#50522-03_head1.

National Disability Team (2005) *Planning a review of provision for disabled students: Guidance and tips for success*
Retrieved 22 February 2006 from
http://www.natdisteam.ac.uk/documents/cbtarticle0805.doc.

Open University (2006) *Making your Teaching inclusive*
Retrieved 4 May 2006 from
http://www.open.ac.uk/inclusiveteaching/pages/inclusive-teaching/field-trips-and-reasonable-adjustments.php.

QAA (1999) *Code of Practice for the Assurance of Academic Quality and Standards in Higher Education. Section 3: Students with Disabilities*
Retrieved 19 April 2006 from
http://www.qaa.ac.uk/academicinfrastructure/codeOfPractice/section3/COP_disab.pdf.

Riddell, S., Tinklin, T. and Wilson, A. (2004) *Disabled Students and Multiple Policy Innovations in Higher Education: Final report to the Economic and Social Research Council.*
Retrieved 4 May 2006 from
http://www.ces.ed.ac.uk/PDF%20Files/Disability_Report.pdf.

Skill (2002) *Some DDA myths uncovered*
Retrieved 19 April 2006 from
http://www.skill.org.uk/info/dda_myths.asp

University of Westminster Diversity Handbook (2003)
Retrieved 5 May 2006 from
http://www.wmin.ac.uk/pdf/Diversity%20Uni%20WorkBook.pdf.

Weedon, E. and Fuller, M. (2004) *What is it like for you? Surveying the learning experiences of disabled students in four HE institutions*
Retrieved 4 May 2006 from
http://www.glos.ac.uk/shareddata/dms/A00E7FB4BCD42A039CDFE2AE830696BB.doc.

APPENDIX 1

General principles

1. Institutions should ensure that in all their policies, procedures and activities, including strategic planning and resource allocation, consideration is given to the means of enabling disabled students' participation in all aspects of the academic and social life of the institution.

The physical environment

2. Institutions should ensure that disabled students can have access to the physical environment in which they will study, learn, live and take part in the social life of their institution.
3. Institutions should ensure that facilities and equipment are as accessible as possible to disabled students.

Information for applicants, students and staff

4. The institution's publicity, programme details and general information should be accessible to people with disabilities and describe the opportunities for disabled students to participate.

The selection and admission of students

5. In selecting students institutions should ensure equitable consideration of all applicants.
6. Disabled applicants' support needs should be identified and assessed in an effective and timely way, taking into account the applicant's views.

Enrolment, registration and induction of students

7. The arrangements for enrolment, registration and induction of new entrants should accommodate the needs of disabled students.

Learning and teaching, including provision for research and other postgraduate students

8. Programme specifications should include no unnecessary barriers to access by disabled people.

9. Academic support services and guidance should be accessible and appropriate to the needs of disabled students.

10. The delivery of programmes should take into account the needs of disabled people or, where appropriate, be adapted to accommodate their individual requirements.

11. Institutions should ensure that, wherever possible, disabled students have access to academic and vocational placements including field trips and study abroad.

12. Disabled research students should receive the support and guidance necessary to secure equal access to research programmes.

Examination, assessment and progression

13. Assessment and examination policies, practices and procedures should provide disabled students with the same opportunity as their peers to demonstrate the achievement of learning outcomes.

14. Where studying is interrupted as a direct result of a disability-related cause, this should not unjustifiably impede a student's subsequent academic progress.

Staff development

15. Induction and other relevant training programmes for all staff should include disability awareness/equality and training in specific services and support.

Access to general facilities and support

16. Students with disabilities should have access to the full range of support services that are available to their non-disabled peers.

Additional specialist support

17. Institutions should ensure that there are sufficient designated members of staff with appropriate skills and experience to provide specialist advice and support to disabled applicants and students, and to the staff who work with them.

18. Institutions should identify and seek to meet the particular needs of individual disabled students.

19. Internal communications systems should ensure that appropriate staff receive information about the particular needs of disabled students in a clear and timely way.

20. Institutions should have a clearly defined policy on the confidentiality and disclosure of information relating to a person's disabilities that is communicated to applicants, students and staff.

Complaints

21. Institutions should ensure that information about all complaints and appeals policies and procedures is available in accessible formats and communicated to students.

22. Institutions should have in place policies and procedures to deal with complaints arising directly or indirectly from a student's disability. Monitoring and evaluation

23. Institutional information systems should monitor the applications, admissions, academic progress and nature of impairment of disabled students.

24. Institutions should operate systems to monitor the effectiveness of provision for students with disabilities, evaluate progress and identify opportunities for enhancement.

CHAPTER THIRTY-ONE

Moving IN FROM THE Margins: FROM Accommodation TO Universal Design

SHERYL BURGSTAHLER AND REBECCA CORY

INTRODUCTION

Universities and colleges are designed for an "average" student—a student who progresses through in a certain time frame, who accesses classes in a "typical way" and who has an age and background of experiences that are within a narrow range. Students who do not have experiences, talents, and backgrounds within the expected range are likely not as well served as those who do. There has been growing interest in creating welcoming environments for underrepresented groups defined by race/ethnicity, age, and gender, but the characteristics of students with disabilities do not often fall within the range of diversity categories considered. Rather, a disability, and the person who has it, is viewed as a "problem." Common solutions to these "problems" are add-on programs—special centers, offices, policies and equipment that accommodate these students—without substantially critiquing or altering the organizational and pedagogical practices of the institution. With growing numbers of students with disabilities attending postsecondary education in the United States (Eudaly, n.d.; Henderson, 2001), it is increasingly important that colleges and universities create a welcoming and accessible environment for them as part of their mission to effectively serve all students. This chapter explores how we create institutions that promote the equality of education for all students, those with disabilities included.

The authors explore how some current college and university policies and procedures serve to reinforce negative stereotypes about people with disabilities and keep them on the margins of the institution. The discussion continues with an approach for creating an inclusive campus that requires a changed mindset about disability and the application of universal design (UD).

NEGATIVE OUTCOMES OF THE ACCOMMODATIONS APPROACH

Typical policies and procedures for providing accommodations for students with disabilities can have some unintended negative outcomes that serve to marginalize students with disabilities. Issues in key areas—attitude, expertise, legislation, documentation, and funding—are discussed below.

Attitude

The perception of some faculty is that including students with disabilities is a burden that somehow weakens program or course rigor (Nelson et al. 1990) is somewhat arbitrary and unfair to other students (Burgstahler & Doe, 2006; Lehmann et al., 2000; Leyser et al., 1998; National Center for the Study of Postsecondary Educational Supports, 2000; Williams & Ceci, 1999), and is done only because the law requires. In reality, *reasonable* accommodations do not lessen academic standards and are only provided to assure fair and equitable access (NJCLD, 1999). Some faculty even suspect that students makeup or exaggerate the impact of disabilities in order to obtain accommodations that advantage themselves (Burgstahler & Doe, 2006; Cope, 2005; Williams & Ceci, 1999; Zirkel, 2000). Articles in both *Academe* (Cope, 2005) and *The Chronicle of Higher Education* (Williams & Ceci, 1999; Zirkel, 2000) reflect a sentiment of some faculty that students will do anything, including "buy" a disability label, in order to gain an advantage in college. Many of these articles single out learning disabilities (LD) as the type that students are likely faking, though other invisible disabilities are cited as well. Some people conclude that because there may be some students who are falsely claiming disability that one cannot trust any student who claims a disability, especially in the case of LD (Williams & Ceci, 1999; Zirkel, 2000). One of the more famous legal cases about disability in higher education came out of Boston University, where the president of the University made up a student who he named "Somnolent Samantha" who fabricated a disability to get out of course requirements (Selingo, 1997). Promoting such stereotypes serves to marginalize students with disabilities, and discourage them from coming forth with disability information (Cory, 2005; Szymanski & Trueba, 1999).

Expertise

Current disability service practices are set up in such a way as to privilege the knowledge of disability service professionals, doctors, and psychologists. Together they are seen as the experts who know what a student needs, after a few conversations and/or the administration of diagnostic tests. Combine the expertise of the disability service staff and medical practitioners with that of the faculty member, who is seen as having the ultimate authority regarding the content and methodology of a specific course, and it creates a situation where student's experiences and expertise on how she or he functions best are often overlooked or undervalued. Many students have a lifetime of living with their disabilities and know how they respond in specific situations and settings. Not valuing self-knowledge serves to further marginalize students with disabilities.

Legislation

Since the passage of the Rehabilitation Act of 1973 and reinforced with the Americans with Disabilities Act of 1990, universities and colleges in the United States have a legal obligation to provide reasonable accommodations for people with disabilities who are qualified for their programs and services. Accommodations (sometimes called academic adjustments) refer to making changes to a product or environment that is not fully accessible to an individual who has a disability. A person with a disability is defined in relevant legislation in the United States as someone who has a physical or mental impairment that limits one or more major life activities, has a record of such an impairment, or is regarded as having an impairment (Americans with Disabilities Act [ADA]; Section 504 of the Rehabilitation Act [Section 504]). Examples of accommodations include providing printed materials in alternate formats (e.g., in Braille), allowing extra time and/or a controlled environment for tests, providing a sign language interpreter, or moving the location of a class to an accessible location. The goal of many institutions is simply to meet their legal obligation to students with disabilities.

Much of the training for students, faculty, and administrators on disability topics, including the professional standards for disability services professional staff (Dukes & Shaw, 1999; Shaw et al., 1997), focus on legal issues surrounding disability (Treloar, 1999; Paul, 2000). Books and articles often start with the legal framework (Bourke et al., 2000; Getzel & Wehman, 2004; Rothstein, n.d). Publications by the Association on Higher Education and Disability (AHEAD), the professional organization for post-secondary disability service personnel, and presentations at the annual AHEAD conference, devote a large part of their discussion to legal obligations (2001a; 2001b). The question "Are we in legal compliance with the Americans with Disabilities Act?" itself suggests that students with disabilities have a marginalized status, that meeting the legal obligation is the goal, and that there is no other guide for action.

Historically, universities have addressed their legal obligations regarding the disabilities of students as an afterthought, designing courses and services for more traditional students and then adding on a disability services office to make needed accommodations for students with disabilities when courses and services are inaccessible to them. Offering an accommodation, because of its very nature, is a way of admitting that a course or program is not accessible to everyone and that some students, as a result of *their* disabilities, need special arrangements that should be made by service units assigned to "take care" of the problems these students have. An institution is sometimes even praised when it serves a large number of students in its disability services office. As long as legal obligations are met, few people ever ask why so many courses and programs on this campus are inaccessible to so many students, and students with disabilities stay on the margins.

Documentation

On many campuses, disabled student service staff play the role of deeming who does and who does not have a disability that requires accommodation. They usually base these decisions on documentation from a third-party professional who outlines diagnostic results and functional limitations, and makes accommodation recommendations. Who is eligible for disability-related accommodations at the university level is a topic discussed at great length in the higher education literature (Gregg & Scott, 2000; Reilly & Davis, 2005; Thoma & Wehmeyer, 2005; Wehman & Yasuda, 2005, Weintraub, 2005). Faculty and administrators want to be assured that there is formal documentation of a disability, especially in the instances of invisible disabilities, such as learning and psychiatric disabilities (Szymanski & Trueba, 1999).

Typically, the first action that a disability services staff member takes when a new student steps into the office is to ask for documentation of the disability (Reilly & Davis, 2005; Thoma & Wehmeyer, 2005; Wehman & Yasuda, 2005). Current AHEAD publications, including the brochures Confidentiality and Disability Issues in Higher Education (2001b) and College Students with Learning Disabilities (2001a), reinforce the need for documentation prior to implementation of services. The College Students with Learning Disabilities brochure tells students how to manage their LD only after saying "If you know you have a learning disability and have documentation on file with the Disabled Student Services office [do these things]." Similarly, the brochure advises faculty to help students with disabilities by first referring them to the disability services office, and second telling students to supply the disability services staff with appropriate documentation. Although administratively the up-front request for documentation seems to make sense for efficient use of time, it sends a message that the medical professional knows the student better than the student knows her or himself. Many campus documentation guidelines are highly structured with details about the age of the documentation, who can conduct an assessment, and how it should be conducted. However, the more rigid the guidelines, the less room there is for variance between disability types or within a disability category. This can be difficult for students to negotiate because what is appropriate for one type of disability may or may not be appropriate for another, and individuals with the same diagnosis may require different accommodations.

An emphasis on documentation is seen in the literature published by AHEAD. AHEAD first published documentation guidelines for students with LD in 1997, and AHEAD members are taught through conference sessions and organizational publications that, especially in the case of an invisible disability, documentation should be the starting point for a relationship with a student (Thomas, 2000). This approach is changing somewhat, as evidenced in the new AHEAD guidelines for documentation that emphasize the case by case nature of accommodation and the interactive process of determining appropriate accommodations (AHEAD, n.d.). In this approach professionals recognize that, with the diverse abilities of people with the same or similar disability labels, it is important to focus less on the label and more on how a student is functioning. For example, students with a learning disability label are often given extended time to complete exams or in-class assignments, no matter what type of learning disability they have. For some students the time is needed and for others it is not. Disability service professionals often argue that accommodations "level the playing field" for students with disabilities while if offered to students without disabilities would not significantly change their performance (Ofiesh, 2000). If this is true, strict accommodation standards based on label are unnecessary, as accommodations would help those who needed them and have no significant difference for those who do not.

An emphasis on documentation promotes the medical model of disability, where disability resides within the person. This approach blames the individual for the inaccessibility of courses and services, without considering the inaccessible design of these products and environments (Burgstahler & Doe, 2004).

What constitutes acceptable documentation continues to be an issue, especially for invisible disabilities like LD, attention deficit disorder, psychiatric illnesses, or chronic pain (Burgstahler & Doe, 2006; Gordon et al., 2002, Weintraub, 2005) where the definition of what constitutes that particular diagnostic label may not even be clear (Lloyd & Hallahan, 2005; Nadeau, 1995). K-12 education provides assessment for LD by school counselors or special education teachers at no cost to the student or family. These evaluations are typically done every few years. When students get to college, they are responsible for providing documentation that is acceptable to the institution, and incur the cost of additional evaluation if the documentation they currently have is not acceptable (Sahlen & Lehmann, 2006). Some students have adequate documentation from high school, but students who were tested too many years earlier, tested by a professional with credentials unacceptable to the postsecondary institution, are returning to college after many years, or have recently acquired or learned of their disability, may be faced with significant out-of-pocket expenses to obtain acceptable documentation.

In 2005 AHEAD issued a revision to previously published guidelines for documentation that includes extending the definition of "current documentation" to be a three–seven year time frame, rather than the previous definition of three years (AHEAD, n.d.). Many colleges have followed suit. However, in practice the emphasis continues to be on requiring that documentation be recent and comprehensive. This situation is complicated by the fact that there is no standard criteria for what constitutes some disabilities, such as LD—at one point a standard discrepancy between IQ and achievement was used; current thinking leans toward a more holistic view of the student (AHEAD, n.d.; Swanson & Howard, 2005) The situation is further complicated by the fact that diagnosing professionals may not fully understand how their evaluation is going to be used by the college or university (Gordon et al., 2002; McGuire et al., 1996).

Szymanski and Trueba (1999) propose that the focus on documentation has had an unintended impact of marginalizing students with disabilities. The system puts people with disabilities, who often are economically disadvantaged (The Henry J. Kasier Family Foundation, 2006), at further disadvantage by requiring that they produce documentation that can be very expensive before they can access the services they need to be on a level playing field with their peers.

Funding

Since disability-related accommodations are only needed for a small portion of the population, students who need them are seen as costly (Collins & Mowbray, 2004; Keim et al., 1996; Rothstein, n.d.). Sometimes the extra cost of disability-related accommodations for a student is presented as a concern because it results in a higher than average cost for this student, without recognizing that other students vary in cost—some above average and some below average in cost. Those who accept the above-average cost of some students—such as those taking science classes with expensive equipment and high-salaried instructors—but are concerned about the additional costs associated with disabilities, send a clear message that members of this group are not valued as highly as other students. In reality, the incremental cost of accommodations for a specific student rarely affects the average cost per student campus-wide. Even so, in an effort to keep costs down, some universities work to limit accommodations to those that are easily obtained, or use less obvious ways of keeping students with disabilities out of programs by providing bureaucratic barriers to access (Szymanski & Trueba, 1999). The perception that students with disabilities are expensive serves as a basis for many to question the rightful place of students with disabilities in higher education, further marginalizing this group (Collins & Mowbray, 2004).

EXPLORATION OF A BETTER APPROACH

The typical model for addressing the needs of students with disabilities in postsecondary education involves a system that emphasizes legislative mandates, documentation, and disability labels; values the expertise of disability services professionals, faculty and medical personnel above the student's knowledge of him or herself; and creates an environment of mistrust of students. A new vision of how to address the needs of students is explored in the remainder of this chapter. It is a vision that creates an inclusive campus where disability issues are not simply addressed as afterthoughts and the need for accommodations is minimized. In this vision, students with disabilities and other students who are typically marginalized are brought in to the university as full participants through UD.

Embracing Diversity and Full Inclusion

Universities and colleges have the opportunity to create intentional communities—ones that value and respect each member's experience and competence, that views the diversity of the campus as an enhancement, and sees resources as going to the places that they are needed to assure equity. Thomson (2006) says the "premise of equality should promote and accommodate the widest possible variety of human forms, functions, and behaviors." Once full inclusion is embraced as a goal on campus and the contributions that people with disabilities make are considered valuable, when different ways of thinking, moving, and accessing the world are seen as a part of human diversity that therefore contribute to the richness of perspectives on campus, it is easier to let go of the tight controls placed on accommodations and consider accessibility in a broader perspective. If the unique perspective of a student who is blind is considered an asset to a seminar discussion, then the cost and effort of creating accessible print materials for him becomes an essential component of the education of a dozen students, and therefore does not seem such a burdensome expense. If interpreters are regarded as facilitating two-way communication between the student who is deaf, the professor, and other students then paying for classroom interpreters is vital for the professor to do his or her job. Changing the location of the accessibility "problem" from an individual to a group makes the solution less personal.

Least Dangerous Assumption

Anne Donnellan (1984) coined the term "least dangerous assumption" (p. 142) when thinking of individuals with autism. The idea of least dangerous assumption is that in situations where it is difficult to immediately assess a person's skills, one should assume competency because it is a "safer" assumption. This idea can be applied to all students. When meeting a student with a disability, why so often is the assumption made, like in the *Academe* article (Cope, 2005) that the individual is *not* able? Why is it often assumed, like in the *Chronicle* articles (Williams & Ceci, 1999; Zirkel, 2000), that students with disabilities are *cheating* the system? Why are accommodation requests often assumed to be *unreasonable*? These assumptions are all quite "dangerous." They create a situation that underestimates a human, where that person is not a full participant in the community, where they are stifled and limited because of the things assumed about them.

The goal of a college education is to create people who participate actively and critically in our society (Lucas, 1994), who are leaders and scholars, who make the world a better place in which to live by offering their unique talents and insights. Students with disabilities should be included in this goal.

Often low achieving students with disabilities are thought to not be working hard enough; they are blamed for their failures and labeled incompetent or poor students. People with disabilities who accomplish something typical are seen as heroes, and as such viewed by some as "super-crips" (Johnson, 1998; Persinger & Tiller, 1999; Rizza & Morrison, 2003). Too often, high achieving students with disabilities are thought to have "overcome" their disabilities and are seen as exceptions, rather than as simply the result when capable people work hard and have full access to curriculum and academic activities.

When the least dangerous assumption is made about students, they are all considered competent. Their academic achievements are considered appropriate for their abilities, skills, and efforts. Students are considered well-intentioned and experts on their own lives. Failure is not because of the disability and success not despite the disability.

Privilege the Lived Experience of Disability

Two common fields from which disability service providers come are special education and rehabilitation counseling (Dukes & Shaw, 2004). In these fields of study, disability is often taught from a functional limitation standpoint, with medicalized descriptions and third-person accounts of the accomplishments of "those" who are disabled. Providing accommodations is in line with the medical model of disability, which focuses on an individual's diagnosis and functional limitations and on making adjustments for the individual in a specific situation (Abberley, 1995; Gill, 1987; Hahn, 1988; Jones, 1996; Swain & Lawrence, 1994). An alternative approach privileges the lived experience of disability as a position of expertise encourages service providers to seek to fully understand the circumstances of the individual and rely on the student's expertise and experiences to help make programmatic decisions.

UNIVERSAL DESIGN: A NEW APPROACH

Universal design has recently emerged in the literature as an approach to address some of the needs of students with disabilities on postsecondary campuses and minimizing the negative impact of the accommodations approach discussed earlier in this chapter (Burgstahler, 2005c; The Center for Universal Design, 1997; National Council on Disability, 2004). Whereas accommodation is a reactive approach to assure access for an individual, UD is a proactive approach to assure access for a large group of potential participants. Proponents of UD support a social model of disability and therefore work to change the environment to make it accessible, rather than changing the person. Here it is argued that many disadvantages associated with disabilities are imposed by the inaccessible design of products and environments (Burgstahler & Doe, 2004; Gill, 1987; Hahn, 1988; Jones, 1996; Swain & Lawrence, 1994).

Originally applied in the field of architecture and later to information technology, UD can provide a philosophical framework for the design of a broad range of educational products and environments, including Web sites, educational software, instruction, and student services. UD offers strategies to redesign colleges in a new way that accounts for the diversity of the students, uses resources effectively, and minimizes the need for accommodations.

The Process of Universal Design

UD is a process, as well as a goal (Story et al., 1998). UD as a process requires taking a macro view of the application being considered, as well as a micro view of subparts of the application. A review of how UD has been applied in a wide variety of settings suggests that the following eight-step process can be used to apply UD in postsecondary education (Burgstahler, 2005d):

1. *Identify the application.* Specify the product or environment (i.e., the service, course, Web site, or other application) to which you wish to apply UD.
2. *Define the universe.* Describe the overall population, for example, students in a course or users of a technology-and then the diverse characteristics of potential members of the population for which the application is described (e.g., with respect to gender; age; size; ethnicity/race; native language; and abilities to see, hear, move and manipulate objects, and learn).
3. *Involve consumers.* Determine how to include people with disabilities and other diverse characteristics in development and implementation of the application.
4. *Adopt UD guidelines/standards/performance indicators.* Create or select existing UD guidelines/standards. Integrate UD practices with other best practices within the field of the specific application.
5. *Apply UD guidelines/standards/performance indicators.* Apply UD along with design standards of good practice within the field to the overall design of the application, subcomponents of the application, and maintenance and procurement processes.
6. *Plan for accommodations.* Develop processes to address accommodation requests (e.g., purchase of assistive technology, arrangement for sign language interpreters) from individuals for whom the design does not automatically provide access.
7. *Train and support.* Tailor and deliver training and support to stakeholders (e.g., instructors, computer support staff, procurement offices, administrators).
8. *Evaluate.* Include UD measures in the evaluation of the application, evaluate the application with a diverse group of users, and make modifications based on their feedback.

Note that *planning* for accommodations (step 6) is included as one aspect of UD; rather than strictly an after-thought, however, in UD the product or environment is created with accessibility in mind and the practitioner is proactive in planning for accommodations that might still be needed by specific students. UD has been applied to many educational products (e.g., Web sites, software, textbooks, lab equipment) and environments (e.g., dormitories, classrooms, student union buildings, library facilities, museums, distance learning courses) (DO-IT, n.d.a; Preiser & Ostroff, 2001). Practicing UD is important in postsecondary education because, unlike accommodations, UD benefits all students, places a high value on diversity and inclusion, and does not marginalize students with disabilities.

An application of UD that is getting a great deal of attention in the educational field is the universal design of instruction—where UD principles are applied in developing and selecting curriculum, arranging physical spaces, and choosing and implementing instructional methods. UD serves to level the playing field so that all students have equal opportunities to reach high standards. To implement the process of UD, an instructor selects multiple strategies for the delivery of instruction and then applies UD to delivery methods, materials, and activities of a class.

Applications of UD allow each student to learn and demonstrate knowledge through multiple channels (e.g., reading, listening, manipulating, experimenting, discussing, participating in art activities). The resulting curricular materials and activities provide built-in alternatives for students with disparities in their abilities, learning styles and preferences, background knowledge, and other characteristics. This flexibility allows all students to learn in ways they learn best.

UD does not require that instructors abandon teaching and learning philosophies, instructional techniques, or quality indicators they have found useful—e.g., student-centered learning, differentiated instruction, collaborative teaching, computer-assisted instruction, constructivism, cooperative learning, guided instruction (e.g., Hall et al., 2003; Kame'enui et al., 2002; Tomlinson, 2001). Instead, UD requires that instructors rethink the mix of strategies they use and assure that implementations of each strategy are accessible to all students.

Fully including all students requires a classroom atmosphere that makes everyone feel welcome and supported, learning areas and activities that are accessible to every student, a variety of teaching methods that engage students with a wide range of characteristics, and testing options that make assessment fair to everyone (e.g., Mason & Orkwis, 2005; McGuire et al., 2003; Mino, 2004; Scott et al., 2003). A working document that lists performance indicators of UD of instruction has been created with input from campuses throughout the United States and is maintained in the document *Equal Access: Universal Design of Instruction* on DO-IT's Web site at the University of Washington (Burgstahler, 2005a). These indicators have been developed through an extensive literature review (Bowe, 2000; Burgstahler, 2005a; Hitchcock & Stahl, 2003; Johnson & Fox, 2003; Mason & Orkwis, 2005; Mino, 2004; Orkwis, 2003; Orkwis & McLane, 1998; Rose & Meyer, 2002; Scott et al., 2001; Silver et al., 1998) and tested and applied at postsecondary institutions with a wide range of characteristics across the United States through a comprehensive project directed by the DO-IT (Disabilities, Opportunities, Internetworking and Technology) Center. Listed below are the seven performance indicator categories, with an example of a goal statement and indicator examples for each (Burgstahler, 2005a).

Universal Design of Instruction

Performance Indicator Categories	Examples of UDI Performance Indicators
1. *Class Climate* Adopt practices that reflect high values with respect to *both* diversity and inclusiveness.	• *Avoid stereotyping.* Offer instruction and support based on student performance and requests, not simply on assumptions that members of certain groups (e.g., students with certain types of disabilities or from specific racial/ethnic groups) will automatically do well or poorly. • *Address individual needs in an inclusive manner.* Make statements on the syllabus and in class inviting students to meet with you to discuss disability-related accommodations and other learning needs.
2. *Physical Access, Usability, and Safety* Assure that activities, materials, and equipment are physically accessible to and usable by all students and that all potential student characteristics are addressed in safety considerations.	• *Arrange instructional spaces to maximize inclusion and comfort.* Arrange seating to encourage participation, giving each student a clear line of sight to the instructor and visual aids and allowing room for wheelchairs, personal assistants, and assistive technology. Minimize distractions for students with a range of abilities to pay attention (e.g., put small groups in quiet work areas). • *Assure safety.* Develop procedures for all students, including those who are blind, deaf, or wheelchair users. Label safety equipment simply, in large print, and in a location viewable from a variety of angles. Repeat printed directions orally.
3. *Delivery Methods* Use multiple, accessible instructional methods.	• *Provide cognitive supports.* Summarize major points, give background/contextual information, provide effective prompting, and provide scaffolding tools (e.g., outlines, study guides, copies of projected materials with room for note taking) and other cognitive supports.
4. *Information Resources* Assure that course materials, notes, and other information resources are flexible and accessible to all students.	• *Select materials early.* Choose printed materials and prepare a syllabus early to allow students the option of beginning to read materials and work on assignments before the class begins and to allow adequate time to arrange for alternate formats, such as books on tape.
5. *Interaction* Encourage effective interactions between students and between students and the instructor and assure that communication methods are accessible to all participants.	• *Promote effective communication with you.* Face the class, speak clearly, use a microphone if your voice does not project adequately for all students, and make eye contact with all students. Use straightforward language and minimize unnecessary jargon and complexity in electronic and written communications. Use student names in communications. Employ interactive teaching techniques. • *Encourage cooperative learning.* Assign group work for which learners must support each other and that places a high value on different skills and roles. Encourage multiple ways for students to interact with each other—e.g., in-class questions and discussion, group work, Internet-based communications.

Performance Indicator Categories	Examples of UDI Performance Indicators
6. *Feedback* Provide specific feedback on a regular basis.	• *Provide feedback and corrective opportunities.* Allow students to turn in parts of large projects for feedback before the final project is due. Give students resubmission options to correct errors in assignment and/or exams.
7. *Assessment* Regularly assess student progress using multiple, accessible methods and tools and adjust instruction accordingly.	• *Provide multiple ways to demonstrate knowledge.* Assess group/cooperative performance as well as individual achievement. Consider traditional tests with a variety of test item formats (e.g., multiple choice, essay, short answer), papers, group work, demonstrations, portfolios, and presentations as options for demonstrating knowledge.
8. *Accommodation* Plan for accommodations for students for whom the instructional design does not meet their needs.	• *Know how to arrange for accommodations.* Know how to get materials in alternate formats, reschedule classroom locations, and arrange for other accommodations for students with disabilities. Make sure that assistive technology can be made available in a computer or science lab in a timely manner.

Although a relatively new concept, UD applications to on-site classes (e.g., Bruch, 2003; McAlexander, 2003; Mino, 2004; Pedelty, 2003), distance learning programs (e.g., Burgstahler et al., 2005), faculty training programs (e.g., Ouellett, 2004), and district and state educational systems (e.g., Abell, 2005) are beginning to appear in the literature. Besides classroom curriculum and instruction, UD principles have also been applied to large-scale assessments (Dolan & Hall, 2001; Dolan et al., 2005; Thompson et al., 2002). Similar to other applications of UD, the result is testing instruments that accurately assess the skills of test takers with a wide range of characteristics.

Universal Design of Student Services

Principles of UD can also be employed to make student services at all academic levels accessible to everyone. These services include libraries, admissions and registration offices, career centers, computer labs, tutoring and learning centers, housing and food services, and student organizations. Applying UD principles minimizes the need for special accommodations for those who use the services, thereby minimizing their negative effect of placing students with disabilities at the margins of the institution.

Performance indicator checklists for student services have been developed and are maintained on a Web site at the University of Washington (Burgstahler, 2005b). They have been tested and applied at postsecondary institutions across

Universal Design of Student Services

Performance Indicator Categories	Examples of Universal Design Performance Indicators
1. *Planning and Evaluation* Consider diversity issues as you plan and evaluate services.	• Include students with disabilities in planning and review processes and advisory committees. • Address disability-related issues in evaluation methods.
2. *Facility and Environment* Assure physical access and safety.	• Assure that there are ample high-contrast, large-print directional signs to and throughout the office. • Keep aisles wide and clear for wheelchair users and protruding objects removed or minimized for the safety of users who are visually impaired.
3. *Staff* Make sure staff are prepared to work with all students.	• Make sure that all staff members are familiar with disability-related accommodations, including alternate document formats, and procedures for responding to requests for accommodations, such as sign language interpreters.
4. *Information Resources* Assure that publications and Web sites welcome a diverse group and that information is accessible to everyone.	• In key publications, include a statement about a service commitment to access and procedures for requesting disability-related accommodations. • Assure that Web resources adhere to accessibility guidelines or standards.
5. *Computers and Assistive Technology* Assure that technology for visitors is accessible to students with disabilities.	• For student service units that use computers as information resources, have available commonly used assistive technology.
6. *Events* Assure that everyone can participate in events sponsored by the organization.	• Assure that events are located in wheelchair-accessible facilities and that information about how to request disability-related accommodations are included in promotional materials.

the United States as pre-post performance measures through a comprehensive project to improve the accessibility of student services throughout the United States. Common categories of issues addressed with examples of guidelines provided in the checklists (Burgstahler, 2005b) are included in the chart below.

DO-IT maintains performance indictors tailored to specific student service units (DO-IT, n.d.a). They include checklists for recruitment and undergraduate admissions, libraries, registration, financial aid, advising, career services, housing and residential life, tutoring and learning centers, computer labs, and student organizations. Preliminary results of this project suggest that implementing UD in student services is easier if specific indicators are given to administrators; even so, measurable change requires staff training, systematic monitoring, and ongoing encouragement. Efforts in implementing accessible and UD are beginning to be reported in the literature (e.g., Kroeger & Schuck, 1993; Sheppard-Jones et al., 2002; Uzes & Connelly, 2003; Wisbey & Kalivoda, 2003).

Practicing UD Campus Wide

Participants in a newly funded DO-IT project are developing campus-wide systemic indicators of an accessible campus. The draft list of performance indicators at the time this chapter was written are (DO-IT, n.d.b):

1. Institution-level mission, vision, and values statements are inclusive of all people, including those with disabilities.
2. Disability is included in campus discussions of and training on diversity and special populations.
3. Policies, procedures, and practices are regularly reviewed for barrier removal and inclusivity of people with a diverse range of characteristics, including disability.
4. Administrators, staff, faculty, and student leaders are trained and empowered to take action around disability and UD issues.
5. People with disabilities are visible (even if their disabilities are not) on campus including in positions of authority (e.g., administrators, faculty, student leaders).
6. Budgeting reflects the reality of the cost of accommodating current and prospective employees, students, and visitors with disabilities.
7. Measures of student success (e.g., retention, course completion, graduation) are the same for all student populations, including students with disabilities, and institutional research includes this data.
8. Campus marketing, publications, and public relations include images and content related to disability.
9. Campus publications and Web sites, including Web-based courses, meet established accessibility standards.
10. Disability issues are regularly included as a component of the curriculum.
11. All campus facilities are physically accessible.

As with the student services and instructional indicators, these performance indicators will continue to be refined with input and practice from postsecondary institutions across the United States. Consult the DO-IT Web site at http://www.washington.edu/doit/Brochures/Academics/access_college.html to keep abreast of and to contribute to this effort.

CONCLUSION

Our universities and colleges are often designed without regard to students with disabilities, creating a situation where such students continue to be marginalized through add-on programs, with negative outcomes as a result of issues related to attitude, expertise, legislation, documentation, and funding. However, the authors of this chapter encourage college and university administrators to rethink and recreate campuses to be fundamentally accessible through the application of UD.

UD is a promising approach for integrating knowledge of gender, racial/ethnic, disability, and other diversity issues into one implementation model that values both diversity and inclusion. It can be routinely applied to all areas of postsecondary education, including instruction and student services. UD is a goal to aspire to, as well as a process that can be employed in all aspects of education. As the group of students pursuing postsecondary education continues to increase with respect to diversity in many ways, the accessibility and usability of courses and student services increases in importance. The field of UD can provide a foundation for campus diversity efforts in order to make this vision a reality.

NOTE

The content in this chapter was supported by the U.S. Department of Education through grants to the University of Washington—grant numbers P333A020044, P333A990042, and P333A50064—from the Office of Postsecondary Education. The opinions, positions, and recommendations expressed in this chapter are those of the authors and do not necessarily reflect the views of the U.S. Department of Education.

REFERENCES

Abberley, P. (1995). Disabling ideology in health and welfare: The case of occupational therapy. *Disability and Society,* 10, 221–232.

Abell, M. (2005). Universal design for learning: A statewide improvement model for academic success. *Information Technology and Disabilities,* 11(1). Retrieved August 22, 2006, from http://www.rit.edu/~easi/itd/itdv11n1/abell.htm.

Americans with Disabilities Act of 1990. (1991). Pub. L. No. 101–336, 104 Stat. 327, 42 U.S.C. §12101 et seq.

Association on Higher Education and Disability (AHEAD). (2001a). *College Students with Learning Disabilities* [Brochure]. Boston, MA.

———. (2001b). *Confidentiality and Disability Issues in Higher Education* [Brochure]. Boston, MA.

———. (n.d.). *AHEAD best practices in disability documentation.* Retrieved August 22, 2006, from http://www.ahead.org/resources/bestpracticesdoc.htm.

Bourke, A. B., Strehorn, K. C., & Silver, P. (2000). Faculty members' provision of instructional accommodations to students with LD. *Journal of Learning Disabilities,* 33(1), January/February 2000.

Bowe, F. G. (2000). *Universal Design in Education*. Westport, CT: Bergin and Garvey.

Bruch, P. L. (2003). Interpreting and implementing universal instructional design in basic writing. In *Curriculum transformation and disability: Implementing universal design in higher education*, (pp. 93–103). Minneapolis, MN: University of Minnesota, Center for Research on Developmental Education and Urban Literacy.

Burgstahler, S. (2005a). *Equal Access: Universal design of instruction*. Seattle, WA: University of Washington, DO-IT. Retrieved August 20, 2006, from http://www.washington.edu/doit/Brochures/Academics/equal_access_udi.html.

———. (2005b). *Equal access: Universal design of student services*. Seattle, WA: University of Washington, DO-IT. Retrieved August 20, 2006, from http://www.washington.edu/doit/Brochures/Academics/equal_access_ss.html.

———. (2005c). *Universal design in education: Principles and applications*. Seattle, WA: University of Washington, DO-IT. Retrieved August 20, 2006, from http://www.washington.edu/doit/Brochures/Academics/ud_edu.html.

———. (2005d). *Universal design: Principles, process, and applications*. Seattle, WA: University of Washington, DO-IT. Retrieved August 20, 2006, from http://www.washington.edu/doit/Brochures/Programs/ud.html.

Burgstahler, S., & Doe, T. (2004). Disability-related simulations: If, when, and how to use them. *Review of Disability Studies*, 1(2), 4–17.

———. (2006). Improving postsecondary outcomes for students with disabilities: Designing professional development for faculty. *Journal of Postsecondary Education and Disability*, 18(2), 135–147.

Burgstahler, S., Corrigan, B., & McCarter, J. (2005). Steps toward making distance learning accessible to students and instructors with disabilities. *Journal of Information Technology and Disabilities*, 11(1). Retrieved August 22, 2006, from http://www.rit.edu/~easi/itd/itdv11n1/brgstler.htm.

The Center for Universal Design. (1997). *About universal design*. Retrieved August 22, 2006, from http://www.design.ncsu.edu/cud/about_ud/about_ud.htm.

Collins, M. E., & Mowbray, C. T. (2004). Higher education and psychiatric disabilities: National survey of campus disability services. *American Journal of Orthopsychiatry*, 75(2), April, 304–315.

Cope, D. (2005). Disability law in your classroom. *Academe*, November/December. Retrieved August 22, 2006, from http://www.aaup.org/publications/Academe/2005/05nd/05ndcope.htm.

Cory, R. C. (2005). Disclosure, identity and support: Issues facing college students with invisible disabilities. Unpublished dissertation. Syracuse University.

DO-IT. (n.d.a). Applications of Universal Design. Seattle. Retrieved August 20, 2006, from http://www.washington.edu/doit/Resources/udesign.html.

DO-IT. (n.d.b). AccessCollege Systemic Change for Postsecondary Institutions. Seattle, WA. Retrieved August 20, 2006, from http://www.washington.edu/doit/Brochures/Academics/access_college.html

Dolan, R. P., & Hall, E. (2001). Universal design for learning: Implications for large-scale assessment. *IDA Perspectives*, 27(4), 22–25.

Dolan, R. P., Hall, J. E., Banerjee, M., Chun, E., & Strangman, N. (2005). Applying principles of universal design to test delivery: The effects of computer-based read-aloud on test performance of high school students with learning disabilities. *Journal of Technology, Learning, and Assessment*, 3(7). Retrieved August 22, 2006 from, http://escholarship.bc.edu/jtla/vol3/7/.

Donnellan, A. M. (1984). The criterion of the least dangerous assumption. *Behavioral Disorders*, 9, 141–150.

Dukes, L. L., & Shaw, S. F. (1999). Postsecondary Disability Personnel: Professional Standards and Staff Development. *Journal of Developmental Education*, 23(1), 26-31, Fall.

Dukes, L. L., & Shaw, S. F. (2004). Perceived personnel development needs of postsecondary disability services professionals. *Teacher Education and Special Needs, 27*(2), 134–146.

Eudaly, J. (n.d.). *A rising tide: Students with psychiatric disabilities seek services in record numbers.* Washington, DC: GW HEATH Resource Center.

Getzel, E. E., & Wehman, P. (Eds.) (2004) *Going to college: Expanding opportunities for people with disabilities.* Baltimore, MD: Paul H. Brookes Publishing.

Gill, C. J. (1987). A new social perspective on disability and its implications for rehabilitation. In F. S. Cromwell (Ed.), *Sociocultural implications in treatment planning in occupational therapy* (pp. 49–55). New York: Haworth Press.

Gordon, M., Lewandowski, L., Murphy, K. & Dempsey, K. (2002). ADA Based accommodations in higher education: A survey of clinicians about documentation requirements and diagnostic standards. *Journal of Learning Disabilities, 33*(4), July/August, 357–363.

Gregg, N. & Scott, S. S. (2000). Definition and documentation: Theory, measurement, and the courts. *Journal of Learning Disabilities, 33*(1), 5–13, January/February.

Hahn, H. (1988). The politics of physical differences: Disability and discrimination. *Journal of Social Issues, 44*(1), 39–47.

Hall, T., Strangman, N., & Meyer, A. (2003). *Differentiated instruction and implications for UDL implementation.* Wakefield, MA: National Center for Accessing the General Curriculum. Retrieved August 22, 2006, from http://www.cast.org/publications/ncac/ncac_diffinstructudl.html.

Henderson, C. (2001). *College freshmen with disabilities: A biennial statistical profile.* Retrieved August 22, 2006, from http://www.heath.gwu.edu/PDFs/collegefreshmen.pdf.

The Henry J., & Kasier Family Foundation. (2006) Rate of disabilities higher among U.S. residents with low income, study finds. August 17. Retrieved August 22, 2006, from www.kaisernetwork.org.

Hitchcock, C., & Stahl, S. (2003). Assistive technology, universal design, universal design for learning: Improved learning opportunities. *Journal of Special Education Technology, 18*(4). Retrieved August 22, 2006, from http://jset.unlv.edu/18.4/hitchcock/first.html.

Johnson, D. M., & Fox, J. A. (2003). Creating curb cuts in the classroom: Adapting universal design principles to education. In J. Higbee (Ed.), *Curriculum transformation and disability: Implementing universal design in higher education* (pp. 7–22). Minneapolis, MN: University of Minnesota, Center for Research on Developmental Education and Urban Literacy.

Johnson, M. (1998). The "super-crip" stereotype: Press victimization of disabled people. *FineLine: The Newsletter On Journalism Ethics*, 1(4), July 1989, 2. Retrieved August 22, 2006, from http://www.journalism.indiana.edu/gallery/ethics/sup_crip.html.

Jones, S. R. (1996). Toward inclusive theory: Disability as social construction. *NASPA Journal, 33*, 347–354.

Kame'enui, E. J., Carnine, D. W., Dixon, R. C., Simmons, D. C., & Coyne, M. D. (2002). *Effective teaching strategies that accommodate diverse learners* (2nd ed.). Upper Saddle River, NJ: Pearson Prentice Hall.

Keim, J., McWhirter, J. J., & Bernstein, B. L. (1996). Academic success and university accommodation for learning disabilities: Is there a relationship? *Journal of College Student Development, 37*(5), 502–509.

Kroeger, S., & Schuck, J. (1993). *Responding to disability issues in student affairs.* San Francisco, CA: Jossey-Bass.

Lehmann, J., Davies, T., & Laurin, K. (2000). Listening to student voices about postsecondary education. *Teaching Exceptional Children, 32*(5), 60–65.

Leyser, Y., Vogel, S., Wyland, S., & Brulle, A. (1998). Faculty attitudes and practices regarding students with disabilities: Two decades after implementation of Section 504. *Journal of Postsecondary Education and Disability, 13*(3), 5–19.

Lloyd, J. W., & Hallahan, D.P. (2005). Going forward: How the field of learning disabilities has and will contribute to education. *Learning Disability Quarterly, 28*, 2, 133–136.

Lucas, C. J. (1994). *American higher education: A history.* New York: St. Martin's Griffin.

Mason, C., & Orkwis., R. (2005). Instructional theories supporting universal design for learning—Teaching to individual learners. In Council for Exceptional Children (Ed.), *Universal design for learning: A guide for teachers and education professionals.* Upper Saddle River, NJ: Pearson Prentice Hall.

McAlexander, P. J. (2003). Using principles of universal design in college composition courses. In J. Higbee (Ed.), *Curriculum transformation and disability: Implementing universal design in higher education* (pp. 105–114). Minneapolis, MN: University of Minnesota, Center for Research on Developmental Education and Urban Literacy.

McGuire, J. M., Scott, S. S., & Shaw, S. F. (2003). Universal design for instruction: The paradigm, its principles, and products for enhancing instructional access. *Journal of Postsecondary Education and Disability, 17*(1), 11–21.

McGuire, J. M., Madus, J. W., Litt, A. V., & Ramirez, M. O. (1996). An investigation of documentation submitted by university students to verify their learning disabilities. *Journal of Learning Disabilities*, 29, May, 297–304.

Mino, J. (2004). Planning for inclusion: Using universal instructional design to create a learner-centered community college classroom. *Equity and Excellence in Education, 37*(2), 154–160.

Nadeau, K. G. (1995). Diagnosis and assessment of ADD in postsecondary students. *Journal on Postsecondary Education and Disability*, 11(2).

National Center for the Study of Postsecondary Educational Supports. (2000). *Postsecondary education and employment for students with disabilities.* Honolulu, HI: University of Hawaii.

National Council on Disability. (2004). *Design for inclusion: Creating a new marketplace.* Washington, DC: Author. Retrieved August 22, 2006, from http://www.ncd.gov/newsroom/publications/2004/online_newmarketplace.htm#afbad.

Nelson, J., Dodd, J., & Smith, D. (1990). Faculty willingness to accommodate students with learning disabilities: A comparison among academic divisions. *Journal of Learning Disabilities, 23*(3), 185–189.

NJCLD. (1999). Learning disabilities: Issues in higher education. *Learning Disability Quarterly, 22*(4), 263–266, Fall.

Ofiesh, N. S. (2000). Using processing speed tests to predict the benefit of extended test time for university students with learning disabilities. *Journal of Postsecondary Education and Disability, 14*(1), 39–56.

Orkwis, R. (2003). *Universally designed instruction.* ERIC/OSEP Digest # E641. Arlington, VA: ERIC Clearinghouse on Disabilities and Gifted Education. Retrieved August 22, 2006 from, http://searcheric.org/scripts/seget2.asp?db=ericft&want=http://searcheric.org/ericdc/ED475386.htm.

Orkwis, R., & McLane, K. (1998). A curriculum every student can use: Design principles for student access. *ERIC/OSEP Topical Brief.* Reston, VA: ERIC/OSEP Special Project. (ERIC Document Reproduction Service No. ED423654). Retrieved August 22, 2006, from http://www.cec.sped.org/osep/udesign.html.

Ouellett, M. L. (2004). Faculty development and universal instructional design. *Equity and Excellence in Education, 37*, 135–144.

Paul, S. (2000). Student with disabilities in higher education: A review of the literature. *College Student Journal,* 34(2), 200–210.

Pedelty, M. (2003). Making a statement. In J. Higbee (Ed.), *Curriculum transformation and disability: Implementing universal design in higher education* (pp. 71–78). Minneapolis, MN: University of Minnesota, Center for Research on Developmental Education and Urban Literacy.

Persinger, M. A., & Tiller, S. G. (1999). Personality not intelligence or educational achievement differentiate university students who access special needs for "learning disabilities." *Social Behavior and Personality,* 27(1), 1–10.

Preiser, W. F. E., & Ostroff, E. (eds.) (2001). *Universal Design Handbook.* New York: McGraw Hill.

Reilly, V. J., & Davis, T. (2005). *Understanding the regulatory environment.* In E. E. Getzel and P. Wehman (Eds.), *Going to college: Expanding opportunities for people with disabilities.* Baltimore, MD: Paul H. Brookes Publishing Co.

Rizza, M. G., & Morrison, W. F. (2003). Uncovering stereotypes and identifying characteristics of gifted students and students with emotional/behavioral disabilities. *Roeper Review,* Winter, 73–77.

Rose, D. H., & Meyer, A. (2002). *Teaching every student in the digital age: Universal design for learning.* Alexandria, VA: Association for Supervision and Curriculum Development (ASCD).

Rothstein, L. (n.d.). Students with disabilities and higher education: A disconnect in expectations and realities. *HEATH Resource Center.*

Sahlen, C. A. H., & Lehmann, J. P. (2006). Requesting accommodations in higher education. *Teaching Exceptional Children,* January/February.

Scott, S., McGuire, J., & Shaw, S. (2003). Universal design for instruction: A new paradigm for adult instruction in postsecondary education. *Remedial and Special Education,* 24(6), 369–379.

Section 504 of the Rehabilitation Act of 1973. 29 U.S.C. § 794.

Selingo, J. (1997). Judge says Boston U. violated rights of learning disabled. *Chronicle of Higher Education.* September 5, 1997. Retrieved August 22, 2006, from www.chronicle.com.

Shaw, S. F., McGuire, J. M., & Madaus, J. W. (1997). Standards of professional practice. *Journal of Postsecondary Education and Disability,* 12(3), 26–35.

Sheppard-Jones, K., Krampe, K., Danner, F., & Berdine, W. (2002). Investigating postsecondary staff knowledge of students with disabilities using a Web based survey. *Journal of Applied Rehabilitation Counseling,* 33(1), 19–25.

Silver, P., Bourke, A., & Strehorn, K. C. (1998). Universal instructional design in higher education: An approach for inclusion. *Equity & Excellence in Education,* 31(2), 47–51.

Story, M. F., Mueller, J. L., & Mace, R. L. (1998). *The universal design file: Designing for people of all ages and abilities.* Retrieved August 22, 2006, from http://www.design.ncsu.edu/cud/pubs_p/pud.htm.

Swain, J., & Lawrence, P. (1994). Learning about disability: Changing attitudes or challenging understanding? In S. French (Ed.), *On equal terms: Working with disabled people* (pp. 87–102). Oxford: Butterworth Heinemann.

Swanson, H. L. & Howard, C. B. (2005). Children with reading disabilities: Does dynamic assessment help in the classification? *Learning Disability Quarterly,* 28, 17–34.

Szymanski, E. M., & Trueba, H. T. (1999). Castification of people with disabilities: Potential disempowering aspects of classification in disability services. In R. P. Marinelli, & A. E. Dell Orto, (Eds.), *The psychological and social impact of disability* (pp. 195–211). New York: Springer Publishing.

Thoma, C. A., & Wehmeyer, M. L. (2005). *Self-determination and transition to postsecondary education.* In E. E. Getzel and P. Wehman (Eds.), *Going to college: Expanding opportunities for people with disabilities.* Baltimore, MD: Paul H. Brookes Publishing Co.

Thomas, S. (2000). College students and disability law. *The Journal of Special Education,* 33(4), 248–257.

Thompson, S. J., Johnstone, C. J., & Thurlow, M. L. (2002). *Universal design applied to large-scale assessments* (NCEO Synthesis Report 44). Minneapolis, MN: University of Minnesota, National Center on Educational Outcomes.

Thomson, R. G. (2006). Welcoming the unbidden. Public address at the University of Washington, February 9.

Tomlinson, C. A. (2001). *How to differentiate instruction in mixed-ability classrooms* (2nd ed.). Alexandria, VA: ASCD.

Treloar, L. L. (1999). Lessons on disability and the rights of students. *Community College Review*, 27(1), Summer.

Uzes, K. B., & Connelly, D. O. (2003). Universal design in counseling center serviced areas. In J. Higbee (Ed.), *Curriculum transformation and disability: Implementing universal design in higher education* (pp. 241–250). Minneapolis, MN: University of Minnesota, Center for Research on Developmental Education and Urban Literacy.

Wehman, P., & Yasuda, S. (2005). *The need and the challenges associated with going to college.* In E. E. Getzel and P. Wehman (Eds.), *Going to college: Expanding opportunities for people with disabilities*. Baltimore, MD: Paul H. Brookes Publishing Co.

Weintraub, F. (2005). The evolution of LD policy and future challenges. *Learning Disability Quarterly.* 28, Spring.

Williams, W. M., & Ceci, S. J. (1999). Accommodating learning disabilities can bestow unfair advantages. *The Chronicle of Higher Education.* August 6, 1999. Retrieved August 22, 2006, from http://chronicle.com/weekly/v45/i48/48b00401.htm.

Wisbey, M. E., & Kalivoda, K. S. (2003). Residential living for all: Fully accessible and "livable" on-campus housing. In J. Higbee (Ed.), *Curriculum transformation and disability: Implementing universal design in higher education* (pp. 215–230). Minneapolis, MN: University of Minnesota, Center for Research on Developmental Education and Urban Literacy.

Zirkel, P. A. (2000). Sorting out which students have learning disabilities. *The Chronicle of Higher Education.* December 8, 2000. Retrieved August 22, 2006, from http://chronicle.com/weekly/v47/i15/15b01501.htm.

CHAPTER THIRTY-TWO

Adapting Disability Studies WITHIN Teacher Education IN Singapore

LEVAN LIM, THANA THAVER, AND KENNETH POON

INTRODUCTION

For decades, students with and without disabilities in Singapore have been perceived as belonging to the special education and mainstream education (the equivalent term to general or regular education that is used in Singapore) systems respectively. This is because Singapore has long maintained a distinct dual system of education where its mainstream education system has remained separate from its special education system, which comprises largely of special schools run by voluntary welfare organizations headed by the National Council of Social Service instead of the Ministry of Education (Lim & Nam, 2000; Lim & Quah, 2004). As a result, many Singaporeans have grown up with little or no personal knowledge and experience with people with disabilities that, in turn, have significantly contributed to the reproduction of current societal attitudes and beliefs about people with disabilities (Lim & Tan, 2004). This is reflective of many of our preservice and inservice mainstream teachers whom we teach at the National Institute of Education (NIE), Singapore's sole teacher education body.

The dual system of education has also spawned separate teacher education programs for mainstream teachers and special education teachers at the NIE. Mainstream teachers are employed by the Ministry of Education and receive higher salaries than their special education counterparts who are employees of the voluntary welfare organizations that manage the special schools. Moreover, special education teachers, unlike mainstream education teachers, are not required to undergo preservice teacher education before they can begin teaching. These discrepancies constitute structural inequalities that stem from systemic arrangements that are grounded upon fundamental views of and beliefs about disability in Singaporean society.

These discrepancies, produced by a dual system of education, have contributed to the differential treatment of disabled and nondisabled persons in society as well as shaped the epistemological frameworks implicit in teacher education. In catering to the needs of special education teachers working in special schools, the focus of our teacher education program has largely been on equipping them with the strategies and intervention techniques to work effectively with their students in special school settings. This approach to teachers' appropriation and dispensing of technical special education knowledge within separate settings for both teachers and students alike has not only justified the dominance of a technical-rational framework of special education (Skrtic, 1986) at the teacher education level in Singapore but also made acceptable segregated placements (Kauffman, 1995). A corollary of this narrow interpretation and application of special education knowledge is that disability has been disavowed from being part of mainstream educational discourse in Singapore until recently.

Recent major developments in Singapore concerning its vision as an inclusive society and its place in the world have, however, presented unprecedented opportunities for disability to be introduced as part of mainstream discourse and consciousness. This chapter provides a historical contextualization of disability in Singapore as a peripheral priority until the emergence of recent developments in education and society that have made it possible to adapt disability studies within mainstream teacher education program at the NIE. Disability Studies in Education (DSE), as an interdisciplinary field of study that offers the "meta-language" and "meta-view" to understand the social construction and interpretation of disability, stimulated us to think about and articulate ways to introduce change within teacher education to interrupt current attitudes among our teachers toward disability. This chapter therefore also describes how we have adapted DSE within a new core module covering disability that has, for the first time at the NIE, been made compulsory for all preservice teachers.

CONTEXTUALIZING THE PRIORITY OF DISABILITY IN SINGAPORE

The dual system of education in Singapore has left generations of Singaporeans with little or no direct exposure or experience with their peers with disabilities. Hence, people with disabilities, whilst gaining increasing coverage in the mass media and government support, remain apart from their nondisabled peers. This separation of people with disabilities from the rest of the populace in the education system can be attributed to Singapore's sociohistorical and sociopolitical context. As a consequence, unlike many developed countries around the world, Singapore has yet to formally embrace inclusion as an educational agenda.

Singapore's predominant approach toward students with disabilities can be described more as integration rather than inclusion. Although there have been increasing numbers of students with disabilities enrolled in mainstream schools in the recent past, they have been expected to fit into and cope with the mainstream curriculum. Moreover, the choice for integrating into less segregated environments is quite limited other than special schools since there are few other options, such as special education classes within mainstream schools. Without the availability of special education classes or facilities within mainstream school environments, children with higher support needs are not able to access these environments and are instead relegated to special schools where there are few or no opportunities to meet and interact with their mainstream peers.

The concept of education as a basic right for all children, including children with disabilities, has yet to be fully acknowledged in compulsory educational policies. The compulsory education report, published in 2000 (Ministry of Education, 2000) highlighted the need for at least six years of compulsory education in order to prepare citizens for the needs of the knowledge economy. Compulsory education, however, was defined to mean schooling in mainstream schools.

On the international platform, Singapore has yet to formally embrace the inclusion movement that has swept many countries around the world, including the Asia-Pacific region where Singapore is located, for example, Brunei Darussalam (Koay, 2004), the Philippines (Inciong & Quijano, 2004), Hong Kong (Poon-McBrayer, 2004), China (Deng & Poon-McBrayer, 2004), and Australia (Gillies & Carrington, 2004). Singapore is not a signatory of the Salamanca Statement, the most prominent and explicit international initiative on inclusion ever issued, which calls for inclusion to be the norm for the education of all children with special needs (UNESCO, 1994). It is also one of the few countries in the developed world where little exists in terms of legislative mandates, protection or considerations for its citizens with disabilities. As recently as in 2004, the prospects for inclusion in Singapore looked rather bleak because of clear and longstanding differential treatments of people with and without disabilities (Lim & Quah, 2004).

The relative lack of discourse and awareness of disability as a social issue in Singapore society can be traced back to economic and educational priorities during Singapore's formative years as a nation. Since independence in 1965, Singapore's national advancement plan has been to pursue peace, stability and economic growth, and education has been central to these priorities. With education as the "blue chip" investment of economic growth in Singapore's formative years, schools were entrusted with the task of preparing a skilled pool of human resource. Concomitantly, the school infrastructure, the allocation of resources, and the offering of courses have been driven by the practicalities of responding to the latest trends in technology or projected economic needs in identified niches in the foreseeable future.

This efficiency-based model has long characterized Singapore's approach to education, especially during the 1970s and 1980s, where students were "streamed" by their ability level in order to mass produce skilled workers who were in demand by the labor market. Lured by generous tax incentives, a disciplined work force, adequate infrastructure and a stable political environment, many international multinational companies set up bases in Singapore to serve the region and beyond, thereby bolstering the labor market. To ensure the supply of skilled labor, a meritocratic educational system was established and has evolved within the context of labor-intensive industrialization in the 1970s to the new rules of the knowledge-based world economy.

With these economic and educational priorities in mind since independence, Singapore's founding fathers and subsequent successors have deftly navigated its direction and fortunes through decades of accelerating global change to become one of the most successful and prosperous countries in the world. Without the blessings of any natural resources, except for its people and the strategic location of its port, Singapore is an economic miracle borne out of a strong necessity to survive by excelling in the highly competitive global stage of business and commerce.

Set against this backdrop of Singapore's determination, especially in its formative years, to succeed in its economic aspirations that were viewed as vital to its future security, academic ability has been the de facto basic criterion for the placement of students within the education system. By default, however, students with disabilities or special needs have been sidelined and marginalized, with the option of either failing in the mainstream system if they cannot cope with the highly rigorous and inflexible mainstream curriculum or referred to a special school.

Disability as an emerging priority in the Singapore of today can be said to be another default—this time in response to Singapore's reinvention of itself in the new millennium as a world-class city which local denizens and foreigners would be proud to call home and stake their futures. After having attained economic prosperity, political stability, and affluence, Singapore realizes that unless its citizens succeed in valuing and practicing a cohesive spirit and rooting themselves, their families, and their future in Singapore, the nation's capability to meet future challenges will be seriously compromised. The government responded to this challenge by engaging greater participation of its citizens in reenvisioning Singapore along the lines of promoting social cohesion as well as honoring the individual and collective aspirations of Singaporeans in the late 1990s.

In August 1997, the former prime minister Goh Chok Tong launched the Singapore 21 Committee, which was comprised of Singaporeans from all walks of life, to dialogue on issues aimed at strengthening the "heartware" of Singapore in the twenty-first century. He defined "heartware" as the intangibles of society—social cohesion, political stability, and the collective will, values, and attitudes of a people (Government of Singapore, 1999). In striving for new ideals and redefining success, Singapore 21 reaffirmed the creation of opportunities for each individual as "every Singaporean matters" (Government of Singapore, 1999, p. 4) by developing the full potential of every citizen through educational opportunities regardless of family, financial or social background. More importantly, the notion of success was broadened beyond academic excellence in Singapore 21 through the recognition of many different talents among Singaporeans and the need to create multiple social pathways to honor diverse abilities.

Correspondingly, new educational priorities, initiated in the late 1990s till the present, reflect and support the ethos of Singapore 21. For instance, "National Education" (Ministry of Education, 1997) and the "Thinking Schools, Learning Nation Framework" (Goh, 1998) emphasize social cohesion, emotional attachment to Singapore, and a sense of identity and pride as Singaporeans. The "Desired Outcomes of Education" document (Ministry of Education, 1998) encourages the nurturing of the whole individual and the development of qualities such as graciousness, caring and compassion, as well as getting along with relating with diverse others. More recent educational priorities build on these initiatives by emphasizing socioemotional development, thinking and problem-solving skills, community service, the broadening of postschool options, multiple pathways for different abilities and talents, more differentiated learning experiences for students; in short, a clear shift from an efficiency-based model of education to an ability-driven and holistic educational paradigm.

These societal and educational trends proved to be a harbinger to what was to become the first official announcement of the vision of Singapore as an inclusive society. In 2004, the prime minister, Lee Hsien Loong, in his inauguration speech, proclaimed the vision of a "Government that will be open and inclusive in its approach, toward all Singaporeans, young and old, disabled and able-bodied. ..." (Ibrahim, 2004). Approximately a month later, the prime minister called for greater efforts to integrate people with mild disabilities into mainstream society, beginning with the integration of students with disabilities into mainstream schools (Teo, 2004).

New schemes for supporting increasing numbers of students with disabilities within mainstream schools were subsequently launched in 2005. Special Needs Officers (SNOs) were introduced into mainstream primary and secondary schools beginning 2005 to support students with either mild to moderate dyslexia or high functioning autism spectrum disorder (Ministry of Education, 2005). These SNOs complement the mainstream teachers in the support of these students through inclass supports, small group interventions, and relevant administrative duties. Initially starting with a small number of schools, this scheme will be gradually expanded such that by 2010 all primary schools will have at least one SNO.

Another scheme that involves the training of mainstream teachers in special needs also began in 2005. Under this scheme, 10 percent of all mainstream teachers in Singapore will be trained in special needs at the NIE between 2005 and 2010 so that they can better support students with disabilities in their schools. Also, in 2005, all preservice mainstream teachers, for the first time at the NIE (approximately 1,800), were introduced to the topic of disability under the auspice of a core module on individual differences. Although, there were only twelve hours allocated for disability to be covered as a topic, the fact that the curriculum for all preservice mainstream teachers now includes understanding disability through a social interpretivist lens is truly a milestone in teacher education in Singapore.

THE RELEVANCE OF DISABILITY STUDIES IN EDUCATION

These swift and exciting changes in special education becoming an increasing part of mainstream education appear to be aligned with the Singapore government's vision of an inclusive society. The explicit mention of the disabled in Singapore's vision of becoming an inclusive society heralds new possibilities for change and reform in current educational and social arrangements that limit the participation of both the disabled and nondisabled in each other's lives. For the first time in mainstream teacher education, there is the legitimate and sanctioned space to involve a significant mainstream audience to recognize the presence and visibility of persons with disabilities in Singaporean society, and to understand their own individual and society's responses to the experience of disability.

In designing our module on introducing disability to the preservice mainstream teachers within the limited credit hours, we decided against adopting a strong technical-rational approach where these teachers would search outside of themselves for skills and strategies to define the very nature of their impending work with individuals they had little or no personal knowledge and experience with (Gallagher, 2005). Such an approach would reinforce the notion of disability as a deficit residing within the individual to be dealt with through the use of specialized expertise and resources, without exploring the external factors such as cultural, social, political and economic conditions that contribute toward how people with disabilities are treated (Gabel, 2005).

It is precisely these external factors that DSE highlights for exploring the influence of meanings about disability held by people in society on the experience of disability itself. These external factors cast foregrounding influences on fundamental ways of knowing about the experience of disability in society which are often unquestioned and taken for granted. Through our interactions with our teachers, we realized that even though many have not had any or little direct and personal experiences with persons with disabilities, they carried within themselves particular perceptions and attitudes (usually negative) that were unconsciously bred from the societal context they grew up in. These perceptions and attitudes are significant because, individually and collectively, they contribute to the level of acceptance and welcome people with disabilities experience in Singaporean society. At the school level, these perceptions and attitudes of the teachers toward disability are fundamental to the inclusion of children with disabilities.

Our task then was to address teachers' attitudes, which formed the basic thrust in the design of our module. Such change begins first with awareness raising through an honest examination of one's own personal attitudes, knowledge, beliefs and understandings (Stubbs, 1997). Our role as teacher educators was to facilitate our teachers to examine and become aware of their own positioning, and the influence of society's position on their own, in relation to the experience of disability as they understand it. The importance of looking inward, and in the process of doing so, engage in serious and intense intellectual and personal inquiry, is essential to teachers' understandings of their own epistemologies (how they know what they know) and fundamental beliefs and meanings they hold about the purpose of their work (Gallagher, 2005).

OUR MODULE: DECONSTRUCTING DISABILITY

This section describes the key ideas of how we adapted disabilities studies within the compulsory core module on introducing disability to the preservice mainstream teachers at the NIE. For the twelve hours allocated for this module, there were four sets of one-hour lectures followed by two hour tutorials each week. The focus of the module was for the preservice teachers to explore their own implicit theories, meanings, beliefs, values, and assumptions that have influenced their understanding of and position to the experience of disability, and a workbook was developed for this purpose (Lim et al., 2005). Hence, the focus of the module was on the preservice teachers exploring and "restorying" (Ware, 2005), in hindsight, their personal life journeys into how they saw disability through gaining a critical awareness and understanding of how society has constructed its position to disability and how the self has participated through its own positioning.

Our underlying pedagogy for the module positioned the *self* as the site for educational learning and change, in that the preservice teachers were guided to enter into a personal encounter with their own attitudes toward disability. To prepare them for this unsettling task, the inevitable questions of *Why do I have to think about disability?* and *What does disability have to do with my life?* were confronted with and referenced to the current realities of increasing numbers of students with disabilities in mainstream schools; more Singaporean parents, especially the younger ones, wanting their children with disabilities to grow up and be educated in mainstream settings; greater supports within mainstream schools for accommodating special needs; and the vision of an inclusive society that explicitly mentions the disabled. They were also informed that this module offered them the space to engage in critical self-reflection, thinking, and learning to prepare for what might be inevitable in their teaching career—having a child with a disability in their classroom.

We also prepared the preservice teachers by exploring with them their possible learning trajectories when it came to learning new, unfamiliar, challenging, or uncomfortable topics or experiences, especially with the *other*, a reference to what they did not know, understand, have not experienced and whose presence poses questions that challenge and even contradict one's own ways of knowing, assumptions and worldviews.

Understanding ahead that their learning trajectories would bring them to a place where learning is uncomfortable, challenging, disorganized, confusing, and even painful, helped normalize their acceptance of their learning encounters with their own attitudes toward disability (which surfaced especially with the showing of relevant videos on persons with disabilities living desirable and fulfilling lives within the community). To help the preservice teachers situate and understand their personal learning encounters with their own attitudes within the context of Singaporean society, we adapted a model of human learning and action from Butler's (1996) model of human agency for them to deconstruct how they arrived at their own positions toward disability (Lim et al., 2005). Figure 32.1 illustrates the components of this model.

There are two core interfacing domains in the model that influence one's learning and positioning in relation to disability: the self and social context of one's experiences in Singapore. The domain of the self comprises two components: personal, practical knowledge and worldview. Within the domain of the social context are the two components of public knowledge and human action. In

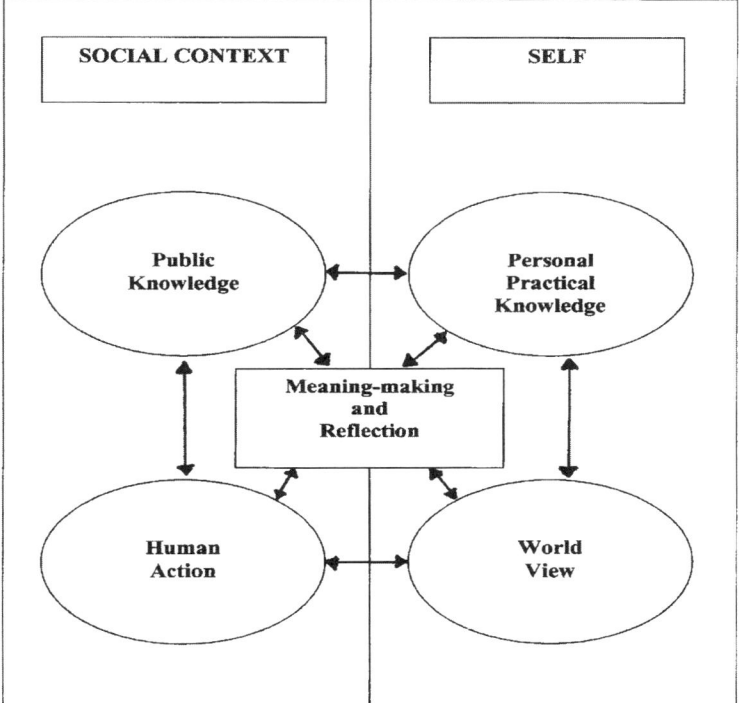

Figure 32. 1. A model of human learning and action.

the center of the figure is the component of reflection and meaning-making, which refers to the process of making sense and meaning in understanding and relating to the various components of the model. Each of these components is described below followed by a list of questions that the preservice teachers were asked to reflect upon and discuss during their tutorial sessions (Lim et al., 2005).

PERSONAL AND PRACTICAL KNOWLEDGE

Personal and practical knowledge about disability refers to the knowledge and understanding gained through *lived* experience with persons with disabilities. The example of parents of children with disabilities having personal, practical knowledge about disability, gained through direct experiences with their children, was used to illustrate this component of the model. Personal and practical knowledge is "real" knowledge admitted into the self through experiential learning and is also powerful knowledge because it contains personal significance and emotional depth. Since personal knowledge is grounded upon authentic experience, it is also "potent" knowledge that is more likely to lead to personal change and transformation. Learning personal knowledge about disability may, however, not be easy, because it involves confronting personal assumptions, beliefs and values about the experience of disability. For example, many parents, in having children with disabilities, go through much unlearning, and in so doing, earn invaluable personal knowledge along their learning trajectories about the meaning of disability and society's position in response to disability.

The preservice teachers reflected on the following questions to gauge and understand their personal, practical knowledge about disability.

- Do you personally know any person(s) with disabilities?
- If you do, what type of disability or disabilities does this person or persons have and how did you come to know him or her or them?
- Where there were moments of contact and/or interaction, what meanings did you construct in your mind about disabilities?

PUBLIC KNOWLEDGE

Public knowledge refers to what abounds in social contexts outside the self that can directly or indirectly influence the experience of disability. Public knowledge about disability is strongly influenced by different cultures and societies (Gartner et al., 1991), and can manifest in the form of common beliefs and assumptions, ideologies, folklore, superstitions, cultural perceptions, stereotypes, societal expectations and attitudes, media reports, policies, social structures, and so on. As an illustration, public knowledge about disability in Singapore regarding schooling has traditionally declared that the responsibility of educating children with disabilities falls mainly under the purview of the special education system rather than mainstream education.

Public knowledge about disability regarding postschool adult life in Singapore is commonly associated with the social welfare and charity-based vernacular. Much of this public knowledge is conveyed through media images and reports and reinforced by the informal cultural discourse about disability within home and community settings. As a result, many Singaporeans have grown up with such "second-hand" knowledge that has affected their attitudes toward people with disabilities. Such knowledge thus provides the social "input" about disability to the public (hence, the term "public knowledge").

After being introduced to this component, the preservice teachers were asked to think about the public sources of information related to disability that they had encountered in Singapore through which they acquired their ideas and knowledge about disability. They were then asked to reflect on:

- What images and thoughts come to your mind in association with the word "disability?"
- How has "public knowledge" influenced your perceptions of persons with disabilities?

WORLDVIEW

An individual's worldview, in a broad sense, refers to one's own way of looking at the world. It is derived from historical, cultural, institutional, and contextual processes and experiences, and provides a map to negotiate practice and moral concerns and actions as well as the progress of one's life (Butler, 1996). Our wordviews are linked to our personal assumptions and beliefs that influence our thoughts, feelings, and actions. Worldviews can be clarified or modified through self-reflection of new experiences.

We provided an illustration of a teacher who had taught primary one–level children for many years for the preservice teachers to understand this component. When approached by a parent to include her child with Down syndrome in her classroom, this teacher agreed even though she had never taught a child with a disability. The child's entry into her classroom provided a very new and different challenge to her worldview of education and pedagogical beliefs about how children learn and develop individually and with others. Through including this child, this teacher learned in greater depth what it meant to meet the individual educational needs of every student in her classroom, regardless of ability level, while building a sense of community, interdependence and belonging among her students. Not only did this teacher's own beliefs about children with disabilities change but also her personal worldviews about education, her role as a teacher, and fostering classroom community.

To guide the preservice teachers' exploration of the meaning of worldview pertaining to disability within Singaporean society, we posed the following aphorism for them to reflect on and asked the subsequent questions.

> We exclude because we don't understand …
> We don't understand because of limited contact …
> We lack contact because we exclude.

- What do you make of this?
- Who do we exclude and how do we exclude?

- What are some assumptions and beliefs we make on the basis of exclusion?
- Where do these assumptions and beliefs come from?

We also asked the preservice teachers to reflect on why they chose to be a teacher and share their worldviews about the meaning and purpose of education, teaching, and their choice of wanting to become a teacher.

HUMAN ACTION

Human action is the "output" of how people behave as a result of the interaction between the other three interrelated components of public knowledge, personal and practical knowledge, and worldview. It is the expression of the individual and collective positions regarding disability that is evident in the social, physical, and institutional landscape and activities—the gawks that people with disabilities may receive in public; the lack or benefit of attention to the physical infrastructure in public facilities in accommodating disability; the dual system of education; the lack of mainstream preparation in disability hitherto at the NIE.

These "human actions" do not come about by accident. They are the product of individual and collective thoughts, values, beliefs, and assumptions. They are the evidence or fruit of a particular discourse about disability within a society, and they influence how many Singaporeans actually have the opportunity on a daily or regular basis to meet and interact with persons with disabilities. To understand this component of the model, the preservice teachers were asked to reflect on the following questions:

- Do daily or regular experiences afford you the opportunity to meet and interact with persons with disabilities?
- If you answered "yes" to the question, tell us about it. If you answered "no," why do you think this is the case?

After applying this model and its components to themselves, the preservice teachers were encouraged to share their responses with their tutorial groups. Many realized that their learning journey into disability began long before they came into the course, and long before they ever became conscious that they were actually learning, without any design but through sheer living, about how to relate and position themselves to the experience of disability. For them to deconstruct this learning journey so far was to reflect on making sense of how they arrived at their own positions as well as develop a reflexive and critical awareness of the implicit assumptions that underlie society's position toward disability.

At this phase of their learning journey, the preservice teachers were probably more aware of their positions in relation to disability than they had ever been before in their lives. Awareness, however, can be liberating or unsettling because it clarifies that all in society are, to a certain degree, culpable or complicit in participating in the social construction of disability within society. Liberating, because one becomes aware and enlightened that somehow, one can play a part, no matter how small, in direct or indirect capacities, to affect the experience of disability in Singapore. Unsettling in that awareness ushers in the realization that "experience is never innocent" (Avis, 1995, p. 185). Awareness negates the space to occupy the position of "It's-none-of-my-business-because-it-does-not-concern-me" because in taking up this stance of indifference, one already will have participated. The awareness gained by the preservice teachers surfaced various reactions from different individuals. Feedback from the tutors revealed that while there were many preservice teachers who were willing to welcome and accept students with disabilities in their future classrooms, there were others who were honestly resistant. Even though there were these preservice teachers who showed clear resistance and prejudice, the module accomplished its objective of raising to awareness their own attitudes toward disability, which, in itself, is an important outcome to arrive at … to be dealt with over a lifetime.

The last part of the module concluded with the sharing of research conducted with successful local mainstream teachers on how they came to terms with including students with disabilities and how they catered to these students within their classrooms and schools. This part of the module was designed to help the preservice teachers to envision and reconstruct new possibilities for themselves as teachers in working with students with disabilities. The model of human learning and action was used to illustrate the learning journey of these successful teachers as they gained more personal and practical knowledge of students with disabilities which then changed their worldviews and led them to refute incorrect public knowledge and commit to human actions that improved the quality of support for students with disabilities in their schools. Practical strategies used by these teachers were also shared with the preservice teachers.

CONCLUSION

The movement toward inclusion in Singapore has never been more apparent than in the present. This has been made possible by the evolution of Singapore in its deliberate consideration of how best to forge ahead as a nation to meet the challenges of an unpredictable and rapidly changing world. The announcement by the government of the vision of an inclusive society for Singapore, which explicitly mentions the disabled, presents the long-awaited opportunity to entertain, contemplate, and consider possibilities to translate such a vision into reality for Singaporeans with disabilities.

The articulation of possibilities, however, needs to be grounded upon the analysis and critique of the status quo within Singapore that impacts upon the experience of disability. Since there are encouraging exhortations from within Singapore for its citizens to engage in thinking about their collective future (e.g., Fernandez, 2004), it is indeed timely for reflection, dialogue and discourse about disability issues to extend beyond pathologizing the individual to society's role in reifying meanings about disability simply because "disability cannot be abstracted from the social world which produces it; it does not exist outside the social structures in which it is located and independent of the meanings given to it" (Oliver, 1992, p. 1).

This is where the contribution of disability studies lies—to highlight the dynamic interplay between disability, culture, and society so that Singaporeans can explore, examine, and interrogate how society has invested itself in response to its full range of humanity (Ware, 2005). That we were able to engage a particular significant segment of Singaporeans, namely our preservice teachers, in this task (and will continue to do so in subsequent semesters) is fortuitous and very exciting in our teacher education arena. The deconstruction of the preservice implicit beliefs and attitudes toward disability, through the module we conducted, raised serious questions about the nature of existing society, its status quo, the purpose of education, and the kind of society Singaporeans desire to build. This is precisely the type of engagement needed of its citizens to begin participating to shape the future of Singapore to be inclusive of all.

REFERENCES

Avis, J. (1995). The validation of learner experience: A conservative practice? *Studies in the Education of Adults, 27*, 173–186.

Butler, J. (1996). Professional development: Practice as text, reflection as process, and self as locus. *Australian Journal of Education, 40*, 265–283.

Deng, M., & Poon-McBrayer, K. F. (2004). Inclusive education in China: Conceptualisation and realization. *Asia-Pacific Journal of Education, 2*, 143–156.

Fernandez, W. (2004). *Thinking allowed? Politics, fear and change in Singapore*. Singapore: SNP International.

Gabel, S. (2005). Introduction: Disability studies in education. In S. L. Gabel, & S. Danforth (Eds.), *Disability studies in education: Readings in theory and method* (pp. 1–19). New York: Peter Lang.

Gallagher, D. J. (2005). Searching for something outside of ourselves: The contradiction between technical rationality and the achievement of inclusive pedagogy. In S. L. Gabel, & S. Danforth (Eds.), *Disability studies in education: Readings in theory and method* (pp. 139–154). New York: Peter Lang.

Gartner, A., Lipsky, D. K., & Turnbull, A. P. (1991). Culture and disability. In A. Gartner, D. K. Lipsky, & A. P. Turnbull (Eds.), *Supporting families with a child with a disability: An international outlook* (pp. 17–56). Baltimore, MD: Paul H. Brookes.

Gillies, R. M., & Carrington, S. (2004). Inclusion: Culture, policy and practice: A Queensland perspective. *Asia-Pacific Journal of Education, 2*, 117–128.

Goh, C. T. (1998). Shaping our future: Thinking schools, Learning nation. In M. L. Quah, & W. K. Ho (Eds.), *Thinking processes: Going beyond the surface curriculum* (pp. 1–6). Singapore: Prentice-Hall.

Government of Singapore (1999). *Singapore 21: Together we make the difference.* Singapore: Singapore 21 Committee c/o Prime Minister's Office (Public Service Division).

Ibrahim, Z. (2004, 13 August). Let us shape our future together. *The Straits Times,* p. 1.

Inciong, T. G., & Quijano, Y. S. (2004). Inclusion of children with disabilities: The Philippines experience. *Asia-Pacific Journal of Education, 2*, 173–191.

Kauffman, J. M. (1995). Why we must celebrate a diversity of restrictive environments. *Learning Disabilities Research and Practice, 10*, 225–232.

Koay, T. L. (2004). Inclusive education in Brunei Darussalam. *Asia-Pacific Journal of Education, 2*, 129–142.

Lim, L., & Nam, S. S. (2000). Special education in Singapore. *The Journal of Special Education, 34*, 104–109.

Lim, L., & Quah, M. M. (2004). Foresight via hindsight: Prospects and lessons for inclusion in Singapore. *Asia-Pacific Journal of Education, 24*, 193–204.

Lim, L., & Tan, J. (2004). Learning and diversity. In L. Lim, & M. M. L. Quah (Eds.), *Educating learners with diverse abilities* (pp. 1–28). Singapore: McGraw-Hill.

Lim, L., Thaver, T., & Slee. R. (2005). *Deconstructing special needs: A personal learning encounter.* Singapore: McGraw-Hill.

Ministry of Education, Singapore (1997). The launch of National Education. Retrieved 31 May 2006 from http://intranet.moe.gov.sg/ne/keyspeeches/may17-97.htm.

——— (1998). *Desired outcomes of education.* Singapore: Author.

——— (2000). *Report of the committee on compulsory education in Singapore.* Singapore: Author.

——— (May, 2005). *Greater support for students with special needs in selected schools in 2006.* Retrieved 14 June 2005 from http://www.moe.gov.sg/press/2005/pr20050520_print.htm.

Oliver, M. (1992). Changing the social relations of research production? *Disability, Handicap & Society, 7*, 101–114.

Poon-McBrayer, K. F. (2004). Equity, elitism, marketisation: Inclusive education in Hong Kong. *Asia-Pacific Journal of Education, 2*, 157–172.

Skrtic, T. M. (1986). The crisis in special education knowledge: A perspective on perspective. *Focus on Exceptional Children, 18*, 1–16.

Stubbs, S. (1997). *The rights of children with disabilities* (Manchester, Enabling Education Network). Available online at www.eenet.org.uk.

Teo, L. (2004, 19 September). $220m school aid for disabled kids. *The Straits Times,* p. 1.

UNESCO (1994). *The Salamanca statement and framework for action in special needs education.* World Conference on Special Needs Education: Access and Quality. New York: UNESCO.

Ware, L. (2005). Many possible futures, many different directions: Merging critical special education and disability studies. In S. L. Gabel, & S. Danforth (Eds.), *Disability studies in education: Readings in theory and method* (pp. 103–124). New York: Peter Lang.

CHAPTER THIRTY-THREE

Disability Narratives, Social Models, AND Rights Perspectives AS Higher Education Imperatives

CHRISTOPHER JOHNSTONE, ALEX LUBET, AND LEONARD GOLDFINE

INTRODUCTION[1]

The field of Disability Studies (DS) is historically situated as a deliberate challenge to deficit-oriented perceptions of disability. DS scholars have challenged medical and deficit models of disability to broaden and reassign societal views of disability. The perspective that the challenges posed by living with a disability reside in the disabled individual's deficits rather than failures of social justice are common not only in medicine but in such fields as (special) education and social work. To this end, scholars of DS tend to refer to the deficit model as the "medicalization" of disability in all contexts.

DS scholars engage in a variety of research methods, including personal narrative, critical theory, and historical reviews to challenge marginalizing constructions of people with disabilities (PWD). In doing so, the field of DS promulgates information and analysis to students, scholars, and beyond, creating opportunities for providing participating universities to enter a world with more diverse perspectives than are typically found in fields that specialize in service delivery of "cure" protocols for PWD. These relatively new perspectives on disability tie neatly into the historical and broad-based goals of higher education. In this chapter, we specifically focus on higher education goals of the United States.

The philosophical underpinnings of American higher education are marked by one constant: change. For example, the landmark 1828 Yale report emphasized liberal education, noting that subjects such as ancient languages would help students develop mental acuity. The Morrill Acts of 1862 and 1890 established land-grant universities that "were among the first institutions of learning in the United States to welcome applied science and the mechanic arts and to give these subjects a recognized place in the college curriculum" (Brubacher & Rudy, 1997, p. 64). The passing of the Servicemen's Readjustment Act of 1944 (the GI Bill of Rights) opened the door for colleges to be a universal resource rather than one strictly for elites. Although these are milestones in the history of American higher education, they do not impart a complete picture of its philosophical ebbs and flows. For every two steps forward toward inclusion and universal access that American higher education institutions have made, there has always been one step back. Progress toward egalitarian higher education has been slow and incremental. Nevertheless, uneven progress has been made. As a contemporary example, this chapter traces the uneven development of DS curricular perspectives in a U.S. higher education institution at a large public university, chronicling the proceedings of the all-university Disability Studies Committee in understanding DS as a field, as well as related developments in DS beyond the committee's purview. Future directions are proposed for colleges and universities hoping to broaden their disability-related theoretical and methodological base to include the social model of disability.

LIBERAL GOALS OF HIGHER EDUCATION

Among the most influential schools of thought in American higher education are the Cornell Model and the Wisconsin Idea. Cornell University's vision of an "All Purpose Curriculum," was nonsectarian (though not antireligious), emphasized equality between different courses of study, the importance of scientific study, and the application of scientific method to every field of knowledge. The Cornell model was intended to be adaptive to "the American people, to American needs, and to the requirements of modern times" (Brubacher & Ruby, 1997, p. 160). This model opened the door for universities to offer a broad, secular education that prepared students for life in a variety of specialized and technical fields, not just a limited number of "gentlemanly" fields such as law and medicine. Besides technical training, this model emphasized substantial "cultural" content along with more utilitarian preparation.

The Wisconsin Idea is similar to the Cornell Model, with the added notion of community service. The framers of the Wisconsin model assumed that the universities should be institutions for all the people of the state. The close proximity of the University of Wisconsin's (UW) physical campus to state government facilitated their close partnership, though the UW plan was not limited to its main, Madison campus. To meet the state's agrarian needs, Wisconsin combined the main central campus with a university extension system. In this way, the university attempted to meet the needs of the people of the state it served who supported it through taxes and tuition. While the philosophies of the Wisconsin Idea and the Cornell Model serve as examples of the increasing roles of "all-purpose" and "service" oriented higher education, one should note that these concepts were not the sole property of these respective institutions:

> As the state universities grew and became established on a firm foundation they came to stand in the American public mind for two dominant ideas. The first was the 'all purpose' curriculum; the second was faithful service to the needs of the community. Most state universities were active in both fields, but the first concept came to be most dramatically associated with Cornell University, and the second was most frequently connected with the University of Wisconsin.
>
> —(BRUBACHER & RUDY, 1997, P. 161)

It is important to acknowledge these two models when making the case for the importance of DS. The university that we use as our example—hereafter, State University—is a large, land-grant, research institution. Like UW, State University is metropolitan and based near the state capital, in proximity to state government. The charter for this university was modeled on the UW's.

In U.S. contemporary higher education, one means of ascertaining public needs is to study populations. In an effort to meet a diverse public's needs, university faculty often lobby their institutions to advocate for academic study of the cultures within the society, especially underrepresented groups. Typically, minority perspectives are represented by "ethnic" or "population" studies programs.[2] Most ethnic studies programs study populations that have historically needed to overcome institutionalized discrimination, such as racial and sexual/gender minorities. In these programs there is often academic freedom for *emic* perspectives to be shared and studied. DS is—or should be—no different. As evidenced through legislative advances such as Section 504 of the Vocational Rehabilitation Act of 1973 and the Americans with Disabilities Act of 1990, discrimination against persons with disabilities has entered the lexicon of American higher education. The study of social reform and empowerment of PWD has emerged, challenging the focus on rehabilitation and cure in the curriculum. Increasing numbers of students with disabilities themselves are enrolling in DS programs that focus on culture, social organization, and rights. As evidence of this trend, State University even has a "Disabled Student Cultural Center."

As with a growing number of increasingly outspoken PWD in higher education and beyond, disability is increasingly on the radar of university administrators. Understanding the logistical, infrastructural, and learning needs of students with disabilities, however, is only a small component of DS. DS, while concerned with broader issues of inclusion, social justice, and accommodation, is not necessarily engaged with service provision. DS scholars operate, though guardedly, upon the assumption that any confluence or dissidence between DS theory and service provision is guided by the policies and epistemologies embraced by service providers. DS, however, is a far broader field than this, and not always well understood by faculty and administration. This failure of understanding is a major source of challenge in program development.

DISABILITY STUDIES

As reliable scientific knowledge about the human body increased, so did perceptions of disability. From the 1500s to the present day, medical researchers have attempted to understand the workings of the human body and mind. Advances in research led to assumptions about the normative functioning of the body and mind. People with impairments under this model have been viewed as sick or as carrying a pathogenic condition. Historically, the place of PWD in this model has been that of client or patient (Minnesota Governor's Council on Developmental Disability, 1998). Goffman (1963) first explored the stigma attached to the perpetual client status that people with disabilities often endure. A sociologist, Goffman found that service professionals in disability-related fields actually promulgated stigma, because disability service organizations needed PWD to be dependent upon them to maintain their professional status.

In the 1930s–1970s, social movements by and for persons with disabilities challenged the notion that disability status was solely a medical issue and confronted the role of dependency fostered by service organizations (Longmore, 2003). Activists with disabilities and their nondisabled allies challenged notions of deficit and dependence. Disability rights advocates believed that economic and social barriers experienced by people with disabilities were a result of cultural and institutional factors, not individual deficits (Shapiro, 1993).

With social and empowerment models of disability gaining credence, DS arose as an alternative discourse to research that primarily defined PWD as patients (Linton, 1998) or defectives (Oliver, 1990; Thompson, 1997). The challenge to deficit models of disability is this social model of disability. Lubet (2002) noted that the social model of disability found in DS programs "privileges the sociocultural over the scientific." In practice, this is realized in multiple "social models," insofar as social model principles have been applied across the full range of disciplines, both theoretical and applied, including even the "hard" sciences, where scientists themselves sometimes interrogate discourse in their fields to unveil implicit cultural biases.[3] Research is often multidisciplinary, contemplating disability through various humanistic and social science/policy lenses. DS scholars are working in fields ranging from medical service professions to anthropology, education, and the arts.

DISABILITY STUDIES: DIVERGENT DISCOURSES

Introduction

The complicated issues related to perspectives of disability are described here in a case study of an institution we call State University. Issues were faced by an all-university committee, representing faculty, staff, and students from many programs. Committee work aimed at creating a DS program started and fizzled throughout the 1990s and 2000s until the committee was re-formed in 2002, charged with the task of designing and implementing a DS program at the university, a large "Doctoral Research University-Extensive"[4] state-supported, land-grant institution (The Morrill Land-Grant Colleges Act of 1862). The idea for the Disability Studies Committee originated in the all-campus Disability Issues Committee, which is appointed by the Faculty Senate, but whose membership is appointed independent of senate membership and is comprised of faculty, staff, and students, with administrators from Disability Services and Equal Opportunity serving as ex officio members. Members of the Disability Issues Committee comprised the majority of the Disability Studies Committee, but additional members were recruited from beyond its ranks. The committee included six key players: a high-level administrator of a disability-related office who volunteered to host and chair the meetings, two non-physician health sciences personnel, an educator, a doctoral student who worked on disability issues, and a liberal arts faculty member with a significant record of publication in DS (the only member of the committee able to make such a claim). The original committee was formed as a result of discussions in a university senate meeting that noted the lack of a disability studies program at the university. All members had interest in and longstanding and extensive commitment to disability issues, and all participated faithfully in the committee meetings from 2002 to 2005 (in 2006 the committee was expanded again to include a variety of new constituents for reasons described below). Understandings and misunderstandings of DS as a field circulated throughout the years of committee meetings. These understandings, misunderstandings, and other events were qualitatively coded into major themes:

- Disability Studies as an Existing Entity at State University;
- Disabilities Studies versus Disability Studies;
- Disability Studies as a Necessary Perspective for a Highly Ranked Medical University;
- Disability Studies as a Field that May Compliment or Oppose and Contrast Other Disability-Related Fields.

For the remainder of this chapter, themes are laid out sequentially in a way that exemplifies paradigmatic approaches to PWD and the field of DS. Understandings and misunderstandings revolved around social and empowerment models of disability and possible conflicts that arise when such models are conflated with medical or deficit models. The themes were selected by the authors in an effort to describe the philosophical approaches of higher education personnel that may guide a nascent DS program. They are reported below in an effort to capture contemporary thinking about disability and DS from those familiar and unfamiliar with the field. The themes present are case-specific, but represent how the words "Disability Studies" may be understood by higher education faculty and staff. Such understandings appear to have emerged from a university culture rich in scientific research but lacking in social interpretations of disability. Such understandings may be common in other institutions of higher education with similar attributes. The brief introductions of each of the themes below are followed by substantive conversations about each theme.

(1) Disability Studies as an Existing Entity at State University. Support of this position emerged from a constituency that defined DS literally—as any and all study of disability, regardless of theoretical foundations—and maintained thus that the current curriculum, grounded in deficit models of disability, and its decentralized structure, dispersed among fields such as psychology, special education, and public health, was adequate to call a "Disability Studies" program. Advocates for this position were unclear about social and empowerment models of disability and generally understood disability as deficit without amendment or augmentation.

(2) Disabilities Studies versus Disability Studies. The constituency for a "Disabilities Studies," as opposed to a "Disability Studies" program, supported the deficit model perspectives available in the extant curriculum, while advocating for their incorporation into an interdisciplinary major with limited, if not "token," inclusion of social model perspectives. Specifically, advocates of a "Disabilities Studies" program were interested in developing a program that prepared future

practitioners in disability-related fields. Introductory courses in the "Disabilities Studies" program would relate to the etiology of disability, either in body or mind. This particular position remains a popular position among some at State University and other institutions that, however, call their programs "Disability Studies." As the reader will see, exigencies at State University as well as idiosyncrasies of its administrative culture motivated this position as much or more than any particular educational philosophy.

(3) Disability Studies as a Necessary Perspective for a Highly Ranked Medical University. This position, advocated from an administrative rather than a faculty perspective, shares with *Theme 2* its support for an interdisciplinary "Disabilities Studies" program which might potentially permit more space and time for social model perspectives. Its justification, however, is more utilitarian/instrumental than philosophical. Here, a DS program, its methodological content and theoretical principles essentially undefined, is seen as an essential "cutting-edge," "next big thing" accoutrement of a major research university. The only nod to DS perse—as opposed to any other curricular innovation, was its rhetorical placement alongside State University's storied accomplishments in the health sciences, which, of course, explicitly sanction the medical/deficit model of disability.

(4) Disability Studies as a Field Of Study That May Complement or Oppose and Contrast Other Disability-Related Fields. This is the position advocated by proponent of profoundly interdisciplinary while firmly social model adherent DS program. Cognizant that the social model approach not only contrasts but largely opposes deficit perspectives, its advocates regard the dialogue that would surely ensue from the presence of such a program on campus as the literal realization of the fundamental principles of university education, that is, one dedicated to a universe of inquiry. While the social model was ultimately widely accepted in the committee at least as one possible approach to the study of disability, the strategies and contexts through which the social model might be implemented were highly contested.

A fuller synopsis of the two years of discussions among the committee follows, under the four topic headings described above, plus a fifth theme describing the current status of the program. The depth of contestation and intensity of feelings was at times of an intensity that threatened the committee's continuation, and indeed, the all-campus DS initiative morphed into a very different structure, with the nature of a potential DS program still a work-in-progress.

Theme #1: Disability Studies as an Existing Entity at State University

As noted above, the first theme that arose was that DS was already present on campus and was thus not necessary as a new and autonomous program. According to this rationale, DS was represented in the Medical School, Allied Health Sciences (including therapy programs), in the College of Education (including special education), and in a strong student disability services program on campus. Therefore, some believed that what was present was sufficient, a notion that carries the implicit subtext that if people study disability, it must be DS.

Such thinking highlights an important distinction in higher education. There is frequently confusion between service-, rehabilitation-, and therapy-oriented studies of disability and DS. The former conflation, a lexical inversion—"study of disability" versus DS—evokes a world of difference in culturally mediated meaning.

Such confusion is explicable, as many DS programs reside in professional schools of health or education. Further, any comprehensive discussion of disability includes services, medical issues, and body dynamics. DS, however, privileges the study of disability within a *sociocultural* context, distinct from programs which study disability solely as a question of individual deficit. Therefore, the cobbling together of extant service-based programs may create a program of broad-based disability services, but it does not promulgate DS social and anthropological models of disability.

This has obvious ramifications. Disability service providers are characteristically stakeholders in the deficit model of disability and thus widely seen in DS as "part of the problem" that the social model seeks to address (Lubet, 2002). An analogous link between services to gender, ethnic, or sexual minorities and corresponding academic disciplines would never be contemplated, at least at a major research university.

Even the most adamant social model advocates have never argued for the elimination of service-oriented studies of disability—which, naturally, benefit greatly from a DS perspective, but are tragically flawed by restricting the study of disability to deficit models. The problematic nature of Theme #1 is rendered utterly obvious by applying that same model to an ethnic or gender studies field, at which point its racism and/or sexism would be undeniable.[5] For DS, an exclusively deficit model curriculum translates into an academic agenda that promotes the idea of disability as inferiority, an attitude of ableism.

While we would be reticent to deny the good intentions of those who have dedicated their careers to addressing the challenges of lives with disabilities through deficit model methods, the move described above amounts to a form of intellectual colonialism. Not only are deficit models of disability long entrenched in academia and the professions that train there (although DS is significantly older than many acknowledge),[6] they represent a paradigm example of an outsider perspective—that of the nondisabled "expert"—seeking to own through specialized knowledge—that is, to represent the disabled "insider."[7]

Theme #2: Disabilities Studies versus Disability Studies

In the first year of committee meetings, service-oriented committee members the committee used the term "Disability Studies" to describe a program that would introduce future medical health sciences professionals to various impairments and to impairment-related clinical and law/policy issues. Advocates for a service-oriented "Disabilit*ies* Studies" proposed that the new "DS" program explore the etiology, pathology, and curability of disability. This curriculum was seen as a "feeder" program (an undergraduate course of study leading to a different graduate major) for professional studies programs in disability-related fields. Some committee members ascribed client status to people with disabilities, as objects of, rather than participants in, research and learning. In this type of program, the voice of advocacy, expression, and pride by people with disabilities would fall silent, yielding to a more scientific and clinical approach to impairment. Such perspectives reject the social model distinction between impairment and disability.

Issues of the institutional home of the "DS" program were a concern, but not as much as curriculum. Disability Studies programs throughout the United States are sometimes housed in professional studies departments, and other times not housed in any academic unit. The Ohio State University undergraduate minor is housed in seven different colleges across campus. Syracuse University's program is centered in that university's School of Education and has a complementary program in Law. The University of Illinois-Chicago's program is housed in the Allied Health Sciences. The university for which the program in question resided required a departmental home for administrative purposes. A departmental home in the medical or educational sciences seen as somewhat of an issue, but less one than the teaching and learning issues of the proposed curriculum. The service-based approach, which was intended to rely heavily upon existing courses missed the perspectives of contemporary DS scholarship found both in leading journals such as *Disability and Society*, *Disability Studies Quarterly*, and the *Review of Disability Studies: An International Journal* and in DS research found in books in fields such as literature and history. A fully interdisciplinary program without a departmental base, such as the DS program at Ohio State University, was not an option at State University. State's administrative structure in general, its traditions of budget management in particular, and especially its concern for who gets what tuition revenue, make such profound interdisciplinarity a distant goal at best. The desire for the sort of extensive transformation of institutional administrative culture that would be required to facilitate such interdisciplinary conversations have long been a theme of many discussions at State.

Unforeseen circumstances lent the idea of DS as a "feeder" program a sense of urgency during the following year. Under the university's latest, much-vaunted strategic plan, a medical science (rehabilitation) program whose faculty included a DS committee member, was targeted to close. In an effort to save the program, an initiative to move it to another academic unit was begun. The field in question required an undergraduate "feeder program." It was thus proposed that the new DS program would reside in the same unit as the newly relocated rehabilitation program. DS majors would thus be undergraduates preparing for graduate study in a rehabilitation field. Opponents of this program fought this idea because it was pedagogically inimical to traditional DS curriculum and was in principle questionable because the program (according to its representative) was hesitant to enroll persons with certain impairments who would be unable to undertake all the necessary tasks of the program. Theme 2 represented a "borrowing" or "stealing" of the name DS in order to promote a program that lacked a title or name.

In summary, Theme 1 represented a case of intellectual colonialism, while Theme 2 was an attempt at misappropriation of resources. The rubric, and possibly even some of the substance of, DS would be exploited to train professionals for a field that simultaneously, if ironically, serves but excludes people with disabilities. Once more, the depths of inappropriateness of such a move are well illustrated by analogy to another area studies field. Imagine the outrage were the name Women's Studies used to describe premedical "feeder program" courses for gynecology—even if the latter would benefit from such an arrangement.

Theme #3: Disability Studies as a Necessary Perspective for a Highly Ranked Medical University

Theme 3 emerged because State University has a prestigious medical program. Its researchers have pioneered numerous medical devices and procedures, thus improving the lives of many people with and without disabilities. As discussion ensued, the entire committee ultimately accepted the validity of personal narrative, first-person accounts, and multidisciplinary, and sociocultural approaches to the study of disability—as a counterbalance to scientific research that often took place in laboratory conditions. Over time, the committee members all began to understand the philosophical underpinnings of DS and to see the field's value as necessary to the myriad of disability perspectives found on campus and as part of a larger contribution to higher education. There was a general acceptance that DS coursework and research would be a valuable addition to existing disability service programs even though there was skepticism from some committee members regarding the merit and validity of DS research.

One compromise approach that was proposed was to introduce the social model into current medical model curricula as simply another perspective or unit; a "breath of fresh air."[8] Such an assertion ignores the incompatibility of these highly epistemologically opposed views and DS largely, even ontologically adversarial relationship to the disability professions, at least as they are sometimes practiced. There was also concern raised that social model perspectives on healthcare in general and disability in particular would become co-opted in a (lucrative) medical environment. As an example, one committee member observed that the fields of biomedical ethics and healthcare policy have at times become so invested in their relationship to the health sciences that needed dissent was nonexistent (Lubet, 2004).

As in Theme 2, DS becomes indentured to deficit modeled perspectives. The analogy between the "breath of fresh air" and the "court jesters" of old—escape valves for oppressive regimes—comes to mind. Alternative examples are to be found in the many higher education curricula in music which provide only token coverage of world musics and American vernacular and minority traditions; just enough to remind students that these cultures are far less important than the Western classics that form the canonic core curriculum. It is not unrealistic to speculate that the traditions of the "Other" would be better served by being skipped entirely, rather than being addressed as clearly if implicitly unimportant. The compromise was tabled and discussions continued. Discussions in Theme 3 demonstrated progress toward a full-fledged program and of the growing acceptance of DS perspectives, but still minimized the role of DS and narratives as part of the liberal education of *all* higher education students

Theme #4: Disability Studies as a Field of Study that may Complement, Oppose or Contrast Other Disability-Related Fields.

Scholars dedicated to DS approaches remained committed throughout the process to the notion that DS is indeed a legitimate field of study and is a field whose theoretical and methodological tenets must be defined from within the field itself (Linton, 1998). The committee members supported the idea that the underpinnings of DS can both complement and challenge the assumptions of deficit model fields and promote diversity initiatives at the University. If present, acknowledging or even forthrightly teaching these differences would be welcomed. Differing or adversarial perspectives would exemplify what is best in university life: the academic enterprise in general and liberal education in particular.

Philosophical discussions raised important issues about the appropriate underpinnings of the study of disability. There were some who assumed that social model perspectives could simply be appended to a fundamentally medical/deficit model course, as perhaps but a single, brief unit taught by faculty who are stakeholders in service professions. Missing from the discussion of "adding on" DS to such programs was any evidence of committee members' substantive inculcation into the field of DS and the social model; an almost total paucity of knowledge of DS's major figures, canonic texts, important journals, successful programs, or the primacy of the Society for DS in setting national and international agendas for the field.

The level of comfort with which committee members spoke as if from authority about DS while lacking the usual and customarily expected qualifications appears to owe primarily from two factors, neither of these unique to State University, though perhaps carried to extremes there. The first of these is the refusal to acknowledge the existence of a field called DS that is radically interdisciplinary yet firmly grounded in a particular set of principles, these emanating from the social model of disability. In effect, committee members denied the existence of DS as anything more than an empty vessel awaiting any disability content the future faculty chose, though this would inevitably be dominated by the deficit model disciplines that have long thrived on the campus and which were well-represented on the committee. Additionally, over the years the committee met, it became increasingly apparent that no serious attempt was made by committee members ignorant of DS principles and scholarship to learn anything; indeed, that there was no need to learn more.

That faculty and staff of deficit model disability curricula that thrive in a university system aspire also to own for themselves the name of DS as well should concern not only DS scholars and the disability community, but anyone concerned for the future of liberal education. More than once after this committee morphed into something larger but hardly less troubling, administrators participating in the "disability studies initiative" made statements to the effect that "Disability Studies at State University would be what State University decides." This is what members of the earlier committee had been saying all along, though with less authority. It is also identical in structure what the proponents of "intelligent design" such as the Board of Education of the state of Kansas are saying; that in Kansas, science will be religion. The ascendancy of such fundamentalist newspeak, medical and religious, should frighten everyone.

The second reason that traditional academic authority based on scholarship was undermined in this committee resulted from a tendency within universities to grant the privilege and responsibility of authoritative voice in matters concerning protected classes such as women, racial and sexual minorities, and people with disabilities, to the offices that provide services to these groups. The administrators of these programs are frequently not academic and lack anything resembling the requisite qualifications to guide or even advise curriculum. To be sure, there are numerous disability services personnel (including people with disabilities) who are active participants in the field of DS as teachers and scholars, but services and studies must never be conflated. Once that had taken place, it became clear that all reasonable academic standards had been abandoned and that the committee could include nonteaching staff and faculty from deficit model curricula as well. That there was so little interest in DS in a major university system obviously made the knowledge vacuum even worse.

Also fundamentally problematic was the failure of many on the committee to consider the research mission of the university. No discipline can thrive on a Doctoral Research University-Extensive campus simply as a teaching field. A fully articulated and appropriately respected DS presence at the university would require the presence of scholars committed to the furthering the knowledge base of the field. Only an explicit and demonstrated commitment to the propagation of the social model of disability—perhaps best achieved through the addition of new faculty lines in DS—can assure the successful integration of this important, relatively new epistemological and methodological perspective. Within the committee, advocates for a "social model of disability" were not wed to a unitary approach of examining DS through social lenses, but were committed to opening a program that investigated disability through a variety of lenses and disciplines tied together by broad-based ideas about the lived experience and empowerment of people with disabilities.

In addition to philosophical differences, practical matters arose. The committee discovered through its proceedings that a logistical problem was the paucity of tenure-track professors with knowledge of the field of DS at State. This dearth of faculty committed to DS holding tenure-track academic positions appears to apply to the field of DS in general, which has an extraordinarily high rate of participation by scholars without academic affiliations.[9] University guidelines prevented programs from being run by academic staff, yet the bulk of tenured professors who were interested in this program had no record of DS research.

Further discussion in the committee concerned the most appropriate disciplinary home for DS (university policy required that an academic unit house the program). One view was that the importance of having any DS program, regardless of its methodological base, was paramount and that the particular academic home was utterly irrelevant. Even music was suggested.[10] Implicit and explicit in this position was the notion that the programmatic location of DS would have no ramifications whatsoever with regard to curriculum or personnel, a view that would certainly never be expressed by an experienced faculty member in any field. This position ignores or disregards that every academic program has a document of principles that includes a clear mission statement, one that would invariably define its relationship—including, perhaps, little or none—to DS.

Related to the question of programmatic home was the much-discussed issue of the credential(s) to be awarded by the new DS program. Currently there are programs in the United States, Canada, and the United Kingdom that offer credentials. These include undergraduate minors, undergraduate and graduate "concentrations," master's, doctoral, and postdoctoral "certificates," and master's and doctoral degrees.[11] In large part to explore the range of options at the university, a conference was held, whose distinguished guest was a well-known Liberal Arts and DS scholar from a similar large public university that had just initiated a DS minor. Discussions continued for months. Philosophical differences emerged, with members attempting to find a home for DS in various departments. Although the College of Liberal Arts appeared to be the most logical choice for a field of study that examined societal and cultural interpretation of disability, discussions never reached consensus.

Theme #5: Disability Studies finds an Unlikely Home

Change often occurs as a result of reculturing an organization (Fullan, 2001) and happenstance events (Mitchell et al., 1999). In the case of State University's Disability Studies program, change occurred because of a gradual acceptance by Disability Studies Committee members related to the philosophical and epistemological underpinnings of Disability Studies Committee members and events that were unexpected by all parties involved.

As a result of cost-cutting and strategic positioning at State University, two programs were slated for reconfiguration or termination in 2006. The first was the abovementioned therapeutic program previously housed in the health sciences. The second was a "school within a school" developmental education unit that sought to provide first-generation college students and students who needed additional support and academic preparation before entering the university at large.

The first (therapeutic) program's faculty proposed a new DS program, but talks stalled when the proposal's themes reflected those found in *Theme 1 (Disability Studies as an Existing Entity at State University)*and *2 (Disabilities Studies versus Disability Studies)* of this chapter. Talks reemerged, however, when an open letter from the State Consortium of Citizens with Disabilities (an organization that is comprised of disability service providers, some with PWD in leading roles) challenged the university to take an integrated approach to the study of disability that privileged interdisciplinary study and built on the university's research strengths. This integrated approach attempted to merge the perspectives that had been at odds in the committee for years.

At present, a proposal for a DS program has nearly emerged, and found an academic home in what appears to be a compromise between competing medical and social model advocates. The "school within a school" unit mentioned above that prepared undergraduate students for the university-at-large was subsumed into the College of Education. Tenured faculty in the "school within a school" were expected to develop innovative ways to draw new students and replace college preparation courses which were no longer deemed to be a part of State University's mission.

As of this writing, DS appears to have found its negotiated home in the College of Education. As such, the field has taken on a character different from that of a Liberal Arts–based program. At the same time, the programmatic foci of diversity, societal critique, and public engagement (which have been keystones for all "school within a school" programs) appear as if they might usefully temper the purely service-based approaches called for by advocates of "disabilities studies" discussed in *Themes 1* and *2*. The hybrid model, in theory, attempts to balance the frequently contradictory messages coming from medical-model and social model research. This tentative balance appears to address concerns of the Consortium of Citizens with Disabilities, but has several challenges that lie ahead, including staffing the program with knowledgeable faculty, attempting to mend hegemonic perceptions of persons with disabilities frequently found in medical-model research, and promoting examination of disability through art, literature, history, social sciences, and politics while remaining relevant to the College of Education's mission. The urgent need for a social model DS program with a philosophical and methodological approach that is currently poorly represented in State University's curriculum,[12] is a significant challenge that lies ahead. It is unknown if the faculty and staff related to this program will be able to match the high quality DS programs in other institutions. The present level of programmatic ambiguity demonstrates that administrative placement is only one of many considerations for academic programs in postsecondary education. Further decisions around curriculum, core courses, and core faculty are still being contested in committee meetings.

Disability Studies as an Imperative for Higher Education in the Twenty-First Century

Despite challenges, there appears to be a necessity for universities to include DS approaches in higher education endeavors. Indeed, the cultural perspectives embodied by DS literature and DS research provide students an opportunity to view disability from a first-person perspective. In keeping with the citizen-oriented approaches of higher education population and ethnic studies programs, DS provides learners with valuable perspectives that apply to future endeavors as both professionals and citizens. DS programs fall squarely into the liberal goals of American higher education, by educating the citizens of a state about its populace. In this case, DS provides an educative tool for scholars to educate society at large about barriers and empowerment issues related to disability, societal responses to disability, artistic expressions, representations of people with disabilities, and policy issues.

IMPLICATIONS

The case of State University carries an important message for DS scholars in institutions with emerging programs. An important lesson learned from State University is that the field "Disability Studies" is diverse, but has many common assumptions, such as an intellectual interest in social and empowerment model approaches to disability. The understandings of "Disability Studies" presented by some committee members at State reflected exactly the opposite of generally accepted notions related to *emic* perspectives, barrier reduction, and empowerment of people with disabilities. Disability-related services are a necessary function in society and research related to these services serves an important need. Studying the professions, however, is not necessarily "Disability Studies."

Disability Studies, as a field, does not have a standard set of approaches that can be used in program development. Rather, program development in higher education settings may go in a variety of directions. Such are the lessons learned from State University. Within the iterative process of program development, however, several philosophical tenets may guide future actions in colleges and universities across the United States and around the world.

First, DS scholars have noted that DS is not simply any scholarly activity related to disability. While the term "canonical" DS is somewhat problematic, readers in the field should note that DS as a field departs from research meant to "cure" and "fix" people with disabilities and rather seeks emic perspectives to "empower" and "remove barriers." The line between these distinctions may at times be vague, so committees seeking to develop DS programs are best served by persons familiar with the historical writings of authors who have used the term DS to distinguish their research from deficit-oriented research.

Second, DS may take on a variety of forms. The hybrid program proposed at State University is grounded in social models of disability but reflects the diverse research foci of the University. In theory, DS programs should allow for individualization and not be constrained by dogmatic requirements, but programs that veer too far from social model approaches may lose so much DS perspective that they become something else (see the above examples of Women's Studies and Women's Medicine). Because strict rules of adherence on DS programs do not exist, it is relevant for DS activists to understand the nature of other DS programs and literature and be grounded in the liberal goals of higher education.

To conclude, higher education as an institution, since the Wisconsin Idea and Cornell Model, has had the historically lofty goals of educating the populace for the greater good of society. Cultural studies are germane to the understanding of the broader populace and commonplace in higher education settings. DS provides an opportunity for scholarly pursuit of disability-related issues from a variety of lenses, all of which seek to engage societal understandings of disability. DS, however, differs from research that specifically aims to "cure" the person with a deficit. Such research will always be present in higher education settings, but is not appropriately labeled if it uses the moniker "DS." Evidence from State University indicates that the DS label may be used as a tool for program marketing, program development, and courses without having any social model perspectives at all. While there is no consensus statement on what is and what is not DS, this case study demonstrated that scholars dedicated to DS may want involve themselves in conversations around program development to ensure that at least some semblance of social model inquiry is part of the process. Such participation may ensure that the lofty goals of higher education and citizen learning are met.

NOTES

1. This chapter chronicles the history of an evolving process at State University. To the extent possible, the anonymity of all participants in the all-campus Disability Studies Committee (its real name) has been protected, through a process that combines broad description of their professional appointments with limited ascription of comments and actions. In the interest of having the activities and actions within the committee judged on their merits and not their titles, the same strategy of broad description has been applied there as well. If, nonetheless, any identities are transparent despite our efforts, please know that we have done our best and that, disagree as we might with certain views and machinations, we intend no challenge to the professional integrity of any of the parties involved, all of whom consistently behaved in good conscience and with the best of intentions.
2. The distinction between area studies and ethnic studies may be subtle, but it is significant on a variety of levels. Area studies programs focus on individual ethnicities, such as African American or Latino. Their curricula include courses whose perspectives are multi- and interdisciplinary. Ethnic studies programs typically combine the ethnicities that would be found in several area studies programs, sometimes in inter- or panethnic courses and theoretical courses on ethnicity. The former tend to be organized around topic, the latter methodology. From the perspective of administration, area studies offers more autonomy, while ethnic studies offers obvious "top-down" advantages in reduced staffing and flexibility in faculty hiring. Ethnic studies units, with their more methodological and thus research-oriented perspective, are also more likely to have graduate programs. For further reference, see "Area Studies Graduate Schools," http://www.gradschools.com/programs/area_studies.html (retrieved June 16, 2005) and "Ethnic Studies Programs," http://www.amherst.edu/~dtf/ethnic/programs.html (retrieved June 16, 2005). There are also both women's and feminist studies programs, as well as men's, queer, and gender studies programs. The distinctions between women's and feminist studies as subject versus methodology/undergraduate versus graduate are strikingly parallel to those between area and ethnic studies. For further reference, see "Women's Studies Programs Worldwide," http://research.umbc.edu/~korenman/wmst/programs.html#outside (retrieved June 16, 2005) and "CAFS Center

for Advanced Feminist Studies" (University of Minnesota), http://cla.umn.edu/cafs/links.html (retrieved June 16, 2005).
3. Although she works on social and cultural constructions of sexuality rather than disability, Stanford University population biologist Joan Roughgarden's (2004) *Evolution's Rainbow* is an excellent example of a scientist's application of social model principles to discourse in her field.
4. Administrators at State University often compare the institution to a cohort of "top 30 Research I Universities and the top 15 public research universities." The category "Research I" was used by the Carnegie Foundation in its 1994 report and has since been replaced with "Doctoral Research University-Extensive."
5. The conflation of disability with race, sex, sexuality, or ethnicity is far more than the analogy offered here. Historian Douglas Baynton (2001) has demonstrated convincingly that throughout American history, the rationale for denial of rights for any of these classes has always been because of their perceived defects.
6. The twentieth annual meeting of the Society for Disability Studies was scheduled for June 2007.
7. This is not to deny the presence of people with disabilities in the disability professions and some of these individuals, as well as some nondisabled professionals who appreciate social model perspectives, have contributed to reforming their fields through social model perspectives. Psychologist Carol Gill of the University of Illinois-Chicago may be the foremost example. But an individual's disability or other minority identity by itself is, of course, wholly inadequate to transform a deficit model professional principles and practice.
8. We owe the "breath of fresh air" analogy to Dr. Tammy Berberi, professor of French and DS scholar, University of Minnesota-Morris.
9. A very simple and admittedly rough instrument was devised to confirm this hypothesis. The conference program of the 2005 Society for Disability Studies meeting was tallied according to those presenters who hold tenured/tenure-track appointments (or their equivalents in foreign universities) versus all others. The count was fifty-two in the tenure stream versus 154 others (The many who presented multiple times were each counted only once.). The survey was rendered somewhat crude by some necessary reliance on guesswork concerning the tenure status of participants and made somewhat less effective by the "all others" group including students as well as workers. However, the extremely low number of tenure stream faculty relative to others is remarkable, insofar as both the incentives and the infrastructure—travel funds, leave time, tenure/merit pay credit—for presenting is so much greater for tenure stream faculty. Even a rough ratio of PWD versus able-bodied participants would also have been highly valuable, but neither data nor reasonable grounds for an educated guess exist.
10. There are, of course, music fields whose relevance to deficit model studies of disability are obviously relevant, including music therapy and music education, for the latter its special education subfield in particular. And while we maintain that all fields that are strongly related to the human condition are easily capable of incorporating DS perspectives, there is simply too much of DS that falls beyond the purview of music to consider such an academic marriage.
11. See "Academic Programs or Centers of Disability Studies" (Society for Disability Studies Homepage), http://www.uic.edu/orgs/sds/links.html#academic (retrieved June 20, 2005).
12. The handful of faculty at State University who are committed to social model DS in their research are also deeply wedded to the disciplines of their training, where their other assigned teaching duties leave little time for disability studies. Creating openings in the teaching schedules of faculty engaged in DS research—to say nothing of adding faculty lines for DS scholars—is an issue that has been raised little if at all. This seems most unusual in an effort to build a new curriculum.

REFERENCES

Baynton, D. (2001). Disability and the justification of inequality in American history. In P. Longmore & L. Umanski (Eds.), *The new disability history: American perspectives* (pp. 33–57). New York: New York University Press.

Brubacher, J.S. & Rudy, W. (1997). Professional education. In L.F. Goodchild & H.S. Weschler (Eds.), *The history of higher education* (2nd ed., pp. 379–393). Needham Heights, MA: Simon & Schuster.

Fullan, M. (2001). *The new meaning of educational change* (3rd ed.). New York: Teachers College Press.

Goffman, E. (1963). *Stigma: Notes on the management of spoiled identity.* Englewood Cliffs, NJ: Prentice Hall.

Linton, S. (1998). *Claiming Disability: Knowledge and Identity.* New York: New York University Press.

Longmore, P. (2003). *Why I Burned My Book and Other Essays on Disability.* Philadelphia, PA: Temple University Press.

Lubet, A. (2002). "Disability Studies and Performing Arts medicine." *Medical Problems of Performing Artists, 17 (2),* 59–62.

——— (2004). "Can Disability Studies survive and prosper within medically-modeled curricula?" *Disability Studies Quarterly, 24 (4).* http://www.dsq-sds.org/2004_fall_toc.html (retrieved September 25, 2007).

Minnesota Governor's Council on Developmental Disability (1998). *Making your case.* St. Paul, MN: Author.

Mitchell, K.E., Levin, A.S., & Krumboltz, J. (1999). "Planned happenstance: constructing unexpected career opportunities." *Journal of Counseling and Development, 17 (2),* 115–124.

The Morrill Land-Grant Colleges Act of 1862 (Public Law 37–108). U.S. Congress.

Oliver, M. (1990). *Politics of disablement.* London: Macmillan.

Rehabilitation Act of 1973, Pub. L. No. 93–112, 87 Stat. 394 (Sept. 26, 1973), codified at 29 U.S.C. § 701.

Roughgarden, J. (2004). *Evolution's Rainbow: Diversity, Gender, and Sexuality in Nature and People.* Berkeley, CA: University of California Press.

Servicemen's Readjustment Act of 1944 (GI Bill of Rights). Retrieved March 5, 2008 from http://www.higher-ed.org/resources/GI_bill.htm.

Shapiro, J. (1993). *No pity.* New York: Times Books.

Thompson, R.G. (1997). *Freakery: Cultural spectacles of the extraordinary body.* New York: New York University Press.

Appendix A

WORLD DECLARATION ON EDUCATION FOR ALL:
MEETING BASIC LEARNING NEEDS

Education for all: The purpose

Article I—meeting basic learning needs

1. Every person—child, youth and adult—shall be able to benefit from educational opportunities designed to meet their basic learning needs. These needs comprise both essential learning tools (such as literacy, oral expression, numeracy, and problem solving) and the basic learning content (such as knowledge, skills, values, and attitudes) required by human beings to be able to survive, to develop their full capacities, to live and work in dignity, to participate fully in development, to improve the quality of their lives, to make informed decisions, and to continue learning. The scope of basic learning needs and how they should be met varies with individual countries and cultures, and inevitably, changes with the passage of time.

2. The satisfaction of these needs empowers individuals in any society and confers upon them a responsibility to respect and build upon their collective cultural, linguistic and spiritual heritage, to promote the education of others, to further the cause of social justice, to achieve environmental protection, to be tolerant towards social, political and religious systems which differ from their own, ensuring that commonly accepted humanistic values and human rights are upheld, and to work for international peace and solidarity in an interdependent world.

3. Another and no less fundamental aim of educational development is the transmission and enrichment of common cultural and moral values. It is in these values that the individual and society find their identity and worth.

4. Basic education is more than an end in itself. It is the foundation for lifelong learning and human development on which countries may build, systematically, further levels and types of education and training.

Education for all: An expanded vision and a renewed commitment

Article II—shaping the vision

To serve the basic learning needs of all requires more than a recommitment to basic education as it now exists. What is needed is an "expanded vision" that surpasses present resource levels, institutional structures, curricula, and conventional delivery systems while building on the best in current practices. New possibilities exist today which result from the convergence of the increase in information and the unprecedented capacity to communicate. We must seize them with creativity and a determination for increased effectiveness.

As elaborated in Articles III–VII, the expanded vision encompasses:

- Universalizing access and promoting equity;
- Focussing on learning;
- Broadening the means and scope of basic education;
- Enhancing the environment for learning;
- Strengthening partnerships.

The realization of an enormous potential for human progress and empowerment is contingent upon whether people can be enabled to acquire the education and the start needed to tap into the ever-expanding pool of relevant knowledge and the new means for sharing this knowledge.

Article III—universalizing access and promoting equity

1. Basic education should be provided to all children, youth and adults. To this end, basic education services of quality should be expanded and consistent measures must be taken to reduce disparities.

2. For basic education to be equitable, all children, youth and adults must be given the opportunity to achieve and maintain an acceptable level of learning.

3. The most urgent priority is to ensure access to, and improve the quality of, education for girls and women, and to remove every obstacle that

hampers their active participation. All gender stereotyping in education should be eliminated.

4. An active commitment must be made to removing educational disparities. Underserved groups: the poor; street and working children; rural and remote populations; nomads and migrant workers; indigenous peoples; ethnic, racial, and linguistic minorities; refugees; those displaced by war; and people under occupation, should not suffer any discrimination in access to learning opportunities.

5. The learning needs of the disabled demand special attention. Steps need to be taken to provide equal access to education to every category of disabled persons as an integral part of the education system.

Article IV—focussing on learning

Whether or not expanded educational opportunities will translate into meaningful development—for an individual or for society—depends ultimately on whether people actually learn as a result of those opportunities, i.e., whether they incorporate useful knowledge, reasoning ability, skills, and values. The focus of basic education must, therefore, be on actual learning acquisition and outcome, rather than exclusively upon enrolment, continued participation in organized programmes and completion of certification requirements. Active and participatory approaches are particularly valuable in assuring learning acquisition and allowing learners to reach their fullest potential. It is, therefore, necessary to define acceptable levels of learning acquisition for educational programmes and to improve and apply systems of assessing learning achievement.

Article V—broadening the means and scope of basic education

The diversity, complexity, and changing nature of basic learning needs of children, youth and adults necessitates broadening and constantly redefining the scope of basic education to include the following components:

- *Learning begins at birth.* This calls for early childhood care and initial education. These can be provided through arrangements involving families, communities, or institutional programmes, as appropriate.
- *The main delivery system for the basic education of children outside the family is primary schooling.* Primary education must be universal, ensure that the basic learning needs of all children are satisfied, and take into account the culture, needs, and opportunities of the community. Supplementary alternative programmes can help meet the basic learning needs of children with limited or no access to formal schooling, provided

that they share the same standards of learning applied to schools, and are adequately supported.
- *The basic learning needs of youth and adults are diverse and should be met through a variety of delivery systems.* Literacy programmes are indispensable because literacy is a necessary skill in itself and the foundation of other life skills. Literacy in the mother-tongue strengthens cultural identity and heritage. Other needs can be served by: skills training, apprenticeships, and formal and non-formal education programmes in health, nutrition, population, agricultural techniques, the environment, science, technology, family life, including fertility awareness, and other societal issues.
- *All available instruments and channels of information, communications, and social action could be used to help convey essential knowledge and inform and educate people on social issues.* In addition to the traditional means, libraries, television, radio and other media can be mobilized to realize their potential towards meeting basic education needs of all.

These components should constitute an integrated system—complementary, mutually reinforcing, and of comparable standards, and they should contribute to creating and developing possibilities for lifelong learning.

Article VI—enhancing the environment for learning

Learning does not take place in isolation. Societies, therefore, must ensure that all learners receive the nutrition, health care, and general physical and emotional support they need in order to participate actively in and benefit from their education. Knowledge and skills that will enhance the learning environment of children should be integrated into community learning programmes for adults. The education of children and their parents or other caretakers is mutually supportive and this interaction should be used to create, for all, a learning environment of vibrancy and warmth.

Article VII—strengthening partnerships

National, regional, and local educational authorities have a unique obligation to provide basic education for all, but they cannot be expected to supply every human, financial or organizational requirement for this task. New and revitalized partnerships at all levels will be necessary: partnerships among all subsectors and forms of education, recognizing the special role of teachers and that of administrators and other educational personnel; partnerships between education and other government departments, including planning, finance, labour, communications, and other social sectors; partnerships between government and non-governmental organizations, the private sector, local communities, religious groups, and families. The recognition of the vital role of both families and teachers is particularly important. In this context, the terms and conditions of service of teachers and their status, which constitute a determining factor in the implementation of education for all, must be urgently improved in all countries in line with the joint ILO/UNESCO Recommendation Concerning the Status of Teachers (1966). Genuine partnerships contribute to the planning, implementing, managing and evaluating of basic education programmes. When we speak of "an expanded vision and a renewed commitment," partnerships are at the heart of it.

Education for all: The requirements

Article VIII—developing a supportive policy context

1. Supportive policies in the social, cultural, and economic sectors are required in order to realize the full provision and utilization of basic education for individual and societal improvement. The provision of basic education for all depends on political commitment and political will backed by appropriate fiscal measures and reinforced by educational policy reforms and institutional strengthening. Suitable economic, trade, labour, employment and health policies will enhance learners' incentives and contributions to societal development.

2. Societies should also insure a strong intellectual and scientific environment for basic education. This implies improving higher education and developing scientific research. Close contact with contemporary technological and scientific knowledge should be possible at every level of education.

Article IX—mobilizing resources

1. If the basic learning needs of all are to be met through a much broader scope of action than in the past, it will be essential to mobilize existing and new financial and human resources, public, private and voluntary. All of society has a contribution to make, recognizing that time, energy and funding directed to basic education are perhaps the most profound investment in people and in the future of a country which can be made.

2. Enlarged public-sector support means drawing on the resources of all the government agencies responsible for human development, through increased absolute and proportional allocations to basic education services with the clear recognition of competing claims on national resources of which education is an important one, but not the only one. Serious attention to improving the efficiency

of existing educational resources and programmes will not only produce more, it can also be expected to attract new resources. The urgent task of meeting basic learning needs may require a reallocation between sectors, as, for example, a transfer from military to educational expenditure. Above all, special protection for basic education will be required in countries undergoing structural adjustment and facing severe external debt burdens. Today, more than ever, education must be seen as a fundamental dimension of any social, cultural, and economic design.

Article X—strengthening international solidarity

1. Meeting basic learning needs constitutes a common and universal human responsibility. It requires international solidarity and equitable and fair economic relations in order to redress existing economic disparities. All nations have valuable knowledge and experiences to share for designing effective educational policies and programmes.

2. Substantial and long-term increases in resources for basic education will be needed. The world community, including intergovernmental agencies and institutions, has an urgent responsibility to alleviate the constraints that prevent some countries from achieving the goal of education for all. It will mean the adoption of measures that augment the national budgets of the poorest countries or serve to relieve heavy debt burdens. Creditors and debtors must seek innovative and equitable formulae to resolve these burdens, since the capacity of many developing countries to respond effectively to education and other basic needs will be greatly helped by finding solutions to the debt problem.

3. Basic learning needs of adults and children must be addressed wherever they exist. Least developed and low-income countries have special needs which require priority in international support for basic education in the 1990s.

4. All nations must also work together to resolve conflicts and strife, to end military occupations, and to settle displaced populations, or to facilitate their return to their countries of origin, and ensure that their basic learning needs are met. Only a stable and peaceful environment can create the conditions in which every human being, child and adult alike, may benefit from the goals of this Declaration.

We, the participants in the World Conference on Education for All, reaffirm the right of all people to education. *This is the foundation of our determination, singly and together, to ensure education for all. We commit ourselves to act cooperatively through our own spheres of responsibility, taking all necessary steps to achieve the goals of education for all. Together we call on governments, concerned organizations and individuals to join in this urgent undertaking. The basic learning needs of all can and must be met.*

There can be no more meaningful way to begin the International Literacy Year, to move forward the goals of the United Nations Decade of Disabled Persons (1983–92), the World Decade for Cultural Development (1988–97), the Fourth United Nations Development Decade (1991–2000), of the Convention on the Elimination of Discrimination against Women and the Forward Looking Strategies for the Advancement of Women, and of the Convention on the Rights of the Child. There has never been a more propitious time to commit ourselves to providing basic learning opportunities for all the people of the world. We adopt, therefore, this **World Declaration on Education for All: Meeting Basic Learning Needs** *and agree on the* **Framework for Action to Meet Basic Learning Needs**, *to achieve the goals set forth in this* **Declaration***.*

Appendix B

THE SALAMANCA STATEMENT ON PRINCIPLES, POLICY AND PRACTICE IN SPECIAL NEEDS EDUCATION

— Reaffirming the right to education of every individual, as enshrined in the 1948 Universal Declaration of Human Rights, and renewing the pledge made by the world community at the 1990 World Conference on Education for All to ensure that right for all regardless of individual differences,
— Recalling the several United Nations declarations culminating in the 1993 United Nations Standard Rules on the Equalization of Opportunities for Persons with Disabilities, which urges States to ensure that the education of persons with disabilities is an integral part of the education system,

Noting with satisfaction the increased involvement of governments, advocacy groups, community and parent groups, and in particular organizations of persons with disabilities, in seeking to improve access to education for the majority of those with special needs still unreached; and recognizing as evidence of this involvement the active participation of high level representatives of numerous governments, specialized agencies and intergovernmental organizations in this World Conference,

1. We, the delegates of the World Conference on Special Needs Education representing ninety-two governments and twenty-five international organizations, assembled here in Salamanca, Spain, from 7–10 June 1994, hereby reaffirm our commitment to Education for All, recognizing the necessity and urgency of providing education for children, youth and adults with special educational needs

within the regular education system, and further hereby endorse the Framework for Action on Special Needs Education, that governments and organizations may be guided by the spirit of its provisions and recommendations.

2. We believe and proclaim that: every child has a fundamental right to education, and must be given the opportunity to achieve and maintain an acceptable level of learning, every child has unique characteristics, interests, abilities and learning needs, education systems should be designed and educational programmes implemented to take into account the wide diversity of these characteristics and needs, those with special educational needs must have access to regular schools which should accommodate them within a child-centred pedagogy capable of meeting these needs, regular schools with this inclusive orientation are the most effective means of combating discriminatory attitudes, creating welcoming communities, building an inclusive society and achieving education for all; moreover, they provide an effective education to the majority of children and improve the efficiency and ultimately the cost-effectiveness of the entire education system.

3. We call upon all governments and urge them to: give the highest policy and budgetary priority to improve their education systems to enable them to include all children regardless of individual differences or difficulties, adopt as a matter of law or policy the principle of inclusive education, enrolling all children in regular schools, unless there are compelling reasons for doing otherwise, develop demonstration projects and encourage exchanges with countries having experience with inclusive schools, establish decentralized and participatory mechanisms for planning, monitoring and evaluating educational provision for children and adults with special education needs, encourage and facilitate the participation of parents, communities and organization of persons with disabilities in the planning and decision-making processes concerning provision for special educational needs, invest greater effort in early identification and intervention strategies, as well as in vocational aspects of inclusive education, ensure that, in the context of a systemic change, teacher education programmes, both preservice and inservice, address the provision of special needs education in inclusive schools.

4. We also call upon the international community; in particular we call upon: governments with international cooperation programmes and international funding agencies, especially the sponsors of the World Conference on Education for All, the United Nations Educational, Scientific and Cultural Organization (UNESCO), the United Nations Children's Fund (UNICEF), United Nations Development Programme (UNDP), and the World Bank:

— to endorse the approach of inclusive schooling and to support the development of special needs education as an integral part of all education programmes;

- the United Nations and its specialized agencies, in particular the International Labour Office (ILO), the World Health Organization (WHO), UNESCO and UNICEF;
- to strengthen their inputs for technical cooperation, as well as to reinforce their cooperation and networking for more efficient support to the expanded and integratedprovision of special needs education; non-governmental organizations involved in country programming and service delivery;
- to strengthen their collaboration with the official national bodies and to intensify their growing involvement in planning, implementation and evaluation of inclusive provision for special educational needs; UNESCO, as the United Nations agency for education;
- to ensure that special needs education forms part of every discussion dealing with education for all in various forums,
- to mobilize the support of organizations of the teaching profession in matters related to enhancing teacher education as regards provision for special educational needs;
- to stimulate the academic community to strengthen research and networking and to establish regional centres of information and documentation; also, to serve as a clearinghouse for such activities and for disseminating the specific results and progress achieved at country level in pursuance of this Statement;
- to mobilize funds through the creation within its next Medium-Term Plan (1996–2002) of an expanded programme for inclusive schools and community support programmes, which would enable the launching of pilot projects that showcase new approaches for dissemination, and to develop indicators concerning the need for and provision of special needs education.

5. Finally, we express our warm appreciation to the Government of Spain and to UNESCO for the organization of the Conference, and we urge them to make every effort to bring this Statement and the accompanying Framework for Action to the attention of the world community, especially at such important forums as the World Summit for Social Development (Copenhagen, 1995) and the World Conference on Women (Beijing, 1995).

Adopted by acclamation, in the city of Salamanca, Spain

Appendix C

WORLD DECLARATION ON HIGHER EDUCATION
FOR THE TWENTY-FIRST CENTURY: VISION AND ACTION

Preamble

On the eve of a new century, there is an **unprecedented demand for and a great diversification in higher education, as well as an increased awareness of its vital importance for sociocultural and economic development,** and for building the future, for which the younger generations will need to be equipped with new skills, knowledge and ideals. Higher education includes "all types of studies, training or training for research at the post-secondary level, provided by universities or other educational establishments that are approved as institutions of higher education by the competent State authorities." Everywhere higher education is faced with great challenges and difficulties related to financing, equity of conditions at access into and during the course of studies, improved staff development, skills-based training, enhancement and preservation of quality in teaching, research and services, relevance of programmes, employability of graduates, establishment of efficient co-operation agreements and equitable access to the benefits of international co-operation. At the same time, higher education is being challenged by new opportunities relating to technologies that are improving the ways in which knowledge can be produced, managed, disseminated, accessed and controlled. Equitable access to these technologies should be ensured at all levels of education systems.

The second half of this century will go down in the history of higher education as the period of its most spectacular **expansion:** an over sixfold increase in student enrolments worldwide, from 13 million in 1960 to 82 million in 1995. But it is also the period which has seen the gap between industrially developed, **the developing countries** and **in particular the least developed countries** with regard to access and resources for higher learning and research, already enormous, becoming even wider. It has also been a period of increased socio-economic stratification and greater difference in educational opportunity within countries, including in some of the most developed and wealthiest nations. Without adequate higher education and research institutions providing a critical mass of skilled and educated people, no country can ensure genuine endogenous and sustainable development and, in particular, developing countries and least developed countries cannot reduce the gap separating them from the industrially developed ones. Sharing knowledge, international co-operation and new technologies can offer new opportunities to reduce this gap.

Higher education has given ample proof of its viability over the centuries and of its ability to change and to induce change and progress in society. Owing to the scope and pace of change, society has become increasingly **knowledge-based** so that higher learning and research now act as essential components of cultural, socio-economic and environmentally sustainable development of individuals, communities and nations. Higher education itself is confronted therefore with formidable challenges and must proceed to the most radical **change and renewal it has ever been required** to undertake, so that our society, which is currently undergoing a profound crisis of values, can transcend mere economic considerations and incorporate deeper dimensions of morality and spirituality.

It is with the aim of providing solutions to these challenges and of setting in motion a process of in-depth reform in higher education worldwide that UNESCO has convened a World Conference on Higher Education in the Twenty-First Century: Vision and Action. In preparation for the Conference, UNESCO issued, in 1995, its *Policy Paper for Change and Development in Higher Education*. Five regional consultations (Havana, November 1996; Dakar, April 1997; Tokyo, July 1997; Palermo, September 1997; and Beirut, March 1998) were subsequently held. The Declarations and Plans of Action adopted by them, each preserving its own specificity, are duly taken into account in the present Declaration—as is the whole process of reflection undertaken by the preparation of the World Conference—and are annexed to it.

*   *   *

We, participants in the World Conference on Higher Education, assembled at UNESCO Headquarters in Paris, from 5 to 9 October 1998,

Recalling the principles of the Charter of the United Nations, the Universal Declaration of Human Rights, the International Covenant on Economic, Social and Cultural Rights, and the International Covenant on Civil and Political Rights,

Recalling also the Universal Declaration of Human Rights which states in Article 26, paragraph 1, that "Everyone has the right to education" and that "higher education shall be equally accessible to all on the basis of merit," and *endorsing* the basic principles of the Convention against Discrimination in Education (1960), which, by Article 4, commits the States Parties to it to "make higher education equally accessible to all on the basis of individual capacity,"

Taking into account the recommendations concerning higher education of major commissions and conferences, *inter alia*, the International Commission on Education for the Twenty-First Century, the World Commission on Culture and Development, the 44th and 45th sessions of the International Conference on Education (Geneva, 1994 and 1996), the decisions taken at the 27th and 29th sessions of UNESCO's General Conference, in particular regarding the Recommendation concerning the Status of Higher-Education Teaching Personnel, the World Conference on Education for All (Jomtien, Thailand, 1990), the United Nations Conference on Environment and Development (Rio de Janeiro, 1992), the Conference on Academic Freedom and University Autonomy (Sinaia, 1992), the World Conference on Human Rights (Vienna, 1993), the World Summit for Social Development (Copenhagen, 1995), the fourth World Conference on Women (Beijing, 1995), the International Congress on Education and Informatics (Moscow, 1996), the World Congress on Higher Education and Human Resources Development for the Twenty-First Century (Manila, 1997), the fifth International Conference on Adult Education (Hamburg, 1997) and especially the Agenda for the Future under Theme 2 (Improving the conditions and quality of learning) stating: "We commit ourselves to ... opening schools, colleges and universities to adult learners ... by calling upon the World Conference on Higher Education (Paris, 1998) to promote the transformation of post-secondary institutions into lifelong learning institutions and to define the role of universities accordingly,"

Convinced that education is a fundamental pillar of human rights, democracy, sustainable development and peace, and shall therefore become accessible to all throughout life and that measures are required to ensure co-ordination and co-operation across and between the various sectors, particularly between general, technical and professional secondary and post-secondary education as well as between universities, colleges and technical institutions,

Believing that, in this context, the solution of the problems faced on the eve of the twenty-first century will be determined by the vision of the future society and by the role that is assigned to education in general and to higher education in particular,

Aware that on the threshold of a new millennium it is the duty of higher education to ensure that the values and ideals of a culture of peace prevail and that the intellectual community should be mobilized to that end,

Considering that a substantial change and development of higher education, the enhancement of its quality and relevance, and the solution to the major challenges it faces, require the strong involvement not only of governments and of higher education institutions, but also of all stakeholders, including students and their families, teachers, business and industry, the public and private sectors of the economy, parliaments, the media, the community, professional associations and society as well as a greater responsibility of higher education institutions towards society and accountability in the use of public and private, national or international resources,

Emphasizing that higher education systems should enhance their capacity to live with uncertainty, to change and bring about change, and to address social needs and to promote solidarity and equity; should preserve and exercise scientific rigour and originality, in a spirit of impartiality, as a basic prerequisite for attaining and sustaining an indispensable level of quality; and should place students at the centre of their concerns, **within a lifelong perspective,** so as to allow their full integration into the global knowledge society of the coming century,

Also believing that international co-operation and exchange are major avenues for advancing higher education throughout the world,

Proclaim the following:

MISSIONS AND FUNCTIONS OF HIGHER EDUCATION

Article 1—Mission to educate, to train and to undertake research

We affirm that the core missions and values of higher education, in particular the mission to contribute to the sustainable development and improvement of society as a whole, should be preserved, reinforced and further expanded, namely, to:

(a) educate highly qualified graduates and responsible citizens able to meet the needs of all sectors of human activity, by offering relevant qualifications, including professional training, which combine high-level knowledge and skills, using courses and content continually tailored to the present and future needs of society;

(b) provide opportunities (*espace ouvert*) **for higher learning and for learning throughout life,** giving to learners an optimal range of choice and a flexibility of entry and exit points within the system, as well as an opportunity for individual development and social mobility in order **to educate for citizenship and for active participation in society,** with a worldwide vision, for endogenous capacity-building, and for the consolidation of human rights, sustainable development, democracy and peace, in a context of justice;

(c) **advance, create and disseminate knowledge** through **research** and provide, as part of its service to the community, relevant expertise to assist societies in cultural, social and economic development, promoting and developing scientific and technological research as well as research in the social sciences, the humanities and the creative arts;

(d) help **understand, interpret, preserve, enhance, promote and disseminate national and regional, international and historic cultures,** in a context of cultural pluralism and diversity;

(e) help protect and enhance **societal values** by training young people in the values which form the basis of democratic citizenship and by providing critical and detached perspectives to assist in the discussion of strategic options and the reinforcement of humanistic perspectives;

(f) contribute to the development and improvement of education at all levels, including through the training of teachers.

Article 2—Ethical role, autonomy, responsibility and anticipatory function

In accordance with the Recommendation concerning the Status of Higher-Education Teaching Personnel approved by the General Conference of UNESCO in November 1997, **higher education institutions and their personnel and students** should:

(a) preserve and develop their crucial functions, through the exercise of ethics and scientific and intellectual rigour in their various activities;

(b) be able to speak out on ethical, cultural and social problems completely independently and in full awareness of their responsibilities, exercising a kind of intellectual authority that society needs to help it to reflect, understand and act;

(c) enhance their critical and forward-looking functions, through continuing analysis of emerging social, economic, cultural and political trends, providing a focus for forecasting, warning and prevention;

(d) exercise their intellectual capacity and their moral prestige to defend and actively disseminate universally accepted values, including peace, justice, freedom, equality and solidarity, as enshrined in UNESCO's Constitution;

(e) enjoy full academic autonomy and freedom, conceived as a set of rights and duties, while being fully responsible and accountable to society;

(f) play a role in helping identify and address issues that affect the well-being of communities, nations and global society.

SHAPING A NEW VISION OF HIGHER EDUCATION

Article 3—Equity of access

(a) In keeping with Article 26.1 of the Universal Declaration of Human Rights, admission to higher education should be based on the merit, capacity, efforts, perseverance and devotion, showed by those seeking access to it, and can take place in a lifelong scheme, at any time, with due recognition of previously acquired skills. As a consequence, no discrimination can be accepted in granting access to higher education on grounds of race, gender, language or religion, or economic, cultural or social distinctions, or physical disabilities.

(b) Equity of access to higher education should begin with the reinforcement and, if need be, the reordering of its links with all other levels of education, particularly with secondary education. Higher education institutions must be viewed as, and must also work within themselves to be a part of and encourage, a seamless system starting with early childhood and primary education and continuing through life. Higher education institutions must work in active partnership with parents, schools, students, socio-economic groups and communities. Secondary education should not only prepare qualified candidates for access to higher education by developing the capacity to learn on a broad basis but also open the way to active life by providing training on a wide range of jobs. However, access to higher education should remain open to those successfully completing secondary school, or its equivalent, or presenting entry qualifications, as far as possible, at any age and without any discrimination.

(c) As a consequence, the rapid and wide-reaching demand for higher education requires, where appropriate, **all policies concerning access to higher education** to give priority in the future to the approach based on the merit of the individual, as defined in Article 3(a) above.

(d) Access to higher education for members of some special target groups, such as indigenous peoples, cultural and linguistic minorities, disadvantaged groups, peoples living under occupation and those who suffer from disabilities, must be actively facilitated, since these groups as collectivities and as individuals may have both experience and talent that can be of great value for the development of societies and nations. Special material help and educational solutions can help overcome the obstacles that these groups face, both in accessing and in continuing higher education.

Article 4—Enhancing participation and promoting the role of women

(a) Although significant progress has been achieved to enhance the **access of women** to higher education, various socio-economic, cultural and political obstacles continue in many places in the world to impede their full access and effective integration. To overcome them remains an urgent priority in the renewal process for ensuring an equitable and non-discriminatory system of higher education based on the principle of merit.

(b) Further efforts are required to eliminate all gender stereotyping in higher education, to consider gender aspects in different disciplines and to consolidate women's participation at all levels and in all disciplines, in which they are under-represented and, in particular, to enhance their active involvement in decision-making.

(c) Gender studies (women's studies) should be promoted as a field of knowledge, strategic for the transformation of higher education and society.

(d) Efforts should be made to eliminate political and social barriers whereby women are under-represented and in particular to enhance their active involvement at policy and decision-making levels within higher education and society.

Article 5—Advancing knowledge through research in science, the arts and humanities and the dissemination of its results

(a) The advancement of knowledge through **research** is an essential function of all **systems** of higher education, which should promote postgraduate studies. **Innovation, interdisciplinarity and transdisciplinarity** should be promoted and reinforced in programmes with long-term orientations on social and cultural aims and needs. An appropriate balance should be established between basic and target-oriented research.

(b) Institutions should ensure that all members of the academic community engaged in research are provided with appropriate training, resources and support. The intellectual and cultural rights on the results of research should be used to the benefit of humanity and should be protected so that they cannot be abused.

(c) Research must be enhanced in all disciplines, including the social and human sciences, education (including higher education), engineering, natural sciences, mathematics, informatics and the arts within the framework of national, regional and international research and development policies. Of special importance is the enhancement of research capacities in higher education research institutions, as mutual enhancement of quality takes place when higher education and research are conducted at a high level within the same institution. These institutions should find the material and financial support required, from **both public and private sources.**

Article 6—Long-term orientation based on relevance

(a) **Relevance** in higher education should be assessed in terms of the fit between what society expects of institutions and what they do. This requires ethical standards, political impartiality, critical capacities and, at the same time, a better articulation with the problems of society and the world of work, **basing long-term orientations on societal aims and needs, including respect for cultures and environmental protection.** The concern is to provide access to both broad general education and targeted, career-specific education, often interdisciplinary, focusing on skills and aptitudes, both of which equip individuals to live in a variety of changing settings, and to be able to change occupations.

(b) Higher education should **reinforce its role of service to society,** especially its activities aimed at eliminating poverty, intolerance, violence, illiteracy, hunger, environmental degradation and disease, mainly through an **interdisciplinary and transdisciplinary approach** in the analysis of problems and issues.

(c) Higher education should enhance its contribution to the **development of the whole education system,** notably through improved teacher education, curriculum development and educational research.

(d) Ultimately, higher education should aim at the creation of a new society—non-violent and non-exploitative—consisting of highly cultivated, motivated and integrated individuals, inspired by love for humanity and guided by wisdom.

Article 7—Strengthening co-operation with the world of work and analysing and anticipating societal needs

(a) In economies characterized by changes and the emergence of new production paradigms based on knowledge and its application, and on the handling of information, the links between higher education, the world of work and other parts of society should be strengthened and renewed.

(b) Links with the world of work can be strengthened, through the participation of its representatives in the governance of institutions, the increased use of domestic and international apprenticeship/work-study opportunities for students and teachers, the exchange of personnel between the world of work and higher education institutions and revised curricula more closely aligned with working practices.

(c) **As a lifelong source of professional training, updating and recycling,** institutions of higher education should systematically take into account trends in the world of work and in the scientific, technological and economic sectors. In order to respond to the work requirements, higher education systems and the world of work should jointly develop and assess learning processes, bridging programmes and prior learning assessment and recognition programmes, which integrate theory and training on the job. Within the framework of their anticipatory function, higher education institutions could contribute to the creation of new jobs, although that is not their only function.

(d) Developing entrepreneurial skills and initiative should become major concerns of higher education, in order to facilitate employability of graduates who will increasingly be called upon to be not only job seekers but also and above all to become job creators. Higher education institutions should give the opportunity to students to fully develop their own abilities with a sense of social responsibility, educating them to become full participants in democratic society and promoters of changes that will foster equity and justice.

Article 8—Diversification for enhanced equity of opportunity

(a) Diversifying higher education models and recruitment methods and criteria is essential both to meet increasing international demand and to provide access to various delivery modes and to extend access to an ever-wider public, in a lifelong perspective, based on flexible entry and exit points to and from the system of higher education.

(b) More diversified systems of higher education are characterized by new types of tertiary institutions: public, private and non-profit institutions, amongst others. Institutions should be able to offer a wide variety of education and training opportunities: traditional degrees, short courses, part-time study, flexible schedules, modularized courses, supported learning at a distance, etc.

Article 9—Innovative educational approaches: Critical thinking and creativity

(a) In a world undergoing rapid changes, there is a perceived need for a new vision and paradigm of higher education, which should be student-oriented, calling in most countries for in-depth reforms and an open access policy so as to cater for ever more diversified categories of people, and of its contents, methods, practices and means of delivery, based on new types of links and partnerships with the community and with the broadest sectors of society.

(b) Higher education institutions should educate students to become well informed and deeply motivated citizens, who can think critically, analyse problems of society, look for solutions to the problems of society, apply them and accept social responsibilities.

(c) To achieve these goals, it may be necessary to recast curricula, using new and appropriate methods, so as to go beyond cognitive mastery of disciplines. New pedagogical and didactical approaches should be accessible and promoted in order to facilitate the acquisition of skills, competences and abilities for communication, creative and critical analysis, **independent thinking and team work in multicultural contexts,** where creativity also involves combining traditional or local knowledge and know-how with advanced science and technology. **These recast curricula should take into account the gender dimension and the specific cultural, historic and economic context of each country.** The teaching of human rights standards and education on the needs of communities in all parts of the world should be reflected in the curricula of all disciplines, particularly those preparing for entrepreneurship. Academic personnel should play a significant role in determining the curriculum.

(d) New methods of education will also imply new types of teaching-learning materials. These have to be coupled with new methods of testing that will promote not only powers of memory but also powers of comprehension, skills for practical work and creativity.

Article 10—Higher education personnel and students as major actors

(a) A vigorous policy of staff development is an essential element for higher education institutions. Clear policies should be established concerning higher education teachers, who nowadays need to focus on teaching students how to learn and how to take initiatives rather than being exclusively founts of knowledge. Adequate provision should be made for research and for updating and improving pedagogical skills, through appropriate staff development programmes, encouraging constant innovation in curriculum, teaching and learning methods, and ensuring appropriate professional and financial status, and **for excellence in research and teaching,** reflecting the corresponding provisions of the **Recommendation concerning the Status of Higher-Education Teaching Personnel approved by the General Conference of UNESCO in November 1997.** To this end, more importance should be attached to international experience. Furthermore, in view of the role of higher education for lifelong learning, experience outside the institutions ought to be considered as a relevant qualification for higher educational staff.

(b) Clear policies should be established by all higher education institutions preparing teachers of early childhood education and for primary and secondary schools, providing stimulus for constant innovation in curriculum, best practices in teaching methods and familiarity with diverse learning styles. It is vital to have appropriately trained administrative and technical personnel.

(c) **National and institutional decision-makers should place students and their needs at the centre of their concerns,** and should consider them as major partners and responsible stakeholders in the renewal of higher education. This should include student involvement in issues that affect that level of education, in evaluation, the renovation of teaching methods and curricula and, in the institutional framework in force, in policy-formulation and institutional management. As students have the right to organize and represent themselves, students' involvement in these issues should be guaranteed.

(d) Guidance and counselling services should be developed, in co-operation with student organizations, in order to assist students in the transition to higher education at whatever age and to take account of the needs of ever more diversified categories of learners. Apart from those entering higher education from schools or further education colleges, they should also take account of the needs of those leaving and returning in a lifelong process. Such support is important in ensuring a good match between student and course, reducing drop-out. Students who do drop out should have suitable opportunities to return to higher education if and when appropriate.

FROM VISION TO ACTION

Article 11 – Qualitative evaluation

(a) **Quality in higher education is a multidimensional concept,** which should embrace all its functions, and activities: teaching and academic programmes, research and scholarship, staffing, students, buildings, facilities, equipment, services to the community and the academic environment. Internal self-evaluation and external review, conducted openly by independent specialists, if possible with international expertise, are vital for enhancing quality. Independent national bodies should be established and comparative standards of quality, recognized at international level, should be defined. **Due attention should be paid to specific institutional, national and regional contexts in order to take into account diversity and to avoid uniformity.** Stakeholders should be an integral part of the institutional evaluation process.

(b) Quality also requires that higher education should be characterized by its international dimension: exchange of knowledge, interactive networking, mobility of teachers and students, and international research projects, while taking into account the national cultural values and circumstances.

(c) To attain and sustain national, regional or international quality, certain components are particularly relevant, notably careful selection of staff and continuous staff development, in particular through the promotion of appropriate programmes for academic staff development, including teaching/learning methodology and mobility between countries, between higher education institutions, and between higher education institutions and the world of work, as well as student mobility within and between countries. The new information technologies are an important tool in this process, owing to their impact on the acquisition of knowledge and know-how.

Article 12—The potential and the challenge of technology

The rapid breakthroughs in new information and communication technologies will further change the way knowledge is developed, acquired and delivered. It is also important to note that the new technologies offer opportunities to innovate on course content and teaching methods and to widen access to higher learning. However, it should be borne in mind that new information technology does not reduce the need for teachers but changes their role in relation to the learning process and that the continuous dialogue that converts information into knowledge and understanding becomes fundamental. Higher education institutions should lead in drawing on the advantages and potential of new information and communication technologies, ensuring quality and maintaining high standards for education practices and outcomes in a spirit of openness, equity and international co-operation by:

(a) engaging in networks, technology transfer, capacity-building, developing teaching materials and sharing experience of their application in teaching, training and research, making knowledge accessible to all;

(b) creating new learning environments, ranging from distance education facilities to complete virtual higher education institutions and systems, capable of bridging distances and developing high-quality systems of education, thus serving social and economic advancement and democratization as well as other relevant priorities of society, while ensuring that these virtual education facilities, based on regional, continental or global networks, function in a way that respects cultural and social identities;

(c) noting that, in making full use of information and communication technology (ICT) for educational purposes, particular attention should be paid to removing the grave inequalities which exist among and also within the countries of the world with regard to access to new information and communication technologies and to the production of the corresponding resources;

(d) adapting ICT to national, regional and local needs and securing technical, educational, management and institutional systems to sustain it;

(e) facilitating, through international co-operation, the identification of the objectives and interests of all countries, particularly the developing countries, equitable access and the strengthening of infrastructures in this field and the dissemination of such technology throughout society;

(f) closely following the evolution of the "knowledge society" in order to ensure high quality and equitable regulations for access to prevail;

(g) taking the new possibilities created by the use of ICTs into account, while realizing that it is, above all, institutions of higher education that are using ICTs in order to modernize their work, and not ICTs transforming institutions of higher education from real to virtual institutions.

Article 13—Strengthening higher education management and financing

(a) The management and financing of higher education require the **development of appropriate planning and policy-analysis capacities** and strategies, based on partnerships established between higher education institutions and state and national planning and co-ordination bodies, so as to secure appropriately streamlined management and the cost-effective use of resources. Higher education institutions should adopt **forward-looking management practices** that respond to the needs of their environments. Managers in higher education must be responsive, competent and able to evaluate regularly, by internal and external mechanisms, the effectiveness of procedures and administrative rules.

(b) Higher education institutions must be given autonomy to manage their internal affairs, but with this autonomy must come clear and transparent accountability to the government, parliament, students and the wider society.

(c) The ultimate goal of management should be to enhance the institutional mission by ensuring high-quality teaching, training and research, and services to the community. This objective requires **governance that combines social vision, including understanding of global issues, with efficient managerial skills.** Leadership in higher education is thus a major social responsibility and can be significantly strengthened through dialogue with all stakeholders, especially teachers and students, in higher education. The participation of teaching faculty in the governing bodies of higher education institutions should be taken into account, within the framework of current institutional arrangements, bearing in mind the need to keep the size of these bodies within reasonable bounds.

(d) The promotion of North-South co-operation to ensure the necessary financing for strengthening higher education in the developing countries is essential.

Article 14—Financing of higher education as a public service

The funding of higher education requires both public and private resources. The role of the state remains essential in this regard.

(a) The diversification of funding sources reflects the support that society provides to higher education and must be further strengthened to ensure the development of higher education, increase its efficiency and maintain its quality and relevance. **Public support for higher education and research remains essential** to ensure a balanced achievement of educational and social missions.

(b) Society as a whole must support education at all levels, including higher education, given its role in promoting sustainable economic, social and cultural development. **Mobilization for this purpose depends on public awareness and involvement of the public and private sectors** of the economy, parliaments, the media, governmental and non-governmental organizations, students as well as institutions, families and all the social actors involved with higher education.

Article 15—Sharing knowledge and know-how across borders and continents

(a) The principle of solidarity and true partnership amongst higher education institutions worldwide is crucial for education and training in all fields that encourage an understanding of global issues, the role of democratic governance and skilled human resources in their resolution, and the need for living together with different cultures and values. The practice of multilingualism, faculty and student exchange programmes and institutional linkage to promote intellectual and scientific co-operation should be an integral part of all higher education systems.

(b) The principles of international co-operation based on solidarity, recognition and mutual support, true partnership that equitably serves the interests of the partners and the value of sharing knowledge and know-how across borders should govern relationships among higher education institutions in both developed and developing countries and should benefit the least developed countries in particular. Consideration should be given to the need for safeguarding higher education institutional capacities in regions suffering from conflict or natural disasters. Consequently, an international dimension should permeate the curriculum, and the teaching and learning processes.

(c) Regional and international normative instruments for the recognition of studies should be ratified and implemented, including certification of the skills, competences and abilities of graduates, making it easier for students to change courses, in order to facilitate mobility within and between national systems.

Article 16—From "brain drain" to "brain gain"

The "brain drain" has yet to be stemmed, since it continues to deprive the developing countries and those in transition, of the high-level expertise necessary to accelerate their socio-economic progress. International co-operation schemes should be based on long-term partnerships between institutions in the South and the North, and also promote South-South co-operation. Priority should be given to training programmes in the developing countries, in centres of excellence forming regional and international networks, with short periods of specialized and intensive study abroad. Consideration should be given to creating an environment conducive to attracting and retaining skilled human capital, either through national policies or international arrangements to facilitate the return—permanent or temporary—of highly trained scholars and researchers to their countries of origin. At the same time, efforts must be directed towards a process of "brain gain" through collaboration programmes that, by virtue of their international dimension, enhance the building and strengthening of institutions and facilitate full use of endogenous capacities. Experience gained through the UNITWIN/UNESCO Chairs Programme and the principles enshrined in the regional conventions on the recognition of degrees and diplomas in higher education are of particular importance in this respect.

Article 17—Partnership and alliances

Partnership and alliances amongst stakeholders—national and institutional policy-makers, teaching and **related** staff, researchers and students, and administrative and technical personnel in institutions of higher education, the world of work, community groups—is a powerful force in managing change. Also, non-governmental organizations are key actors in this process. Henceforth, **partnership, based on common interest, mutual respect and credibility, should be a prime matrix for renewal in higher education.**

We, the participants in the World Conference on Higher Education, adopt this Declaration and reaffirm the right of all people to education and the right of access to higher education based on individual merit and capacity;

We pledge to act together within the frame of our individual and collective responsibilities, by taking all necessary measures in order to realize the principles concerning higher education contained in the Universal Declaration of Human Rights and in the Convention against Discrimination in Education;

We solemnly reaffirm our commitment to peace. To that end, we are determined to accord high priority to education for peace and to participate in the celebration of the International Year for the Culture of Peace in the year 2000;

We adopt, therefore, this World Declaration on Higher Education for the Twenty-First Century: Vision and Action. To achieve the goals set forth in this Declaration and, in particular, for immediate action, we agree on the following Framework for Priority Action for Change and Development of Higher Education.

Appendix D

EDUCATION FOR ALL:
MEETING OUR COLLECTIVE COMMITMENTS

Text adopted by the World Education Forum,
Dakar, Senegal, 26–28 April 2000

1. Meeting in Dakar, Senegal, in April 2000, we, the participants in the World Education Forum, commit ourselves to the achievement of education for all (EFA) goals and targets for every citizen and for every society.

2. The Dakar Framework is a collective commitment to action. Governments have an obligation to ensure that EFA goals and targets are reached and sustained. This is a responsibility that will be met most effectively through broad-based partnerships within countries, supported by cooperation with regional and international agencies and institutions.

3. We re-affirm the vision of the World Declaration on Education for All (Jomtien 1990), supported by the Universal Declaration of Human Rights and the Convention on the Rights of the Child, that all children, young people and adults have the human right to benefit from an education that will meet their basic learning needs in the best and fullest sense of the term, an education that includes learning to know, to do, to live together and to be. It is an education geared to tapping each individual's talents and potential, and developing learners' personalities, so that they can improve their lives and transform their societies.

4. We welcome the commitments made by the international community to basic education throughout the 1990s, notably at the World Summit for Children (1990), the Conference on Environment and Development (1992), the World

Conference on Human Rights (1993), the World Conference on Special Needs Education: Access and Quality (1994), the International Conference on Population and Development (1994), the World Summit for Social Development (1995), the Fourth World Conference on Women (1995), the Mid-Term Meeting of the International Consultative Forum on Education for All (1996), the Fifth International Conference on Adult Education (1997), and the International Conference on Child Labour (1997). The challenge now is to deliver on these commitments.

5. The EFA 2000 Assessment demonstrates that there has been significant progress in many countries. But it is unacceptable in the year 2000 that more than 113 million children have no access to primary education, 880 million adults are illiterate, gender discrimination continues to permeate education systems, and the quality of learning and the acquisition of human values and skills fall far short of the aspirations and needs of individuals and societies. Youth and adults are denied access to the skills and knowledge necessary for gainful employment and full participation in their societies. Without accelerated progress towards education for all, national and internationally agreed targets for poverty reduction will be missed, and inequalities between countries and within societies will widen.

6. Education is a fundamental human right. It is the key to sustainable development and peace and stability within and among countries, and thus an indispensable means for effective participation in the societies and economies of the twenty-first century, which are affected by rapid globalization. Achieving EFA goals should be postponed no longer. The basic learning needs of all can and must be met as a matter of urgency.

7. We hereby collectively commit ourselves to the attainment of the following goals:

(i) expanding and improving comprehensive early childhood care and education, especially for the most vulnerable and disadvantaged children;

(ii) ensuring that by 2015 all children, particularly girls, children in difficult circumstances and those belonging to ethnic minorities, have access to and complete free and compulsory primary education of good quality;

(iii) ensuring that the learning needs of all young people and adults are met through equitable access to appropriate learning and life skills programmes;

(iv) achieving a 50 per cent improvement in levels of adult literacy by 2015, especially for women, and equitable access to basic and continuing education for all adults;

(v) eliminating gender disparities in primary and secondary education by 2005, and achieving gender equality in education by 2015, with a focus on ensuring girls' full and equal access to and achievement in basic education of good quality;

(vi) improving all aspects of the quality of education and ensuring excellence of all so that recognized and measurable learning outcomes are achieved by all, especially in literacy, numeracy and essential life skills.

8. To achieve these goals, we the governments, organizations, agencies, groups and associations represented at the World Education Forum pledge ourselves to:

(i) mobilize strong national and international political commitment for education for all, develop national action plans and enhance significantly investment in basic education;

(ii) promote EFA policies within a sustainable and well-integrated sector framework clearly linked to poverty elimination and development strategies; (iii) ensure the engagement and participation of civil society in the formulation, implementation and monitoring of strategies for educational development;

(iii) ensure the engagement and participation of civil society in the formulation, implementation and monitoring of strategies for educational development;

(iv) develop responsive, participatory and accountable systems of educational governance and management;

(v) meet the needs of education systems affected by conflict, national calamities and instability and conduct educational programmes in ways that promote mutual understanding, peace and tolerance, and help to prevent violence and conflict;

(vi) implement integrated strategies for gender equality in education which recognize the need for changes in attitudes, values and practices;

(vii) implement as a matter of urgency education programmes and actions to combat the HIV/AIDS pandemic;

(viii) create safe, healthy, inclusive and equitably resourced educational environments conducive to excellence in learning with clearly defined levels of achievement for all;

(ix) enhance the status, morale and professionalism of teachers;

(xi) harness new information and communication technologies to help achieve EFA goals;

(xii) systematically monitor progress towards EFA goals and strategies at the national, regional and international levels; and

(xiii) build on existing mechanisms to accelerate progress towards education for all.

9. Drawing on the evidence accumulated during the national and regional EFA assessments, and building on existing national sector strategies, all States will be requested to develop or strengthen existing national plans of action by 2002 at the latest. These plans should be integrated into a wider poverty

reduction and development framework, and should be developed through more transparent and democratic processes, involving stakeholders, especially peoples' representatives, community leaders, parents, learners, non-governmental organizations (NGOs) and civil society. The plans will address problems associated with the chronic under-financing of basic education by establishing budget priorities that reflect a commitment to achieving EFA goals and targets at the earliest possible date, and no later than 2015. They will also set out clear strategies for overcoming the special problems facing those currently excluded from educational opportunities, with a clear commitment to girls' education and gender equity. The plans will give substance and form to the goals and strategies set out in this Framework, and to the commitments made during a succession of international conferences in the 1990s. Regional activities to support national strategies will be based on strengthened regional and subregional organizations, networks and initiatives.

10. Political will and stronger national leadership are needed for the effective and successful implementation of national plans in each of the countries concerned. However, political will must be underpinned by resources. The international community acknowledges that many countries currently lack the resources to achieve education for all within an acceptable time-frame. New financial resources, preferably in the form of grants and concessional assistance, must therefore be mobilized by bilateral and multilateral funding agencies, including the World Bank and regional development banks, and the private sector. We affirm that no countries seriously committed to education for all will be thwarted in their achievement of this goal by a lack of resources.

11. The international community will deliver on this collective commitment by launching with immediate effect a global initiative aimed at developing the strategies and mobilizing the resources needed to provide effective support to national efforts. Options to be considered under this initiative will include:

(i) increasing external finance for education, in particular basic education;

(ii) ensuring greater predictability in the flow of external assistance;

(iii) facilitating more effective donor coordination;(iv) strengthening sector-wide approaches;

(v) providing earlier, more extensive and broader debt relief and/or debt cancellation for poverty reduction, with a strong commitment to basic education; and

(vi) undertaking more effective and regular monitoring of progress towards EFA goals and targets, including periodic assessments.

12. There is already evidence from many countries of what can be achieved through strong national strategies supported by effective development cooperation.

Progress under these strategies could—and must—be accelerated through increased international support. At the same time, countries with less developed strategies—including countries in transition, countries affected by conflict, and post-crisis countries—must be given the support they need to achieve more rapid progress towards education for all.

13. We will strengthen accountable international and regional mechanisms to give clear expression to these commitments and to ensure that the Dakar Framework for Action is on the agenda of every international and regional organization, every national legislature and every local decision-making forum.

14. The EFA 2000 Assessment highlights that the challenge of education for all is greatest in sub-Saharan Africa, in South Asia, and in the least developed countries. Accordingly, while no country in need should be denied international assistance, priority should be given to these regions and countries. Countries in conflict or undergoing reconstruction should also be given special attention in building up their education systems to meet the needs of all learners.

15. Implementation of the preceding goals and strategies will require national, regional and international mechanisms to be galvanized immediately. To be most effective these mechanisms will be participatory and, wherever possible, build on what already exists. They will include representatives of all stakeholders and partners and they will operate in transparent and accountable ways. They will respond comprehensively to the word and spirit of the Jomtien Declaration and this Dakar Framework for Action. The functions of these mechanisms will include, to varying degrees, advocacy, resource mobilization, monitoring, and EFA knowledge generation and sharing.

16. The heart of EFA activity lies at the country level. National EFA Forums will be strengthened or established to support the achievement of EFA. All relevant ministries and national civil society organizations will be systematically represented in these Forums. They should be transparent and democratic and should constitute a framework for implementation at subnational levels. Countries will prepare comprehensive National EFA Plans by 2002 at the latest. For those countries with significant challenges, such as complex crises or natural disasters, special technical support will be provided by the international community. Each National EFA Plan will:

 (i) be developed by government leadership in direct and systematic consultation with national civil society;
 (ii) attract co-ordinated support of all development partners;
 (iii) specify reforms addressing the six EFA goals;
 (iv) establish a sustainable financial framework;
 (v) be time-bound and action-oriented;

(vi) include mid-term performance indicators; and

(vii) achieve a synergy of all human development efforts, through its inclusion within the national development planning framework and process.

17. Where these processes and a credible plan are in place, partner members of the international community undertake to work in a consistent, co-ordinated and coherent manner. Each partner will contribute according to its comparative advantage in support of the National EFA Plans to ensure that resource gaps are filled.

18. Regional activities to support national efforts will be based on existing regional and subregional organizations, networks and initiatives, augmented where necessary. Regions and subregions will decide on a lead EFA network that will become the Regional or Subregional Forum with an explicit EFA mandate. Systematic involvement of, and co-ordination with, all relevant civil society and other regional and subregional organizations are essential. These Regional and Subregional EFA Forums will be linked organically with, and be accountable to, National EFA Forums. Their functions will be: co-ordination with all relevant networks; setting and monitoring regional/subregional targets; advocacy; policy dialogue; the promotion of partnerships and technical cooperation; the sharing of best practices and lessons learned; monitoring and reporting for accountability; and promoting resource mobilization. Regional and international support will be available to strengthen Regional and Subregional Forums and relevant EFA capacities, especially within Africa and South Asia.

19. UNESCO will continue its mandated role in co-ordinating EFA partners and maintaining their collaborative momentum. In line with this, UNESCO's Director-General will convene annually a high-level, small and flexible group. It will serve as a lever for political commitment and technical and financial resource mobilization. Informed by a monitoring report from the UNESCO International Institute for Educational Planning (IIEP), the UNESCO International Bureau of Education (IBE), the UNESCO Institute for Education (UIE) and, in particular, the UNESCO Institute of Statistics, and inputs from Regional and Subregional EFA Forums, it will also be an opportunity to hold the global community to account for commitments made in Dakar. It will be composed of highest-level leaders from governments and civil society of developing and developed countries, and from development agencies.

20. UNESCO will serve as the Secretariat. It will refocus its education programme in order to place the outcomes and priorities of Dakar at the heart of its work. This will involve working groups on each of the six goals adopted at Dakar. This Secretariat will work closely with other organizations and may include staff seconded from them.

21. Achieving Education for All will require additional financial support by countries and increased development assistance and debt relief for education by bilateral and multilateral donors, estimated to cost in the order of $8 billion a year. It is therefore essential that new, concrete financial commitments be made by national governments and also by bilateral and multilateral donors including the World Bank and the regional development banks, by civil society and by foundations.

28 April 2000 Dakar, Senegal.

Contributors

Julie Allan is Professor of Education and Deputy Head of Department at the Stirling Institute of Education, University of Stirling, Scotland. She directs the Professional Doctoral Programme, teaches on the undergraduate teacher education programme and is involved in research on inclusion, disability, children's rights and social capital. Her recent book, *Rethinking Inclusion: The Philosophers of Difference in Practice*, is published by Springer.

Marisol Moreno Angarita, is an Associated Professor in The Department of Human Communication, School of Medicine, National University of Bogotá, Colombia. South America. She is a Ph.D. Candidate in Public Health and a Speech and Language Pathologist and Audiologist, with a Magister in Communication. Mrs. Moreno is currently the Chair of the Masters in Disability and Social Inclusion of the School of Medicine at the National University in Bogotá. This is the first program of its kind in Latin America. Mrs. Moreno is also an advisor to the National Consulting Committee on Disability, of the Ministry of Education and of the Secretariat of Health, Education and Social Welfare of the District of Bogotá. Mrs. Moreno has extensive experience in collaborating and consulting with the local school district regarding aspects of disability services and policy, inclusion of children with disabilities in regular classrooms and school activities, early diagnosis of disability, and development of public policy regarding the education of children with disabilities in Colombia, from a social justice perspective. Mrs. Moreno conducted a 5-month visiting scholar sabbatical at the University of Illinois at

Chicago, Department of Disability and Human Development in 2006. She has conducted several studies on several topics on Education, Health, Media and Policies. She can be reached at marisolmorenoa@gmail.com.

Andrew Azzopardi is a Lecturer at the Department of Youth and Community Studies (Faculty of Education) at the University of Malta. His lecturing focuses on sociology, critical pedagogy, disability and multicultural politics, inclusive education, community management, emancipatory research, narrative enquiry, youth and community studies. He has had *papers* published in the applauded journals of disability studies; *Disability and Society* and *The International Journal of Inclusive Education*, had several pieces of work published in an electronic journal of the University of Leeds, reviewed books for the British Educational Research Association (BERA) and co-authored a text, *Developmental Programme for PSD Teachers.* He has recently published a Text called *Career Guidance for Persons with Disability* and a peer reviewed paper on JMER (Journal of Maltese Education Research), *Preventing exclusion of migrant children and young people in our schools.* Dr Azzopardi is co-researching a project called *Educating for open mindedness - Maltese primary schools' multiethnic educational experiences.* He has presented papers at the University of Leeds, University of Lancaster, Manchester Metropolitan University and the University of Manchester. He was also the Advisor of the National Parents Society for Persons with Disability. He can be reached at andrew.azzopardi@um.edu.mt.

Auxilia Badza is a Lecturer in Special Education at Zimbabwe Open University.

Dóra S. Bjarnason is a Professor in Sociology and Disability Studies and the Dean of Special Education for inclusive settings. She is the director of a Research Center for Inclusive education studies at the university. Dóra is borne in Reykjavík, Iceland in 1947 and educated in Britain at Manchester University, Keele University and Reading University. She was a Morris Ginnsberg fellow at the LSE 1977-1978. Her doctorate is from the University of Oslo. She is one of the pioneers in teacher training and researching in the fields of inclusive education and disability studies in Iceland. Dora has published a number of articles and books in her field. Her latest books in English are *School Inclusion in Iceland: The Cloake of Invisibility*, 2003, and *Disability and Young Adulthood: New Voices from Iceland*, 2004. Both books are published by NOVA Science publishers, inc. N.Y. Dora has been a visiting professor at universities in the USA, New Zealand, Australia and Denmark. She sat on committies for the National Federation for People with Learning Disability and is an advocate for the inclusion of disabled people in school and society. Dora is the mother of a young man with severe impairment who lives and works in the community. She can be reached at dora@khi.is.

Eric Broekaert is full Professor and Head of the Department of Special Education at Ghent University, Belgium Prof. Broekaert is a specialist for years in the field of young drug addicts and their treatment in Therapeutic Communities. He has also a strong interest and expertise concerning the theoretical fundaments of Special Education. He can be reached at Eric.Broekaert@UGent.be.

Sheryl Burgstahler directs DO-IT (Disabilities, Opportunities, Internetworking and Technology) and the Accessible Technology division within UW Technology Services at the University of Washington. DO-IT promotes the success of students with disabilities in postsecondary programs and careers. Dr. Burgstahler is also the Director of The Alliance for Access to Science, Technology, Engineering, and Mathematics (AccessSTEM), which is funded by the National Science Foundation to increase the participation of individuals with disabilities in high tech careers. In addition, she directs AccessCollege, a collaboration funded by the U.S. Department of Education Office for Postsecondary Education to make courses and programs atpost-secondary institutions more accessible to students with disabilities. Dr. Burgstahler has published dozens of articles and delivered presentations at national and international conferences that focus on universal design, the full inclusion of individuals with disabilities in postsecondary education, distance learning, work-based learning, and electronic communities. She is theauthor or co-author of six books on using the Internet with pre-college students and the co-editor of a book on universal design in higher education. Dr. Burgstahler has extensive experience teaching at the pre-college, community college, and university levels. She is an Affiliate Associate Professor in the College of Education at the University of Washington. She can be reached at sherylb@u.washington.edu.

David Chakuchichi is Senior Lecturer and Chairperson of the Department of Special Education at Zimbabwe Open University.

Jagdish Chander is a Senior Lecturer (Associate Professor) in the Department of Political Science, Hindu College, University of Delhi, India and doctoral candidate in Disability Studies program At Syracuse University, USA. He is Currently writing his doctoral dissertation on the self-advocacy movement of the blind in India and the biography of Lal Advani, a leading disability rights advocate and father of rehabilitation services for the disabled in India in the 20th century. In 1994, he co-founded the Disability Rights Group, the first cross-disability group in Delhi. He also co-founded the Beyond Compliance Coordinating Committee disabled students' advocacy group at Syracuse University in 2001. His academic interests include disability narratives, disability rights movement in and social construction of disability in cross-cultural settings, self advocacy movement of the blind in India and the United States, comparative study of disability rights legislations, social construction of disability in the context of Karma theory etc. He can be reached at jagdish100@hotmail.com.

Zhaoyang Chi is a fourth year doctoral student in Special Education and Disability Studies at Syracuse University. She received two Masters degrees, one in Teaching and Curriculum and the other in Early Childhood Special Education, all from Syracuse University. She is a graduate of Beijing Normal University with a Bachelors degree in Preschool Education. Her current research interest areas include inclusive education, disability studies, and experiences of Chinese families of children with autism.

Robert Chimedza is an Associate Professor and Pro Vice Chancellor Academic at Zimbabwe Open University.

David J. Connor is an Associate Professor in the Department of Special Education at Hunter College, City University of New York. He is the co-author of *Reading Resistance: Discourses of Exclusion in Desegregation and Inclusion Debates* (Peter Lang, 2006), and author of *Urban Narratives: Life at the Intersections of Learning Disability, Race, and Social Class* (Peter Lang, 2008). His research interests include multiple ways of conceptualizing disability, learning disabilities, race, gender, social class, inclusive education, and developing the practical application of disability studies in education. He can be reached at dconnor@hunter.cuny.edu.

Rebecca Cory is the Research Consultant for DO-IT, Disabilities, Opportunities, Internetworking and Technology at the University of Washington where she is focusing on how to create systemic change for accessibility at institutions of higher education. Dr. Cory holds a PhD in Cultural Foundations of Education and Disability Studies from Syracuse University, where she was a founding member of the Beyond Compliance Coordinating Committee, an advocacy group for individuals with disabilities and their allies. She has served as disability services coordinator at two different colleges and is a teacher, lecturer, and advocate for educational attainment for individuals with disabilities. She is the co-editor of *Universal Design for Higher Education: From Principles to Practice* (Harvard Education Press, 2008). She can be reached at rccory@u.washington.edu.

Scot Danforth is an Associate Professor in the College of Education and Human Ecology at The Ohio State University. With Terry Jo Smith, he co-authored *Engaging Troubling Students: A Constructivist Approach.* He co-edited (with Susan L. Gabel) *Vital Questions Facing Disability Studies in Education.* He is co-editor (with Brenda Brueggemann) of the interdisciplinary journal *Disability Studies Quarterly.* His current book project is an intellectual history of learning disabilities in the United States.

Lisa Dimling is an Assistant Professor in the School of Intervention Services at Bowling Green State University. Her research interests include education of deaf and hard of hearing students with an emphasis on improving reading and vocabulary development.

Kai Felkendorff is a Lecturer and Research Officer at the Zurich University of Teacher Education. His research and teaching focus upon the construction and measurement of disability and on the evaluation of educational settings created for disabled students.

Beth A. Ferri, Ph.D. is Associate Professor in Teaching and Leadership and Cultural Foundations of Education at Syracuse University. She is graduate faculty in Disability Studies and affiliate faculty in the Department of Women's & Gender Studies at Syracuse University. She also coordinates the Masters program in Inclusive (Special) Education (grades 7-12) and the Doctoral Program in Special Education. Her research interests include inclusive education, feminist disability studies, critical pedagogies and methods, and narrative inquiry. As an interdisciplinary scholar, Prof. Ferri has published in a range of journals, including *Disability Studies Quarterly, Disability & Society, Teachers College Record, Journal of Learning Disabilities, Journal of African American History, Women's Studies International Forum, Women's Studies Quarterly, and The Journal of Gender, Race, and Justice.* In 2006 she published a book with David J. Connor, titled *Reading Resistance: Discourses of Exclusion in Desegregation and Inclusion Debates* (Peter Lang), which chronicles through an analysis of archival newspaper sources how problematic rhetorics of race and ability were used to maintain and justify segregated education after the historic *Brown v. Board of Education* decision.

She was recognized in 2003 as an *Outstanding Young Scholar in Disability Studies in Education*.

Susan L. Gabel is a Professor of Special Education and Disability and Equity in Education in the National College of Education. She is the editor of *Disability Studies in Education: Readings in Theory and Method*. With Scot Danforth she is the co-editor of *Vital Questions Facing Disability Studies in Education* and co-editor of the Disability Studies in Education book series with Peter Lang. She identifies as disabled. Her three oldest adult children are disabled and have significant, multiple impairments. She can be reached at sgabel@nl.edu.

Leonard Goldfine is currently an Assistant Director in the Office of Institutional Research, University of Minnesota–Twin Cities. Prior to his appointment in 2007, he served as the Director of Institutional Research in Rochester Community and Technical College Rochester, Minnesota. Leonard's education includes a Bachelor of Music in Composition from Bradley University, a Master of Arts in Music Composition from the University of Minnesota, and a Ph.D. in Educational Policy and Administration from the University of Minnesota. Leonard has worked with numerous research partners including the Minnesota State Colleges and Universities Center for Teaching and Learning, the Center for School Change, the Postsecondary Educational Policy and Studies Center (now called the Postsecondary Educational Research Institute), the Center for Applied Research and Educational Improvement, the Wallace Readers' Digest Fund, the University of Minnesota Office of the President, the University of Minnesota Faculty Senate, and Capella University. His current research is focused on transfer student success, college rankings systems, and equity issues in faculty salaries.

Dan Goodley is Professor of Psychology and Critical Disability Studies at Manchester Metropolitan University. His research focuses upon sociological and critical community psychological theories of disability which work alongside the activism of disabled people and their allies. He can be reached at D.Goodley@mmu.ac.uk.

Liz Gordon is a research manager in Christchurch, New Zealand. Her academic interests are in education policy, bioethics and the law.

Linda Graham is a postdoctoral research fellow in the Faculty of Education and Social Work at The University of Sydney, Australia. Dr Graham specialises in the medicalisation of childhood and other institutional responses to children and young people who are difficult to teach. She can be reached at l.graham@edfac.usyd.edu.au.

Valerie Harwood is a Senior Lecturer in Foundations of Education at the University of Wollongong, Australia. Her work draws on Foucault to critically examine contemporary understandings of youth and youth subjectivities. Her research interests include the uses of Foucault in Education and critique of the psychiatrisation & medicalisation of young people. Her recent book, *Diagnosing 'Disorderly' Children: A critique of behaviour disorder discourses* was published by Routledge in 2006. She can be reached at vharwood@uow.edu.au.

Anna Hickey-Moody is a Lecturer in Creative Arts Education in the Faculty of Education at Monash University. She is a writer, teacher and performance maker. She has taught in universities since 1999 and in community settings since 1996. Anna's university teaching has been in the areas of Gender Studies, Cultural Studies and Education. She is co-author of *Masculinity beyond the Metropolis* (Palgrave Macmillan UK 2006) and co-editor of *Deleuzian Encounters: Studies in Contemporary Social Issues* (Palgrave Macmillan UK 2007). She has published on disability, gender, place and identity, contemporary Australian performance art and youth performing arts, and a number of creative writing pieces. She is currently working on affect, creativity, school spaces, and young people 'at risk' of leaving school early. She can be reached at Anna.HickeyMoody@Education.monash.edu.au.

Judith Hollenweger is a Professor at the Zurich University of Teacher Education and Head of the University's Department of Research and Development. After qualifiying and working as a teacher, she studied Educational Psychology and Special Education at Zurich, where she also received her Ph.D. Her research includes several projects on the construction and measurement of disability in educational systems. She serves as the Swiss representative for the European Agency for Development in Special Needs Education and for an OECD project to improve statistics and indicators concerning disability. She is a consultant to the WHO for the development of a children's version of the International Classification of Functioning, Disability and Health (ICF).

Geert Van Hove is an Associate Professor at Ghent University. His field of work is located in Disability Studies and Inclusive Education. In a structural agreement with the movement of 'Parents for Inclusion' he is looking at different ways to support families, children and schools within inclusion projects. Within research projects he is especially interested in the "basic stories of families of children with special needs" and in the stories of "adults with a label" starting from the idea that the more we dig into stories the more we are confronted with existential questions. Within the theoretical part of his work, he is especially interested in the Freirian basics of dialogue (dialogical theory of action) and of problematising what is taken for granted in grand theories. He can be reached at Geert.VanHove@UGent.be.

Nicoli Humphry is a secondary teacher and PhD student at the University of Wollogong. Through her work she has developed an interest in the ways educational practice frames young people and the implications of this marginalised young people in educational settings. For her doctoral research she is conducting an ethnography of an alternative school in order to investigate the ways in which these alternative education sites engage with young people excluded from regular schooling.

Christopher Johnstone is Director of International Initiatives at the College of Education and Human Development at the University of Minnesota. He is also a Research Associate at the Institute for Community Integration (ICI). As part of his research appointment, Dr. Johnstone Directs ICI's Global Resource Center on Inclusive Education. He has written on a wide variety of topics relevant to disability, disability studies, and special education. His scholarly interest in Disability Studies continually informs his work in education. He can be reached at john4810@umn.edu.

Rebecca Lawthom, PhD, is Principal lecturer in Psychology at Manchester Metropolitan University and convenor of the Social Change and Well Being Research Centre. Her research engages with feminisms, community psychology, and narrative research. She has written extensively on connecting these different perspectives and is currently developing on-line resources for community psychologists. She can be reached at R.Lawthom@mmu.ac.uk

Mieke Leroy is (almost) mother of five children. As an expert in mothering for children with and without special needs she and her husband have chosen for inclusive education for one of their sons who is labelled with Down Syndrome. Whenever she has some time left, Mieke works with and for parents to give them support and respect for their pedagogical choices.

Levan Lim is an Associate Professor at the Early Childhood and Special Needs Education Academic Group, National Institute of Education, Nanyang Technological University, Singapore. He obtained his Ph.D. in special education from Lehigh University in Pennsylvania, and besides Singapore, has worked in the United States and Australia. His areas of teaching, research and community work include disability issues in Singapore, curriculum development, and the inclusion of persons with disabilities within schools and society. He is an editorial board member in several international disability-related journals, such as the *International Journal of Inclusive Education* and *Research and Practice for Persons with Severe Disabilities*. Dr. Lim can be reached at levan.lim@nie.edu.sg

Alex Lubet is Morse Alumni/Graduate & Professional Distinguished Teaching Professor at the University of Minnesota, with appointments in Music and Jewish and American Studies and an affiliate faculty member of the Center on Disability Studies at the University of Hawai'i. At Minnesota, he chairs the Senate Disability Issues Committee. At Hawai'i, he serves as Associate Editor of Review of Disability Studies: An International Journal. His disability studies research emphasizes issues in music, religion, and higher education. He is also a composer and guitarist.

Kim Marshall is a senior lecturer in the School of Law at the University of Westminster in London. She pioneered the teaching of disability law at undergraduate level in the UK in by introducing the first module in the subject 2001. Her current research is on the impact of the new provisions introduced by the Disability Discrimination Act 2005 and the development of the non-discrimination duties in relation to disability and higher education in the UK. She can be reache at marshak@wmin.ac.uk.

Helen McCabe is an Assistant Professor of Education at Hobart and William Smith Colleges in Geneva, NY. She is also Affiliated Faculty in the Asian Languages and Cultures Department. Dr. McCabe's research focuses on special education and disability in China. In particular, she has conducted research on families of children with autism in China, as well as organizations that serve this population. Her most current research looks at issues facing adults with developmental disabilities and their families in China.

Dr. Rod Michalko teaches disability studies in the department of Equity Studies, University of Toronto. He is also adjunct professor in the Critical Disability Studies program at York University. Rod is author of numerous articles and three books, the most recent, *The Difference that Disability Makes* (Temple UP 2002). He is currently in the final stages of completing his forth book in which he explores the cultural connection between disability and the concept of problem. All of Rod's work is committed to the exploration of disability as a cultural phenomenon and his starting point is his own blindness experience. He can be reached at rod.michalko@utoronto.ca.

Emily Mintz is a doctoral candidate in special education at University of California, Berkeley and San Francisco State University. Her areas of study have centered around inclusive education and school reform, disability studies in education, and understanding general education teachers' work in inclusive classrooms. Ms. Mintz is currently conducting her dissertation research, which uses ethnographic methods to understand general educators' conceptions of and commitments to inclusive education. Ms. Mintz is a former special education teacher in inclusive and segregated settings, and works with Bay Area teacher credentialing programs that prepare teachers to work in inclusive settings. She can be reached at eamintz@berkeley.edu.

Kathleen Mortier is a Research assistant and Ph.D. student at Ghent University. In her research projects and practical work she invests a lot of energy in the way "support," and especially "natural support," are organised in inclusive education projects.

Missy Morton is Principal Lecturer, BTchLn Hons & MTchLn Research Coordinator, School of Educational Studies and Human Development, University of Canterbury. She can be reached at missy.morton@canterbury.ac.nz.

Nithi Muthukrishna is Professor in the School of Education and Development, University of KwaZulu-Natal. Her research and teaching interests are in the areas of policy and practice related to social inclusion and exclusion, educating for social justice and equity, and the psychology of learning and teaching, with a particular focus on child health and well-being. Nithi can be reached at School of Education and Development, Faculty of Education, University of KwaZulu-Natal, Private Bag X01, Scottsville 3209 Pietermaritzburg campus South Africa.

Jabulani Ngcobo is principal at a rural primary school in Estcourt, province of KwaZulu-Natal, South Africa. He is currently a PHD student in the School of Education and Development, University of KwaZulu-Natal. His research interests are in the areas of education for social justice and equity, and developing inclusive schools and communities. Jabulani can be reached at School of Education and Development, Faculty of Education, University of KwaZulu-Natal, Private Bag X01, Scottsville 3209 Pietermaritzburg campus South Africa.

Susan Peters is an Associate Professor in the College of Education at Michigan State University. She is the author of two edited books on cross-cultural education. She has been a disability studies scholar and disability advocate for over twenty-five years. Her research focuses on urban education, cross-cultural and comparative education, and inclusive education policy. She can be reached at speters@msu.edu.

Kenneth Poon is an Assistant Professor at the Early Childhood and Special Needs Education Academic Group (ECSE AG), National Institute of Education, Nanyang Technological University, Singapore. He obtained his Ph.D. from the University of North Carolina, Chapel Hill, North Carolina. He is presently the coordinator of in-service programs within the ECSE AG. His current teaching, research and community service interests revolve around improving the quality of service provision and delivery for persons with autism and their families in Singapore.

Justin J.W. Powell, Dr. Phil., is Senior Researcher at the Social Science Research Center Berlin (WZB). Previously, he taught sociology of education and Disability Studies at the University of Goettingen (2005-07) and was Research Fellow of the Max Planck Institute on Human Development in Berlin (2000-05). He received the 2006 Irving K. Zola Award from the Society for Disability Studies and his book *Barriers to Inclusion: Special Education in the United States and Germany* is forthcoming from Paradigm. He can be reached at justinjwpowell@gmail.com.

Griet Roets is an expert in giving support to self advocacy groups. She is doing narrative research that combines Disability Studies and Gender Studies. Griet has also a very strong interest in postmodern and critical science. She can be reached at Griet.Roets@ont.be.

Elisabeth DeSchauwer is a research assistant and Ph.D. student at Ghent University. As a scientist she stands for "praxis" combining coaching of families, teams and children within inclusive education projects. For her research project she is extremely interested in the perspective and participation of children with communication barriers. She can be reached at Elisabeth.DeSchauwer@UGent.be.

Qing Shen was a fourth year doctoral student in Special Education and Disability Studies at Syracuse University when the chapter was written. Her interest areas include early childhood inclusive education, communication for children with special needs, multi-cultural factors in inclusive education and public services for people with disabilities. She now lives in New York City.

Jitka Sinecka is a Ph.D. student in Disability Studies, School of Education, Syracuse University. She graduated from Charles University, Prague, with a Master's degree in Social and Public Policy in 2004, and in Anthropology in 2003. She received her Bachelor's degree in Humanities at CU. Jitka is interested in comparative disability law and policy, deinstitutionalization of people with developmental disabilities, and facilitated communication for nonverbal people with autism. Her interest in disability comes from her grandmother who is Deaf. She has conducted research on families with Deaf young people, school and work inclusion of the Deaf, and disability social and public policies in the Czech Republic and the US. She is involved in disability advocacy on SU campus through the Beyond Compliance Coordinating Committee, and wishes to initiate a change of Czech disability policy when she returns back home. She can be reached at jsinecka@syr.edu.

Roger Slee is Research Chair of Inclusive Education at the Institute of Education, University of London. As well as being the Founding Editor of the *International Journal of Inclusive Education*, he has authored and edited numerous books, journal articles and keynotes on issues pursuant to inclusive education.

Phil Smith describes himself as post labels, but sometimes works as a Critical ethnographer, poet, teacher educator, and artist. Both he and his daughter have disabilities. His research interests cross margins and boundaries, and include the representation of research; ways in which people with disabilities experience choice, control, and power in their lives; normal theory; disability and education policy; and cultural understandings of disability. A transplanted Yankee, he lives in Michigan, where he watches loons and bald eagles on Lake Superior. He can be reached at psmith16@emich.edu.

Thana Thaver is a Lecturer with the Early Childhood and Special Needs Education Academic Group, National Institute of Education (NIE), Nanyang Technological University, Singapore. She has taught both mainstream and gifted secondary school students in Singapore. Before joining NIE, she was with Singapore's Ministry of Education. She was involved in developing the primary school English curriculum for the gifted and working with teachers of the gifted. In recent years, she has expanded her teaching and research work to working with children with special needs. Her research and teaching interests include provisions for diverse learners in the classroom and teacher education.

Tanya Titchkosky's various publications in the field of interpretive disability studies include two books, *Reading and Writing Disability Differently: The Textured Life of Embodiment* (UTP, 2007), and *Disability, Self and Society* (UTP, 2003). Tanya holds the newly established faculty position in Disability Studies in the Department of Sociology and Equity Studies at OISE, University of Toronto. Her research and teaching, informed by her dyslexia, address the interpretive relations that ground disability in everyday life. Currently, with the support of a standard SSHRC grant, she is exploring disability experience as it is expressed in the academy. She can be reached at tanyatitchkosky@oise.utoronto.ca.

Dr. Annemieke van Drenth is senior researcher at the Department of Education at Leiden University in the Netherlands, in the Section Clinical Child and Adolescent Studies. She published articles and edited books on gender and the history of social care and education. With Dr Francisca de Haan, she wrote *The Rise of Caring Power. Elizabeth Fry and Josephine Butler in Britain and the Netherlands* (Amsterdam, 1999). Currently, her research is on the history of special education and women's role in professional developments within the field, themes on which she edited Special Issues of History of Education (2005) and Paedagogica Historica (2008). She can be reached at drenth@fsw.leidenuniv.nl.

Kimberly Wolbers is an Assistant Professor in the department of Theory and Practice in Teacher Education at the University of Tennessee. Her research focuses on educational issues of language, literacy and deafness. She can be reached at kwolbers@utk.edu.

Kathryn Young is a Postdoctoral Fellow at University of Aberdeen, Scotland and a visiting Assistant Professor at Metropolitan State College of Denver. She holds a PhD in Educational Policy. She taught students with and without disabilities in Namibia, North Carolina, and Arizona and teacher education students with and without disabilities in California and Colorado. Her research on the socio-political nature of disability focuses on teaching and teacher education. Her areas of interest include Disability Studies in Education, urban education, and inclusive teacher education. Her work has been published in Teaching and Teacher Education. She can be reached at kathryn.s.young@gmail.com.